BUSINESS & SOCIETY
Ethics, Government, and the World Economy

BUSINESS & SOCIETY
Ethics, Government, and the World Economy

Alfred A. Marcus
University of Minnesota
Carlson School of Management

Homewood, IL 60430
Boston, MA 02116

© RICHARD D. IRWIN, INC., 1993

Senior sponsoring editor: Kurt L. Strand
Developmental editor: Libby Rubenstein
Marketing manager: Kurt Messersmith
Project editor: Jean Lou Hess
Production manager: Ann Cassady
Cover designer   Janet M. Cunniffee
Art coordinator: Mark Malloy
Compositor: Graphic Composition, Inc.
Typeface: 10/12 Palatino
Printer: R. R. Donnelley & Sons Company

Library of Congress Cataloging-in-Publication Data

Marcus, Alfred Allen, date
     Business and society: ethics, government, and the world economy /
Alfred A. Marcus.
         p.   cm.
     ISBN 0-256-08866-7
     1. Business ethics.   2. Social responsibility of business.
     3. Business and politics.   I. Title.
    HF5387.M3454   1993
    174'.4—dc20   92–23081

Printed in the United States of America
2 3 4 5 6 7 8 9 0 DOC 9 8 7 6 5 4 3

To my family: my wife, Judy; and my sons, David and Ariel; my mother Alice; and to the memory of my father James (1912–1992). May the next generation learn: "What is the right path that a person should choose? That which honors the person and brings honor from humankind."

PREFACE

In discussing strategic decisions that managers have to make, this text emphasizes three important topics: ethics, public policy, and global competition. We examine the principles of ethics and the proper sphere of markets and government, and these topics are applied to natural resource and environmental issues. The text considers the impacts of technology and explains the tort system. We include extensive comparative material, especially regarding Japan, but more generally concerning other countries and regions. Cases provide students with practical experience in handling concrete issues where the conceptual material has direct application. Some of the topics covered, and the related cases, are as follows:

Topic:

- Normative and psychological approaches to ethics and social responsibility.
- The rationale for government. The performance of the U.S. economy in international competition.
- Comparative aspects of energy and environmental problems.
- The role of technology in creating economic growth.
- Legal and liability aspects of new-product development.

Selected Cases:

- Dennis Levine.
- Chrysler and Honda.
- General Motors.
- ARCO Solar.
- The Future of Nuclear Power.
- Cochlear Implants.
- Bhopal.
- Auto Safety at Ford.

Why This Text Is Needed. The author feels as if he is standing on the shoulders of giants, and acknowledges a profound debt of gratitude to colleagues whose masterful business-and-society texts have built an impressive field. Why then is another text needed?

- There are many good books that emphasize either ethics or public policy, but few successfully deal with *both topics*.
- None has incorporated the vast changes occurring in *the world economy*.
- None deals extensively with *energy and environmental issues*.
- None provides in-depth coverage of *technology*.

Rather than superficially treating diverse and unrelated topics, this book has a focus—it provides in-depth coverage of strategic areas that have importance for the firm.

Ethics and Public Policy.   The standard ethics and public-policy topics treated in business-and-society courses are found in this book: the debate about social responsibility, corporate governance, business and politics, the historic relationship between business and government, mergers and acquisitions, women, minorities, consumerism, and poverty.

The World Economy.   This book also addresses business practice throughout the globe. It has extensive comparative material—on Japan, the West European nations, the Russian Federation and the former Eastern Bloc states, the oil-producing countries of the Middle East, the rising nations of the Pacific Rim, and developing states such as India. The strategic focus and international dimension mean that this book can be used in business-strategy and international-business courses, as well as business-and-society courses. It covers the world—a requisite for any modern business-and-society text.

Natural Resource and Environmental Issues.   The treatment of natural resource and environmental issues also is comprehensive and up-to-date. The book views these issues in an international context and in light of global competitiveness. Principles relating to ethics and the proper sphere of markets and government are applied in chapters on natural resource and environmental issues.

The Impact of Technology.   This book gives extensive treatment to technology. Managers should be able to derive many practical ideas from this material. We consider the impacts of technology on society, and we explain the tort system, which has had such a profound impact on business practice in recent years, in a way that is meaningful to managers.

Conceptually Rich with Features That Pinpoint Ideas and Cases That Provide Application Opportunities.   This book is very rich conceptually. The special features, which are found in each chapter, pinpoint important ideas. The cases allow you to apply the conceptual material to concrete issues. They provide the full level of argument and evidence needed to adequately debate what a company should do, and they require students to exercise judgment in the type of complex settings that exist in the real business world.

Summary of Special Features.   In summary, the book's features are the following:

1. *Extensive discussion of changes in the world economy.* The discussion of changes in the world economy is far-reaching, extending to sections on ethics and social responsibility and law and public policy ordinarily found in business-and-society texts, as well as to sections where these changes are treated individually. From the outset, we show the connection between social and individual values and economic growth. We include the international dimension in the

discussion of the Lockheed bribery scandal, and we address social responsibility and corporate governance in the Japanese firm.

2. *Normative and social psychological approach to ethics and social responsibility.* The approach to ethics and social responsibility is not only normative; it is also based on social psychology. Some of the important literature in this area (e.g., Millgram and Kohlberg) is summarized, and an individual and organizational context is provided for the discussion of ethical dilemmas in the corporation.

3. *Historical discussion of normative ethics.* We give a clear historical discussion of normative ethics with extensive quotations from classical writings; the deontological (rights-based) tradition of Kant is contrasted with teleological concepts from modern utilitarianism. We discuss the political philosophy of the founders of the American republic and of such contemporaries as Rawls and Nozick. Both the deontological and the teleological traditions are evaluated from the perspective of such moderns as Freud, who stressed the role of passions and instincts in governing human behavior.

4. *The rationale for government.* In this era of diminished expectations about the capabilities of government and reduced means for governments worldwide to accomplish worthy objectives, we give students some perspective on the role economists believe governments should play and the actual roles governments have played in economic development. This approach of contrasting normative economic theory with actual behavior is used in a number of places in the book, for example, when the theory of the firm proposed by economists (agency theory) is contrasted with actual firm behavior observed by management scholars (the behavioral theory).

5. *Different views on the appropriate government role.* We contrast three different views on the appropriate role of govern-

ment—the traditional liberal, the contemporary liberal, and the neoconservative. The discussion is extended with a summary of contemporary ideologies and insights about the conservative views of recent American administrations (Reagan and Bush) and about the controversy surrounding industrial policies that are supposed to make the U.S. economy more capable of competing internationally.

6. *The performance of the U.S. economy in international competition.* We assess how well the U.S. economy is doing in international competition and we consider its strengths and weaknesses in comparison to Japan and other nations in light of recent debates for and against free trade.

7. *Comparative economic performance of nations.* The slump in economic growth affecting the U.S. economy is worldwide, and the impact on Eastern Europe and the Russian Federation is far greater than that on the United States. The formerly communist economies of Eastern Europe are discussed in a wide-ranging analysis of the many important factors, including values, government policies, and an international market orientation, that are necessary for growth.

8. *Reasons for the rise of some economies.* While most of the economies in the world have declined since 1973, some countries (e.g., South Korea and Taiwan) have seen exceptional growth. We address some of the reasons for this growth, as well as the question of whether it can be sustained.

9. *The importance of the natural world.* This book explicitly recognizes the importance of the natural world both in providing businesses with essential raw materials (from nature) and in receiving the wastes generated in the processes of production and consumption (to nature). We emphasize the role governments and markets play in energy and environmental policy, and we consider

the appropriate role for governments, markets, and individual values in light of concepts presented in early chapters of the text.

10. *International and comparative aspects of energy and environmental problems—ethical and managerial dimensions.* The international and comparative aspects of energy and environmental issues are stressed in sections on developments in Western Europe, Japan, and the United States. We tackle the ethical issues raised by the environmental movement and the challenges it poses to business. Finally, management is not ignored as the discussion of energy and environmental issues ends with a list of the actions managers can take.

11. *The role of technology in creating the conditions for economic growth.* We take up the important role of technology in creating the conditions needed for economic growth and prosperity, with emphasis on the international competitive dimensions (e.g., competition with Japanese technology) and obstacles inherent in bringing any new idea to fruition. Few other texts explicitly consider the important role of technology and technological innovation, which are transforming the United States and the world economy.

12. *Managing technological risks.* The text considers the impacts of new technological developments on people. We look at how society manages the potential danger, and the role of the corporation in alleviating the risks and possible harms is taken up in sections that deal with such controversial topics as the risks of everyday life and the valuation of a human life.

13. *Legal and liability aspects of new-product development—the United States and other countries compared.* We discuss the legal and liability aspects of product development and technological innovation in the United States and other countries, especially Japan. We ask students to consider different proposals for reforming the U.S. tort liability system. The text contains a chapter-length comparison of U.S. and Japanese approaches to compensating victims.

14. *Business strategy making—applying theory to real-world cases.* Theory is put into practice in cases that require the students to indicate how they would respond to actual strategy-making situations faced by businesses. The 15 cases include not only classics like Ford Pinto, Bhopal, and the Chrysler bailout but also such new cases as Dennis Levine, Control Data Corporation, Chrysler and Honda, Alliant Techsystems Inc., the future of nuclear power, ARCO Solar, and Cochlear Implants. Whenever an old case has been used, it has been updated (e.g., the Chrysler bailout case is written from the perspective of Citicorp CEO Walter Wriston, an advocate of free markets, whose bank has lent vast sums to Chrysler and who is being asked by the federal government to make bailout concessions and to testify to Congress about the bailout).

Alfred A. Marcus

ACKNOWLEDGMENTS

The supportive atmosphere for studies in business, government, and society, in business strategy, and in organizational theory that exists in the Strategic Management and Organization Department of the Carlson School, University of Minnesota, has been very conducive for the writing of this book. I would especially like to pay tribute to my colleagues Norman Bowie, Bruce Erickson, Andy Van de Ven, Ian Maitland, Stefanie Lenway, Laurent Jacque, Mary Nichols, Stuart Albert, Bala Chakravarthy, Larry Cummings, John Mauriel, Peter Ring, Ray Willis, and Phil Bromiley. This book was completed while I was on sabbatical at the Sloan School of Management at MIT. I would like to thank John Carrol for inviting me to spend time at MIT, and to thank Don Lessard, Michael Cusumano, Rebecca Henderson, and Richard Locke, in the strategy and international group at MIT, who assisted me during my stay. Many colleagues and students have played an important role in helping me to formulate the views found in this book. I would especially like to acknowledge colleagues Barry Mitnick of the University of Pittsburgh; James Post of Boston University; Ed Epstein of the University of California, Berkeley; Rogene Buchholz of Loyola University, New Orleans; Allen Kaufman of the University of New Hampshire; Rich Wokutch of VPI; and Robert Goodman of the University of Wisconsin, Madison. With regard to students, I am indebted to Gordon Rands, Isaac Fox, and Marc Weber. The special contributions of other students are cited in the individual chapters. Libby Rubenstein of Richard D. Irwin creatively managed this project and kept me on a reasonable schedule. John Pipkin of the University of Minnesota, a loyal and devoted word processor operator and talented computer user, solved the many problems I created; his extraordinary efforts helped me complete this project. Mark Jankus wrote or helped write many of the case studies and the teacher's manual. I greatly appreciated his fresh attitude toward the material and his ability to think in an organized fashion and write clearly. He has been an invaluable assistant in completing this project. Others to whom I owe a debt of gratitude are the reviewers of this manuscript for Richard D. Irwin: Robert Chatov, SUNY-Buffalo; Philip Cochran, Pennsylvania State University; Edwin Epstein, University of California, Berkeley; Nancy Hanawa, University of California, Berkeley; Marya Leatherwood, University of Illinois; Barry Mitnick, The Katz Graduate School of Busi-

ness, University of Pittsburgh; Lee Preston, University of Maryland; Kathleen Rehbein, Marquette University; Robert Weight, University of Phoenix; and David Vogel, University of California, Berkeley.

A. A. M.

CREDITS

Chapter 1, material on p. 7, adapted from *Competitive Strategy: Techniques for Analyzing Industries and Competitors* by Michael Porter, copyright 1980, permission granted by the Free Press, a Division of Macmillan, Inc.

Chapter 1, material on pp. 11–15, adapted from "Measuring Strategic Performance" by Bala Chakravarthy, *Strategic Management Journal,* copyright 1986, volume 7, pp. 437–458, permission granted by John Wiley and Sons Limited.

Chapter 3, material on pp. 62–63, reproduced from *The Republic* by Plato, copyright 1967, permission granted by Oxford University Press.

Chapter 3, material on pp. 64–66, adapted from *The Moral Dimension* by Amitai Etzioni, copyright 1988, permission granted by the Free Press, a Division of Macmillan, Inc.

Chapter 3, material on pp., 67–68, adapted from "Deterring Dubious Behavior" by Alfred Marcus, permission granted by *Executive Excellence.*

Chapter 4, material on p. 93, adapted from "Teaching Managers to do Policy Analysis" by I. Mitroff and R. Kilmann, *California Management Review,* copyright 1977, volume 20, no. 1, permission granted by the Regents of the University of California.

Chapter 6, material on p. 124, adapted from "The Organization and Staffing of Corporate Public Affairs" by S. Lusterman, 1987, permission granted by the Confederate Board.

Chapter 6, material on pp. 127–128, reproduced from "The Business Roundtable Statement on Corporate Responsibility" 1981 and "Corporate Governance and American Competitiveness," 1990, permission granted by the Business Roundtable.

Chapter 6, material on pp. 131–135, adapted from "The Causes and Consequences of Leveraged Management Buyouts" by I. Fox and A. Marcus, *The Academy of Management Review,* 1992, permission granted by The Academy of Management.

Chapter 7, material on p. 163, adapted from "The Directory of Federal Regulatory Agencies" by R. Penoyer, 1980, permission granted by the Center for the Study of American Business.

Case IIA, material on pp. 176–177, adapted from *Personality Assessment in Organizations,* edited by H. J. Bernarden and D. A. Bownas, copyright 1985, Praeger Publishers, permission granted by Greenwood Publishing Group, Inc., Westport, CT.

Case IID, material on pp. 197–199, adapted from "Troubleshooter" by D. J. Tice, 1987,

Corporate Report Minnesota, permission granted by *Corporate Report Minnesota.*

Case IIE, on pp. 204–210, written by Jolene Galegher, permission granted by Jolene Galegher.

Chapter 8, material on pp. 218–223, adapted from *Capitalism and Freedom* by Milton Friedman, 1962, permission granted by the University of Chicago Press.

Chapter 8, material on pp. 227–231, adapted from Markets or Government, by Charles Wolfe, Jr., 1988, published by MIT Press, permission granted by MIT Press.

Chapter 9, material on pp. 242–243, adapted from "The Political Pursuit of Competitive Advantage" by J. Gale and R. Buchholz in *Business Strategy and Public Policy,* edited by A. Marcus, A. Kaufman, and D. Beam, 1987, published by Greenwood Press/Quorum Books, permission granted by Greenwood Publishing Group, Inc., Westport, CT.

Chapter 9, material on pp. 248–251, adapted from *The Adversary Economy* by A. Marcus, 1984, published by Greenwood Press/Quorum Books, permission granted by Greenwood Publishing Group, Inc., Westport, CT.

Chapter 9, material on pp. 258–259, adapted from "Industrial Policy" by J. C. Miller, T. F. Walcott, W. E. Kovacic, and J. A. Rabkin, 1984, *Yale Journal on Regulation,* pp. 1–37, permission granted by the *Yale Journal on Regulation.*

Chapter 9, material on p. 259, adapted from "Reindustrialization through Coordination or Chaos," by S. E. Eizenstat, 1984, *Yale Journal on Regulation,* pp. 39–51, permission granted by the *Yale Journal on Regulation.*

Chapter 9, material on pp. 260–261, adapted from "Why It is Difficult to Implement Industrial Policies. . ." by A. Mitroff and A. Kaufman, *California Management Review,* copyright 1986, volume 28, no. 4, permission granted by the Regents of the University of California.

Chapter 11, material on pp. 299–301, 322–323, adapted from "Growth and Slowdown in Advanced Capitalist Societies," by A. Maddison, 1987, *Journal of Economic Literature," p. 649, permission granted by A. Maddison.*

Chapter 12, material on p. 387, and Case IV B, material on p. 484, reprinted from *The Dimming of America,* by Peter Navarro, copyright 1985, Ballinger, permission granted by Harper Collins Publishers Inc.

Chapter 13, material on pp. 420–425, adapted from "Policy Issues in the Natural Environment" by D. Mann and H. Ingram in *Public Policy and the Natural Environment,* pp. 15–47, permission granted by JAI Press.

Chapter 14, material on p. 446, extracted from *War on Waste,* by L. Blumberg and R. Gottlieb, 1989, permission granted by Island Press, Washington, D.C. and Covelo, California.

Case IVA, on pp. 464–479, and Case IVC on pp. 497–506, adapted from *Managing Environmental Issues,* by R. Buchholz, A. Marcus, J. Post, 1992, Prentice-Hall, permission granted by Simon & Schuster.

Case IVB, tables on pages 483, 485, 487–491 reproduced from *The Realities of Nuclear Power* by S. D. Thomas, 1988, permission granted by Cambridge University Press.

Case IVB on pp. 494–496, adapted from "Taking the Fear Out of Nuclear Power" by Ed Faltermeyer, August 1, 1988, *Fortune*, pp. 105–114, permission granted by Time Inc. All rights reserved.

Chapter 15 on p. 511, adapted from "Opening Windows. . ." by G. P. Zachary, *Wall Street Journal*, May 21, 1990, p. A1, permission granted by Dow Jones & Company, Inc. All rights reserved worldwide.

Chapter 16 on pp. 542–543, adapted from "The Perils of Prudence" by J. Morrall, *Regulation*, November/December, 1986, pp. 25–39, permission granted by The American Enterprise Institute for Public Policy Research, Washington, D.C.

Chapter 16 on pp. 556–557, adapted from "How Much Money Is Your Life Worth" by Daniel Seligman, March 3, 1986, *Fortune*, pp. 25–27, permission granted by Time Inc. All rights reserved.

Chapter 16 on pp. 546–56, adapted from "Risk, Uncertainty, and Scientific Judgement" by Alfred Marcus, 1988, 2, *Minerva*, pp. 138–152, permission granted by Minerva Quarterly Review Ltd., 19 Nottingham Road, London SW 17 7 EA, UK.

Chapter 17 on pp. 571–572, adapted from *Liability Perspectives and Policy,* edited by R. E. Litan, 1988, the Brookings Institution, Washington, D.C., permission granted by the Brookings Institution.

Chapter 17 on pp. 572–573, adapted from "The Impact of Product Liability" by E. P. McGuire, 1988, Research Report # 908, permission granted by The Conference Board.

CONTENTS IN BRIEF

CONTENTS

PART II

ETHICS AND SOCIAL RESPONSIBILITY

3   Ethics: Group Norms and the Individual   49

4   Ethical Dilemmas in Business   73

PART V

TECHNOLOGY AND THE LAW

INTRODUCTION
The Strategic Business Environment

1

UNDERSTANDING THE STRATEGIC BUSINESS ENVIRONMENT

The environment of an organization in business, like that of any other organized entity, is the pattern of all external conditions and influences that affects its life and development. The environmental influences . . . are technological, economic, physical, social, and political . . . in all these categories change is taking place at varying rates. Change . . . necessitates continuous monitoring. . . . Executives . . . must be aware of those aspects of their company's environment . . . that will affect their company's future.

Kenneth Andrews, *The Concept of Corporate Strategy.*

Introduction and Chapter Objectives

This text discusses the corporate environment:

- How are changes in values affecting the corporation's relationship to society?
- How are changes in government affecting the corporation's global competitiveness?
- How are resource availability and pollution issues having an impact on the corporation's operations?
- How are legal developments influencing its ability to make technological innovations?

This book starts with a section on ethics and social responsibility (Chapters 3 through 7 and Cases IIA, IIB, IIC, IID, and IIE). It examines government and the international economy (Chapters 8 through 11 and Cases IIIA, IIIB, IIIC, and IIID), business and the natural world

(Chapters 12 through 14 and Cases IVA, IVB, and IVC), and trends in technology and law (Chapters 15 through 18 and Cases VA, VB, and VC).

Chapter 1 discusses the effect of the strategic business environment on the firm. It addresses the extent of the firm's environment and the meaning of performance. Six aspects of the organization's environment are described. This chapter considers performance in terms of financial and nonfinancial characteristics and at several levels of analysis: individual, work unit, and organization as a whole. In addition, the static and dynamic dimensions of performance are presented, including such important elements as fit, nearness to bankruptcy, slack, reputation, innovativeness, and the organization's social performance—its ability to satisfy external constituencies.

The Strategic Business Environment

The key to a successful organization strategy is to match internal strengths and weaknesses to external opportunities and threats.[1] Strength and weakness analysis identifies the organization's distinctive competencies. That is, it highlights the characteristics that allow the organization to successfully compete with other organizations. By matching internal strengths with external challenges, managers can enhance the organization's effectiveness (see Exhibit 1–1).

The acronym for this type of analysis is SWOT, with *S* standing for strengths, *W* for weaknesses, *O* for opportunities, and *T* for threats. Determining an organization's strategy begins with identifying the opportunities and risks that exist in the environment. This text addresses changes in the business environment and strategies firms have for coping with those changes. It is organized to help managers analyze, manage, and cope with environmental change. This book divides the business environment into ethics and social responsibility, government and global competition, business and the natural world, and technology and the law.[2]

Ethics and Social Responsibility

The business system has experienced scandals that have resulted in questions about its integrity and legal and ethical standing. We need to examine the roles of greed and self-interest versus altruism and other-regarding behavior in the economy and in the business system. We also need to consider essential questions: What is the purpose of the firm? Whose interests does it serve? In addition, numerous business dilemmas involve hard choices between means and ends. Moreover, managers are often forced to choose between their responsibility to the individuals in the organization and their responsibility to maintain the

---

EXHIBIT 1–1   Analysis of the Strategic Business Environment

EXTERNAL OPPORTUNITIES AND THREATS

Government and global competition

The natural environment — Internal strengths and weaknesses — Technology and law

Ethics and social responsibility

---

organization. Questions like these require closer scrutiny by business managers.

Government and Global Competition

Government is important both because of the constraints it imposes and the opportunities it generates. For example, trends in government budgets and taxes, trade and antitrust legislation, deregulation, and defense spending have important effects on U.S. companies. Also important have been trends in the international economy: the opening up of formerly communist countries, the relationships between prosperous and poor nations, the redefinition of capitalism and socialism, changes in the military balance and in the regimes of some nations, and other worldwide developments. The rationale for government, the prospects for sustaining worldwide economic development and growth, and the comparative advantages of nations are important topics that managers have to understand.

Business and the Natural World

The relationship between the human population and the physical environment is undergoing fundamental transformation. Problems with consumption of nonrenewable energy, ozone depletion, global warming, and disposal of hazardous and nonhazardous wastes have become apparent. The natural world is the source of critical resources corporations need for production, and it is also the receptacle for the wastes that corporations and consumers generate as by-products of their activities. A better understanding of these issues is essential for management. The consequences of not understanding them will be measured in unrealized gains and avoidable losses.

Technology and the Law

This area is important because scientific discoveries lead to new products (e.g., genetic engineering), new production techniques (e.g., robotics), and new management strategies caused by computer automation. Technology also has a significant impact on such business essentials as transportation, product safety and reliability, and pollution control. However, the promise of technology often is in conflict with people's fears of its unknown dangers. Also, technological innovation is affected by the legal climate in the United States and other countries, which helps to determine how technological risks are going to be managed. Consequently, the innovation process and the liability rules that accompany new product introductions must be better understood by managers.

Environment of the Organization

Thus, the corporate environment consists of the pattern of external conditions and influences that affect its performance. Unfortunately, "a definitive conceptual framework" capable of "guiding and interpreting the full range of economic, technological, social, and political forces" that affect its performance does not exist.[3] The ability to forecast—let alone cope with—large-scale, discontinuous change in the environment is weak, and models of change in an organization's environment contain a number of fundamental differences.

The Broad Approach

The broad approach to environmental analysis describes all of the characteristics of an era in terms of values or ideologies linked to technological change or other structural features of a society.[4] This approach categorizes the culture within which the organization operates, the ideology and dominant values of society, the state of knowledge, the progress and state of technology, and the government agencies involved in setting policies in such areas as antitrust, environmental protection, safety, and antidiscrimination.[5] But however stimulating the broad approach is, it tends not to be well linked to specific industry conditions or managerial tasks.

The Industry Structure Model

In contrast, the industry structure model emphasizes the competitive forces that govern industry behavior: buyers, suppliers, substitute products and services, potential entrants, and strategic groups of directly competing firms (see Exhibit 1–2).[6] These elements establish the opportunities and threats that an organization confronts. However, they are influenced, in turn, by broader forces, including technological innovations, government policies, and social values. Technological innovations, for instance, make production scale economies possible, and these, in turn, make it difficult for competitors to enter an industry and thereby protect an organization from its competitors.

The industry structure model, moreover, is not static. Industries evolve and change. Their emergence typically follows a pattern of fragmentation, consolidation, maturity, and decline accompanied by fierce global competition. As industries mature, managers face many new challenges.

The Cognitive Model

Both the broad model and narrow one assume an objective environment lying outside the organization that managers correctly perceive. However, the extent to which managers correctly perceive external conditions is unclear.[7] Perceptions do not match objective reality because managers' cognitive abilities are limited.[8]

Managers scan the environment selectively, and many factors influence how they perceive threats and opportunities: age, personal history,

EXHIBIT 1–2 Industry Structure Model

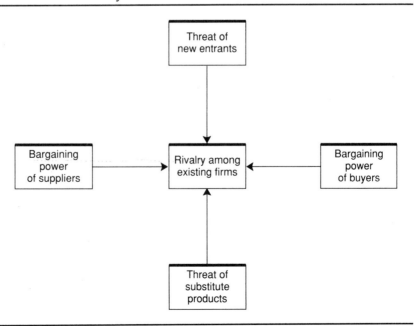

availability of information, indicators the organization uses to judge managerial performance, and the existence of external constituencies that make demands upon them.[9] In addition, cognitive schemes and biases lead managers at different levels in the organization to perceive events differently.[10] Managers categorize events, assess the consequences, and consider appropriate actions based on their different schemes and biases.[11] Environments themselves are perceptual in nature; they depend on information-gathering and -filtering systems of organizations and managers' interpretations of events.[12]

Enactment, Selection, and Retention

Environmental conditions become meaningful to managers through a process of enactment, selection, and retention (see Exhibit 1–3).[13] Enactment refers to the activities that isolate environmental conditions for closer scrutiny. Events that differ from expectations, such as indications of poor employee morale, complaints about product quality, near-accidents, or other incidents, bring conditions to the attention of managers. Selection is the effort to use prior understandings to make sense of these irregularities. Retention is storage of the information. The reformulated knowledge gained after irregularities have been analyzed is retained in the organization's files and in the memories of the individuals in the organization, and it is used when the organization confronts similar situations later.

A Critique of the Cognitive Model

While the role of perception, psychological states, and cognitive processes is important, objective environmental conditions should not be disregarded.[14] Environmental understanding cannot be reduced to "perceptions alone," for then it becomes nothing more than the "psychoanalysis of managers."[15] Indeed, a social reality exists outside managerial cognition[16] that it is not just a reflection of managers' subjective and intersubjective experience.[17]

Managers try "to understand, make sense out of, and respond to" an objective world.[18] But what they face is uncertainty in their knowl-

---

EXHIBIT 1–3   How the Business Environment Becomes Meaningful to Managers

Enactment: Environmental conditions isolated for further scrutiny.
Selection: Use of prior understandings to make sense of the irregularities.
Retention: Storage of the information gained after irregularities have been confronted.

edge of this world, which reflects itself in different ways. For example, managers are unsure of how cause and effect relationships work in the world, they have trouble assigning probabilities to future events, and they cannot know for sure what the outcomes of their decisions will be.[19]

Environmental Uncertainty

Uncertainty affects nearly everything managers do. Its sources are in both insufficient information and the inability to effectively combine and use existing information. In fact, managers may have too much information and thus be unable to discriminate between what is relevant and what is irrelevant.[20] Information overload may make it difficult to understand the environment as a whole and to see how the different parts interrelate. Also, some parts of the environment (e.g., relations with suppliers, competitors, government, or financial institutions) may generate more uncertainty than others.

Three types of uncertainty can be distinguished—state, effect, and response (see Exhibit 1–4).[21] **State** uncertainty refers to incomplete knowledge about environmental components and about the relationships among these components. These elements are in the general environment (e.g., sociocultural trends, demographic shifts, technological developments), in the structure of the industry (e.g., suppliers, competitors, and consumers), and in the organization of stakeholders outside the immediate industry structure (e.g., the government or communities where firms are located).

Effect uncertainty refers to the impact of the components on the organization. That is, information about environmental conditions may be adequate, but managers may not understand how these conditions affect their organization.

Response uncertainty refers to a "lack of knowledge of response options" and/or an "inability to predict the likely consequences of a response choice."[22] The environment and its impact on the organization may be known, but how to respond may be highly uncertain.[23]

Uncertainty generally is assumed to be negative.[24] Thus, managers take steps to overcome it, to reduce or absorb its impacts on the

---

EXHIBIT 1–4 Three Types of Uncertainty about the Business Environment

State:	Incomplete knowledge about environmental components.
Effect:	Uncertainty about the impact of environmental components on the organization.
Response:	Lack of knowledge of response options and/or inability to predict consequences of response choice.

organization. However, managers may sometimes try to increase uncertainty since it opens the possibility for change.[25] With the potential losses and reduced power that come with uncertainty, anxiety among managers runs high. As a result, uncertainty may stimulate creative thinking and help overcome the tendency toward drift and inertia.[26]

The Organizational Field Model

So far the environment has been defined as the broad social forces and narrow competitive conditions that affect the organization. It has been conceived of in objective and subjective terms and has been presented as a major source of uncertainty for managers. Often the uncertainty comes to managerial attention through the actions of other organizations with whom the managers relate. Thus, the environment also should be viewed in terms of these other organizations.

The organizational field model emphasizes the relationships organizations have with each other. Managers contend with external circumstances by making exchanges or having transactions with managers of other organizations.[27] The organizations to whom they relate correspond to the forces in the industrial structure model such as buyers, suppliers, and competitors, but are not restricted to them. Managers relate to trade associations and government regulatory agencies that are not part of this model.

The organization is part of an open system in which it depends on the resources generated by other organizations to survive. It has to negotiate or navigate between the competing demands and expectations of these organizations.[28] Supporters may include organizations that represent customers, suppliers, government agencies, and financial institutions. If unsatisfied, in either an economic or a normative sense, the supporters can switch allegiance to competitors. The relative power of the organization depends upon its ability to forge close ties with supporters so that they do not switch allegiance.[29] To do so, the organization must supply the supporters with what they need. In return, it acquires from the supporters the resources the organization needs to survive.

Environmental Turbulence

Few organizations operate in munificent environments with ample supplies of resources. For most organizations, the environment is rapidly changing, as is the organization's ability to acquire the resources it needs. Fluctuations in the ability to acquire resources is experienced as a wave function (see Exhibit 1–5).[30] With a wave there is velocity of change (its frequency), degree of change over time (the amplitude of this change), and the predictability of change (the extent to which there is directional deviation). Frequency is the number of peaks or valleys

EXHIBIT 1–5 **Flow of Resources over Time**

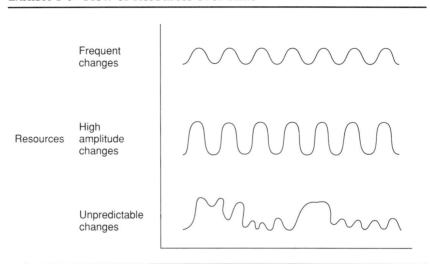

experienced, amplitude is the height and depth of these peaks and valleys, and directional deviation is the sameness in the pattern of the peaks and valleys over time.[31] For most organizations the flow of resources is neither steady nor predictable.

Managers need to cope with rapid changes in the flow of resources.[32] The challenge is compounded because environments differ not only in resource levels. They also differ in their complexity. Some environments are more interconnected and heterogeneous than others; that is, there are more organizations with whom managers have to relate and the pattern of linkages between these organizations is denser and more difficult to understand.

Nonmunificent, complex environments have been described as disturbed, unstable, volatile, and unpredictable. Environmental turbulence is central to models of strategic choice, firm failure, and executive turnover. Extreme turbulence puts the organization in jeopardy, threatens its survival, and takes away managers' opportunities to freely determine the organization's fate. Turbulent environments severely test managers' adjustment capabilities.[33]

The Performance of the Organization

The ability to cope with environmental change is critical to organizational success, but by what measure is this success to be judged? Useful measurements of performance can help assess the quality of a firm's adaptation to its environment, but performance must first be defined.[34]

Although it appears to be a simple concept, performance has been the subject of great debate.[35]

Basic Terminology and Definitions

Performance is at the core of strategic management and is the test of any strategy, but there is little agreement about basic terminology and definitions.[36] Issues such as the following have impeded efforts to achieve a consensus:

1. What is the appropriate *level of analysis*—the individual, work unit, or organization as a whole? Should concern center on the business unit or the corporate entity?

2. How should performance be differentiated from *organizational effectiveness*, which includes nonfinancial aspects of success such as the human and ethical aspects of the organization?[37] The organization has to be judged for meeting broader societal expectations, as well as for meeting the financial goals of investors.

Measurement

Evaluation of measurement approaches should lead to improved understanding of the underlying concept of performance, but still there are difficulties. Two types of basic economic indicators exist. *Accounting* measurement includes sales growth, profitability (return on investment, return on sales, return on equity), and earnings per share. *Financial* measurement (the stock market valuation of the company) includes stock market returns, ratio of market value to book value, and Tobin's Q (ratio of market value to replacement cost of assets). A basic difference between these methods is that while accounting measurement records past performance, financial indicators are meant to capture investors' sense of the company's future potential.[38] For instance, biotech firms often are making no accounting profits, but they have high stock market values because of their potential for future performance.

Economic performance, whether accounting or financial, actually is a result of *operational success* in key areas such as market share, new product introduction, product quality, marketing effectiveness, manufacturing, and technological efficiency. However, concepts of operational success are often hard to measure.

In addition, relying too greatly on *managerial perceptions* leads to problems of bias because it is difficult for managers to truthfully assess their performance. Accounting data, however, also is biased. There is ample scope for manipulation through different depreciation policies and the varied treatment given to certain revenue and expenditure items.[39]

Different performance measures can be combined and analyzed together. A factor analysis of 14 indicators has revealed four performance dimensions.[40] Profitability/cash flow and relative market position capture the *static* elements of performance; change in profitability and cash flow and growth in sales and market share capture the *dynamic* elements. However, combining different dimensions of performance into a unified concept may be misleading since it masks conflicts and trade-offs, for example, the conflict between long-term growth and short-term profitability.

Fit

Based on the idea that performance reflects a match between key organizational characteristics and the environment, the concept of fit can be used to differentiate companies.[41] There is a need to establish fit between (*a*) industry structure and competitive context,[42] (*b*) organizational structure and environment,[43] (*c*) management systems and organizational structure,[44] and (*d*) management style and strategic context.[45] Indeed, it may be necessary to synchronize all of the so-called seven S's—strategy, structure, systems, style, shared values, staff, and skill. However, the concept of matching the organization's strengths with environmental opportunities is very complicated. Defining these different concepts and assessing the fits the organization makes is difficult and time-consuming.

A Financial Screen

In their best-selling book, Peters and Waterman used a simple financial screen to distinguish excellent companies from nonexcellent companies. To make the grade, a firm had to be in the top half of its industry in four of the six measures: compound asset growth, compound equity growth, ratio of market value to book value, average return on total capital, average return on equity, and average return on sales.[46] However, these measures do not capture such important dimensions as the quality of internal processes or the ability to manage external stakeholders.[47]

Innovativeness

Peters and Waterman also relied on a measure of innovativeness.[48] Industry experts were asked to rate companies on their innovation record and on their ability to adapt to changing circumstances. However, the ratings by industry experts capture just a single dimension of performance, and the judgment of experts may be a poor basis for evaluation.

Nearness to Bankruptcy, Slack, and Company Reputation

Chakravarthy distinguished excellent from nonexcellent companies in the computer industry by using measures based on nearness to bankruptcy, slack, and company reputation.[49] Nearness to bankruptcy is assessed using "Z scores." Z scores measure survivability showing the limits below which a firm cannot slip. They are a function of working capital/total assets, retained earnings/total assets, earnings before interest and taxes/total assets, market value of equity/book value of total debt, and sales/total assets.[50]

To examine a company's ability to adapt to future environments, the *generation of slack* and *investment of slack* may be assessed (see Exhibit 1–6).[51] Slack is a measure of the cash remaining after the company has met its obligations to its primary stakeholders (i.e., customers, suppliers, shareholders, employees, etc.). Excellent firms are likely to generate more slack and to invest more than nonexcellent firms. Particularly significant will be the higher investments in research and development and in new product development by the excellent firms.

Corporate reputation may be assessed using *Fortune* surveys of knowledgeable industry experts who have ranked firms based on their ability to satisfy *stakeholders*.[52] The stakeholders are stockholders (quality of management, value as a long-term investment, financial soundness, use of assets), customers (quality of products, innovativeness), em-

---

EXHIBIT 1–6   The Generation and Investment of Slack

Generation of Slack

Profitability:
Cash flow by investment.
Return on sales.
Return on total capital.

Employee productivity:
Sales revenue per employee.

Capital productivity:
Sales revenue per dollar of total assets.

Ability to raise long-term resources:
Market to book ratio.
Debt to equity ratio.

Investment of Slack

Percentage of sales revenues allocated to R&D.
Capital expenditure increases to sales.
Working capital to sales.
Dividend payout ratio.

---

ployees (ability to attract and keep), and community (social responsibility). Reputational rankings may be good at distinguishing excellent from nonexcellent companies.

Social Performance

While admirable in its effort to go beyond mere economic indicators, Chakravarthy's analysis does not go far enough in extending the concept of organizational performance.[53] Businesses generate externalities that affect society and that cannot be captured by limiting assessment to their economic performance.[54] A full understanding of these externalities and their relationship to the firm's economic performance is needed. However, it is very difficult to measure social performance.[55] For example, the social accounting movement in the United States quickly lost momentum not only because of measurement difficulties but also because firms did not want to set up additional accounting systems for which there were no generally accepted standards.

Social performance needs better definition. It has been defined as the organization's ability to meet the demands and expectations of *external constituencies* beyond those directly linked to its product markets (for additional discussion of how various studies have analyzed social performance, see the feature, "Assessing Social Performance"). To operationalize this concept, however, an indicator of constituent satisfaction is needed.[56] For instance, it would be necessary to list all the external constituents and measure their satisfaction, obviously a very complicated task, which is made more complicated because companies are selective in regard to the stakeholders they take into consideration and the actions they take to develop relationships with these stakeholders.[57]

Summary and Conclusions

This book deals with four environmental arenas: ethics and social responsibility, government and global competition, energy and the physical environment, and technological innovation and the law. This chapter has described the environment of organizations and organizational performance. The environment has the following dimensions: (a) the characteristics of an era in terms of values and ideologies, technology, and government; (b) industry structure—buyers, suppliers, substitute products and services, potential entrants, and competitors; (c) the parts of this environment that managers view as relevant at any point in time (i.e., the perceptual, as opposed to the objective, environment); (d) the degree to which managers have certain knowledge about environmental components, their effects on the organization, and which actions the organization should take; (*e*) the relationships with other organizations that provide key resources; and (*f*) the extent to which the provision of these resources is smooth or turbulent.

Assessing Social Performance

In assessing social performance, scholars have employed some of the following methods. First, they have done content analysis of annual reports. However, attention has to be paid to the use of annual reports for purposes of impression management. Those who draft the reports may decide to systematically underrepresent their companies' social involvement because they do not want investors to know about the cost. Or they may decide to systematically overrepresent their companies' involvement to create the impression of sensitivity to nonmarket factors and ward off attacks by social activists. Another reason for overrepresenting social performance is to rationalize poor economic performance by claiming that it is a consequence of events beyond the company's control.[1]

Other scholars have relied on the Council of Economic Priorities (CEP) pollution performance index. The CEP rankings are based on the investigation of company pollution control records. However, they refer to only one aspect of social performance, and companies are selective in regard to the types of social performance they choose to emphasize.[2] Moreover, the CEP rankings are simply the judgments of a particular organization with a point of view (very liberal) that may not be generally shared.

In addition, reputational indexes, which have relied on the perceptions of individuals who are not members of the organization, have also been used to measure social performance. The ratings have been done by an editor of *Business and Society Review* (Milton Moskowitz), and business people and M.B.A. students. Other scholars have used *Fortune* magazine's rating of corporate reputation to measure social performance.[3] Still another method is to see whether companies have social responsibility programs.[4] As can be seen, all of these methods are imperfect. Exhibit 1–7 illustrates an effort to assess corporate social performance of the companies that recruit at the MIT Sloan School of Management. Sloan School M.B.A. students devised the questionnaires; what do you think of this effort?

---

[1] R. W. Ingram and K. B. Frazier. "Environmental Performance and Corporate Disclosure," *Journal of Accounting Research* 18, 1980, pp. 614–22.

[2] B. L. Kedia and E. C. Kuntz, "The Context of Social Performance: An Empirical Study of Texas Banks," in *Research in Corporate Social Performance and Policy 3*, ed. L. E. Preston (Greenwich, Conn.: JAI Press, 1981), pp. 133–54.

[3] J. McGuire, A. Sundgren, and T. Schneeweis, "Corporate Social Responsibility and Firm Financial Performance," *Academy of Management Journal*, 1988, pp. 854–72.

[4] Kedia and Kuntz, "The Context of Social Performance."

EXHIBIT 1–7

January 31, 1992

Dear _____ ,

In recent years, Sloan students have placed an increasing emphasis on personal values when making career decisions. As a result, students have become interested in learning more about prospective employers' organizational policies and sense of social responsibility. To provide students with information along these lines, the Sloan Business Ethics Group has prepared the enclosed Questionnaire on Corporate Policies and Ethics. We invite you to help us in this effort by completing the questionnaire and returning it to Sloan School of Management's Career Development Office by March 3, 1992.

With the support of the Career Development Office, the Sloan Business Ethics Group is sending the Questionnaire on Corporate Policies and Ethics to all companies that recruit at Sloan. The questionnaire covers a variety of topics in which students expressed interest in a schoolwide survey. In order to make the questionnaire manageable to recruiting firms, we have limited it to four pages and worded questions as neutrally as possible. Questions generally require either yes or no answers or simple numerical information. In a few instances, we also request brief descriptions of corporate policies or historical experiences.

The Sloan Business Ethics Group will summarize and publish the results of the questionnaire in a booklet to be available to students in the Sloan Career Development Office. We will publish responses as provided by recruiting firms, without ratings or comment. For comparison, we will accompany responses with the percentage of companies responding yes or no to each question or, for numerical responses, the mean and range of responses by industry, company size, and entire population. Copies of the actual surveys and additional information returned by companies will also be available to students in a separate binder.

The Questionnaire on Corporate Policies and Ethics is an opportunity both to help students make informed career decisions and to help companies attract M.B.A.'s with similar values and goals. We understand that some of the information requested may be sensitive in nature, and that different companies will be willing to provide different levels of information. Any questions left blank will simply be marked "no response." We encourage you to answer as many questions as possible and provide any additional information or comments which you think will be useful to prospective recruits.

If you have any questions about the questionnaire or the Sloan Business Ethics Group, please feel free to call me at (617) 621-1065 or Linda Stantial, Director of the Career Development Office, at (617) 253-6149. We hope you will join us by returning your completed questionnaire by March 3, 1992.

Sincerely,

Scott V. Seidewitz
Co-Director, Sloan Business Ethics Group

EXHIBIT 1–7 *(continued)*

Sloan Recruiter Questionnaire   Company Name:

Sloan Business Ethics Group
Questionnaire on Corporate Policies and Ethics
Please feel free to provide additional information about any question.

I. Company Information

1. General information:
    Company name: _____
    Address: _____
    _____
    Contact person (name): _____
               (title) _____
    Phone: (   ) _____

2. Company size:
    What were your company's sales in the most recent fiscal year $ _____
    What were your company's assets at the end of most recent fiscal year? $ _____
    How many people does your company currently employ? _____

3. Ownership:
    Your company is: Publicly owned _____ Privately owned _____
                    Wholly owned subsidiary of _____
    In what country is your company headquartered? _____

4. Does your company have a mission statement, credo, or other statement of purpose?
    Yes ___ No ___ If yes, please attach a copy.

II. Charitable Contributions and Community Service

1. Does your company make direct charitable contributions? Yes ___ No ___
   Does your company have a charitable foundation? Yes ___ No ___
    If yes to either, what amount of cash contributions did your company and/or
    charitable foundation donate in the latest fiscal year? $ _____
        What percentage of worldwide corporate pretax profits is this? _____
    (Optional) Attach a description of your charitable contributions program, including
    names of recipients and amounts received.

2. Does your company make in-kind contributions (product donations)?
   Yes ___ No ___
    If yes, what was the value of in-kind contributions in the most recent fiscal year? ___
   Does your company perform pro bono work for nonprofit organizations?
    Yes ___ No ___
    If yes, what percentage of client-hours is spent on pro bono work?

3. Does your company match employee contributions to charitable organizations? Yes ___
   No ___
    If yes, at what ratio are they matched? _____ Up to what contribution amount?
    _____

4. Does your company have an employee volunteer or executive loan program?
   Yes ___ No ___
    (Optional) Attach a description of your employee volunteer/executive loan programs.

Please return to Sloan Career Development Office, 50 Memorial Drive, Cambridge, MA 02139

EXHIBIT 1–7 (*continued*)

Sloan Recruiter Questionnaire   Company Name:

III. Environment

1. To what extent does your company have formal programs promoting:

	Company-wide	Only in Specific Locations	None
			___
Recycling	___	___	
			___
Use of recycled office materials	___	___	
			___
Energy conservation	___	___	
Car or van pooling and/or public transportation use	___	___	___
Reuse or recycle of manufacturing inputs (N/A __)	___	___	
Reduction of wastes, emissions, and effluents from manufacturing processes (N/A _____)	___	___	___
Design and production of ecologically sound products (N/A _____)	___	___	___

(Questions 2 and 3 apply only to manufacturing firms. Nonmanufacturing firms may leave blank.)

2. Does your company have a designated corporate environmental official?
Yes ___ No ___
   If yes, what percentage of her/his time is spent on environmental matters? _____

3. Has your company been cited by the EPA or other federal or state agencies for violations of environmental laws or regulations in the past five years? Yes ___ No ___
   If yes, how many times have you been cited in:

	Number of violations	Amount of Fines
Past year	___	___
Past 5 years	___	___

   (**Optional**) Attach a description of the nature of violations and penalties.

IV. WORK FORCE BENEFITS AND POLICIES
(Please limit responses in this section to *U.S. operations* only.)

1. To what extent does your company offer maternity leave benefits?
   Companywide ___ Only at some locations ___ Not offered ___
   If offered, how many weeks of leave do you provide:

	Paid Leave	Unpaid Leave
With current position guaranteed	___	___
With comparable position guaranteed	___	___
With comparable or lesser position guaranteed	___	___

   To what extent does your company offer paternity leave benefits?
   Companywide ___ Only at some locations ___ Not offered ___
   If offered, how many weeks of leave do you provide:

Please return to Sloan Career Development Office, 50 Memorial Drive, Cambridge, MA 02139

EXHIBIT 1–7 (*continued*)

Sloan Recruiter Questionnaire   Company Name:

	Paid Leave	Unpaid Leave
With current position guaranteed	___	___
With comparable position guaranteed	___	___
With comparable or lesser position guaranteed	___	___

2. What type of assistance does your company offer for child and/or elder care?

	Child care	Elder care
Subsidized on-site care, all locations	___	___
Subsidized on-site care, some locations	___	___
Reimbursement	___	___
Referral	___	___
No assistance	___	___

3. To what extent does your company offer the following types of flexibility in hours and work place?

	All Locations	Some Locations	No Locations
Flextime	___	___	___
Reduction of hours following parental leave	___	___	___
Work-at-home arrangements	___	___	___

4. Do you extend the same benefits provided to married employees to unmarried employees who meet defined domestic partner criteria for:
   Unmarried homosexual couples? Yes ___ No ___
   Unmarried heterosexual couples? Yes ___ No ___

5. Does your company have a policy on sexual harassment? Yes ___ No ___
   (**Optional**) If yes, please provide a copy.
   Does your company have a designated person outside of the supervisory hierarchy with whom employees can confidentially discuss concerns about sexual harassment? Yes ___ No ___
   Do you offer awareness training to discourage sexual harassment? Yes ___ No ___
   If yes, what percentage of employees have participated in it? _____

V. ADVANCEMENT OF MINORITIES AND WOMEN

1. Please indicate the percentage representation of minorities in your company:

	African-American	His-panic	Asian	Native American
U.S. work force	___	___	___	___
U.S. management staff (exempt employees)	___	___	___	___
Senior management team (executive or partner level)	___	___	___	___
Board of directors	___	___	___	___

Please return to Sloan Career Development Office, 50 Memorial Drive, Cambridge, MA 02139

EXHIBIT 1–7 (*continued*)

Sloan Recruiter Questionnaire   Company Name:

2. Please indicate the percentage representation of women in your company:
    U.S. work force   _____
    U.S. management staff (exempt employees)   _____
    Senior management team (executive or
        partner level)   _____
    Board of directors   _____

3. Does your company have officially sanctioned support groups for:
    Women? Yes ___ No ___ Lesbians and gays? Yes ___ No ___
    Minorities? Yes ___ No ___

VI. LEGAL/POLITICAL RECORD

1. Have any state or federal government agencies cited your company for major
    violations of labor, occupational safety, product safety, advertising, securities, or
    equal opportunity laws or regulations in:
    Past year? Yes ___ No ___
    Past 5 years? Yes ___ No ___
        If yes, please describe (attach additional sheets, if necessary):

    _____

    _____

2. Does your company sponsor a political action committee (PAC)? Yes ___ No ___
    If yes, how much did it contribute to political campaigns in:
        the 1987–88 election cycle?_____
        the 1989–90 election cycle?_____
    (Optional) Attach a listing of your PAC's contributions for the above election cycles.

VII. INTERNATIONAL OPERATIONS AND INVESTMENTS

1. Does your company have operations outside the U.S.? Yes ___ No ___
    If yes, do the policies described in your answers to this questionnaire apply to
    (check one):
        All international operations   _____
        Some international operations   _____
        U.S. operations only   _____

2. Does your company have operations in non-OECD (less industrialized) countries?
    Yes ___ No ___
    If yes, does your company require that these operations abide by the health and
    safety regulations of:
        The United States? Yes ___ No ___
        Each individual country? Yes ___ No ___

3. Does your company offer the same level of benefits to employees in non-OECD
    countries as given to employees in the U.S.? Yes ___ No ___

4. Please indicate the extent to which your company does business in South Africa:
    Direct operations Yes ___ No ___
    Franchise, licensing, or distribution agreements Yes ___ No ___
        If yes to either of the above, is your company a signatory to the Statement of
        Principles? Yes ___ No ___

Please return to Sloan Career Development Office, 50 Memorial Drive, Cambridge, MA 02139

Organizational performance has the following dimensions: (*a*) financial and nonfinancial performance of the individual, work unit, and the organization as a whole; (*b*) accounting and stock market evaluation; (*c*) operational success; (*d*) managerial perceptions; (*e*) changes in performance; (*f*) fits between strategy, structure, systems, style, shared values, staff, and skill; (*g*) innovativeness; (*h*) nearness to bankruptcy; (*i*) slack; (*j*) reputation; and (*k*) social performance (i.e., the ability to satisfy external constituencies).

Relationships between social and other types of performance are explored in the next chapter.

Discussion Questions

1. What does SWOT stand for? What kind of analysis does it call for? To what extent is this type of analysis useful? How easy is it to carry out?

2. Compare and contrast the notion of the broad environment with the industry structure model. What relationships are likely between these two notions of the organization's environment?

3. What is the point made by those who consider the cognitive environment to be important? What is meant by enactment, selection, and retention? Is there an objective environment? What is your opinion?

4. Some managers complain that they just don't understand what is happening in the environment. Others say that they understand what is happening, but they don't know how it will affect their organization. Still others say that they understand how it is affecting their organization, but they do not know what to do with the information. What do these three statements illustrate? Which type of uncertainty is the most important?

5. What is the organizational field model?

6. Environmental turbulence may be viewed in terms of the velocity, amplitude, and predictability of change in resources. How useful is this depiction?

7. What level of analysis is most appropriate in performance assessment?

8. To what extent is organizational effectiveness synonymous with the financial performance of the organization?

9. Distinguish accounting and financial measures of success.

10. What does the term *fit* imply?

11. How would you determine if a company was innovative?
12. How useful is company reputation as a measure of success?
13. What is meant by the term *slack?* Why is it important?
14. What is social performance? How can it be measured?

Endnotes

1. K. Andrews, *The Concept of Corporate Strategy* (Homewood, Ill.: Richard D. Irwin, 1987).
2. J. Bower, C. Bartlett, C. Christensen, A. Pearson, and K. Andrews. *Business Policy: Text and Cases* (Homewood, Ill.: Irwin Mirror, 1991).
3. R. Lenz and I. Engledow, "Environmental Analysis: The Applicability of Current Theory," *Strategic Management Journal* 7, 1986, p. 340.
4. D. Bell, *The Coming of Post-Industrial Society: A Venture in Social Forecasting* (New York: Basic Books, Inc., 1973); G. Lodge, *The New American Ideology* (New York: Alfred Knopf, 1975).
5. R. Butler and M. Carney, "Strategy and Strategic Choice: The Case of Telecommunications," *Strategic Management Journal* 7, 1986, pp. 161–77.
6. M. Porter, *Competitive Strategy* (New York: The Free Press, 1980).
7. R. B. Duncan, "Characteristics of Organizational Environments and Perceived Environmental Uncertainty," *Administrative Science Quarterly* 17, 1972, pp. 313–27; J. M. Pennings, "Strategically Interdependent Organizations," in *Handbook of Organizational Design 1,* ed. P. C. Nystrom and W. H. Starbuck (New York: Oxford University Press, 1981), pp. 433–55.
8. J. G. March and H. A. Simon, *Organizations* (New York: Wiley, 1958).
9. A. Tversky and D. Kahneman, "Judgment under Uncertainty: Heuristics and Biases," *Sciences* 185, 1974, pp. 1124–31; S. Keisler and L. Sproul, "Managerial Response to Changing Environments: Perspectives and Problem Sensing from Social Cognition," *Administrative Science Quarterly* 37, 1982, pp. 548–70.
10. D. C. Hambrick, "Environmental Scanning and Organizational Strategy," *Strategic Management Journal* 3, 1982, pp. 159–74.
11. R. Ireland, M. Hitt, R. Bettis, and D. De Porras, "Strategy Formulation Processes: Differences in Perceptions of Strength and Weaknesses Indicators and Environmental Uncertainty by Managerial Level," *Strategic Management Journal* 8, 1987, pp. 469–85.
12. W. H. Starbuck, "Organizations and Their Environments," in *Handbook of Industrial and Organizational Psychology,* ed. M. Dunnette (Chicago: Rand-McNally, 1976), pp. 1069–1124.
13. K. Weick, "Enactment Processes in Organizations," in *New Directions in Organizational Behavior,* ed. B. Staw and G. Salancik (Chicago: St. Clair Press, 1977).
14. H. K. Downey, D. Hellreigel, and J. W. Slocum. "Individual Characteristics as Sources of Perceived Uncertainty Variability," *Human Relations* 30, 1977,

pp. 161–74; A. H. Van de Ven, A. L. Delbecq, and R. Koenig, "Determinants of Coordination Modes within Organizations," *American Sociological Review* 41, 1976, pp. 322–38; H. K. Downey, D. Hellreigel, and J. W. Slocum, "Environmental Uncertainty: The Construct and Its Operationalization," *Administrative Science Quarterly* 2, 1958, pp. 409–43.

15. F. Milliken, "Three Types of Perceived Uncertainty about the Environment: State, Effect, and Response Uncertainty," *Academy of Management Journal*, 1987, p. 134.

16. L. Jauch and K. Kraft, "Strategic Management of Uncertainty," *Academy of Management Review* 13, 1986, pp. 777–90.

17. G. Morgan, "Paradigms, Metaphors, and Puzzle Solving in Organization Theory," *Administrative Science Quarterly* 25, 1980, p. 608.

18. Milliken, "Perceived Uncertainty," p. 133.

19. Duncan, "Characteristics of Organizational Environments."

20. W. E. Gifford, H. R. Bobbitt, and J. W. Slocum, "Message Characteristics and Perceptions of Uncertainty by Organizational Decision Makers," *Academy of Management Journal* 22, 1979, pp. 458–81.

21. Milliken, "Perceived Uncertainty."

22. Milliken, "Perceived Uncertainty." p. 137.

23. P. R. Lawrence and J. W. Lorsch, "A Reply to Tosi, Aldag and Storey," *Administrative Science Quarterly* 18, 1973, pp. 397–98.

24. March and Simon, *Organizations*; R. M. Cyert and J. G. March, *A Behavioral Theory of the Firm* (Englewood Cliffs, N.J.: Prentice Hall, 1963).

25. Jauch and Kraft, "Strategic Management"; R. E. Miles and C. C. Snow, *Organizational Strategy, Structure, and Process* (New York: McGraw-Hill, 1978).

26. I. I. Mitroff and R. H. Kilmann, "Teaching Managers to Do Policy Analysis: The Case of Corporate Bribery," *California Management Review* 20 (1), 1977, pp. 47–54.

27. J. Pfeffer and G. R. Salancik. *The External Control of Organizations: A Resource Dependence Perspective* (New York: Harper and Row, 1978); O. E. Williamson, *Markets and Hierarchies: Analysis and Antitrust Implications* (New York: Free Press, 1975).

28. Pfeffer and Salancik, *External Control*; L. J. Bourgeois and W. G. Astley, "A Strategic Model of Organizational Conduct and Performance," *International Studies of Management and Organization* 9, 1979, pp. 40–46; Butler and Carney, "Strategy and Strategic Choice."

29. Butler and Carney, "Strategy and Strategic Choice."

30. D. Wholey and J. Brittain, "Characterizing Environmental Variation," *Academy of Management Review* 16, 1989, pp. 867–82.

31. Ibid.

32. H. E. Aldrich, *Organizations and Environments* (Englewood Cliffs, N.J.: Prentice Hall, 1979).

33. F. E. Emery and E. L. Trist, "The Causal Texture of Organizational Environments," *Human Relations* 18, 1965, pp. 21–32; Aldrich, *Organizations and Environments.*

34. B. Chakravarthy, "Measuring Strategic Performance," *Strategic Management Journal* 7, 1986, pp. 437–58; R. T. Lenz, "Determinants of Organizational Performance: An Interdisciplinary Review," *Strategic Management Journal* 2,

1981, pp. 131–54; J. Child, "Management and Organizational Factors Associated with Company Performance—Parts I and II," *Journal of Management Studies* 2, 1974, pp. 175–89, and 1974, pp. 12–27.

35. Chakravarthy, "Measuring strategic performance."
36. D. E. Schendel and C. W. Hofer, eds., *Strategic Management: A New View of Business Policy and Planning* (Boston: Little, Brown, 1979).
37. P. S. Goodman and J. M. Pennings, eds., *New Perspectives on Organizational Effectiveness* (San Francisco: Jossey-Bass, 1977); R. Steers, "Organizational Effectiveness: A Behavioral View," in *The Goodyear Series in Management and Organizations* (Santa Monica, Calif.: Goodyear, 1977); M. T. Hannan, J. Freeman, and J. W. Meyer, "Specification of Models for Organizational Effectiveness," *American Sociological Review* 41, 1976, pp. 136–43.
38. A. Rappaport, "Selecting Strategies That Create Shareholder Value," *Harvard Business Review* 3, 1981, pp. 139–49.
39. J. McGuire and T. Schneeweis, *An Analysis of Alternate Measures of Strategic Performance,* paper presented at the third annual conference of the Strategic Management Society, Paris, 1983.
40. C. Y. Woo and G. Willard, *Performance Representation in Business Policy Research: Discussion and Recommendation,* paper presented at the 23rd annual national meetings of the Academy of Management, Dallas, 1983. The 14 indicators are return on investment (ROI), return on sales, growth in revenues, cash flow/investment, market share, market share gain, product quality relative to competitors, new product activities relative to competitors, direct cost relative to competitors, product R&D, variations in ROI, percentage change in ROI, and percentage change in cash flow.
41. Chakravarthy, "Measuring Strategic Performance."
42. Porter, *Competitive Strategy;* B. D. Henderson, *Henderson on Corporate Strategy* (Cambridge, Mass.: Abt Books, 1979).
43. P. Lawrence and J. Lorsch, *Organization and Its Environment* (Boston: Harvard University Press, 1967).
44. R. E. Miles and C. C. Snow, *Organizational Strategy, Structure, and Process* (New York: McGraw-Hill, 1978).
45. H. Mintzberg and J. A. Waters, "The Mind of the Strategist(s)," in *The Executive Mind,* ed. S. Srivastava (San Francisco, Calif.: Jossey-Bass, 1983).
46. T. J. Peters and R. H. Waterman, *In Search of Excellence: Lessons from America's Best Run Companies* (New York: Harper & Row, 1982).
47. R. E. Freeman, "A Typology of Enterprise Strategy," in *Strategic Management: A Stakeholder Approach* (Boston: Pitman, 1984), pp. 101–7.
48. Peters and Waterman, *In Search of Excellence.*
49. Chakravarthy, "Measuring Strategic Performance."
50. E. I. Altman, *Corporate Bankruptcy in America* (Lexington, Mass.: Heath Lexington Books, 1971); J. Argenti, *Corporate Collapse: The Causes and Symptoms* (New York: John Wiley, 1976).
51. Chakravarthy, "Measuring Strategic Performance."
52. Ibid.
53. Ibid.
54. K. W. Kapp, *The Social Costs of Private Enterprise* (Cambridge, Mass.: Harvard University Press, 1950); A. C. Pigou, *Economics of Welfare,* 4th ed. (London: Macmillan, 1960).

55. A. Ullman, "Data in Search of a Theory: A Critical Examination of the Relationships among Social Performance, Social Disclosure, and Economic Performance of U.S. Firms," *Academy of Management Review* 11, 1984, pp. 545–57.

56. M. A. Keeley, "Social Justice Approach to Organizational Evaluation," *Administrative Science Quarterly* 23, 1978, pp. 272–92; R. H. Kilmann and R. P. Herden, "Towards a Systematic Methodology for Evaluating the Impact of Interventions on Organizational Effectiveness," *Academy of Management Review* 3, 1976, pp. 87–98.

57. Pfeffer and Salancik, *External Control.*

2

ADJUSTING TO CHANGES IN THE STRATEGIC BUSINESS ENVIRONMENT

Innovative companies are especially adroit at responding to change in their environment. . . . When the environment changes, these companies change too. As the needs of their customers shift, the skills of their competitors improve, the mood of the public perturbates, the forces of international trade realign, and government regulations shift, these companies tack, revamp, adjust, transform, and adapt.

Thomas J. Peters and Robert H. Waterman, *In Search of Excellence.*

Introduction and Chapter Objectives

This chapter examines how corporations adjust to changes in the strategic business environment. We discuss the relationships between a firm's social and financial performance, as well as the strategies managers use to align their companies with forces emanating from the environment. We consider the managerial role in strategic change. Can managers make a difference? How effective can they be in aligning their organizations with environmental change?

Connecting Economic and Social Performance

Matching external opportunities and threats with internal capabilities is a central part of strategy, but it is not all there is to strategy. In developing an overall strategy, the corporation must acknowledge its noneconomic responsibilities to society. These responsibilities go beyond the fiduciary obligations managers owe shareholders. Thus, a corporation's strategy shows what the company stands for—the mission, function, and purpose—in light of both society's standards and managers' values (see Exhibit 2–1).

Four relationships between a firm's economic and social performance are possible:[1]

1. Profitability and social performance are *positively* related: profitable firms are better social performers.
2. Profitability and social performance are *negatively* related: profitable firms are poorer social performers.
3. There is *no relationship* between economic and social performance.
4. There is an *inverted U-shaped* relationship: very profitable and unprofitable firms are not good social performers. Firms in the middle are the best social performers.

Why would a positive relationship (see Exhibit 2–2) exist between economic and social performance (firms that have a good effect on society are also highly profitable)? The direction of causation plays a very important role.

Companies Can Afford to Be Good

If economic performance influences social performance, then well-to-do companies can afford positive social performance. According to this view, a firm's economic performance affects its capability to undertake programs to meet social demands. Thus, firms need excess resources to be good social performers because social performance involves substantial costs, and only firms with these resources are capable of absorbing these costs.[2]

EXHIBIT 2–1   **Factors That Affect Competitive Strategy**

External to the company:

    Industry opportunities and threats (economic and technical).
    Broader societal expectations

Internal to the company:

    Company strengths and weaknesses.
    Personal values of key implementors.

EXHIBIT 2–2   A Positive Relationship between Financial and Social Performance

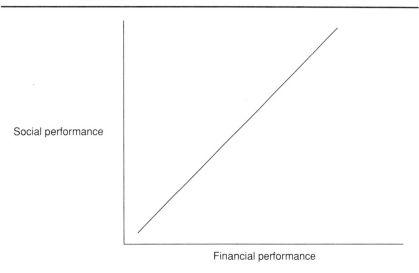

Social performance

Financial performance

It Pays to Be Good

If the direction of causation is reversed, a different interpretation is in order. According to this perspective, good social performance contributes to economic performance, that is, it *pays to be good*.

In what sense can this be true?

1. It is possible that the *quality and skills* of good social management also apply to the economic sphere; that is, management excellence in one area has some bearing upon excellence in the other area. Socially aware and concerned management may possess the skills needed to run a superior company in the traditional financial sense.[3] These skills may be sensitivity to outside forces and creative adjustment to external pressures.

2. Social performance may benefit the corporation by creating *goodwill*, a very important asset because it exerts positive pressure on employees, customers, government officials, bankers, investors, and other important constituencies to be favorably disposed to the corporation.[4]

3. Being perceived as a good social performer may raise *employee morale* and result in increased productivity. Fewer strikes and work stoppages may more than offset the other costs associated with being socially responsible.

4. A reputation for social performance may enhance *customer loyalty*. To satisfy customers' claims for perceived quality may be easier than to satisfy their claims for better products.

5. Goodwill may ease tensions with *government officials*, making it less likely that the corporation will pay large fines and become involved in lengthy suits.

Performance Cycles

Good economic performance may be a precondition for good social performance (if a firm is not profitable, it cannot be a good social performer), and it may be a consequence of good social performance (it pays to be good). *Beneficent cycles* exist when strong economic performance contributes to strong social performance, which in turn contributes to strong economic performance.[5] *Vicious cycles* exist when poor economic performance contributes to poor social performance, which in turn contributes to poor economic performance (see Exhibit 2–3).

Bad Firms That Prosper

If firms that have a bad effect on society are highly profitable, it suggests that there is *a simple trade-off* between social performance and economic performance: firms cannot afford both. The bad firms prosper, achieving their economic success at the expense of society, while the good firms suffer on account of their social performance (see Exhibit 2–4). Accordingly, social performance is detrimental to economic performance because it imposes costs. Paying these costs puts the firm at a disadvantage

---

EXHIBIT 2–3   Beneficent and Vicious Cycles: Positive and Negative Feedback Loops

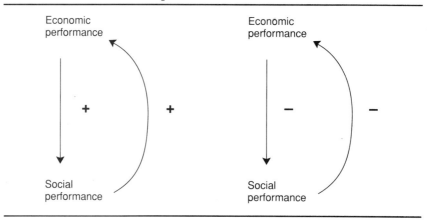

EXHIBIT 2–4   **A Negative Relationship between Financial and Social Performance**

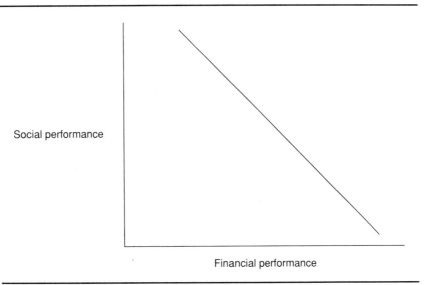

Social performance

Financial performance

---

in comparison to its competitors. For example, Milton Friedman argues that firms should not volunteer social performance activities because their primary obligation is to shareholders.[6]

Neither Good nor Bad

Of course, it is also possible that there is no relationship between social and economic performance, or that the relationship is not a linear one. A nonlinear relationship implies that too much or too little social performance is detrimental to the firm's economic performance. This condition is illustrated by an inverted U-shaped curve (see Exhibit 2–5), where a firm's economic performance is likely to be enhanced only if its social performance is somewhere *in the middle*. In this scenario, firms in deep economic trouble are most likely to cut back on their social spending, and firms with an extremely positive economic performance may have achieved their success at the expense of society.

Other Factors to Consider

Understanding the relationship between a company's social and economic performance must take into account industry, company size, availability of slack resources, age of assets, the firm's age, and other factors.[7] For example, the specific risk and performance patterns in an

EXHIBIT 2–5   **An Inverted U-Shaped Relationship between Financial and Social Performance**

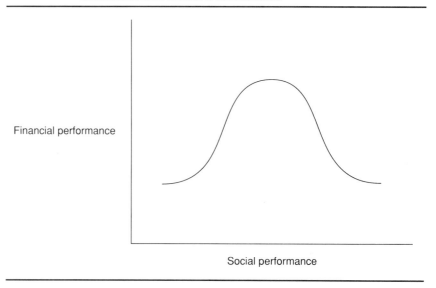

Financial performance

Social performance

industry are likely to be important. Also, stakeholders often focus their demands on the most conspicuous industries and firms, often the largest in an industry. At the same time, however, large companies also are likely to have financial, managerial, and technical know-how and are likely to be able to achieve economies of scale or scope in social performance. They also are likely to have more bargaining power with government officials and may be more able to obtain concessions that can result in delays in implementing social demands. In comparison, older firms are likely to have higher costs of upgrading old facilities for such purposes as pollution control. They may also have more rigid organizational structures, permitting less managerial flexibility in responding to social demands (see "Corporate Crime" on page 37).

The Effects of Strategy

A company's business strategy influences its social performance, and its social performance affects its business strategy (see Exhibit 2–6). Strategies, the patterns of resource allocations that managers make over time, reflect the organization's responses to volatile environments.[8] Strategy *content* refers to the specific decisions about the corporation's goals, scope, and competitive approaches.[9] Strategic *process* refers to how these decisions are made. *Content* results in a *position* that shows the firm's choices about its product and markets and how it is trying to achieve

EXHIBIT 2–6   The Effect of Strategy on Social Performance

competitive advantage in relation to firms offering similar goods and services. *Process* is a *perspective* "through which problems are spotted and interpreted and from which streams of decisions flow."[10]

Content

Content decisions are made at both the corporate and business levels. At the *corporate* level, managers select the firm's products and markets. They define the businesses in which it will operate and the companies against whom it will compete.

An important content issue is the degree of business diversification and the relatedness of the businesses in which a firm operates. On the one hand, managers must decide if there is less risk in being in unrelated businesses—the appeal of the conglomerate structure. On the other hand, they must decide if economies of scale, scope, or learning are to be realized through specialization. They must weigh the advantages of horizontal and vertical integration. What can the firm gain from upstream or downstream acquisitions or mergers, and so on?

At the *business* level, the questions are different. Once managers decide which environments the firm will call its own, the issues are how to compete in those environments. Within product and market domains, managers must decide price and quality. Then they have to deploy resources in functional areas to reflect these choices. Marketing and sales, manufacturing, R&D, accounting, and control have to be aligned to support the competitive strategies the managers have chosen.

Strategic Typologies

Typologies are commonalities in business strategies that are similar across organization types, technologies, and industries.[11] Three types of typologies will be discussed.

1. Adaptation.   The major strategic categories in this framework are defenders, prospectors, analyzers, and reactors (see Exhibit 2–7). When the organization's environment is stable, the appropriate strategy is to be a *defender.* The organization then adopts a single core technology that

EXHIBIT 2–7 **Adaptation**

	Defender	Prospector	Analyzer
Environment	Stable	Expanding	Stable/expanding
Technology	Cost-effective	Flexible	Cost-effective/ flexible
Planning	Centralized	Opportunistic search	Centralized/oppor- tunistic search
Organization	Mechanistic	Organic	Mechanistic/ organic

Reactor: Fails to align technology, planning, and organization with the environment

is highly cost-effective. It engages in intensive planning and centralized control to maintain stability. A mechanistic (rigid, control-oriented, bureaucratic) structure is necessary.[12]

When the organization's environment is broad and continuously expanding, the appropriate strategy is to be a *prospector.* The organization then monitors a wide range of environmental conditions in search of new product and market opportunities. It relies on flexible technologies with a relatively low degree of routinization. Under these conditions an organic (loose, innovative, unbureaucratic) structure is necessary.[13]

In a mixed domain, the appropriate strategy is to be an *analyzer.* The organization attempts to locate and exploit new product and market opportunities, while clinging to its base of traditional products and customers. It develops a dual technical core representing stable and flexible components and a dual structure reflecting mechanistic and organic elements.

The *reactor* fails to appropriately take into account environmental conditions, whether they are stable or changing. It does not align itself to its environment, and as a result it stresses neither cost effectiveness, new products and markets, nor some combination of the two. Alignment between strategy, environment, technology, and structure is not made, and therefore performance deteriorates.

2. Uniqueness.   According to Porter, performance depends upon the firm's ability to influence the forces in its environment that determine its profitability.[14] These forces are the threat of new competitors, rivalry among existing competitors, the threat of substitute products, bargaining power of buyers, and bargaining power of suppliers (see the last

---

EXHIBIT 2–8   **Uniqueness**

Focus: Degree of specialization, width of product lines, target customer
                        segments, geographic markets

Low cost: Price, high volume, homogeneous product, experience curve effects,
                        investment in cost minimizing facilities and equipment, economies of
                        scale and scope in production, advertising, distribution, and
                        procurement

Differentiation: *Customer:* advertising and sales force, brand identification with
                        customer, distribution channel, company-owned outlets, specialty
                        outlets, broad line outlets, extent of company-owned forward
                        integration, extent of company-owned service network, engineering,
                        credit

                        Supplier: product quality, raw materials, specifications of product,
                        tolerances, special features, captive supplier (extent of backward
                        integration)

---

chapter). The firm can influence these forces by generating strategic advantage through uniqueness, which derives from overall cost leadership, differentiation, or focus (see Exhibit 2–8).

Cost leadership signifies high market share and/or favorable access to raw materials. The firm typically adopts an aggressive strategy of construction of efficient-scale facilities, tight cost and overhead control, avoidance of marginal customer accounts, and cost minimization in areas such as R&D, service, sales force, and advertising.[15]

Differentiation means that the firm offers products or services that are unique along several dimensions such as brand image, technology, features, customer service, or dealer network. These unique features attract a premium price. The attributes can be varied in quantity or combined in different ways to differentiate the product. In consumer goods industries, advertising is the most obvious method of achieving differentiation.

Focus signifies that the firm has a narrow strategic target. It emphasizes a particular consumer group or segment of a product line. Cost leadership and differentiation can be combined with focus.

Being "stuck in the middle" is the low profitability strategy. The tendency of organizations is to move toward the middle, and therefore strong leadership is needed to prevent firms from drifting in this direction. The generic strategies imply specific organizational arrangements, control procedures, and incentive systems that are different from each other. Implementing them successfully requires the ability to use particular resources and skills. A firm cannot be successful at two strategies at once. The resources and skills needed to succeed at one are not interchangeable with those required by another.

Corporate Crime

Studies of white-collar crime provide important insights and raise interesting questions:

Are managers rational about corporate crime? Do they calculate the benefits of illegal activities and compare them to the probability of detection times the costs of getting caught?[1] If managers are rational actors, then the way to reduce corporate crime is to change the cost-benefit calculus, to impose more onerous consequences on the offenders (large fines, more public shame and humiliation), and to increase the likelihood of getting caught (larger enforcement budgets).[2]

Do declining economic conditions affect the performance of illegal acts? When there is a downturn in organizational performance, depression within an industry, or general recession, organizational crime should go up.[3] Criminal acts appear more attractive as the environment becomes constrained. As economic pressure on the firm increases, managers get desperate, and they feel justified in committing illegal acts. They exaggerate the benefits of carrying out illegal acts and underestimate the costs. Studies suggest that illegal behavior increases in a scarce (nonmunificent) environment characterized by poor prior industry performance (measured by return on equity and return on sales). Violating firms are less profitable than firms in general but not less profitable than other firms in their industry.[4]

What is the role of ethical climate in illegal behavior? Not surprisingly, financial strain often appears as a rationale for dubious behavior.[5] Violations can increase sales and profits or improve market share and can help cut costs. But are not all firms motivated by the desire to improve their economic performance? Does the additional stress of economic decline really make a difference in a firm's decision to commit unethical acts? According to Yeager, the relationships between economic performance and corporate illegality are generally weak.[6] Other factors seem to explain the differences between violating

---

[1]P. Bromiley and A. Marcus. "The Deterrent to Dubious Corporate Behavior," *Strategic Management Journal* 10, 1989, pp. 233–50.

[2]G. Geis and R. F. Meier, *White-Collar Crime: Offenses in Business, Politics and the Professions* (New York: The Free Press, 1977).

[3]E. Szwajkowski, "Organizational Illegality: Theoretical Integration and Illustrative Application," *Academy of Management Review*, 1985, pp. 558–67.

---

[4]Ibid.

[5]P. C. Yeager, "Analyzing Corporate Offenses: Progress and Prospects," *Corporate Social Performance and Policy*, 1986, pp. 93–120; P. Asch and J. J. Seneca, "Is Collusion Profitable?" *The Review of Economics and Statistics*, 58, 1976, pp. 1–12.

[6]Yeager, "Analyzing Corporate Offenses," pp. 93–120.

3. Life Cycle.   Product life cycle might be the most significant environmental factor in formulating a successful strategy (see Exhibit 2–9). According to this framework, the first strategy is to *develop* a new product or service.[16] The interest of the organization is in long-term growth through exploiting new market opportunities. The organic structure prevails and marketing, technology, and R&D are stressed. The organization seeks out and appraises opportunities. Investment in launching

Corporate Crime continued

from nonviolating firms, including "different ethical climates."[7]

Although environmental stress is a motive for dubious activities, it should not be viewed as its cause. For that, one must turn to the organizational climate and the control mechanisms that permit illegal activity in an organization, and the personality and character of the individuals involved. In the final analysis illegal behavior is a matter of free choice (see Case IIA, concerning Dennis Levine). Situations do not cause it.

Criminal behavior is learned in isolation from the rest of society and in close association with those who define such behavior favorably.[8] This theory of criminal behavior is called referent group theory. In some companies, employees so completely identify with the company's production, profit, growth, and other goals that they subordinate their individual values to the company. They lose a sense of their own identity. Their values and personality structure are fragile and are broken by strong company pressures and other stresses.

Case studies suggest that corporate illegalities become a way of life in organizations.[9] When organization members are asked to give their own reasons why corporate crime takes place, they rarely mention economic pressures. Instead, they point to the ethical climate and the influence of leadership.[10] Also, highly mobile leaders who are more interested in financial results and in advancing their careers than in the firm's reputation create in their employees' eyes a weak climate for resisting corporate illegality.

In addition, size can make a difference. For instance, dominant companies in uncompetitive industries may be able to pass on costs to consumers and therefore be more compliant.[11] And in large organizations where hierarchical relations prevail, lower level employees may feel that they are supposed to achieve profit and growth targets without regard to ethical and legal considerations. In large complex organizations, illegalities can occur because the division of labor keeps upper level persons protected by a "veil of ignorance." Superiors do not want to know how results have been obtained so long as the results are achieved.

---

[7]Ibid., p. 99.

[8]E. H. Sutherland, *White Collar Crime* (New York: Holt, 1949), p. 234.

[9]Geis and Meier, *White-Collar Crime.*

[10]M. B. Clinard, *Corporate Ethics and Crime: The Role of Middle Management* (Beverly Hills: Sage, 1983).

[11]P. C. Yeager, *The Politics of Corporate Social Control: The Federal Response to Industrial Water Pollution,* unpublished Ph.D. dissertation. University of Wisconsin, Madison, 1981; P. C. Yeager, *Structural Biases in Regulatory Law Enforcement,* paper presented at the annual meetings of the Society for the Study of Social Problems, Washington, D.C., 1985.

and developing new products and processes is high. The organization engages in extensive market development and pursues market share. Flexibility of operations and technological risk taking are the hallmarks of this strategy. The aim is to generate long-term earnings, not short-term profits.

The second strategy is to *stabilize* the market. If the organization operates in a homogeneous market, it competes through price/cost

---

EXHIBIT 2–9   The Life-Cycle Typology

Develop	New markets, technological risk taking
Stabilize	Cost leadership or differentiation
Turnaround	Survival, reverse cash flow problems
Harvest	Wind down, sell, or liquidate

---

margins. It pursues a cost leadership approach using tight mechanistic structures and efficient manufacturing processes and procedures to produce a limited set of products. Another stabilization strategy is differentiation. The organization creates a niche, making it difficult for competitors to penetrate. It defends its brand name or other product characteristics. It emphasizes specialization, high quality and distinctive service, convenient distribution, or close customer contact. By focusing on the consumer's specific needs regarding the product, profitability is maintained in a mature market.

The third strategy is *turnaround*. Survival is the goal. The company has an urgent need to reverse cash flow problems; it has to stop the hemorrhaging and rebuild. After a tightening of operations, there can be a redirection of the organizations and units worth saving. Thus, cost efficiency and controls are introduced, and the organization rationalizes product lines by phasing out unprofitable assets, units, and products. Reorganization through diversification, expansion, acquisition, merger, or integration may follow. The temptation to use white collar crime to turn around the company may be strong.

The final strategy is to *harvest*. The company decides to wind down, sell, or liquidate assets that are not meeting performance criteria, such as ROA. It eliminates assets that are incompatible with the core business, culture, or perceived expertise of company, or that do not fit with the strategic direction. Harvesting can be imposed by the situation, it can be planned, or it can be emergent, that is, a decision made after trial-and-error efforts to change the situation. There may be significant exit barriers that affect the ability to carry out this strategy, including legislative, social, and moral issues, as well as management issues of pride and competitiveness.

Process

In addition to making strategic decisions, firms must also make process decisions about the types of formal and informal management control systems and structures they will have. Within this realm, the systems for data collection, event reporting, tracking, monitoring, guiding, and controlling are important.[17]

The organization records past events and compares them with what it plans to accomplish. These efforts produce "alert" messages. When something goes wrong, the organization takes actions to correct deficiencies. It exercises control when these actions have not been taken. Documents and reports produced as events occur show how the firm corrects error and aligns its expectations with reality.

Managers use the organization's processes to steer it through troubled environments. As they move forward, managers test environments for obstacles not originally anticipated. How managers handle discrepancies shows something about the long-standing norms that govern the organization's relationships to its employees and the outside world. They represent the organization's culture, ideology, and basic paradigm of interpreting and interacting with the world. The values that the processes represent, in turn, help determine how the firm chooses its domain and how it chooses to compete within that domain.

Strategic Change

This book is dedicated to helping managers make better choices. The basic premise of the text is that organizational effectiveness depends on the ability of the organization to adapt to its environment. The strategies management chooses constitute the means by which it adapts. Thus, environmental change should lead to changes in organizational strategies.

In the real world, change in organizational environments is rampant. For example, globalization has yielded intense competitive pressures, and government policies have shifted the conditions under which industries and firms operate. Also, government has provided and taken away incentives for investment; it has introduced and then removed import, export, and trade barriers, duties and quotas, health and safety standards, and antitrust regulations. Its macroeconomic policies have influenced economic growth, employment, and the inflation rate. Deregulation and technological discontinuities have had major effects on such industries as telecommunications, banking, and airlines. Changes in strategy should be able to influence organizational performance by restoring or improving the organization's alignment with its environment.

Can Managers Make a Difference?

This book is designed to give managers better environmental-scanning capabilities. Daft et al. find that executives in high performing companies scan the environment "more frequently and more broadly than their counterparts in low performing companies.[18] But with better information can managers make a difference?

One important school of thought on organizations, the organizational ecology school, views the environment as determining organizational success and survival.[19] According to this view, managers have little influence. Instead, the availability of capital and financial resources, technological innovation, the expansion of market opportunities, and the political stability needed to engage in future-oriented behavior originate in the organization's environment, and they determine its success. Evidence for this viewpoint comes from biological analogies, taken from the evolution of species. Variation, selection, retention, and survival are environmentally determined as organizations pass through inevitable cycles of creation, growth, and decline.

In contrast, institutional theorists take the point of view that managers can influence the fate of organizations by achieving harmony with existing environmental contingencies.[20] Certainly, the environment imposes constraints on organizations, but managers choose how to respond to the constraints. They learn by copying what other organizations do; they may use the constraints for winning attention, gaining approval, and achieving legitimacy. Of course, the environment also offers incentives, and managers decide to take advantage of them. But they are not at the mercy of environmental forces; they mold the environment as well as being shaped by it. They interact with the environment and change the conditions that affect organizational survival.

Managers face different situations with respect to environmental determinism and choice (see Exhibit 2–10): (1) there can be high determin-

---

EXHIBIT 2–10   Choice and Determinism

		Choice	
		High	*Low*
Determinism	*High*	Analyze: Some options open	Defend: Few options available
	Low	Prospect: Many options open	React: Failure to grasp available options

ism and low choice (the classic natural selection approach, where choice is severely restricted); (2) there can be low determinism and high choice (the classic strategic choice situation, where managers have numerous options open to them); (3) there can be high determinism and high choice (where some options in some areas have been foreclosed, but other options remain open); and (4) there can be low determinism and low choice (where options are available, but managers fail to grasp them as they muddle along as if they had no choices).[21]

The different situations require different strategies. In the first setting, managers must be *defenders* of an existing niche or position. In the second, they can be *prospectors* continually searching for new profit-making opportunities. In the third, they can be *analyzers* defending existing strengths and selectively looking for new opportunities. The fourth situation is the weakest, and managers become *reactors* who fail to take the initiative when they can. The last two situations are the most common that managers face—neither totally free nor totally determined.

Aligning the Organization with Multiple Contingencies

Strategy, then, is the alignment of environmental opportunities and threats with the organization's internal strengths and weaknesses. This alignment must be matched by a linking of managerial values and ideals with society's values and expectations. There is no best way to accomplish the alignment; it depends on managerial judgment, values, and the environmental context.[22] Organizational performance is the result of a fit between numerous factors, including context, structure, systems, style, culture, technology, reward systems, tasks, and personnel.

Managers have to match the context with the organization's strengths. If the fit is good, the organization functions effectively. If it is poor, then the organization does not. Macrocongruence should prevail between the external environment and organizational structure, and microcongruence between the internal structure and individual behavior.

For example, it is not enough for a CEO to declare that the goals of the organization are ethical behavior, international expansion, environmental responsibility, and technological innovation. The organization has to be aligned internally to accomplish these goals. Otherwise, the goals cannot be accomplished. There will be a gap between goals and what is actually carried out; intention will not reflect reality.

Since organizations operate in contexts of multiple and conflicting contingencies, managers must recognize that there are multiple, equally effective organizational strategies and designs for coping with these contingencies.[23] Multiple and conflicting contingencies create the possibility for choice: the greater the number of equally effective options, the greater the opportunities for choice. Performance, then, may be subject to equifinality; "that is, the same outcomes can be achieved in multiple ways."[24] The same outcomes can be achieved from different starting points by different methods.

Continuous and Discontinuous Change

Strategic change is not a simple function of strategic choice in a placid environment. It depends on realigning the organization with rapidly changing environmental conditions. In every organization, small adjustments in magnitude "tend to be interspersed with periods of discontinuous shifts in pattern."[25] In some circumstances, the fundamental shifts are smooth. They occur incrementally, the result of accumulated, common everyday experience. Their significance is not appreciated until after the fact. What seems trivial at the moment, only tactical, in the end proves to be strategic and of the utmost importance.

While major shifts are hardly noticed in some situations, in others they are like earthquakes—disruptive interruptions in strategic direction that cannot be ignored. Discontinuous change occurs infrequently, but when it does take place, it has great impact on the organization.[26] It creates havoc. People are laid off, divisions are sold, established patterns of doing business are done away with, and nearly everything that has been comfortable and familiar is turned topsy-turvy. The memory of the cataclysmic event lies embedded in the collective conscious of organizational members. Referred to constantly as a point of comparison, it helps define what the organization then becomes.

Pressures for Change

The basic idea of this book is that environmental forces create pressures for strategic change. A firm no longer aligned with its environment will be ineffective if it continues with its current strategy. The forces that create pressure for change, however, must overcome the forces of inertia. A good example is General Motors, which faced a vastly different environment but was unable to adjust because the forces of inertia were so strong. For change to occur, the costs of being mismatched with the environment have to be greater than the costs of change. Mere awareness that a misalignment or gap needs redress is insufficient. Strategic change does not occur unless there is both the capacity and desire for change. Resources must be available for change, and stakeholder groups must believe that the change is fair and just to overcome possible opposition.

Summary and Conclusions

This chapter has discussed a number of possible relationships between corporate social and financial performance: positive, negative, no relationship, and inverted U-shaped relationship. It has given reasons why these relationships might exist. It has also explored the effects of corporate strategy on social performance, and the effects of social performance on corporate strategy.

Strategy has been defined as corporate adjustments to volatile environments. Distinctions have been drawn between strategy content and process and between strategy at the corporate and business levels. Three strategic typologies have been presented in this chapter: adaptation, uniqueness, and the life cycle.

The differing views of organizational ecologists and institutional theorists about whether managers can make a difference have been examined. Microcongruence, it has been argued, has to match macrocongruence if managers are to make a difference. If microcongruence does not match macrocongruence, managers are unlikely to have much impact. The next chapters discuss the alignment between the corporation and various societal forces.

How the Text Is Organized

Four types of alignments are discussed in Part II:

- Alignments between individual and organizational values and economic growth (Chapter 3).
- Alignments between managers, shareholders, and other stakeholders (Chapter 4).
- Alignments between the corporation and public policy (Chapter 5).
- Alignments between the corporation and women and minorities (Chapter 6).

Part III of this book deals with alignments between the corporation and the changing conditions of international competition; Part 4 deals with the necessary alignments between the corporation and the natural world; and Part 5 deals with the alignments between the corporation, technological innovation, and the rules of legal liability.

Discussion Questions

1. Why might there be a positive relationship between corporate social and financial performance?
2. Why might there be a negative relationship between corporate social and financial performance?
3. Why might there be an inverted U-shaped relationship?
4. Why might there be no relationship?
5. What practical difference would it make if these relationships prevailed? Is it not the case that people should do what is right regardless of the consequences?
6. What is strategy?
7. What is the difference between strategy content and strategy process?
8. What is the difference between corporate and business strategy?
9. Distinguish between defenders, prospectors, analyzers, and reactors.
10. Distinguish between cost leadership, differentiation, and focus. Do you agree that the low-profit strategy is to be stuck in the middle?
11. What is the product life-cycle approach to strategy? How does it differ from other approaches?
12. How do organizational ecologists answer the question, Can managers make a difference? How do institutional theorists? Which view, in your opinion, is correct?
13. What is the difference between macrocongruence and microcongruence? Why are both needed?
14. What does *equifinality* mean? What does it imply for organizational behavior?
15. Why does corporate crime take place? What can be done to prevent it?

Endnotes

1. A. Ullman, "Data in Search of a Theory: A Critical Examination of the Relationships among Social Performance, Social Disclosure, and Economic Performance of U.S. Firms," *Academy of Management Review,* July 1985, pp. 545–57.
2. R. Cyert and J. March, *A Behavioral Theory of the Firm* (Englewood Cliffs, NJ, 1963).

3. G. Alexander and R. A. Buchholz, "Corporate Social Responsibility and Stock Market Performance," *Academy of Management Journal* 21, 1978, pp. 479–86.

4. B. Cornell and A. Shapiro, "Corporate Social Responsibility and Financial Performance," *Academy of Management Journal* 27, 1984, pp. 42–56.

5. A. Marcus, "Responses to Externally Induced Innovation: Their Effects on Organizational Performance," *Strategic Management Journal* 9, 1988, pp. 387–402.

6. M. Friedman, "The Social Responsibility of Business Is to Increase Its Profits," in *The Management of Values*, ed. Charles S. McCoy (Boston: Pitman, 1985), pp. 253–60.

7. P. L. Cochran and R. A. Wood, "Corporate Social Responsibility and Financial Performance," *Academy of Management Journal* 27, 1974, pp. 42–56.

8. H. Mintzberg and J. A. Waters, "The Mind of the Strategist(s)," in *The Executive Mind*, ed. S. Srivastava (San Francisco, Calif.: Jossey-Bass, 1983).

9. A. Ginsberg, "Measuring and Modeling Changes in Strategy: Theoretical Foundations and Empirical Directions," *Strategic Management Journal* 9, 1988, pp. 559–75.

10. Ibid.

11. T. Herbert and H. Deresky, "Generic Strategies: An Empirical Investigation of Typology Validity and Strategy Content," *Strategic Management Journal* 8, 1987, pp. 135–47; N. Venkatraman and J. Grant, "Construct Measurement in Organizational Strategy Research," *Academy of Management Review* 13, 1986, pp. 71–87.

12. J. Woodward, *Industrial Organizations* (Oxford: Oxford University Press, 1965); J. Woodward, "Management and Technology: Problems of Progress in Industry," Series No. 3, Her Majesty's Stationery Office, London, 1958; R. E. Miles and C. C. Snow, *Organizational Strategy, Structure, and Process* (New York: McGraw-Hill, 1978).

13. Woodward, *Industrial Organizations;* Woodward, "Management and Technology."

14. M. Porter, *Competitive Strategy* (New York: The Free Press, 1980); Woodward, *Industrial Organizations.*

15. E. Segev, "A Systematic Comparative Analysis and Synthesis of Two Business Level Strategic Typologies," *Strategic Management Journal* 10, 1989, pp. 487–505; Porter, *Competitive Strategy;* C. Hill, "Differentiation versus Low Cost or Differentiation and Low Cost: A Contingency Framework," *Academy of Management Review* 15, 1988, pp. 401–12; A. Murray, "A Contingency View of Porter's 'Generic Strategies,'" *Academy of Management Review* 15, 1988, pp. 390–400; R. Wright, "A Refinement of Porter's Strategies," *Strategic Management Journal* 8, 1987, pp. 93–101.

16. T. Herbert and H. Deresky, "Generic Strategies: An Empirical Investigation of Typology Validity and Strategy Content," *Strategic Management Journal* 8, 1987, pp. 135–47.

17. S. Kotha and D. Orne, "Generic Manufacturing Strategies: A Conceptual Synthesis," *Strategic Management Journal* 10, 1989, pp. 211–31.

18. R. Daft, J. Sormunen, and D. Parks, "Chief Executive Scanning, Environmental Characteristics, and Company Performance," *Strategic Management Journal* 9, 1988, pp. 123–39.

19. D. Wholey and J. Brittain, "Organizational Ecology: Findings and Implications," *Academy of Management Review* 13, 1986, pp. 513–33.

20. W. Scott, "The Adolescence of Institutional Theory," *Adminstrative Science Quarterly* 32, 1987, pp. 493–511.

21. M. Lawless and L. Finch, "Choice and Determinism: A Test of Hrebiniak and Joyce's Framework on Strategy-Environment Fit," *Strategic Management Journal* 10, 1989, pp. 351–65; L. G. Hrebiniak and W. F. Joyce, "Organizational Adaptation: Strategic Choice and Environmental Determinism," *Administrative Science Quarterly,* Sept. 1985, pp. 336–49.

22. A. Van de Ven and R. Drazin, "The Concept of Fit in Contingency Theory," *Research in Organizational Behavior,* 1985, pp. 333–65.

23. N. Venkatraman, "The Concept of Fit in Strategy Research: Toward Verbal and Statistical Correspondence," *Academy of Management Review* 16, 1989, pp. 423–44; L. Fry and D. Smith, "Congruence, Contingency, and Theory Building," *Academy of Management Review* 14, 1987, pp. 117–32; D. Hambrick and D. Lei, "Toward an Empirical Prioritization of Contingency Variables for Business Strategy," *Academy of Management Journal* 12, 1985, pp. 763–88; A. Ginsberg and M. Venkatraman, "Contingency Perspectives of Organizational Strategy: A Critical Review of the Empirical Research," *Academy of Management Review* 12, 1985, pp. 421–34.

24. Hrebiniak and Joyce, "Organizational Adaptation," p. 338.

25. A. Ginsberg, "Measuring and Modeling Changes in Strategy: Theoretical Foundations and Empirical Directions," *Strategic Management Journal* 9, 1988, pp. 559–75.

26. M. L. Tushman and E. Romanelli, "Organizational Evolution: Interactions between External and Emergent Processes and Strategic Choice, in *Research in Organizational Behavior,* ed. B. M. Staw and L. L. Cumminigs (Greenwich, Conn.: JAI Press, 1985).

II

ETHICS AND SOCIAL RESPONSIBILITY

3

ETHICS

Group Norms and the Individual

If the hypothesis were offered us of a world in which . . . millions kept permanently happy on the one simple condition that a certain lost soul on the far-off edge of things should lead a life of lonely torture, . . . even though an impulse arose within us to clutch at the happiness so offered, how hideous a thing would be its enjoyment when deliberately accepted as the fruit of such a bargain.

William James, "The Moral Philosopher and the Moral Life."

Introduction and Chapter Objectives

This chapter introduces you to conflicts between the good-and-bad and the right-and-wrong moral traditions. For instance, according to utilitarianism, in a good-and-bad system, what is paramount is the greatest good for the greatest number; however, according to Immanuel Kant, the 18th-century German philosopher, it is right to treat each person with dignity and respect. This chapter also deals with the relationships between ethical values and economic growth and the conflicts that can arise between individual ethical standards and group norms. Since people have to learn to justify themselves ethically, it is important to understand issues surrounding the changing ethical standards of society. The sources of altruism and of an ethical personality are considered, as is the role of self-interest in business management.

Reasoning about Ethical Dilemmas

The ethical choices managers face are difficult. They involve questions of right and wrong and good and bad. Chapters 3 and 4 provide some of the concepts that are needed to reason better about ethical dilemmas.

A brief analysis of the problem posed in the opening quotation is an appropriate place to start. While it may not be *right* to allow an individual to suffer, can it be justified by the *good* achieved—the happiness of the group? To achieve noble *ends*—"millions kept permanently happy"—can one rely on nasty *means*—that a single person "should lead a life of lonely torture"? William James points to the tragic character of this dilemma. Even if the group decides that its happiness justifies an individual's suffering, can the group easily live with its decision? Its happiness is muted by the consciousness of the unhappy bargain it has struck.

This situation illustrates some of the core issues of ethics. Do the ends justify the means? Does the happiness of the collectivity override that of the individual? While not as extreme as the dilemma just discussed, ethical choices in business are often tragic in character. They involve bitter trade-offs between apparently irreconcilable values. Right and wrong often must be balanced against good and bad.

Balancing Right and Wrong against Good and Bad

The following examples further illustrate the trade-offs mentioned above. Surely, genuinely valid *ends* are served by agents of the Central Intelligence Agency (CIA) in protecting the liberty, freedom, and integrity of the institutions of American society; nonetheless, the CIA, in pursuing these desirable ends, routinely relies on *means* (lying, deception, and outright violence) that violate generally accepted canons of right and wrong. On the other hand, the ends of Nazi soldiers certainly were vile—to conquer other nations and impose upon them a system that systematically brutalized and subordinated elements of their population. Nonetheless, in pursuing these ends the Nazi soldiers may have adhered to some of the principles of common morality (fidelity, love, and sympathy) in their dealings with each other (thus showing that even thugs may have to treat each other fairly to accomplish their purposes).

Many common situations in business present similar dilemmas. Ends conflict with means (see Exhibit 3–1). What is good or bad conflicts with what is right and wrong.[1] The right-and-wrong tradition in ethics (in the next chapter, a more technical term will be used) teaches that people have a responsibility to do what is right and to avoid doing what is wrong. They should love their neighbors as themselves and treat others with ultimate respect because all people are human beings with inalienable rights (to life, liberty, and the pursuit of happiness, as in the

EXHIBIT 3–1   **Ends versus Means: A Classic Ethical Dilemma**

		Means	
		Right	*Wrong*
Ends	*Good*	Acceptable actions	Unclear ? ? ?
	Bad	Unclear ? ? ?	Unacceptable actions

Declaration of Independence, and to property, security, and freedom from oppression, as in the Declaration of the Rights of Man). According to Immanuel Kant, the 18th-century German philosopher, people should apply universal rules to their conduct; they should act only how they would want *everyone* to act under the circumstances.[2] For example, unless they believe that *everyone* should be cruel and harsh, and that society could not function unless people generally conducted their lives in this way, then they have no right doing so.

Questions of right and wrong force people to examine their *intentions*, but in so doing, they may miss the *consequences* of their actions.[3] That is, they may not estimate the significance of their actions by forecasting probable results. Thus, a separate ethical tradition exists (the good-and-bad tradition) that requires that people assess the consequences. Rather than limiting its account to what is right and wrong, it asks what are the ends worth seeking in human life?

Indeed, what is the *summum bonum,* or ultimate good, for which all else is worth sacrificing? For the classical philosophers in the tradition of Plato and Aristotle, the ultimate end is wisdom, which should produce virtuous character and behavior.[4] For modern thinkers, the ultimate end is more likely to be some calculus of pleasure and pain best summarized by the phrase "the greatest good for the greatest number."[5] However, this utilitarian precept has obvious drawbacks, not the least of which is determining how to measure pain and pleasure. But the concern for the greatest good for the greatest number has another serious limitation, which was alluded to earlier: the concern for the greatest good can prevent a person from taking individual rights seriously. As in the William James example, to what extent must the greatest good for the greatest number be built upon individual pain and suffering?

Reasons for Not Thinking Ethically

People need to vigorously ask themselves both ethical questions: to what extent are their actions right and wrong *and* to what extent are they good and bad? Nonetheless, people give many reasons why they do not reason about ethical matters.[6] They may argue, from the standpoint of *relativism,* that since there is no single method for deciding whether actions are moral, there is no need for further reflection. They believe that all paths are equivalent, so it is meaningless to choose among them. Accordingly, people should merely do what feels best, with no requirement to justify themselves to others.

Along with relativism, there is *cynicism:* a tendency to believe that ethical arguments can neither be won nor lost, that they are neither scientific, factual, nor subject to proof and counterproof, but are based solely on feeling and illogical convention. In the end, according to the cynics, ethical analysis comes down to *egoism.*[7] Most people are selfishly pursuing only their own interests; they do not care about others. Thus, giving to others takes place only when people feel that it is necessary to do so to get what they want. As well, people love only because they want to be loved, and only love those that love them; they hate or are indifferent to the rest of humanity.

According to such views, people do not have a capacity for ethical action because their behavior is *instinctual.*[8] Since they act on instinct, neither are they free nor can virtue be taught. Simply, what occurs in most cases is that might equals right and ethics are a rationalization, an ideological justification created by those in power to keep those who do not have power at a distance.

No Choice but to Reason Ethically

The premise of this book is that moral nihilism misses the point that people must seek ethical justification for their actions. Doing so is not simply a duty; people have *no choice.* Each person has to marshall facts and construct theories to justify actions taken or intended to be taken.[9] Indeed, all people have to reason ethically and test their actions by ethical standards. Why? Because everyone's beliefs are subject to challenge and to justification by reasoned argument.[10]

The need to reason ethically is great especially for managers, who are in a position where conflicting rights are at stake and different parties are affected by the decisions they make. Managers make everyday ethical judgments that require justification and refinement through the use of moral principles and theories.[11] In a particular case, they must inquire about who has rights, who will be affected, and how they will be affected. Moreover, they need to know the ethical theories that can enable them to justify their actions because their legitimacy and credibility are affected by their capacity for ethical reasoning. Of course, it would be wrong to become so familiar with various ethical systems that any action could be justified after-the-fact, even when the manager knows the action is wrong and bad.

Changing Ethical Values

Businesses operate in a context of changing ethical standards. For instance, polls have shown declining public confidence in business.[12] The 1980s have been portrayed as a period of rampant greed and social irresponsibility, and the 1990s are supposed to have a different focus.[13] These assessments provoke the question, where do values come from?

People receive their values from family, school, and neighborhood. They obtain ethical grounding from religious institutions, and they learn to behave also from peers and popular culture—from music, the movies, and television. However, as mobility increases and the community's influence declines, people are presumed to have become more inward seeking.[14] That is, as less of their validation comes from external sources, self-fulfillment and self-gratification are supposed to be playing a greater role.

The shift from the community to the individual means that the purpose in life for many people is to feel good rather than to do good or be good. Therefore, good feelings may come, for example, from the thrills and pleasures of drug taking and from alcohol consumption. And virtue may come not from treating others kindly or contributing to the common good, as it should have when institutions like family, school, and neighborhood had sway. Instead, virtue may be an expression of exercising, eating right, and appearing fit.

When feeling good is a higher value than doing and being good, then business ethics may be questioned. It may be argued that expediency is as necessary as virtue for success. It may be said that people are driven to pursue what appear to be the good things in life (money, power, and sex) rather than things that are intrinsically good. (But are not money, power, and sex intrinsically good?) Business ethics may be viewed as an oxymoron (i.e., a contradiction in terms, like *military intelligence*).

Cynicism about business ethics was common in the 1980s. Prior to receiving a three-year prison term for insider trading, Ivan Boesky said in a commencement address to University of California at Berkeley M.B.A.'s that "greed is all right . . . I want you to know that. I think greed is healthy. You can be greedy and feel good about yourself."[15] Dennis Levine, also convicted of insider trading, said: "Greed is a nice religion; if you are really greedy, you are going to keep your shoes polished, you won't run around on your wife or get drunk. You will do what it takes to maximize your lifetime income, and that doesn't leave time for messing up."[16] Insider trading, illegal campaign contributions, bribery, and other scandals contributed to a sense that corporate leaders evaded by illicit means the market discipline to which they publicly professed.

Ethical Values and Economic Growth

The sociologist Daniel Bell relates the ethical values of a society to the competitiveness of its economic institutions (see Exhibit 3–2). He discerns a movement in American values "from the Protestant ethic to the psychedelic bazaar." The Protestant ethic and Puritan temper were based on "work, sobriety, frugality, sexual restraint, and a forbidding attitude toward life." They were the result of an agrarian, small-town way of life where clergymen held sway and a person was expected to "scrutinize himself and hold himself to account." In this context, a person got ahead by thrift, self-improvement, and industry, by avoiding the "temptations of the flesh" and devoting oneself to the "sanctity of work" and to other "higher pursuits."[17]

In 20th-century America, however, this ethic has been eroded by a consumption ethic of hedonism, pleasure, and play. Autos, movies, and radio eliminated rural isolation and created a common culture devoted to spending money and gaining material possessions. Items once considered luxuries, such as automobiles, television sets, air conditioners, and dishwashers, diffused down to the middle and lower classes. People showed they succeeded not by saving and abstinence but by lavishly displaying the life-styles they were able to acquire. Gratification of the impulses, rather than their suppression, became the norm.

EXHIBIT 3–2   Ethical Values and Economic Growth

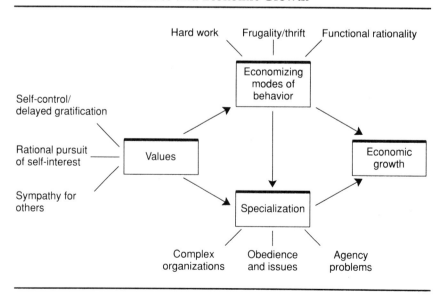

There is conflict between the effectiveness of American business and these new values of self-gratification. Effective business practice requires a reliance on economizing, efficiency, optimization, and functional rationality, which may conflict with the new tradition of consumption. In newly industrializing nations, one finds greater adherence to the traditional tenets of the Protestant ethic. People in these nations value hard work, thrift, frugality, honesty, and self-sacrifice for the purpose of economic success. Thus, the question of ethical values is a broader one than the personal salvation of individual managers. It concerns economic growth and the competitiveness of U.S. business in the world economy.

Self-Interest and Economic Growth in Adam Smith

Adam Smith was the first person to systematically address the connection between economic growth and individual values. Smith published *The Wealth of Nations*, which became the foundation for modern economics, in 1776, the year the American republic was formed.[18] Its founders assumed that individuals were driven to pursue their own self-interest.[19] In the Constitution, they established a system of checks and balances as a protection against the pursuit of self-interest. Adam Smith, too, felt that this pursuit is inevitable. In fact, he considered it virtuous; he believed that the more you pursued self-interest, the more you would unwittingly (by means of the "hidden hand") enrich society:

> Every individual . . . neither intends to promote the public interest, nor knows how much he is promoting it. . . . By directing his industry in such a manner as its produce may be of the greatest value, he intends only his own gain, and he is in this, as in many other cases, led by an invisible hand to promote the end which was not part of his intention.[20]

Thus, the individual promotes the interests of society (does good) by doing well (promoting his or her own interest).

Smith believed that in economic activity people do not think about right or wrong or good and bad but about bottom-line concerns, productivity and efficiency, that contribute to profitability. Profit, according to Smith, is the engine that drives economic progress. The incentive to make a profit stimulates people to offer a valuable good or service to sell to others. The competition between people in the marketplace then increases the wealth of a society and makes all citizens better-off.

Because of competition, people have to innovate and specialize. The market's calling, in elevating people above the miserable conditions to which they otherwise would be subject, is noble. People in the societies that have not adopted the principles of liberty that adhere to the market, Smith believed, are destined to live primitively with vast inequality.

Adam Smith as a Moral Philosopher

Adam Smith is a moral philosopher.[21] In his era, neither economics nor economists existed; rather, there were moral philosophers. In the *Theory of Moral Sentiments*, published in 1759, Smith discussed how people acquire sympathy for the distress of others by imagining how they would feel in the other's situation. As revealed in this oft-quoted passage from the *Wealth of Nations*, a deep sympathy for and understanding of others is necessary for success in a capitalist system:

> Man has almost constant occasion for the help of his brethren, and it is in vain for him to expect it from their benevolence only. He will be more likely to prevail if he can interest their self-love in his favour and show them that it is for their advantage to do for him what he requires of them. Whoever offers to another a bargain of any kind, proposes to do this. Give me that which I want, and you shall have this which you want, is the meaning of every such offer.[22]

To succeed in a capitalist system, a person must think of the other person's needs and desires. A concern for the other's advantage is needed to satisfy one's own needs and fulfill one's own desires.

In addition, the pursuit of individual gain must be tempered by proper moral virtues, according to Smith.[23] It cannot be accomplished without self-restraint and delayed gratification. The character traits of parsimony are necessary for an individual to advance and for the economy to grow; people have to keep themselves from prodigality. They have to save, invest, and postpone gratification. If they become too wealthy, Smith is worried that they might lose these admirable traits.

Smith was also aware of the dangers of specialization. To increase society's wealth, workers must concentrate on narrow tasks, which they perform very proficiently. But this concentration on simple, repetitive tasks dulls their intelligence. Thus, by requiring a high degree of specialization, capitalism inflicts damage on workers in modern factories and organizations.

Smith's Defense of Capitalism

Smith's defense of capitalism was based on certain assumptions about a perfectly (or nearly perfectly) functioning market. No one has undue market power to limit supply or raise prices. Each person functioning in the market is relatively equal and each has nearly complete information. Moreover, there are few if any external effects (effects on others) when two people make a deal. When free and equal persons possessing good information complete a transaction, both are better off, no one is worse off, and society is improved. These conditions may apply in the aggregate to real-world market situations, but they can be breached in particular instances.

With the liberation of Eastern Europe and the Soviet Union from nonmarket rule, few maintain that there are viable alternatives to market-based economies as systems for generating economic growth. However, the meaning of the capitalism practiced in different countries is a matter of dispute. In what senses are market-based economies of the United States, Japan, Germany, South America, and the Scandinavian countries similar? In what senses are they different? What is the significance of these differences? These issues will be addressed later in this book.

Different Levels of Ethical Discourse

For now, it is enough to say that there are different levels of ethical discourse:

1. The level of the individual, where the concern is with personal and professional behavior and the meaning of such terms as trust, honesty, and integrity.
2. The level of the organization, where the survival of the organization can come into conflict with individual standards of ethical conduct.
3. The level of society, where the justness and appropriateness of specific policies in areas such as child care, defense procurement, and national security must be debated.
4. The level of the system, that is, whether capitalism as it is practiced in the United States and other countries is just and appropriate and whether alternative economic systems are more just and better able to meet people's needs.

Conflicts between the individual and the organization are an important part of ethical dilemmas. What rights do individuals have in relation to the entity for which they work? What obligations do they have to this entity, what obligations does the entity have to them, and what obligations do specific individuals have to the other employees?

Adam Smith pointed out that employees in modern organizations have to carry out orders whose sense they cannot completely understand.[24] The separation between the order givers and those who carry out the orders creates what today is called agency problems.[25] Since the order givers cannot fully observe if their orders have been faithfully carried out, they have a tendency to say to employees that they do not care what methods are used to get the job done so long as the job is successfully accomplished. The tendency of the employees, who cannot fully comprehend what they have been commanded, is to maintain that they are just following orders, regardless of whether they know if what they are doing is right or wrong. These views blunt moral responsibility and invite people in large organizations to blame others when moral standards are violated.

Millgram's Experiments on Obedience to Authority

In a series of experiments conducted in the late 1950s, the social psychologist Stanley Millgram considered the tension between organizational requirements and individual conscience.[26] Over 1,000 subjects were involved in these experiments, which were repeated in numerous universities. The basic situation involved telling an individual to inflict punishment upon another person whenever the other person made apparent learning errors. As the other person gave what seemed to be an incorrect answer, the subject in the experiment was instructed to increase the level of electric shock the person was to receive.

The purpose was to determine how far people would go in inflicting increasing pain on a protesting victim. The victim was a professional actor and the subject was a randomly chosen individual who had volunteered for the experiment. Would people stop inflicting pain after hearing grunts, verbal complaints, demands to be released, vehement and emotional protests, or agonizing screams from the victim?

As it turned out, a substantial portion of the subjects, although they might display obvious distress and express outrage to the person in authority who was conducting the experiment, continued to inflict pain on the victims. They continued to increase the level of electric shocks no matter how much pleading they heard from the victim to be released.

Millgram infers from these experiments that people are unlikely to defy authority even in the face of an obvious moral imperative. Normal and otherwise reasonable people have a capacity for abhorrent, immoral acts committed simply because they are obeying authority.

What explains the apparent willingness of one person to inflict pain upon another? First, people appear to be committed to doing their jobs and to doing them well (in this case, the job is to inflict pain when the victim makes an incorrect answer) even when the destructive consequences of what they are doing is clear to them. People want to be viewed as competent performers. They understand that society consists of persons who are carrying out narrow and specialized jobs. They believe that the broader tasks of setting goals and assessing the morality of situations are entrusted to others—someone else oversees what is taking place and assumes responsibility.

Second, while people may recognize that they are doing wrong, they have trouble carrying out the values they hold. "Binding factors," such as a desire to uphold the promise to conduct the experiment and the awkwardness of a withdrawal, lock people into the situation. They then become consumed by the narrow technical details of their job and lose sight of the broader implications.

Third, as they become involved in the task, people lose a sense of responsibility. They see themselves simply as the agents of an external authority; they feel like they are simply carrying out their duty. This point of view is adopted by people operating in large organizations where they are locked into a subordinate status in the authority structure. Such people tend to believe that the activities of the organization are benevolent and useful to society and justify the inconvenience that any particular person suffers. Quite simply, the ends of the organization, defined for them by others, justify the organization's means.

Finally, once having caused suffering to the victim, the people start to see the victim as unworthy. The victim deserves punishment because the victim is unable to answer the question that has been given. The subject gradually perceives the victim as having some basic defect in intellect or character. This stereotyping of the victim has very broad implications for how disadvantaged minorities are treated in our society.

Being Ethical in an Organizational Context

People sometimes have to rebel against outrageous orders. Being ethical in an organizational context, however, poses difficult dilemmas. Should a person contribute to unethical organizational behavior, or should the person resist the behavior and try to end it?[27] By opposing unethical behavior, the person is likely to suffer unpleasant consequences—punishment, dismissal, shunning by colleagues, and banishment to distant locales or uninteresting and unchallenging assignments. The person can be someone working against other employees and against the organization itself to end unethical behaviors, or someone who is part of the organization and who is trying to bring about change. There are many ways to follow one's conscience and defy unethical or unreasonable authority (see Exhibit 3–3). Before publicly blowing the whistle on unethical practices, a person can inform or threaten a higher level manager. If this does not work, the person can conscientiously object to, quietly refrain from, or sabotage the implementation of unethical behavior.

While actions taken against the organization can be effective, they have important limitations. First, the person might be wrong about whether the organization's actions are indeed unethical. Second, the person is likely to damage organizational relationships by coercing people into doing things they otherwise would not do. Even if the

EXHIBIT 3–3   Confronting Unethical Behavior

		Voice	
		Yes	No
Loyalty	Yes	Work with others to change behavior	Accept behavior
	No	Blow the whistle	Exit the organization

person is right, the organization can be hurt unnecessarily. The person's actions can create a climate in the organization in which others feel that might makes right. By using coercion to compel people to end the unethical practice, the person may contribute to a climate in which people believe that the only way to get things done in the organization is to act by means of force.

Thus, a person might want to consider changing the organization by being a part of it rather than against it. "The self," according to the Protestant theologian Paul Tillich, "affirms itself as participant in the power of a group."[28] This model is more like the one found in Japan, where a person brings about change by being a part of the group. The U.S. style is for the individual to take on the lonely but romantic fight against the organization.

Working with people in the organization, however, has its limitations. First, it requires achieving compromises that are satisfactory to contending parties. Of course, doing so may not be possible. It also requires a strong capacity for leadership. However, not all persons have this capacity. Moreover, in some organizations, no matter how hard one tries to change them from within, doing so is impossible. This is because some organizations have very strong cultures that resist change (whether they are run by consensus or are authoritarian does not seem to matter). Thus, a person is left with the dilemma of deciding whether to compel change as an individual separate from the organization or to lead change as a part of the organization.

The Sources of Altruism

Why would a person be willing to challenge the organization? The sources of altruistic behavior (bad for the person but good for society) have been investigated by many scholars; however, their explanations

---

EXHIBIT 3–4   Reasons to Challenge Authority on Ethical Grounds

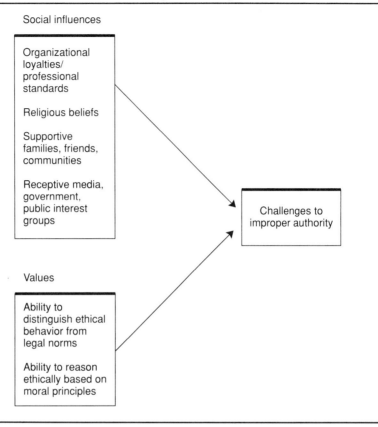

Social influences

Organizational
loyalties/
professional
standards

Religious beliefs

Supportive
families, friends,
communities

Receptive media,
government,
public interest
groups

Challenges to
improper authority

Values

Ability to
distinguish ethical
behavior from
legal norms

Ability to reason
ethically based on
moral principles

---

provide no simple answers as to why a person would be willing to make sacrifices to challenge unjust authority (see Exhibit 3–4).

Whistle-blowers, who challenge their organizations for the sake of some higher value, tend to be conservative people. They are highly devoted to their work and to their organization.[29] However, they have been asked to violate what they consider to be the standards of appropriate workplace behavior. They then feel that they are defending the true mission of the organization, that in engaging in some form of courageous dissent or protest they are the true organizational loyalists. Whistle-blowers engage in protest against the organization at great personal cost. They face harsh reprisals, blacklistings, dismissals, transfers, and personal harassment. What sustains them is their professional ethics, religious beliefs, supportive friends, families, and communities, a receptive media and government, and public interest groups that are willing to take them seriously.[30]

Since ethical behavior requires self-sacrifice, a person's behavior when tested by moral challenges cannot be easily predicted. Ethical behavior may require breaking the rules of society that are otherwise functional in that they permit people to live with each other. Ethical behavior and legal norms are not necessarily equivalent. Ethical behavior requires more than the determination of whether a particular action is legal.

It might not be possible to teach this type of behavior. Theory and practice do not always coincide. Simple people sometimes meet ethical challenges better than people with immense learning (consider the German philosopher Martin Heidegger, who supported the Nazis). One may be an ethical person and never have studied ethics. On the other hand, a person who has devoted a lifetime to ethical study may not act always ethically.

Some people appear to be naturally good. It is part of their make-up. They cannot be otherwise. But is natural goodness the highest level of ethical behavior? If the reasons cannot be articulated, to what extent is the behavior ethical? Take the example of a tree that cannot help but grow in a particular manner. Its growth gives pleasure to others, but it has no control over its growth and deserves no special merit on account of it. To be deserving of merit, actions require the probing reflection and the ability to choose of which a tree is not capable.

Ethical reasoning and reflection distinguish humans from natural objects. To maintain their integrity, humans need to be able to reflect about ethics. In *The Ethics of the Fathers,* a collection of rabbinic sayings, Hillel maintains: "If I am not for myself, who will be for me"; but, he also says: "If I am only for myself, what am I?" Another of the rabbinic sages holds that "the right path that a person should choose" is one that "honors the person who does it, but which also brings honor from humankind." Reflection upon the principles articulated in the great ethical works of humankind is apt to make people more sensitive to the meaning and consequences of their actions.

Unrestrained Egoism: Socrates' Answer

What do the great works say about why a person should restrain his or her egoism? One of the classic efforts to reply to the challenge of unrestrained egoism is given by Socrates in *The Republic.* The form of the dialogue is one in which someone poses a question and Socrates attempts to answer. The question posed by Thrasymachus, classical cynic, is remarkably contemporary:

> Is not injustice more profitable than justice? Innocent as you are yourself Socrates you must see that a just man always has the worst of it. Take a private business: when a partnership is wound up, you will never find that the more honest of the two partners comes off with the larger share; and in

> their relation to the state, when there are taxes to be paid, the honest man will pay more than the other on the same amount of property; or if there is money to be distributed the dishonest will get it all. . . . So true is it Socrates, that injustice, on a grand scale, is superior to justice . . . and 'right' . . . means simply what serves the interest of the stronger party; 'wrong' simply means what is for the interest and profit of oneself.[31]

Socrates responds:

> I am delighted with your answer, Thrasymachus; . . . Please add to your kindness by telling me whether any set of men—a state or an army or a band of robbers or thieves—who were acting together for some unjust purpose would be likely to succeed, if they were always trying to injure one another. Wouldn't they do better if they did not?[32]

Thrasymachus is then forced to answer, "Yes, they would." To which Socrates retorts: "Because, of course such injuries must set them quarreling and hating each other. Only fair treatment can make men friendly and of one mind."[33]

Socrates wins the argument by shifting the focus of discussion from the individual to the group. He suggests that the success of the collectivity requires fair treatment of the individuals that compose it. Even a band of thieves have to treat each other fairly. Injustice undermines the cooperation between people that is necessary for social interaction to take place. If unrestrained egoism prevails, neither the individual nor society benefit.

Developing a Moral Personality

Thus, personal integrity, empathy, and virtue play an important role in society. They engender the trust between people that make social interaction possible. They foster the cooperation and coordination that is needed so that each person is better-off than he or she would be alone. But from whence does an ethical bearing spring? Contemplating ethical writing can take us only so far. A person's behavior is not simply a matter of sensitivity to ethical values; it is a consequence of character, which develops from one's natural endowments and the influences of home, schooling, and community. The willingness to sacrifice for the collective good must have a source in a person's early training and upbringing.

According to the psychologist Lawrence Kohlberg, ethical sensitivity requires an appreciation for collective interests, for rules and laws that promote long-run community interests.[34] This type of appreciation develops as the person matures. A child has no sense of communal interests. Influenced by praise and displeasure, the child is affected mainly by reward and punishment. Concerned with personal gratification and affected by authority, the child has no sense that it is obeying rules because they promote the common good.

An adolescent, however, has a changed perspective. The adolescent focuses on the group and group norms. In trying to conform to the expectations of parents and peers, of home, school, and church, adolescents learn proper behavior from the surrounding groups. But adolescents, too, conform without knowing why. They obey rules because rules are there to be obeyed, not because they have an intrinsic understanding of their purpose.

According to Kohlberg, only adults with a universal orientation and the need for justification based on moral principles reach the pinnacle of moral sensitivity. These adults are at the "post-conventional, autonomous stage" because they are willing to accept rules, not merely because society says so, but because they understand their function and purpose. They understand what the rules mean and what they are trying to accomplish. They can give a rational defense of their actions and are not likely to obey authority simply because obedience is expected.

Reasons for Optimism: People Are (at Least Sometimes) Altruistic

In surprising and unanticipated ways, people are indeed altruistic. They take into account interests broader than their own selfish ends. In an important book called *The Moral Dimension,* Amitai Etzioni provides many examples.[35] Experiments have shown that people mail back lost wallets to strangers with the cash intact.[36] They return lost contributions to a charity, declining to take the money for themselves and going to the trouble of paying for the postage and for the mailing of the contribution back to its original intended donor.[37] Even a high proportion of people in the streets of New York asked to aid a person in distress did so.[38] People tend to support public television. They do not always cheat even when there is little chance of getting caught. They vote even when they know that their vote will make no difference.

Throughout history people have risked their lives for the sake of others, from non-Jews who saved Jews in Nazi Germany to freedom riders who demonstrated against segregation in the American South. The main reward to these people was "the inner sense of having done what is right."[39]

Even purely economic behavior cannot be completely understood if the propensity for self-sacrifice is not considered. Saving, for instance, is of prime importance to economics (see Exhibit 3–5). Savings and investment are key attributes of social development and what makes society prosperous. Long-run prosperity is impossible without saving and investment. Nonetheless, saving cannot be explained purely in terms of individual self-interest. The economic explanation is that it is a consequence of the size of a person's income (the more income, the more saving), the desire for financial security in retirement, and the level of the

---

EXHIBIT 3–5   Reasons for Saving

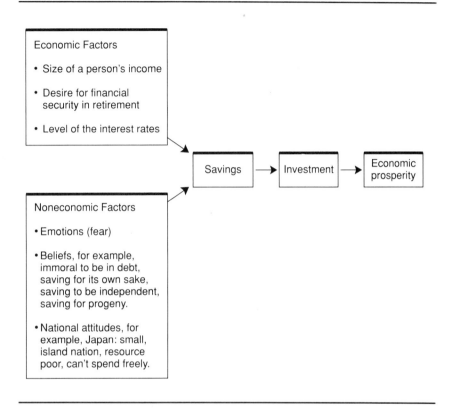

interest rate (the higher the interest rate, the more the saving). Economists are the first to admit that these factors do not explain all the variance observed, that something is missing in their explanation of saving.

Emotional factors (fear) and moral and societal values lead a person to save. The decision is not simply a calculation of rational self-interest. People may believe that it is immoral to be in debt, that one should save for its own sake, that one should save to be independent of the welfare system and independent from one's children, and that one should save because of the obligation to one's progeny (they deserve an easier start in life).

In addition, certain national attitudes lead to the propensity to save. The Japanese, for instance, perceive themselves to be the crowded inhabitants of a resource-poor island that has few economic endowments. If they do not judiciously save and invest, they, their children, and their children's children will be doomed to poverty. A concern for unborn future generations is not necessarily an expression of rational self-interest, which says it is better to consume now than to worry about what happens long after one is dead.

Without moral commitments, there are insufficient incentives and penalties to save, and without savings a market economy would not prosper. Clearly, many of the relationships needed to develop an economy depend on noneconomic feelings and ethical norms. People may not be able to articulate why they follow ethical norms, which become a matter of habit. However, if they failed to obey the contracts and implicit promises that are upheld by moral commitments, the whole system would collapse. Indeed, if everybody acted as if promises and contracts had no meaning, prolonged economic activity could not take place.

Distinguishing between Psychological Egoism and Prudential Altruism

Certainly, the desire to gain at someone else's expense is a powerful motive. Egoism cannot be denied, but distinctions have to be made about what egoism means. Some people are strict psychological egoists who try to reduce all behavior to self-interest. According to their view, even obvious saints and heroes are denounced as promoting unselfish appearances (e.g., Ralph Nader) to promote their selfish and parochial ends. Even if people mistakenly overlook what is in their best interests and behave altruistically, the strict egoist view insists that the main motivation is selfishness. If people love others, for example, it is only because they expect to be loved themselves.

This viewpoint is consistent with the perspective of prudential altruism. The desire for distinction and recognition, if not monetary and other rewards, can lead a person to do good. If, in treating others well, people are acting only to make their own lives more agreeable, who is to fault them if they achieve positive results. If kindness is merely the result of a fear of anarchy (Hobbes' solitary, poor, nasty, brutish state of nature), then the fear of this condition is beneficial.[40] It is in people's interests to behave properly because it makes everyone's situation more secure and stable. Everyone is better-off if they are allowed to pursue their self-interest within limits, that is, without threatening the social order.

Self-interest surely is relevant, but it may not be the only factor affecting people. People may be simultaneously "under the influence of two major sets of factors—their pleasure, and their moral duty . . . [and] there are important differences in the extent each of these sets of factors is operative under different historical and societal conditions, and within different personalities under the same conditions."[41]

Self-interest should not be the main motivation in every situation. There are instances when the motivation should be principled (see the feature below, "The Stock Market as a Deterrent to Dubious Behavior"). It should be based on the fact that something is inherently right. Why? Because, if people do everything purely for selfish reasons, when the selfish reasons disappear, they will reduce their level of commitment to the behavior. However, if they are acting because the action is inherently right, they will continue with the behavior regardless of how their interests are affected. They will continue "in the face of opposition" because they have "internalized the values that justify their actions." [42]

Summary and Conclusions

This chapter has tried to show the following:

- Most serious ethical dilemmas involve conflicts between ends (e.g., the greatest good for the greatest number) and means (e.g., treating each person with respect).
- The characteristic values prevalent in a society are likely to influence the pattern of economic growth and prosperity of that society. Saving rates, particularly important for economic growth, are affected by values about thrift and frugality and orientations toward the future; they cannot be explained in purely economic terms.
- Individuals working in an organization may face conflicts between adhering to their personal ethical values and carrying out the policies of the organization. What is common practice in the organization may conflict with the individual's ethical point of view; the individual then may have to choose between being loyal to the organization and struggling for change from within it or exiting the organization and fighting for change from without.
- Self-interest is a powerful motivating force promoting economic growth; however, if it is totally unrestrained, it can lead to a war of all against all and to social anarchy. Thus, most people realize that it is in their self-interest to control self-interest; that is, they believe prudentially that it needs to be controlled as well as unleashed. For nations to prosper in the long run, we need a modicum of social harmony, built upon commonly shared values of respect for each person.
- There are times when each person must put aside self-interest for the sake of some higher principle.

The Stock Market as a Deterrent to Dubious Behavior

The classic theory of the firm is based on the idea that managers are the agents for the owners. So assessing managers' success in increasing shareholder wealth, according to this theory, is the appropriate way to judge managerial behavior.[1] Negative stock market returns, therefore, should discourage managers from engaging in dubious behavior.[2] They should function as a deterrent. Thus, the prudent manager will not engage in ethically dubious behavior because of a concern for the possible impact on shareholders.

Indeed, many studies demonstrate negative stock market returns following exposure to ethically dubious behavior.[3] Researchers have found abnormal reductions in stock market returns following accusations of bribery, fraud, and illegal political contributions. In addition, they have found abnormal reductions in stock market returns after automobile recalls, following the Three Mile Island and the Bhopal tragedy, and in the aftermath of major airline accidents. If managers acted as the true agents of their shareholders, they would not allow their companies to fall into these predicaments of possible ethical compromise.

These findings and the theory that supports them, however, raise interesting issues that cannot be easily answered. The first has to do with the *effectiveness* of negative stock market returns as a deterrent to ethically dubious behavior. If negative returns are to be an effective deterrent, then it is necessary for managers to be aware of what is likely to take place and to protect shareholder interests accordingly. But how strong is the signal that shareholders send to managers? And how capable are managers of perceiving the negative reaction that springs from shareholder interests? Managers may employ a number of different perspectives (an aggregate perspective, the perspective of their industry, of their company, or of their industry and company in a specific time period) in es-

[1]M. Friedman, "The Social Responsibility of Business Is to Increase Its Profits," in *The Management of Values,* ed. Charles S. McCoy (Boston: Pitman, 1985), pp. 235–60.

[2]A. A Marcus, "Deterring Dubious Business Behavior," *Executive Excellence,* Sept. 1990, pp. 11–12.

[3]G. Jarrel and S. Peltzman, "The Impact of Product Recalls on the Wealth of Sellers," *Journal of Political Economy* 83, 1985, pp. 512–36; A. A. Marcus and R. S. Goodman, "Corporate Adjustments to Catastrophe: A Study of Investor Reaction to Bhopal," *Industrial Crisis Quarterly* 3, 1989, 213–34; P. Bromiley and A. Marcus "The Deterrent to Dubious Corporate Behavior: Profitability, Probability and Safety Recalls," *Strategic Management Journal* 10, pp. 233–50; W. N. Davidson, P. R. Changey, and M. Cross, "Large Losses, Risk Management and Stock Returns in the Airline Industry," *Journal of Risk and Insurance* 57, 1987, pp. 162–72; W. N. Davidson and D. L. Worrell, "The Impact of Announcements of Corporate Illegalities on Shareholder Returns," *Academy of Management Journal* 31, 1988, pp. 195–200;

A. A. Marcus and R. S. Goodman, "Compliance and Performance: Toward a Contingency Theory," *Research in Corporate Social Performance and Policy* 8, 1986, pp. 193–221; A. A. Marcus, and R. S. Goodman, "Victims and Shareholders: The Dilemmas of Presenting Corporate Policy during a Crisis," *Academy of Management Journal* 2, 1991, pp. 281–305.

The Stock Market as a Deterrent to Dubious Behavior cont.

timating the impact of their dubious acts on stock prices. In each instance, the results may be different. Therefore, the signals from shareholders to investors are not completely clear.

However, a more fundamental issue is the appropriateness of viewing shareholder returns as a deterrent to dubious behavior. The classic theory of the firm emphasizes the stock market valuation of the company. Despite being principally an investor's model, it fully acknowledges the firm's responsibility to act legally and ethically.[4] Thus, serving shareholder interests, if properly understood, can be consistent with other claims so long as the interests of shareholders are not violated by paying attention to the other claims.

If these other claims violate shareholder interests, then the classic theory provides no guidance. A different ethical standard, derived from religion, such as the Sermon on the Mount, or from philosophy such as Immanuel Kant's formulation of the categorical imperative, would demand an unconditional devotion to what is right regardless of shareholder interests. Under these systems if shareholder interests conflict with other claims, then the needs of shareholders would have to be sacrificed.

Indeed, one can readily imagine situations facing managers where behavior that would be likely to increase shareholder returns will conflict with ethical standards. In these circumstances, shareholder reaction is an inducement, not a deterrent, to dubious activities. The responsibility to increase

shareholder returns says one thing; the requirements of ethical behavior say to do something else. It is up to the managers to decide which interest to favor—that of their shareholders or that of their ethical conscience. Under these conditions, the classic theory provides no guidance. Although it asserts that managers should maximize shareholder returns within the bounds of laws and ethics, it does not say how to reconcile the possible conflicts between ethics and profits.

Thus, managers are likely to face situations where they must lay prudence aside and adopt a more rigorous ethical standard that may be at odds with shareholder interests. When facing these situations, it is appropriate to ignore stockholders and put other considerations first. Managers cannot rely solely on shareholder returns as a guide to ethical behavior.

Stockholders' interests should not necessarily be the sole determinant of the goodness of a particular policy. Indeed, if the rational pursuit of self-interest always comes before moral duty, then humanity is the great loser. The only dependable deterrent to dubious behavior is moral duty, which is an awareness of the consequences of one's actions and an attention to ethical process. People should be treated with ultimate respect, as ends and not as means, and as autonomous creatures free of managerial coercion. In some cases, these standards need to apply regardless of the short-term impact on shareholders.[5]

---

[4]Friedman, "The Social Responsibility of Business Is to Increase Its Profits."

[5]Kant, "Foundations of the Metaphysics of Morals"; D. Vogel, "Ethics and Profits Don't Always Go Hand in Hand," *Ethics: Easier Said Than Done* 1, 1989, p. 60.

Discussion Questions

1. If faced with the William James hypothesis of "millions kept permanently happy" on the condition of one person leading "a life of lonely torture," what would you do? What if the one person were a "statistical person," for example, 1 chance of excess cancer in 10,000; what would you do? How would you justify your decision?

2. Reasons people give for not thinking ethically are relativism, cynicism, egoism, and the argument that behavior is instinctual. Do you agree with these reasons? How would you refute them?

3. What effect has the decline of such institutions as schools, families, neighborhoods, and religious institutions had on individual values? To what extent do people actually adhere to a "feel good" rather than "do good" or "be good" ethic?

4. To what extent have people working in the Asian economies of the Pacific Rim taken on the values of thrift, hard work, and self-control that used to be associated with the Protestant ethic? To what extent have these values aided their economic growth?

5. To what extent do people in the Asian economies strive for self-interest, and to what extent do they strive for group success? If their goal is group success, does this challenge Adam Smith's views about the importance of individualism in explaining economic success?

6. To what extent does Adam Smith's model of capitalism match the real conditions that exist in capitalist economies?

7. In the Millgram experiments, why did people obey authority? What do you think of these reasons? Are they good ones?

8. Even in the face of an obvious organizational wrong, what are some of the reasons for not being a whistle-blower? What are some alternatives to blowing the whistle?

9. Can ethics be taught? Can it be learned?

10. Is Socrates' answer to Thrasymachus convincing? Why or why not?

11. Are you convinced by the examples of altruistic behavior provided by Etzioni? What about voting? If their individual votes are not likely to make a difference in the outcomes, why do people vote?

12. Distinguish between psychological egoism and prudential altruism?

Endnotes

1. T. L. Beauchamp and N. E. Bowie, *Ethical Theory and Business,* 2nd ed. (Englewood Cliffs, N.J.: Prentice Hall, 1983); R. T. DeGeorge, *Business Ethics,* 2nd ed. (New York: Macmillan, 1986); K. E. Goodpaster, *Some Avenues for Ethical Analysis in General Management,* Harvard Business School Paper No. 383–007, 1982; O. A. Johnson, *Ethics: Selections from Classical and Contemporary Writers,* 3rd ed. (New York: Holt, Rinehart, and Winston, 1974).
2. I. Kant, "Foundations of the Metaphysics of Morals," in *Ethics: Selections from Classical and Contemporary Writers,* 3rd ed., ed. O. A. Johnson (New York: Holt, Rinehart and Winston, 1974).
3. J. Dewey, *Ethics* (1908, reprint Carbondale, Ill.: Southern Illinois University Press, 1978).
4. R. McKeon, *Introduction to Aristotle* (New York: Random House, 1947); Plato, *The Republic,* trans. M. Cornford (New York: Oxford University Press, 1967); L. Strauss, *Natural Right and History* (Chicago: The University of Chicago Press, 1953).
5. J. Bentham, "An Introduction to the Principles of Morals and Legislation," in *Ethics: Selections from Classical and Contemporary Writers,* 3rd ed., ed. O. A. Johnson (New York: Holt, Rinehart, and Winston, 1974), pp. 228–39.
6. R. E. Freeman and D. R. Gilbert, Jr., *Corporate Strategy and the Search for Ethics* (Englewood Cliffs, N.J.: Prentice Hall, 1988); G. A. Steiner and J. F. Steiner, *Business, Government, and Society: A Managerial Perspective* (New York: McGraw-Hill, Inc., 1991).
7. N. E. Bowie, *Challenging the Egoistic Paradigm,* discussion paper No. 142, Strategic Management Research Center, University of Minnesota, 1990.
8. R. H. Frank, *Passions with Reason: The Strategic Role of the Emotions* (New York: W. W. Norton & Company, 1988); S. Freud, "From Civilization, War and Death," in *The University of Chicago History of Western Civilization, Topic X: Problems of the Twentieth Century* (Chicago: The University of Chicago Press, 1964).
9. B. A. Ackerman, *Social Justice in the Liberal State* (New Haven, Conn.: Yale University Press, 1980).
10. Beauchamp and Bowie, *Ethical Theory and Business;* Freeman and Gilbert, *Corporate Strategy and the Search for Ethics.*
11. B. L. Toffler, *Tough Choices* (New York: John Wiley & Sons, 1986).
12. H. C. Bunke, "Should We Teach Business Ethics?" *Business Horizons* 4, 1988, pp. 2–8; W. Shapiro, "What's Wrong: Hypocrisy, Betrayal and Greed Unsettle the Nation's Soul," *Time,* May 25, 1987, pp. 14–17.
13. R. Henkoff, "Is Greed Dead?" *Fortune,* Aug. 14, 1989, pp. 40–49; C. Hutton, "Greed Really Turns Me Off," *Fortune,* January 2, 1989, p. 69.
14. R. N. Bellah, *Habits of the Heart: Individualism and Commitment in American Life* (Berkeley, University of California Press, 1985).
15. Bunke, "Should We Teach Business Ethics?"
16. Ibid.
17. D. Bell, *The Cultural Contradictions of Capitalism* (New York: Basic Books, 1976), pp. 54–57; D. Vogel, "Business Ethics Past and Present," *The Public Interest* 102, 1991, pp. 49–64.

18. A. Smith, *The Wealth of Nations* (New York: The Modern Library, 1965).
19. A. Hamilton, J. Madison, and J. Jay, *The Federalist Papers* (New York: The New American Library, Inc., 1961).
20. Smith, *The Wealth of Nations.*
21. J. Q. Wilson, "Adam Smith on Business Ethics," *California Management Review* 1, 1989, pp. 59–72.
22. Smith, *The Wealth of Nations.*
23. Wilson, "Adam Smith on Business Ethics."
24. Ibid.
25. K. M. Eisenhardt, *Agency Theory: An Assessment and Review* (Stanford, Calif.: Department of Industrial Engineering and Engineering Management, Stanford University, 1988); C. G. Luckhardt, "Duties of Agent to Principal," in *Business Ethics: Corporate Values and Society,* ed. M. Snoeyenbos, R. Almeder, and J. Humber (New York: Prometheus Books, 1983), pp. 115–21; W. W. Manley and W. A. Shrode, *Critical Issues in Business Conduct: Legal, Ethical, and Social Challenges for the 1990s* (New York: Quorum, 1990); J. W. Pratt and R. J. Zeckhauser, eds., *Principals and Agents: The Structure of Business* (Boston: Harvard Business School Press, 1985).
26. S. Millgram, *Obedience to Authority* (New York: Harper & Row, 1975).
27. R. P. Nielsen, "Changing Unethical Organizational Behavior," *The Academy of Management Executive* 3, no. 2, 1989, p. 123.; M. Velasquez, D. J. Moberg, and G. F. Cavanagh, "Organizational Statesmanship and Dirty Politics: Ethical Guidelines for the Organizational Politician," *Organizational Dynamics,* Autumn 1983, pp. 65–80.
28. Cited in R. P. Nielsen, "Changing Unethical Organizational Behavior."
29. M. P. Glazer and P. M. Glazer, *The Whistle-Blowers: Exposing Corruption in Government and Industry* (New York: Basic Books, 1989); J. P. Near, "Whistle-blowing: Encourage It!" *Business Horizons* 1, 1989, pp. 2–6.
30. Glazer and Glazer.
31. Plato, *The Republic,* trans. M. Cornford (New York: Oxford University Press, 1967).
32. Ibid.
33. Ibid.
34. L. Kohlberg, "Moral Development," in *International Encyclopedia of the Social Sciences,* vol. 10, ed. D. L. Sills (New York: Macmillan & Free Press, 1968); L. Kohlberg, *Moral Stages: A Current Formulation and Response to Critics* (New York: Karger, 1983).
35. A. Etzioni, *The Moral Dimension: Toward a New Economics* (New York: The Free Press, 1988).
36. H. A. Hornstein, *Cruelty and Kindness* (Englewood Cliffs, N.J.: Prentice Hall, 1976).
37. Ibid.
38. Latane and Darley, 1970; H. A. Hornstein, H. N. Masor, and K. Sole, "Effects of Sentiment and Completion of a Helping Act on Observer Helping," *Journal of Personality and Social Psychology* 17, 1971, pp. 107–12.
39. Etzioni, *The Moral Dimension.*
40. DeGeorge, *Business Ethics.*
41. Etizioni, *The Moral Dimension,* p. 63.
42. Ibid.

4

ETHICAL DILEMMAS IN BUSINESS

Every rational being exists as an end in himself and not merely as a means to be arbitrarily used by this or that will. In all his actions, whether they are directed to himself or to other rational beings, he must always be regarded at the same time as an end . . . i.e., . . . an object of respect.

Immanual Kant

Introduction and Chapter Objectives

This chapter contains some preliminary advice about the questions to ask and the principles to consider in handling ethical dilemmas. A more detailed analysis of what ethics consists of will follow, and an understanding of the two ethical traditions, the right and wrong and good and bad, is developed. The sources for this discussion are some of the ideas of the classic thinkers about ethics, including Immanuel Kant. The chapter ends with a dicussion of the Lockheed bribery incident, where the clash between the two ethical traditions is very striking.

Ethical Challenges

The United States is a scandal-plagued society. In recent years, there have been many scandals, including influence peddling by top political appointees, television evangelists cheating their congregations, collusion among military contractors, and bribery at the Pentagon.[1] The ethical situations managers face, are often less dramatic than these well-publicized cases. A high percentage of them may have to do with personnel issues and involve decisions about firing employees, promoting them, and taking them on and off projects.[2] Why do personnel issues acquire such significance? Hard work is supposed to result in success, a sign of election by God according to the Protestant ethic; however, in modern bureaucratic organizations, the connection between hard work and success may not be clear. Success often depends on "the interpretive judgments of shifting groups in an ever-changing social structure."[3] In evaluating the person's contribution to the organization's performance, people believe that the capriciousness of a person's superiors and fellow-workers may play a role.

Commonplace and even ordinary, the ethical dilemmas found in organizations are extremely troubling nonetheless. They consist of relationships between people that involve the possibility of causing harm.[4] Harm is central to any definition of an ethical dilemma.

Situations consisting of actual or potential harm to others constitute the essence of ethical predicaments.[5] Ethical dilemmas involve actions that affect the freedom and well-being of others.[6] They also arise when one wants to do the right thing but does not know what it is or if one has the power to carry it out.[7] They exist, too, when there are conflicts between values, between means and ends, and between groups and individuals to whom one is obligated.

Handling Business Dilemmas

The business world presents many dilemmas with ethical implications (see Case IB). The following questions may be helpful in dealing with these dilemmas:

> What principles are involved?
>
> Who has a stake (what groups/and or individuals) in the outcome?
>
> Whom are you as a manager serving?
>
> Whom might you as a manager injure? And how badly?
>
> What principles should you use in making a decision?
>
> Are these principles clear? Could you describe them to the company's board of directors? To your family? Could you explain them in court? Could you explain them to the media? Could you explain them to your fellow workers?
>
> Would the decision you make seem right a year from now?
>
> Would it seem right 20 years from now when someone wrote a history of the company?

Moral Muteness

Unfortunately, managers may be reluctant to ask ethical questions even when situations have obvious ethical dimensions.[8] They tend to discuss issues as if their motivations are solely practical and they are concerned with organizational interests and economic good sense. The situations are labeled as judgment calls, professional matters, or strategic concerns rather than ethical ones.

Managers may be exceptionally mute when it comes to ethical discussion.[9] They may prefer to avoid the use of ethical language and to define conflicts they face in nonethical terms. Serious negative consequences—undue managerial stress and decreased influence for ethics—arise from this failure to directly confront ethical issues.[10]

Relativism

Thus, managers should try to reason about situations in terms of the ethical issues involved. However, in its application to day-to-day behavior, the problem of relativism makes it difficult to do so. Individuals use many different principles to justify their behavior, and these principles often are in conflict. Some people argue that conventions should govern: in business, do as others do or risk financial loss. Others hold that might equals right: seize what advantage is possible without regard to ordinary social laws and customs. Still others have an intuitionist ethic; they believe in doing what feels right. In short, people seek to justify their behavior in many different ways.[11]

Some companies have ethical codes that employees may invoke to justify what they do. For instance, IBM's guideline of business practice asks employees to inquire of themselves, if under the "full glare of examination by associates, friends, and family they would remain comfortable with their decisions."

Common Sense

Moral common sense can be a starting point in reasoning about ethical issues.[12] Certainly, a person should try to:

· Avoid harm to others.
· Respect others' rights.
· Avoid lying or cheating.
· Keep one's promises and contracts.
· Obey the law.
· Prevent harm.

· Help those in need.
· Be fair.

But how does a person reconcile conflicts among these principles? What do the principles mean when they are applied to specific situations? For instance, what if avoiding harm to others requires lying and cheating? To save lives threatened by terrorists, is it not acceptable to lie, cheat, and even to strike back violently against the terrorists? But would it be right to kill a healthy individual and distribute the person's body parts to save the lives of a dozen people needing transplants? How should values be weighed against values in a particular instance?

These problems cannot be easily overcome. They make ethical discourse necessary. Philosophers believe that people should reason about ethical issues and that with practice their judgment can be improved. Some background about ethical philosophy can help people make better ethical decisions. The remainder of this chapter elucidates concepts that may have bearing on the judgments people make.

Ethics Defined

Ethics has been defined as systematic inquiry into human conduct.[13] The purpose is to discover both the rules that ought to govern human action and the goods that are worth seeking in human life. As indicated, two different but related questions are central to this pursuit: What is right or wrong? And what is good or bad? The history of ethical study has examples of thinkers who have been primarily concerned with the question of action and its rightness and wrongness, and thinkers who have been primarily concerned with the ends or goals of action *and* their goodness or badness. The first of these traditions is called the *deontological,* because it concerns duty. It is associated with the great Western religions, Judaism and Christianity. The second tradition is called *teleological,* because it concerns the purposes of action. It is associated with classical Greek thought.

No fine line can be drawn between these two traditions, however. Greek writers such as Plato are concerned with duty, and religious writers have been concerned with ends. An interest in ethics requires reflection on both these elements—what is right and wrong *and* what is good and bad.

Metaethics

Modern ethical thinkers have moved away from normative ethical concerns, that is, what ought to be done, and are more preoccupied with questions of metaethics, that is, problems of meaning, method, and knowledge. These problems include the following types of questions:

- Just what do the main ethical concepts like *good* and *right* mean? Can these concepts be defined?
- By what process does a person reach a conclusion about an ethical dilemma? Is the conclusion based on empirical evidence, authority, intuition, moral insight, revelation, or established social practice?
- Is it possible to reach ethical conclusions that overcome the relativism and disagreement about values? Are there answers to ethical dilemmas that would be universally accepted?

Doing What Is Right

On the surface, ethical standards differ, yet there is a core of similarity that runs through ethical systems that negates claims of total relativism. The Golden Rule—do unto others as you would have them do unto you—is a universal idea with origins in both Judaism and Christianity as well as in non-Western religions such as Buddhism and Confucianism. In Buddhism, it is expressed as, "Hurt not others with that which pains yourself." The excellent companies in Peters and Waterman's bestselling book often displayed this type of behavior, as the managers tried to treat their employees, customers, suppliers, shareholders, and other stakeholders with the same respect that they would have liked to have received.[14]

All but the most extreme cynics believe that humans should do what is right by treating others with dignity. People have a duty, a moral obligation, to do so. In everyday discussion, this duty is signified by the word *ought.* In the Judeo-Christian tradition this ought is positively expressed as the Golden Rule: people are obligated to love their neighbors as themselves.

Going beyond the Golden Rule

The Golden Rule may not be a sufficient guide to action. In fact, starting with the New Testament, it has been criticized (see Exhibit 4–1). In the

---

EXHIBIT 4–1   The Golden Rule and Its Critics

The Golden Rule	*Critiques of the Golden Rule*
"Love your neighbor as yourself."	What about your enemies? Are they not deserving of love?
	If a person loves being harmed, can the person harm others?

Sermon on the Mount, Jesus was more demanding of people. He said that they should not simply love their neighbor as themselves:

> I say unto you love your *enemies,* bless them that curse you, do good to them that hate you, and pray for them that despitefully use you and persecute you. . . . For if you love those who love you, what reward have you? Do not even the common people do the same? . . . Be you therefore perfect.

The 18th century German philospher, Immanuel Kant, was also a critic, however friendly, of the Golden Rule.[15] For example, he was concerned that it might be applied perversely by wicked people. A sadomasochist, for instance, believes that it is right to harm others and to be harmed by them because hurting and being hurt are how such a person wants to be treated. A business person too might believe that inflicting harm and being the recipient of such harm was acceptable; it was part of the natural order of the dog-eat-dog business world. "Do unto others before they do it unto you" might be this person's motto. Such a person would claim that he or she was not opposed to hurting or being hurt and saw no reason why others should be opposed to the infliction of harm by people on each other. Kant formulated the famous categorical imperative in his 1785 treatise on *The Metaphysics of Morals* at least partially to combat the possibility that people would use the Golden Rule in such a perverse way.

Treating Others with Respect

Kant went beyond the Golden Rule by positing that the moral ought is unconditional—it is binding regardless of a person's wishes, desires, or interests. The word *ought* has many connotations.[16] Some of them do not concern morals. There is a logical ought used in mathematical statements to indicate necessity, and a prudential ought usually used in statements about money and riches, for example, "Hard work and thrift make a person wealthy."

As Kant expressed it, the duty to regard other human beings with respect is unconditional. Be just in your dealings with your fellow human beings, he argued, treat them as ends and not merely as means. This principle cannot be abrogated. It exists regardless of whether we want to treat others with respect or not, whether it helps or harms us, whether it is prudential to do so and we receive financial gain or suffer financial loss.[17] His teaching is referred to as the categorical imperative in that it is binding and permits no exceptions.

Kant taught that people should be treated as ends-in-themselves and not merely as means to ends or as objects of manipulation by others. But his idealism does not rule out the possibility that people will to a degree treat others as objects of manipulation. Note he says, "not merely"; he admits that people will inevitably treat others as means to some extent. But he argues that they should not be treated merely as means.

Universalism

Kant's imperative also requires that a person ask if a proposed action is consistent with universal standards of conduct. Would a person be willing to live in a world where *everyone* behaved in the manner contemplated? For example, would a person be willing to live in a world where everyone inflicted harm and was a victim of the harm inflicted by others? Would a person be willing to live in a world where everyone's ends are achieved by violent means, where everyone lied, cheated, bribed, or discriminated against persons of a different race or religion? If one person lies, according to the imperative, that person must permit everyone to lie. If everyone lied, of course, it would be impossible to tell if anyone were telling the truth, and it would be impossible for society to function. Similarly, if everyone cheated, bribed, or discriminated, social order would disintegrate. Transactions between persons would be impossible.

If you are unwilling to permit others the right to a particular type of behavior, then you may not make an exception, reasoning that for yourself the behavior is permitted but for others it is forbidden. For example, before cheating on an exam, consider whether you would want to live in a world where everyone cheated?[18] On simple, pragmatic grounds, the answer is no, for if everyone cheated, the exam would have no meaning and one could gain no particular advantage by cheating. Condemning the behavior on universal grounds takes away the rationale for engaging in the behavior.

Autonomy

Kant also believed in people's autonomy; they should knowingly submit themselves to universally valid moral principles.[19] People are not animals, nor are they subject to blind instincts and sensations. They are rational and can control their passions. They are free, rational entities who are distinctive because of their ability to formulate universal laws and to abide by them. Thus, they should only act such that their actions should become the basis for a universal law.

Unalienable Rights

Kant lived at the time of the revolutions in America and France, and his ideas are largely in accord with those expressed by these revolutions' leaders. For example, people were deserving of respect, Thomas Jefferson held, because certain "truths" are "self-evident, . . . [that is, that] all men are created equal." People, according to Jefferson, "are endowed by their Creator with . . . unalienable rights" and "among these are life, liberty, and the pursuit of happiness." The leaders of the French Revolution, similarly, proclaimed that human beings have natural rights consisting of the rights to "liberty, property, security, and resistance to oppression."[20] Liberty is defined as "the power to do anything that does not injure others." People also should have the right to freedom of religion and of opinion "provided that their manifestation does not disturb the public order established by law."[21] They should be guaranteed the right to "freely speak, write, and print subject to responsibility for the abuse of this freedom."[22] For the makers of the French Revolution, property also was "an inviolable and sacred right."[23] No one can be deprived of property "unless legally established public necessity obviously demands it and upon condition of a just and prior indemnity."[24]

The rights, or entitlement, model of ethics, represented by Kant and the leaders of the American and French revolutions, holds that individuals have a right to be treated in ways that ensure their dignity, autonomy, and respect. All persons have basic rights to respect as free and rational individuals. They have rights to free consent, privacy, freedom of conscience, freedom of speech, and due process.

Kant's Rationality and Human Instinct: Are They Compatible?

Although a critic of the Golden Rule, Kant is a friendly critic who merely emphasizes the universal aspect of the Biblical injunction to love your neighbor as yourself. The self in the Bible is based on a belief that people are created in the divine image. For Kant, the unique aspect of people that gives them their potential for morality is their rationality, their ability to articulate reasons for their actions, and their freedom, their ability to engage in autonomous action based on the reasons they give. Kant's image of humanity is similar to that in the Bible. If a person reasons ethically and is free to act on the results of reflection, the person is unlikely to conclude that "hurt me and I will hurt you" is an acceptable model for how people should treat one another.

In contrast, 20th-century thinkers commonly view people as driven by impulses beyond their control and incapable of freedom (see Exhibit 4–2). Thus, sadomasochism would be viewed as a destructive drive, as an urge that some people would be unable to control or resist. Compare Kant's notion of humanity with that of Sigmund Freud, the founder of psychoanalysis, who wrote that "the inmost essence of human nature consists of elemental instincts, which are common to all men and aim at the satisfaction of certain primal needs."[25] Humans, according to this view, are driven by impulses, not reflection: "We assume that human

---
EXHIBIT 4–2   **The Categorical Imperative and Its Critics**

Kant's Categorical Imperative	Critiques of the Imperative
Treat others with respect: an unconditional principle	Are people rational, and worthy of respect?
Universalism: everyone should behave in this manner	Is an ethics based on intentions, not consequences, adequate?
Human autonomy: people knowingly submit themselves to universal laws.	Are people free to do what they want?

---

instincts are of two kinds: those that conserve and unify which we call erotic or else 'sexual' and secondly the instincts to destroy and kill which we associate as the aggressive or destructive instincts."[26] These impulses represent the desire to love and hate. They are too complex to be called either good or bad. According to Freud, "in themselves [they] are neither good nor evil. . . . They are inhibited, directed toward other aims and departments, become commingled, [and] alter their objects."[27]

Indeed, Freud believed that each of the instincts is "every whit as indispensable as its opposite" and that "an instinct of either category can operate but rarely in isolation. . . . Only exceptionally does an action follow on the stimulus of a single instinct. . . . As a rule several motives . . . concur to bring about an act."[28] Even ideal motives, according to Freud, are made up of contradictory elements and often are just camouflages "for the lust of destruction."[29]

The Betrayal of the Intellectuals?

This tendency to denigrate rationality and to view humans as bundles of elementary drives and instincts has been criticized by post—World War II European intellectuals. For instance, the Dutch thinker Julien Benda wrote about "the teaching of modern metaphysics which exhorts man to feel comparatively little esteem for the truly thinking portion of himself and to honor the active and willing part of himself"; he complains that modern thinkers tend to assign "a secondary rank to the mind."[30] He condemned "a whole literature [that] has assiduously proclaimed the superiority of instinct, the unconscious, intuition, the will as opposed to intelligence."[31]

The Nobel Prize winning economist Friedrich Hayek in *The Road to Serfdom* wrote that the instinctual element in behavior was harnessed by totalitarian dictatorships to impose their will. Since in a totalitarian society, a person does not choose to do good or evil, but is forced to do so, Nazi and Communist totalitarianism deprived people of their autonomy and took away their ability to exercise moral judgment. In these societies Hayek believed that people "have no title to praise." His view was that

> outside the sphere of individual responsibility there is neither goodness nor badness nor opportunity for moral merit. . . . Only where we ourselves are responsible for our own interests and are free to sacrifice them has our decision moral value . . . morals . . . can exist only in the sphere in which the individual is free to decide for himself and is called upon voluntarily to sacrifice personal advantage to the observance of a moral rule.[32]

Hayek rested his defense of capitalism on a Kantian foundation. Before human beings could be ethical, they had to be free.

Intentions and Consequences

Another criticism of Kant is that he stressed motives but neglected consequences. Kant taught that other people should be treated with respect, that one should have goodwill toward them. However, does appropriateness of *motives* (as Kant believed and as the Christian tradition taught) make an action right, or is it the goodness of *consequences* (as utilitarians propose)?

John Dewey, the 20th-century American philosopher, argued that motives—the intention to treat people with respect—are less important than deliberation on consequences: "We are reasonable when we estimate the import or significance of any present desire or impulse by forecasting what it would come or amount to if carried out."[33] Dewey advises that people should deliberate about the proposed action by means of an "imaginative rehearsal." They should consider the result of their actions in terms of their "likes and dislikes, . . . desires and aversions," developing within themselves "a running commentary" based on their values of "good or evil."[34] In the mind, we give way to some impulse or try some plan. Following its "career through various steps, we find ourselves in imagination in the presence of the consequences that would follow; and as we then like and approve, or dislike and disapprove, these consequences, we find the original impulse or plan good or bad."[35]

Kant's views are deontological; they focus on the rightness or wrongness of actions in themselves. Dewey's views are teleological in that they focus on the purpose of actions; moral worth is determined by a consideration of the action's consequences, not the actor's intentions.

Considering an action's consequences puts a great burden on an actor's time and analytical capabilities. The person must develop many options, consider who might be affected directly and indirectly, both positively and negatively, if the options were carried out, and weigh the total results. The person should consider whether an action is good or bad in light of its manifold consequences, a difficult task.

Good and Bad

But what constitutes a good or bad result? The word *good* is used in so many different senses—a good job, a good movie, a good apple, a good feeling, and so on.[36] No one would maintain that any of these uses indicates a highest good. One must distinguish between things valued for what they are good for and final goods, things valued for themselves. Philosophers refer to the former classification as *extrinsic* goods because they are instrumental in character; they are valued only for what they provide. Final goods are denoted as *intrinsic* goods because they have inherent value; they are the ultimate goods, the reason that all other goods are worthwhile.

Aristotle distinguishes between intrinsic and extrinsic goods as follows:

> If then there is some end of the thing which we desire for its own sake (everything else being desired for the sake of this), and if we do not choose everything for the sake of something else (for at that rate the process would go on to infinity, so that our desire would be empty and vain), clearly this must be the good and the chief good. Will not the knowledge of it, then, have a great influence on life?[37]

Extrinsic goods are means to an end, rather than being ends in themselves. Thus, we go to the dentist not because doing so is a final good but because it allows us to achieve some other, more important aim. We may go to college because we want a higher paying job, not because we value a college education in itself. We may earn money because we seek to provide for our children and improve the quality of our lives, not because we value the money in itself and seek to accumulate it simply for the sake of accumulating. (Surely, such a person is a miser.)

Intrinsic goods have the highest value, but how do we determine what is the highest good? Again, moral theory is challenged by the problem of relativism. The answer to this question—what is the highest good—that comes from both modern and classical views is *happiness*. But what is happiness and how can it be achieved? And what does the answer to this question imply for how we should live our lives? What should we be seeking, and how?

Wisdom and Virtue versus Pleasure and Pain

Classic philosophers such as Plato and Aristotle believed that the highest good is wisdom, and that virtuous behavior is the product of wisdom. Aristotle felt that virtue is "concerned with passions and actions and in these there is excess, defect, and the intermediate."[38] He believed that "excess and defect are characteristic of vice, and the mean of virtue."[39] He said that a person can "fail in many ways . . . while to succeed is possible only in one way" and "to miss the mark easy, to hit it difficult."[40] Accordingly, a person must act as if he or she were an archer trying to hit a target. "Shall we not, like archers who have a mark to aim at, be more likely to hit upon what is right?"[41] Virtuous behavior requires great precision.

Unlike the ancients who sought to understand virtue, many modern thinkers focus on pleasure and pain and are hedonists who believe that the highest good is pleasure and the greatest evil is pain. The 19th-century English philosopher Jeremy Bentham wrote: "Nature has placed mankind under the governance of two sovereign masters, pain and pleasure. It is for them alone to point out what we ought to do as well as to determine what we shall do."[42] Understand clearly that he is saying that right and wrong amount to nothing more than pleasure and pain: "On the one hand the standard of right and wrong, on the other hand the chain of causes and effects are fastened to [pain and pleasure's] throne. They [pain and pleasure] govern us in all we do, all we say, all we think."[43]

Community interests are simply the aggregation of the pleasures and pains experienced by individuals. In other words, Bentham is arguing that what is in the interests of the community is the "greatest good for the greatest number."[44] Or as John Stuart Mill articulated it in his "greatest happiness" principle, something is good in proportion to its tendency to promote pleasure and the absence of pain and bad in proportion to its tendency to promote displeasure and pain.[45]

Bentham suggests that people as a society should add together quantitative units of happiness and subtract quantitative units of unhappiness to arrive at a measure of total happiness or total pain and pleasure (the so-called hedonic calculus). Then society can make more rational decisions about what to do. In doing these calculations, economists are at an advantage because for them a quantitative analytical unit exists: money. Thus, economists have produced indicators of national economic performance like the gross national product (GNP). They have advocated the use of procedures like cost-benefit analysis before proceeding with individual policies and programs. These quantitative techniques are simply systems of national accounts that aggregate at the level of the nation information that business people routinely gather about their firms.

Undoubtedly, these indicators and procedures are quite useful. Nevertheless, they have a concreteness that prevents people from grappling with more fundamental questions. For instance, what exactly is happiness? Does it consist of friendship, knowledge, courage, and beauty in addition to material things which have obvious value in units of currency?

Is happiness the same as quantified units of pleasure? What about a dissatisfied Socrates, according to a famous question asked by John

Stuart Mill; is he or not better off than a satisfied hog? Should our subjective preferences as reflected in the price system be the sole criteria for assessing pleasure and pain (see Exhibit 4–3)?

The Tyranny of the Majority

Utilitarianism aims to maximize happiness, pleasure, and welfare for all people in society. But in paying attention to overall happiness, it can disregard the fate of individuals and specific groups. What happens to the rights of individuals and groups when the majority (or some benevolent utilitarian dictator claiming to represent the majority) has decided what the greatest good for the greatest number is? Would the rights of individuals and groups be trampled?

American democracy seems to have been designed to deal with this question. The founders of the American republic in the *Federalist Papers* are sensitive to the potential abuses brought on by the tyranny of majority. As this famous passage from the *Federalist Papers* reveals, to assure that individual and group rights are not violated, the founders established a complex system of governance designed to protect minority interests. They maintain that there are "points of difference between a democracy and a republic" and that these differences protect citizens from the abuses of the majority:

> First, the delegation of the government . . . to a small number of citizens elected by the rest; secondly, the greater number of citizens and greater sphere of country over which the latter may be extended. . . . Extend the sphere and you take in a greater variety of parties and interests; you make it less probable that a majority of the whole will have a common motive to invade the rights of other citizens; or if such a common motive exists, it will

---

EXHIBIT 4–3   Utilitarianism and Its Critics

Utilitarianism	*Critiques of Utilitarianism*
Consider consequences	Are people capable of forecasting the consequences of their actions?
Aim for happiness	What is happiness?
Seek pleasure, avoid pain	Is there a better way to establish what happiness is than in monetary terms?
Try to achieve the greatest good for the greatest number	What about wisdom, virtue, courage, friendship, and beauty—do they get counted?
	What happens to the rights of individuals and groups?

be more difficult for all who feel it to discover their own strength and to act in unison with each other.[46]

The cure for the brute force of the majority is representative government, not direct democracy, and a large and diverse country, big enough to prevent any single faction from imposing its view on the rest.

In an organization, similar principles can be applied to promote plural views and protect minority interests. If diverse interests are represented, it is likely that minority rights will be protected. However, with diversity of interests comes the problem of disruptive, cantankerous, and potentially destructive factions, about which the founders of the American republic also had much to say (see the feature on page 90, "The Destructive Potential of Factions").

Justice and Liberty

Can a person be happy in an unjust society? The relationship between individual well-being and the collective good is taken up by the modern political philosophers John Rawls and Robert Nozick. Rawls justifies inequality only if it is "reasonably expected to be in everyone's advantage and attached to positions and offices open to all." His principles of justice are:

> First: each person is to have an equal right to the most extensive basic liberty compatible with a similar liberty for others. Second: social and economic inequalities are to be arranged so that they are both (*a*) reasonably expected to be to everyone's advantage, and (*b*) attached to positions and offices open to all.[47]

These principles, he maintains,

> are a special case of a more general conception of justice that can be expressed as follows. All social values—liberty and opportunity, income and wealth, and the bases of self-respect—are to be distributed equally unless an unequal distribution of any, or all, of these values is to everyone's advantage.[48]

Another modern political philosopher, Robert Nozick, takes a different view. He stresses liberty and the rights of people to acquire property. He maintains that "a person who acquires a holding in accordance with the principle of justice is entitled to that holding" regardless of the implications for equality or inequality:[49]

> If the world were wholly just, the following inductive definition would exhaustively cover the subject of justice. . . .
>
> 1. A person who acquires a holding in accordance with the principle of justice in acquisition is entitled to that holding.

2. A person who acquires a holding in accordance with the principle of justice in transfer, from someone else entitled to the holding, is entitled to the holding.
3. No one is entitled to a holding except by repeated applications of 1 and 2.[50]

While the highest good for Rawls is some form of justice, for Nozick it is liberty, the ability of people to forge their own destinies and reap the consequences without communal interference. Nozick writes:

> We might say: From each according to what he chooses to do, to each according to what he makes for himself (perhaps with the contracted aid of others) and what others choose to do for him and choose to give him of what they've been given previously. . . . So as a summary and great simplification . . . we have: From each as they choose, to each as they are chosen.[51]

Summing up So Far

Five principles for addressing ethical dilemmas have been discussed (see Exhibit 4–4).[52] The principles emanating from the deontological tradition should be familiar by now. The intent of a person must be to treat others with *respect*. An act has moral value only if all people have been treated as possessing dignity and worth. People have the right to be treated with dignity because they are human beings with inalienable rights to such things as life, liberty, and the pursuit of happiness. The other principle from the deontological tradition is *universalism*. An act can be justified only if it can be universally applied. A person has to be consistent with regard to moral choices and be prepared to argue that all

EXHIBIT 4–4 **Deontological and Teleological Ethics Combined**

		Means	
		Respect for the Individual	Universalism
	Greatest Good for the Greatest Number		
Ends	Justice		
	Liberty		

people with the same information facing the same circumstances should act in the same way.

The important thing from the deontological perspective is a person's motives, not the consequences of the person's actions; a person cannot possibly foresee and evaluate all possible consequences of actions that might be taken. The teleological tradition stresses outcomes, not motives. From it, the *utilitarian* principle that actions should result in the greatest good for the greatest number is derived. The additional principles from the teleological tradition are *justice* and *liberty:* an act is good if the least advantaged in society enjoy a better standard of living because of it, and it is good if the members of society enjoy greater freedom because of it.

Means and Ends: A Basic Moral Dilemma

Juxtaposed against each other, the two major ethical traditions pose a dilemma. On the one hand, right and wrong questions are those of means, of proper conduct. Good and bad questions are those of ends, of the purposes such conduct serves, whether it is the greatest good for the greatest number, justice, or liberty. Means and ends come into conflict; their conflict constitutes the core of most ethical dilemmas.

For instance, consider individual goals, like being successful in life, not failing, and not being humiliated. They are not universal principles on a par with the greatest good, justice, and liberty. Yet they are the types of goals that often motivate people.[53]

People may engage in ethically dubious behavior because they want to achieve these goals. They rationalize their actions by claiming that the ends justify the means; simply, they hold that success justifies the dubious behavior that is necessary to achieve that success. The fear of humiliation that comes with failure is as important as succeeding. Sometimes this fear is based on very realistic concerns, such as a concern about economic security. At other times, the fear is simply not wanting to look bad or be wrong. Fears such as these often drive people to ethically dubious acts.

People often define themselves in terms of achievement in their jobs and careers. If they do not attain the success they seek, they open themselves to ethical compromise. The end—to maintain their self-worth—justifies the means. To those so defining themselves, it is worth it to commit dubious acts to maintain self-esteem.

Another manifestation of ends conflicting with means is how people at different levels in an organization view the issues the organization faces (see Exhibit 4–5). Typically, people lower in the hierarchy stand for a deontological ethics that calls for treating people with respect.[54] People higher in the organization stand for a teleological ethics that emphasizes the greatest good for the organization as a whole. People lower in the

---

EXHIBIT 4–5   Ethical Principles at Different Levels in the Organization

		Typical Ethical Principle
Organizational Level	*Executives*	Greatest good for the greatest number
	Employees	Welfare of individual employees

---

hierarchy frame ethical questions as helpful or hurtful to the welfare of individuals in the organization. They care about their friends and colleagues who may be hurt by decisions made at the top. For instance, they are reluctant to carry out layoffs that involve people they know and respect. But people higher in the organization do not have the same reluctance about these cuts. They can justify the layoffs in terms of the organization's survival. They frame ethical questions as broad policy issues that involve the organization's welfare, not the welfare of the individuals who have been harmed. The ends the organization serves justify the means it has to use to accomplish its objectives.

The Lockheed Bribery Case: Do the Ends Justify the Means?

The Italian political philosopher Niccolo Machiavelli argued in his 1513 book *The Prince* that worthwhile ends justify efficient means; that is, when ends are of overriding importance, unscrupulous means may be used to achieve them. Almost everyone would agree with Machiavelli that under some circumstances, ends do justify the means. For example, when asked by a terrorist where a child is hiding, one is permitted to lie. However, deciding in a particular case that the ends justify the means is not as easy as in this example. For instance, one of the most difficult dilemmas faced by American businesses operating abroad is the question of illegal payments. Should American companies engage in this activity when it is accepted business practice, albeit illegal? Should they engage in it when it seems necessary to obtain contracts and to open up new business? The Lockheed bribery scandal of the mid-1970s is an interesting example of this dilemma.

Because of Lockheed's desperate straits as a company—it had just been bailed out by a federal government loan guarantee—the company's existence was at stake.[55] Many jobs would be lost if the company did not

The Destructive Potential of Factions

The founders of the American republic were aware that democratic government could be hurt by competing factions:

> A factious spirit has tainted our public administration. . . . By a faction I mean a number of citizens whether amounting to a majority or minority of the whole who are united and actuated by some common impulse of passion, or of interest, adverse to the rights of other citizens, or to the permanent and aggregate interests of the community.[1]

The roots of faction are in the different capabilities of human beings. Differing capabilities yield different economic circumstances. From the different capabilities result "unequal distribution of property."[2] Unequal distribution yields different "sentiments,"

---
[1]*The Federalist Papers* (Garden City, N.Y.: Anchor Books, 1966).
[2]Ibid.

and different sentiments produce the division of society into different groups and interests:

> Those who hold and those who are without property have ever formed distinct interests in society. Those who are creditors and those who are debtors . . . a landed interest, a manufacturing interest, a mercantile interest, a moneyed interest, with many lesser interests grow up of necessity in civilized nations and divide them into different classes actuated by different sentiments and views.[3]

The division of society into classes with different interests is dangerous but it cannot be avoided. The rights of contending factions have to be protected, according to the founders of the American republic:

> There are . . . two methods of removing the causes of faction: the one by destroying the lib-

---
[3]Ibid.

obtain a sufficient number of orders for its L-1011 Tristar commercial aircraft. Was it right for Lockheed to bribe foreign officials in an effort to get them to buy its aircraft?

Below are some of the details as they relate to the decision of Carl Kotchian, Lockheed's president to pay $3.8 million in bribes to Japanese officials. Kotchian did not go to Japan intending to bribe Japanese officials. Although directly responsible for the negotiations for the sale of the planes, he did not speak Japanese and had to rely on advice and representation from executives of a Japanese trading company that had been retained as an agent for Lockheed. The negotiations extended over a period of 70 days, during which Kotchian stayed in a hotel room in downtown Tokyo. He was subject to hurried meetings and continued suggestions that the decision would soon be made except that something, an unnamed something, was not in place.

Kotchian had no firm knowledge of whether his competitors had

The Destructive Potential of Factions continued

erty which is essential to its existence, the other by giving to every citizen the same opinions, the same passions, and the same interests. . . . The first remedy . . . [is] . . . worse than the disease. . . . The second expedient is as impracticable as the first would be unwise. As long as the reason of man continues fallible, and he is at liberty to exercise it, different opinions will be formed.[4]

Since the causes of faction cannot be removed, relief can be sought only "in the means of controlling its effects."[5]

Karl Marx, the founder of Communism, contributed greatly to our understanding of classes. In *The Communist Manifesto,* he wrote:

The history of all hitherto existing society is the history of class struggles. Freeman and slave, patrician and plebeian, lord and serf, guild-

master and journeymen, in a word, oppressor and oppressed, stood in constant opposition to one another, carried on an uninterrupted, now hidden, now open fight, a fight that each time ended either in a revolutionary reconstitution of society at large, or in the common ruin of the contending classes. . . . The modern bourgeois society that has sprouted from the ruins of feudal society has not done away with class antagonisms. It has but established new classes, new conditions of oppression, new forms of struggle in place of the old ones.[6]

Unlike the founders of the American republic, Marx saw no reason why classes should survive. He looked for the establishment of a classless society where factions would be eliminated. He envisioned a dictatorship of the proletariat that would do away with private property and the exploitation of one class by another.

[4]Ibid.
[5]Ibid.

[6]K. Marx, from "The Communist Manifesto," in *Views on Capitalism,* ed. R. Romano and M. Leiman (Beverly Hills, Calif.: Glencoe Press, 1970), pp. 328–46.

supplied that unnamed something, but he suspected that they had or would be willing to do so. The trading company represented Lockheed in all deliberations with the prime minister and the prime minister's office, and Kotchian did not have direct contact with the government officials who would make the actual decision. His contact was limited to the technical and functional representatives of Japan's airlines.

Lockheed had failed to obtain contracts for the L-1011 from Italy, Germany, and Sweden, and a large order was essential to bring unit sales close to the break-even point and to repay at least partially the expense of designing and building the aircraft. If the Nippon order, which meant more than $430 million in revenues, was not forthcoming, it would be another blow to sales momentum, which would mean a slowdown in new design projects and the necessity to lay off engineers and production workers. There was a large work force in Burbank, California, which Kotchian felt it his duty to protect. If Lockheed lost its fourth foreign order in a row, not only would the jobs of these workers in Burbank be in danger but Kotchian's own job also would be in jeopardy. Kotchian felt that 0.8 percent of the face value of the order as a bribe was a small price to pay when so much else was at stake.

Breaking Prima Facie Rules in Some Circumstances

Mark Pastin, a business ethicist at the University of Arizona, justifies Kotchian's decision.[56] He argues that most ethical rules are not categorical. Even rules that people should keep their promises (or not lie, cheat, bribe, and violate the law) have clear exceptions: "a sound ethics requires that rules sometimes be broken."[57] Almost everyone would agree that a person could break a promise to sell to a friend a patent that the friend would give to Iraq to make advanced guided missiles.

Categorical rules are those that "cannot be violated under any circumstances. . . . Prima facie rules," however, may be "violated in favor of more pressing obligations."[58] Prima facie rules should not be violated if other things are equal; however, in the "complex circumstances of international business," situations "do not conform to simple maxims."[59] Under these circumstances, "violating an ethical rule may be ethical or ethically required."[60]

According to Pastin, the Lockheed situation should be assessed from a utilitarian perspective. Using this perspective, it is clear that the positive ends outweigh the negative means. The decision to bribe Japanese officials is ethical. The costs are moral ones. A corporation engages in lying, covering up, and cheating to get what it wants. It takes unfair advantage of its competitors. However, there are other considerations: the health of American businesses that engage in international trade, the overall health of the U.S. economy, and the benefits of the sale to management, stockholders, and employees. The $400 million that Lockheed would receive for the planes would go a long way toward restoring Lockheed's fiscal health and provide savings to taxpayers in the form of revenues generated and unemployment benefits avoided. Management has an obligation to stockholders to earn a reasonable return, to employees to try to assure job security, and to society at large to promote U.S. economic well-being through the success of the company.

Certainly, the company would be doing harm by helping corrupt officials stay in power. Also, the costs of the bribe would be passed along to consumers, and it might result in inferior and possibly dangerous products on the market. But somebody else probably would have paid the bribes, and Lockheed believed that the Tristar was an acceptable, if not technically superior, plane. From the standpoint of an "endpoint" ethics, Pastin argues that "such payments are ethical if the product is good and someone else would have made the bribe anyhow."[61] The rules against bribery are only prima facie rules. Bribery cannot be condemned in all situations.

Of course, today the Foreign Corrupt Practices Act 1977 (FCPA) is in place, and it is a crime to offer payments to foreign officials to obtain or retain business. A company can be fined up to $1 million. Officers of the company who participate in or have reason to know of violations can be fined up to $10,000 and receive up to five years in prison. However, Pastin feels that it is an unnecessary law that is hurting American business in international competition.[62]

Probing More Deeply

In contrast, Professors Ian Mitroff of the University of Southern California and Ralph Kilmann of the University of Pittsburgh argue that the only way to defend Lockheed is to cite necessity, that the company had no other choice because of the economic factor.[63] The company cannot be defended based on the moral factor or the rightness or wrongness of its decision. These professors maintain that to prevent bribery from taking place, certain questions should be posed in a "dialectical" style in a company. The company should consider:[64]

1. What is worst thing that can happen if it engages in bribery?
2. What will be the effect on future business?
3. What will be the effect on the company's image?
4. How will it affect the corporation's philosophy of management?
5. How will it affect the control managers have over the corporation?
6. How will it affect the kind of employees the company attracts?
7. How will it affect the company's customers?
8. How will it affect the company's relationships with competitors?
9. What will it do to the managers as human beings? Will it erode their moral fibre?
10. How will it affect the status and quality of products, R&D, and innovation in the company?
11. Is this the kind of practice with which the company wants to be identified?

If these questions are asked, and the probing with respect to them is deep and substantial, Mitroff and Kilman are convinced that managers will not engage in bribery.[65]

Final Considerations

This chapter ends as it began. Ethical dilemmas are difficult; they involve conflicts between deeply held and often opposing principles. There is no easy way out and yet one must still give an account for what one has done. One must provide a justification.

With respect to how to resolve the difficult choices that exist, a few final pieces of advice may be useful. First, if two apparently irreconcilable principles are in conflict, one should make sure that there really is an ethical dilemma. Might there not be some ingenious way out that will allow one to proceed without violating any moral rule? Consider all the facts then rethink the problem. Try to redefine the situation before caving in on moral principles. If it is necessary to compromise on moral grounds, then establish firm limits and stick to them with respect to how far to go in making ethical compromises.

A second piece of advice is to make distinctions. The distinction between prima facie and categorical rules already has been introduced. Another is the distinction between "act" utilitarianism and "rule" utilitarianism.[66] Act utilitarianism calls for actions that are always in accord with the greatest good for the greatest number. Thus, if one person has to die so that an individual's body organs can be shared by five persons needing transplants, the act of killing the person to preserve the lives of the five others is justified. Breaking the rules, lying, and engaging in other types of ruthless behavior including killing are justified if the greater good is served.

A rule utilitarian looks at such situations differently. Certain rules cannot be violated under any circumstances because they guarantee the existence of society. The ultimate justification for them is an appeal to social utility. Without these rules (e.g., the prohibition against murder), society could not maintain itself.

Some situations, however, cannot be resolved either through a redefinition or the use of sophisticated distinctions. They are indeed tragic. A person can do only one thing: carefully give reasons why some principles take precedence over others. Thereafter, provide justifications for the actions one has taken.[67] And understand that the moral rules still have meaning, that their violation is an unfortunate exception. Do not give into absolute relativism, pure anarchy, to the inability to make all moral distinctions and judgments. Even permit oneself some guilt and remorse for engaging in a necessary but still wrong action.

It is not easy for humans to be just and to preserve a sense of integrity in an imperfect world. The 20th century, for all it material progress, has been a brutal period with wars and mass slaughter and the degradation of the human spirit. The question posed by the Christian theologian Reinhold Neibuhr is relevant: in situations where a person's survival is at stake and people are acting unjustly, can the person maintain a sense of integrity? Can a person be moral in an immoral society?

Summary and Conclusions

This chapter may be summarized as follows. Ten moral principles from the writings of various ethical philosophers have been shown to exist. Some of these are deontological principles relating to right and wrong and some are teleological relating to good and bad. The ten principles are:

1. Treat others with respect (Kant).
2. Investigate the consequences of one's actions (Dewey).
3. Evaluate one's actions in terms of a higher good (Aristotle).
4. Aim to behave in a virtuous manner (balanced with precision between states of extreme) (Aristotle).
5. Strive to maximize pleasure and minimize pain (Bentham, Mill).
6. Assess actions in terms of the greatest good for the greatest number (Bentham, Mill).
7. Avoid causing unnecessary suffering to individuals and groups (James).
8. Take a broad range of interests into account when deciding (the founders of the American republic).
9. Tolerate inequality only when it is in everyone's interest and it arises under conditions where opportunities are open to all (Rawls).
10. Encourage people to forge their own destinies as long as they do not infringe on the rights of others (Nozick).

These principles can be applied to many business decisions.

Discussion Questions

1. Define ethics. What does it mean? What is an ethical dilemma?
2. Why are managers reluctant to discuss ethical issues? Why do they insist on referring to them as organizational or economic matters?
3. Are all ethical principles relative? Explain.

4. What is the difference between the deontological tradition in ethics and the teleological?

5. What is metaethics?

6. Explain Kant's critique of the Golden Rule.

7. To what extent did Kant envision any exceptions to his rule of treating others with respect? Can this rule really be unconditional and absolute?

8. To what extent are people rational? To what extent are they controlled by passion and instinct? What do you think (or feel)? What difference does your answer make?

9. In your view, which is more important—motives or consequences? Why?

10. What is the difference between an intrinsic good and an extrinsic good?

11. How would you answer the criticisms raised against utilitarianism?

12. Can a person be happy in an unjust society? What do you think (or feel)?

13. In the controversy about the Lockheed bribery, who is right—Pastin or Mitroff and Kilmann? Why?

Endnotes

1. W. Shapiro, "What's Wrong: Hypocrisy, Betrayal and Greed Unsettle the Nation's Soul," *Time,* May 25, 1987, pp. 14–17.

2. K. E. Kram, P. C. Yeager, and G. E. Reed, "Decisions and Dilemmas: The Ethical Dimension in the Corporate Context, in *Research in Corporate Social Performance and Policy* (Greenwich, Conn.: JAI Press, Inc., 1989), pp. 21–54.

3. R. Jackall, *Moral Mazes: The World of Corporate Managers* (New York: Oxford University Press, 1988), p. 197.

4. B. L. Toffler, *Tough Choices* (New York: John Wiley & Sons, 1986).

5. R. A. Cooke, *Ethics in Business: A Perspective* (Chicago: Arthur Andersen & Co., 1988).

6. K. Goodpaster, *Ethics in Management* (Boston: Harvard University Graduate School of Business Administration, 1984).

7. Toffler, *Tough Choices.*

8. F. B. Bird and J. A. Waters, "The Moral Muteness of Managers," *California Management Review* 1, 1989, p. 73.

9. Kram, Yeager, and Reed, "Decisions and Dilemmas."

10. Bird and Waters, The Moral Muteness of Managers.

11. G. A. Steiner and J. F. Steiner, *Business, Government, and Society;* (New York: Random House, 1988).

12. Goodpaster, *Ethics in Management.*

13. O. A. Johnson, ed., *Ethics: Selections from Classical and Contemporary Writers,* 3rd ed. (New York: Holt, Rinehart and Winston, 1974).

14. T. J. Peters and R. H. Waterman, *In Search of Excellence: Lessons from America's Best Run Companies* (New York: Harper & Row, 1982).

15. T. L. Beauchamp and N. E. Bowie, *Ethical Theory and Business,* 2nd ed. (Englewood Cliffs, N.J.: Prentice Hall, 1983).

16. Johnson, *Ethics: Selections from Classical and Contemporary Writers.*

17. I. Kant, "Foundations of the Metaphysics of Morals," in *Ethics: Selections from Classical and Contemporary Writers,* 3rd ed., ed. O. A. Johnson (New York: Holt, Rinehart and Winston, 1974), p. 205.

18. Beauchamp and Bowie, *Ethical Theory and Business.*

19. R. T. DeGeorge, *Business Ethics,* 2nd ed. (New York: Macmillian, 1986.

20. "Declaration of the Rights of Man and Citizen," in *The University of Chicago History of Western Civilization, Topic VIII: The French Revolution, Liberalism, Nationalism* (Chicago: The University of Chicago Press, 1964).

21. Ibid.

22. Ibid.

23. Ibid.

24. Ibid.

25. S. Freud, "Civilization, War and Death," in *The University of Chicago History of Western Civilization, Topic X: Problems of the Twentieth Century* (Chicago: The University of Chicago Press, 1964).

26. Ibid.

27. Ibid.

28. Ibid.

29. Ibid.

30. J. Benda, "The Betrayal of the Intellectuals," in *The University of Chicago History of Western Civilization, Topic X: Problems of the Twentieth Century* (Chicago: The University of Chicago Press, 1964).

31. Benda, "The Betrayal of the Intellectuals."

32. F. Hayek, "Excerpts from the Road to Serfdom," in *The University of Chicago History of Western Civilization, Topic X: Problems of the Twentieth Century* (Chicago: The University of Chicago Press, 1964).

33. J. Dewey, *Ethics* (1908, reprint Carbondale, Ill.: Southern Illinois University Press, 1978).

34. Ibid.

35. Ibid.

36. O. A. Johnson, ed., *Ethics: Selections from Classical and Contemporary Writers,* 3rd ed. (New York: Holt, Rinehart and Winston, 1974).

37. Aristotle, "The Nicomachean Ethics," in *Ethics: Selections from Classical and Contemporary Writers,* 3rd ed., ed. O A. Johnson (New York: Holt, Rinehart and Winston, 1974), pp. 47–76.

38. Ibid.

39. Ibid.

40. Ibid.

41. Ibid.

42. J. Bentham, "An Introduction to the Principles of Morals and Legislation, in *Ethics: Selections from Classical and Contemporary Writers,* 3rd ed., ed. O. A. Johnson (New York: Holt, Rinehart and Winston, 1974), pp. 228–39.

43. Ibid.
44. Ibid.
45. J. Mill, *Utilitarianism* (Oxford: Blackwell, 1986).
46. *The Federalist Papers* (Garden City, N.Y.: Anchor Books, 1966).
47. J. Rawls, *A Theory of Justice* (Cambridge: Harvard University Press, 1971).
48. Ibid.
49. R. Nozick, *Anarchy, State and Utopia* (New York: Basic Books, 1975).
50. Ibid.
51. Ibid.
52. L. T. Hosmer, *The Ethics of Management* (Homewood, Ill.: Irwin, 1987).
53. M. Josephson, "Ethics in Business: An Overview," *Ethics: Easier Said Than Done* l, no. 2, 1989, pp. 40–43; J. Sigler and J. Murphy, "Business Ethics: Action Needed," *Ethics: Easier Said Than Done* 1, 1989, p. 60; W. Smithburg, "Corporate Ethics," *Ethics: Easier Said Than Done* 1, 1989, p. 60.
54. Kram, Yeager, and Reed, "Decisions and Dilemmas."
55. B. Pendergast, *Note on Lockheed Aircraft Corporation* (Boston: Harvard Business School Case 9–372–013, Rev. November 1976).
56. M. Pastin, "Case: International Bribery," in *The Hard Problems of Management: Gaining the Ethics Edge* (San Francisco: Jossey-Bass Publishers, 1986), pp. 117–23.
57. Ibid.
58. Ibid.
59. Ibid.
60. Ibid.
61. Ibid.
62. Ibid.
63. I. I. Mitroff and R. H. Kilmann, "Teaching Managers to Do Policy Analysis: The Case of Corporate Bribery," *California Management Review* 20, no. l, 1977, pp. 47–54.
64. Ibid.
65. Mitroff and Kilmann, "Teaching Managers to Do Policy Analysis."
66. DeGeorge, *Business Ethics.*
67. B. A. Ackerman, *Social Justice in the Liberal State* (New Haven, Conn.: Yale University Press, 1980).

CHAPTER

5

SOCIAL
RESPONSIBILITY
Managers and Shareholders[1]

*In a free-enterprise, private property system, a corporate executive is an
employee of the owners of the business. He (or she) has direct responsibility to
his (or her) employers. That responsibility is to conduct the business in accord
with their desires, which generally will be to make as much money as possible
while conforming to the basic rules of society, both embodied in law and those
embodied in ethical custom.*

Milton Friedman, "The Social Responsibility of Business Is to Increase Its Profits."

Introduction and Chapter Objectives

Thus far, the text has stressed the ethical decisions of individuals. Although we have noted the pressures that the organization places on the
individual in making decisions, a theory of the organization is needed.
To whom is the corporation responsible? Who is affected by what it
does? This chapter and the next review the debate about corporate social
responsibility. What does corporate social responsibility mean?[2] Why
has this debate aroused controversy? Although various perspectives are
discussed, this chapter focuses on theories that stress managers' obligation to shareholders (agency theory), theories that stress managers' control of the corporation for their own benefit (managerialism), and theories that emphasize recognition of a wide array of forces inside and
outside the firm affecting managerial choices (behavioral theory).

The Meaning of Responsibility

The term *responsibility* is relatively new, first appearing in the *Federalist*, Paper 64, by Alexander Hamilton, in 1787.[3] Responsibility implies that actors are accountable for their actions. They can be subject to praise, blame, reward, and punishment, but only for voluntary actions that are susceptible to deliberation and choice and of which they are a free cause. When injury occurs from external accident that is contrary to reasonable expectation, it is a mistake (e.g., an industrial accident) for which the organization can claim that it is not responsible.

Responsibility has both internal and external aspects (see Exhibit 5–1). Internally, the members of the organization have responsibility for choosing criteria that bear upon their choices and taking into account the consequences of what they do. However, people in the organization may arbitrarily designate what pleases them as good and what displeases them as evil. They call something good simply because they desire it. Thus, responsibility needs an external dimension—standards and sanctions that come from society. The government establishes penalties to rectify or prevent irresponsible acts—crimes, misdemeanors, breaches of contract, and negligence. John Stuart Mill holds that "responsibility means punishment."[4] However, the state may be designed to secure the interests of the mighty, the powerful, or the rich. It may be an instrument to protect the privileged. Thus, responsibility needs more than external sanctions; it has to have an internal component. Society structures and orders values, and governments apply sanctions when people do not live up to these values. People, however, must determine their level of compliance. They are responsible to society *and* to their beliefs about what is right and wrong and good and bad.

Corporate Social Responsibility

Corporate social responsibility means that the corporations have obligations.[5] For instance, managers should work for the social betterment.[6] Without doing away with the need for profits, they should respond to claimants other than shareholders.

Questions arise about this obligation:

EXHIBIT 5–1   Two Dimensions of Corporate Responsibility

External: To the laws of society.
Internal: To values and beliefs.

---

1. *Is the obligation voluntary?* Is it volunteered by managers because they are devoted to various principles (religious, democratic, or humanistic), or does it come from law and the threat of punishment?

2. *Of what does the obligation actually consist?* Does it involve philanthropy or does it consist of an obligation to use the corporation's technical skills and resources to solve social problems? Were Westinghouse's efforts to enter the field of public transportation, Control Data's attempts to develop software packages to help underprivileged youth, or Du Pont's programs to recycle waste and sell its pollution control expertise examples of corporate responsibility? (See the case at the end of Part II regarding Control Data Corporation.)

3. *Why should managers be socially responsible?* Is it because of a concern about government encroachment on private decision making? Do managers desire to be good citizens of their communities? Or do they fear violence and social disruption if they do not try to achieve broad public acceptance?

The lives of two American businessmen of the 19th century—Andrew Carnegie and Julius Rosenwald—illustrate different approaches to social responsibility (see Exhibit 5–2). Carnegie's approach was to be profitable in order to be philanthropic.[7] By contrast, Rosenwald's was to identify social needs as the basis for profitable business opportunities. Peter Drucker is of the opinion that "in the years to come, the most needed and the most effective—indeed perhaps the only truly effective—approach to 'social responsibility' " will be identifying social needs as the basis for profitable activities.[8]

Both approaches show enlightened self-interest. The corporation is profitable, and therefore able to be socially responsible (Carnegie); or social responsibility is a way for the corporation to be profitable (Rosenwald). The corporation can benefit from socially responsible behavior in many ways. By providing consumers with safe products, it assures their loyalty. By granting employees pleasant and safe working conditions, it reduces absenteeism and turnover, and productivity increases. By being a good corporate citizen, by supporting the arts and charitable organizations, the corporation enhances the quality of life and attracts a better quality work force. The aspects of an organization that make it socially

---

EXHIBIT 5–2 Two Views of Corporate Social Responsibility

Carnegie: Be profitable to be philanthropic.
Rosenwald: Find profitable opportunities in meeting society's social needs.

responsible—sensitivity to changing societal expectations and attentiveness to detail—are ones that make it a better financial performer.

Does It Pay to Be Good?

But does it actually pay for the corporation to be good? In a review of fourteen studies, Ullman found the following:[9]

- Seven studies showed a positive relationship between social and financial performance.
- Three studies showed a negative relationship between corporate social performance and corporate financial performance.
- One study showed a positive relationship between female promotions and financial performance and a negative relationship between charitable contributions and financial performance.
- One study showed a U-shaped relation: extreme social performance (whether extremely good or bad) was negatively related to financial performance.
- Two studies found no effect.

At a minimum, the studies found no payoff in being bad. However, it is difficult to operationalize and measure social performance, and the means for assessing financial performance varied in the different studies (see the special feature in Chapter 1).

Recent work continues to support the positive relationship between social responsibility and profitability. Wokutch and Spencer used corporate crime (Federal Trade Commission violations) and philanthropy as measures of corporate social responsibility and correlated them with return on assets (ROA) and return on sales (ROS) for the 500 largest corporations in the United States between 1979 and 1982.[10] They found that five-year ROA and ROS measures were significantly lower for companies with a high crime rate and a low rate of philanthropy. It was unclear, however, if firms with more crimes and less philanthropy suffered financially, or if firms that committed more crimes and made smaller contributions did so because of poor financial performance.

McGuire and Schneeweis tried to clarify whether financial performance follows or precedes social performance.[11] Using *Fortune* magazine's survey of corporate executives and analysts as the measure of social performance, they found that a company's previous financial record, measured by stock market and accounting figures, influences its subsequent social performance ratings. The relationship between prior social responsibility ratings and subsequent financial performance is positive but not statistically significant. The authors concluded that good financial performance is a precondition for good social performance, but good social performance is not necessarily a precondition for good financial performance.

While a company must be profitable to be good, being good does not guarantee profitability; not all actions that are socially responsible contribute to corporate profitability. The moral responsibilities of individuals cannot be contingent upon expected gain. Some activities have to be pursued even at financial cost simply because they are right.[12]

Managers as Agents of Shareholders

We now turn to three theories of managerial responsibility, starting with the normative view of corporate social responsibility articulated by economists such as Frederick Hayek and Milton Friedman. Hayek and Friedman see managers as the trustees or agents of shareholders. Shareholders are the principals whose interests the managers must serve. The duties of an agent to a principal are termed *the fiduciary relation.*

The Fiduciary Relation

One person or entity (the agent) consents to act in behalf of, or in the interests of, another person or entity (the principal). Ideally, the principal would be able to carry out the action, but for some reason (e.g., time, expertise, or distance) it is not in a position to do so. Therefore, it appoints the agent to act in its behalf with the intent that the agent carry out the principal's wishes as precisely as possible.

Although the agent can voluntarily agree to act for the principal, it usually receives monetary remuneration. Agency-principal relations are common and are critical to all kinds of economic activity. Employers and employees, doctors and patients, and aircraft pilots and passengers have agency-principal relationships. Whenever someone is hired to fulfill a function for another, the person hired is the other person's agent.

The main question with regard to fiduciary relations is that although the agent is supposed to act for, or on behalf of, the principal, the agent is likely to have other interests of its own that may take precedence over the interests of the principal. How is the principal to monitor the agent's behavior to assure that the agent carries out the will of the principal? How is it to determine that the agent acted in good faith in pursuing its interests?

The agency relationship is "a contract under which one or more persons (the principal[s] engage another person [the agent]) to perform some service on their behalf which involves delegating some decision making authority to the agent."[13] Since the interests of the agent do not always coincide with the interests of the principal, there is good reason to believe that the agent will not always act in the best interests of the principal. The principal can limit divergences in the agent's actions by establishing appropriate incentives for the agent and by incurring costs for monitoring designed to limit the agent's discrepant behavior. But it is virtually impossible for the principal to guarantee that the agent always will make decisions that are optimal from the principal's viewpoint. This is because incentive and monitoring instruments are limited by time and by the costs that the principal must incur.

Inevitably, there is some discrepancy between what the principal considers to be its interests and what the agent has done. In law, this problem leads to complicated contractual issues and legal disputes before and after the deals have been made. The agent has to consent to act for the principal, and the principal has to consent to have the agent act for it. If the agent does not perform its duties as called for in the agreement between the agent and the principal, the principal has the right to take away its consent and end the agreement.

The agent grants the principal the right to direct and control its activities. The agent must obey the instructions given by the principal, but obedience is not the only basis for the fiduciary relation. Trust and faith (from the Latin *fidere*) are important. Care, loyalty, and obedience are the major obligations the agent owes to the principal.

The agent has a duty to refrain from knowingly violating the reasonable directions of the principal. For violation of reasonable directions the agent can lose its job and incur liability. However, if the principal's instructions are unreasonable, the agent has no duty to obey. By unreasonable, we usually mean instructions (*a*) that are illegal, unethical, and contrary to public policy; (*b*) that threaten the physical well-being of the agent; (*c*) that violate ordinary business custom; (*d*) that are impossible or impractical to carry out; and (*e*) that conflict with other contractual duties or other duties of the agent.

The normative view of such economists as Frederick Hayek and Milton Friedman is that managers are responsible to the shareholders who own the corporation.[14] They are the agents of the shareholders. Other corporate constituencies and stakeholders such as employees, customers, and residents of the communities where a corporation is located are important only insofar as they affect the relationship between the owners and the managers. The managers' main responsibility is to add to shareholder wealth. Other claimants' rights to the corporation's resources are limited because in the event of bankruptcy the shareholders are the last to be paid. They are the residual claimants who are the most at risk. Managers are trustees for stockholders upon whom the risk for the decisions they make ultimately falls.

Hayek's View

Hayek starts with the legal definition of the corporation that it is chartered under the various laws of the different American states to pursue economic activities that are meant to benefit shareholders *and* society.[15] In law, the corporation is a legal person capable of entering contracts. Its owners have limited liability, which means that not all their property is at risk, only what they have invested in the corporation. This arrangement is very effective for raising the large sums of capital needed by modern industry. It means that shareholders readily move their capital toward attractive, wealth-creating opportunities. The result is the efficient use of capital.

However, limited liability also is a privilege in return for which the corporation is expected to serve the public. The corporation's social role is to use the resources it has to increase social output.[16] Managers are obligated to put the corporation's resources to their most productive uses.

In putting the corporation's resources to their most productive uses, managers serve shareholders. Even though the goal is profit, generally accepted rules of decency and even charity are binding on the corporation, as are strict rules of law.[17] The purpose the corporation should serve is to secure the highest long-term return on capital, given the legal and moral rules that prevail in society.

According to this view, the tendency to compel corporations to use resources for specific ends other than long-term maximum return on capital is likely to produce "undesirable results."[18] And the doctrine that corporate policy should be guided by "social considerations" is mistaken.[19] For one thing, the range of such considerations is very wide. Many different political, charitable, educational, and other ends can be brought under its heading. To allow managers to use corporate funds in ways that managers believe are socially appropriate would "create centers of uncontrollable power never intended by those who provided the capital."[20] It would vest powers over social, cultural, political, and moral decisions in people selected for their capacities in an entirely different field, that is, for their abilities to use resources efficiently in production.

Hayek admits that the actual influence of shareholders is often slight. Moreover, it is not unusual that their capital is used for purposes other than those they would choose.[21] Shareholder interests, for instance, are served by maximizing profits per unit of capital invested, while that of the managers may be served by maximizing aggregate profits. The separation of ownership and control places shareholders in a subordinate position, with managers often dictating to shareholders rather than acting on the basis of their recommendations.

Friedman's Position

Milton Friedman's view is that businesses do not have responsibilities, only people, that is, individual proprietors and managers.[22] The proprietors have the right to do with their money as they please. If they wish to spend it on what they consider to be socially beneficial projects, that is their prerogative. However, managers are employees of owners to whom they are responsible. They have to make as much money as possible for shareholders while conforming to the basic rules of society embodied in law and ethical custom.

In an eleemosynary institution (a nonprofit) such as a hospital or school, the goal of the managers may be other than profit, but in the corporation, managers are responsible to the owners. They are the agents of the owners of the corporation and their primary responsibility is to them. Thus, managers have no right to "tax" shareholders for social purposes. The tax function has been vested by the constitution in public authorities who have been elected by the people.

While citizens are the principals to whom public officials owe their allegiance, the principals to whom managers owe allegiance are shareholders. Managers have been chosen by the shareholders for one purpose alone, to run the company effectively, to produce a product, finance it, and sell it. As individuals outside of the corporation, managers may take on other responsibilities (to church, family, conscience, or whatever), but as employees of the owners, they have no right to exercise these responsibilities. To do so would be to spend someone else's money and to reduce the profits due the shareholders. If corporate profits are to be spent on charity, the underprivileged, the environment, or other worthy causes, the money should be spent freely and separately by owners, not by managers acting for them.

In any event, how are the managers to decide how this money is to be spent? What specific expertise do they have in the area? Moreover, if the managers decide to spend the money on purposes the shareholders have not authorized, the shareholders will be likely to abandon the company. The company's stock price may decline precipitously, and the managers will probably be fired for being derelict in their duties. The system, according to Friedman, prevents managers from "exploiting" shareholders even for "unselfish" social purposes.[23] It requires that if managers wish to do good, they do so "at their own expense."[24]

Nonetheless Friedman admits that if the managers can increase the profits of the firm by spending the shareholders' money for social purposes then doing so surely is legitimate. Thus, if, by providing amenities to a community, it is possible to attract better quality employees, who are more loyal to the corporation and willing to work harder, then this activity is appropriate. Similarly, if the managers reduce the corporation's tax burden by making charitable donations, then this activity too is appropriate. Friedman accepts enlightened self-interest as being a legitimate activity of managers.[25] But he expresses disgust for managers who cloak their profit-making motivations behind an aura of social responsibility and who suggest that their real intentions are altruistic when they are not.

Individual Liberty and Economic Growth

Ultimately, Friedman opposes "social responsibilities in any sense other than the shared values of individuals."[26] His ideal is the market where "no individual can coerce any other, all cooperation is voluntary, [and] all parties to such cooperation benefit or they need not participate."[27] By contrast, politics, no matter what kind, requires conformity; an individual must serve a more general interest determined by some political authority, whether the church, a dictator, or a democratic majority. For Friedman, markets are to be preferred, even to democratic decision making, because even in a democracy, once the people have voted in the political realm, everyone must conform.[28]

Friedman's final justification for shareholder dominance therefore is somewhat different from Hayek's. Hayek's main justification is that shareholder dominance maximizes output and contributes to the economic well-being of society, but Friedman's main justification is that it is consistent with individual liberty; that is, shareholder dominance maximizes voluntarism and noncoercion in society.

Managerial Control

Analysts and commentators such as Berle and Means have tried to change the focus of the debate from what ought to be to what is (see Exhibit 5–3).[29] They argue that in reality managers dominate shareholders. As we already indicated, even Hayek admits that what should be is not what is, that while shareholders should be dominant, often they are not, and that often managers control the corporation.[30]

These concerns go back at least as far as Adam Smith, who in *The Wealth of Nations* had identified the potential problems that could arise with the separation of ownership from control:

> The directors of . . . [joint stock] companies, however, being the managers rather of other people's money than of their own, it cannot well be expected, that they should watch over it with the same anxious vigilance with which the partners in a private copartnery frequently watch over their own. Like the stewards of a rich man, they are apt to consider attention to small

---

EXHIBIT 5-3   Main Questions Posed and Answered by Agency, Managerial, and Behavioral Theories

Agency Theory	*Managerial Theory*	*Behavioral Theory*
Who should dominate? Shareholders	Who does dominate? Managers	Who does dominate? A shifting coalition of interests internal and external to the firm
Why? Maximizes social output/increases individual liberty	What are the consequences? Self-seeking behavior by the managers (the search for their own security, perks, salary, and power at the expense of the shareholders)	What are the consequences? Goals other than profits show up in what the corporation does Complex, short-run behavior by the corporation that is not perfectly rational

---

> matters as not for their master's honour, and very easily give themselves a dispensation from having it. Negligence and profusion, therefore, must always prevail, more or less, in the management of the affairs of such a company.[31]

Smith believed that the managers would watch over other people's money with less vigilance than they used for their own.

In their classic work *The Modern Corporation and Private Property,* Berle and Means hold that the modern corporation draws its capital from an increasingly dispersed group of investors, while at the same time concentrating greater economic power in the hands of relatively few managers.[32] They stated the dilemma as follows:

> Those who control the destinies of the typical corporation own so insignificant a fraction of the company's stock that the returns from the running of the corporation profitably accrue to them in only a very minor degree. The stockholders, on the other hand, to whom these profits of the corporation go, cannot be motivated by those profits to a more efficient use of the property, since they have surrendered all disposition of it to those who control the enterprise.[33]

If the managers act in a rational, self-interested fashion, they will use the corporate property under their control to benefit themselves rather than to benefit the shareholders. They will maximize their own personal income rather than the value of the firm.

Variations on the Managerialist Premise

There are many variations to the argument that managers maximize their own wealth at the expense of shareholders. One view states that since managers' salaries are at least partially based on the firm's growth, they may be motivated to expand firm size beyond the level that maximizes shareholder wealth. Once the constraints of the shareholder are satisfied, the managers can use the retained earnings to maximize growth, choosing a growth rate greater than the one that would maximize shareholder value.[34]

Another view is that managers use discretionary profit, that is, profit above the necessary minimum required by stockholders, to increase staff and administrative expenses and to raise the level of perks and emoluments; managers spend more on staff and perks than would maximize shareholder value because doing so provides them with the salary, status, prestige, and security they seek.[35] Still another view is that managers maximize their lifetime income by avoiding risk and making decisions that produce stable financial results.[36] Thus, managers would attempt to achieve steady growth in sales and earnings even though better investment opportunities might, with added risk, provide a higher return to the owners.

Risk-Averse Managers

A very strong theme in the managerialist argument is that managers are likely to be more risk-averse than shareholders. For example, John Kenneth Galbraith maintains that managers are conservative and risk-averse in their efforts to earn returns; they "put prevention of loss ahead of maximum return."[37] While managers agree that achieving planned results is desirable, they believe that avoiding unplanned disasters is even more important.

Managers seek to avoid unnecessary risks that might diminish their direct control. Mainly interested in their own survival, they seek to retain power and their special status. To ensure demand for the corporation's products, they engage in extensive advertising and support government policies that maintain full employment. To ensure stable prices for labor and raw materials, they seek long-term contracts with suppliers. They prefer to finance through retained earnings rather than through debt, paying dividends as expected and trying to generate adequate cash flow for reinvestment while avoiding the constraints that would exist if they borrowed funds.[38]

Managers, according to this view, are not as interested in maximizing returns to shareholders as in maximizing their survival and security at shareholder expense. Their goal is the highest growth in sales at an acceptable level of risk, which, if achieved, should provide them with job security, frequent promotion, and adequate pay.

Why are managers likely to be risk-averse? The answer is that investors, whether individual or institutional, are more diversified than managers. Individual investors may not hold diversified portfolios, but institutional investors, which dominate the marketplace, do:

> Once shareholders have diversified their portfolio, they are in theory largely immune from firm-specific risk, both because no individual stock will have that material an impact on their portfolios' performance and because their portfolios will include countercyclical stocks whose price movements will offset each other.[39]

Managers' most important possession, on the other hand, is likely to be their jobs, from which they expect a discounted earnings stream until retirement. With the job also come firm-specific assets, fringe benefits, and stock options that cannot be easily transferred and that make lateral mobility costly and difficult, as well as firm-specific risks that managers may have to bear in the form of personal liability in case of insolvency and financial distress.

Conglomerate growth may be viewed as an effort by managers to protect their own interests via diversification, but such growth is not likely to be in the interests of shareholders, who can diversify on their own. Since managers cannot spread their risks or escape them as easily as investors, they are likely to be more firmly tied to the company's fortunes and consequently more risk-averse than shareholders.

Criticisms of the Managerialist Premises

A number of criticisms of the managerialist premises have been made, and empirical support for it does not appear to be especially strong.[40] For example, the sample used by Berle and Means had a large proportion of regulated firms. Also, empirical work done in the 1980s suggests that they might have underestimated the degree of ownership and family control that existed in their sample. The neglect of the power of financial institutions as a vehicle for centralizing control also has been raised.

After examining the power exercised by family owners, institutional investors, lenders, and government regulators, Herman supported Berle and Means. He concluded that active power and control does in fact lie with managers. However, he did acknowledge that other parties, as well as the board of directors, had latent power that could serve to constrain managerial discretion.[41] Latent power was "exercisable within limits, under constraints, and on a contingent basis."[42]

Schwartz examined the role of average investors in exercising corporate control, and concluded that the barriers to decisive shareholder participation in elections, approval of major transactions, and policy initiatives was so great as to render greater shareholder involvement largely a vain hope.[43] Heard noted, however, that institutional investors had been able in some cases to defeat antitakeover proposals made by management or secure the removal of such proposals before a vote, following discussions with management.[44] This exercise of power by shareholders appeared to be consistent with Herman's notion of latent power. And Mizruchi suggested that such instances were clear examples of control by shareholders.[45] Further, he argued that the ability of the board to use unobtrusive control to set the boundaries within which management makes decisions was an example of true control.[46]

The Board of Directors

These studies bring up an important point: The board of directors is supposed to control managers in the name of the shareholders. It has six primary functions:[47]

1. Select, regularly evaluate, and, if necessary, replace the chief executive officer.
2. Determine management compensation and review succession planning.
3. Review and, where appropriate, approve the financial objectives, major strategies, and plans of the corporation.
4. Provide advice and counsel to top management.
5. Select and recommend to shareholders for election an appropriate slate of candidates for the board of directors; evaluate board processes and performance.
6. Review the adequacy of systems to comply with all applicable laws/regulations.

Supported by data regarding board ouster of CEOs, Mizruchi argued that boards did exercise a great deal of real control, even if it was through the holding of latent power.[48]

Control by the Market

Fama has argued that managers are controlled by the market for managerial jobs.[49] The outside labor market for jobs controls managers. It prevents potential agency problems because managers are being evaluated on the basis of the firm's performance, and managers acting in self-interest want to maximize their compensation and future job flexibility. Factors in addition to competitive labor markets for executive talent that are likely to induce managers to adopt a shareholder orientation are a relatively large managerial ownership position; compensation that is tied to shareholder returns; and the threat of takeovers, which make managers anxious about their continued job security if they do not meet shareholders' expectations (see discussion in the next chapter on corporate restructuring).

The Behavioral Theory: Plural Interests

The behavioral theory, developed at Carnegie-Mellon University in the late 1950s and early 1960s, is empirical as opposed to normative in nature; that is, it intends to study how decisions are made, not to prescribe how they should be made.[50] It holds that the corporation, being a coalition of groups with different goals and interests, makes decisions at different points in time which favor different groups. The origins of behavioral theory are described in the following sections.

Goals Other than Profits

Some economists question whether profits are even possible: "In the long run, under pure competition, pure profit will be zero as competition will force output to the point at which no factor can earn more than its opportunity cost."[51] However, this zero profit situation is only true for a static system under pure competition. In a changing world with imperfect competition and uncertainty, profits will continually arise. Profits may be earned from monopoly or monopsony power, or they may be a result of innovation. Brand names, copyrights, patents, and trade secrets can also be used to generate profits. Finally, profits can come into being as a consequence of windfall gains and losses over the business cycle.

In the finance literature, the goal of the firm is not accounting profits. It is to maximize the value per share earned by the shareholders (see the feature on page 114, "Creating Shareholder Value").

Most economic theories of the firm leave little question that companies are influenced by the profit motive. The possibility of profit directs the enterprise in many ways.[52] It is an essential condition for bringing a firm into being and a factor in the ability of the firm to attract new capital. Its increase may lead to reorganization or change, and its absence may result in the firm's demise. The business organization provides goods and services to society under the incentive of profit, which is its reason for being. It tries to produce products of unique qualities that capture a market because they cannot be duplicated by competitors.

Even those who assume that businesses have goals other than profit assume that these goals ultimately have to be subservient to profit. Thorsten Veblen for example, held that other goals were at best understood as a "constraint on pecuniary advantage."[53] They did not constitute an "abrogation." Thus, the firm that ended up serving its customers and the community to the exclusion of profit faced ultimate failure.

Under certain circumstances, however, managers may sacrifice profit for prestige, stability, and liquidity.[54] According to the behavioral theory, the objective of business is not necessarily profit maximization, but rate of return on net worth, total assets, or sales in comparison with other firms in the industry and based on historical performance.[55]

Satisfactory Profits

According to economics Nobel prize winner Herbert Simon, the search for what he calls satisfactory financial success takes precedence over simple profit maximization.[56] Even if managers are not strict profit maximizers, they have targets for financial well-being. Thus, short-run behavior depends on the firm's *pattern* of decision making, which is often neglected in discussions by economists.

Depictions of decision making as the rational pursuit of predetermined objectives (whether profit, growth, or competitive advantage) are not descriptively accurate; and the view that assumes that "corporate management has considerable discretion, is analytical and rational, and can plan comprehensively" is too narrow.[57]

Multiple Centers of Power

The behavioral theory assumes that firms have multiple centers of power.[58] Groups from within and without (such as managers, workers, stockholders, suppliers, bankers, customers, lawyers, accountants, and regulatory officials) have different subgoals that they pursue simultaneously. At least five internal subgoals (production, inventory, sales, market share, and profit) and sometimes many more are involved. The actual goals of the organization as a whole are ambiguous. They reflect the bargaining among various internal units, as well as pressures from society.

Pressure is exerted by customers, suppliers, and regulatory agencies. For the firm's survival, the search for customers is critical. A major reason for business failures is inattention to markets. From suppliers the firm must obtain labor, materials, and equipment. They are important because they influence costs and prices. Regulatory agencies impose constraints by legal action or by the implied threat of legal action. As E. A. Grefe comments: "If the chief executive officer's attention is focused solely on share of the market, the market itself could vanish or be severely restricted by regulation. Witness the experience of any number of industries: nuclear power, tobacco, candy, cereal, bottling, chemicals, paper, oil, to name but a few."[59] However, regulatory agencies also provide opportunities for competitive advantage and improving public image.

Creating Shareholder Value

Northwestern University finance professor Alfred Rappaport argues that a focus by management on accounting numbers like growth in earnings per share will not necessarily lead to maximum returns for shareholders. Returns to shareholders are defined as dividends plus increase in the company's share price.[1]

Managers should use discounted cash flow techniques, which are the essential means for analyzing shareholder value creation, not only for buying and selling businesses, but also for planning and performance monitoring of all business strategies on an ongoing basis. The essence of this approach is to estimate the economic value of an investment by discounting forecasted cash flow by the cost of capital.

Rappaport shows how "basic value drivers"—sales growth rate, operating profit margin, and working and fixed capital investment—are incorporated into shareholder value calculations. For example, estimating the cost of capital (debt plus equity)

> is essential for establishing the minimum acceptable rate of return or hurdle rates that management should require on new investment proposals. Investments yielding returns greater than the cost of capital will create shareholder value, while those yielding less than the cost of capital will decrease shareholder value.[2]

Complications arise, such as growth strategies that involve spending on product devel-

opment, and marketing, which may increase long-term cash flows but hurt immediate cash flow. Liquidation caused by erosion in market share may free up short-term working capital, but it lowers long-term growth potential. There are difficulties and uncertainties, too, in making estimates (e.g., of future sales growth rates, income tax rates, and equity risk premiums). However, according to Rappaport, only the market fully includes information from the company and other sources in its valuation of the company's future prospects.[3] Thus, market prices are "a signal to the company about the level of expected accomplishments needed if shareholders are to earn the required rate of return on the company's shares."[4]

Rappaport argues that "one of the most destructive canards in business is the notion that the stock market has a short time horizon," which has led many companies to a preoccupation with short-term performance.[5] He admits that the "financial community is obsessed with its own short-term performance"; however, he believes it essential to distinguish between the scurrying of investors and the fundamental forces that determine market prices.[6] That is, investors often see long-term implications in current information, and the market is often willing to pay a premium for companies providing evidence of sustainable competitive advantage.

---

[1]A. Rappaport, "Selecting Strategies That Create Shareholder Value," *Harvard Business Review* 3, 1981, pp. 139–49; A. Rappaport, "Corporate Performance Standards and Shareholder Value," *The Journal of Business Strategy* 4, 1983, pp. 28–38.
[2]Ibid.

[3]Ibid.
[4]Ibid.
[5]Ibid.
[6]Ibid.

In a large corporate organization, numerous groups participate, each having a different status, job assignment, geographic location, educational background, career aspiration, attitude toward the firm, and expectations. Boards of directors have direct authority, but their power may be limited. At Exxon, for example, the board has been a large group that meets relatively infrequently. It has been a forum for the exchange of information, not an arena for challenging the decisions of internal management.[60]

Rather, the corporation experiences pressures stemming from the existence of different coalitions of interests in its internal and external environments. The inherently different interests of these groups lead to a diversity of sometimes opposing forces that affect managerial decisions.

Complex Short-Run Behavior

According to the behavioral theory, although ultimately motivated by profits and other indicators of financial success, firm behavior in the short run is a complex amalgam of many forces. Stockholders, employees, and the community play a role; internal and external coalitions with different interests and goals affect outcomes; and leadership may make a difference. The firm is, in a sense, a political entity, as conflicting goals and limited information influence outcomes.[61] Decision making involves groping for solutions gradually over a considerable period of time, and avoiding the pitfalls without necessarily changing policies in a radical way.

Summary and Conclusions

Milton Friedman has argued that the primary responsibility of managers is to maximize returns to shareholders within the confines of laws and ethical principles (see Exhibit 5–4). According to this theory, the objective of the firm is to reward owners subject to the constraints that managers obey the laws of society and follow ethical norms.

Social responsibility is more than simply charity. Consistent with Friedman's theory, it may involve efforts to identify social needs as the basis for profitable activities. Most studies show that the corporation's interests are served by its being socially responsible. Many benefits accrue to the socially responsible corporation. These include better motivated employees, more loyal customers, and more supportive communities. When these benefits are realized, even Milton Friedman would agree that corporations should be socially responsible.

EXHIBIT 5–4   **The Impact of Three Types of Responsibility on Managerial Behavior**

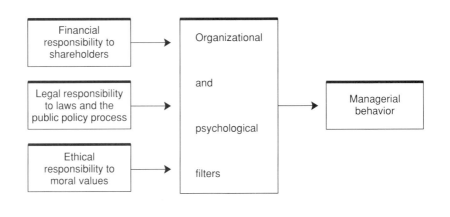

Different theories of managerial responsibility have been reviewed in this chapter. Agency theory holds that the corporation's main responsibility is to shareholders. Managers have a fiduciary obligation to maximize returns subject to laws and prevailing ethical mores. Agency theory is contradicted by managerial theory, which maintains that managers run corporations in their own interests. The managers take actions that are less risky than owners would take on their own, because their assets are specialized and more closely tied to the corporation than those of the owners, who usually have diversified portfolios. The managers also focus on growth rather than profitability and provide themselves with perks that the owners probably would not want them to take.

Managerialist premises, however, have been challenged by scholars who have shown that boards play a role and that other forces, such as takeovers and the market for managerial talent, limit managerial discretion.

In messy situations in the real world, managers often face conflicting fiduciary, legal, and ethical demands. Their behavior is a function of different sets of responsibilities that influence their actions. These factors work through an organizational and psychological screen best described by the behavioral theory (see Exhibit 5–4). The behavioral theory holds that neither shareholders nor managers control the corporation; rather, a shifting coalition of interests is in charge. This shifting coalition biases decisions in unique ways.

Corporate social responsibility has been viewed as the obligation to shareholders, social norms embodied in laws and statutes, and community values. The previous two chapters discussed ethical criteria for decision making. The next chapter focuses on laws and the public policy process.

Discussion Questions

1. What does corporate social responsibility mean?
2. Why should managers be socially responsible?
3. To what extent is social responsibility obligatory?
4. To what extent is social responsibility legally binding?
5. To what extent is the obligation to be socially responsible in the corporation's economic interest?
6. Elaborate on the fiduciary relationship. What problems does the principal face in controlling the agent's behavior? When is the agent justified in not obeying the principal?
7. Compare and contrast Hayek's view of the corporation with that of Milton Friedman.
8. What is meant by the phrase *separation of ownership from control?* What practical difference does it make if ownership is separated from control?
9. Can boards of directors exert effective control over the corporation? How else do shareholders control the corporation?
10. What role does profit play in the firm?
11. What is the right way to know if the firm is making profit for the owners?
12. Which groups influence a firm's decision making? How do they exert this influence? What effect does it have?

Endnotes

1. I would like to acknowledge the assistance of the following Ph.D. students at the University of Minnesota who contributed to parts of this chapter and the next: Linnea Van Dyne, Isaac Fox, Kent Miller, Gordon Rands, and Doug Schuller.
2. H. R. Bowen, *Social Responsibilities of the Businessman* (New York: Harper, 1953).
3. R. McKeon, "The Development and the Significance of the Concept of Responsibility," *Extrait de la Revue Internationale de Philosophe*, 1957, pp. 1–30;

A. Hamilton, J. Madison, and J. Jay, *The Federalist Papers* (New York: The New American Library, Inc., 1961).

4. McKeon, "The Development and the Significance of the Concept of Responsibility."

5. L. E. Preston, "Corporation and Society: The Search for a Paradigm," *The Journal of Economic Literature* 13, 1975, pp. 434–53; Bowen, *Social Responsibilities of the Businessman.*

6. W. C. Frederick, From CSR_1 to CSR_2: *The Maturing of Business-and-Society Thought,* working paper No. 279, Graduate School of Business, University of Pittsburgh, 1978.

7. P. Drucker, "The New Meaning of Social Responsibility," *California Management Review,* Winter 1984, pp. 53–63.

8. Ibid., p. 55.

9. A. Ullman, "Data in Search of a Theory: A Critical Examination of the Relationships among Social Performance, Social Disclosure, and Economic Performance of U.S. Firms," *Academy of Management Review,* July 1985, pp. 545–57.

10. R. Wokutch and B. Spencer, "Corporate Saints and Sinners: The Effects of Philanthropic and Illegal Activity on Organizational Performance," *California Management Review,* Winter 1987, pp. 62–78.

11. J. McGuire and T. Schneeweis, *An Analysis of Alternate Measures of Strategic Performance,* paper presented at the third annual conference of the Strategic Management Society, Paris, 1983.

12. C. G. Luckhardt, "Duties of Agent to Principal," in *Business Ethics: Corporate Values and Society,* ed. M. Snoeyenbos, R. Almeder, and J. Humber (New York: Prometheus Books, 1983), pp. 115–21.

13. M. Jensen and W. Meckling, "Theory of the Firm, Managerial Behavior, Agency Costs and Ownership Structure," *Journal of Economics* 3, 1976, pp. 305–60.

14. M. Friedman, "The Social Responsibility of Business Is to Increase Its Profits," in *The Management of Values,* ed. Charles S. McCoy (Boston: Pitman, 1985), pp. 253–60; F. Hayek, "The Corporation in a Democratic Society: In Whose Interests Ought It and Will It Be Run?" in *Business Strategy,* ed. H. I. Ansoff (New York: Penguin, 1977), pp. 225–39.

15. Hayek, "The Corporation in a Democratic Society."

16. Ibid.

17. Ibid.

18. Ibid.

19. Ibid.

20. Ibid.

21. Ibid.

22. Friedman, "The Social Responsibility of Business."

23. Ibid.

24. Ibid.

25. Ibid.

26. Ibid.

27. Ibid.

28. Ibid.

29. A. Berle and G. Means, *The Modern Corporation and Private Property* (New York: Harcourt, Brace and World, 1967); J. K. Galbraith, "The Goals of an Industrial System," in *The New Industrial State* (Boston: Houghton Mifflin Co., 1967), pp. 166–78.

30. Hayek, "The Corporation in a Democratic Society."

31. A. Smith, *The Wealth of Nations* (1776, Cannan edition, New York: Modern Library, 1937), p. 700.

32. Berle and Means, *The Modern Corporation and Private Property*; M. Weidenbaum and M. Jensen, *Introduction to the Modern Corporation and Private Property,* working paper no. 134, Center for the Study of American Business, St. Louis, September 1990; L. S. Zacharias and A. Kaufman, *The Problem of the Corporation and the Evolution of Social Values,* working paper MG 87/88 no. 2, Management Research Center, School of Management, University of Massachusetts at Amherst, 1987.

33. Berle and Means, *The Modern Corporation and Private Property,* pp. 8–9.

34. R. Marris, *The Economic Theory of 'Managerial' Capitalism* (London: Macmillan, 1964).

35. O. Williamson, *The Economics of Discretionary Behavior* (Chicago: Markham, 1967); Marris, *The Economic Theory of 'Managerial' Capitalism.*

36. W. Baumol, *Business Behavior, Value and Growth* (New York: Harcourt, Brace and World, 1959).

37. Galbraith, *The New Industrial State,* p. 215.

38. G. Donaldson and J. Lorsch, *Decision Making at the Top* (Basic Books, New York, 1983).

39. J. C. Coffee, Jr., "Shareholders versus Managers: The Strain in the Corporate Web," in *Knights, Raiders, and Targets: The Impact of the Hostile Takeover,* ed. J. C. Coffee, Jr., L. Lowenstein, and S. Rose-Ackerman (New York: Oxford University Press, 1988), p. 83.

40. E. S. Herman, *Corporate Control, Corporate Power* (Cambridge: Cambridge University Press, 1981); G. Bentsen, "The Self-serving Management Hypothesis: Some Evidence," *Journal of Accounting and Economics* 7, 1985, pp. 67–84; R. D. Kosnik, "Greenmail: A Study of Board Performance in Corporate Governance," *Administrative Science Quarterly* 32, 1987, pp. 163–85.

41. Herman, *Corporate Control, Corporate Power.*

42. Ibid., p. 23

43. D. E. Schwartz, "Corporate Governance," in *Corporations and Their Critics,* ed. T. Bradshaw and D. Vogel (New York: McGraw-Hill, 1981); D. E. Schwartz, "Shareholder Democracy: A Reality or Chimera?" *California Management Review* 25, no. 3, 1983, pp. 53–67.

44. J. E. Heard, "Pension Funds and Contests for Corporate Control," *California Management Review* 29, no. 2, 1987, pp. 89–100.

45. M. S. Mizruchi, "Who Controls Whom? An Examination of the Relation between Management and Boards of Directors in Large American Corporations," *Academy of Management Review* 8, no. 2, 1983, pp. 426–35.

46. Ibid.

47. *"Corporate Governance and American Competitiveness"* The Business Roundtable, New York, March, 1990, p. 7; I. Kesner, "Directors Characteristics

and Committee Membership: An Investigation of Type, Occupation, Tenure and Gender," *Academy of Management Journal* 31, no. 1, 1988, pp. 66–84; A. Stalnaker, *The Board of Directors and the Chief Executive Officer,* Formal Publication No. 74, Center for the Study of American Business, St. Louis, June 1986.

48. Mizruchi, "Who Controls Whom?"
49. E. Fama, "Agency Problems and the Theory of the Firm," *Journal of Political Economy* 88, 1980, pp. 288–307.
50. R. M. Cyert and J. G. March, *A Behavioral Theory of the Firm* (Englewood Cliffs, N.J.: Prentice Hall, 1963); L. Gomez-Mejia, H. Tosi, and T. Hinkin, "Managerial Control, Performance, and Executive Compensation," *Academy of Management Journal* 30, no. 1, 1987, pp. 51–71.
51. J. Herendeen, "Goals of the Enterprise," in *The Economics of the Corporate Economy,* ed. J. B. Herendeen (New York: Dunellen, 1975), p. 36.
52. W. R. Dill, "Business Organizations," in *Handbook of Organizations,* ed. J. G. March (Chicago: Rand McNally, 1965), pp. 1071–1114.
53. T. Veblen, *The Theory of the Business Enterprise in Recent Times* (New York: B. W. Heubsch, Inc., 1904).
54. M. H. Spencer and L. Siegelman, *Managerial Economics* (Homewood, Ill.: Irwin, 1959).
55. Dill, "Business Organizations," p. 1074; N. W. Chamberlain, *The Firm: Microeconomic Planning and Action* (New York: McGraw-Hill, 1962).
56. H. Simon, "On the Concept of Organizational Goal," *Administrative Science Quarterly* 9, June 1964, pp. 1–22.
57. E. A. Murray, "Strategic Choice as a Negotiated Outcome," *Management Science,* May 1978, pp. 960–72.
58. Cyert and March, *A Behavioral Theory of the Firm.*
59. E. A. Grefe, *Fighting to Win: Business Political Power* (New York: Harcourt Brace Jovanovich, 1981), p. 13.
60. A. J. Parisi, "The Men Who Rule Exxon," *New York Times Magazine,* August 3, 1980, pp. 19–25.
61. H. Mintzberg, D. Raisinghani, and A. Theoret, "The Structure of Unstructured Decision Processes," *Administrative Science Quarterly,* June 1976, pp. 246–75.

6

PUBLIC RESPONSIBILITY AND STAKEHOLDERS

More than ever, managers of corporations are expected to serve the public interest as well as private profit. . . . Management must be measured for performance in noneconomic and economic areas alike. . . . Corporations operate within a web of complex, often competing relationships which demand the attention of corporate managers. The decision-making process requires an understanding of the corporations many constituencies and their various expectations.

The Business Roundtable, 1981.

Introduction and Chapter Objectives

This chapter examines the view that managers are responsible to the public policy process (the theory of public responsibility) and the view that they freely choose a group of interests they favor (stakeholder theory). In the 1980s, the debate about corporate social responsibility was influenced by the wide-scale restructuring of corporate institutions that took place in the United States, that is, by the rash of takeovers, mergers, and management buyouts that occurred. It also was influenced by the growing competition between American companies and those in other parts of the world, particularly Japan. At the end of this chapter, the corporate social responsibility debate is examined in the context of these recent developments.

The Principle of Public Responsibility

The growth of government involvement in the economy in the post–World War II period led to a theory of public responsibility in which corporations are supposed to be responsible to the processes by which public policy is formulated.[1] Analysts argued for a principle of public responsibility that limits the scope of managerial responsibility and defines it in terms of primary and secondary areas. The primary area consists of the organization's "functional role," its "exchange relationships with the market."[2] The secondary area consists of the "consequences of production and sales activities," the "impact of procurement and employment," the "neighborhood effects" of the business activities, and the "use by others of the merchandise and services sold."[3]

Managerial responsibility is supposed to extend no further than the secondary involvements. Managers are "not expected to improve social conditions" or "resolve social problems regardless of their character or cause."[4] Nor does public responsibility consist of being sensitive to the complaints of all social groups.[5] Rather, it requires that managers pay attention to the "rules of the game, as reflected and modified within the broad framework of public policy."[6] Doing so should provide "a guide for managerial behavior [that is] more objective than individual moral or ethical insights."[7]

Public policy is understood to mean the spirit as well as the letter of the law. Public policy reflects a changing environment, a moving target that extends from "accepted standards" to "specific laws and requirements" and "newly emerging viewpoints and issues."[8] The corporation and the public policy process form interpenetrating systems.[9] The corporation, it is assumed, is neither completely controlled by the public policy process nor does it completely control the process. Rather, it influences public policy and is influenced by it.

This model moves the debate about corporate social responsibility from what the corporation is obligated to do to how corporations should respond to changing societal expectations.[10] The question is no longer one of defining the values that make up social responsibility or of exploring the meaning of business's contribution to social betterment. Instead, the public policy process is taken as a given that defines corporate social responsibility, and the question becomes one of responding to it (how, to what extent, and with what effect).

The object of management is to overcome the internal and external constraints on the corporation's ability to respond. These constraints include the organization's structure and leadership, its ability to measure and reward managers for their contribution to social performance, and the financial formulas used in making decisions.

Responsiveness rests on the idea that what a corporation is obliged to do is relatively straightforward and clear. The response processes consist of different stages (see Exhibit 6–1).[11] The corporation's responsibilities are not based on individual conscience or moral judgment. They are not primarily economic, nor are they bound to a set of corporate constituencies, although both have roles to play. Rather, laws and the public policy process are the ultimate arbiters of communities' expectations about corporate behavior. Laws and the public policy process are what define corporate responsibility.

Regulatory Growth

Regulatory growth in the late 1960s and early 1970s was the embodiment of the focus on laws and public policies. It signified a so-called managerial revolution.[12] The first revolution was the shift from owners managing their enterprises to the joint stock company, where ownership and management were separated (see the discussion of managerialism in the last chapter). The second revolution meant that government decision makers had vast powers and increasing control over key areas of managerial decision making, including manufacturing and the introduction of new products and services. The critical challenge for management was how to respond to the public control that emanated from government officials and the shifting public policy process.

Special Public Affairs Departments or Units

In the 1970s and 1980s, many firms developed and enhanced their capabilities for responding to the public policy process by creating special public affairs departments or units. Varying with the needs of an industry and individual companies, these departments or units brought many important activities together (see Exhibit 6–2).[13]

EXHIBIT 6–1 Response Stages

---

1. **Awareness:**
   Managers recognize the existence of a problem. They can be *early* or *late* in their ability to detect an emerging public policy issue and can lead or lag in their response to an issue.
2. **Commitment:**
   Managers decide on *a course of action*. There are different actions that they can choose from attempting to buffer the corporation's internal operations from emerging public policy issues to altering both a company's internal operations and the external environment.
3. **Implementation:**
   Managers organize to carry out the course of action they have chosen. They attempt to *achieve goals* they have set for their organizations.

EXHIBIT 6–2 **Activities of Public Affairs Units**

---

1. Issues Management. Public affairs departments help to identify important social, political, economic, and technological developments and to integrate this information into strategic planning.

2. Government Relations (federal, state, and local). Public affairs departments monitor legislative and regulatory developments, assess their implications, and try to affect the course of public policy.

3. Public relations. Public affairs departments communicate information about the firm to the media.

4. International relations. Public affairs departments promote company interests in foreign capitals and in international forums.

5. Investor and stockholder relations. Public affairs departments often take charge of company communications with investors, brokerage houses, and other financial institutions.

6. Corporate contributions. Frequently, public affairs departments coordinate company contributions to the community.

7. Institutional advertising. To heighten public awareness, public affairs departments often engage in image building through such means as nonproduct, corporate advertising.

8. Employee communications. Public affairs departments also may produce newsletters and other communications that help gain the support of employees, stockholders, customers, and local citizens for the corporation.

A successful public affairs program should enhance a firm's credibility, facilitate a timely and appropriate response to issues, and have a positive financial impact.[14] From 1982 to 1985, the average number of employees in public affairs grew from 8.7 to about 15 persons per firm despite declining regulation and a sympathetic administration in Washington.[15]

Additional Steps to Enhance Public Affairs Management

In recent years corporations have taken additional steps to enhance public affairs management. In the 1970s and 1980s, they created many corporate political action committees, or PACs.[16] The purpose of PACs is to make donations to political candidates. Under reforms to federal election laws passed after the Watergate scandals, companies are allowed to solicit funds for candidates from their employees, subject to limitations on the amount that an individual employee can give to a particular candidate and various other reporting and disclosure requirements.

Firms made grass roots efforts to motivate their employees, stockholders, customers, suppliers, and local citizens to become politically active.[17] The actions that were sought might include writing a letter to a member of congress or local politician, signing a petition, marching in a demonstration, or expressing an opinion on a television or radio talk show.

Another change that took place in the way corporations managed the political and social environment was the involvement of chief executive officers in national political organizations. The Business Roundtable claimed to speak for the entire business community.[18] It was made up of the chief executive officers (CEOs) of the largest corporations in America. In the 1970s, CEOs became directly involved in establishing a political agenda for the American business community, taking positions on issues of vital concern, and personally lobbying Congress and government officials (for an example of chief executive involvement see the feature: "William McGowan—Effective Corporate Public Affairs Leader").

Public Policy Advocacy Advertising

Another notable development was the use of public policy advocacy advertising by corporations, that is, their use of advertising space on the editorial pages of major newspapers and magazines to promote their viewpoints. The purpose of advocacy advertising is for a corporation to present a particular position on matters of public policy.

It is not a new idea; corporate views on public policy issues have been presented to the public throughout this century. However, in 1969, when Rawleigh Warner Jr. was elected chairman and CEO of Mobil, he inaugurated, along with Bill Tavoulareas, the company's president, a new program to directly reach the public through a newspaper campaign.[19] A young labor lawyer, Herbert Schmertz, was appointed head of public affairs with the direct responsibility to make this campaign successful.

Mobil's intention was not only to inform the public about Mobil's particular needs. It wanted to deal with public interest matters. For example, when *The New York Times* opened its editorial pages to advertising copy, Mobil bought the space and used it to argue for a better transportation system and for improved health care, policies that would appeal to liberal opinion. In March 1975 when WNBC in New York produced a mini-series on the oil industry that Mobil thought was slanted against the oil companies, Mobil responded with full-page ads in *The New York Times* and *The Wall Street Journal*. These ads, entitled "Whatever Happened to Fair Play?" complained that the TV series was inaccurate and unfair.

Surveys by Lou Harris and other pollsters showed that because of advocacy advertising Mobil was regarded more favorably by the general public than other oil companies. However, although the ads were very visible to public policymakers, the policymakers felt that the ads were of little or no use to them in formulating policy on issues that concerned the oil industry.

Other developments in corporate public affairs were the proliferation of ad hoc coalitions and the increased involvement of intermediaries such as specialized consulting firms and lobbying groups.[20]

Stakeholder Theory

Stakeholder theory derives its name from the groups such as shareholders, suppliers, customers, and employees that surround the corporation.[21] Joining together the concerns of business strategy and social responsibility, stakeholder theory maintains that the managers must decide what they stand for. Then they must formulate and carry out a strategy based on the interests they intend to favor.

Generic strategies are meant to be broad descriptions of what the corporation stands for and how it intends to make trade-offs about stakeholder concerns. Exhibit 6–3 lists some of the generic strategies managers might choose: a narrow stakeholder strategy, and financial, utilitarian, social justice, and social harmony strategies.[22]

Company Statements of Stakeholder Interests

Many firms have made statements of their stakeholder strategies. For example, Hewlett-Packard is dedicated to the dignity and worth of its individual employees; Aetna Life and Casualty believes that tending to the broader needs of society is essential to fulfilling its economic role;

EXHIBIT 6–3   Generic Stakeholder Strategies

Narrow stakeholder strategy:
　Maximize benefits to one or a small set of stakeholders (management, labor, suppliers, shareholders, governments, customers, affected communities, and others).

Financial strategy:
　Maximize benefits to stockholders.
　Maximize benefits to all financial stakeholders, including banks and analysts.

Utilitarian strategy:
　Maximize benefits to all stakeholders (greatest good for the greatest number).
　Maximize average welfare level of all stakeholders.
　Maximize benefits to society.

Social Justice Strategy
　Raise the level of the worst-off stakeholder.

Social Harmony Strategy
　Maintain or create social harmony.
　Gain consensus from society.

and J.C. Penney Company tests every policy, method, and act so that it is right and just.[23]

Perhaps, the most famous example of a statement of a corporation's stakeholder strategy is Johnson & Johnson's (see Exhibit 6–4).[24] Johnson and Johnson consistently receives the highest rankings for community and social responsibility in *Fortune*'s annual surveys of top business officials.

The Business Roundtable Statement on Stakeholders

In 1981, the Business Roundtable issued a statement on stakeholder strategy. Below are some excerpts:

> Customers have a primary claim for corporate attention. Without them, the enterprise will fail. . . .
>
> Employees expect not only fair pay but also such conditions as equal opportunity, workplaces that protect health and safety, financial security, personal privacy, freedom of expression, and concern for the quality of life. Experience has shown that employees will perform well for corporations

---

EXHIBIT 6–4   Johnson & Johnson's Stakeholder Strategy

We believe our first responsibility is to the doctors, nurses and patients, to mothers and all others who use our products and services. In meeting their needs everything we do must be of high quality. We must constantly strive to reduce our costs in order to maintain reasonable prices. Customers' orders must be serviced promptly and accurately. Our suppliers and distributors must have an opportunity to make a fair profit.

We are responsible to our employees: the men and women who work with us throughout the world. Everyone must be considered as an individual. We must respect their dignity and recognize their merit. They must have a sense of security in their jobs. Compensation must be fair and adequate, and working conditions clean, orderly and safe. Employees must feel free to make suggestions and complaints. There must be equal opportunity for employment, development, and advancement for those qualified. We must provide competent management and their actions must be just and ethical.

We are responsible to the communities in which we live and work and to the world community as well.

We must be good citizens—support good works and charities and bear our fair share of taxes. We must encourage civic improvements and better health and education.

We must maintain in good order the property we are privileged to use, protecting the environment and natural resources.

Our final responsibility is to our stockholders. Business must make a sound profit. We must experiment with new ideas. Research must be carried on, innovative programs developed, and mistakes paid for. New equipment must be purchased, new facilities provided, and new products launched. Reserves must be created to provide for adverse times.

When we operate according to these principles, the stockholders should realize a fair return.

William G. McGowan—Effective Corporate Public Affairs Leader[1]

In the 1960s, technological changes began to radically transform the telecommunications industry. Companies wanted to connect their telephone lines to computers in order to transmit and process information from different plant locations. They wanted to share leased lines. But AT&T was not being responsive to their requests. Microwave Communications Incorporated (MCI), a new company, proposed to take advantage of microwave technology to set up a private line between Chicago and St. Louis. This line would be more flexible than the ones provided by AT&T, but AT&T resisted and in a long drawn out regulatory proceeding that lasted from 1963 to 1969 it blocked MCI from proceeding.

---

[1] D. Yoffie, "Corporate Strategies for Political Action: A Rational Model," in *Business Strategy and Public Policy,* eds. A. Marcus, A. Kaufman, and D. Beam (Greenwood Press: Westport, Conn., 1987) pp. 43–60.

In 1968, William G. McGowan joined MCI. A hard-driving executive from Scranton, Pennsylvania, McGowan had received his M.B.A. from Harvard and had a successful career working as a consultant and executive for many firms. McGowan's first move as chief executive officer was to relocate corporate headquarters to Washington, D.C. In Washington, he looked for political allies to fight AT&T but could find none. No trade association in the telecommunications industry was willing to take on the industry behemoth. Telephone users, even large ones, were afraid to offend AT&T. The financial backers of MCI were small entrepreneurs who had little political clout or sophistication. In developing an opposition to AT&T, McGowan had to act alone. His aim was no less than to divest AT&T of its local subsidiaries, and he marketed his ideas to policy makers in much the same way a company would market its product to consumers.

that have earned their loyalty, rewarded their performance, and involved them in the decision making process . . .

Corporations most closely touch people's lives in the individual communities where they operate. Here they are expected to be concerned with local needs and problems—schools, traffic, pollution, health, recreation. . . .

The corporation's first responsibility to society is to maintain its economic viability as a producer of goods and services, as an employer, and as a creator of jobs. . . .

Shareholders have a special relationship to the corporation. . . . The corporation must be profitable enough to provide shareholders a return that will encourage continuation of investment. . . . The expectation of near-term gain can exert pressure to subordinate long-term objectives to more immediate profit considerations. Despite such expectations, management needs to maintain a long-term perspective.

Balancing the shareholder's expectations of maximum return against

William G. McGowan continued

McGowan found that a group of officials in the Federal Communications Commission, the White House, and the Justice Department were willing to listen. They too felt that competition in the telecommunications industry would have benefits—additional innovation would result from an effective check on AT&T's monopoly power and consumers would have lower telephone rates. McGowan articulated his objectives in terms of broad social goals. He established with a number of other small companies the Ad Hoc Coalition for Competitive Telecommunications (ACCT) in 1976 to pursue these goals.

McGowan's efforts in building MCI involved (1) maintaining venture capital, (2) lobbying, (3) exploiting loopholes in the laws that would allow MCI to expand its services, and (4) providing telecommunications services to existing customers. He did not regard the initial FCC decisions that opened the door for MCI, especially the Specialized Carrier Decision of 1971, as being sufficient.

He constantly pushed at the FCC to broaden the frontiers of competition. Finally, in 1974 MCI started an antitrust suit against AT&T. This suit lasted for nearly 10 years, during which time McGowan heightened visibility for his firm by portraying AT&T in a negative manner.

McGowan's political strategy was essential to his company's business success. He needed access to government officials and he obtained it. By the middle of the 1970s it was impossible to resolve a telecommunications issue without first hearing from McGowan. McGowan's persistence paid off because one of the important outcomes was permission for MCI and others to compete in offering long-distance telephone service. When deregulation took place, McGowan used his visibility as spokesperson for the procompetition forces to enhance the image of MCI and make it a leader in the long-distance telephone market. He was a master at combining the individual interest of his firm with the broader public interest in telecommunication's deregulation.

other priorities is one of the fundamental problems confronting corporate management. The shareholder must receive a good return but the legitimate concerns of other constituencies also must have the appropriate attention.[25]

The Business Roundtable's statement was attacked by the economist Paul MacAvoy.[26] In an article in *The New York Times*, MacAvoy maintained that a concern with constituencies "implies that the large corporation is a political entity subject to the votes of interest groups, rather than an economic organization subject to the market test for efficient use of resources."[27]

MacAvoy argued that "the corporation should be using its resources to maximize investment returns, so as to stimulate the investment required to produce the largest amount of goods and services for which consumers are willing to pay."[28] He maintained that "unless social and charitable activities reduce long-run marginal costs or increase consumer demand, then they divert resources from the social goals inherent in maximum production."[29]

The Business Roundtable replied in *The New York Times* on December 27, 1981, that it recognized that a corporation's first responsibility was "to make available to the public quality goods and services at fair prices, thereby earning a profit that attracts investment to continue and enhance the enterprise, provide jobs, and build the economy."[30] However, "chief executive officers who have been out there facing reality know that they are surrounded by a complicated pattern of . . . expectations . . . [and] . . . they have to be concerned not only about shareholders but about . . . constituent groups."[31]

Revision of the Business Roundtable Position

In 1990, the Business Roundtable issued a statement on "Corporate Governance and the American Economy," which appeared to revise its original position on stakeholders in light of the competitive challenges U.S. companies faced abroad.

> As an economic entity chartered by the state, each corporation finds itself in heavy competition not only with other U.S. corporations but also with the products and services of foreign corporations, and with business organizations that are as diverse as individual entrepreneurs to nations or consortiums of nations. . . .
>
> Corporate governance is sometimes erroneously compared to political governance. Although surface similarities exist between the election of boards of directors and the election of legislative bodies, the fundamental purposes of the corporation as an economic entity are quite different from those of a political body. . . . A corporation has as its prime purpose the long-term optimization of economic outcomes. . . .
>
> It is important that all stakeholder interests be considered, but impossible to assure that all will be satisfied.[32]

The Business Roundtable position was different because the conditions governing business were different at the end of the 1980s.

Corporate Restructuring

The stakeholder debate has been reflected in the argument about corporate restructuring. For example, some have supported hostile takeovers on the grounds that they contribute to shareholder wealth (agency theory), while others have opposed such restructuring on the grounds that it damages the interests of the corporation's other stakeholders (stakeholder theory).[33]

Boone Pickens was a leading advocate of shareholder rights.[34] Many eminent, academic economists supported his views.[35] They argued that restructuring was good because it removed entrenched management that stood in the way of economic progress.

The opponents to this way of thinking often were managers whose jobs were threatened (managerial theory). However, it was not only the managers whose jobs were in jeopardy. To finance hostile takeovers, the new owners took on risky, high-interest debt (called junk bonds), and to service the debt they often had to divest the company of some (or all) of operations. Blue-collar workers typically were the first to be laid off, local economies lost their vitality, factories closed, and communities suffered. Opposition to hostile takeovers came not only from the managers of the target companies but also from the residents of the communities where companies were located (see the Dayton Hudson case at the end of Part II).

The debate about takeovers has had broad ramifications. After a takeover, the firm might have less money to spend on research and development (R&D) and other so-called nonessential business functions. The scarcity of cash not only would influence the firm's economic future; it would impact the entire economy, which depended on a steady stream of improvements that emanated from R&D spending.[36]

Takeover Results

Research showed that the stockholders of firms that had been taken over reaped substantial gains. The stockholders of the acquiring firms tended to lose money in the short run, but the losses did not negate the overall shareholder benefit.[37] Roll suggested that the acquirers systematically overbid the price of target companies because they thought they were smarter than the market: the managers exhibited "hubris."[38]

Ravenscraft and Scherer relied on accounting rather than market data to evaluate the postmerger performance of merged entities.[39] They showed that average performance declined after mergers, acquisitions, and tender offers. The only area where significant improvement occurred was for mergers of two relatively equal sized firms.

Leveraged Management Buyouts

A growing proportion of takeover activity was in the form of leveraged management buyouts (LBOs).[40] By 1986, LBOs accounted for 20 percent of all takeover activity in the United States.[41] In a typical buyout, a management group in association with a specialist firm such as Kohlberg, Kravis, and Roberts (KKR) would buy the outstanding public stock in a company in exchange for cash and or debt. The firm would no longer be traded on public stock markets or be subject to public disclosure and scrutiny requirements. As a privately owned entity, it would have greater freedom than publicly traded firms.

The specialist firm was needed to carry out the transaction because managers typically did not have the personal wealth or the access to financing to purchase the firm on their own. They therefore used the specialist firm to arrange for the financing through the sale of debt. In the newly private firm, the specialist firm had a very important role. It was a major equity holder, financial adviser, and board member.

Most LBOs were financed through a combination of senior debt, subordinate debt, and equity. The senior debt generally was secured with fixed assets, inventory, and accounts receivable. It was held by banks, insurance companies, leasing companies, and LBO venture-capital limited partnerships. The subordinate debt, or "mezzanine money," often was in the form of high-yield bonds, otherwise known as junk bonds. Junk bonds were senior to common equity but junior to secured debt. Generally, similar groups held both the senior debt and the junk bonds. The equity typically belonged to management, the specialist firm which helped finance the deal, and employee stock ownership plans (ESOPs).[42] In firms subject to LBOs, debt increased dramatically. In 76 buyouts that occurred between 1980 and 1986, the median book value of debt to total capital jumped from 18 percent to 88.4 percent.[43]

After a buyout, managers had a large personal stake in the success of the business. The problems emanating from the separation of ownership and management that have been described should have been reduced. The pressure of debt along with the increased personal stake provided a strong incentive to increase efficiency. Peter Magowan, CEO of Safeway, wrote that after the LBO involving his company, the "transformation from [being] managers to being co-owners" was a "powerful stimulus" since "after all" it was "now . . . our money too."[44]

Eliminating Free Cash Flow

Free cash flow is cash "in excess of that required to fund all of a firm's projects that have positive net present values when discounted at the relevant cost of capital."[45] Many economists believe that, to enhance the efficiency of the firm, excess free cash should be paid to shareholders.[46] However, because of the separation of ownership and control, managers have strong incentives not to pay it to the shareholders. "The problem," according to Jensen, "is how to motivate managers to disgorge the cash rather than to invest it at below the cost of capital or to waste it through organizational inefficiencies."[47]

Management buyouts, then, must be seen as part of a larger phenomenon—the market for corporate control—that has assisted in the process of disgorging free cash (see Exhibit 6–5). Corporate restructuring came about because of contests among management teams for the control of corporate assets.[48] These contests had the effect of limiting

EXHIBIT 6–5   The Economic Perspective on LBOs

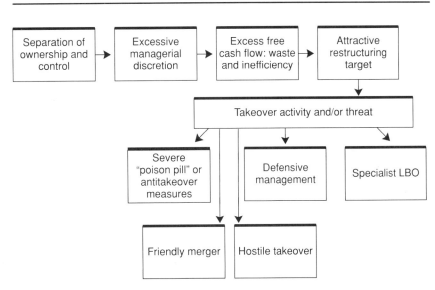

managerial discretion, since ineffective management, incapable of putting assets to their highest valued use, was likely to be replaced.

LBOs had some unique characteristics and some characteristics in common with other types of corporate restructuring. They were unique in that they explicitly aligned the interests of managers and stockholders. Managers became an important, if not the most important, equity holder. However, like other types of restructuring, this aligning of the interests of managers and stockholders was accomplished through the expansion of debt, which tended to subject the managers to new standards of discipline and control and to reduce their discretionary use of the company's funds.

With the firm highly leveraged, the fear of bankruptcy was a powerful motivator; managers had little choice but to run the firm efficiently. This fear constrained them from investing in discretionary projects that might have negative net present value. Rather, after the buyout there often were significant asset sales to get rid of unrelated or unprofitable operations or to reduce the debt burden or both.

Tax Benefits

Perhaps unwittingly, the government through the tax code subsidized this movement from equity to debt.[49] Three types of expected tax savings stimulated corporate restructuring. First, by issuing added debt, firms increased their interest deductions. Second, they reaped depreciation benefits: they could step up the value basis, from historical cost to the purchase value of equity plus outstanding debt, that might be depreciated over time. Third, both the principal and the interest on loans incurred by ESOPs were tax deductible. Also, the ESOP could buy the shares of the company by borrowing from a commercial bank. The Tax Reform Act allowed lenders to exclude from income up to 50 percent of the interest paid.[50]

Controversy about LBOs

LBOs became not only important but also controversial. Defenders saw them as a new organizational form with powerful efficiency enhancing and agency cost reduction potential.[51] According to this view, the increased managerial and investment banker equity holdings and the added debt load increased the alignment between managerial and stockholder interests and reduced the incentives for wasteful managerial spending. With the concentration of ownership, too, the monitoring costs of the board declined and the monitoring effectiveness of the board went up. However, the critics contended that LBOs were fraught with

EXHIBIT 6–6   **The Causes and Consequences of LBOs**

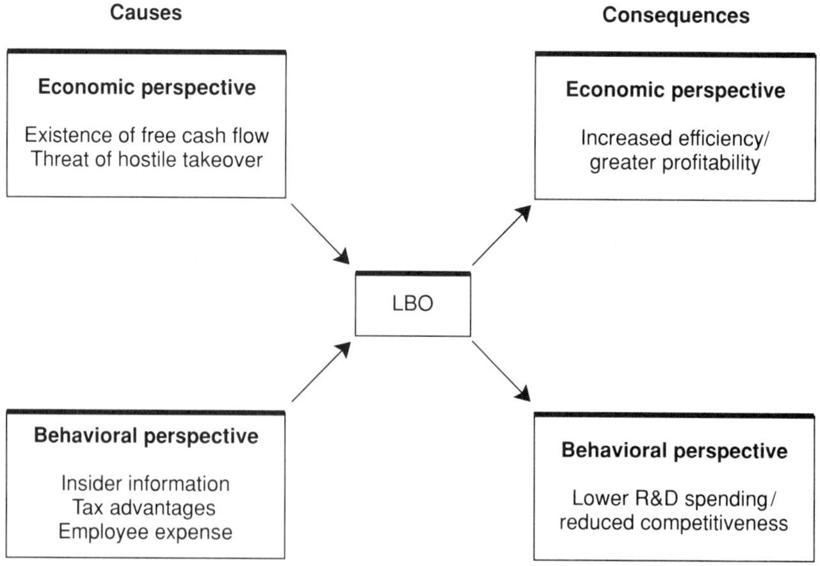

ethical problems and were at best merely redistributive (see Exhibit 6–6).

For example, the critics maintained that the inherent informational asymmetries between insider managers and outsider stockholders created a severe conflict of interest between management's fiduciary responsibility to sell at the highest possible price and its natural self-interest to buy at the lowest possible price.[52] However, a variety of legal safeguards were available to the stockholders. Since 1979, SEC rules required firms to make statements on the fairness of the transaction. These statements included questions about whether there were independent valuations and independent parties negotiating for the stockholders. They also included questions about whether the deal had the support of either a majority of outside directors or a majority of nonparticipating shareholders. Litigation remedies also existed.

As buyouts frequently occurred in response to hostile tender offers or rumors of them, the ultimate protection for shareholders was the overall market for corporate control.[53] Between 1980 and 1983, 28 percent of all LBOs were accompanied by a competing bid or takeover speculation; during the four years from 1984 to 1987, this figure had jumped to 48.6 percent.[54] The very fact that an LBO bid had been made and that the structure of the bid was known provided important information about insider valuations.[55]

Redistributional Arguments

The redistributional arguments about LBOs were that the buyout premiums to existing stockholders, averaging around 40 to 50 percent, were due to tax savings and lower value on existing debt, and constituted a significant redistribution from society as a whole to the shareholders.[56] This argument had several aspects. First, bondholders suffered because existing debt was more risky.[57] There was widespread downgrading of bonds by Moody; 83 percent lost their investment-grade-or-better status because of a perceived increase in the risk of default.

Other stakeholders also were damaged. Employees faced greater uncertainty, layoffs, and lower wages. After the Safeway LBO, the company closed its Dallas area division, taking away jobs from nearly 9,000 employees with average length of service of 17 years.[58] It fired the employees without notice, eliminated in as little as two weeks their health insurance, and provided severance pay for only eight weeks. Safeway introduced incentives and quotas that were designed to make the remaining employees more entrepreneurial and accountable, but the employees referred to the incentive system as the "punishment system," and claimed that "mass panic" and "burnout" were yielding a "grind of tension and overwork" with little real benefit to the firm.[59]

The drive for cost cutting and increased efficiency also altered relationships with customers and suppliers. Since many LBOs were financed by junk bonds, the risk of bankruptcy during a recession grew.

However, of one thing there was no doubt: corporate restructuring was remaking American corporations. The impact was likely to be complex, with gains offset by losses and the overall effect on society at large and on specific stakeholders being highly uncertain.

Social Responsibility in the Japanese Firm

Managers, politicians, academicians, and others have been fascinated with the strength of the Japanese firm. Voluminous accounts attempt to explain this success and to show how the factors behind it might be transferred to other countries.[60] Much of the rest of this book will deal with this topic in one way or another.

The risks of discussing Japan, however, are great because as analyses of the Japanese economy proliferate, there is a tendency for writers to find in Japan what they already value. Many factors have contributed to the Japanese economic miracle, but few analysts see it as a totality. Rather, they focus on a particular area. Thus, Japanese success is attributed to low defense spending, a long-run perspective, easy access to capital, a high educational level, low levels of unionization, labor-management cooperation, lifetime employment, decision making by consensus, workplace democracy, job rotation, quality circles, robotics, kanban inventory systems, a high savings rate, low interest rates, low taxes, industrial policies, trade protection, and many other factors. By contrast, this discussion will center on corporate governance in Japan and the social performance of Japanese corporations. Later chapters will take up additional features. In an effort to move the study of the strategic business environment beyond its parochial moorings in U.S. society, it is necessary to begin the process of comparing the United States with other countries with which it is competing on a global level.

Corporate Governance

Corporate governance in Japan is very different from U.S. practice. Agency theory is the prime theory of the firm in the United States.[61] The firm is conceived of a nexus of contracts. Principals (shareholders) delegate decision making for realizing their objectives to agents (managers), who may have greater expertise or better site-specific information but different preferences and interests. The principals, therefore, have to devise means to control the agents' actions.

Ultimately, discrepancies arise between the desires of the principals and what the agents do. Management is regarded largely as a hierarchical control problem with each level of agents delegating some of their duties down to lower levels. When not viewed simply as a hierarchical control problem, then management becomes a problem of dealing with potentially antagonistic aspects of government and of building an effective consensus among diverse interests.

In Japan, however, the structure of the corporation is different. Banks, not shareholders, are the main providers of capital. Subject to regulation and administrative guidance by the government's Ministry of Finance, they are allowed to hold up to a maximum of 5 percent of the stock of nonfinancial companies. Banks and other financial institutions own about 40 percent of the stocks of listed companies. Individual shareholders own only about 30 percent of total equities (see Exhibit 6–7).

Close Banks Ties

The companies and the banks have very close ties in Japan that cannot be matched in the United States because of legal requirements (both antitrust and banking laws prevent these ties from developing).[62] In Japan, six large enterprise groups exist, consisting of an alliance of a main bank and a group of industrial and financial firms. Within the enterprise group (which would be illegal in the United States), there is a strong information exchange that manifests itself through business group executive committees, temporary transfers of personnel between banks and member firms, interfirm business ventures, and substantial leveraging within the group (e.g., the bank will loan funds to an insurance company, which will loan to a manufacturing company, with all of them being members of the same group).[63]

Controlling interests of stock are held by the management of other members of the enterprise group who are sympathetic to the firm's man-

---

EXHIBIT 6–7   A Comparison of the U.S. and Japanese Firm

U.S. Firm	*Japanese Firm*
Agency theory: 　Firm is nexus of contracts.	Banks provide most of the capital: 　Close coordination with government and other firms.
Shareholders' need to control managerial behavior.	Central banks plan, industrial groups support.
Banks without control when firm in distress.	Banks control when firm in severe financial distress.
"Maximize returns to shareholders subject to laws and ethics."	"Maximize income per employee after fixed payment to shareholders."

agement. Typically, about 20 to 30 percent of the common stock is controlled by the enterprise group with the understanding that these are long-term holdings that are not to be traded.[64] As a result, only about 25 percent of the shares listed on the Tokyo exchange are available for trading, and takeovers and other types of corporate restructuring are very uncommon.[65] The close ties that Japanese firms have with the banks is one of the reasons that they can obtain loans at a higher debt/equity ratio than U.S. firms, resulting in ratios five or six times larger than for typical U.S. firms.

However, some analysts dispute the significance of the good information ties and resultant high debt to equity ratio. They claim that most loans are secured by assets and that accounting practices in Japan are more conservative than in the United States, thus understating assets and increasing net worth, which would increase debt over equity.[66]

Bank Control under Conditions of Distress

Unlike banks in the United States, which are prohibited from doing so under the Glass-Steagal Act, Japanese banks can assume managerial responsibilities. This includes not only the rescheduling of loan payments and the granting of emergency loans but also taking active control by advising which assets to liquidate, which business opportunities to pursue, which managers to hire or fire, and which reorganizations to carry out.[67]

In well-run companies, the control of policy and the selection of managers is not a function that the banks readily assume. Company management enjoys substantial autonomy. The threat of extensive intervention exists only if a company finds itself in financial difficulty.

Because of the strength of their economy, Japanese companies have been run by their managers subject to the constraint that the managers would lose control to the banks only if the financial condition of their companies should dramatically deteriorate. In practice, this situation has meant that the Japanese firm "chooses the amount of output and the amounts of labor and capital input so as to maximize income per employee . . . after the payment of a fixed share of profits to stockholders."[68] In fact, maximizing income per worker, rather than return to shareholders, has been a major objective of Japanese companies because of their special system of governance.

Japanese Capital Markets

A critical factor in Japan's success has been the nature of its capital markets. Japanese firms have enjoyed a competitive advantage over U.S. firms because of the low rates at which they have been able to secure funds. For instance, comparative studies of U.S. and Japanese firms in the semiconductor business have shown significantly lower costs of debt financing in Japan.[69]

Besides the close ties between banks and firms, what makes this possible is that Japan has had an excess of savings over investment. Individuals have been encouraged to save through many means, including tax incentives. There are no capital gains taxes for individuals (up to a certain high amount) and interest on savings is nontaxable. Since the Japanese government is averse to running fiscal deficits, the bulk of these savings have been invested in industry.

The Bank of Japan (BOJ) and the Ministry of Finance (MOF) play an important role in this process. BOJ and MOF help keep interest rates below market rates, thus creating a demand for funds, which results in considerable government control over the banks. Through the mechanism of artificially low interest rates the government has been able to direct capital flows into industries targeted for development, and industry has been the recipient of numerous tax incentives and depreciation allowances to encourage investment.

A Comparison with West Germany

West German firms, too, have relied on debt financing more heavily than equity financing and have also had creditors that take an active role in the management of the company. Relatively few West German companies are publicly traded; many firms are fairly small. Firms with 500 or fewer employees accounted for half of the country's gross domestic product (GDP) and more than half of the patents issued.[70] Capitalism in the Anglo-Saxon countries—the United States, Britain, Australia, and Canada—is to be contrasted with capitalism in Japan and West Germany.

However, the situation for Japanese and West German firms has changed since the mid-1980s. The companies have used part of their substantial cash inflows to lower their debt burdens and invest heavily in the equity markets, and new laws have reduced the proportion of a company's stock that a creditor can hold, lessening the banks' control over the firm.

Social Performance

With regard to social performance, the record of Japanese firms is very mixed (see Exhibit 6–8).[71] For example, Japan is South Africa's largest trading partner. In addition, the country has a long and successful history of opposition to immigration. Prejudice against minorities is common.

Social movements in Japan have not had the strength they have had in the United States. The strongest social movement is in the environ-

---

EXHIBIT 6–8 **Social Performance: Japanese and U.S. Firms**

Japan	*The United States*
• Prejudice against minorities.	• Attempts to eliminate prejudice.
• Weak women's movement.	• Strong women's movement.
• Strong environmental movement.	• Strong environmental movement.
• Few pressures for corporate philanthropy.	• Strong pressures for corporate philanthropy.
• Harmonious labor-management relations.	• Labor-management strife.
• Duty and loyalty to the group.	• Pursuit of personal interests.
• High-quality health and safety programs in companies with lifetime employment (e.g., automotive industry).	• Lower quality health and safety programs in major companies.
• Very few occupational injuries.	• Many more occupational injuries.

---

mental area. But there are no significant minority movements, the women's movement is weak, the consumer movement has had little impact, and labor-management relations for the most part have been free of serious conflict. Pressures for corporate philanthropy do not exist in Japan. Yet Japanese companies have established a much greater identification between themselves and their employees. Japanese companies provide extensive welfare-like benefits to employees, including the right to use company hospitals, housing, and recreational facilities.

In individual ethics, Japanese norms are unlike those in Western countries. Conflicts between the expectations of society and the dictates of a person's conscience are less of a factor. Japanese values tend to come from the group and to be based on personal relationships. A sense of duty and loyalty to the group precedes the pursuit of personal interests. Identification with the company tends to be strong and to dominate over other duties such as those to family and even in some cases to obeying the law.

A Major Emphasis on Employees

Japanese companies obtain this loyalty because of their commitment to their employees. In firms with lifetime employment (about a quarter of the economy), the interests of the permanent employees are the major concern. This concern is reflected in extremely high-quality health and safety programs in such industries as the automotive industry, where lost work days due to injury rates are 67 times less than the equivalent American rates.[72]

In industries where accidents can cause serious disruption to operations, they are viewed as a form of inefficiency that must be weeded out. Workers therefore do their utmost to keep accident rates low. Indeed, because of a sense of shame and loyalty to the group, they may even hide injuries. However, smaller firms where the bond between employee and employer is less strong achieve less impressive worker safety records. Nonetheless, in occupational safety and health, whether large or small, Japanese firms outperform American firms.

Summary and Conclusions

In Chapters 5 and 6, five theories of social responsibility (agency, managerialism, behavioral, public responsibility, and stakeholder) have been reviewed. The debate about corporate restructuring and the character of the Japanese firm have been discussed in light of these theories. The discussion is summarized as follows.

The corporate social responsibility debate took on a new significance for companies in the 1970s as society turned its attention to issues like equal opportunity, pollution control, energy and natural resources, and consumer and worker protection. Advocates of corporate social responsibility maintained that corporations had a broader array of responsibilities that went beyond the mere production of goods and services at a profit. They argued for a long-run, enlightened view of self-interest.

This view was appropriate for at least two reasons: not only does a company have to accommodate itself to social change to survive; advantages can accrue to it for being socially responsible. For example, it can acquire an enhanced public reputation and avoid unnecessary and costly regulation if it is perceived as socially responsible. Some advocates of social responsibility even maintained that society's problems should be viewed as business opportunities, and that profits could be made from systematic and vigorous corporate efforts to solve these problems.

The Critics

On the other hand, critics of the social responsibility doctrine argued that in a capitalist society economic performance was a corporation's primary social responsibility. If the corporation did not serve shareholders first, it would be unable to serve society. Society relied on the profit incentive to motivate corporations to provide jobs and make investments;

without these investments, economic growth was impossible. If the firm did not single-mindedly strive for economic success in a highly competitive national and international climate, it might fail, and its failure was not in society's interests.

Moreover, the critics contended that there was no legal or ethical basis for a broader definition of social responsibility. Who would hold managers accountable for using corporate resources if these resources were not spent to maximize shareholder returns? Also, placing too much latitude in the hands of managers was irresponsible. What some might see as acts of charity and responsibility, others would view as managerial perks and undue managerial discretion. Was it not better to have hundreds of individual investors decide what to do with profits they had earned because they have risked their money than to have a committee of executives decide for them that the executives' favorite causes should be supported?

Assessment of managerial economic performance, while still crude in certain respects, certainly was more advanced than the art of accounting for a firm's social performance. There were no generally accepted social performance standards and to the extent that there were standards, operationalization and measurement were extremely difficult. Accounting in the social performance realm was not sufficiently advanced to determine if managers were doing a good job.

The critics also maintained that government officials, not corporate executives, had the legal authority and responsibility to wrestle with social problems. Managers were hired because of their business acumen, not their social problem-solving abilities. Government officials, not business managers, were given a legal mandate to address social problems. Moreover, through its oversight and budgetary functions, Congress had a mechanism to hold government officials accountable, but managers lacked official sanction and thus accountability.

Maximize Profits While Conforming to Ethical and Legal Standards

The classic view of corporate social responsibility was stated by Milton Friedman: the social responsibility of managers is to increase shareholder profits within legal and ethical constraints.[73] The basis for his statement was that when managers act as executives, they are the *agents* of shareholders who own the corporation. The relationship of managers to owners is a *contractual* one based on fiduciary norms implicit in agency relationships.

Moreover, the standard that shareholders use to judge managers, return on investment, is straightforward. Managers are hired because they are expert at running the company—at producing, marketing, and financing. They are not hired to fulfill a social need such as reducing unemployment, hiring minorities, or lowering prices. Politicians act in the name of the public to pursue these ends, but the goals of managers are more narrow. According to Friedman, as individual citizens, managers can take on additional social responsibilities, but when acting for shareholders, they have the primary responsibility, to increase profits.

Friedman, nonetheless, emphasized that the pursuit of profit *had to* conform with the requirements of law and ethics. If ethical custom, for example, required that firms donate to charity, then the donations, as long as they were accurately reported to shareholders, were legitimate. In making donations, firms should admit that they want to improve the quality of life in a particular region in order to attract better employees and more loyal customers and make larger profits. To emphasize anything other than profits, according to Friedman, was to take away the corporation's credibility.

Thus, when it pays to do good, according to Friedman, there is no reason why corporations should not be good. Questions arise only when managers' good actions have no obvious effect on the corporate bottom line or when their bad actions seem to improve their performance.

Virtue, However, Not Contingent

Nonetheless, as indicated in earlier chapters, according to Kant, virtue is not contingent; it is universal and should apply in all circumstances regardless of the consequences.[74] Enlightened self-interest is only one form of virtuous behavior. A higher form involves self-sacrifice. Thus, a prudential ethics, based only on self-interest, is inadequate. In some situations, managers have to choose between profitability and values that are more important.

Discussion Questions

1. What is the principle of public responsibility? Why did it come to prominence? How does it differ from the principle of social responsibility?
2. In what ways did corporations enhance their capabilities for public affairs management in the 1970s and early 1980s?
3. What do you think of the way William McGowan founded MCI? Would H. Ross Perot be another example of a corporate executive who used the public policy process to serve his company's interests? To what extent are there other opportunities for using the public policy process to create new businesses?

4. Is business involvement in the political process fair? Are important nonbusiness interests unrepresented or underrepresented in the public policy process because they do not have the resources that businesses can command? Should the laws be reformed to reduce business involvement in politics?

5. Compare and contrast the five generic stakeholder strategies. Why would any company choose a social-justice strategy?

6. What would Milton Friedman say about Johnson and Johnson's stakeholder strategy? Would you agree with him?

7. Who won the debate between the Business Roundtable and Paul MacAvoy? What are your reasons for thinking so?

8. Why has the Business Roundtable modified its statement?

9. Are takeovers good for the economy? Why or why not?

10. Are leveraged management buyouts good for the economy? Why or why not?

11. Compare the U.S. and Japanese firm with respect to corporate governance.

12. Compare the U.S. and Japanese firm with respect to corporate social performance.

13. Why are U.S. and Japanese firms so different along these two dimensions?

Endnotes

1. L. Preston and J. Post *Private Management and Public Policy,* (Englewood Cliffs: Prentice Hall, 1975), pp. 14–43, 94–106.
2. Ibid.
3. Ibid.
4. Ibid.
5. Ibid.
6. Ibid.
7. Ibid.
8. Ibid.
9. Ibid.
10. W. Frederick, "Toward CSR-3: Why Ethical Analysis Is Indispensable and Unavoidable in Corporate Affairs," *California Management Review* 2, 1986, pp. 126–41; R. E. Freeman, *Strategic Management: A Stakeholder Approach* (Marshfield, Mass.: Pitman, 1984); A. A. Marcus, *The Adversary Economy: Business Responses to Changing Government Requirements* (Westport, Conn.: Quorum Books, 1984).
11. R. W. Ackerman, *The Social Challenge to Business* (Cambridge, Mass.: Har-

vard University Press, 1975); R. W. Ackerman, "How Companies Respond to Social Demands," *Harvard Business Review,* July–August 1973, pp. 88–98.

12. W. Lilley, and J. C. Miller, "The New Social Regulation," *The Public Interest,* Spring 1977, pp. 49–62; R. J. Penoyer, *Directory of Federal Regulatory Agencies—1982 Update* (St. Louis: Center for the Study of American Business, 1982), p. 1; P. Weaver, "Regulation, Social Policy, and Class Conflict," *The Public Interest,* Winter 1978, pp. 45–64; M. L. Weidenbaum, "The Future of Business-Government Relations in the United States, in *The Future of Business,* ed. M. Ways (New York: Pergamon, 1979), p. 49.

13. S. Lusterman, *The Organization and Staffing of Corporate Public Affairs* (New York: The Conference Board, 1987); J. A. Sonnenfeld, *Corporate Views of the Public Interest: Perceptions of the Forest Products Industry* (Boston: Auburn House Publishing Company, 1981); G. Starling and O. Baskin, "Pfizer Corporation: Strategy, Organization, and Implementation in the Public Affairs Function," in *Issues in Business and Society: Capitalism and Public Purpose* (Boston, Mass.: Kent Publishing, 1985), pp. 29–51; A. Kaufman, E. Englander, and A. Marcus, *Structural Aspects of Issues Management: Transaction Costs and Agency Theory,* paper presented at the Eastern Academy of Management Meeting, 1987.

14. P. Andrews, 1986, "The Sticky Wicket of Evaluating Public Affairs: Thoughts about a Framework," *Public Affairs Review* 6, pp. 94–105; A. M. Kaufman, E. J. Englander, and A. A. Marcus, "Structure and Implementation in Issues Management: Transaction Costs and Agency Theory," *Research in Corporate Social Performance and Policy* 11, 1989, pp. 257–71; A. Marcus and A. Kaufman, "The Continued Expansion of the Corporate Public Affairs Function," *Business Horizons* 31, 1988, pp. 58–62.

15. A. Marcus and M. Irion, "The Continued Growth of the Corporate Public Affairs Function," *The Academy of Management Executive,* August 1987, pp. 249–52.

16. R. E. Cohen, "Congressional Democrats Beware—Here Come the Corporate PACs," *National Journal,* August 9, 1980, p. 1305; M. Glen, "The PACs Are Back Richer and Wiser to Finance the 1980 Elections," *National Journal,* December 24, 1979, pp. 1982–84; A. Matasar, *Corporate Responsibility Gone Away? The Corporate Political Action Committee,* paper presented at the 1981 annual meeting of the American Political Science Association, New York, September 3–6, 1981; J. S. Shockley, *Corporate Spending in the Wake of the Bellotti Decision: National Implications,* paper presented at the American Political Science Convention, New York, 1978.

17. G. Keim and C. Zeithaml, "Corporate Political Strategy and Legislative Decision Making," *Academy of Management Review* 11, no. 4, 1986, pp. 828–43; A. A. Marcus, *The Adversary Economy: Business Responses to Changing Government Requirements* (Westport, Conn.: Quorum Books; 1984); Keim and Zeithaml, "Corporate Political Strategy and Legislative Decision Making."

18. K. McQuaid, "The Roundtable: Getting Results in Washington," *Harvard Business Review,* May–June 1981, pp. 114–23.

19. R. Buchholz, W. Evans, and R. Wagley, *Management Response to Public Issues* (Englewood Cliffs, N.J.: Prentice Hall, 1987), pp. 186–200.

20. Keim and Zeithaml, "Corporate Political Strategy and Legislative Decision

Making"; R. E. Cohen, "The Business Lobby Discovers that in Unity There Is Strength," *National Journal,* June 28, 1980, pp. 1050–55; R. Reich, "Regulation by Negotiation or Confrontation?" *Harvard Business Review,* May–June 1981, pp. 82–92.

21. Freeman, *Strategic Management: a Stakeholder Approach.*

22. Ibid.

23. The Business Roundtable, *Corporate Ethics: A Prime Business Asset* (New York: The Business Roundtable, 1988); J. Dresang, "Companies Get Serious about Ethics," *USA Today,* Dec. 9, 1986, p. B1.

24. The Business Roundtable, *Corporate Ethics: A Prime Business Asset;* R. W. Johnson, *Johnson & Johnson: Our Credo.*

25. The Business Roundtable, *Statement on Corporate Responsibility* (New York: The Business Roundtable, October 1981).

26. P. W. MacAvoy, "The Business Lobby's Wrong Business," in *Business and Society,* ed. T. G. Marx (Englewood Cliffs, N.J.: Prentice Hall, 1981), pp. 158–64.

27. P. W. MacAvoy, "The Business Lobby's Wrong Business," *The New York Times,* December 20, 1981.

28. Ibid.

29. Ibid.

30. A. C. Sigler, "Roundtable Reply," in *Business and Society: Economic, Moral, and Political Foundations,* ed. T. Marx (Englewood Cliffs, N.J.: Prentice Hall, 1985).

31. Sigler, "Roundtable Reply."

32. Business Roundtable, *Corporate Governance and American Competitiveness* (New York: The Business Roundtable, March, 1990).

33. R. Caves, "Effects of Mergers and Acquisitions on the Economy: An Industrial Organization Perspective," in *The Merger Boom,* ed. L. Browne and E. Rosengren (Boston: Federal Reserve Bank of Boston, 1987); J. C. Coffee, L. Lowenstein, and S. Rose-Ackerman, *Knights, Raiders and Targets* (New York: Oxford University Press, 1988); A. Auerbach, *Corporate Takeovers: Causes and Consequences* (Chicago: University of Chicago Press, 1989).

34. P. T. Boone Pickens, "Professions of a Short-Termer," *Harvard Business Review,* May–June 1986, pp. 75–80; and W. Law, "A Corporation Is More Than Its Stock," *Harvard Business Review,* May–June 1986, pp. 80–84.

35. M. Jensen, "The Takeover Controversy Analysis and Evidence," in *Knights, Raiders and Targets,* ed. J. Coffee et al; M. Jensen, "The Free Cash Flow Theory of Takeovers: A Financial Perspective on Mergers, Acquisitions and the Economy," in *The Merger Boom,* ed. L. Browne and E. Rosengren (Boston: Federal Reserve Bank of Boston, 1987); M. Weidenbaum and S. Vogt, "Takeovers and Stockholders: Winners and Losers," *California Management Review,* Summer 1987, pp. 157–69.

36. B. H. Hall, "Effects of Takeover Activity on Corporate Research and Development," in *Corporate Takeovers,* ed. A. Auerbach (Chicago, University of Chicago Press); B. H. Hall, *The Impact of Corporate Restructuring on Industrial Research and Development,* working paper 89–129 University of California at Berkeley, 1989; C. W. L. Hill, M. A. Hitt, and R. E. Hoskisson, "Declining U.S. Competitiveness: Reflections on a Crisis," *Academy of Management Executive* 2, no. 1, 1988, pp. 51–60; National Science Foundation, *An Assess-*

ment of the Impact of Recent Leveraged Buyouts and Other Restructurings on Industrial Research and Development Expenditures, report prepared for the Subcommittee on Telecommunications and Finance, House Committee on Energy and Commerce, February, 1989.

37. M. Bradley, A. Desai, and E. H. Kim, "Synergistic Gains from Corporate Acquisitions and Their Division between the Stockholders of Target and Acquiring Firms," *Journal of Financial Economics* 21, 1988, pp, 3–40; D. Dennis and J. J. McConnel, "Corporate Mergers and Security Returns," *Journal of Financial Economics* 10, 1986, pp. 143–87; I. Krinsky, W. D. Rotenberg, and D. B. Thornton, "Takeovers—A Synthesis," *Journal of Accounting Literature* 7, 1988, pp. 243–79; R. E. Hoskisson, and M. A. Hitt, "Strategic Control Systems and Relative R&D Investment in Large Multiproduct Firms," *Strategic Management Journal* 9, 1988, pp. 605–21; Weidenbaum and Vogt, "Takeovers and Stockholders: Winners and Losers."

38. R. Roll, "The Hubris Hypothesis of Corporate Takeovers," *Journal of Business* 59, 1986, pp. 197–216; R. Roll, "Empirical Evidence on Takeover Activity and Shareholder Wealth," in *Knights, Raiders and Targets,* ed. J. Coffee et al.

39. D. Ravenscraft and F. M. Scherer, *Mergers, Selloffs and Economic Efficiency* (Washington, D.C.: The Brookings Institution, 1987).

40. J. C. Easterwood, A. Seth, and R. F. Singer, "The Impact of LBOs on Strategic Direction," *California Management Review* 32, no. 1, pp. 30–43; J. P. Newport, "LBO's: Greed, Good Business, or Both?" *Fortune,* January 2, 1989, p. 66; T. Pouschine, P. Berman, and M. B. Grover, "The Takeover Game Isn't Dead, It's Just Gone Private," *Forbes,* October 1, 1990, pp. 63–74; I. Fox and A. Marcus, "The Causes and Consequences of Leveraged Management Buyouts," *Academy of Management Review,* January 1992.

41. S. Kaplan, *Management Buyouts, Efficiency Gains or Value Transfers,* Working Paper 244, University of Chicago, 1988.

42. K. Lehn and A. Poulsen, *Free Cash Flow and Stockholder Gains in Going Private,* Transactions, manuscript, University of Georgia, 1988; K. Lehn and A. Poulsen, "Leveraged Buyouts: Wealth Created or Wealth Redistributed," in *Public Policy toward Corporate Takeovers,* ed. M. Weidenbaum and K. Chilton (New Brunswick: Transaction Books, 1988).

43. Kaplan, *Management Buyouts, Efficiency Gains or Value Transfers.*

44. P. A. Magowan, "The Case for LBOs: The Safeway Experience," *California Management Review* 1, 1989, pp. 13–14.

45. M. Jensen, "Agency Costs of Free Cash Flow, Corporate Finance, and Takeovers," *American Economic Review* 76, no. 2, 1986, p. 323.

46. M. Friedman, *Capitalism and Freedom* (Chicago: University of Chicago Press, 1962).

47. Jensen, "Agency Costs of Free Cash Flow, Corporate Finance, and Takeovers."

48. E. Fama, "Agency Problems and the Theory of the Firm," *Journal of Political Economy* 88, 1980, pp. 288–307.

49. A. Auerbach and D. Reishus, "The Efforts of Taxation on the Merger Decision," in *Corporate Takeovers,* ed. A. Auerbach (Chicago, University of Chicago Press, 1988); H. Leland, "LBOs and Taxes: No One to Blame but Ourselves?" *California Management Review* 32, no. 1, pp. 19–29;

L. Lowenstein, "Management Buyouts," *Columbia Law Review* 85, 1985, pp. 730–84.

50. Lowenstein, "Management Buyouts."
51. H. DeAngelo, L. DeAngelo, and E. Rice, "Going Private: Minority Freeze Outs and Stockholder Wealth," *Journal of Law and Economics*, October 1984, pp. 367–401; H. DeAngelo, and L. DeAngelo, "Management Buyouts of Publicly Traded Corporation," *Financial Analysts Journal*, May–June 1987, pp. 38–48; M. Jensen, "Is Leverage an Invitation to Bankruptcy, *The Wall Street Journal*, February 1, 1989, p. 29; Jensen, "The Takeover Controversy Analysis and Evidence"; Jensen, "The Free Cash Flow Theory of Takeovers"; Kravis Kohlberg, Roberts & Co., *Presentation on Leveraged Buyouts*, paper presented at the Conference on Corporate Governance, Restructuring, and the Market for Corporate Control, Salomon Brothers Center for the Study of Financial Institutions, May 22–23, 1989; Lowenstein, "Management Buyouts"; T. Ricks, "Two Scholars Blast KKR Buy-Out Study That Reached Pro-Takeover Conclusions," *The Wall Street Journal*, May 10, 1989; F. Rohatyn, "The Debt Addiction," *New York Review of Books*, April 13, 1989, pp. 39–42.
52. L. Lowenstein, "Management Buyouts"; R. Bruner and L. Paine, "Management Buyouts and Managerial Ethics," *California Management Review*, Winter, 1988, pp. 89–106.
53. Lehn and Poulsen, *Free Cash Flow and Stockholder Gains in Going Private*; R. Morck, A. Shleifer, and R. Vishny, "Characteristics of Hostile and Friendly Takeover Targets," in *Corporate Takeovers*, ed. A. Auerbach (Chicago: University of Chicago Press, 1988).
54. Lehn and Poulsen, *Free Cash Flow and Stockholder Gains in Going Private*.
55. DeAngelo, DeAngelo, and Rice, "Going Private: Minority Freeze Outs and Stockholder Wealth"; Y. Huang and R. Walking, "Target Abnormal Returns Associated with Acquisition Announcements: Payment, Acquisition Form, and Managerial Resistance," *Journal of Financial Economics* 19, 1987, pp. 329–49; N. Stoughton, "The Information Content of Corporate Merger and Acquisition Offers," *Journal of Financial and Quantitative Analysis* 23, 1988, pp. 175–97.
56. A. Shleifer and R. Warner, "Management Buyouts as a Response to Market Pressure," in *Mergers and Acquisitions*, ed. A. Auerbach (Chicago: University of Chicago Press, 1988), A. Shleifer and L. Summers, "Breach of Trust in Hostile Takeovers," in *Corporate Takeovers: Causes and Consequences*, ed. A. Auerbach (Chicago: University of Chicago Press, 1988.).
57. Lowenstein, "Management Buyouts."
58. S. C. Faludi, "Safeway LBO Yields Vast Profits but Exacts a Heavy Human Toll," *The Wall Street Journal*, May 16, 1990, p. 1.
59. Ibid.
60. J. C. Abegglen and G. Stalk, *Kaisha: The Japanese Corporation* (New York: Basic Books, 1985); A. Murray and U. C. Lehner, "U.S., Japan Struggle to Redefine Relations as Resentment Grows," *The Wall Street Journal*, June 13, 1990, p. A1; R. T. Pascale and A. G. Athos, *The Art of Japanese Management: Applications for American Executives* (New York: Simon and Schuster, 1981); D. Garvin, "Quality Problems, Policies, and Attitudes in the U.S. and Japan: An Exploratory Study," *Academy of Management Journal* 19, December

1986, pp. 653–74; D. Encarnation, "Cross-Investment: a Second Front of Economic Rivalry," *California Management Review,* Winter 1987, pp. 20–49; D. Dunphy, "Convergence/Divergence: A Temporal Review of the Japanese Enterprise and Its Management," *Academy of Management Review* 14, July 1987, pp. 445–59.

61. K. M. Eisenhardt, *Agency Theory: An Assessment and Review,* manuscript, Department of Industrial Engineering and Engineering Management, Stanford University, 1988; J. W. Pratt and R. J. Zeckhauser, eds., *Principals and Agents: The Structure of Business* (Boston: Harvard Business School Press, 1985).

62. "Toward an Economic Model of the Japanese Firm," *Journal of Economic Literature* 28, 1990, pp. 1–27; W. C. Kester, "Capital and Ownership Structure: A Comparison of U.S. and Japanese Manufacturing Corporations," in *International Competitiveness,* ed. A. M. Spence (Cambridge, Mass.: Ballinger, 1988).

63. D. Encarnation, "Cross-Investment: A Second Front of Economic Rivalry," *California Management Review,* Winter 1987, pp. 20–49.

64. "Capitalism: In Triumph, in Flux," *The Economist,* May 5, 1990, p. 6 of special section, "Punters or Proprietors?"

65. Ibid.

66. Abegglen and Stalk, *Kaisha: The Japanese Corporation.*

67. W. Ouchi, *The M-Form Society: How American Teamwork Can Recapture the Competitive Edge* (Reading, Mass.: Addison-Wesley Publishing Co., 1984).

68. Komiya, "Structural and Behavioristic Characteristics of the Japanese Firm"; Ouchi, *The M-Form Society,* p. 115.

69. Ouchi, *The M-Form Society.*

70. "Capitalism: In Triumph, in Flux."

71. R. E. Wokutch, "Corporate Social Responsibility Japanese Style," *Academy of Management Executive* 4, no. 2, 1990, pp. 56–74.

72. L. S. Zacharias and A. Kaufman, *The Problem of the Corporation and the Emergence of the 'Managerial Thesis', 1920–1960,* proposal for NEH collaborative grant, Management Research Center, School of Management, University of Massachusetts at Amherst, 1987.

73. M. Friedman, "Social Responsibility of Business," in *Business and Society: Economic, Moral, and Political Foundations,* ed. T. Marx (Englewood Cliffs, N.J.: Prentice Hall 1985), pp. 145–50.

74. I. Kant, "Foundations of the Metaphysics of Morals," in *Ethics: Selections from Classical and Contemporary Writers,* ed. O. A. Johnson (New York: Holt, Rinehart and Winston, 1974).

WOMEN AND MINORITIES

Imagine a hundred-yard dash in which one of the two runners has his legs shackled together. He has progressed 10 yards, while the unshackled runner has gone 50 yards. How do they rectify the situation? Do they merely remove the shackles and allow the race to proceed? Then they could say that "equal opportunity" now prevailed. But one of the runners would still be forty yards ahead of the other. Would it not be the better part of justice to allow the previously shackled runner to make up the forty yard gap; or start the race all over again.

Lyndon Johnson[1]

Introduction and Chapter Objectives

This chapter discusses discrimination and what companies are being called upon to do to end it. It distinguishes between equal protection under the law and affirmative action, and considers some of the ethical isses these subjects raise. We then examine what the movement of women and minorities into the workplace has meant for business, discussing the attitudes of men and women, sexual harassment, equal pay for equal work, and the economic status of women and minorities. We review the public policies that have been created, the 1964 Civil Rights Act and the executive orders leading to affirmative action, as well as some of the important court cases that have been decided (e.g., *Griggs* and *Bakke*). The chapter concludes with a brief description of what companies might do to respond to these challenges.

Discrimination

The essence of discrimination is that individuals are not free to compete on the basis of their abilities.[2] They are judged for belonging to a particular group and are subjected to negative stereotypes associated with that group; for instance, negative stereotypes that all group members are lazy, violent, dangerous, and irresponsible, or negative stereotypes that all group members are timid, meek, self-effacing, overly sensitive, and emotional. People are treated negatively because of the supposed qualities of the group rather than being judged on their own merits.

In business relationships, people should be judged as individuals on their own merits. They should be judged according to what they have to offer as employees, suppliers, and customers, not in terms of the group to which they belong. If a person offers a superior or unique blend of talents, products, and services, or if a person's talents, products, and services are on a par with those of others, then the person should be allowed to offer those talents, products, and services regardless of who the person is or where the person came from, or the color of the person's skin. No person should be excluded from taking part in business transactions because of the group to which he or she belongs.

When there are grounds for mutually advantageous deals that make the parties better-off, but the deals are not consummated because one of the parties belongs to a group that is discriminated against, then not only are the deal makers losers. The interests of society as a whole are not served. The basis of business relationships should not be who you are or the group you belong to: gender, race, and national origin should have no bearing. The basis should be the special blend of skills, products, and services the parties to a deal have to offer. A society that consistently violates this principle is likely to remain in a backward and primitive condition. Transactions in such a society are not based on the need to improve, innovate, and provide better products and services, but on the basis of who the parties to a deal are and on the groups to which the parties to a deal belong. The market in these societies is not a perfect market; it is not working to maximize the wealth of those living in society.

Thus, gender-free and racially and ethnically blind business transactions advantage not only women, people of color, and people of different national origins who have suffered discrimination and been excluded from full and equal participation in the economy in the past. They benefit all of society, as they unleash the talents and energy of the people who have not been allowed to fully participate, and promote the social and economic development of the whole society. On purely utilitarian grounds, society has very strong reasons for ending discrimination.

What Companies Are Being Called upon to Do to End Discrimination

To end discrimination, companies are subject to two sets of legal demands.[3] First, they must conform to the laws of equal employment opportunity and not discriminate on the basis of sex, race, ethnicity, religion, handicap, age, or veteran status. They must treat each person as an individual, not as a member of a group. Each person must be dealt with similarly regardless of the group (or groups) to which the person belongs.

Second, companies are expected to carry out affirmative action programs. They must give groups that have suffered historical discrimination special treatment. As these groups have suffered from stereotypes, prejudice, hostility, and outright oppression in the past, they have a special status, and have been accorded rights to preferential treatment.

The demand to treat people alike, as individuals regardless of their sex, race, ethnic background, religion, or any other characteristic, comes from the 1964 Civil Rights Act. This act states very clearly that discrimination of any kind is illegal. The requirement to accord special treatment to the historically disadvantaged originated in a 1965 Executive Order issued by President Johnson. This executive order states that employers must favor historically disadvantaged groups through affirmative action.

Court cases support both doctrines. Companies have to do both—treat all people as individuals and accord special status to groups that have suffered past discrimination. The courts have not invalidated either principle.

One of the reasons that both principles continue to have standing is that the first principle, equality of opportunity, by itself will not produce equality of results. Historically disadvantaged groups suffer not only from prejudice, which has kept them from fully participating in the economy. They also suffer from the results of this prejudice, a lower socioeconomic status than the population as a whole. Those whose equality of opportunity was guaranteed with the passage of the 1964 Civil Rights Act were not on an equal footing with the rest of the population when the act was passed. Not being on an equal footing to start with, they were bound to have trouble successfully competing. Giving them the opportunity to compete equally did not guarantee that they could achieve better living conditions. Even if allowed to fully participate in economic transactions, their economic status might not improve. Indeed, it actually could decline (and to some extent did). Though no one can be prevented from advancing to the top, an equal proportion of people from different groups cannot be expected to do so when some groups start from a better position than others (see the quotation from Lyndon Johnson opening the chapter).

Disadvantaged people do not begin at the same level. The oppression and discrimination they have suffered means that many of them start the race with poor background and weak skills. Without the special treatment offered by affirmative action, they might not be able to catch up. This special status continues to set them apart and accords them status as members of groups, not as individuals. It contradicts the main idea of equal protection under the law, but it may be necessary to raise the social and economic status of women and minorities so that they can compete on an equal footing.

But if some are given this type of treatment, there is bound to be resentment among those who do not receive it. When a woman or a person of color appears to be favored over a white Protestant male, when the woman or person of color is hired or promoted in a tight economy and the white Protestant male with similar or even better background and qualifications is not, then the white Protestant male is bound to be upset. Even if, in the abstract, he sympathizes with the struggle women and minorities have had to undergo to obtain equal protection, even if he also has the compassion to feel that according them special status so that they can compete on an equal footing is justified, when *his* job is involved, *his* economic welfare and standing in society, he is upset.

This resentment has created a backlash against the movement for women's and minorities' rights. The backlash has been considerably stronger than it might otherwise have been because of the relatively weak U.S. economy in the 1970s and 1980s. And it has been a very important feature in defining the politics of the United States in the 1970s and 1980s.

Ethical Dilemmas

The striving for equality raises serious dilemmas that can be considered in an ethical framework. The framework for ethical analysis, developed in earlier chapters (see Chapters 3 and 4), can be applied, but with a cautionary note that what is offered here is only a beginning. To grapple fully with these issues requires much careful thought and reflection.

William James's paradox (see Chapter 3) is a good starting point. James warns that people should think about the rights of specific individuals and groups when pursuing the greatest good for the greatest number. In a market economy, the greatest good for the greatest number can be achieved only if people are treated as individuals in terms of what they have to offer each other in market transactions. People cannot be dealt with in terms of their sex, race, religion, or national origin. But what about specific groups that have suffered historic discrimination and have been left unable to compete adequately in a market economy. Do they have the right to preferential treatment? We must consider both the rights of groups that have suffered despite society's overall progress and the rights of those that might be harmed because of the need to give these groups special treatment.

Kant held that people must show respect for the dignity of everyone. We must restore the dignity of people who were excluded because they belonged to particular groups. We must show them the same dignity as everyone else; their rights, too, have to receive equal protection under the law. But should society go further and show them more than equal protection? Should it try to redress historic wrongs? Is compensating for past harms the only way to show full respect for the dignity of each person in these groups? Or is putting a person into a group category, for any reason, even to benefit that person, denigrating to the person? For instance, what happens when women or minority group members are hired because of affirmative action programs? What happens to their dignity? Is their sense of self-worth and self-esteem diminished because they realize they have not been accepted according to the standards that apply to the rest of society but have received special treatment?

The standard of universalism requires that people consider whether they would want to live in a world where all people were permitted to behave in certain ways. For instance, would one want to live in a world where everyone lied? Then truth telling would have no meaning, people could not trust each other, and many normal transactions that depend on trust could not take place.

Few people would want to live in a world where discrimination was routinely permitted. One day they might be in the majority, but the next they might be in the minority and subject to the same discrimination they inflicted on others. Also, most people want to live in a world where efforts are made to redress historic wrongs. They accept as universal the need to extend compassion to previously exploited groups. However, few would accept the proposition that previously exploited groups should advance at the expense of those who have caused them no direct harm.

Utilitarianism stands for the greatest good for the greatest number, and discrimination can only have a bad effect on the gross national product of a society. Discrimination confers no quantitative gain on all people in society. If market transactions are to maximize economic welfare, economic considerations, not a person's identity or group affiliation, have to prevail. Indeed, preferential treatment retards productivity if it means, for example, that less well qualified children of alumni are admitted to elite educational institutions like Harvard, Yale, and Princeton. Graduates of these institutions are accorded high status, and they may be offered prestigious jobs that affect the whole economy. If they accept important jobs for which they are unqualified, they can cause considerable social harm, negatively impacting the lives of many. If preferential treatment in any way requires that companies hire unqualified persons, then it can adversely affect national output.

Conceptually, preferential treatment for the formerly disadvantaged is in the same category as preferential treatment for the sons and daughters of Ivy League alumni. From a utilitarian perspective, they both do harm to the economy. But if preferential treatment for the formerly disadvantaged provides for the development of the confidence and capabilities of these people, if, for instance, it gives hope to unhappy, unemployed, people who have been poor, then might it not also serve the greatest good by preserving the social order? Might it not serve the greatest good by preventing riots and social disruption? It would seem that society has to make a trade-off between how much GNP it wants and how much social order, not an easy trade-off to make because there is no quantitative calculus by which it can be carried out.

Rawls argues that inequality is justified only if it is in the interests of everyone and is attached to positions open to all. Clearly, for there to be justice, positions have to be open to all. People cannot be excluded because of their race, gender, or national origin. But what about inequality? When can it be justified? Inequality may be in everyone's interest under the following conditions: if every person receives the same (or roughly the same) reward, people would not strive beyond a certain point, and without the incentive to strive for more, the social product would diminish. But preferential treatment for women and minorities might prevent them from making the extraordinary striving needed to catch up with everyone else. If they are given equality of result, they will not try to achieve it on their own.

The extraordinary striving of lower status groups formerly excluded from the mainstream of society can be very beneficial to society in general. Often, for example, it has been the extraordinary striving of outsiders, groups that were on the margins of society because of recent immigration, that has played a vital role in opening new sectors of the economy, innovating, and stimulating economic growth.

However, if the resentment of groups that have suffered past discrimination is so great that they would be unwilling to make extraordinary efforts, should they not be helped by society so that they can more easily move into the mainstream? Can this help be justified because it helps preserve social order, which is a necessary precondition for wealth-maximizing activity? Or does giving special assistance to particular groups actually decrease social order because of the resentment it causes among relatively more privileged portions of the population that have not received this special status and whose position in society now is in jeopardy?

Nozick maintains that one should be able to do what one wants so long as others are not harmed. People should be able to realize their potential without interference from others, so long as they do not harm anybody else. But women and members of minority groups are kept form realizing their full potential because of discrimination. Thus, people who discriminate should not be allowed to do so because they harm women and minorities. According to Nozick's standards, as is the case of all other ethical systems considered, discrimination clearly is wrong and bad. Preferential treatment, on the other hand, helps one group while doing harm to another. If it is foisted on people against their will, it violates the libertarian tenets for which Nozick stands.

As is the case of all ethical systems, antidiscrimination policies clearly are proper, but affirmative action policies are open to question. However, the fact that they are open to question does not mean that they are necessarily wrong or bad (see the special feature on p. 159, "Managerial Questions about Discrimination").

The Movement of Women and Minorities into the Workplace

The post–World War II movement of women and minorities into the workplace in the United States has been extraordinarily important. This movement will be examined, along with the public policies that have been created and the court cases that have been decided.

Women

An unprecedented number of women moved into the workplace after World War II (see Exhibit 7–1), and this phenomenon accelerated during the 1970s and 1980s. It affected relationships between people, work, family, marriages, and politics. After World War I, about 20 percent of the workforce in the United States was female, after World War II it was about 25 percent, and today it is over 45 percent. Over 40 percent of management positions are occupied by women, although a majority of

---

EXHIBIT 7–1   Women in the Workforce[4]

	1990	*1985*	*1980*
Percentage of workers who are women	45.4	44.4	42.4
Number of corporate CEOs	3	3	2
Percentage of corporate boards with women directors	56	45	36
Percentage of women-owned sole proprietorships	30.4	28.1	26.1
Percentage of self-employed women	35.9	33.3	30.0

women are at lower levels in the corporation. Only three CEOs of Fortune 500 companies are women. But more than a quarter of all M.B.A. students in the United States are women, and their participation in management will grow in the future.

The Harvard sociologist Orlando Patterson, commenting during the controversy over Judge Thomas's nomination to the Supreme Court, wrote that "we must face certain stark sociological realities: in our increasingly female, work-centered world, most of our relationships, including intimate ones, are initiated in the workplace; gender relations . . . are complex and invariably ambiguous."[5] Surveys suggest that 80 percent of the people in companies are aware of romantic affairs that have developed in the workplace, and 90 percent see the affairs as negative.[6] They cause gossip, create hostilities, and strain relationships. When couples are both high-level managers, there are special complications. The partners to the relationship may not be able to confront each other, or they may form powerful alliances against others. When the couples break up, it puts a strain on the entire organization.[7]

Sexual Harassment

Most men (66 percent) think sexual harassment at work is grossly exaggerated, but most women (32 percent) do not.[8] In a 1988 study of business school graduates, 46 percent of the men surveyed thought women would be flattered by behaviors that 95 percent of the women thought were unacceptable. A *Harvard Business Review* study found that 24 percent of women are annoyed at men who stare at them, while only 8 percent of the men consider it inappropriate.[9] A relatively high percentage of women, more than 20 percent in one survey, feel that they have been harassed (i.e., that unwanted advances have been made, where a refusal on the woman's part would have led to a loss of promotion, raise, or job). Many more women resent the subtle forms of harassment such as off-color jokes, unnecessary touching, and references to them as "sweetie" or "honey."

Unwanted propositions, lewd remarks, and even physical assault can become a problem in any office. A study found that 42 percent of women who worked for the federal government felt that they had been sexually harassed between 1985 and 1987.[10] Most of it was in the form of suggestive looks, touching, pressure for dates, and unwanted love letters.

Lower Pay for the Same Work

Women not only feel harassed by traditional male behaviors. They also receive less pay for similar work. Overall, they earn about 65 percent of what men earn (see Exhibit 7–2). A 1983 study by *Common Cause* reported that women did not equal men's average pay in any of the 259

Managerial Questions about Discrimination

Managers are responsible to shareholders, laws, and ethical standards. They should pay attention to economic considerations, consider legal obligations, and examine ethical issues. They might want to ask these questions about discrimination:

- Are discrimination and affirmative action simply legal and economic matters, or do they entail broader voluntary activities on the part of the corporation? What can the corporation do, for instance, to be a better place for women and minorities to work, and in so doing be a better place for everyone? Managers need to go beyond the way women and minorities are supposed to be treated by government decree and even by corporate personnel policies. They must overcome differences between official doctrines and informal attitudes and opinions. They must pay attention to how women and minorities are actually treated in their firms. Managers must grapple with both the official doctrines and the insidious biases, the quiet sexism and racism of which people are hardly aware.

- How should the corporation contribute to the public policy–making process? How should it respond to the process and influence it? The public policy issues with respect to discrimination and affirmative action are very contentious. The corporation has a very influential role to play. What should it do? For instance, affirmative action is not the only way to overcome past discrimination. A need exists in society to invest in education, to produce better elementary schools and more qualified and able people. A need exists to reex-

amine welfare and health policies, and to strengthen drug prevention. Can the corporation play a role in these areas?

- Many corporations have mission statements or credos like that of Johnson & Johnson (see Chapter 6). How should women and minorities be treated in the credo? Are women and minorities separate stakeholders like consumers, employees, communities, or should they be considered part of other groups? What does it take to become a corporate stakeholder and to be included in the corporate mission statement? And why would either women or minorities want to be included in the mission statement?

- What are the implications of women and minority issues for global competitiveness and for the vitality of American business in the international marketplace? The United States is a heterogeneous society with strict legal guidelines against discrimination, which is not true of all the nations with whom the United States competes. Other countries may have weaker laws, or their laws may be less well enforced. How can the United States harness its heterogeneity for the good of its people and its economy? Investment in people, as well as in opportunities to participate in the world economy, clearly are needed. Appreciation for other people and cultures can be a competitive strength if it is fostered. The link between U.S. citizens and their countries of national origins can give U.S. citizens an international orientation they might otherwise not have.

EXHIBIT 7–2   **Women's Median Weekly Earnings As a Percentage of Men's**

	1990	*1985*	*1983*
Engineers/architects/surveyors	89	79	82
Mathematical and computer sciences	79	80	75
Executives, administrative, managerial jobs	65	66	64

SOURCE: Adapted from "Women in the Workplace," *The Wall Street Journal,* October 18, 1991, p. B3.

---

different job categories that were examined.[11] The women were not promoted as rapidly, and fewer were found in top echelon positions in corporations.

Men tend to view these differences as the fault of the women.[12] They often claim that women are unwilling to relocate, unwilling to accept more responsibility, and may be doing only part-time work. But women see the differences as examples of discrimination based on stereotypes about their being too emotional, not tough enough, not aggressive, and lacking the ambition or career drive to succeed because of pregnancy, child rearing, and the fact that the women have to meet family needs.[13]

However stereotypes of women do not fit the reality. For instance, a survey of 1,460 managers by the American Management Association found that 60 percent of the women, as opposed to 37 percent of the men, consider their careers to be the primary source of satisfaction in their lives, and 50 percent of women, as opposed to 48 percent of the men were willing to move their families for the sake of a higher paying job.[14]

In some professions women have made great advances, while in others they remain underrepresented (see Exhibit 7–3). The women's numbers in managerial ranks rapidly moved upward from 32 percent of executive, administrative, and managerial jobs being held by women in 1983 to 40 percent in 1990. The number of self-employed women also went up to 36 percent of the total self-employed in 1990, and women in 1990 owned 30 percent of the sole proprietorships in the United States. Nineteen percent of the physicians and 21 percent of the lawyers found in the United States in 1990 were women. However, women were underrepresented in science and engineering. Although they were about 36 percent of the mathematical and computer scientists, they were only about 8 percent of the 2 million engineers in the United States, and only about 12 percent of the 225,000 physical scientists.

EXHIBIT 7–3   **Percentage of Professionals Who Are Women**

	1990	*1985*	*1983*
Executive, administrative, managerial jobs	40	36	32
Engineers	8	9	6
Mathematical and computer scientists	36	31	30
Physicians	19	17	16
Lawyers and judges	21	18	16

SOURCE: Adapted from "Women in the Workplace," *The Wall Street Journal*, October 18, 1991 p. B3.

Minorities

At least five minority groups traditionally have experienced discrimination in the United States: blacks, Hispanics, native Americans, Asians, and Jews. Only the former three groups have been seriously economically disadvantaged. Average black family income in the United States, for instance, is about half that of average white family income.[15] The gap has grown in recent years. Part of reason it is so large is the disproportionate number of young people in the black population and the fact that many blacks still live in the South where incomes are lower. Still, the personal wealth of blacks is only about 36 percent of that of whites. Blacks are 12 percent of households, but they own only about 4 percent of U.S. wealth. More than twice the number of blacks have been unemployed, compared to whites (see Exhibit 7–4), and the median income of black families is only about 60 percent of the median income of white families.

Educated blacks usually get off to a good start, but their careers often lag behind those of their white counterparts. Studies have shown that although black MBAs received higher starting salaries than white MBAs, they did not advance as quickly in the organization. The majority of black MBAs were still in entry level positions after 5 years, while the majority of white MBAs had advanced to middle management positions or better.[16]

Another problem blacks faced was more danger on the job. They had a 37 percent greater chance of occupational illness or injury and a 20 percent greater chance of dying from accidents.[17]

Even white managers have acknowledged that blacks face serious work-related obstacles. In one survey, 89 percent of the white managers admitted that blacks faced such obstacles; 54 percent believed that the blacks confronted explicit racism; and 60 percent of the white managers

EXHIBIT 7–4   Black and White Unemployment: Selected Years

| | Unemployment Rate | | |
Year	Black and Other Races	Whites	Unemployment Ratio: Black-White
1948	5.9	3.5	1.7
1960	10.2	4.9	2.1
1969	6.4	3.2	2.1
1975	13.8	7.8	1.8
1978	11.9	5.2	2.3
1984	14.4	6.5	2.2

SOURCE: W. J. Wilson, *The Truly Disadvantaged* (Chicago, University of Chicago Press, 1987), p. 101.

who responded to the survey were found to have some stereotyped views about blacks.[18]

The equal employment and affirmative action programs that exist have tended to help only the better educated, more upwardly mobile blacks. They have done little for the hard-core underclass of unskilled, unemployed blacks who have little working background or useful work experience and who are often unprepared to hold a job. Also, this group has been hurt the most by structural changes in the economy that have led to fewer unskilled manufacturing jobs. The riots in Los Angeles point to the giant challenge all of American society faces in rebuilding its core urban areas, providing training, and opening opportunities for meaningful work.

Public Policies and Court Cases

The public policies and court cases that deal with the problems of women and minorities are numerous. The following sections review the major civil rights legislation, affirmative action programs, and antidiscrimination court cases.

Equal Employment Opportunity

The 1964 Civil Rights Act was landmark legislation that forbid discrimination in employment based on race, color, religion, sex, or national origin: "It shall be an unlawful . . . practice for an employer . . . to discriminate against any individual . . . with respect to his compensation, terms, conditions, or privileges of employment because of such individual's race, color, sex, or national origin."[19]

As amended, it requires all companies with 15 or more employees to report each year the number of women and minorities on each step of the employment ladder in the company. It also contains a stipulation against preferential treatment:

> Nothing contained in this title shall be interpreted to require any employer . . . to grant preferential treatment to any individual or to any group because of the race, color, religion, sex, or national origin of such individual . . . or . . . on account of an imbalance which may exist with respect to the total number or percentage of persons of any race, color, religion, sex, or national origin employed.[20]

The Civil Rights Act also upholds an employer's right to "apply different . . . conditions . . . of employment pursuant to a bona fide seniority or merit system . . . provided that such differences are not the result of an intention to discriminate."[21]

EEOC and Sexual Harassment

The Equal Employment Opportunity Commission (EEOC), which administers the Civil Rights Act, can investigate, conciliate, and litigate charges of discrimination (see Exhibit 7–5). One of the most important things that the EEOC has done is to issue guidelines on sexual harassment. It has defined harassment as "unwelcome sexual advances,

---

EXHIBIT 7–5   The Equal Employment Opportunity Commission

Purpose:	To enforce 1964 Civil Rights Act (Title VII) provision regarding discrimination based on race, sex, color, religion, or national origin in hiring, promotion, firing, wages, testing, training, apprenticeship, and all other conditions of employment.
Activities:	1. Issues guidelines on employment discrimination. 2. Investigates charges of discrimination and makes public its decisions. 3. Litigates noncompliance cases.
Established:	1964.
Enabling legislation:	1964 Civil Rights Act. Equal Pay Act of 1963. Age Discrimination Act of 1967. Rehabilitation Act of 1973. Executive orders relating to equal employment.
Organization:	Five commissioners appointed by president with the advice and consent of the Senate.
Budget:	$175 million (approximately).
Staffing:	3200 employees (approximately).

SOURCE: Adapted from R. J. Penoyer, *Directory of Federal Regulatory Agencies,* 2nd ed. (St. Louis: Washington University Center for the Study of American Business, 1980), p. 28.

requests for sexual favors, and other verbal or physical conduct of sexual nature" that are a condition of employment or that create an intimidating, offensive, or hostile work environment.[22]

The two classes of harassment defined under this provision are supervisor requests for sexual favors for job benefits and a hostile work environment. The courts in the *Meritor Savings Bank* v. *Vinson* case in the mid-1980s accepted the principle that an atmosphere of sexual aggression, even without economic injury, constitutes harassment.

Affirmative Action

President Kennedy's 1961 Executive Order 10925 established a national commission on equal employment opportunity and it made the first official pronouncement about affirmative action. What it meant was that minority members had to be informed of job openings so that they had an equal chance to be hired.

In 1965, Lyndon Johnson issued Executive Order 11246. It required federal contractors to take affirmative action to ensure against job discrimination. The Labor Department, which administered the Executive Order, required in 1971 that federal contractors determine if they were utilizing minorities in the same proportion as they were found in the area labor force.[23] If not, the contractors would have to establish government-approved goals with respect to hiring, retention, and promotion, and they would have to set up timetables for achieving these goals.

The standard for minority employment used by the Labor Department is the proportion of minorities living in an area or in the Standard Metropolitan Statistical Area (SMSA) surrounding a business. If the area where a plant is located has 20 percent black workers or residents, the company is supposed to aim for a work force that is 20 percent black, at all levels and not just the lowest. A substantial discrepancy between the minority percentage in the population at large and the minority percentage in the company constitutes evidence of discrimination. If a company hires minorities at a rate of at least 80 percent of the rate at which it hires from the demographic group that provides most of its employees (usually white males), then it is likely that the federal government will not issue a complaint, but this is not assured. The concentration of minority employees at lower echelons in a company also can be evidence of discrimination.

The Reagan administration came out very strongly against affirmative action, maintaining that it believed in the concept but not in the "police approach" developed by Carter administration officials.[24] W. Bradford Smith, head of the Justice Department's Civil Rights Division under Reagan said that "racial and sexual preferences are at war with the American ideal of equal opportunity for each person to achieve whatever his or her industry and talents warrant."[25] Attorney General Edward Meese said, "The idea that you can use discrimination in the form of racially preferential quotas, goals, and set asides to remedy the lingering social effects of past discrimination [is] nothing short of a legal and constitutional tragedy."[26]

Other Laws against Discrimination

Laws were passed in 1967 against age discrimination (i.e., discrimination against people between the ages of 40 and 70); in 1973 providing for affirmative action in the hiring of the handicapped; in 1974 providing for affirmative action in the hiring of Vietnam veterans; and in 1978 against discrimination toward pregnant women. This legislation covered a large number of people. Approximately 40 million Americans were between the ages of 40 and 70, 40 million were women, 10 million were blacks, 6 million were Hispanics, 2.5 million were native Americans, 6 million were handicapped, and three quarters of a million were Vietnam vets.

Court Cases

Landmark court cases have affected the way antidiscrimination and affirmative action laws have been implemented. Companies first learned to take these laws seriously in 1971 when in the case of *EEOC* v. *AT&T*, AT&T was found guilty of discrimination and made a $45 million settlement to cover back wages. Also, 1971 was the year of *Griggs* v. *Duke Power*, in which the Supreme Court found that a high school education and the passing of tests not related to a job were not relevant employment characteristics.[27] "The Civil Rights Act," the Court said, "proscribes not only overt discrimination but also practices that are fair in form, but discriminatory in operation. The touchstone is business necessity. If an employment practice which excludes Negroes cannot be shown to be related to job performance, the practice is prohibited."[28]

In 1981, the Ninth Circuit Court of Appeals reaffirmed the basic thinking in *Griggs*. In *Fernandez* v. *Wynn Oil Co.* a woman did not get the job as director of international relations because the company believed that men in South America would not feel comfortable dealing with a woman in a position of responsibility. The court did not accept that there was any relationship between job performance and gender in this case.

Connecticut v. *Teal* decided by the Supreme Court in 1982 had a similar outcome. In this case, 23 percent of black employees had been promoted to be supervisors of a welfare department, while only 14 percent of white employees had been promoted. To be promoted, all employees had to take a test, which 46 percent of the blacks failed and only 20 percent of the whites failed. Supervisors then picked who was to be promoted on the basis of seniority, letters or recommendations, and past performance reviews. Winnie Teal failed the test, but claimed that it was not job-related. The Supreme Court supported her contention.

There have been four major affirmative action cases. Undoubtedly the most famous is the 1976 *Bakke* v. *University of California* decision.[29] A white male applicant to medical school at the University of California at Davis charged reverse discrimination against the university because it reserved 16 out of 100 places in its medical school class for minorities. Bakke claimed that he had superior qualifications to many of the minorities admitted, and the Supreme Court agreed that he had been a victim of reverse discrimination. It ordered Bakke admitted and prohibited quota admissions of minorities and separate evaluations of minorities without comparison to other applicants. However, in a very important qualification, it did allow race to be considered as a factor in admissions. The court said that a "properly devised admissions program" can involve "the competitive consideration of race and ethnic origins."[30]

A second important affirmative action case was decided in 1979 in *Weber* v. *Kaiser Aluminum*.[31] Brian Weber was a white male worker in a Kaiser Aluminum plant in Louisiana. Like Bakke, he charged the company with reverse discrimination. He said that he had applied for entrance into a training program sponsored by the company and the United Steel Workers that would have doubled his pay and given him a better job. The program called for selection of 50 percent blacks. At Kaiser prior to 1974 less than 2 percent craft workers were black even though blacks constituted 39 percent of the labor force in the area. Weber was not chosen despite the fact that he had more seniority than the blacks who had been selected. Even so, the Supreme Court decided against Weber, holding that Kaiser's affirmative action program was not court-ordered. It was voluntary and private and within the "spirit of the law." The program did not discharge any white workers and did not create a total obstacle to their promotion. The program was simply a temporary measure to eliminate a serious racial imbalance and therefore was acceptable.

A third important case was decided in 1983 in *Firefighters* v. *Stotts,* when the Supreme Court decided that 15 blacks hired by the Memphis Fire Department could be laid off during a budget crisis using a seniority rule that laid off the last hired first, even though this rule meant that disproportionately more blacks than whites would be laid off. After arguments were heard from attorneys appointed by the Reagan administration, the Court held that the Civil Rights Act did not require seniority systems to be changed to remedy past discrimination.

The final case, *Crosson* v. *Richmond,* was decided in 1989. The Richmond City Council, five of whose nine members were black, took actions that the Supreme Court ruled were unacceptable. Half of the city of Richmond is black, but less than 1 percent of the city's prime construction contracts had gone to black businesses. The city council set aside 30 percent of prime contracts to be subcontracted to minority businesses. Crosson Co., a white-owned mechanical plumbing and heating company, lost a bid to supply toilets to the city jail because it was unwilling to use a minority-owned subcontractor. It then challenged the city council's requirement, and the Supreme Court sustained the challenge. The Court accepted that the ordinance violated the white contractor's right to equal protection under the law. The court said that laws favoring blacks over whites had to be judged by the same constitutional test as laws favoring whites over blacks. Justice Sandra Day O'Connor wrote that racial discrimination even for "laudable purpose" is not "benign," and that "racial classifications" even with "assurances of good intention" are "suspect."[32]

Corporate Policies

With respect to hiring, companies should try to work within the following framework:[33]

1. Standards should not be lowered.
2. Unqualified people should not be hired.
3. However, standards used to evaluate people clearly should be job-related.
4. If a woman or minority person is better qualified, then clearly pick the woman or minority person; not doing so is an example of discrimination.
5. If a woman or minority person is equally qualified, and if the woman or minority person is underrepresented in comparison to the working population in the area, then again it is clear— pick the minority person; doing so is in the spirit of affirmative action requirements.
6. However, what if a woman or a minority person was clearly qualified, but a majority person was more qualified, then what should a company do? Are minimum-or-above standards of qualification sufficient when another candidate is more qualified. Under these circumstances, it is important for the company to consider:
    a. The degree to which the woman or minority person is underrepresented in the job in question.
    b. The extent of the gap in the qualifications level between the woman or minority person and the majority person.

c. The degree to which the woman or minority person could rapidly grow in the job to the point where that person would quickly catch up with and perhaps surpass the more qualified majority person.

d. The degree to which the company can devote the time, energy, and attention to the woman or minority person to assure that such rapid progress was possible.

e. The job's immediate importance for the safe and efficient operation of the business.

f. The side-benefits to the company from having a woman or minority person, in terms of employee understanding and acceptance of diversity, community relations, and/or fulfilling legal mandates and requirements without compromising product quality or integrity.

Sexual Harassment Policies

Judicial decisions in the 1980s made an employer financially responsible for harassment by its employees, unless the company had taken action to prevent the offenses and had responded vigorously when they occurred. Still, K. C. Wagner, a consultant to businesses on sexual harassment, stated that "it's the unique company that takes [sexual harassment] seriously enough to spend time to train their work force to let them know about the policy instead of just tacking it to the bulletin board."[34] Some companies, however, were doing more (see Exhibit 7–6).[35] General Motors had a one-day workshop that all supervisors had to attend. Du Pont had a four-hour workshop called "A Matter of Respect"; 65,000 workers have attended. Honeywell, Corning, and Du Pont have 24-hour hotlines. At Du Pont, workers who call the hotline do not have to identify themselves, confidentiality is assured, and calling does not mean bringing charges. Every complaint filed must receive an immediate response, if not from the employee's supervisor then from someone in the personnel office.

If an investigation is warranted, then there is the difficult problem of establishing the facts of the case. Since there are usually no witnesses or physical evidence and it is difficult to show that the advances were unwanted, fact finding is complicated. For example, it is important to know if the victim repeatedly told the accused person that he or she did not welcome the advances. In any case, resolution of these cases has to be quick. At Du Pont the policy is to resolve most cases in 3 to 20 days. When allegations prove to be true, the company either transfers or terminates the offender.

EXHIBIT 7–6   AT&T's Policy toward Sexual Harassment

AT&T's sexual harassment policy prohibits sexual harassment in the workplace, whether committed by supervisory or nonsupervisory personnel. Specifically, no supervisor shall threaten to insinuate, either explicitly or implicitly, that an employee's submission to or rejection of sexual advances will in any way influence any personnel decision regarding that employee's employment, wages, advancement, assigned duties, shifts, or any other condition of employment or career development.

Other sexually harassing conduct in the workplace that may create an offensive work environment, whether it be in the form of physical or verbal harassment, and regardless of whether committed by supervisory or nonsupervisory personnel, is also prohibited. This includes, but is not limited to, repeated offensive or unwelcome sexual flirtations, advances, propositions, continual or repeated verbal abuse of a sexual nature, graphic verbal commentaries about an individual's body, sexually degrading words being used to describe an individual, and the display in the workplace of sexually suggestive objects or pictures.

Sexual harassment in the workplace by any employee will result in disciplinary action up to and including dismissal and may lead to personal, legal, and financial liability.

Employees are encouraged to avail themselves of AT&T's internal equal opportunity complaint procedure if they are confronted with sexual harassment. Such internal complaints will be investigated promptly, and corrective action will be taken where allegations are verified. No employee will suffer retaliation or intimidation as a result of using the internal complaint procedure.

SOURCE: AT&T Policy Statement, 1992.

Summary and Conclusions

This chapter has defined discrimination as those conditions under which individuals are not free to compete based on their abilities. We have argued that discrimination is wrong because it hinders the occurrence of worthwhile economic transactions. We have distinguished between equal employment opportunity programs, which require that companies treat all people as individuals, and affirmative action programs, which require that companies treat people as members of groups. Equal employment opportunity and affirmative action have been discussed from the perspective of different ethical systems. We considered some of the important issues that arise with the rapid entry of women and minorities into the workplace, including office romance, sexual harassment, and pay differentials between men and women and between whites and blacks. We noted the major provisions of civil rights legislation and administrative orders that guide public policies, and we reviewed some of the major court cases in these areas. We provided some guidelines for corporate hiring policies and some examples of exemplary corporate sexual harassment programs.

Discussion Questions

1. Define discrimination. Why is it wrong?

2. Distinguish between equal opportunity and affirmative action. Why have both of these principles guided federal policies?

3. What is white backlash? Why has it come into existence?

4. Pick your favorite deontological and teleological standards. Discuss equal employment opportunity and affirmative action from the perspective of these standards.

5. How can managers eliminate subtle workplace biases? Is there anything they can do?

6. What should corporations do to affect public policies about women and minorities? You are the public affairs officer for a major corporation; write a memo.

7. How should women and minorities be treated in corporate mission statements?

8. What is your feeling about office romance? Are you for it or against it? Why?

9. Why do you think women receive lower pay for the same work? What should be done about it?

10. How large is the economic gap between black and white Americans? What responsibilities do corporations have to decrease this gap?

11. What does the 1964 Civil Rights Act say about preferential treatment?

12. Define sexual harassment.

13. What do you think about Reagan administration opposition to affirmative action? Was it justified?

14. What principles were established in the *Griggs, Bakke, Weber,* and *Richmond* cases? As a corporate personnel officer, what should you learn from them?

15. What kind of hiring policies should companies have with respect to women and minorities?

16. What kind of policies should they have with respect to sexual harassment?

Endnotes

1. In R. K. Fulwinder, *The Reverse Discrimination Controversy* (Totowa, N.J.: Rowman and Littlefield, 1980), p. 95, as cited by G. A. Steiner, and J. F. Steiner, *Business, Government, and Society*, 4th ed. (New York: Random House, 1985), p. 545.

2. P. Mason, *Race Relations* (London: Oxford University Press, 1970).

3. Steiner and Steiner, *Business, Government, and Society*, p. 540.

4. "Women in the Workplace," *The Wall Street Journal*, October 18, 1991, p. B3.

5. O. Patterson, "Race, Gender, and Liberal Fallacies," *The New York Times*, Op-Ed, Oct. 20, 1991, p. 15.

6. R. E. Quinn, "Coping with Cupid," *Administrative Sciences Quarterly*, March 1977.

7. E. Collins, "Managers and Lovers," *Harvard Business Review*, September–October 1983.

8. E. Collins and T. B. Blodgett, "Sexual Harassment . . . Some See It . . . Some Won't," *Harvard Business Review*, March–April 1981.

9. A. Deutschman, "Dealing with Sexual Harassment," *Fortune*, Nov. 4, 1991.

10. "Hands Off at the Office," *U.S. News & World Report*, August 1, 1988, p. 56.

11. "It Pays to Be a Man," *Common Cause*, March/April 1983.

12. B. Rosen, S. Rynes, and T. Mahoney, "Compensation, Jobs, and Gender," *Harvard Business Review*, July–August 1983.

13. J. Fernandez, *Racism and Sexism in Corporate Life* (Lexington, Mass.: Lexington Books, 1981).

14. W. Schmidt and B. Posner, *Managerial Values and Expectations* (New York: American Management Association, 1982).

15. T. Schellhardt, "Data on Average Wealth of Blacks Suggests Economic Gap with Whites Is Widening," *The Wall Street Journal*, June 20, 1983, p. 11.

16. D. Ford, "Blacks in Management," *UTD Advance*, March 1984, p. 3.

17. Steiner and Steiner, p. 533.

18. Fernandez, *Business, Government, and Society*, p. 65.

19. Committee on Labor and Public Welfare, U.S. Congress, Senate Subcommittee on Labor, *Compilation of Selected Labor Laws Pertaining to Labor Relations, Part III* (Washington, D.C.: U.S. Government Printing Office, 1974), p. 591.

20. Ibid., p. 610.

21. Ibid., p. 612.

22. 29 C.F.R. 1604. 11 (a) 1987.

23. U.S. Equal Employment Opportunity Commission, *Affirmative Action and Equal Employment: A Guidebook for Employers, Vol. 1* (Washington, D.C.: U.S. Government Printing Office, 1974).

24. "The New Bias on Hiring Rules," *Business Week*, May 25, 1981, p. 123.

25. L. Denniston, "Changes in Affirmative Action Policy," *Boston Globe*, January 5, 1982.

26. S. Taylor, "Breaking New Ground on Affirmative Action, *The New York Times,* May 21, 1986, p. A28.
27. *Griggs* v. *Duke Power,* 401 U.S. 424, 1971.
28. Ibid.
29. *Allan Bakke* v. *The Regents of the University of California,* 553, p.2d 1152, 1976.
30. Ibid.
31. *United Steelworkers of America* v. *Weber,* 99 S.Ct. 2721, 1979.
32. Cited in L. Greenhouse, "Court Bars a Plan Set up to Provide Jobs to Minorities," *The New York Times,* January 24, 1989, p. A1, 16, 19; also see E. A. Bronner, "Plan to Help Minority Firms Is Struck Down," *Boston Globe,* January 24, 1989, pp. 1, 7.
33. Steiner and Steiner, *Business, Government, and Society,* p. 546.
34. Quoted in S. Strom, "Harassment Rules Often Not Pushed," *The Wall Street Journal,* October 20, 1991, p. 1.
35. Deutschman, "Dealing with Sexual Harassment."

Case IIA
Recruiting Ethical
Employees
Shearson-Lehman and Dennis Levine[1]

Jane Martin sat down at her desk and opened the file of background materials her consulting firm's client, Shearson-Lehman, had provided. The personnel department of Shearson-Lehman had a problem. In the wake of the insider-trading scandal that had swept Wall Street beginning in 1986 with the arrest of former Shearson-Lehman employee Dennis Levine, the reputation of the financial services conglomerate, like the rest of the major investment banking houses, was suffering. This was a matter of concern because a reputation for integrity, trustworthiness, and confidentiality, which can inspire confidence in potential clients, was an essential asset for a bank.

Further, tradition was at stake. Bankers like to believe that theirs is a gentlemanly profession, a profession with an ethical code that demands honesty and strict observance of banking rules and regulations by those fortunate enough to find a place in the field. The widely publicized account of how a network of important figures in the financial community, including Levine, noted arbitrageur Ivan Boesky, investment banker Martin Siegel, financier Michael Milken, and others, had used highly confidential information about upcoming mergers and acquisitions to amass personal fortunes had shredded the reputation of the investment banking community as a whole.[2]

The question facing Shearson-Lehman was what, if anything, could or should be done to modify the company's recruitment process. Part of the problem, however, was that the ambition that had driven people like Levine to illegal acts in order to enrich themselves was also a part of the psychological makeup of the most successful employees. In order to prosper in the highly competitive mergers and acquisitions (M&A) field, a person had to be aggressive, driven, and ambitious enough to put in long hours and thrive under the mental pressure generated by billion-dollar deals, where clients might earn tens or hundreds of millions of dollars and the investment banks involved might earn millions in fees. Zeal and ambition were welcome commodities in a new employee, but the Levine episode seemed to demonstrate that an employee's ambition had to be tempered with a respect for the rules and with at least a minimum measure of honesty.

Shearson-Lehman was considering whether to require all prospective employees to take a pencil-and-paper honesty test.[3] A variety of such tests were available, but their use was controversial. Questions about an applicant's attitudes towards theft, for example, could be seen by some as an invasion of privacy and could be considered offensive by potential employees. The validity of the tests was also in question. Perhaps there were other, better methods for ensuring that only reasonably honest people were hired. Somehow the firm had to find a way to balance the need for aggressive, ambitious employees with the equally important need to maintain a good reputation.

The Rise and Fall of Dennis Levine

The history of the Levine episode is as follows.[4] At the time of his arrest in May 1986, Dennis Levine was well on his way to achieving his lifetime goal of wealth and power. At 33 he already was a managing director in the M&A department of Drexel Burnham Lambert, at that time the hottest investment banking house on the Street. His $1 million annual salary plus the $11.5 million in insider trading profits he had racked up had given him a solid start towards achieving his goal of *real* wealth, which he personally pegged at $100 million. In early 1986, it had seemed like everything was going his way. A year later, he was trading cigarettes for contraband plates of linguini with clam sauce behind bars at a federal prison camp.

Levine himself described the personality trait that got him in trouble as an inability to set limits.[5] Born to a solidly middle class family and raised in a working-class neighborhood in Queens, Levine was an unremarkable high school student academically, but had a knack for making people believe in him. He learned salesmanship by making cold calls for his father's home renovation business, but it wasn't until his junior year at City University of New York's Baruch College that he found a field that excited him enough to make him want to really apply himself: the high-stakes, get-rich-quick world of investment banking.

His idols were the dealmakers, the people who worked behind the scenes putting together mergers and acquisitions and who made millions in the process.[6] An investment banker could be making $500,000 a year or more before he was thirty, could drive Porsches and live at the best addresses in Manhattan, could dine every night at the most fashionable restaurants and ride to work in a limo. Levine was captivated by the promise of such a life-style and threw himself into the pursuit of a job in the field with a vengeance.

After taking an M.B.A. at Baruch in 1976, Levine hit the Street in his banker's pinstripes and began putting his charm to work. He came up empty-handed in his search for an entry-level position in the investment banking field. Having no useful social connections, no degrees from Ivy League schools, and coming from a solidly middle-class background, Levine had none of the necessary tickets for admission, not even a track record of success in the business that might persuade someone he was worth a try.

Levine took a position in the corporate counseling department of Citibank to gain the real-world experience that was the only shortcoming on his resume about which he could do anything. After a year of developing hedging strategies for clients with foreign currency exposures, Levine tested the investment banking waters again and moved another step closer to his goal when Smith Barney Harris Upham & Co. hired him in 1978. After spending a year working in corporate finance at the firm's branch in Paris, Levine was made an associate in the firm's M&A department on his return to New York in 1979.

It was at Smith Barney that Levine first began to regularly capitalize on the inside information he was privy to as a member of one of the investment banking teams that companies first approach when they consider an acquisition. In 1980, he flew to the Bahamas and opened a secret brokerage account in the name of "Mr. Diamond" with Bank Leu, a branch of a Swiss bank. Under cover of the Bahamian privacy laws, Levine felt sure that his clandestine trading activity would be undiscovered, and he began placing regular buy and sell orders for the stocks of companies that he learned were takeover targets.

By this time, Levine had already established a network of contacts with whom he traded information on upcoming mergers and acquisitions. He was particularly eager to develop relationships with the lawyers on the Street, since they, like the investment banks, were usually among the first parties approached by CEO's interested in a takeover attempt. These lawyers thus had two commodities prized by Levine: potential clients to be won for his employer, and information to be used for his personal profit.

It was partly to improve the quality of information available to him that Levine began looking for another position in 1981. Smith Barney wasn't really one of the major M&A firms on the Street, and besides, Levine had antagonized his superiors at Smith Barney, and it appeared doubtful he would ever be promoted to the partnership he coveted. He didn't have to search for greener pastures long: Lehman Brothers Kuhn Loeb, then the major M&A house and desperate for people with experience, snapped him up within a few weeks after he made his interest in moving known.

Levine began to cash in on his inside information in earnest while at Lehman Brothers. Between 1982 and 1984 he made 22 illegal trades, the most profitable of which involved a tender offer made by Lehman client American Stores for the Jewel Companies. After learning in early 1984 that American Stores intended to make an offer, Levine began buying Jewel stock through his Bank Leu account, gradually accumulating 75,000 shares at $49.45 apiece. When American Stores went public with a tender offer of $70 per share, Levine racked up $1,206,275 in profits. During his tenure at Lehman Brothers, he took in about $5 million through his illegal trades.

In early 1984, Shearson American Express bought Lehman Brothers. Within a year, Levine began to look for another job. Now that Lehman was no longer a privately held company, there were no partnerships to be had, and consequently no chance for Levine to share directly in the firm's profits. Moreover, Levine's aggressive style and lack of social credentials did not play well with some of the firm's top management. In February 1985, he was hired by Drexel Burnham Lambert, the acknowledged up-and-coming M&A business in town. The Drexel partners knew of Levine's reputation as someone who had reliable and profitable ties to Wall Street's information network, and they agreed to his terms of employment: $1 million a year to start and a position as managing director in the Drexel M&A department.

The Drexel culture suited Levine well. Drexel employees were expected to produce results, and how they managed to do so was not a matter of great interest. Levine continued to develop his network of contacts and bring in business for the firm.

May 1985 was an important month in Levine's life for two reasons. First, he scored his biggest insider profit, taking in $2.7 million on 150,000 shares of Nabisco Brands that he bought when he learned Nabisco and R. J. Reynolds were planning a merger. Second, the Securities and Exchange Commission (SEC) began a series of investigations that ultimately led to his downfall.

Although Levine denies that he was aware of the fact, the bank official that he dealt with at Bank Leu was making personal trades based on Levine's information, buying and selling the stocks in question when "Mr. Diamond" did. The Bank Leu official wasn't the only person "piggybacking" on Levine's trades. A Merrill Lynch broker in Caracas, Venezuela, through which Bank Leu executed many of Levine's trades, also picked up some money by taking advantage of the apparently faultless timing demonstrated by the Bahamian bank as it executed Levine's trades.

In May 1985, the SEC received an anonymous letter tipping them off to the Caracas broker's trading activities. The broker led the SEC to Bank Leu, and after 10 months of investigations and negotiations, Bank Leu was given special permission by the Bahamian government to violate its privacy laws and expose Levine. In return, Bank Leu was granted immunity from prosecution.

When the arresting officials showed up at Drexel to take Levine away, he left the building before they could take him into custody and drove around the city in his BMW, making calls to his family and attorney before finally turning himself in to the authorities.[7] Levine pleaded guilty to two counts of tax evasion, one count of securities fraud, and one count of perjury. To reduce his sentence, he agreed to expose his accomplices. In order to help trap Ivan Boesky, Levine made tape-recorded calls to the arbitrageur to get Boesky to implicate himself. It worked. Boesky in turn exposed others, including Michael Milken, who had single-handedly popularized the junk-bond-funded takeover.

Levine spent 15 months in the Lewisburg federal prison camp in Pennsylvania. After his release he began developing a business advising companies about raising money or executing deals. Levine has also lectured at several top business schools on the subject of ethics, and professes remorse for his trespasses: "I will regret my mistakes forever. . . . I've gained an abiding respect for the fairness of our system of justice: For the hard work and creativity I brought to my investment banking career, I was well rewarded. When I broke the law, I was punished. The system works."[8]

Drexel Burnham Lambert was itself made the subject of SEC investigations and eventually pleaded guilty to six felony counts related to securities fraud. The firm paid a record $650 million fine, and eventually filed for bankruptcy protection in February 1990.[9]

Honesty Tests: Are They Useful?

Pencil-and-paper honesty tests are designed primarily to help employers identify job applicants that may be a bad risk for theft of company property.[10] Employee theft costs business around $10 billion per year. At least 5,000 companies use honesty tests; dozens of different honesty tests are on the market. However, a number of question types are common to most honesty tests:

- Questions inquiring into the applicant's attitude towards theft and other illegal activity.
- Questions probing beliefs about the frequency and extent of theft in our society.
- Questions examining the applicant's punitive attitudes towards theft.

- Questions dealing with whether the applicant has considered theft, how easy they believe it would be to accomplish, and how likely they think it is that they would be caught.
- Questions that ask applicants to assess their own honesty.
- Questions that ask outright whether the applicant has engaged in employer theft previously.
- Questions designed to detect whether the applicant's answers are lies, which involves counting the number of socially desirable but implausible answers to questions like, "Have you ever told a lie?" (The socially desirable but implausible answer would be no.)

Studies of the validity of honesty tests have been inconclusive. Depending on the cutoff used by the firm, anywhere from 25 to 75 percent of applicants will fail an honesty test.[11]

Critics of the tests point out that there is no irrefutable link between a person's performance on a test and their actual behavior on the job. Still, experts in the field note that the tests incorporate psychologists' best strategies for assessing honesty, and contend that "while it is acknowledged that each of the validity strategies used to date has flaws, what stands out is the consistency of positive findings across tests and across validity strategies."[12]

These experts also note that not everyone agrees that the best way to curb employee theft is improved screening procedures. Some argue that the problem lies in the culture and norms of the organization and that the solution is to be found in developing a more positive and honest climate.

Minicases for Assessing Employee Suitability

An alternative to using honesty tests to screen new employees is to present them with minicases and to see how they will respond.[13] A recruiter then can assess an applicant's judgment to see if the person will fit into the highly competitive yet morally demanding securities industry. Here are some examples of the types of minicases that Shearson-Lehman could use:[14]

- You take a break from work and go to lunch with a friend. When you mention what you have been working on, you begin a discussion about the ethics of the financial services industry. Your friend cannot understand why insider trading is illegal. Even though a person trading on inside information is enjoying an advantage the rest of the investing public does not have, your friend reasons, no one is forced to sell them any shares. Whoever decides to sell the shares has done so freely and presumably has received about what they expected to get for them. Who is really hurt, your friend asks. How should you answer?
- You are a securities analyst, responsible for advising a pool of investors who put their trust in your advice. You get a call from an acquaintance who works for a company whose stock some of your clients hold. He tells you that the company has just filed a certain type of report, and tells you that "there's some information on page 76 you might be interested in." You know from experience that the type of report in question is very long and

filled with technical detail that few analysts bother to fully examine. If the information indicates that it would be prudent for your clients to sell their holdings in the company, should you act on the tip?

· Later that evening you are at a party, trying to relax and put the ethical questions of the day behind you. You begin a conversation with a reporter from a major financial publication, who tells you that he has written a story detailing the self-serving behavior of the top management of a company whose stock you've been recommending to clients. The reporter says he expects the story to be published within a week. This is the first you've heard of any alleged improper dealings by that management team, and you're not sure the allegations are true, but you do know the company's stock price is likely to be affected. By extension, so will your clients who own the stock. Would it be ethical to use this information? Are there circumstances where it clearly would or would not be ethical to use it?

· You are a vice president of a brokerage house that provides both investment banking services to corporate clients and brokerage services for retail customers. You learn that one of your corporate clients has suffered a large, unreported loss. Unfortunately, the client corporation is on your "recommended buy list" and your brokers have been advising your retail customers to purchase the stock. If you do nothing, the brokers will continue advising clients to buy stock in a company you know is in trouble. If you act to protect the retail customers, you may be using confidential information improperly. Are there any steps you could take to protect your retail customers that would not be unethical?

Shearson-Lehman's Statement

All new Lehman employees including Dennis Levine had been required to sign the following statement:[15]

Confidential Nature of Information
It is essential that all information concerning any business carried on in this office, whether security transactions or otherwise, should be kept completely confidential. The stock-in-trade of a banker is his integrity and his respect for the confidence that others place in him. There can be no excuse for failure to observe this fundamental principle.

Signing such a statement had not prevented Dennis Levine from trading confidential information with others in his network of contacts. It seems doubtful that requiring employees to sign such oaths was actually much of a deterrent to unethical or illegal activities.

Should Shearson Lehman adopt a form of honesty testing to weed out dishonest job applicants? How far did the company's responsibility in this respect extend? Were there other steps the company could take to ensure ethical behavior by its employees without stifling the ambition and initiative necessary in an effective investment banker? The company needed some recommendations.

The Other Major Players in the Insider-Trading Scandals

More than 60 insider-trading cases have been prosecuted since the mid-1980s, involving people linked to the financial services industry in a variety of ways, from investment bankers to lawyers to reporters. The stories of some of the most publicized cases are summarized below.

Martin Siegel.   Dennis Levine wasn't the only Drexel Burnham Lambert investment banker who had a history of illicit financial arrangements with Ivan Boesky.[16] Martin Siegel, co-head of Drexel's M&A department and an expert in defense-oriented takeover maneuvers, had taken a total of $575,000 in payments from Boesky in return for inside information on several deals Siegel worked on while employed by Kidder, Peabody & Co. in the mid-1980s. When Boesky began cooperating with SEC investigators in order to lighten his sentence, he turned in Siegel.

Siegel came from a modest background marked by financial problems. His father had filed for bankruptcy protection when Siegel was a young man, and the experience had made an impression on him. He was frugal and lived modestly for years after he began earning large salaries, saving most of his money. When he remarried in 1981 and soon afterwards had a child and built a new home, his personal expenditures began to outdistance his income. It was during that vulnerable period that he began trading information for payoffs from Boesky.

Terrified of being caught, Siegel insisted that Boesky pay him in cash. Boesky couriers would meet Siegel in a public place and hand over a suitcase full of greenbacks, which Siegel would use for household expenses and pocket money.

During 1983 and 1984, Siegel supplied Boesky information on upcoming M&A deals involving Diamond Shamrock and Natomas, Inc., Getty Oil and Texaco, and Carnation and Nestle, among others. Eventually, fearful that he would be caught, Siegel ceased giving Boesky leads, and after moving to Drexel in early 1986, Siegel gave up his illegal activities altogether.

His past caught up with him when Boesky turned him in. Siegel pleaded guilty to two felony counts and agreed to pay a $9 million fine. In addition, he was permanently barred from working in the securities industry.

Michael Milken.   The "Mozart of the money markets" was, like the musical genius, interested in his field from an early age.[17] Michael Milken was helping his accountant father prepare clients' tax returns at age 10. By the time he graduated from the Wharton business school, he had already begun developing expertise in the area of finance he almost single-handedly made a household word: junk bonds.

Milken was the founder and head of the High Yield and Convertible Securities Department at Drexel. He specialized in helping Drexel clients (both companies and corporate raiders like T. Boone Pickens) who were unable or unwilling to raise capital by borrowing from banks or insurance companies to do so via junk bonds. Milken and his subordinates would earn handsome fees by finding a pool of investors willing to buy the less-than-investment-grade debt issued by these companies.

Milken made himself a billionaire and Drexel one of the richest and most powerful investment firms on Wall Street, but along the way he engaged in several violations of the federal securities, tax, and mail fraud laws, among others. Working with Boesky, Milken arranged to have the Boesky organization buy stock that a Drexel client wanted to sell. By quietly selling the stock to Boesky, who subsequently sold it at a loss (made up by Drexel), the client was able to make more on the sale than it would have if the public had learned the sale was occurring. On other occasions Boesky asked Drexel to buy stock Boesky wanted to sell for the same purpose. A Drexel employee kept track of the profits and losses on these transactions, and if Drexel owed Boesky some money, Milken would engineer some bond trades that would benefit Boesky.

One of Milken's other violations involved defrauding the investors of the Finsbury Fund, an investment fund for foreign investors managed by a Drexel client. In order to reimburse Drexel for the commissions it paid its salesmen for selling the fund, Milken arranged with the client to overcharge Finsbury Fund shareholders on their transactions. In another violation, Milken engaged in securities transactions designed to allow the same client to generate short-term losses in order to reduce his personal income tax liability.

In April 1990, Milken pleaded guilty to six charges and agreed to pay a $200 million fine and $400 million in restitution to benefit defrauded investors and clients.[18] Under the terms of the agreement, he was permanently barred from the securities industry. He faced up to 28 years in prison on the charges. Even with the $600 million fine, Milken's personal fortune was still estimated at more than $1 billion.

Ivan Boesky.   Ivan Boesky made his living as an arbitrageur, a financier who steps in when deals are announced or rumored and buys the stock at a lower price than the raider has offered.[19] Stockholders who would rather not wait until the tender offer is actually made sell to the arbitrageur, who then racks up hefty profits if and when the deal actually goes through. Boesky commanded more than $3 billion in buying power and legitimately earned more than $100 million for himself this way.

For some reason, his legitimate earnings weren't enough. Boesky developed a network of contacts throughout the financial community, including Levine, Siegel, and Milken, with whom he traded inside information on upcoming deals. When Levine turned him in to the federal investigators, Boesky pleaded guilty to one count of conspiring to file false statements with the SEC and paid a $100 million fine. In December, 1987, he was sentenced to three years in prison.

Discussion Questions

1. What should Jane Martin recommend to Shearson Lehman?
2. How would you answer the dilemmas posed by the minicases?
3. Why did the financial scandals in which Dennis Levine and others were involved take place?

Endnotes

1. This case was prepared by Mark Jankus under the editorial guidance of Alfred Marcus.
2. L. P. Cohen, "Milken Pleads Guilty to Six Felony Counts and Issues an Apology," *The Wall Street Journal,* April 25, 1990, p. A1; L. P. Cohen, "How Michael Milken Was Forced to Accept the Prospect of Guilt," *The Wall Street Journal,* April 23, 1990, p. A1; G. Crovitz, "Milken's Tragedy: Oh How the Mighty Fall before RICO," *The Wall Street Journal,* May 2, 1990, p. A15; M. Milken, "Text of Michael Milken's Statement in Court," *The Wall Street Journal,* April 25, 1990, p. A12.
3. P. R. Sackett and M. M. Harris, "Honesty Testing for Personnel Selection: A Review and Critique," in *Personality Assessment in Organizations,* ed. H. J. Bernardin and D. A. Bownas (New York: Praeger Publishers, 1985), p. 236–76.
4. D. B. Levine, "The Inside Story of an Inside Trader," *Fortune,* May 21, 1990, pp. 80–89; M. Stevens, *The Insiders: The Truth Behind the Scandal Rocking Wall Street* (New York: G. P. Putnam's Sons, 1987).
5. M. Stevens, *The Insiders.*
6. Ibid.
7. Levine, "The Inside Story of an Inside Trader."
8. Ibid.
9. B. D. Fromson, "The Last Days of Drexel Burnham," *Fortune,* May 21, 1990, pp. 90–96; J. B. Stewart and D. Hertzberg, "SEC Accuses Drexel of a Sweeping Array of Securities Violations." *The Wall Street Journal,* September 8, 1988, p. A1.
10. Sackett and Harris, "Honesty testing for personnel selection."
11. Ibid.
12. Ibid.
13. J. L. Casey, *Ethics in the Financial Market Place* (N.Y.: Scudder, 1988).
14. Ibid.
15. Stevens, *The Insiders.*
16. Fromson, "The Last Days of Drexel Burnham"; Stewart and Hertzberg, "SEC Accuses Drexel of a Sweeping Array of Securities Violations."
17. Cohen, "Milken Pleads Guilty to Six Felony Counts and Issues an Apology"; Cohen, "How Michael Milken Was Forced to Accept the Prospect of Guilt."
18. Crovitz, "Milken's Tragedy: Oh How the Mighty Fall before RICO."
19. J. Fierman, "The Paranoid Life of Arbitragers," *Fortune,* November 9, 1987, pp. 97–109.

CASE IIB
FIFTEEN ETHICAL DILEMMAS

This case provides you with fifteen ethical dilemmas confronted in business situations.[1] Think about how you would respond to these dilemmas. What would you do, and why? Consider the ethical principles involved in the dilemmas. What conflicts between principles do the dilemmas illustrate? How would you resolve the conflicts? What reasons would you give for what you would do? How would you justify your actions?

1. After looking for a job for six months, a new college graduate finally has a chance to obtain the kind of work she has been seeking. It feels to her as if this is a once-in-a-lifetime opportunity. She can get in on the ground floor in a new and expanding business that promises all the challenges, excitement, and monetary remuneration she wants. Since the job pays extremely well for an entry position, she finally will be able to get an apartment for herself and live without the restrictions imposed by parents and roommates. The catch is that the job is in a very sensitive industry where standards of personal conduct have to be very high. The job demands a high degree of creativity but also a high degree of personal integrity. The company offering her the job recently was hurt by a scandal involving an irresponsible employee who took actions that embarrassed the company and hurt its image. Image is critical in the industry that the company is in. As a result of this experience, the company now requires that all new employees take a personality test, and it carefully scrutinizes the results. The new graduate admittedly is an eccentric, who has carefully cultivated an odd-ball life-style that makes her stand out from others. She is independent-minded and nonconformist and resents it when anyone tries to tell her how to behave. She knows that if she guesses at the average responses on the personality test so as to appear normal, she is less likely to be questioned by the company's psychologist and more likely to be hired immediately. She has nothing but contempt for the personality test and does not see how it would relate to her job performance, which she is certain would be beyond reproach. However, she can't take the pressure anymore of being out of work. What should she do?

2. Thefts are rampant in a particular area in your company. One of the five security guards with access to the area has a prison record. You make all the guards take a lie detector test, and the one with a prison record has some questionable answers. However, you know that studies show error rates of 40 to 50 percent with lie detector tests. What should you do?

3. Finally, you are in a position to promote the person you consider a star employee to the vice presidency of your company. However, the personnel manager does a routine background check and finds that the employee has not finished her M.B.A., as claimed on her resume. What should you do?

4. An inexperienced customer calls and asks for an item that is fairly specialized. The customer has no idea what the standard price is. Should you add a little extra to the standard price for this particular customer?

5. You work for a small but very prestigious and well-respected marketing research firm. An attorney from a firm that represents the cigarette manufacturer's association calls your boss and asks that he conduct a study of the academic literature on risk perception. This request is a bit odd, for it is not the kind of work your company usually does. Moreover, your boss is a bit reluctant about working for a firm that represents the cigarette manufacturers. So he tells the attorney to look elsewhere and gives him recommendations about who might be better suited to do this type of work. But the attorney persists and says that he wants your firm to do it. Your boss then demands a huge fee, expecting that the attorney will back off. Surprisingly, the attorney gives in to the boss's requests. Your firm certainly could use the business, because right now is a down cycle in the economy. In discussing the issue, your boss complains that "if his wife only

knew" that he was accepting this job, she would be extremely upset. Her father, to whom she was very close, smoked two packs a day and died at the age of 50 from lung cancer. However, your boss rationalizes that it is "only an academic survey" that he is agreeing to do and that he won't get further involved if asked to testify at a court trial. You know from your brother, an attorney, that the issue your firm has been asked to address is a hot topic in the courts and that your boss could easily get involved in a trial. The cigarette manufacturers have escaped paying damages to people who have contracted diseases from smoking because of the warning label on the package, which shifts the burden of proof to the smoker, who is assumed to know the risks and to have voluntarily assumed them. If ever an attorney for a smoker who has been harmed could show that the warning label was an inadequate way of communicating the risk, the cigarette manufacturers could face huge liabilities. You are asked to do the literature review, and your boss also suggests that you take the lead role in contacting the client. For you this may be a chance to develop some business on your own and to create an independent reputation. However, you realize that the evidence you provide the law firm could be very helpful to it. From your brother's cynicism about the legal process, you have little faith that what you write will be used in any other way but to further the interests of the cigarette manufacturers. You are uncertain about how you feel about all this: if someone wants to smoke and risk getting cancer, then it is their business. What should you do?

6. Your company has developed a device that reduces pollution by 70 percent but that costs $1,000 more per product. The average cost of the product already is $20,000 and the industry is extremely competitive. The Japanese and Korean manufacturers are driving down prices, which is not only affecting your company but also the national economy because of the negative effect on the balance of payments. Should you wait till Congress requires that you introduce the new pollution control device or should you introduce it on your own?

7. After a year long search for a job, you finally have employment in the industry you have been trying to enter. The industry has high status, is dynamic, and has super growth potential. Landing this job makes you the envy of the graduates in your M.B.A. program. However, you see that your company is using a recently banned chemical as a cleansing agent and that it is flushing it down the drain. When you ask why the company is acting in this fashion, you are told that it has a large amount of the chemical in storage and that it is only using the remaining amount. Management believes that to waste what is left would be silly. But to dispose of it safely is a bother, and the alternative compound the government is proposing the company use is very expensive. Moreover, you are told that company officials believe the government has been overly cautious in banning the chemical inasmuch as the company has had no reported health problems with it in the past. What should you do?

8. A young engineer has been offered a promotion to be the leader of a team developing a new recreational vehicle with a harsh ride and few amenities but that can travel at high speeds and take people on trips to places "where highways dare not go." The vehicle would be marketed to young people interested in thrills and adventure. The engineer knows that the product will have to sell for a low price and that there will be severe limits on the engineering costs and the costs for the materials and that perhaps there will be safety problems with the vehicle. However, the company has been having financial difficulties because of

foreign competition and it is betting that this product will be very profitable. Taking the promotion would put the engineer in the enviable position of being next in line for a top management spot. Should the engineer take the job?

9. The manager of an airport is receiving noise complaints from angry citizens. He could disclose to the press contingency plans about a possible airport expansion, knowing full well that the expansion plan is highly unlikely to be implemented. The only purpose would be to gain a bargaining chip with the citizens. He then would be able to guarantee them no airport expansion in exchange for an end to their protest. What should the manager do?

10. After having lunch with a customer, a salesperson alleges sexual harassment. She claims that the customer made unwanted and unwelcome offensive comments followed by physical contact to which she objected. She expects legal action to be taken by her company. If her company fails to protect her, she will sue. When confronted, the customer with whom she had lunch claims "boys will be boys," that what happened was "nothing more than a joke," an "innocent flirtation," and perhaps a "chance for a relationship." This customer constitutes one quarter of the company's business. The company discovers that in her previous employment the salesperson also complained of sexual harassment. What should the company do?

11. You are the research director for a pharmaceutical company. You believe that its claims for a product you participated in developing, though not actually false, are exaggerated and perhaps even could endanger the lives of the people it is supposed to help. You are also aware that the pharmaceutical company is no longer growing as rapidly as it once was, that it has had few major products reach the market in recent years, and, as an insider in the industry, that exaggerations of all kinds are typical. Moreover, it takes millions of dollars in income from successful products to recoup the losses from unsuccessful ones. Product development is a very expensive proposition and the misses outnumber the hits by a very wide margin. Only by making substantial profits from its few successful products can the company afford the research that is needed to keep your research team adequately funded; but that is not the only issue. Only by keeping the research team that you are leading adequately funded, do you believe your company can benefit society (you feel that your research team may be near a fundamental breakthrough in the fight against AIDs). What should you do?

12. You work together with three other brokers. The four of you are very tight. You have strong personal ties going back to college and childhood. You grew up with these people, knew their families, went to the same elementary schools, and to the same church. You have been working together with them for at least 15 years. Your families regularly visit each other and send gifts during the holidays and other important occasions. In a surprise to all of you, one of the brokers reveals that he has been successfully trading on tips he has been receiving from an unmentioned source. You know that this person has been having some personal financial difficulties, but that things seemed to be improving. Now you think you know why. This person then invites you and the other brokers you work with to join him in the trades based on the tips he has obtained. You too face financial challenges as your children come of college age and they apply to high-priced private schools. Your parents are aging and their financial situation is deteriorating. You have been quite concerned lately as you have had to dip into your savings merely to meet your monthly living expenses. One of

the brokers you work with eagerly accepts the offer to trade based on the tips, but the second says that doing so is probably against the law. She is quite agitated and goes on to say that it is not worth the risk of getting caught, that she is in no way interested in hurting her family or career, and that she is uncertain if she would participate in a cover-up if an investigation occurred. The broker who has been engaging in the trades then explains his scheme. It seems foolproof, but of doubtful legality. Nonetheless, the risks of getting caught appear minimal. What should you do?

13. You are the owner of a bank and your best employee is president of a local environmental group. Recently, the group has been conducting vigorous protests against a hazardous waste dump that is owned by a company that is a subsidiary of your most important client. You feel that the environmental group's campaign against your client has been grossly unfair. It has been a sensationalized campaign based on all kinds of blatant lies and distortions and not based on a true estimate of the risks involved in the situation. You are inclined to tell your employee that she is fired if she does not quit leading that environmental group in such an irresponsible direction. Last year you were embarrassed by the media when they barged into one of your banks to interview an employee who was heavily involved in the antiabortion campaign. At that time, you explicitly said to all employees that they had to keep their private causes to themselves and away from the workplace. What should you do?

14. You have just received your M.B.A. and are appointed to the post of statistician in a company that is having talks about a proposed merger with another firm. You are approached by the director of the company, who tries to enlist your support in "polishing the company's image" for the upcoming merger talks. What she asks for is "some terrific forecasts of industry growth and market share" to give her "some leverage" in the talks. You are not naive. You know that the figures that you choose to use as the basis for the forecasts and the approach and techniques you employ can influence the results. On the one hand, the data could be massaged to paint a fairly rosy picture of the company's future. On the other hand, they could be also analyzed to show pitfalls ahead and the prospects of rough going. Standards among statisticians vary. The rules for developing the numbers a person brings to the table in merger talks are pretty grey. You like the job, the people, the company, even the director. What should you do?

15. Five smokers and five nonsmokers work in the same office. The nonsmokers complain that they have a right to be protected from "sidestream" smoke. The smokers claim they have a right to smoke. What should the supervisor do?

Discussion Questions

Analyze the dilemmas in terms of the following considerations:
1. What principles are involved?
2. Who has a stake (what groups/and or individuals) in the outcome?
3. Whom are you as a manager serving?
4. Whom might you as a manager injure, and how badly?
5. What principles should you use in making a decision?

6. Are these principles clear?
   a. Could you describe them to the company's board of directors? to your family?
   b. Could you explain them in court?
   c. Could you explain them to the media?
   d. Could you explain them to your fellow workers?
7. Would the decision you make seem right a year from now?
8. Would it seem right 20 years from now?

Endnotes

1. J. R. Glenn, Jr., *Ethics in Decision Making* (New York: John Wiley & Sons, 1986); L. T. Hosmer, *The Ethics of Management* (Homewood, Ill.: Irwin, 1987); G. A. Stiener and J. F. Stiener, *Business, Government, and Society* (New York: Random House Business Division, 1988); J. L. Casey, *Ethics in the Financial Marketplace* (New York: Scudder, 1988).

CASE IIC
DAYTON-HUDSON
The Social Responsibility of a Takeover Target[1]

We are not in business to make maximum profit for our shareholders. We are in business . . . to serve society. Profit is our reward for doing it well. If business does not serve society, society will not long tolerate our profits or even our existence.

Kenneth Dayton, chairman, Dayton-Hudson Corporation, October 30, 1975.[2]

Dayton-Hudson (DH) had a history of social responsibility activism, but in June of 1987 its policies were challenged. While its net earnings per share were declining (from $2.89 in 1985 to $2.62 per share in 1986), its stock price was escalating on the basis of takeover rumors.[3] The company's history of social activism had to be reexamined in light of the takeover threat.

How should DH respond to the takeover attack? How should it balance its obligations to its shareholders with its commitments to its employees, customers, and the local community? In an era of corporate restructuring, did its policies of social responsibility continue to make sense?

DH's History

Originally a family-owned retailer established in Minneapolis in 1902, DH went public in 1967 and in 1969 merged with Hudson, a department store chain in Detroit. In 1987, it was the seventh largest retail company in the United States, earning $494.2 million before taxes in 1986 on revenues of $9.259 billion.[4]

Still headquartered in Minneapolis, the company consisted of four chains operating in 22 states. It had 37 department stores in the Midwest, but the largest chain was Target, a discount retailer. Target had 246 stores throughout the country. The only area where Target stores were not found was the East. Mervyns was the second largest chain, with 175 stores in the West, and Lechmere was the smallest with 17 stores in the East. Mervyns was mainly responsible for the 1986 drop in profitability.

DH's 1986 revenues and operating profits are presented below:[5]

	Revenues	*Operating Profit* *(in millions)*
Target	$4,354.9	$ 311.0
Mervyns	2,862.3	160.2
Lechmere	475.6	19.5
Dayton Hudson	1,566.3	165.8

Since 1983 DH had been under the leadership of Kenneth Macke.[6] Macke was 48 years old in 1987. He had spent his entire career with the company. He was credited with expanding Target from 49 stores in 9 states to more than 100 stores in 19 states and with turning the company around. Unlike members of the founding family, Macke was a very private person who did not like to give speeches and was not involved in politics or political appearances.

Social Responsibility at DH

The Dayton Foundation was set up by the Dayton Family in 1917 (in 1969 the name was changed to the Dayton-Hudson Foundation) to promote "the welfare of mankind everywhere in the world."[7] In 1976, when the family still reportedly owned about 40 percent of the common stock, Kenneth Dayton commented: "Our current practices grew out of a private sense of social obligation that my grandfather had when he started this company. He was a very charitable man who made substantial contributions to the community." Bruce Dayton, another member of the founding family, said: "Business can take the initiative in addressing the priority needs of our society."[8]

Like other companies, DH's stated goal was growth and return on equity: "to grow and earn at a rate commensurate with the best in the industry."[9] However, it also had a policy of using 5 percent of its federal taxable income "to improve the quality of life" in the communities in which the corporation and its operating companies are located.[10]

Conservative shareholders mocked such practices. Evelyn Davis, a dissident shareholder, maintained that the higher profits belonged to shareholders who had the right to use them for whatever they wanted.[11]

In 1973, DH was virtually the only American company giving five percent. It took a leadership role in encouraging other Twin Cities companies to set up such programs. In 1976, the Chamber of Commerce formally set up a "Five Percent Club" for Twin City firms.

DH's contribution policies were somewhat different from other companies' in that they emphasized social action and the arts, not health, welfare, and education (see the appendix to this case, which provides further details on DH's community involvement expenditures).[12] The formula for computing and allocating funds to institutions was quite complicated. Some of the funds were given by operating companies directly to their local communities.

In 1986, the $20,781,500 DH gave was broken down as follows:[13]

Dayton Hudson Community Giving in 1986	
State	*Amount*
Minnesota	$ 9,023,500
California	3,442,800
Texas	1,502,600
Michigan	1,401,700
Colorado	554,400
Indiana	378,400
Arizona	355,600
Iowa	298,700
Wisconsin	220,700
Massachusetts	196,100
Other States	3,407,000
Total	$ 20,781,500

In 1974, when profits fell and the company's stock reached an all time low, the contribution program was reviewed, but the company decided to maintain its "unique leadership posture." (see Table 1 at end of case).[14]

DH also had formal programs in equal employment and advancement, consumerism, energy conservation, environmental impact, and community development.[15] In 1973, the board of directors of the corporation added a Committee on Social Responsibility, designed to focus the attention of all operating units on corporate citizenship. It monitored the progress of the corporation in the areas of charitable contributions, consumerism, affirmative action, environmental protection, and community development. Each year, the heads of the operating companies had to report on their social responsibility programs, and about 5 percent of their incentive compensation was based on it.

DH's department stores were known for offering quality goods. Its discount stores were known for offering low-price goods that were equal, if not superior, to the goods offered by its competitors. Its reputation for service was superb, having been built on a willingness to allow returns of merchandise for virtually any reason. In 1984, it won the prestigious University of California School of Business Administration award for being "the best managed company in America." Cited for "unusual dynamism . . . entrepreneurial zeal . . . and . . . uncompromising ethical standards," it was committed to excellence in all areas.[16]

DH employed more than 34,000 people in its Minnesota stores. Nearly two thirds of its Minnesota employees were part-time workers and DH had been criticized for lobbying against minimum wage legislation. DH also had been heavily criticized for closing the Hudson Store in downtown Detroit. Around 1,000 jobs were lost, and Detroit Mayor Coleman Young said, "I don't think Hudson's demonstrated any sense of responsibility or citizenship after growing in this city and off this city for almost 100 years."[17]

The Takeover

Rumors of the takeover began on June 10, 1987, when DH was the second most actively traded stock on Wall Street. The DeBartolo Corporation, an Ohio based shopping center developer, was supposed to be involved, as was the Revlon Group, the Limited Group, and the Dart Group. By July 1, 1987, DH stock was up 22 percent and more than 39 percent of its shares had been traded. On June 23, the value of the stock escalated by nearly $1 billion for a few hours on false rumors that a $6.8 billion cash tender offer was being made by a wealthy Ohio family.[18]

The board of the company already had attempted to protect the company from unfriendly takeovers.[19] It had approved a requirement for a super-majority vote in the case of an uninvited tender offer, given the company the right to issue large amounts of new stock to buyers that would side with current management, established rules that all shareholders had to receive the same prices in a tender offer, and offered golden parachutes worth more than $12 million to its top 14 employees.

DH's management gradually became aware that the Dart Group was behind the takeover activity.[20] Owned by Herbert Haft and his son Robert, the Dart Group Incorporated (DGI) was the major participant in buying DH stock. The elder Haft had started with one drug store in Washington, D.C., which he built into a chain of discount stores. His son, Robert, a Harvard M.B.A., had been responsible for building the 445 Crown Book discount store chain. In 1984, DGI sold its drug stores, bought an auto parts business (Trak Auto), and began buying stock in larger companies, threatening entrenched management, and obtaining "greenmail" payments for backing off.

To remove DGI from the scene, the boards of threatened companies authorized buy-back plans of stock held by DGI at higher prices than what was offered to other shareholders. In 1986, the Hafts made $97 million in this manner after buying stock in Safeway. They also made substantial amounts by raids on Beatrice, Jack Eckerd Corporation, May Department Stores, and Supermarkets General.

Unlike other "greenmailers," the Hafts generally bought into businesses in which they had experience (i.e., in retailing, especially discount retailing), and they claimed that they actually wanted to run these companies. Their claim was that they could run them well and in shareholders' interests if only given a chance.

The Haft management style was to cut expenses, eliminate waste, and distribute the profits to the rightful owners, the shareholders, who were short-changed in companies run to please managers. The Hafts were called "the most feared family in retailing." Kenneth Macke and the Board of DH had to decide what to do. (see Table 2 at end of case).[21]

Appendix: Details on Dayton-Hudson's Community Involvement Expenditures

These details on DH's community involvement expenditures come from the 1986 Community Involvement Annual Report:

We concentrate our community involvement on programs that offer the potential for achieving results and demonstrating leadership.

We do 80 percent of our giving in two focus areas where we believe we can have significant impact: Social Action and Arts. The other 20 percent of our giving responds to social community needs and opportunities.

Social Action: 40 percent of community giving funds are contributed to programs and projects that result in (*a*) the economic and social progress of individuals, and/or (*b*) the development of community and neighborhood strategies that respond effectively to critical community social and economic concerns.

Arts: another 40 percent of community giving funds are contributed to programs and projects that result in (*a*) artistic excellence and stronger artistic leadership in communities, and/or (*b*) increased access to, and use of, the arts as a means of community expression.

Miscellaneous: 20 percent of community giving funds are contributed to programs and projects outside Social Action and the Arts that result in (*a*) our responsiveness to special community needs and opportunities, and/or (*b*) innovative partnerships with other community leaders.

1986	
Social action giving	$8,279,436
Arts giving	$8,754,319
Miscellaneous giving	$3,747,783
Total giving:	$20,781,538

Discussion Questions

1. How appropriate is it for a company to give charity? How much should it give? To whom should it give this money? For what purpose?
2. Assess Dayton-Hudson's corporate giving.
3. To what extent is Dayton-Hudson a socially responsible company?
4. What should Kenneth Macke and Dayton-Hudson do to respond to the takeover attempt by the Haft family? What considerations should govern the decision it makes?

Endnotes

1. This case was prepared by A. A. Marcus and is partially based on information contained in *Dayton-Hudson Corporation,* case of the Harvard Business School, 9–377–079, 1976; and J. W. Ellwood, *Who Will Get Custody of Santabear?* case from the Amos Tuck School of Business Administration, Dartmouth, College, 1988.
2. *Dayton-Hudson Corporation.*
3. Ellwood, *Who Will Get Custody of Santabear?*
4. *Dayton-Hudson Corporation.*
5. Ellwood, *Who Will Get Custody of Santabear?*
6. Ibid.
7. *Dayton-Hudson Corporation.*
8. Ibid.
9. Ibid.
10. Ibid.

TABLE 1 Some Examples of Dayton-Hudson Grants
from the 1986 Community Involvement Annual Report

Social Action

Organization	Program	Grant Awarded
American Indian Opportunity Industrialization Center	General support for employment training program	$15,000
American Variety Theatre Company	General support for youth development program	10,000
	Van purchase	7,500
Anishinabe Council of Job Developers	General support for job development and placement	15,000
Association for the Advancement of Hmong Women	Improved capacity to aid refugees in becoming self-reliant	8,000
Bridge for Runaway Youth	General support for family crises program	8,250
Catholic Charities	Employment program for hard-to-employ people	20,000
	One-time grants for North Side Child Development Center	12,500
Cedar Riverside Project Area Committee	General support for community planning process	10,000
Center for Community Action	General support for youth employment program	9,000
Central Neighborhood Improvement Association	Completion and implementation of youth plan in Minneapolis	6,500
Centre for Asians and Pacific Islanders	Employment assistance for Asian refugees	10,000
Centro Cultural Chicano	General support for employment and advocacy program	13,000
Centro Legal Inc.	General support for immigration, family, and other legal assistance cases	10,000

Arts

Actors Theatre of St. Paul	Capital renovation	$70,000
	General support for 1987 season	30,000
Artspace Projects Inc.	Feasibility and planning study of shared media arts facility	25,000
	General support for special development projects	25,000
At the Foot of the Mountain	Management consultant	19,000
	General support for 1987 season of multiracial women's theater	13,000
Brass Tacks Theatre	Three-year program to employ national directors	11,000
	General support for 1987 season of new plays	7,500
Children's Theatre Company and School	General support for 1987 season	49,200
	General support for 1986 season	38,400
	Executive director search	5,000
College of St. Catherine	1987 O'Shaughnessy Dance Series	5,000
COMPAS	Screenwriters-in-the-Schools Program with JV Films	25,000
Creation Production Company	Production of *Propaganda* at the Southern Theatre	5,000
The Cricket Theatre	General support for 1986 season	10,000
	Artistic director search	2,500

Miscellaneous

American Public Radio	Start-up administrative costs	$25,000
Central Community Housing Trust	General support for preservation and replacement of low-income housing	500
Charities Review Council of Minnesota	General support for information services on Minnesota charities	1,000
Chicanos Latinos Unidos En Services	Spanish speaking seniors program	15,000
Citizens League of Minneapolis	General support for 1986 membership	20,000
Commission on the Economic Status of women	Reprint "A Woman's Place" resource guide	5,000
Community Administrative Services	General support for management assistance program	10,000
Community-Based Industries	Market development project	13,000
Decade of Light	Tenth anniversary of Minnesota program for victims of sexual assault	6,000

TABLE 2 Dayton-Hudson's Financial Statement, 1973–1986

(millions of dollars, except per-share data)	1986	1985	1984(a)	1983	1982	1981	1980	1979	1978(a)	1977	197
Revenues:	$9,259.1	8,255.3	7,519.2	6,518.2	5,286.4	4,623.6	3,777.9	3,174.9	2,787.5	2,356.7	2,01
Cost of retail sales, buying and occupancy	$6,705.2	5,908.3	5,392.1	4,642.5	3,721.7	3,278.3	2,678.7	2,218.1	1,943.7	1,643.8	1,41
Selling, publicity and administrative	$1,538.1	1,365.9	1,234.4	1,080.5	901.8	826.9	690.1	590.4	508.5	417.9	35
Depreciation	$ 182.7	158.2	144.9	123.1	99.4	85.1	62.4	46.8	37.5	34.1	2
Interest expense, net	$ 117.5	99.8	97.7	86.1	64.9	47.1	13.6	5.4	14.2	15.1	1
Earnings from continuing operations before income taxes and extraordinary charge:	$ 494.2	517.8	453.5	415.9	358.1	261.2	230.0	223.0	18.37	173.7	14
Income taxes	$ 239.2	237.3	207.9	189.1	165.6	116.2	103.1	106.8	95.1	88.8	7
Net earnings:											
Continuing	$ 255.0	180.5	245.6	226.8	192.5	145.0	126.9	116.2	88.6	84.9	6
Discontinued (b)	$ 87.3(c)	3.1	13.7	18.7	14.2	28.4	19.8	75.9	176.3	13.0	
Extraordinary charge	$ (32.3)	—	—	—	—	—	—	—	—	—	—
Consolidated	$ 310.0	283.6	259.3	245.5	206.7	173.4	146.7	192.1	264.9	97.9	7
Per common share:											
Net earnings:											
Continuing	$ 2.62	2.89	2.54	2.35	2.00	1.51	1.33	1.23	.93	.91	
Discontinued (b)	$ .90(c)	.03	.14	.19	.15	.30	.21	.80	1.87	.13	
Extraordinary Charge	$ (.33)	—	—	—	—	—	—	—	—	—	
Consolidated	$ 3.19	2.92	2.68	2.54	2.15	1.81	1.54	2.03	2.80	1.04	
Cash dividend declared	$ .86	.785	.695	.625	.575	.525	.475	.425	.375	.325	
Shareholders' investment	$ 22.38	20.04	17.90	15.91	13.98	12.41	11.14	10.09	8.50	6.10	5
Return on beginning equity (shareholders' investment):											
Continuing	13.1%	16.2	15.9	16.8	16.1	13.6	13.2	14.4	15.3	17.0	1
Consolidated	15.9%	16.3	16.8	18.2	17.3	16.3	15.2	23.8	45.7	19.6	1
Capital Expenditures	$ 940.9	403.0	336.1	320.7	268.2	238.1	247.2	201.8	147.9	100.4	7
Consolidated year-end financial position:											
Working capital	$1,192.8	1,130.2	972.8	868.6	718.3	508.9	381.3	438.8	427.6	309.4	2
Property and equipment, net	$2,402.3	1,655.7	1,418.6	1,306.8	1,139.0	978.1	826.7	596.3	451.0	363.6	3
Property under capital leases, net	$ 114.9	114.7	114.7	115.8	97.9	93.9	100.4	67.2	70.9	57.0	5
Total assets	$5,282.0	4,417.5	3,799.9	3,594.9	2,985.3	2,555.2	2,155.2	1,793.2	1,637.5	1,411.4	1,2
Long-term capital lease obligations	$ 131.6	128.1	125.2	123.9	102.4	96.3	103.3	73.0	76.8	62.0	5
Long-term debt	$1,244.9	794.5	625.4	626.8	529.3	331.8	213.8	117.6	94.3	116.8	1
Shareholders' investment	$2,179.5	1,947.4	1,736.5	1,540.2	1,348.8	1,192.7	1,066.4	962.6	808.4	579.8	4
Average common shares outstanding (millions)	97.3	97.1	96.9	96.6	96.2	95.8	95.2	94.8	94.4	94.0	9

The financial comparisons should be read in conjunction with the financial statements.

Per-share amounts and shares outstanding reflect two-for-one common stock splits effective July 1983 and November 1981.

(a) Consisted of 53 weeks.

(b) Discontinued operations include discontinued real estate through 1981 and B. Dalton Bookseller for all years.

(c) Includes the gain on sale of B. Dalton Bookseller.

192

Business Segment Comparisons (millions of dollars)	1986	1985	1984*	1983	1982
Revenues:					
Target	$4,354.9	$3,931.5	$3,550.1	$3,118.4	$2,412.4
Mervyn's	2,862.3	2,527.0	2,141.1	1,688.9	1,335.8
Department stores	1,566.3	1,447.9	1,547.8	1,483.9	1,350.2
Lechmere	475.6	348.9	280.2	227.0	188.0
Total	$9,259.1	$8,255.3	$7,519.2	$6,518.2	$5,286.4
Operating profit:					
Target	$ 311.0	$ 277.8	$ 235.6	$ 176.8	$ 150.1
Mervyn's	160.2	245.0	223.3	184.5	152.3
Department stores	165.8	12.18	106.7	155.7	114.4
Lechmere	19.5	19.8	20.2	18.8	12.0
Total	656.5	664.4	585.8	535.8	428.8
Interest expense, net:	117.5	99.8	97.7	86.1	64.9
Corporate and other	54.2	57.2	47.4	40.2	10.2
Corporate and interest expense absorbed by discontinued operations	(9.4)	(10.4)	(12.8)	(6.4)	(4.4)
Earnings from continuing operations before income taxes and extraordinary charge	$ 494.2	$ 517.8	$ 453.5	$ 415.9	$ 358.1
Operating profit as a percent of revenues:					
Target	7.1%	7.1%	6.6%	5.7%	6.2%
Mervyn's	5.6	9.7	10.4	10.9	11.4
Department stores	10.6	8.4	6.9	10.5	8.5
Lechmere	4.1	5.7	7.2	8.3	6.4
Assets:					
Target	$2,178.6	$1,518.8	$1,374.9	$1,257.8	$1,056.2
Mervyn's	1,817.4	1,614.5	1,328.9	1,064.2	821.3
Department stores	738.6	737.9	727.2	863.3	819.5
Lechmere	317.5	209.9	151.0	105.4	89.2
Discontinued operations	—	221.4	204.0	185.7	152.6
Corporate and other	229.9	115.0	13.9	118.5	46.5
Total	$5,282.0	$4,417.5	$3,799.9	$3,594.9	$2,985.3
Depreciation:					
Target	$ 76.3	$ 70.0	$ 65.7	$ 56.4	$ 42.1
Mervyn's	67.5	54.5	42.7	30.0	23.6
Department stores	28.0	27.3	31.9	33.0	31.2
Lechmere	7.8	4.5	3.1	2.0	1.8
Corporate and other	3.1	1.9	1.5	1.7	.7
	182.7	158.2	144.9	123.1	99.4
Less: Depreciation on capital	8.1	8.0	8.1	7.7	7.9
Total	$ 174.6	$ 150.2	$ 136.8	$ 115.4	$ 91.5
Capital expenditures:					
Target	$ 598.0	$ 138.3	$ 109.8	$ 143.4	$ 137.5
Mervyn's	243.5	176.6	165.4	138.3	95.7
Department stores	30.5	36.8	33.5	26.5	27.8
Lechmere	48.6	42.1	24.5	5.7	2.9
Corporate and other	20.3	9.2	2.9	6.8	4.3
	940.9	403.0	336.1	320.7	268.2
Less: Expenditures on capital leases	9.1	7.9	10.5	25.6	11.9
Total	$ 931.8	$ 395.1	$ 325.8	$ 295.1	$ 256.3

*consisted of 53 weeks.
Department stores include Diamond's and John A. Brown through September 29, 1984.

11. Ibid.
12. *Annual Report, 1986* (Minneapolis: Dayton-Hudson Corporation, 1986); *Community Involvement Report, 1989* (Minneapolis: Dayton-Hudson Corporation, 1989); *Dayton-Hudson Corporation Grants List, 1989* (Minneapolis: Dayton-Hudson Corporation, 1989).
13. *Annual Report, 1986; Community Involvement Report, 1989; Dayton-Hudson Corporation Grants List, 1989.*
14. *Dayton-Hudson Corporation.*
15. Ibid.
16. Ellwood, *Who Will Get Custody of Santabear?*
17. Ibid.
18. Ibid.
19. Ibid.
20. J. B. Mathews, K. E. Goodpaster, and L. Nash, *Policies and Persons: A Casebook in Business Ethics* (New York: McGraw Hill, 1991).
21. T. Fiedler, "Dayton-Hudson's Pyrrhic Victory," *Corporate Report Minnesota*, September 1987, pp. 59–64.

CASE IID
SOCIAL RESPONSIBILITY AND MANAGERIAL SUCCESSION AT CONTROL DATA CORPORATION[1]

One of the great delusions of our time is that government alone is primarily responsible for meeting the major needs of society. Unfortunately, that has proven to be neither achievable nor realistic because our society has been going downhill. . . . Deterioration in our society will continue unless and until substantial corporate resources are invested to help meet major needs as profit-making opportunities in cooperation with government and other sectors.
William Norris, founder, Control Data Corporation, 1986.[2]

There is no measurement of earnestness per share or trying per share or good intentions per share. Only earnings per share count.
Larry Perlman, president, Control Data Corporation, 1987.[3]

In late 1987, Larry Perlman was named as the new president and chief operating officer of Control Data Corporation (CDC). He had to make some decisions about its social responsibility policies. CDC was a company in deep financial and business trouble. It was losing large amounts of money and yet had to cope with the visionary ideas of its founder and dominant figure, William Norris.

Control Data Corporation's History

CDC was started in July 1957 when William Norris and 11 other engineers defected from Univac (Sperry-Rand Corp.).[4] The company initially was capitalized at $600,000, and by 1986 had grown to a size of $2.6 billion in assets and $3.3 billion in sales, making it one of the major players in the computer business. CDC was recognized as a BUNCH member (Burroughs, Univac, NCR, CDC, Honeywell) chasing industry leader IBM.

The primary business of CDC was computing hardware, peripheral equipment, and computer services. CDC's initial expertise evolved around developing computing power for the scientific, engineering, aerospace, and defense markets. It pioneered a program in which it built the world's first supercomputer under the guidance of Seymour Cray, but Cray later left CDC and started his own company.

Industry pressures forced CDC to diversify from hardware to computer services in the early 1960s.[5] CDC's first diversification moves were to enter markets for general peripheral products (for the original-equipment manufacturer market) and data services. The peripheral products division grew rapidly, fueled by the growth of minicomputers and to some extent microcomputers in the 1960s and 1970s. By 1982, peripherals were a billion-dollar business, and with nearly half of the disk drive market, CDC dominated the peripherals industry.[6]

CDC used its mainframe capabilities to establish time-sharing and data processing services. Engineering and professional services also became important revenue sources for CDC. In addition, CDC provided support services for these programs. Perhaps CDC's most ambitious endeavor in the nonhardware area was the development of the PLATO system. PLATO utilized minicomputers to run software for training and educational programs for businesses and government agencies, as well as primary and secondary school students. By late 1987, the company's investment in PLATO was nearing $1 billion, yet the operation had never covered its costs.[7]

Commercial Credit Corporation (CCC) was a large independent financing company that CDC purchased in 1968 to provide leasing arrangements for purchasers of large mainframe systems. While providing the needed cash infusion and leasing services that CDC required in the late 1960s and early 1970s, CCC was never successfully assimilated into CDC's businesses. In 1986, a significant portion of CCC was sold and in 1987 the company's final 18.3 percent stake in CCC was given up.[8]

The year leading up to these sales was not a happy one for CDC. In 1985, CDC posted a record loss of $567.5 million on sales that had been lower than 1984. Its problems developed against the backdrop of a general slump in the computer industry, but were exacerbated by its poor performance within the industry.[9]

The peripheral products group, once CDC's "cash cow," was hit hard by competition from Japan and lower margins per unit.[10] Gross margins on sales and rentals of computer equipment dropped 12 percent from the year before. Lenders refused to advance more money, and the company had to sell some assets to raise money.

Declining product quality was another contributor to CDC's troubles.[11] The company did not spend enough money to stay on the leading edge of computer

[handwritten margin notes: "Didn't manbare need there was not a demand for it" and "They didn't do any market research for it... PLATO was there a need"]

technology. CDC also did not anticipate the proliferation of personal computers, which was detrimental to its computer service businesses. Demand for mainframes was flat, and the development of a new supercomputer by a subsidiary, ETA Systems, drained the company's resources.[12]

Despite these difficulties, many critics focused on the controversial views of its founder William Norris. They criticized his autocratic management style, citing it as a contributing factor in CDC's downturn. He was said to "manage by intuition," refusing to allow market research on the need for PLATO before it began operations.[13] His comment about why he did not allow marketing research before launching PLATO was that it would just "uncover all the problems" and "we'd never go into it."[14]

Business Week said that CDC had to dispose of some assets and that William Norris was one of them.[15] In the early days, decisions had been made at the lowest possible level. These decisions were supported by upper management, which created an entrepreneurial environment. However, when Norris moved away from involvement in day-to-day operations toward involvement in social responsibility programs, the company's financial performance began to deteriorate.

William Norris's Vision

William Norris became known for his vision, not his financial acumen.[16] Business was to address society's needs, according to Norris, and unmet social needs represented potential future markets. CDC possessed unique resources, notably technology, to meet these needs. The challenge was to find ways to convert society's unmet needs into profitable business opportunities.

Norris was confident that he was aiming Control Data in a strategic direction that would position it strongly for the next quarter century. Business should take the lead in addressing society's ills. CDC's *1978 Social Responsibility Report* stated that "what is required is a fundamental change in which business takes the initiative and provides the leadership for planning and managing the implementation of programs meeting . . . [society's] needs."[17]

Norris believed government and charities were limited in the amount of social amelioration they could accomplish.[18] Government was relegated to a support role for CDC, coming in as a partner in projects in which the market had been unable to supply the appropriate level of the social good.

Norris believed that the government should provide incentives (i.e., enterprise zones, tax breaks) to encourage the private sector to participate in social programs.[19] However, he also believed that business social programs should not be handouts. He was quoted as saying that such programs must "be a business success before [they] can be a social success."[20] By 1979, a 15-member committee at the company had a $3 million annual budget to develop programs to address social problems.

Cooperation between business, government, and societal groups was part of the business strategy of CDC, and it was involved with the government in a number of social ventures.[21] Some of CDC's ventures with the government can be traced to the military background of its founders, but some resulted from rising technology transfer and diffusion in the world.[22]

Norris believed that CDC should work in a consortium with other firms and the government to maximize knowledge transfer and thus problem solving. He said that "with widespread cooperation to achieve more efficient use of existing intellectual, physical, and financial resources to vastly expand innovation addressing major unmet needs as profitable business opportunities, the decline [of society] can be arrested and gradual improvement can follow."[23]

Technology, he believed, was the means to meet social needs.[24] Unemployment was at the root of many social problems, and technical innovation was the wellspring of new jobs. Applied technology was supposed to be the means that CDC would use to address social problems.

In short, Norris's strategy was to address society's needs as profitable business opportunities. CDC was supposed to look for social needs and determine if it had the capabilities to profitably address them. Cooperative arrangements with other firms and the government would facilitate the achievement of social projects. Applying technological know-how for job creation would help society alleviate many social problems.

"Does Control Data Have a Future?"

Robert Price, who succeeded Norris as Chairman and CEO in January 1986, summarized the company's new tough-mindedness: "We don't have any 'visions'; we have a damn job to do."[25] "Does Control Data Have A Future?" read the headlines in 1985.[26] Many changes had been made, including Norris's reduced role in management. Still, CDC appeared to be sticking to its philosophy that business must address society's unmet needs. The 1985 annual report spoke solemnly about a "narrowing of the company's focus," but added, "some, but certainly not all, unmet needs represent major opportunities for the Corporation's technology and products."[27]

CDC had trimmed its operations, including some of its social ventures, to achieve a strategic fit with its computer business. There was a renewed emphasis on product quality and minimizing manufacturing costs. Financial performance was improving through 1987, but investors were still cautious.[28]

Larry Perlman's Vision

Larry Perlman, the new president of CDC as of December 1987, was known as a troubleshooter for his ability to turn companies around.[29] An intensely competitive person, he was aware that he was operating in a very difficult situation. His assignment as CDC's president was the toughest assignment he had to face.

A St. Paul native, Perlman earned a law degree from Harvard after doing his undergraduate work at Carleton College. For 14 years he had practiced law before becoming general counsel at Medtronic, a medical device manufacturer in the Twin Cities. When Medtronic's U.S. pacemaker division was suffering from product quality problems, declining credibility, and dwindling market share, he was asked to head the division. He did so successfully for three years before returning to private law practice.

Perlman was a small, compact person who looked like the skier, runner, fly fisherman, and squash and tennis player that he was.[30] There was "something efficient about him."[31] He seemed "to contain no unnecessary material, nothing lanky or bulky."[32] Yet in a speech he made in 1985 he condemned the "lone ranger style of management—the classic male tough guy, solitary and imperturbable," and he blamed the problems women were having in reaching upper management positions on men's inability "to accept the female characteristics they themselves have—sensitivity, intuition, and eagerness to cooperate as well as compete."[33]

Perlman joined CDC in 1980 first as general counsel and then as head of Commercial Credit Corporation. CCC had gotten into trouble when it ventured into too many businesses, since its expenses were higher than those of its competitors. Perlman cut back CCC and restricted it to the businesses where it did well. Then he recommended that CDC sell the division, arguing that as a computer manufacturing and service company, it could not successfully compete in the financial industry. The decision to sell Commercial Credit was controversial as CCC had in the past been an important contributor to CDC's earnings. In the 1970s, CDC's computer business netted just $75.4 million out of total earnings of $500 million.[34] What permitted the company to survive was Commercial Credit.

As executive vice president of the company and president of its Data Storage Products Group (DSP), his next assignment, Perlman learned what it meant to battle for survival. In 1985, DSP had $800 million in assets and 20,000 employees. He cut both in half, firing three quarters of DSP's upper level executives in the process. Perlman, however, did not view himself as a "hatchet man."[35] He believed that the work force reductions were "necessary to get expenses down."[36]

DSP formerly was called Peripheral Products. It marketed memory storage devices called disk drives. From 1980 to 1985 it had provided about $1 billion a year in revenues to CDC, about a third of its total revenues. In 1985, when CDC started to lose money seriously, most of the losses came from DSP. DSP lost $350 million that year, 62 percent of the corporate total. Of the 13,000 workers CDC had laid off since 1985, nearly 10,000 were DSP employees.

DSP originated in a CDC middle manager's idea that the company could make disk drives as well as IBM could. In 1963, William Norris, despite the objections of many in the company, allowed CDC to pursue this idea. In the early 1980s, computer earnings took off and DSP bolstered the company's profits. Nonetheless, DSP was basically a manufacturing operation in a company that was becoming increasingly committed to providing computer services. The time-sharing data processing services for which CDC had such high hopes also fell victim to the personal computer revolution. DSP made many computer products, from printers and floppy disks to high-performance, high-capacity disk drives for scientific and engineering computing systems, but what the public really wanted was more memory in smaller disk drives at lower prices, something DSP could not provide, but competitors could.

CDC's dominance in disk drives peaked at about 55 percent of the market in 1980. Japanese competition, a sluggish bureaucracy, and delays had hurt its business before Perlman arrived and attempted to turn things around.

Perlman cut CDC out of the low end of the market of floppy diskettes, computer tapes, and other peripherals, and concentrated on the high-performance, high-capacity end of the market. Even here the competition was intense and the margins low. CDC had to become a high-volume manufacturer, to go from producing 150 drives a day to more than 1,000.[37] This meant reducing the total number of vendors, holding those that remained to higher standards, emphasizing statistical quality control, introducing just-in-time inventory practices, and opening plants in the Far East to take advantage of less-expensive labor.

Perlman's efforts revived the DSP division. His name was often mentioned as a possible successor to Robert Price as chairman and CEO. As the new president and chief operating officer, he understood that he would have to be a change agent; the old culture was no longer adequate to meet today's realities.

Perlman would have to make rapid changes, but not so rapid that the company could not adapt. A big question was the place of Norris's philosophy of social responsibility in the new CDC. It was a hallmark of CDC's strategy in the past, but what place did it have in CDC's future?

Control Data's Social Ventures

CDC was involved in numerous and varied socially responsible ventures (see Table 1). The unifying theme was that by taking the high moral ground, CDC could make profits simultaneously with alleviating social disorders. Four of its social responsibility programs are described below.

TABLE 1   Control Data's Social Ventures

Program	Goal
ACET (Advanced Career Employment Training)	Job placement
Adult Learning Center	Education
AgTech	Agriculture
BAI (Business Advisors, Inc.)	Human resource management services
Business and Technology Centers	Small business development
Career Outreach	Job placement
City Venture Corporation	Urban renewal
Control Data Institutes	Vocational, technical, educational
EAR (Employee Advisory Resource)	Personal counseling services
Earth Energy Systems	Renewable energy
Employment Readiness Program	Job formation
Fair Break (a.k.a. Job Readiness)	Job training, education
Farm Technology Consortium	Technology for agriculture
HELP (Health Evaluation through Logical Processing)	Health care services
Homework Program	Work and training for homebound employees
Indian Health Management, Inc.	Health care at Rosebud Sioux Reservation
Job Creation Network	Job formation
LOGIN (Local Government Information Network)	Productivity improvement, municipal services, energy management
Minnesota Wellspring	New business and job creation

Northside Manufacturing Facility—Minneapolis.   Two events occurred in 1967 that seemed to compel Norris to proceed with his social vision. One was

Norris's encounter with Whitney Young, head of National Urban League, and the other was the rioting in the Northside area of Minneapolis.[38] These events impressed upon Norris the need for more jobs, to achieve social justice. CDC located a new manufacturing facility in the economically depressed Northside area of Minneapolis in 1968. The Northside facility manufactured peripheral controllers, which were vital to CDC's business. Norris purposefully gave this plant an important function to reaffirm CDC's commitment to social ills.

CDC claimed that its inner-city plants were as profitable as its other manufacturing operations. However, CDC had to expend a great deal of resources to bring its inner-city operations on line. They required special recruiting practices, aid and counseling for workers, and substantially more training than comparable CDC plants. A special child-care facility had to be established. CDC went so far as to have an attorney show up at the city jail on Monday mornings to bail out employees who had been arrested during the weekend. Most of the special programs were phased out over time, and after three years the Northside plant was as productive as other CDC manufacturing facilities.

PLATO and Fair Break.   Norris had proclaimed: "PLATO is the future of Control Data."[39] From its inception in 1961 until 1985, CDC expended over $900 million to develop PLATO. The returns were significantly less, although CDC still believed that high growth was possible. A strong impetus for the program was Norris's belief that the American educational system was inadequate. "Computer technology," he wrote, "provides the only practicable means of bringing to education the quality, equality, and productivity improvement that is so sorely needed."[40] He envisioned the computer raising the level of classroom education of groups with no access to the existing system.

CDC did not limit PLATO to the education and training markets. It became pervasive throughout the organization. The Fair Break program was an example of how CDC utilized PLATO to promote social concerns. Fair Break was started in 1977 primarily to aid unemployed youths.[41] Through PLATO, it taught basic educational, vocational, and life-management skills. Fair Break centers were established in predominantly depressed areas of the country (there were 45 centers as of November, 1986). The aim was to teach skills integral to the local economy that could elevate its users out of joblessness. Two related programs, Advanced Career Employment Training and Career Outreach, were also set up.

The primary difficulty with Fair Break and the two other programs was financial. Implementing the programs, especially on a large scale, was extremely expensive in capital and labor costs. Government assistance was necessary to recover the training costs. Otherwise it was doubtful whether business could be involved in these programs.

City Venture Corporation.   Urban revitalization had been a concern of CDC since the opening of the Northside plant. In 1968, CDC embarked on a more ambitious plan, the City Venture Corporation. Its goal was nothing less than the revitalization and renewal of rundown urban areas.[42] City Venture was set up as a for-profit corporation. It worked in cooperative arrangements with civic and religious groups, cities, states and federal agencies, to foster economic, educational, and cultural development in the affected area. City Venture was to be the consultant in the establishment of new (or reestablishment of previously existing) enterprises. In certain cities, CDC used its Business and Technology Centers (a CDC venture to promote small business development) to implement its agenda.

The results of City Venture were mixed. Certain cities, notably Toledo, experienced some success. But City Venture proved to be a failure in other areas, including Minneapolis. City Venture committed many political blunders and alienated the groups it was supposed to be assisting. Critics complained the only change sought was in who ran the show.[43]

Rural Ventures Inc.   Family farms concerned Norris, possibly because that was where he grew up. He considered small and medium-sized farms to be job creators that were ignored by the federal government in its agricultural programs. He felt that information technology was the key to raising farm productivity, and he developed a farm data base called AgTech to disseminate vital information. In 1979, Rural Ventures Inc. (RVI) was established, an agriculture cooperative akin to City Venture. The goal of RVI was to increase the productivity and profitability of family farms and to improve the standard of living in farm communities. The means to this end was through joint projects with governmental and nonprofit agencies in which RVI supplied business and engineering consulting services, PLATO training, education, health care, and other services.

RVI was marginally effective. Norris blamed RVI's poor performance on the government for its lack of support. However, it seemed equal blame rested with RVI's management, which was criticized for failing to deliver the technical assistance it had promised.

Control Data Financial Highlights, 1983–1987
(dollars in millions, except per share data)

	1987	1986	1985	1984	1983
Revenues	$3,366.5	$3,346.7	$3,679.7	$3,692.6	$3,407.8
Earnings (loss) before income taxes and other items	57.4	(280.6)	(484.0)	(50.0)	189.7
Net earnings (loss): Computer business before extraordinary items*	21.5	(311.1)	(562.7)	(44.5)	132.1
Commercial Credit†	3.5	42.6	(4.8)	49.6	29.6
Net earnings (loss before extraordinary items	25.0	(268.5)	(567.5)	5.1	161.7
Extraordinary items‡	(5.7)	4.0	—	—	—
Total	$19.3	$(264.5)	$(567.5)	$5.1	$161.7

Control Data Financial Highlights, 1983–1987 *(continued)*

	1987	1986	1985	1984	1983
Earnings (loss) per share of common stock:					
Before extraordinary items	$.59	$(6.58)	$(14.56)	$.12	$4.20
Including extraordinary items	$.45	$(6.48)	$(14.56)	$.12	$4.20
Average common shares outstanding	41,505	40,912	39,022	38,520	38,338
Dividends declared per common share	—	—	.54	.66	.60
Balance sheet data:					
Total assets	$2,638.6	$2,594.9	$3,072.5	$3,489.2	$3,153.5
Debt obligations	440.6	556.0	744.2	747.5	526.5
Stockholder's equity	1,047.5	991.1	1,202.6	1,758.8	1,825.5
Stockholder's equity per common share	$24.85	$23.72	$29.21	$45.63	$47.59
Number of computer business employees§	34,500	35,500	39,500	48,000	47,000

*Includes operation and restructure charges (credits) of $107.6 for 1987, $162.2 for 1986, $274.8 for 1985, and $130.2 for 1984. Restructure includes a gain of $136.2 in 1987 and a loss of $6.9 in 1986 from sales of Commercial Credit stock.

†Includes 100% of Commercial Credit earnings (losses) through October 1986, when Control Data participated in a public offering of Commercial Credit stock, and 18.3% thereafter, until and including September 1987, when the company commenced the sale of its remaining ownership interest.

‡Included in extraordinary items for 1987 are losses of $6.5 from early retirement of debt and gains of $0.8 ($4.0 in 1986) from utilization of international tax loss carryforwards.

§Included in the number of computer business employees are additions for December acquisitions of approximately 2,000 and 500 for the years 1987 and 1986, respectively.

Source: 1987 annual report.

Discussion Questions

1. What do you think of William Norris's social vision? To what extent is his social vision related to Control Data's declining financial performance?

2. How does Larry Perlman differ from William Norris? What situation does he confront? What changes should he make at Control Data?
3. What should Control Data do about the legacy of William Norris, given its current financial troubles? What role should Norris's vision of social responsibility now play in the company?

Endnotes

1. This case was prepared by Alfred Marcus and Douglas Schuller with assistance from Mark Jankus.
2. W. C. Norris, "Applying Technology: The Key to the Future," *The Journal of Business Strategy* 6, 1986, pp. 38–46.
3. D. J. Tice, "Troubleshooter," *Corporate Report Minnesota*, Sept. 1987, pp. 72–77.
4. F. S. Worthy, *William C. Norris: Portrait of a Maverick*, (Cambridge, Mass.: Bollinger, 1987).
5. Ibid.
6. Ibid.
7. Value Line, *Value Line Investment Survey, November 6, 1987*, p. 1089.
8. Standard & Poor Corporation, *Company Profile Report, Control Data Corporation, October 22, 1987*, pp. 1–4.
9. R. Broderick, "Corporate Culture: Norris at Colonnus," *Corporate Report Minnesota*, February 1986, p. 126.
10. D. Hertzberg, "As GAF Pursues, Will Carbide Adopt Pac Man Defense?" *The Wall Street Journal*, December 10, 1985, p. 3; P. Houston and G. Bock, "Control Data's Struggle to Come Back from the Brink," *Business Week* 14, 1985, pp. 62–63.
11. Broderick, "Corporate Culture: Norris at Colonnus."
12. Worthy, *William C. Norris: Portrait of a Maverick.*
13. F. S. Worthy, "Does Control Data Have a Future?" *Fortune*, December 23, 1985, pp. 24–26.
14. E. J. Savitz, "The Vision Thing," *Barron's*, May 7, 1990, p. 10; Worthy, "Does Control Data Have a Future?"
15. G. Bock, "Has the Street Given up on Control Data?" *Business Week* 30, 1985, pp. 48–49.
16. D. Kelly, "Doing Well Doing Good," *Corporate Report Minnesota*, December 1981, pp. 106–108.
17. Control Data Corporation, *1978 Social Responsibility.*
18. Norris, "Applying Technology: The Key to the Future."
19. Ibid.
20. Worthy, *William C. Norris: Portrait of a Maverick*, p. 114.
21. J. P. Shannon, "Choose Partners and Dance," *Corporate Report Minnesota*, June 1983, p. 158.
22. Norris, "Applying Technology: The Key to the Future."
23. Ibid, p. 46.
24. Worthy, *William C. Norris: Portrait of a Maverick.*
25. Savitz, "The Vision Thing."
26. Worthy, "Does Control Data Have a Future?"
27. Control Data Corporation, *1985 Annual Report.*
28. Control Data Corporation, *1986 Annual Report*; Value Line, *Value Line Investment Survey, November 6, 1987*, p. 1089.
29. Tice, "Troubleshooter."
30. Ibid.

31. Ibid.
32. Ibid.
33. Ibid.
34. J. Dubashi, "The Do-Gooder," *Financial World,* June 27, 1989, pp. 70–74; Tice, "Troubleshooter."
35. Tice, "Troubleshooter."
36. Ibid.
37. Ibid.
38. Worthy, *William C. Norris: Portrait of a Maverick.*
39. Broderick, "Corporate Culture: Norris at Colonnus."
40. Control Data Corporation, *1978 Social Responsibility,* p. 2.
41. Ibid.
42. Worthy, *William C. Norris: Portrait of a Maverick.*
43. E. Winninghoff, "Corporate Givers under the Gun," *Corporate Report Minnesota,* March 1982, pp. 72–77.

CASE IIE
CHILD CARE AT ATLANTIC INFORMATION SYSTEMS[1]

Only 10 percent of U.S. households fit the mold in which the husband is the sole supporter of both the wife and children. In 40 percent of households, both spouses work, and another 6 percent of all households is composed of single parents. Sixty-six percent of the women who work have children under the age of 18; 59 percent have children under the age of 6.[2]

About 2,599 U.S. companies now are helping employees with their child care needs.[3] The help ranges from being direct providers of day care, to arrangements with independent agencies for modified work schedules. The reasons companies give are that doing so aids in recruiting, morale, productivity, and quality. It is also supposed to lower accident rates, absenteeism, worker stress, tardiness, and turnover.

For instance, Control Data Corporation compared its employees who took advantage of in-house child care with those who did not and found a lower rate of absenteeism (4.4 percent as opposed to 6.0 percent) and turnover (1.8 percent as opposed to 6.3 percent). The effects are greater in companies with large numbers of women employees.

Often companies become involved because of employee initiative. Employees ask or tell the company through various mechanisms (e.g., confidential letter writing, requests to employee assistance programs, or special advisory committees) that they seek child care assistance. Companies respond because of their sense of obligation to employees. They want to help employees with their problems. It is a way to create a family environment and sustain close personal ties between employer and employee.

A large group of companies, though, have not become involved. They are skeptical about the gains and worry about the costs, the insurance arrangements, parents' complaints, quality control problems, and the issue of equity.

This case is about the dilemma faced by Atlantic Information Systems when a group of its employees requested that the company provide child care.

The Company

Atlantic Information Systems Inc. is a medium-size firm with two complementary lines of business. Its 700 professionals advise other organizations about data storage and processing systems. They also produce and market customized software systems for a variety of business functions. In addition to its professional staff, the firm includes 100 employees whose work is administrative, clerical, or janitorial.

When Lester Barks, the founder and CEO of Atlantic, started his business, he recognized that he would require employees with both high-level technical skills and sophisticated communication skills. Thus, he chose to locate his firm in southern New Hampshire. By locating there, he knew that he would be able to recruit his staff from the high-quality labor pool made up of the many distinguished graduates from business schools in the New England area. Barks' analysis proved to be correct. He recruited well and was able to infuse the staff with his own energy and appetite for work. As a result, the firm grew rapidly, developing a strong reputation for innovative designs and good customer service.

From the beginning, Barks had believed in rewarding people for their work, but had also tried to keep fixed costs to a minimum. Thus, although he had established a generous profit-sharing plan, he tried to hold the line against the expansion of employee benefits programs. This policy had been working reasonably well. As long as the company's young, well-educated employees kept getting their substantial paychecks, they seemed content to solve their own personal and career problems.

As the firm and its employees matured, however, sentiment toward the firm's personnel policies seemed to shift. The people who had the skills and experience Barks needed to run his business also had young families to care for. The conflicting demands of jobs and families were proving to be problematic for many people. In particular, the firm's location outside the urban mainstream made it difficult for employees to find high-quality care for their preschool children.

The Request that Atlantic Provide Child Care

Recently, several employees had approached Barteau Weber, the vice president for personnel, with a strongly worded request that Atlantic examine its personnel policies with a view toward adopting practices that were more in keeping with the needs of the work force. In particular, they asked that Atlantic consider opening a company-sponsored child care center. They argued that the company should establish and support a high-quality child care center as a way of reducing demands on their time and concentration that detracted from their ability to focus on their jobs. In addition, they pointed out that predicted changes in the structure of the work force were likely to make such a center a prerequisite for recruiting and retaining qualified employees in the future.

Weber knew that this request was not the product of a few overly demanding whiners. Indeed, the request had been put together by a self-appointed committee consisting of half a dozen of the firm's most respected employees and had been signed by more than 50 people. Furthermore, Weber knew that, within just the past three months, two highly valued senior systems designers had resigned. Rather than returning to work after the six-week parental leave the company allowed, they quit because they were unable to arrange for suitable child care. Weber had overheard many informal conversations focusing on these concerns, and, of course, there was always a certain amount of absenteeism that could be attributed to people staying home to take care of sick children.

Weber was aware that many companies around the nation were establishing child care centers, but he had little technical knowledge of how they were structured or how much they cost. Moreover, he felt certain that Barks would resist the idea of getting involved in such a venture. Nevertheless, he felt that it was his responsibility to bring the matter to Barks' attention.

Barks' Opposition

As he expected, Barks said he was not in favor of having the company get involved in providing solutions to employees' personal problems. As they discussed the matter further, Barks said, "It's not the start-up costs I'm concerned about. We've got space here, and we can afford the initial investment. But this is not a one-time thing. The operating costs are likely to be high, and they'll go on and on. What will we do if times get hard? If we start this, it's going to be difficult to shut it down if we decide we can no longer afford it." Weber acknowledged that there would be some expense involved, but observed that maintaining the firm's competitive position depended on retaining its highly qualified employees, an observation that could hardly be contested in a knowledge-intensive firm such as Atlantic. He said the problem was too important to ignore, and was likely to become even more important in the years ahead.

Barks said: "That may be true, but this problem only affects a part of our work force. Some people don't have children at all, and others have children that they managed to raise without any help from us. How are they going to feel if they see the company spending its money on an expensive program that benefits only a few employees?" Weber said it would probably be a good idea to survey the company to see how people felt about the issue, but pointed out that he'd never heard anyone say anything negative about it.

After some further grumbling, Barks eventually acknowledged that it might be worthwhile to "do something," and asked Weber what he would recommend. Weber hesitated, saying that he'd need some time to gather information about costs. He also pointed out that since other companies already had programs in place, it might be useful to find out about their experiences. Barks agreed to the delay, but said: "I want to see a full analysis of the problem and your recommendations within two weeks. If this is as important as you say it is, we might as well get moving on it. We should find out what everybody thinks about this idea. We can't act without finding out how serious this problem is, and how people who don't have kids feel about it. So do some investigating, and get back to me with your ideas about what you think we should do and why. Even if we start now, it's going to be some time before we can make a decision on this because I'll want to talk it over with the executive committee. You'd better draft a statement on this that we can distribute to everyone. Tell them we're working on it and will get back to them."

Weber's Assignment

Weber accepted the assignment, went back to his office, and sighed. He was enthusiastic about day care, but already overburdened, and did not see how he could gather all the information he needed and come up with a recommendation in two weeks. The only way to meet Barks' deadline was to hand off the task to an assistant.

He made a few quick phone calls to find out how to approach the problem. Then he called Eliot Beckman into his office and said: "I have a great assignment for you. Mr. Barks wants us to figure out whether we should set up a company day-care center. We'll need to look into the pros and cons and figure out how much it will cost. I've done a little bit of background work, but I need you to do some further analysis and put together a set of recommendations. He's looking for us to help him figure out what the company's policy should be. Of course, you know he didn't get where he is today by just waving his hands at problems. He's going to want all the details laid out so that he can judge the situation for himself."

Continuing his instructions, Weber said: "The first thing you'll need to do is get some sense of how big this issue is. You can use electronic mail to ask people whether they have preschool kids, and, if so, whether they would be interested in having a day-care center at work. And ask them for any other questions, concerns or ideas they have about the topic."

Eliot turned to leave, but Weber called him back saying: "We'll need to let people know what we're up to. Give them a few days to respond to your E-mail message, and then draft a memo to go to everybody under my signature. We want to let them know we're studying this issue. Some people are getting pretty hot about this, so we need to cool down the fires a little while we figure this out. Be careful how you say it, though. We want to let the people who are concerned about this know that we're taking them seriously, but we don't want to give the impression that we're caving in to the demands of a few complainers. If we decide to go ahead with this, we want people to think it's a good idea for the company as a whole."

Eliot's Task

Eliot began his work by sending off an E-mail message to everyone on the staff. In the message, he asked people to tell him whether they had preschool kids and whether they would be interested in a company-sponsored child care center. He also invited them to send any comments or questions they had about the idea. After some research, he learned that there were a variety of issues to consider besides cost.

After reviewing the research, he was ready to draft his memos. The memo to the staff had to:

- Announce that the company was studying the problem and explain the rationale for the investigation.
- Describe the investigation itself.
- Acknowledge the viewpoints of all employees with regard to the child care issue.
- Invite comment.

The memo to Mr. Barks had to:

- Acknowledge that some employees opposed employer-sponsored child care.
- Present the expense analysis for both high- and medium-quality centers.
- Make an argument about what the company should do.

Eliot's research suggested the following about (*a*) the costs of day care and (*b*) the personnel of Atlantic. He also had (*c*) the results of the employee survey with which to work and (*d*) estimates of child care fees and estimated usage levels.

(*a*) Annual Costs for Day-Care Centers Designed to Accommodate up to 96 Children

Estimates are based on current costs in the mid-Atlantic region, and include all operating expenses but exclude the capital costs of construction/renovation and equipment. The medium-quality center meets state licensing standards. The high-quality center meets standards established by the National Association for the Education of Young Children. The data were from Resources for Child Care Management of Morristown, New Jersey, a national organization.

Food includes food, supplies, and staff necessary to serve breakfast, lunch, and an afternoon snack.

Medium- and high-quality centers: $46,000.

Supplies includes diapers, medical supplies, and other disposable, nonclassroom items.

Medium-quality center: $10,000.
High-quality center: $12,000.

Transport includes the annual cost of a 17-passenger school bus.

High-quality center only: $8,000.

Classroom supplies includes consumables (paper, paint, etc.), replacement toys, games, books, and so on.

High-quality center: $9,200.
Medium-quality center: $7,500.

Insurance provides $5 million comprehensive liability and student accident insurance.

Medium- and high-quality centers: $11,040.

Enrichment covers specialists (dance, music, etc.) and field trips.

High-quality center only: $5,000.

Management includes an annual management fee (based on an average of $50,000 annually).

Space includes opportunity cost, maintenance and utilities at $20 per square foot.

Medium-quality center: 5,000 sq. ft.
High-quality center: 10,000 sq. ft.

Fringe includes taxes and a cafeteria benefits plan for day-care staff.

Medium-quality center: $54,341.
High-quality center: $83,204.

Staff Development includes outside workshops, tuition reimbursements, conferences, and materials.

High-quality center: $4,000.
Medium-quality center: $2,000.

Staff Salaries for High-Quality Center.   Assumes four lead teachers at $23,000, three teachers at $21,000, seven assistant teachers at $16,000, 31 hours/week of part-time help at $6.50/hour, one director at $35,000, one assistant director at $30,000, one secretary at $20,000, one nurse at $30,000, and one nurse's aide at $14,000 (for sick-child care staff).

Staff Salaries for Medium-Quality Center.   Assumes four lead teachers at $19,000, two teachers at $17,000, five assistant teachers at $14,000, 31 hours/week of part-time help at $5.00/hour, one director at $25,000, one assistant director at $20,000, and one secretary at $15,000.

(b) Personnel Data—Atlantic Information Systems

Average cost to recruit a professional employee: $15,000.
Average cost to recruit a nonprofessional employee: $1,000.
Average salary for professional staff, one to five years of service: $75,000.
Average salary for professional staff, 6–10 years of service: $87,000.
Average salary for administrative staff: $44,000.
Average salary for clerical and janitorial staff: $28,000.
The average parent misses five days of work per year per child due to a child's illness or the breakdown of childcare arrangements.

Turnover attributable to childcare problems is eight professionals/year; child care–related turnover of nonprofessionals was not measured.

(c) Results of Employee Survey

Number of parents of preschool children in the current work force: 215.

Number of children/parents who will be using center: 1.

Percentage of parents interested in employer-sponsored child care program: 45 percent.

Percentage of parents interested in employer-sponsored child care of professional rank: 65 percent; percentage nonprofessional: 35 percent.

Number of employees who oppose employer-sponsored child care: 15.

(d) Child Care Fees and Anticipated Usage Level

Anticipated fees employees would pay for childcare: $75/week for professional employees; $50/week for nonprofessional employees.

Anticipated level of use of childcare center: 49 weeks/year/child.

Discussion Questions

1. What should Eliot Beckman say in his memo to Atlantic Information System's employees?
2. What should Eliot Beckman say in his memo to Mr. Barks?
3. Should corporations provide day care for their employees? Why or why not?

Endnotes

1. This case was written by Jolene Galegher.
2. D. Friedman, "Child Care for Employees' Kids," *Harvard Business Review* 86, 1986, pp. 28–34.
3. J. D. Auerbach, *In the Business of Child Care* (New York, Praeger, 1988).

GOVERNMENT AND GLOBAL COMPETITION

CHAPTER

8

THE PURPOSE OF THE STATE

We hold these truths to be self-evident, that all men are created equal, that they are endowed by their Creator with certain unalienable Rights, that among these are Life, Liberty, and the pursuit of Happiness. That to secure these rights, Governments are instituted among men deriving their just powers from the consent of the Governed.

The Declaration of Independence

We the people of the United States, in Order to form a more perfect Union, establish Justice, insure domestic Tranquility, provide for the common defence, promote the general Welfare, and secure the Blessings of Liberty to ourselves and our Posterity, do ordain and establish this Constitution for the United States of America.

The Constitution of the United States

Introduction and Chapter Objectives

The social responsibility debate has moved between two poles, both of which are relevant. An emphasis on the ethical obligations of the corporation to society as fashioned by corporate managers has been the main focus of Part II. Now, the focus is on the obligations of the corporation as fashioned by the public policy process. Public policy comes from governments, but why are governments needed? The arguments from the Declaration of Independence and the Constitution are that they protect liberty and promote the common welfare. From economics the arguments start with the premise that markets are a superior means to organize production, and governments are needed to correct market defects.

Most economists agree that governments perform critical functions that cannot be adequately performed by markets (e.g., providing police protection, administering justice, and preventing pollution). Economists, however, have debated about whether governments should be involved in the redistribution of income and whether they should act to smooth the business cycle.

Economists acknowledge that government actions are not always called for in the face of market defects: the gains from correcting the defects have to be balanced against the costs of administering the government programs. This chapter compares the arguments made by classic liberals, contemporary liberals, and neoconservatives about why governments are needed.

The Need for Government

For business managers, hounded by unnecessary regulation and red tape, the question of why governments are needed is of real concern. Socialists and communists, when these ideologies had appeal, would have asked the opposite question—why are markets needed? Today, governments' unhealthy role in stifling the economic growth of the formerly centrally planned economies of Eastern Europe is recognized by all. The question asked by citizens of formerly communist countries is how these nations can move rapidly and efficiently from central planning to market control. Making such a transition, though, is proving to be very difficult.

To the founders of the American republic, it was obvious that governments were needed, but they were divided about why. The Declaration of Independence starts with the individual's right to life, liberty, and the pursuit of happiness, which government has to protect. If government becomes "destructive of these ends," then people have the right to "alter or abolish it" and to institute a new government. In contrast, the framers of the Constitution start with collective interests: the purposes of government are to perfect the union, to promote justice and order, and to provide for the common defense and welfare.

These great documents reflect the movement in American history from rebelling against Great Britain (the Declaration of Independence) to establishing a new state (the Constitution). They also reveal an enduring tension among Americans about why governments exist. Some people start from the premise that individual rights are paramount and governments exist to protect liberty, while others start from the premise that collective welfare is paramount and governments exist to further justice. Almost all U.S. politicians are pragmatic. They could not survive for long by dogmatically adhering to either of these positions. To reach solutions to problems, they draw on arguments from both schools of thought.

In Economic Theory

The question of how economic theory views government involvement is as interesting as the question of how politicians do. The strongest body of theory on the appropriate role of government comes from economics. Economists generally prefer decentralized decision making by consumers in the marketplace (individualism) to the centralized control of the government. This preference is based on the efficiency advantages of markets, but it is broader than that and includes economic and technological progress, a rising standard of living, social mobility, and political freedom.[1]

Markets have a number of efficiency advantages. First, they tend to achieve particular purposes at lower costs than government, or they accomplish these purposes better for the same costs. In this way, they outperform government in static efficiency terms. However, they also outperform it in terms of dynamic efficiency, that is, they are better than government at promoting new technologies, improving product quality, and creating new products.[2] Finally, they outperform government by stimulating organizational improvements, increasing worker and management motivation, and enhancing business decision making. This capability has been referred to as X-efficiency to distinguish it from the static and dynamic efficiency advantages mentioned above.[3]

Market Defects

One of the main proofs that markets outperform government comes from the experience of the newly industrialized economies of Asia, which have done so much better than the formerly state-centered economies of Eastern Europe and the Soviet Union. Nonetheless, almost all economists admit that markets are imperfect, that they have certain defects or shortcomings that should be corrected by government action (see Exhibit 8–1). For instance, economic efficiency requires that there be competitive factor and product markets; that is, there must be no obstacles to the free entry of new market participants, full market knowledge, and full market power by existing producers and consumers. But these conditions are rarely met fully by markets.[4] Another defect of markets is that they may not adequately protect future rights and interests. Government intervention may be justified because private and public perspectives on the valuation of the present and future differ.

EXHIBIT 8–1   Why Governments Are Needed

The Declaration of Independence:	To preserve liberty.
The Constitution:	To promote the common welfare.
Economic Theory:	To provide for public goods.
	To handle market defects, for example:
	Entry barriers
	Insufficient consumer knowledge.
	Insufficient consumer power.
	Insufficient protection.
	of future interests.
	To deal with spillovers and externalities.

Public Goods

Further, economists admit that even if markets are operating as they are supposed to in theory, they do not provide certain types of public goods, the need for which is felt collectively and not individually. Since the ownership of public goods cannot be limited to persons who pay for them but is shared broadly throughout society, such goods would not be provided in sufficient quantities were it not for government intervention. For instance, when a given air quality improvement is achieved, the resulting gain is available to all who breathe. Those who pay for the benefit cannot exclude others from enjoying it. This condition applies also to other public goods, such as national defense, police protection, national parks, and highways. All members in society, not just those who buy the good, are in a position to benefit. The people who pay cannot exclude those who do not pay. The private market incentive to provide such goods, therefore, is deficient, even if the preference for them is high.

Spillovers and Externalities

Private market activities also create so-called spillovers or externalities. A positive spillover or externality exists when a producer cannot appropriate all the benefits of the activities it has undertaken. An example would be research and development that yields benefits to society (e.g., employment in subsidiary industries) that the producer cannot capture. Thus, the producer's incentive is to underinvest in the activity unless government subsidizes it. With positive externalities, too little of the good in question is produced; with negative ones too much is made. Negative externalities like air pollution occur when the producer cannot be charged all the costs. Since the external costs do not enter the calculations the producer makes, the producer manufactures more of the good than is socially beneficial. In both instances, that of positive and negative externalities, market outcomes need correction to be efficient.

Other Market Defects

Many, but not all, economists accept that two additional market defects exist. First, to correct for apparent instabilities in the business cycle, the government can implement a variety of fiscal and monetary policies. By themselves, markets may not guarantee a high level of employment, price stability, and a socially desired rate of growth. While Milton Friedman accepts the earlier justifications for government intervention, he contests these Keynesian premises.[5]

Second, market outcomes may violate cherished values about equality and justice. In the market, a person's distribution of goods depends on factor endowments (skill and inherited wealth) and the relative prices they command. Society, however, may consider this distribution neither fair nor just. Thus, government may redistribute income via the tax code and other means such as altering inheritance laws.

Libertarians reject this argument for two reasons. First, on moral grounds, they claim that what someone earns belongs to the person and government has no right to take it away. Second, on practical grounds, they argue that if government routinely redistributes income, then the incentive to earn will decline. If this acquisitive instinct diminishes, society is worse-off. The economy does not grow as fast.[6]

Imperfect Governments

In all of these instances where a rationale exists for government involvement, it does not necessarily follow from the rationale that the government is capable of effectively correcting the defect. While markets are imperfect, governments too are imperfect. They have shortcomings, and their ability to correct market imperfections is limited.[7]

In each instance of a market defect, it is necessary to weigh whether the proposed government action would make things better. A helter-skelter approach, where the government tries to correct all that is wrong with markets without carefully analyzing what it can and cannot do to correct the defects, is as dangerous to the economy as the existence of the defects in the first place. The many unintended consequences of this approach would tend to complicate matters and would make the situation worse rather than better. Below, three different views of the appropriate role for government—the classic liberal, contemporary liberal, and neoconservative—are briefly summarized and contrasted.

The Classic Liberal View

The best representative of this school is Milton Friedman. His 1962 book *Capitalism and Freedom,* considered extreme in the 1960s, nearly became the standard wisdom during the Reagan years.[8] Friedman views himself as a classic liberal, not a conservative, as he is commonly seen today, because his starting point, like that of Adam Smith's, is in opposition to traditional societies that restricted individual liberty.

In traditional societies, people's ability to influence their future is affected by the group to which they belong and the beneficence of the state. The modern revolutions, which ushered in capitalism, stripped away the importance of inherited categories and ascribed statuses such as peasant and aristocrat, Christian and Jew, or Caucasian and Hispanic. Market economies gave people the right to make deals without being limited by these restrictions (see Chapter 7).

Friedman has written about this quality of a market society:

> No one who buys bread knows whether the wheat from which it was made was grown by a Communist or a Republican, by a Constitutionalist or a Fascist, or by a Negro or a White. This illustrates how an impersonal market separates economic activities from political views and protects men from being discriminated against in their economic activities for reasons that are irrelevant to their productivity—whether these reasons are associated with their views or their color.[9]

No central state, no matter what higher purpose it appeals to, should block the individual from striving to achieve what the person wants. No central state should stand in the way of economic liberty. The emancipation of individual talent, energy, and initiative is critical to achieving the economic growth, which is synonymous with modern societies.

Friedman believes that a market system provides this freedom for the individual. In a market, people do business with one another, not because of some social status to which they belong, but because they offer each other a valuable good or service. It does not matter who is offering the good or service just so long as it has high quality, low price, or some other desirable feature.

If forced to choose, Friedman's primary allegiance is to the individual freedom that the market provides, even above economic prosperity. Since individual freedom is his primary value, Friedman's position has been labeled libertarian to distinguish it from economists who defend markets on utilitarian grounds, that is, because they yield prosperity. Individual freedom, according to Friedman, is not a means for achieving some other end, but an end in itself.[10] Markets are a superior means of social organization because they allow for voluntary cooperation based on free discussion, which is the purpose of a liberal society (see Exhibit 8–2).

EXHIBIT 8–2   **The Classic Liberal View**

Markets are superior because they promote liberty:

> Grant right to make deals as individuals.
> Permit free discussion/voluntary cooperation.
> Not binding on those not subject to deals
>   (unlike government).

Governments needed when markets are not practical:

To protect people and the nation from coercion: "civil order."
To resolve disputes between conflicting parties: "rule maker and umpire."
To protect consumers from excessive market power: "technical monopoly."
To protect individuals from the actions of others: "neighborhood effects."
To act for those incapable or incompetent to act for themselves: "paternalism."

Governments in pursuing above should not restrict freedom of entry:

Retards technological innovation.

Governments should limit themselves to areas of technical competence:

Even with obvious market defect like pollution.

Democratically elected governments, according to Friedman, have deficiencies that markets do not have.[11] For instance, when a democratically elected government makes a decision passed by a majority, all citizens have to obey, even those who opposed the measure. Once made, the decision is binding on everyone. Everyone has to comply. In contrast, each person in the market decides if and how much of a particular good or service to acquire. Each chooses whether to buy, sell, or stay out of the market altogether. The individual makes this choice without being bound by the community's interests as represented by the will of a political majority. (Of course, the person may be limited in making this choice based on how much money the person has.)

A politically made decision about national defense spending compels all citizens to conform to its mandate. No longer is each citizen in a position to weigh the evidence and choose how much national defense the person might need or want. Friedman notes that a person "cannot get the amount of national defense [the person wants] and you, a different amount. With respect to such indivisible matters we discuss, and argue, and vote. But having decided we must conform."[12] Friedman recognizes that in the case of indivisible matters such as "protection of the individual and the nation from coercion," reliance on the market is not practical.[13] If each person or group chose the type of protection it wanted (its own weapons and weapon systems, private armies, and security forces), there would be anarchy. Society would be like the frontier society of the wild West or like tragic Beirut, which fell into such chaos, a war of all against all.

No settled society is possible under such conditions, nor can the orderly selling and buying necessary for the exercise of free choice in a market exist. So Friedman accepts the cost of relying on government to preserve civil order even if it strains the social fabric. He argues that since there is a cost, reliance on government should be limited to the issues where people have common views and there are no feasible alternatives. A good example is that nearly all people agree about the need for police for internal security and for armies for external defense.

Appropriate Areas for Government

Thus, Friedman believes government has an appropriate role to play in some areas. Besides domestic order and defense, it has an appropriate role as *rule maker and umpire*.[14] The interactions that take place in a market are like a game where the players have to respect the rules. These rules have to be interpreted, enforced, and modified. When individuals have disputes, someone has to resolve them. A judicial system is needed.

People's freedoms come into conflict. One person's right to live, for instance, comes into conflict with another's desire to kill. The government has to guarantee that the freedom of the person to maintain life takes precedence. Another example of conflicting rights where the government is the arbiter is between the freedom to combine and the freedom to compete. The European tradition has been to favor the freedom to combine. The United States has been more inclined to favor the freedom to compete. In Europe, competitors have had the right to fix prices, divide up markets, and take other actions to keep out potential competitors. In the United States, they have been restricted from doing so and have had to compete by selling better products.

Still another case where freedoms conflict concerns the definition of property rights. For instance, does title to a piece of property give owners the right to the minerals in the ground below it, and the right to control what goes on in the air above it? Can owners charge a nuisance price for noise if someone flies an airplane above their property, or must the owners pay the airplane pilots to stop them from making the noise? These are the kinds of questions the judicial system attempts to resolve.

Friedman includes the government's constitutional responsibility "to coin money" and maintain a monetary system as part of the responsibility to be a rule maker and umpire.[15] Friedman, the most outstanding economist in the "monetarist" school, who has demonstrated that overall economic activity closely follows the amount of money in circulation times the speed of its circulation, does not favor using monetary policies for the purposes of stabilizing economic activity. According to Friedman, the government should increase the money supply in accord with the historic growth rate of the economy (about 3 percent per year), and should not have discretionary authority to adjust the money supply to stimulate or suppress economic activity. Consistent with its role as rule maker and umpire, the government should be neutral with regard to the money supply.

Friedman believes that the government has other legitimate roles. For example, he considers it appropriate for government to take on the role of correcting certain market defects.[16] The first of these defects is *technical monopoly:* one company might gain total dominance because it is technically more proficient than its competitors. It might legitimately acquire some advantage—economies of scale or scope—that drive all competitors from the market. Then, the government faces a difficult dilemma. Markets are based on the premise that consumers have choice; they have more than one option from which to choose. But a technical monopoly reduces their options. The dominant firm, if no substitutes exist for what it sells, can withhold product from the market and arbitrarily raise its prices. It can use its monopoly power to hurt consumers.

In many industries, it is possible for firms to gain market dominance via some type of technical advantage. In such industries as electric utilities, the argument that technical monopolies exist has been used to justify regulating utility prices and entry to the industry. Prices are regulated to prevent the monopolist from gaining unfair advantage over consumers. In exchange for limitations on the monopolist's profits, it is guaranteed entry restrictions. No firm can challenge its position as the government does not let potential challengers compete with the dominant firm.

The United States has favored regulation to deal with technical monopoly situations. In many European nations, the answer to this problem has been public ownership. Friedman offers a third alternative—allowing the monopoly to exist without government controls.[17] He reasons for the free market solution on the following grounds. As long as the government does not enforce entry restrictions, the monopolist must always be on guard against the possibility that a competitor will arise and contest its position. The monopolist must be vigilant against the threat of a technological challenge from a latent rival. If regulation were in place, it would not have to face this challenge. Entry barriers make its markets uncontestable, but they also shield it from technological change that can bring benefits to the public. So Friedman holds that free markets work when a firm has gained uncontested dominance through technical means so long as rivals are not excluded entry through regulation. His point is that with public regulation, technological stagnation is likely. The stagnation can be avoided if there is freedom of entry. Policymakers often unthinkingly take a regulatory route when there is a market defect, when this route can be counterproductive.

However, freedom of entry in an industry as capital intensive as electric utilities is extraordinarily difficult. Friedman's argument, while conceptually valid, may be impractical.

Another type of market defect that Friedman believes it is appropriate for the government to try to correct is what he calls a *neighborhood effect.*[18] The classic neighborhood effect is pollution. The premise of a free market is that when two people voluntarily make a deal, they both benefit. If society gives everyone in society the right to make deals, society as a whole will benefit. It becomes richer from the aggregation of the many mutually beneficial deals that have been made. However, what happens if mutually beneficial deals cause a waste product or a by-product (e.g., hazardous waste) that society has to clean up? The two parties to the deal are better-off, but society as a whole has to pay the costs: "the actions of individuals have effects on other individuals," Friedman writes, "for which it is not possible to charge or recompense them."[19]

Friedman's answer to this dilemma is simple: society must charge the parties to the deal the costs of the cleanup because they are responsible.[20] Whatever damage they generate has to be internalized in the price of the transaction. By doing so, the market defect (the price of pollution, which is not counted in the transaction) is corrected. The market price reflects the true social costs of the deal and the parties have to adjust accordingly. Thus, only deals that are truly in the social interest, and not just in the private interest of the parties to the deal, will be consummated.

However, the tendency of the U.S. government has not been to solve this dilemma by supplementing the price system, as Friedman suggests, but by regulating the polluter. Friedman maintains that whenever government intervenes in business activity, there is a cost in reduced freedom. He questions whether government has the technical competence to correct the market defect.[21] Even if it were to impose a tax or charge on the polluting parties, it would have to determine what damage has been caused by the transaction. It would have to give a monetary value to the damage and collect, in the process setting up a burdensome administrative apparatus. When pollution is involved, the damage is often long term (increased sickness and disease) and intangible (reduced visibility). In cases such as these, Friedman believes that the government may be incapable of appropriately levying the tax or charge on the polluters:

> Neighborhood effects impede voluntary exchange because it is difficult to identify the effects on third parties and to measure their magnitude, but this difficulty is present in governmental activity as well. It is hard to know when neighborhood effects are sufficiently large to justify particular costs in overcoming them and even harder to distribute the costs in an appropriate fash-

ion. Consequently, when government engages in activities to overcome neighborhood effects, it will in part introduce an additional set of neighborhood effects by failing to charge or to compensate individuals properly. Whether the original or the new neighborhood effects are the more serious can only be judged by the facts of the individual case, and even then, only very approximately. Whenever government acts, questions must be asked about whether it is capable of achieving what it intends. Well-intentioned government actions to correct market defects, if such actions are not thoroughly examined, can only make matters worse.[22]

A final area where government intervention is appropriate, according to Friedman, is to act on *paternalistic* grounds for those who are incapable or incompetent to act for themselves.[23] The word *paternalism* is an anachronism: remember Friedman wrote his book in 1962. Markets demand a high level of capability and competence. People have to be able to reason about their self-interest, absorb information pertaining to it, and then successfully make deals that make them better-off. Not everybody is up to this task. Children and psychotics certainly do not have the qualities needed. They are not able to make good decisions for themselves.

However, the market presupposes that the people involved are rational and capable of caring for themselves, that if given the freedom, they can use it to further their self-interest. Only rational, informed people who are capable of caring for themselves can make mutually beneficial deals. Thus, Friedman provides the rationale for welfare state-like activities that involve protecting people who are otherwise unable to care for themselves.

Friedman's rationales for government activities, even with these qualifications, are extensive. The government has a role to play in defending the nation, providing for law and order, defining property rights, adjudicating disputes, enforcing contracts, preserving competition, establishing a monetary framework, countering technical monopolies and neighborhood effects, and supplementing private charity by helping people who cannot otherwise help themselves. Friedman admits that his list of appropriate government functions is quite large, but not as large as the actual list of programs that the government of the United States carries out. For many functions of the U.S. government, he can find no justification (see Exhibit 8–3).[24]

The Contemporary Liberal View

A good representative of this school is the Harvard economist Richard Musgrave, who along with his wife Peggy Musgrave has written an important textbook in public finance.[25] Contemporary liberals like the

---

EXHIBIT 8–3   Federal Government Actions that Classic Liberals Cannot Justify

---

Price supports for agriculture.
Tariffs on imports or restrictions on exports.
Rent controls.
Wage and price controls.
Minimum wages.
Maximum interest rates.
Detailed regulations of particular industries.
Mandatory social security, old-age, and retirement programs.
Occupational licensing.
Public housing.
Military conscription.
The creation and maintenance of national parks.
The public delivery of mail.
Publicly owned and operated toll roads.

Musgraves also have a preference for decentralized decision making and individual choice by consumers in the marketplace. To create a rationale for government activity, they need to justify instances that depart from these premises. Their justifications rest on a variety of market imperfections with which classic liberals would be in agreement. These include:

1. *Uncompetitive factor and product markets.* There must be no obstacles to free entry, full market knowledge, and market power on the part of producers and consumers. Government is needed to assure competition and to expand the knowledge of producers and consumers. Thus, it is not only appropriate for government to endeavor to prevent monopoly, but it is also appropriate for it to require that warning labels be attached to cigarettes and other products if citizens otherwise would be unaware of the full risks.

2. *Public goods.* It is appropriate for the government to provide such public goods as national defense, education, roads and canals, which would not be provided in ample quantities were it not for government intervention. These goods would not be provided in ample quantities because the benefits can be enjoyed by everyone, while the costs must be borne by specific groups of providers. The providers could not appropriate sufficient benefits for themselves to justify creating the amount demanded by the public were it not for government involvement.

Contemporary liberals differ from classic liberals in adding the following justifications to their list of reasons for government intervention (see Exhibit 8–4):

EXHIBIT 8–4   The Contemporary Liberal View

Governments needed to deal with market defects:

    Uncompetitive factor and product markets.
    Public goods.
    Justice and equality.
    Employment, price stability, and growth.

---

1. *Justice and equality.* These cherished values may be violated by the market. Thus, government has to make adjustments in the distribution of income via the tax systems and other means such as changes in the laws of inheritance.

2. *Employment, price stability, and growth.* The market system may not guarantee a high level of employment, price stability, and a socially desired rate of growth without government intervention to secure these objectives. To correct for instability in the business cycle, the government should decide to use a variety of fiscal (budgetary) and monetary policies to smooth the cycle.

Even contemporary liberals, however much they are committed to a larger scope for government, admit that governments, no less than private markets, can err and be inefficient in attempting to remedy these market defects.

Three Functions

Contemporary liberals like the Musgraves have divided the appropriate functions of government into three categories: allocation, distribution, and stabilization.[26] Conflicts can exist among these functions and resolving them is a major challenge that governments face.

With respect to *allocation* there is little to distinguish the position of the classic and the contemporary liberals. Both accept the concept of public goods, the need for certain goods that is felt collectively as opposed to individually. These goods cannot be provided by the market system because their ownership is not limited to the individual who pays for them but is shared broadly throughout society. All members of society, not just those who purchase the good, enjoy the benefits. With national defense, police protection, and other goods provided by the government, the resulting gain is available to everyone. If a single person or group of people paid for the benefits, they could not internalize the gain; they could not exclude others from enjoying these goods. Therefore, the goods are called nonrival goods. For example, in the area of defense, each person would have to develop his or her own private army and weapons (as in Beirut) and each person would have to make sure to use the arms and arsenal only for their own gain so as to keep others from being "free-riders" and benefiting. How can one person assure that when he or she unleashes a Trident missile, another person is not to benefit, that others are not to achieve greater security for themselves?

The private market incentive for providing for such public goods is not great, even if the preference for them is high, unless government intervenes. In this instance, voting by ballot replaces free market decision making.

A distinction, however, must be made between public provision of goods and public production.[27] While in all countries in the world—both those with large public and those with large private sectors—the public provision of goods is relatively high (at least 20 percent), in only some countries is there a large degree of public production.[28] The United States is roughly equivalent to other countries in the world with regard to the provision of public goods, but ranks low in public production (only 12 percent). Most public goods (e.g., weapons and weapons systems) in the United States are purchased from the private sector (i.e., the defense industry).[29]

Distribution is a government function contemporary liberals accept but classic liberals reject. Unlike classic liberals, contemporary liberals argue that some alteration in the pattern of inequality is necessary. Contemporary liberals critique one of the major tenets of welfare economics that defines economic efficiency in terms that exclude distributional considerations. The Pareto rule used in welfare economics holds that a change in economic conditions improves the welfare of society when it makes the situation of Person A better without Persons B or C becoming worse-off. The rule is that "someone gains, but no one loses."

However, this rule implies that Person A may make stupendous gains and that the gains for Person A are justified so long as Persons B or C are not worse-off. Person A can advance way beyond Persons B or C in accumulated wealth. This may mean that excessive concentrations of wealth exist at the top of the scale and inadequacy of income exists at the lower end. The blight of poverty then affects nearly everyone in society as it spawns crime, drug addiction, and numerous other social problems. People are worse-off because of the great gains by Person A even if at first Persons B or C have not been directly affected. Thus, contemporary liberals call on governments to make tax transfers, taxing the wealthiest more than the poor and using the money to subsidize low-income households either directly or by means of various social programs. The cost, to the extent that there is a cost, is in so-called deadweight losses, that is, it arises from the inefficiencies of administering government programs. Another cost is reduced efficiency for the economy-as-a-whole as the wealthy tend to choose leisure over work when they realize they cannot keep as much of their marginal earnings.[30]

Another government function over which contemporary and classic liberals disagree is *stabilization*. There are substantial fluctuations in the business cycle; contemporary liberals believe that it is the role of government to try to control these cycles.[31] Unemployment and inflation may plague society unless government acts to change the level of aggregate demand by means of its taxation and consumption capabilities. Of course, government action in this area also may be mistake-prone, and if it is so, it can be destabilizing. This is the essence of Friedman's main critique of macroeconomic policies.

Another problem with these policies is that economies do not operate in isolation but are linked to other economies by means of trade and capital flows. These flows have been rapidly increasing in the post-World War II period. They make it difficult for any single national government to control its economy via macroeconomic stabilization. International cooperation among all major economies is needed, and this cooperation is hard to achieve. Nonetheless, there has been substantial agreement in all countries in the world that governments should act to try to stabilize the business cycle by means of monetary and fiscal policies.

The Neoconservative View

Many people who formerly were contemporary liberals became neoconservatives after the failure of such government programs as the War on Poverty and such government activities as the War in Vietnam. The views of neoconservatives have been elegantly summarized by Rand Institute economist Charles Wolfe, Jr.[32] Classic and contemporary liberals both admit that government failure is possible, and neoconservatives also emphasize this possibility, but they do not treat government shortcomings as systematically as market shortcomings.

Economists discuss government shortcomings in terms of the self-interest of politicians and bureaucrats, but neoconservatives tend to think that this analysis is too limited. The analysis of government failures has to be expanded to include the following:

1. The fact that the government often is the exclusive provider of public goods and has near monopoly status.
2. The uncertainty that surrounds the means of providing these public goods (e.g., on education, what constitutes good teaching and on defense, what is needed to guarantee national security).

3. The unanticipated results of government activities (e.g., good intentions to provide for the poor may result in welfare dependence).

Neoconservatives ask that the shortcomings of the government be compared with the shortcomings of the market before proposals to remedy market defects are carried out (see Exhibit 8–5).

Neoconservatives judge both markets and governments on the basis of two criteria, efficiency and equity. In their emphasis on equity as well as efficiency as standards for judging the market, they are like contemporary liberals. Classic liberals view individual liberty as the highest value; they do not believe that markets are means for other ends (i.e., equity or efficiency) but are ends unto themselves, because they promote liberty. Neoconservatives, however, have looked very closely at what equity means. It has many definitions and connotations. Rawlsian notions of equity favor the lot of the least advantaged in society before the lot of the most advantaged. Marx would distribute to each person according to the person's needs and demand from each according to the person's abilities. Neoconservatives tend to favor equality of opportunity over equality of outcome.

Like classic and contemporary liberals, neoconservatives accept public goods arguments for government intervention. For instance, Wolfe emphasizes that because there may be positive externalities from government investment in research and development, benefits not appropriable by firms operating in the private market, such investment is justified.[33] Another case of underinvestment, if only private market forces are operating, is philanthropy, where the benefits are available to society at large (less crime, drug addiction, and fewer social problems) but the costs are borne exclusively by the donor.

In some cases traditionally labeled market failure, neoconservatives are skeptical of why government should be involved. Their arguments about technical monopoly, for instance, are similar to the ones made by Milton Friedman. So-called technical monopoly situations may not require government intervention if there are potentially contestable markets (think of the airlines). If new entrants can challenge the monopoly, its status is temporary. If a firm has to be constantly on guard against this situation, then it cannot exploit consumers. Potential competitors

---

EXHIBIT 8–5   **The Neoconservative View**

Compare government shortcomings with market shortcomings:

Government exclusive provider.
Uncertain technology for providing goods.
Unanticipated results.

---

are as good as actual competitors. In cases of government involvement, neoconservatives ask if the government can really make things better. The simple fact of a market imperfection does not guarantee that the government can fix it.

Acceptable Government Involvement

Neoconservatives accept a broad range of government involvement. First, government action is justified in providing regulatory services in such areas as the environment (where there are externalities), food and drug controls (where consumers lack information), and radio and television licensing (where there otherwise would be a monopoly). Second, it is justified in producing pure public goods such as national defense, police protection, and the administration of justice. These goods cannot be provided by the private sector. Third, the government is justified in producing quasi-public goods such as education, postal services, and health research. These goods may also be provided by the private sector (so there is some competition), but not in the quantities required by the public. Finally, some transfer programs such as social security and welfare are justified; here is where neoconservatives part company with classic liberals like Friedman because their justification for the transfer programs is on equity grounds—not on grounds of paternalism.

Neoconservatives believe that in theory these activities are justified, but in practice these offerings have proliferated too greatly.[34] Wolfe, for instance, argues that demand for government intervention is inflated for a variety of reasons (see Exhibit 8-6).[35]

Decoupling of Burdens and Benefits

To explain the inflation in demand, neoconservatives emphasize the decoupling of burdens and benefits in government programs.[36] Decoupling explains why some programs like gun control never get passed.

EXHIBIT 8–6   Reasons that Demand for Government Programs Is Inflated

---

- Increased public awareness of market shortcomings.
- Less tolerance for these shortcomings.
- Greater degree of political organization and enfranchisement.
- The rewards to legislators and government officials to publicize problems and find solutions.
- Legislators' need to show that they are taking dramatic actions so that they will be reelected.
- The decoupling of burdens and benefits.

The public that would benefit is large and dispersed, while those that would bear the burden—the gun lobby—are concentrated and well organized. On the other hand, some programs help specific groups, while the burden is widely dispersed throughout the public. The specific groups have a large incentive to organize and to appropriate the benefit, while the broad public, where each person may lose only a few dollars, has little incentive to organize and to oppose the program. Thus, farmers and retirees are formidable political blocs capable of winning substantial gains through the political process because of the decoupling of burdens and benefits. These two types of decoupling the neoconservatives call microdecoupling.[37]

Another type of decoupling occurs when the vast majority enjoys the benefits of government programs, such as progressive taxation (because the vast majority is relatively poor), while a small minority bear the burden (the small minority that provides most of the tax base). As long as political power is based on majority rule, there is a danger of the majority exploiting a minority in a democracy. This type of decoupling the neoconservatives call macrodecoupling.[38]

Government Incapacity

These factors (increased demand and the decoupling of benefits and burdens) are used by neoconservatives to explain why government has grown. However, their argument does not stop with government growth. They also stress the incapacity of government to effectively manage the programs that have been created.[39] Conditions such as the following lead to ineffective management:

1. Without competition, it is hard for the government to achieve adequate levels of efficiency and quality in the provision of services.
2. It is difficult to define and measure the output of government programs.
3. There is no bottom-line termination mechanism.

In a market, the costs of producing or sustaining an activity are linked to the prices charged for it. The link is provided by consumers who decide what to buy. In the government, revenues come from nonprice sources (i.e., taxes) that are only indirectly linked to the services that are provided. Tax payers do not directly obtain goods and services for their tax dollars. All they can do to express their dissatisfaction is to vote out of office the politicians who supported the programs they opposed. However, these politicians probably also have voted for other programs that the taxpayers favored. The taxpayers cannot unbundle their support for politicians in the same way they unbundle their decisions to buy goods and services in the market place.

The result is that government agencies have less need than businesses to justify their actions. The standards they use to manage day-to-day operations, including evaluating personnel and determining salaries, promotions, and perquisites, can be vague. Private internal goals (what Wolfe calls internalities) may dominate and take precedence over the agencies' explicit public goals.[40]

Additional problems affect the supply of government services.[41] First, the systems government is attempting to influence are very complex. Efforts to correct market failures in one area may create unanticipated consequences in another. In addition, although inequality of income is less of a problem, inequality of power and privilege among government officials can be equally problematic. When one group has the right to command and coerce another, abuses are likely.

Government in Practice

Government policies are not crafted by economic theoreticians, whether they be classic or contemporary liberals or neoconservatives, but by politicians, and fathoming what politicians do and why they do it is a complicated matter. The deliberations that determine political outcomes are influenced by the constitutional system of checks and balances instituted by the founders of the American republic. The founders imagined a large country with diverse interests. Fearful of powerful majority, they tried to create a system where no single faction could dominate. The participants in political controversies, therefore, are wide-ranging and diverse. They include citizens, interest groups, corporations, trade associations, environmental organizations, federal bureaucrats, and the media. Different professional groups—scientists, physicians, engineers, and lawyers—provide expert opinion. Sages, seers, and pundits of all kinds testify in front of congressional committees, appear on talk shows, and write columns for newspapers. Policy is affected by factual information, theory, beliefs, values, attitudes, conjectures, statistics, and anecdotes. When economists are consulted, if at all, they are simply a part of this process.

Moreover, the economists who are consulted often disagree. Among economists there is a broad consensus that, everything else being equal, markets are superior to government in achieving efficient outcomes. Among them, there is also an equally broad consensus about market defects that might justify government intervention to guarantee the efficient outcomes that the market is incapable of producing. However, when it comes to actually applying these principles to particular instances, disagreements exist.

Traditional Conservatives

Moreover, another group not discussed so far, traditional conservatives, do not share the individualistic premises of the economists.[42] They do not value individual freedom as the highest good, and do not see free markets, inviolable property rights, and limited governments as the means to assure that freedom. Rather, they follow in the footsteps of Sir Edmund Burke, the 19th-century British philosopher, who was a critic of the French Revolution and individual rights. The traditional conservatives argue that institutions like the family, church, and state are important in stabilizing the social order. These collective institutions, which help protect the delicate fabric of society and promote law and order, come before individual rights.

The Fusionist Conservative Coalition

Both classic liberals and traditional conservatives have found a home in the modern Republican party, but their viewpoints are different. The fusionist conservative coalition which elected Ronald Reagan and George Bush appealed to both classic liberals and traditional conservatives. Reagan, as a representative of this coalition, showed his hostility to big government and favored market forces. At the same time he supported large increases in defense expenditures and maintained that the family and church should be relied upon to mitigate social problems. The eclectic forces brought together in the Republican coalition helps explain its inconsistencies on an issue like abortion, which classic liberals permit and traditional conservatives prohibit.

　If their viewpoints are so different, how could classic liberals and traditional conservatives find a common home in the Republican party? An important reason is that they both vigorously opposed communism, the classic liberals for communism's repressing individual rights and markets, and the traditional conservatives for communism's atheism and its opposition to organized religion.[43] With the decline of communism, the fusionist conservative coalition also may come apart (an example is the 1992 Republican primary challenge to President Bush by Pat Buchanan).

Summary and Conclusions

Economic theory is one of the main foundations for contemporary ideology about the state. Economists believe that markets are the superior means for organizing a nation's economic life; their preference is for a minimal state. Most believe that the individual consumer should be sovereign. Economists contrast *consumer sovereignty* with rule by government. Consumers should govern because individuals are best able to judge their needs and preferences through the deals they make in the marketplace. Through the invisible hand of the marketplace, where individual consumers are able to freely consummate deals that are in their best interests, society prospers. Reflective of those deals are the laws of the market, supply and demand, which move the goods of a society to their most productive uses. No central planning agency of government can achieve with the same wisdom and foresight what freely cooperating consumers accomplish on their own.

With regard to government, economists, however, are not anarchists. They see it as playing an important role. Most economists accept that government should provide for the common defense (the armed forces), establish domestic order (police), make laws and settle disputes (legislatures and the courts), regulate unfair business practices, protect citizens from monopoly and the undesired side-effects (externalities) of market activities, and provide them with some of the collective goods (e.g., highways) they seek but which their voluntary behavior does not provide. The question is not so much one of permitting or not permitting government activity, but of determining the proper mix of government and markets in a well-functioning system.

Although economists are critical of many aspects of government, their rationales for government activity justify the expenditure of vast sums on such government programs as defense, education, and the building of roads and highways and give ample room for the emergence of huge government deficits.

Even though economists share a preference for markets and recognize that government has a role to play in correcting market defects, they divide with regard to the following points:

1. Classic liberals emphasize individual liberty and believe that big government is the gravest threat. They prefer a minimal state in which the functions and size of government are severely limited. Every infringement by government on individual rights is to be avoided. However, even classic liberals recognize that government inevitably has to perform certain functions, including providing for the common defense, assuring domestic order, settling disputes, correcting market defects, and aiding people (such as minors and the insane) who are unable to compete in the market.

2. Contemporary liberals have a different starting point as they begin with community values, such as justice and the common welfare, instead of individual happiness. To promote community goals, they accept that the government should try to smooth the business cycle and that its programs should redistribute income from the wealthy in society to the less advantaged (see the feature below, "On Property and Poverty"). It is appropriate for government to provide people with certain basic needs such as jobs, food, clothing, and shelter. In this way, all people are on a more equal footing in the competition that goes on in the marketplace.

3. While neoconservatives share the same ends as contemporary liberals, they are more skeptical of the government's abilities to achieve them. They emphasize that whenever the government acts, unanticipated side-effects can occur, which run counter to what the government intends. Thus, in trying to provide for aid to the disadvantaged, the gov-

---

On Property and Poverty

It is interesting to note that classic liberals and contemporary liberals both can appeal to John Locke's views on property.[1] Locke believed that property was the result of people's hard work, applied skills, and unusual talent and that therefore they were entitled to the fruits of their labor. On the other hand, he felt that no person should own more property than that person could properly use. According to this "spoilage principle," the government had the right to redistribute any excess.

With regard to poverty, the classic liberal would like to see problems like poverty solved by the voluntary actions of private charities and social welfare agencies, but recognizes that government might have to play a role. The contemporary liberal stresses that in an increasingly interdependent society, it is impossible for people to participate in the economy in isolation from each other. Whenever voluntary deals are made, they are likely to affect others who are not immediate parties to the deals. The right to freedom, moreover, is not sufficient if one does not also possess the means, that is, the resources and educational attainments, to express that freedom. Thus, government must give the disadvantaged a place to start in life so that they can catch up with the more advantaged.

All three ideologies agree that unless the problems of the disadvantaged are addressed, society will face more crime, social conflict, and discord, which will hurt everyone. The neoconservatives simply emphasize that there may be little that government can effectively do in this area.

---

[1]P. Navarro, *The Policy Game* (New York: John Wiley & Sons, 1984).

ernment may stifle individual initiative. While its aims are noble, the government's capabilities to remake society are limited.

Discussion Questions

1. Compare the views found in the Declaration of Independence and the Constitution as to why government is needed? Are these views really so different?
2. Why do economists prefer markets to governments?
3. What is a market defect? Give some examples.
4. What is a spillover? Give an example of a positive and a negative spillover.
5. Are governments perfect? What difference would it make if they were?
6. Friedman cites the benefits of an "impersonal market." What are they?
7. What's wrong with democracy, according to Friedman? Why are markets superior?
8. Why can't the armed forces be privatized? Why can't the police (after all, aren't there already many good private security agencies?)? Wouldn't the justice system work better if it were privatized (e.g., people could rely on private conflict resolution centers)? Wouldn't jails and schools be better run if they were privatized? Isn't Friedman really a big government liberal?
9. What do you think about Friedman's argument about contestable markets (freedom of entry) in the case of technical monopoly?
10. Do you think pollution taxes are a good idea? Why or why not?
11. Why doesn't Friedman's paternalism argument justify social security?
12. What is a public good? Why does the government have to intervene to provide it?
13. How do the views of contemporary liberals differ from the views of classic liberals like Friedman?
14. How do the views of neoconservatives differ from the views of classic liberals like Friedman?
15. How do the views of neoconservatives differ from the views of contemporary liberals?
16. What does microdecoupling mean? What does macrodecoupling mean?

17. Why is government not better at providing goods and services to the public? Why is it not more efficient?
18. What is the fusionist conservative coalition?

Endnotes

1. M. Friedman and R. Friedman, *Free to Choose: A Personal Statement* (New York: Avon Books, 1979, 1980).
2. "Dear Landlord," *The Economist,* February 9, 1991, pp. 75–76 (a review of "Directly Unproductive Profit-seeking Activities," by J. Bhagwati, in *Journal of Political Economy,* 1982, 90); C. Wolf, Jr., *Markets or Governments: Choosing between Imperfect Alternatives* (Cambridge, MA: The MIT Press, 1988).
3. H. Leibenstein, "A Branch of Economics Is Missing: Micro-Micro Theory," *Journal of Economic Literature* 17, 1979, pp. 477–502.
4. R. Musgrave and P. Musgrave, "Fiscal Functions: An Overview," in *The Politics of American Economic Policy Making,* ed. P. Peretz (Armonk, N.Y.: M. E. Sharpe, Inc., 1987), pp. 3–22.
5. M. Friedman, *Capitalism and Freedom* (Chicago: University of Chicago Press, 1962).
6. G. Gilder, *Wealth and Poverty* (New York: Basic Books, 1981).
7. C. Wolfe, Jr., *Markets or Governments: Choosing Between Alternatives* (Cambridge, MA: MIT Press, 1988).
8. Friedman, *Capitalism and Freedom.*
9. Cited by P. Navarro, *The Policy Game* (New York: John Wiley & Sons, 1984).
10. Friedman, *Capitalism and Freedom.*
11. Ibid.
12. Ibid., p. 23.
13. Ibid.
14. Ibid.
15. Ibid.
16. Ibid.
17. Ibid.
18. Ibid.
19. Ibid.
20. Ibid.
21. Ibid.
22. Ibid., pp. 31–32.
23. Ibid.
24. Ibid.
25. R. Musgrave and P. Musgrave, "Fiscal Functions."
26. Ibid.
27. Ibid.
28. Ibid.
29. Ibid.
30. Ibid.

31. Ibid.
32. Wolfe, *Markets or Governments.*
33. Ibid.
34. Ibid.
35. Ibid.
36. Ibid.
37. Ibid.
38. Ibid.
39. Ibid.
40. Ibid.
41. Ibid.
42. Ibid.
43. Ibid.

9 | INDUSTRIAL POLICIES

Laissez-faire should be the general practice; every departure from it, unless required by some great good, is a certain evil.

John Stuart Mill

Introduction and Chapter Objectives

Many people maintain that the U.S. government should be doing more to promote the international competitiveness of U.S. business. This chapter provides historical perspective on the relationship between government and business in the United States and examines the debate about what the government should be doing for business today.

Historically, two different views have contested for dominance: Jeffersonians have believed in a noninterventionist state and Hamiltonians in an active central government that promotes the nation's commerce. The reality is that government policies and programs have affected U.S. businesses in many ways, changing the size and structure of markets and the costs of doing business. Post–World War II policies were dominated by two innovations in the role of government–business cycle management and the growth of the new social regulation (e.g., occupational safety, pollution prevention, and affirmative action). These were followed by a wave of deregulation of formerly controlled industries (e.g., airlines and banks). Government in the United States undoubtedly has grown, but it is not out of proportion with what is found in other industrialized nations. The United States has more government than Japan, but less than most nations of Western Europe.

The current debate focuses on whether the United States should have industrial policies like those found in Japan and Western Europe. This chapter shows that U.S. political traditions are very different from both the Japanese and the European. It would be hard to formulate and carry out industrial policies in the United States. Nonetheless, a need exists for more coordination of U.S. policies, reciprocity legislation and other means to open foreign markets, better means to evaluate petitions for trade relief, and better ways to help people in distressed industries.

The Call for Industrial Policies

Some claim that in a world of increasing international economic competition, the U.S. government has to take an active role in enhancing national competitiveness. They point to the example of the Japanese government and its powerful Ministry of International Trade and Industry (MITI) which, it is argued, played a major role in that country's success.

Governments in other nations of the world routinely try to stimulate specific industries to promote exports (e.g., South Korea and textiles) and protect industries that are in decline (e.g., West Germany and automobiles). These countries may engage in national planning (e.g., France) or create complex systems of tariffs and subsidies that distort free markets. They try to win advantage in international trade by pegging their currencies to the dollar in a way that lowers export or import prices.

Another way to gain advantage is by manipulating capital markets to encourage savings. If the flow of capital across international boundaries is restricted, the people in a country have to accept low rates of return, but industries benefit from low interest rates that stimulate investment and the modernization of industrial facilities. Governments can then use the influence they have on the financial system to direct investments toward industries they favor.

U.S. firms, it is argued, simply cannot compete against subsidized and protected foreign firms unless the U.S. government has similar policies. The argument made by advocates of industrial policies is that governments throughout the world provide their business sectors with special assistance, and that it is only appropriate that the U.S. government should do the same. U.S. government officials should focus national efforts on the "sunrise" industries of tomorrow (e.g., biotech) and help ease the nation out of the "sunset" industries (e.g., smokestack industries such as steel and coal) of yesterday.

Whereas the opponents of industrial policies maintain that government officials are incapable of making such decisions and that the market is best capable of deciding which industries have long-term potential, the advocates argue that the government has no choice but to become involved. They point to the many areas where the U.S. government already is influencing the competitiveness of U.S. business (e.g., a host of federal rules and regulations that distort the operations of a free market). They call, at a minimum, for more coordinated government policy making.

This chapter provides perspective on this issue, giving a historical survey of the role the U.S. government has played in the nation's economic development and exploring the controversy about industrial policies.[1]

Government's Role in U.S. Economic Development

The United States became a nation in 1776, the same year that *The Wealth of Nations* was published. Smith warned against a system of industrial policies, one that endeavors

> either by extraordinary encouragements to draw towards a particular species of industry a greater share of the capital of the society than what would naturally go to it; or, by extraordinary restraints to force from a particular species of industry some share of the capital that would otherwise be employed in it.[2]

Thomas Jefferson envisioned a nation of small proprietors and farmers, each with the liberty to conduct their own affairs as they saw fit:

> The way to have good and safe government is not to trust it all to one but to divide it among the many distributing to everyone exactly the function he is competent to [perform]. . . . It is by dividing and subdividing [the powers of government] . . . until it ends in the administration of every man's farm by himself; by placing under every one what his own eye may superintend, all will be done for the best.[3]

The Federalists, and the Whig party, in opposition to Jefferson, promoted a vision of a strong central government that was heavily involved in the nation's economic activities. They believed that government had to play an active role in the nation's economic development.

Alexander Hamilton, a leader of the Federalists, believed that the dispersed power that Jefferson advocated would disrupt commerce and prevent the nation from making economic progress. Concentrating power in national institutions like a national bank would help further economic development. According to Hamilton, the easing of credit by the bank would help "the operations of commerce among individuals." Industry would be increased, commodities multiplied, and agriculture and manufacturers flourish, and "herein consists the true wealth and prosperity of a state."

Since Hamilton's time, the federal government has helped in the building of railroads, canals, and harbors. It created roads and highways. It employed public funds to construct airports. It has placed, at certain periods, high import taxes on products brought into the United States to protect American business. Indeed, the 1896 platform of the Republican party proclaimed its

> allegiance to the policy of protection as the bulwark of American industrial independence and the foundation of American development and prosperity. This true American policy taxes foreign products and encourages home industry. . . . It secures the American market for the American producer.[4]

Today, the federal government extends loans to the private sector with the Small Business Administration, extending credit to small businesses, and the Federal Home Loan Bank system, to financial institutions for home construction. In times of trouble, particular companies (e.g., Lockheed and Chrysler) have received government loans to bail them out (see the case on the Chrysler bailout at the end of Part III). In addition, agriculture has been the recipient of a well-developed price support system. The U.S. government also provides weather information and other navigational aids to the airline industry. Many businesses either could not have started, would have failed, or would have been less profitable had it not been for the government.

Assisting and Constraining Business

In the United States there is a broad array of policies that both assist and constrain business. The three general effects of these policies are that they change the size of markets, the structure of markets, and the costs of doing business in an industry.[5] These effects exist because government shifts the rules governing commerce. They also exist because government influences businesses more directly, simply by changing its purchases, since nearly a quarter of the nation's product is consumed by government (see the case on Alliant Techsystems at the end of Part III).

The Size of Markets.   Government's direct impacts come from the purchase of products or services (e.g., the defense industry). Indirect effects occur through policies that affect complements or substitutes for the products an industry sells. For the auto industry, a critical complement is gasoline, whose price is affected by government policies (see Chapter 12 on energy policies). Another complement of the auto industry affected by government policies is highways. A substitute for auto travel is mass transit, which depends heavily on federal subsidies.

The Structure of Markets. The markets businesses serve are affected by the government. The patent system rewards innovation by granting a temporary monopoly, which is, in effect, a legal barrier to entry. Public regulation of gas and electric utilities has prevented competition and denied freedom of entry. Trade protection and anti-trust actions have favored one industry over another. The extent of competition and the type of competition in an industry are influenced by government policies.

The Costs of Doing Business. Government policies also affect the costs of doing business. They vary the costs of inputs (raw materials, labor, and capital) thereby changing the overall cost structure. For instance, as well as increasing the costs of all companies that rely on pollution-producing technologies, pollution requirements impact competitors—with different plant and equipment configurations—differently. In so doing, they create competitive advantage for some firms and competitive disadvantage for others. Subsidy policies, in contrast, lower the cost structure in industries by reducing capital and other costs. Indirect subsidies, such as accelerated depreciation and tax credits, abound in the tax codes. These subsidies affect industries differently; with some being favored over others. Likewise, government aid to education or sponsorship of R&D lowers the costs of firms and industries that require this aid.

Government policies have a large role to play in directing free-market forces. Porter's model of business strategy identifies five forces that should be analyzed: rivalry among firms in an industry, the threat of new entrants, the threat of substitute products or services, the bargaining power of suppliers, and the bargaining power of buyers (see Chapter 2). According to Porter, the impact of these forces determines the ultimate profit potential of an industry. However, Porter admits that "no structural analysis [of an industry] is complete without a diagnosis of how present and future government policy, at all levels, will affect structural conditions."[6]

The Amount and Type of Involvement

Some scholars argue that from the time of the American Revolution until about 1929, government involvement in the U.S. economy was minimal.[7] U.S. businesses enjoyed relatively little interference, and as a consequence they flourished. The reality, however, is that government involvement in the U.S. economy, even if greater today than previously, always was an important factor.

Not only was it important, it also was controversial. Politicians were divided about how much involvement and what type of involvement the

United States should encourage.[8] Two different views had an impact. Some politicians cherished the competitive system and its individual values and feared a powerful state. Others welcomed concentrated state power. Believing that government agencies would be staffed by a professional elite capable of making objective and scientifically neutral decisions in the public interest, those who adhered to the view that favored state power felt that its exercise was essential for economic growth.

First Stirrings of Regulation

These different philosophies have been reflected in different policies that the government has enacted. For instance, at about the time that the federal government passed the first national regulatory legislation, the 1887 Interstate Commerce Act (which ultimately would restrict competition in the transportation industry via price fixing and entry restrictions in railroads and trucking), it also passed the 1890 Sherman Anti-trust Act, which was designed to prevent monopoly and promote free markets (see Exhibit 9–1).

During the 1912 national elections, Theodore Roosevelt's Progressive party stood for centralized policies that would force businesses to serve national objectives. Roosevelt hoped that the government would establish a national regulatory agency with the power to control virtually all aspects of commerce. This agency would fix prices for goods made by dominant firms in an industry. It would force companies to publish detailed accounts of their transactions, control the issuance of

---

EXHIBIT 9–1   A History of U.S. Government Involvement in Economic Activities

1887	Interstate Commerce Act
1890	Sherman Anti-Trust Act
1914	Clayton Act and Federal Trade Commission Act
World War I	War Industries Board
Hoover presidency	Associationalist Policies
1933	National Industrial Recovery Act
1935	National Recovery Administration (found unconstitutional)
Late New Deal	Selective regulation of key industries (e.g., airlines, communication, power)
1948	Employment Act
Early 1970s	Growth of new social regulation (e.g., EPA, OSHA, EEOC)
Late 1970s	Demise of Old Economic Regulation (e.g., airlines, trucking, banking)
1980s	Debate about industrial policies

securities, and investigate all business activities. It also would have power over hours, wages, and the other conditions of labor.

In opposition to Roosevelt stood the Democratic party of Woodrow Wilson, which continued to adhere to its Jeffersonian roots. Wilson argued that it was not appropriate for government to try to dictate to businesses how they should run their affairs. Since the business community was very powerful, it would try to capture government if government tried to dictate to it. Large trusts would take control of government and rob people of their independence.

Influential commentators like Walter Lippman criticized Wilson's ideas as appealing to the "planless scramble of little profiteers."[9] Lippman favored big business over the rising class of entrepreneurs, to whom Wilson appealed. According to Lippman, the country needed more concentrated state power, not antitrust policies that would break up industries and restore the economy to "primitive competitive-like conditions."[10] He wrote that the "anti-trust people" were "engaged in one of the most destructive agitations that America has known"; if they succeeded, they

> would be . . . thwarting the possibility of cooperation. . . . They would make impossible any deliberate and constructive use of our natural resources, they would thwart any effort to form the great industries into coordinated services, they would preserve commercialism as the undisputed master of our lives, they would lay a premium on the strategy of industrial war.[11]

The controversy between Wilson and Roosevelt focused on the purposes the nation's antitrust legislation would serve. In 1914, the Clayton Act and the Federal Trade Commission Act were offered as extensions to the Sherman Act. Under Wilson's economic program, called the New Freedom, the purpose of these laws would be to specify which business practices were unfair and uncompetitive and to give a new antitrust commission wide powers to investigate and prosecute. However, those opposed to Wilson hoped that the new legislation would be used to set up a regulatory agency with broad powers to control virtually all aspects of commerce.

A Stronger Federal Role

This battle was won by Wilson, but the proponents of a stronger federal role had other chances to implement the policies they favored. During World War I, the War Industries Board (WIB) gained sweeping control over the national economy. Headed by financier Bernard Baruch, its purpose was to give business leaders the chance to benefit from "combination, cooperation, and common action with their natural competitors."[12]

WIB decisions influenced the production priorities, resource allocations, and pricing decisions of all businesses.

This philosophy of business combination later flourished under the leadership of Secretary of Commerce, and then President, Herbert Hoover. Hoover encouraged businesses to form trade associations and professional societies that would work in close cooperation with government. He then used the FTC to implement his "associationalist" ideas. Business leaders would meet, ostensibly for the purpose of outlawing or suppressing unscrupulous forms of business practice. In reality, the codes devised under FTC authority would often foster collusion; they failed to protect consumer interests. Business leaders used the cover of the federal meetings to fix prices and restrict output.

Ironically, after the Second World War, the Hoover associationalist movement became the model for postwar reconstruction. French statesman Jean Monnet called it "indicative planning" and tried to apply it throughout the European Community. Corporatist and neocorporatist policies have had a stronger hold on the European continent than they have had in the United States, where they have been tried, but only sporadically.[13]

Planning

During the Great Depression, yet another effort to engage in business planning took place in the United States. The New Deal of Franklin Roosevelt was skeptical of the individualism of the past, which it blamed for the country's distress. It therefore sought increased collective action to turn around the nation's ailing economy.

One of its first initiatives was the National Industrial Recovery Act, which Congress passed in 1933. Under this legislation, the federal government set up the National Recovery Administration (NRA). It resuscitated the idea of establishing industry codes meant to cover business practices. The codes covered output, prices, wages, working conditions, investment, and trade practices. By 1934, the NRA had written 450 codes that extended to 5 million companies and 23 million employees.[14]

Although consumer and labor interests were represented on the NRA, the dominant group was business. Through its powerful trade associations, it was able to cast the NRA codes as it wanted. Labor was given increased wages in exchange for industry's being able to raise prices and restrict output. Consumers got nothing except the promise of economic recovery, which did not materialize during the NRA's existence. The other group that was underrepresented on the NRA was small business. The rising entrepreneurial class in the United States had no role to play, and it complained bitterly.

In 1935, the NRA was effectively abolished by a Supreme Court decision that declared it unconstitutional. The Supreme Court included Louis Brandeis, a former adviser to Woodrow Wilson, and his protege Felix Frankfurter, both of whom opposed the movement toward consolidated state power because the party of Jefferson appeared to be suppressing the individualism for which it previously stood.[15]

Regulating Particular Sectors

With the passing of the NRA, the New Deal lost its authority to comprehensively regulate economic activity. It concentrated instead on regulating prices and entry in particular sectors. Rather than broad and comprehensive codes that were meant to cover every industry in the economy, New Deal policies that controlled business were selective. Separate regulatory agencies were established in a number of important industries that were just emerging at the time. In effect, protection was afforded to the high tech, infant industries of the period. The New Deal's efforts may be seen as industrial policies as they covered aviation (the Civil Aeronautics Board), communications (the Federal Communications Commission), and natural gas (the Federal Power Commission). The companies in these industries were shielded from competition in an early period in their existence.

The deregulation movement of the late 1970s brought to an end the regulatory protection of these industries. They were now mature, and the agencies that had been set up during the New Deal to promote new technology and innovation now stifled innovation. They prevented the dynamic adaptation of these industries to new competitive conditions. With deregulation came vast changes in the industries that had been regulated during the depression.[16]

Business Cycle Management

After World War II, the government was expected to play an active role in smoothing the business cycle. The Keynesian revolution was in full swing, and it was believed that through the use of fiscal and monetary policies the government could gain effective control over rates of growth, employment, and prices.[17] It could prevent a depression from occurring again in the United States.

The Council of Economic Advisers (CEA) was created in the White House to assist the president in devising appropriate macroeconomic policies to influence overall economic activity. The Employment Act of 1948 gave the federal government explicit responsibility to maintain economic growth, keep employment up, and assure that price levels were stable. President Kennedy's tax cuts, inspired by CEA director Walter

Heller, directly applied Keynesian principles and helped start the longest continuous period of growth in American history.

When Richard Nixon assumed the presidency, he announced, "We are all Keynesians now." Economists believed that the basic economic problem—business cycle instability—had been solved.[18] They felt that the "level of misery" in society, that is, the combined unemployment and inflation rates, was constant. Thus, fiscal and monetary policy tools simply gave partisan administrations a choice about whether to tolerate more unemployment or more inflation: tight-money Republicans tolerated more unemployment, while Democrats had to worry about a working-class constituency and favored less unemployment.[19] In 1970, no one anticipated, that both the unemployment rate and the inflation rate could increase simultaneously, that the economy again could get so out of control after the advances made by the Keynesians.

The New Social Regulation

Another role for government that gained ground in the post-World War II period was protecting people from the unintended by-products of business activities, including the degradation of the environment, erosion of health, and exclusion of minorities. A new type of regulation, called social regulation, rose in importance.[20] It was far less acceptable to business than the old economic regulation, because it often involved government control over production and the quality of goods and services, not just government control over prices and entry (see Exhibit 9–2).

The new social regulation differed from earlier regulation in two other ways. First, the new agencies often had lengthy, specific laws rather than vague statutes. The Environmental Protection Agency (EPA), for example, had precise pollution reduction targets and timetables, which allowed little room for discretion. In contrast, the Federal Trade Commission, which had no specific timetable for eliminating unfair methods of competition, had great latitude for discretionary behavior. In addition, the new agencies were often organized along functional lines. The EPA, for example, regulated the pollution of all firms, unlike the FCC or the ICC, which were limited to a particular industry. The new agencies, as a result, were less likely to have sympathy with those they regulated. They were more resistant to domination by forces within a single industry.

According to Murray Weidenbaum, who served in the Reagan administration as head of the CEA, these changes signified a "second managerial revolution."[21] The first revolution had involved a shift in decision-making power from the formal owners of business corporations to professional managers. The second revolution, Weidenbaum maintained, shifted power from corporate management to government

---
EXHIBIT 9–2   Federal Regulatory Agencies

New Social	*Old Economic*
1948: Federal Aviation Administration (FAA)	1887: Interstate Commerce Commission (ICC)
1964: Equal Employment Opportunity Commission (EEOC)	1890: Anti-Trust Division (ATD)
	1914: Federal Trade Commission (FTC)
1966: National Transportation Safety Board (NTSB)	1920: Federal Power Commission (FPC)
1970: Environmental Protection Agency (EPA)	1931: Food and Drug Administration (FDA)
1970: Occupational Safety and Health Administration (OSHA)	1933: Federal Deposit Insurance Corporation (FDIC)
1972: Consumer Product Safety Commission (CPSC)	1934: Federal Communications Commission (FCC)
1973: Nuclear Regulatory Commission (NRC)	1934: Securities and Exchange Commission (SEC)
1973: Mining Enforcement and Safety Administration (MESA)	1938: Civil Aeronautics Board (CAB)
1973: Federal Energy Administration (FEA)	

---

planners and regulators, who influenced and controlled key managerial tasks.[22] Weidenbaum argued that the second managerial revolution was responsible for a fundamental change in the nature of society, with the distinction between private power and public power having become increasingly unclear.[23]

Government Growth

Growth in the new social regulation, however, must not be confused with growth in government generally.[24] The new social regulation constitutes less than 3 percent of total federal spending and employment. Rising defense expenditures, transfers to state and local governments, and interest payments on the federal debt dwarf the amount of money spent on regulation.

Though growth in the new social regulation is not its main cause, growth in government is undeniable. To get a sense of its magnitude, it is useful to compare 1929 statistics with current ones. In 1929, there were 68,000 civilian federal employees in Washington, and 500,000 federal civil servants in the nation, of whom 300,000 worked for the Post

Office.[25] Nonetheless, the federal government was smaller than companies such as United States Steel, General Motors, and Standard Oil. By 1940, however, there were a million federal employees, and by 1970 nearly three million (see Exhibit 9–3). The government far surpassed most corporations in number of employees.

Why Government Has Grown

Theories on why government has grown are plentiful.[26]

Economic Development.   In undeveloped nations, taxes and social security contributions typically account for a much lower percentage of gross national product (GNP) than in developed nations. The "law of increasing state activity" attributes growth in government to the complex social changes associated with industrialization. People live closer together, their lives are more connected, and government is more needed both to coordinate their activities and to protect them from one another and from the hazards of industrialization.

Party Politics.   Whether a nation's government is controlled by left-wing or right-wing parties also provides a strong key to the relative degree of change in government spending. There is a strong positive correlation between the size of increases in the public sector and measures of economic equality.

Voting.   Alexis de Tocqueville, in his classic formulation, attributed the expansion of government expenditures to the spread of the franchise and an increase in economic equality.[27] As the franchise is extended, the income of the median voter declines. The median voter, then, has the ability to take income from the rich and redistribute it.

The Supply of Revenues.   Economic development, party politics, and voting are demand-side theories. Other theories focus on the supply side. They explain government growth in terms of the public revenues that can be sustained through taxation. The bracket creep explanation of

---

EXHIBIT 9–3   **Growth of Government in the United States**

Federal Employees	
1929	568,000
1940	1 million
1970	3 million

government growth, for example, holds that a progressive income tax, with inflation and unindexed brackets, moves taxpayers into higher marginal brackets, and leads to increased revenues and a real increase in public expenditures. Decreases in self-employment lead to increases in taxable earnings, as employees are less able to underreport income than are the self-employed.

Legislative Decision Making.   Other explanations for increased government expenditures focus on institutions. For example, in a simplified world, legislators are likely to favor all bills benefiting their own districts. When the costs of such bills are allocated across all districts, legislators agree to pass all bills, provided passage of bills benefiting their own districts is guaranteed.

Bureaucratic Process.   Another theory is that the size and the structure of the budget are the inadvertent result of bureaucratic drift.[28] How bureaucrats solve year-to-year problems influences the problems and sets of solutions available in subsequent years. Short-sighted yearly decisions lead to cumulative long-term problems.

The size and scope of governments in countries with different systems vary a great deal (see Exhibit 9–4). The United States is behind many other countries in total taxes as a percentage of gross national product. The relative size of the government sector is lower in the United States than in any other major developed country except Japan. Federal civilian employment, which peaked at 2.7 million in 1969, has been virtually unchanged since then. No theory provides definitive guidance about what the size and scope of government should be in countries with various social, political, and cultural systems.

Industrial Policies in Other Nations

Today, the debate about government's role concerns industrial policies, which are meant to improve a country's international competitive position by fostering the growth of "strategic" industries.[29] These policies rely on the government to offer incentives and impose constraints. Incentives are intended to cause the occurrence of transactions that would not occur if market forces alone were operating. Constraints are meant to prevent transactions that would occur if market forces alone were operating. The proponents of industrial policies argue that the American economy, which has been threatened by raw materials shortages, rapid inflation, rising unemployment, and economic stagnation, is in decline (see the next chapter). The Japanese, along with other international rivals, have been eroding the economic strength of the United States.

EXHIBIT 9–4   Size of Government in Major Industrial Nations
General Government Expenditures as a Percentage of Gross
Domestic Product (GDP)

	Italy	France	W. Germany	Canada	U.K.	U.S.	Japan
1985	54.6	52.4	48.5	48.5	46.0	36.7	32.6
1979	42.9	45.4	48.0	40.2	41.4	33.0	30.2
1975	41.0	42.5	49.5	41.3	44.5	36.0	25.9
1970	32.5	38.2	39.1	36.4	36.6	32.8	18.2
1965	32.8	37.5	33.8	29.9	33.8	28.1	18.5

SOURCE: Adapted from International Monetary Fund, *World Economic Outlook, April 1985,* p. 109.

Thus, the decline in the American economy justifies a new type of government involvement.

General or nonselective industrial policies available to all industries can be distinguished from sector-specific industrial policies. One example of a sector-specific policy has been the government's long-term efforts to shape the development of American agriculture through production quotas, prices, and income policies. Another example has been its use of price controls, taxes, direct regulation, and research and development to shape energy development (see Chapter 12). On the other hand, the bailouts of Lockheed, Boeing, Continental Illinois, and other companies, are examples of short-term, firm-specific policies. Any intensive long-term effort designed to alter the basic structure of a specific sector may be considered an industrial policy.

These policies raise two separate, but related, issues: the economic issue of whether in the United States it is possible to select the strategic sectors that are worth promoting, and the political issue of whether it is possible to administer a national policy designed to help these sectors.

Have Industrial Policies Helped Other Nations?

Opponents of industrial policies maintain that the extent to which they have actually helped economic development in other countries is exaggerated.[30] For instance, in Japan, MITI has tried but failed to coordinate firm behavior in industries such as cotton spinning, automobiles, and computers. These industries remain intensely competitive despite efforts by MITI to limit competition. In fact, it is possible that MITI's policies have inadvertently spurred competition as firms entered the market in anticipation that they could earn cartel-like profits.

In industries where Japan has the most domestic competitors (e.g., pocket calculators) it has been the most successful. In industries where MITI has been active (e.g., shipbuilding), Japan has confronted overcapacity. MITI has had to play a role in downsizing these industries.

According to the opponents of industrial policies, "Japan, Inc.," which is supposed to thrive on close business-government relations, is largely a myth. In the early stages of industrialization, when a nation is building heavy industry and infrastructure (an example would be the Soviet Union), centrally coordinated industrial policies may be effective. But in later stages, when a nation is involved in worldwide competition in high tech areas, such as integrated circuits and microprocessors, relying on government-coordinated industrial policies is a disadvantage. In this stage, industries have to be prepared for rapid change. They have to be sensitive to market signals and cannot take orders from slow-moving government bureaucracies whose orientation is as much political as it is economic.

The Role of Industrial Policies in France and West Germany

The performance of industrial policies in France and West Germany is open to question.[31] The French indicative planning model, taken from Hoover's associationalism, had as its purpose to "construct a series of national champions" that would compete in international markets. Industrial policies were necessary because of a belief that the scale and efficiency of French industry were not adequate for world competition.

The implementors of these policies were a group of elite civil servants who had been trained in the best institutions of higher learning in France. Insulated from political pressures, they were supposed to be mainly responsive to industry. Their mission was to regulate competitive forces without input from trade unions, consumer groups, small businesses, or farmers, who were excluded from their forums.

French industrial policies came together in national plans. The first four national plans in the post–World War II period had little impact. Nonetheless, after the War the French economy flourished, along with those of other nations, and many attributed its success to these plans. However, only the fifth and sixth plans, formulated in 1968 and 1970, were tests of whether national industrial policies would work; both involved comprehensive efforts at resource allocation, including incomes policies for labor and specific investments for business.

However, they failed and were not completely carried out. No group—neither business, government, nor labor—was willing to cooperate fully. Notable ways in which the plans failed were the efforts to build an internationally competitive computer industry and a commercially viable supersonic aircraft, the Concorde, in cooperation with Britain. In both cases, where government dictates took precedence over market forces, the industries created were uncompetitive.

West German industrial policies, although not leading to national plans, suffered similar setbacks. They did not really get off the ground until the late 1960s when industries like steel, coal mining, and building declined and industries like computers and nuclear power needed to be rejuvenated.

After 1973, the economies of all the West European nations slowed. While their post-World War II performance prior to 1973 surpassed that of the United States, in the rest of the 1970s and in the early 1980s, their economic growth rates slipped behind the United States. Their unemployment rates soared, while the United States created new jobs to absorb the baby boom generation, new immigrants, and women entering the work force for the first time.

Of course, factors besides reliance on industrial policies (e.g., the OPEC oil embargo) contributed to the relative decline of the West European economies (see Chapter 12). However, from the experience West European leaders concluded that the way to create jobs and stimulate economic growth was not to rely on government. Instead, it was to draw on the strengths of entrepreneurs and the market. In a world in which technology and markets were changing rapidly, deregulation was being hailed as the solution to the problems that ailed the Western European economies. It was accepted even in socialist France after a short, but unsuccessful, experiment in increased public ownership. In Eastern Europe and what was once the Soviet Union, there was little doubt that a movement toward a freer economy was needed (see the discussion of the Soviet Union and the East European economies in Chapter 11).

The Japanese Economy

The success of the Japanese economy cannot be explained by industrial policies. A more careful examination starts with two factors: the Japanese banking system and close cooperation among Japanese corporations (compare with Chapter 6).

The Japanese Banking System

Debt has been less expensive in Japan than in the United States and interest rates lower. Japanese firms have had a higher percentage of their capital in debt than in equity. Japanese investors, however, have expected less of a premium for purchasing shares in highly leveraged companies. Capital costs in Japan therefore have been lower than capital costs in the United States.

The providers of capital have been more patient because the structure of banking is different. Savers accept lower rates of interest than U.S. savers. They have not had the wide array of instruments, such as money funds and mutual funds, that have been available to U.S. savers. As a result, they have ended up subsidizing Japanese economic development.

Japan has an extremely well-developed banking system.[32] Three long-term credit banks specialize in long-term loans, and there are 7 trust banks, 11 government banks, and 13 city banks. Also, over 1,000 smaller financial institutions with numerous branch offices offer loans to small businesses. Post offices accept individual savings accounts and offer tax-free interest. Even though a large number of institutions still exist, the government has encouraged consolidation to reduce risk.

The Japanese government extends or withholds credit depending upon whether it believes the banks are investing in industries that will help Japanese economic development. The government-run Bank of Japan provides "window guidance" to the major banks meeting with them every three months and listening to their lending plans. Bank examiners also seek detailed information about the banks' strategies.

In Japan, banks by law are permitted to hold equity in a company and to offer loans. In the United States, they are not allowed to do so. They must establish holding companies, and the holding companies cannot hold too much equity lest they arouse the concern of regulatory bodies. In 1865, a federal court ruled that because the law did not explicitly grant banks the right to own nonbank equities, they were not permitted to do so. And the Glass-Steagall Act of 1933 set up the so-called Chinese Wall between bank trust departments and their commercial banking activities.

A U.S. bank that takes an active role in managing a company (e.g., by removing a manager) faces the prospect of losing its legal status of lender and becoming a shareholder, with all the limitations that entails. If banks expect to retain their status of priority over equity holders in case of default, they cannot exercise effective control. Their risk is less and so is their reward, but they cannot interfere in management. Investors in the United States expect a higher return because they are "residual claimants," the last to be paid back in case of bankruptcy. Officially, they are the company's owners and have hierarchical control.

The institutions that provide money to business in Japan have been very well informed about how the capital is being used. The banks get good information on a regular basis on how the divisions are doing so that annual accounting data are less important. They have intimate knowledge of the people and customers and how product development is progressing, which is more valuable than crude accounting data.

In the United States, banks legally have to have an arm's-length relationship with the companies to whom they lend money. They are not allowed to get to know them intimately and cannot take a vigorous role in managing their affairs. Japanese banks, because the government lets them own equity, do not suffer from such limitations. They can make larger loans at lower interest rates because they are better informed *and* have more power. They can play an active role in knowing and managing the company.

During the mid-1970s recession, U.S. semiconductor manufacturers were forced to cut back on capital spending, but Japanese firms NEC, Hitachi, and Toshiba did not face the same constraint. They were able to continue to invest heavily in new production capacity, and when the recession ended they had the capacity to supply a growing market.

As capital markets in the world have become more open, Japanese savers have been attracted by higher rates of return outside Japan. They have purchased large amounts of assets (such as real estate and U.S. Treasury bonds) on international markets. Similarly, foreign firms have been attracted by the low rates of interest offered by Japanese banks and have sought to obtain loans from these banks. Thus, these banks have grown into the largest in the world. Thus, with the free flow of capital across international boundaries, the distinctive advantages of Japan's banking system may be receding in importance.

Cooperation among Japanese Corporations

Ownership in Japan is much more concentrated than it is in the United States. In a sample of 585 U.S. companies, only about half had single owners with 5 percent or more of shares, while in a sample of 135 Japanese firms all but 6 had a single shareholder with this kind of holding. Whereas the large U.S. owner was likely to be a founding family, in Japan it was likely to be an interlocking group of banks, insurance companies, and manufacturing concerns.

Mitsubishi Bank, for instance, owns significant portions of Mitsubishi Trust Bank, Tokyo Marine, Mitsubishi Heavy Industries, Mitsubishi Corporation (the trading company), Mitsubishi Electric, Asahi Glass, Kirin Beer, Mitsubishi Chemical, and NYK. These companies in turn owned more than a quarter of Mitsubishi Bank's stock.

By contrast, U.S. equity is held by investors. Small ones cannot possibly know a company's true potential—its long-run needs to invest in new technology, to train people, and to keep loyal and committed people working for the company during an economic slowdown. Large investors such as insurance companies, pension funds, and bank holding companies are legal trustees; they cannot engage in actions that may put the funds of their beneficiaries at "unreasonable risk." They must sell off holdings at the first sign of trouble.

Thus, Japanese firms have evolved a system of cooperation that distinguishes them from U.S. firms.[33] Believing that funds and managerial skills are limited, they have pooled their resources. Corporations lacking experience overseas and needing natural resources from abroad join an industrial group.

Earlier industrial groups were called *zaibatsu*. They were pyramid-like structures in which a family held a business that in turn controlled other businesses, which also controlled subsidiaries and affiliated firms. Prior to World War II, the dominant *zaibatsu* in Japan were Mitsui, Mitsubishi, Sumitomo, and Yasuda. After the war, 7 new *zaibatsu* were established, and 16 smaller ones, that operated on a local level, came into existence. Today, the dominant *zaibatsu* are Mitsui, Mitsubishi, and Sumitomo and the banks Fuji, Sanawa, and Dai-ichi Kang. The latter concerns came into existence in their present form after 1965.

Earlier *zaibatsu* derived their power from their commercial might. They were large trading companies, particularly good at helping Japanese businesses penetrate foreign markets. Today's *zaibatsu* obtain their power from their financial clout. They are organized around large banks and insurance companies.

The leaders of the earlier *zaibatsu* were typically very autocratic. Today member companies in the *zaibatsu* have much more independence. *Zaibatsu* today carry on much less of their commerce with other members of the *zaibatsu* (typically less than 30 percent). Goods are bought from nonmember companies if these goods are offered at lower prices.

Still, members of the *zaibatsu* are very highly interconnected. They own stock in each other, have various kinds of financial relations, sometimes share or exchange top managers, and have other types of business ties. The interlocking stock holdings contributed to the stabilization of stock prices. The easy availability of funding during Japan's rapid economic growth was very advantageous to the *zaibatsu* members. The sharing of managerial know-how aided an economy where employees did not usually move from firm to firm. Companies could obtain information about technology and markets that otherwise might not be available to them.

Cooperative ventures have been primarily in importing energy resources, introducing new technologies, launching new businesses, and exporting large turnkey projects. However, new startup high-technology companies have generally found the *zaibatsu* stifling and have not been heavily involved. The *zaibatsu* mainly function in capital-intensive, big projects that can result in large economies of scale. Of course such cooperation among American firms would be prohibited by antitrust laws.

Why Carrying Out Industrial Policies in the United States Is Difficult

The U.S. political tradition makes it difficult to formulate and implement industrial policies. National crises, like war, might be able to unify the American people temporarily, but the Constitutional system is built on checks and balances and divided power.[34]

The American Political Tradition

Four characteristics of the American system that make it difficult to carry out industrial policies should be noted:

1. *A profusion of interest groups.* The founders of the American republic embraced the idea that numerous interests should exist. Diversity reflects the different backgrounds of the American people and the dynamic character of U.S. society. The existence of many interests dilutes the strength of any particular one. Indeed, no single organization represents business or labor in the United States as it does in other countries. Thus, policies favored by one business group are likely to be opposed by another business group. Entrepreneurism in politics, as well as in economics, is a feature of American society that inhibits the creation of coordinated government policies.

2. *The accessibility of political institutions.* No one ever seems to permanently lose a political battle in the United States. Frustrated interests always have appeal to other governmental units. State and local governments exist alongside the federal government. The federal government has three branches (the executive, legislative, and judicial), which in turn are not unified in a coherent and logical way. The executive branch, for instance, has departments that represent diverse interests—business and labor, environmentalists and developers, and so on. Congress too is divided into numerous committees and subcommittees. Even after it has enacted a law, there is no assurance that the law can be effectively carried out, as the bureaucracy is likely to face an array of competing interests with which it must contend when implementing the legislation.

3. *The absence of a neutral administrative elite.* No trusted, professionally based, neutral civil service exists in the United States on the scale that it exists in such Western European nations as France. The U.S. bureaucracy, particularly at its upper reaches where the appointments are almost all political, is more partisan than the bureaucracy in other nations. An impartial bureaucracy would be needed to make decisions about where resources should be spent if industrial policies were implemented.

4. *Activist courts.* Attorneys and judges play a larger role in economic policy making in the United States than they do in other countries. Losers in economic battles can appeal through the courts where their cases may be reexamined by judges sensitive to legal questions of precedent or fairness. The legal system in the United States is particularly protective of the rights of minorities, which is less true of the legal system in other nations.

These obstacles do not mean that industrial policies cannot be carried out in the United States. They simply mean that the U.S. political system has not been designed that it would be easy to do so. An enduring sense of national peril would be necessary if private groups were to permit the government to exercise the kind of authority needed to carry out industrial policies effectively.

The Need Still Exists

The proponents of industrial policies grant that these obstacles exist. Nevertheless, they hold that industrial policies are still necessary.[35] They point to four reasons:

· First, the federal government already is extensively involved in making industrial policy. It is playing a role in a whole variety of industries, but the role it is playing is inadvertent and lacks coherence. For instance, the U.S. tax code favors some industries over others. Federal R&D constitutes nearly half the R&D conducted but federal R&D policies lack clear priorities. They have been formulated without carefully considering their overall effects. At a minimum, the proponents of industrial policies hold that the U.S. government should coordinate the many policies it already has.

· Second, the nature of international competition is such that other nations are providing assistance to their industries—promoting them through subsidies, favorable exchange rates, low-interest rate loans, and in other ways. Thus, the U.S. government also needs to provide help. In some circumstances, it should implement reciprocity legislation to open foreign markets. In others, it could strengthen the role of the Export-Import Bank to make financing arrangements for the purchase of American goods more competitive.

· Third, when industries ask for trade relief, the government needs to have formal criteria to evaluate the claims already in place. It cannot engage in ad hoc policy making in which the claims are evaluated separately, according to unique circumstances. Moreover, in exchange for the relief it grants, the government has to be in a position to demand concessions, for example, that will force industries seeking relief to modernize. It has to be able to compel them to reduce excess capacity, invest in new plant and equipment, lower wages, and change work rules.

· Fourth, as some industries lose competitiveness and others gain competitiveness, the government has to play a role in easing the transition. It should copy what countries like Japan have done. Japan's Depressed Industries Law provides for the retraining of workers who might otherwise have trouble finding new jobs. Displaced workers need training and assistance so that they can find new jobs. Skills in the industries that are gaining in competitiveness have to be built up so that the emerging industries will have the kind of people they need to sustain an advantage.

Synfuels: An Unsuccessful Industrial Policy

The Carter administration introduced its synfuels program with much fanfare. Declaring the "moral equivalent of war," it proposed to spend some $88 billion dollars in the 1980s to speed the development of synthetic fuels.

The initial proposal called for raising this money through taxes on oil-company windfall profits. The program would be administered by a private corporation, later called the Synthetic Fuels Corporation (SFC). Chartered and initially financed by the federal government, the corporation would be given the freedom to exercise its judgment on the most prudent investment of its capital. It would be the nation's wealthiest corporation, with assets more than twice those of Exxon. Its goal would be to create the equivalent of 2.5 million barrels of oil daily by 1990, at a price of between $200 and $400 billion.

Carter's action was supported by advisers such as Paul Ignatius, Lloyd Cutler, and Eugene Zuckert, who had distinguished themselves in the New Deal. Felix Rohatyn, the investment banker noted for urging large-scale public/private enterprises, also promoted synfuels development. These advisers argued that reliance on markets had caused the United States to become energy dependent, and thus markets could not be expected to restore the nation's energy independence.

Constraints   Accompanying the government proposals to offer incentives for synfuel development were constraints,[1] many of which had arisen in the 1970s and were associated with the new social regulation. These constraints were especially important because to justify investment in synfuels, the world price of oil in real terms would have had to nearly double from its 1970 level.

Given this fact, a sponsor of a synthetic fuel project faced the possibility that price controls, environmental constraints, permit delays, and court actions could radically change the economics of a project. An example was the energy industry's concern about future energy rate regulation. Companies were reluctant to invest because the future return might not justify the large risks. They were unwilling to take the downside risks, because they perceived a probable government floor on their upside potential.

Another impediment resulted from environmental policies. For example, would standards be promulgated only after plants became operational or would these standards be known in advance? This question was important because it involved the issue of whether the plants would need retrofitting after they were in use. It therefore affected estimates of project costs and expected profitability. Given the uncertainty, it was difficult for companies to determine if they should proceed with specific projects.

---

[1]H. D. Johnson, "Financing Synthetic Fuel Projects: An Overview," *University of Pittsburgh Law Review* 43, 1981, p. 103.

Synfuels continued

Antitrust regulation created an additional uncertainty. A synthetic fuel producer needed access to raw materials, the ability to transport the raw materials to a production facility, basic production capacity, and the means of transporting and marketing the fuels produced. Few companies were able to carry out all these functions; most preferred to share the risks by entering into joint ventures with other concerns. At a minimum, an integrated oil and gas company would supply the site, a part of the market, and the capital equipment. The engineering company would provide the know-how and other necessary management services. The contemplated joint venture, however, would be closely scrutinized under Section 7 of the Clayton Act as to its effects on competition.

These regulatory uncertainties made it extremely difficult for companies to plan. Instead of a willingness to participate, companies hesitated because of the unknown impact of government policies on future income.[2] Firms were unable to accurately assess risk and opportunity and thus make the trade-offs necessary for investment in synfuels development.

A Slow Start   Even during the Carter administration, the program to produce 2 million barrels of oil a day by 1992 got off to a slow start. The SFC's performance during the Reagan administration was downright abysmal, perhaps justifiably so. As of Janu-

ary 1984, the SFC had made only two financial awards for a total of $520 million to projects that promised to produce about 15,000 barrels of oil per day equivalent (boed) by 1985.

These figures were obviously way below the original 500,000 boed by 1987 prescribed in the Energy Security Act (ESA). No doubt, economic circumstances contributed to the SFC's performance. Corporate enthusiasm for synfuels evaporated by 1981 as the world economy tumbled into its worst recession since the 1930s.[3] As demand for oil dwindled, the energy companies unexpectedly discovered that oil was in oversupply— at least in the short run—so that the price for a barrel of oil fell from $35 in 1980 to $29 in 1984.

With projected profitability for synfuels based on oil prices of about $40 to $70 a barrel, many firms canceled projects either scheduled for or already under construction. By 1982, over half the sponsors for SFC funding under its first solicitation had rescinded their applications.

The case of synfuels shows that the ability of the U.S. government to carry out strongly interventionist, long-term industrial policies is severely limited. It should serve as a warning to those who have called for such policies. Centrally directed development efforts, such as the synfuels program, often go awry. Their goals are not achieved.

---

[2]A. A. Marcus, "Policy Uncertainty and Technological Innovation," *Academy of Management Review* 6, 1981, pp. 443–48.

---

[3]Y. M. Ibrahim, "Latest Oil Uncertainty Concerns Drop in Price rather than Big Rise," *The Wall Street Journal* March 8, 1982; "Synfuel Baby Is Thrown Out with the OPEC Bathwater," *Economist*, March 13, 1981, pp. 182–94.

Institutional Arrangements to Implement These Policies

The proponents of industrial policies believe that institutional arrangements have to be created to implement these policies. They imagine a Council on Industrial Competitiveness in the White House, which would function similarly to the Council of Economic Advisers. In the same way that the CEA is supposed to coordinate the federal government's macroeconomic decisions, the Council on Industrial Competitiveness would coordinate the microeconomic decisions of the federal government.

For proponents of industrial policies, federal government involvement in macroeconomic matters is insufficient. Since the government is already involved in microeconomics, proponents say, it should be more careful about what it is doing. Given the realities of international competition, it has to coordinate its efforts.

In addition, proponents imagine that there would be a Bureau of Industrial Analysis in the Commerce Department, which would provide industry analyses to the federal government in the same way that the Bureau of Labor Statistics provides analyses of conditions in labor.

Opponents of industrial policies believe that these additional government bureaucracies are unnecessary and unwarranted, that they extend the scope of government far beyond what can be defended in economic theory. They believe that the industrial decisions government bureaucrats would be asked to make are best left to the market. Even if coordinated industrial policies have facilitated economic growth in other nations, they would not succeed in the United States with its special political traditions.

An Aborted Effort to Carry Out an Industrial Policy

An analysis of the origins and the development of the synfuels program suggests why it is difficult to establish and execute long-term, strongly interventionist industrial policies in the United States.[36] The synfuels program was part of the larger and flawed effort to create a national energy policy.[37] For a short period in 1979, it was the cornerstone of this policy. However, the synfuels policy failed (for more detail, see the feature on the previous pages, "Synfuels: An Unsuccessful U.S. Industrial Policy").

In carrying out industrial policies in the United States four problems stand out:

- During the course of carrying out a policy, market perceptions about the relative costs and benefits of a policy change.
- Division within government (e.g., between prodevelopment and antidevelopment forces or between politicians with different views of the proper role of government) occurs.

- Industry disagreement (e.g., about whether a program should exist and how extensive it should be) takes place.
- Lack of consensus about the appropriate means to achieve the policy goals exists.

These factors suggest inherent difficulties that are likely to affect any effort to initiate and carry out long-term, strongly interventionist industrial policies in the United States. Only overwhelming mass support for such policies, based on clear and compelling reasons (e.g., national defense), are likely to overcome these obstacles.

Summary and Conclusions

This chapter has portrayed the history of business-government relations in the United States in terms of the debate about centralized planning. This debate has a long history, going back to colonial times and the period of Jefferson and Hamilton.

The U.S. government has provided practical assistance to American businesses in many ways. Its policies affect the size and structure of markets and the costs of doing business. Government policies are of strategic importance to all firms.

Among the most important changes in the role of government in the post-World War II period was its involvement in fiscal policy management, its expanded role in social regulation, and its diminished role in economic regulation. In the 1980s, the debate about government shifted: given the realities of the new international competition, what should it do? Proponents of industrial policies maintained that the U.S. government should play an active role, like that of the governments of successful nations—Japan, France, and West Germany. Opponents held that the U.S. government was incapable of playing a larger role. Also, government efforts were impeded by a profusion of interest groups, access to political institutions, the absence of a neutral administrative elite, and activist courts. Nonetheless, more government involvement was needed in areas such as coordinating its policies, opening foreign markets, modernizing industries seeking trade relief, and aiding people in distressed industries.

Discussion Questions

1. Give some examples of what governments do to promote business. Should the United States carry out similar policies?

2. How would you distinguish the views of Jefferson and Hamilton on the role of government in economic development? Has the United States evolved in a more Jeffersonian or more Hamiltonian direction?

3. Give examples of the way the U.S. government influences business. What strategic importance do these influences have?

4. Describe the controversy surrounding the passage of the 1914 FTC Act.

5. Explain why you would or would not agree with the statement that the Democrats always have been the party of big government and the Republicans always have been the party of small government.

6. What was the NRA? What was it designed to accomplish? Why was it declared unconstitutional?

7. Distinguish between the new social regulation and the old economic regulation.

8. Discuss the major innovations in U.S. government policy vis-à-vis business after World War II.

9. Governments throughout the world have grown in the post–World War II period. Why?

10. Is the growth of government in the United States out of line with the growth of government in other nations in the world? How much government does the United States require?

11. To what extent have industrial policies been successful in Japan, France, and West Germany?

12. Describe the banking system in Japan. What advantages does the system provide the Japanese economy?

13. Describe industrial groups in Japan. What advantages do these groups provide the Japanese economy?

14. Why is it so difficult to formulate industrial policies in the United States?

15. What does the synfuels example show?

16. In your opinion, should the United States have industrial policies? If yes, what kind of industrial policies should it have?

Endnotes

1. P. Navarro, *The Policy Game* (New York: John Wiley & Sons, 1984).
2. A. Smith, *The Wealth of Nations* (New York: The Modern Library, 1965), p. 650.
3. K. Prewitt and S. Verba, *An Introduction to American Government* (New York: Harper and Row, Publishers, 1974).
4. Ibid., p. 27.
5. J. Gale, R. A. Buchholz, and A. A. Marcus, *Achieving Competitive Advantage through the Political Process: Business Strategy and Legitimacy,* discussion paper No. 75, The Strategic Management Research Center, The University of Minnesota, 1987; J. Gale and R. A. Buchholz, "The Political Pursuit of Competitive Advantage: What Business Can Gain from Government," in *Business Strategy and Public Policy,* ed. A. A. Marcus, A. M. Kaufman, and D. R. Beam (Westport, Conn: Greenwood Press, 1987), pp. 31–41.
6. M. E. Porter, "The Competitive Advantage of Nations," *Harvard Business Review,* March-April 1990, p.28.
7. M. Friedman and R. Friedman, *Free to Choose: A Personal Statement* (New York: Avon Books, 1979, 1980).
8. A. Kaufman, L. S. Zacharias, and A. Marcus, "Managers United for Corporate Rivalry: A History of Managerial Collective Action," *Journal of Policy History* 2, 1990, pp. 56–97; T. K. McCraw, "Mercantilism and the Market: Antecedents of American Industrial Policy," in *The Politics of Industrial Policy,* ed. C. E. Barfield and W. A. Schammbra (U.S.A.: American Enterprise Institute, 1986), pp. 33–62; J. C. Miller, T. F. Walcott, W. E. Kovacic, and J. A. Rabkin, "Industrial Policy: Reindustrialization through Competition or Coordinated Action?" *Yale Journal on Regulation* 2, 1984, pp. 1–37.
9. Cited in Miller et al., "Industrial Policy,"
10. Ibid.
11. Ibid., p.10.
12. Ibid. p. 124.
13. Ibid.
14. Kaufman, et al., "Managers United for Corporate Rivalry"; Miller, et al., "Industrial policy."
15. T. K. McCraw, *Prophets of Regulation: Charles Frances Adams, Louis D. Brandeis, James M. Landis, Alfred E. Kahn* (Cambridge, Mass.: Harvard University Press, 1984)
16. A. Marcus, "Business Demand for Regulation: An Exploration of the Stigler Hypothesis, "*Research in Corporate Social Performance and Policy* 7, 1985, pp. 25–46; A. Marcus, "Airline Deregulation, Business Strategy, and Regulatory Theory," in *Public Policy and Economic Institutions* (Greenwich, Conn.: JAI Press, 1990); A. Marcus, "Airline Deregulation: Why the Supporters Lost Out," *Long Range Planning* 20, no. 1, 1987, pp. 90–98; B. Mitnick, *The Political Economy of Regulation* (New York: Columbia University Press, 1980).

17. Kaufman et al., "Managers United for Corporate Rivalry."

18. J. D. Gwartney and R. L. Stroup, *Economics: Private and Public Choice* (Harcourt Brace Jovanovich, 1987).

19. A. Marcus and B. Mevorach, "Planning for the U.S. Political Cycle," *Long Range Planning* 21, 1988, pp. 50–56; P. Young, A. Marcus, R. S. Koot, and B. Mevorach, "Improved Business Planning through an Awareness of Political Cycles," *Journal of Forecasting* 9, 1990, pp. 37–52.

20. W. Lilley and J. C. Miller, "The New Social Regulation," *The Public Interest*, Spring 1977, pp. 49–62; P. Weaver, "Regulation, Social Policy, and Class Conflict," *The Public Interest*, Winter 1978, pp. 45–64; A. A. Marcus, *The Adversary Economy: Business Responses to Changing Government Requirements* (Westport, Conn.: Quorum Books, 1984).

21. M. L. Weidenbaum, "The Future of Business/Government Relations in the United Sates," in *The Future of Business: Global Issues in the 80s and 90s*, ed. M. Ways (New York: Pergamon Press, 1979), pp. 48–76.

22. Ibid.

23. Ibid.

24. Marcus, *The Adversary Economy.*

25. B. D. Porter, "Parkinson's Law Revisited: War and the Growth of American Government," *The Public Interest*, Summer 1980.

26. P. Larkey et al., "Theorizing about the Growth of Government," *Journal of Public Policy*, May 1981, p. 167; D. R. Cameron, "The Expansion of the Public Economy: A Comparative Analysis," *American Political Science Review* 72, 1978, pp. 1243–61; J. B. Kau and P. H. Rubin, "The Size of Government," *Public Choice* 37, no. 2, 1981, pp. 261–74; A. Meltzer and S. Richard, "A Rational Theory of the Size of Government," *Journal of Political Economy*, October 1981, pp. 914–27; A. T. Peacock and J. Wiseman, *The Growth of Public Expenditures in the United States* (Princeton, N.J.: Princeton University Press, 1961).

27. A. De Tocqueville, *Democracy in America* (Oxford: Oxford World Classics, 1935).

28. C. E. Lindblom, "The Science of 'Mudding Through,' " in *Business Strategy*, ed. H. I. Ansoff (New York: Penguin Books, 1977, pp). 41–60.

29. J. L. Badaracco and D. B. Yoffie, " 'Industrial Policy': It Can't Happen Here," *Harvard Business Review*, November-December 1983, pp. 97–105; C. E. Barfield and W. A. Schammbra, eds., *The Politics of Industrial Policy* (U.S.A.: American Enterprise Institute, 1986), pp. 187–205; A. T. Denzau, *Will an 'Industrial Policy' Work for the United Sates?* formal publication No. 57, Center for the Study of American Business, Washington University, 1983; A. A. Marcus and A. M. Kaufman, "Why It Is Difficult to Implement Industrial Policies: Lessons from the Synfuels Experience," *California Management Review* 28, 1986, pp. 98–114; P. Norton, "A Reader's Guide to Industrial Policy," in *The Politics of American Economic Policy Making*, ed. P. Peretz (Armonk, NY: M. E. Sharpe, Inc., 1987), pp. 126–27; K. Phillips, *Staying on Top: The Business Case for a National Industrial Strategy* (New York: Random House, 1984); C. L. Schultze, "Industrial Policy: A Solution in Search of a Problem," *California Management Review* 25, 1983, pp. 5–15.

30. G. Gilder "A Supply-Side Economics of the Left," *Public Interest*, Summer

1983, pp. 29–43; A. Etzioni, "The MITIzation of America," *Public Interest,* Summer 1983, pp. 44–51.

31. S. S. Cohen, S. Halimi, and J. Zysman, "Institutions, Politics, and Industrial Policy in France," in *The Politics of Industrial Policy,* ed. C. E. Barfield and W. A. Schammbra (U.S.A.: American Enterprise Institute, 1986), pp. 106–27; D. C. Mueller, ed., *The Political Economy of Growth* (New Haven, Conn.: Yale University Press, 1983).

32. L. L. Jacque and H. V. Perlmutter, *Global Financing for Multinational Corporations: The Quest for Geocentric Advantage,* advanced management practices paper No. 4, Strategic Management Research Center, December 1987; W. Ouchi, *The M-Form Society: How American Teamwork Can Recapture the Competitive Edge* (Reading, Mass.: Addison-Wesley Publishing Co., 1984); D. P. Quinn and R. Jacobson, "Industrial Policy through the Restriction of Capital Flows: A Test of Several Claims Made about Industrial Policy," *American Journal of Political Science* 33, 1989, pp. 700–736; C. Rapoport, "Japan's Big Knack for Coming Back," *Fortune,* November 6, 1989, pp. 131–38.

33. L. C. Thurow, ed., *The Management Challenge: Japanese Views* (Cambridge, Mass.: The MIT Press, 1985).

34. Badaracco and Yoffie, "Industrial Policy: It Can't Happen Here"; A. Wildavsky, "Industrial Policies in American Political Cultures," in *the Politics of Industrial Policy,* ed. C. E. Barfield and W. A. Schammbra (U.S.A.: American Enterprise Institute, 1986), pp. 15–32.

35. S. E. Eizenstat, "Reindustrialization through Coordination or Chaos?" *Yale Journal on Regulation* 2, 1984, pp. 39–51.

36. Marcus and Kaufman, "Why It Is Difficult to Implement Industrial Policies."

37. R. D. Hershey, "Synthetic Fuels: Program Lags," *The New York Times,* May 12, 1983, p. 430; R. D. Hershey, "Energy: Blessing or Boondoggle?" *The New York Times,* September 21, 1980; A. Kaufman, "Public Policy and Synthetic Fuels: Challenges to Business Solidarity, 1984," in *Research in Corporate Social Performance and Policy* 6, ed. L. Preston (Greenwich, Conn.: JAI Press, 19); P. Nulty, "The Tortuous Road to Synfuels," *Fortune,* September 8, 1980, pp. 58–64; R. H. K. Vietor, *Energy Policy in America since 1945: A Study of Business-Government Relations* (New York: Cambridge University Press, 1984).

10

GLOBAL COMPETITION

While America's commitments steadily increased after 1945, its share of world manufacturing and of world gross national product began to decline, at first rather slowly, and then with increasing speed . . . ; there is the country's industrial decline relative to overall world production, not only in older manufacturers, such as textiles, iron and steel, shipbuilding, and basic chemicals, but also . . . in robotics, aerospace technology, automobiles, machine tools, and computers. . . . The uncompetitiveness of U.S. industrial products abroad . . . [has] . . . produced staggering deficits in visible trade.

Paul Kennedy, *The Rise and Fall of the Great Powers.*

Introduction and Chapter Objectives

This chapter explores opposing views about recent trends in the world economy and America's role in it. The U.S. economy is supposed to be in decline; manufacturing capabilities are said to have eroded, and the United States is no longer as strong as it once was in high-technology industries like supercomputers and semiconductors. Causes include low investment and high capital costs. By contrast, Japan has been able to sustain a higher level of savings and investment than the United States. The apparent decline of the U.S. economy has led some to question the principles of free trade. We will review the arguments for free trade and we will compare the strengths and weaknesses of the world's major industrial nations—West Germany, Japan, Great Britain, and the United States. This chapter also includes some recommendations about what the United States can do to improve its competitiveness.

The Decline of the U.S. Economy

The arguments made in the opening quotation from Paul Kennedy are by now very familiar.[1] The Japanese, along with other international rivals, are supposed to be eroding U.S. economic strength. Some of the following points have been made about the U.S. economy:[2]

· American manufacturing is held back by a proliferation of rules and unnecessary control systems. It is well suited to making mass items in a predictable and routinized fashion, but it is not well suited to flexible manufacturing that involves skilled labor and rapidly changing technologies in knowledge intensive industries.

· Having been hurt by declining mathematical scores among students, a glut of attorneys, and a shortage of machinists and skilled laborers, the productivity of U.S. manufacturing has fallen seriously behind that of other nations.

· Too many American managers lack hands-on knowledge of technologies and production. They are experts in the arts of financial manipulation, mere "paper entrepreneurs," who have no understanding of what happens on the factory floor.

Some believe that "U.S. industry's loss of competitiveness . . . has been nothing short of an economic disaster."[3] It is no longer true that each generation of Americans will be able to look forward to more comfortable conditions than its predecessors experienced.

However, this dim view of U.S. economic prospects is not shared by everyone.[4] Some feel that the relative decline of the United States was inevitable, natural, and indeed beneficial; certainly, it was not something to cause alarm. The easy superiority achieved by the United States after World War II simply was not sustainable.

Indeed, U.S. intentions have been to help other nations achieve greater equality with itself. After World War II, the United States contributed to the recovery of the Western European and Japanese economies, because it needed strong trading partners. And it helped create them through such programs as the Marshall Plan and the promotion of free trade.

According to economic theory, each nation should specialize in what it does best; through free trade, the wealth of all nations will increase.[5] In the short term, all economies including that of the United States have to undergo adjustments, which include bankruptcies and the restructuring of industries, but in the long term all nations will benefit.

The Performance of the U.S. Economy

How well is the U.S. economy doing? A 1985 report by President Reagan's Commission on Industrial Competitiveness claimed that U.S. ability to compete internationally was facing unprecedented challenges
from abroad.[6] U.S. world economic leadership was at stake, as was its
ability to provide Americans with the standards of living and opportunities to which they aspired.[7] Contrary to these views, however, a 1984
New York Stock Exchange report stated that, with the exception of selected industries, the U.S. economy remained competitive with the
economies of Japan and Western Europe.[8]

In some areas, the U.S. economy was performing very well.[9] Living
standards in the U.S. continued to be equal to or above those in Western
Europe and Japan. Social mobility was high. Almost half the top quarter
of earners in the United States fell from that position every seven years,
and nearly half the bottom quarter moved up. In comparison to Western
Europe and Japan, the U.S. economy was a powerful job creator. It absorbed the "baby boom" generation and nearly 12 million legal and illegal immigrants and created over 22 million jobs in the 1970s. The West
European economies, in contrast, had net job losses and high rates of
unemployment. From 1960 to 1980, 30 million new jobs were created in
the United States, but only 7.5 million in Japan and 2.5 million in Western Europe (see Exhibit 10–1).

Service Sector Jobs

Nearly 70 percent of the U.S. economy was part of the service sector;
that meant that millions of new jobs had been created in labor-intensive
service industries such as health care and fast foods.[10] Manufacturing employment in the United States had declined from 26.4 percent
of total employment in 1960 to under 20 percent in 1980. Historically,

EXHIBIT 10–1 Unemployment Rates in Major Industrialized Nations

	1990	1985	1980	1970	1960
Japan	2.1	2.6	2.0	1.2	1.7
United States	5.5	7.2	7.1	4.9	5.5
United Kingdom	5.9	11.2	7.0	3.1	2.2
West Germany	7.1	7.2	6.4	.5	1.1
Canada	8.1	10.5	7.5	5.7	6.5
France	10.2	10.4	6.4	2.5	1.5

SOURCE: Adapted from Directorate of Intelligence, Central Intelligence Agency, *Handbook of Economic Statistics* (Washington, D.C.: Government Printing Office, 1991).

productivity had grown most rapidly in manufacturing; technological progress had been achieved through automation and economies of scale. The service industries depended more upon personal relations (e.g., medicine or hairstyling) than manufacturing, and they resisted the introduction of factors that were responsible for manufacturing's gains. Only some service industries continued to see annual gains in productivity rates, and even those that were improving were not doing so at the same rate as manufacturing industries.

Many service industries such as finance, process engineering, and consulting, moreover, depended upon manufacturing to create demand for what they had to offer. They needed a strong manufacturing base to thrive. Furthermore, service industries such as medical care, education, transportation, and government offered few opportunities for export. A main indicator of declining U.S. competitiveness was the merchandise trade balance. It became negative for the first time in the 20th century in 1971, and since then it continued along a negative path, reaching record low levels (see Exhibit 10–2).

Manufacturing Decline

The decline of the U.S. economy was most evident in capital-intensive manufacturing industries such as automobiles, steel, electronics, and home appliances. In these industries, investment in capital and growth in productivity were very important. However, in the U.S. capital

---

EXHIBIT 10–2   Trade Balances and Other Data on Major Industrialized Nations in 1990

In Billions of Dollars	United States	United Kingdom	France	Canada	Japan	West Germany
Trade balance	− 122.3	− 37.6	− 17.8	6.8	52.2	65.2
Imports	516.2	222.8	234.4	124.8	235.4	354.8
Exports	393.9	185.2	216.6	131.7	287.6	420.0
Population (millions)	250	57.4	56.4	26.5	123.6	63.0
Per capita purchasing power (thousands of U.S. dollars)	21.8	14.9	15.5	19.5	17.1	16.1
GNP per capita (thousands of U.S. dollars)	21.0	14.3	20.1	16.8	22.9	19.5

SOURCE: Adapted from Directorate of Intelligence, Central Intelligence Agency, *Handbook of Economic Statistics* (Washington, D.C.: Government Printing Office, 1991).

formation per employed person was declining, and growth in productivity was slowing. Between 1960 and 1983, gross fixed capital formation in the U.S. as a percentage of gross domestic production (GDP) was 18 percent, compared to 32 percent in Japan and 21.5 percent in Western Europe. U.S. manufacturing productivity increased at an average annual rate of only 2.5 percent, while it grew by 8.3 percent in Japan and by 4.0 percent in Western Europe.[11]

Slow Investment

The rate of investment in the United States was lower than in other countries. Investment depended upon savings and interest rates, but savings in the United States lagged behind savings in other countries (see Exhibit 10-3). American businesses, like those in Great Britain—another industrial power that had declined—depended more heavily on equity financing than did businesses in Japan or West Germany. Equity holders assumed a part ownership position, and the additional risks it entailed, because they expected higher returns. This expectation put pressure on managers to produce short-term profits.

High U.S. Capital Costs

Capital costs in the United States appeared higher than in other countries. Capital-intensive industries were in high tax brackets, while

EXHIBIT 10–3   **Personal Savings and Annual Growth in Labor Productivity in Manufacturing**

	United States	United Kingdom	France	Canada	Japan	West Germany
Personal Savings (Savings as a Share of Disposable Personal Income)						
1960	6.2	6.6	15.2	3.9	17.4	8.6
1970	8.3	9.2	18.7	5.6	18.2	13.8
1980	7.3	13.5	17.6	13.6	17.9	12.7
1985	4.5	9.7	14.0	13.3	16.0	11.4
1990	4.6	8.7	12.8	10.8	15.9	13.7
Labor Productivity (Output per Hour)						
1961–70	2.8	3.7	6.7	4.1	10.8	5.9
1971–80	2.3	2.4	4.5	2.7	6.6	4.1
1981–85	3.5	5.6	3.7	3.7	5.6	2.8
1986–89	3.8	5.1	3.6	0.4	5.0	1.6

SOURCE: Adapted from Directorate of Intelligence, Central Intelligence Agency, *Handbook of Economic Statistics* (Washington, D.C.: Government Printing Office, 1991)

service industries such as retailing, finance, airlines, utilities, commercial banks, and railroads, had low effective tax rates.[12] Thus, the tax code was biased against investments in capital-intensive industries.

In the 1980s, the United States had the highest capital costs of any of the industrialized nations. The weighted average debt and equity costs after taxes in the United States was about 5.5 percent, in West Germany 4 percent, in Great Britain 3.5 percent, and in Japan 3 percent.[13] Given that the Japanese cost of capital was only about half that of the United States, it was no surprise that annual gross investment per factory worker in Japan was higher than in the United States. The gap widened from a 40 percent lead from 1972 to 1982 to an 85 percent lead from 1982 to 1986 (see Exhibit 10–4).[14]

A high cost of capital meant that U.S. managers had to be extremely careful about the types of investments they made. They had to be able to demonstrate on a project-by-project basis that they could maximize returns, or the projects would not be approved. The discount rate estimates used in projections favored less risky projects that promised immediate paybacks over long-term projects that promised gradual returns.

Dow Chemical estimated that its international competitors, which control 32 percent of the chemical market, pay three percentage points

EXHIBIT 10–4   Declining Domestic Investment: United States
Net Domestic Investment as a Percentage of GNP

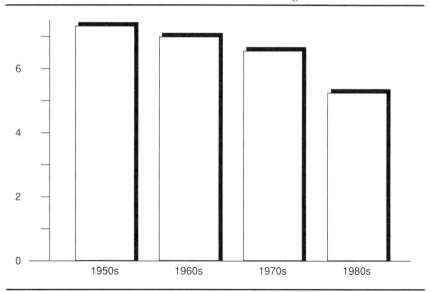

SOURCE: Council on Competitiveness. Based on Commerce Department data.

less for borrowed money and six points less for equity financing.[15] Therefore, Dow has had to concentrate its long-term spending on a select group of technologies, including engineering thermoplastics and pharmaceuticals. Its long-term investments must be related areas that complement each other and add up to more than the sum of the parts. Dow can wait only five years for its R&D investments to start showing a payback.

High-Tech Weakness

U.S. weakness in manufacturing did not pose a serious threat if the nation assumed leadership in high technology, but the U.S. advantage in this area also deteriorated. The United States lost market share in such high-technology industries as semiconductors, scientific and medical equipment, robotics, advanced fiber optics, and composite materials. Invention remained high, but the commercialization of new ideas into competitive products fell behind that of other nations (see Chapter 15).

Altered Supercomputer Plans

High capital costs plagued computer giants like Control Data and Cray Research, which had to alter long-term plans to develop U.S. supercomputer technology.[16] Control Data abandoned its supercomputer investments in 1989 after spending $350 million. To make its project self-financing it would have had to spend at least $150 million more, but its bankers and shareholders were not willing to wait for a possible payback. Cray Research also needed from $150 to $200 million to complete its supercomputer projects; and such a commitment was a very difficult undertaking for a company with just $756 million in annual sales.

Rather than abandon the project, Cray created a separate company for the venture called Cray Computer Corporation, headed by Cray's founder, Seymour Cray. This turbulence in the American computer industry, brought about by these financing problems, placed Japan's computer giants (Hitachi, Fujitsu, and NEC) which had no such problems in a position to gain dominance in an important technology.

Semiconductor Problems

High capital costs have hurt technological development in particularly critical areas like semiconductors, which are components to many other products. DRAMs are the semiconductor memory chips used in products from digital watches to supercomputers. The Japanese have gained control of 85 percent of this market. A major advantage they have is a lower cost of capital, which has enabled them to continue with high levels of investment even during downturns in the business cycle, something that no American manufacturer has been able to do.[17] While U.S. companies rely on the equity market to fund development and early manufacturing, the Japanese companies borrow at one quarter of the cost.

U.S. companies hope to overcome this disadvantage by forming a new joint venture. Called Memories, it includes Intel, National Semiconductor, Advanced Micro Devices, LSI Logic, IBM, Digital Equipment Corporation (DEC), and Hewlett-Packard. Memories tried to raise $1 billion in capital, half in equity from the member companies and the rest in debt. IBM, DEC, and Hewlett-Packard would be major consumers of the new companies' output, which would reduce much of the risk that chipmakers standing alone previously faced.

Selling Technology Rights Abroad

The rights to promising technologies are being sold to overseas concerns because U.S. companies cannot afford the development costs. Allied-Signal Corporation's Bendix Electronics Groups was an innovator in the development of engine sensors and antilock brakes. However, to fully exploit these technologies the company would have had to make a five-year investment of $1 billion.[18] The West German electronics giant Siemens, which operates under better financial conditions, was more willing, and able, to tolerate this expense. It purchased Bendix from Allied-Signal. Siemens' goals for the company were less driven by its monthly cash flow and more by what Bendix was doing to become a global leader in the technological areas where it excelled.

The Japanese Economy

As shown, the success of the Japanese economy depends upon many factors including:[19]

- · A high savings rate.
- · An extremely well-educated and motivated work force.
- · Employment security and participative management in its largest corporations.
- · An emphasis on total quality control.
- · A dedication to commercial, as opposed to government sponsored, research and development.
- · Closer supplier relations, represented by the just-in-time system of inventory control.

Each of these factors in isolation might be copied by U.S. companies. However, for U.S. companies to reproduce all the conditions that led to the Japanese success would be impossible. Many of the underlying conditions that produced this success were beyond the control of individual managers. They depended upon long-standing social relations, such as the Japanese family structure, as well as on specific government policies.

Japan's Government

Political analysts differ about the role that Japan's government has played in its economic success (see previous chapter), but continuity of government policies is one advantage Japan has had over the United States. Since the end of World War II, Japan has been ruled by the Liberal Democratic Party. The Japanese system of government, like the parliamentary democracies in Western Europe, does not divide power between branches. Thus, the common situation in the United States of having a president from one party and a Congress controlled by another party was not possible in Japan. Also, Japan has a stronger and more professional bureaucracy than the United States, and Japanese civil servants have a very decisive influence on policy making.

MITI

Japan's Ministry of International Trade and Industry (MITI) helps craft policies to keep Japanese interest rates low. The average Japanese family has strong reasons to save.[20] It needs money to buy a house (there is no standard mortgage deduction) or to tide it over in case of loss of employment, illness, or old age (welfare benefits are low). Interest-bearing accounts are not taxed as they are in the United States. Moreover, individuals do not receive deductions for going into debt to purchase expensive consumer items.

With savings high and interest rates low, MITI has been able to direct investment toward particular sectors of the economy. It has done so symbolically through its publications, research reports, and industry conferences and practically through its influence on the nation's financial institutions and banking system.

However, MITI's efforts to consolidate Japanese industry into giant conglomerates—to create national champions, Japanese equivalents of GM and Ford in the auto industry—failed (see Chapter 9). The core of the Japanese economy is built on a foundation of intense domestic competition. Japan has 12 auto firms, 12 integrated steel producers, 48 producers of calculators, and 147 robotics companies. There is rapid small business formation, with seven times the growth in the number of small manufacturing firms as in the United States.

Political Pressure

The Japanese government is not as large as governments in the United States and Western Europe and is generally less intrusive in the affairs of business. The relation between government and business is different in Japan than it is in the United States and other nations. Japan has lower tax rates, welfare benefits, and government spending. The Japanese government, nonetheless, like its counterparts in the United States, Western Europe, and other parts of the world, often bows to political pressure.[21] It does not always direct funds toward Japan's most advanced industrial sectors. It has extended aid to less competitive industries and less developed areas. The system of subsidies has led to market distortions that have made the Japanese economy less efficient than it otherwise would have been.

Japanese agriculture is heavily subsidized by the government because of a concern that as an agriculturally poor country Japan should try to produce a high percentage of its food. Small, unproductive farms are protected, and foreign agricultural products have been prevented from entering Japanese markets.

Another highly inefficient sector, which the government has done nothing to change, is the distribution system. Japan has more wholesalers per capita than any other advanced industrial nation. Often when someone retires, with little government support and a slim pension, the person takes over a small wholesale outlet. If a foreign discount chain wants to operate in Japan, it has to receive permission from existing outlets. This system stops foreign chains from entering Japanese markets. It also means that goods made in Japan often sell at lower prices in the United States.

The U.S. Economy

U.S. Policies Affecting Business

Japanese policies affecting business have been more consistent than U.S. policies, longer term, and more predictable, thus providing businesses with a more stable environment around which to make long-term investment decisions. In contrast, U.S. policies have lacked a sense of order, have been hodgepodge with different groups of policies helping different sectors in different ways, but with little overall coordination or sense of purpose.[22] For instance:

- Import restrictions mainly aided the steel, textiles and apparel, and motor vehicle industries.

- Federally subsidized loans mainly helped the home construction industry and the agricultural sector.
- The federal government financed roughly a half of U.S. R&D, but much of it went to defense-related businesses and a high proportion to the aerospace industry.

The patchwork of federal policies, created incrementally over time in response to specific contingencies, reflect lobbyist and special interest influence.

The outcomes of the policy-making process are highly unstable. What is done by one Congress or administration may be undone by another; laws are amended and reamended in rapid succession. Changes in party, in administration, and in intellectual fashion bring new policies to the forefront, and with them new conditions with which business managers have to contend. For instance, with a complete overhaul of the tax system occurring twice during the 1980s, business managers cannot be certain that today's tax policies will remain in place in the future. The investments they make today may not have payoffs in the future when the political environment may be vastly different.[23] The surest way to succeed, then, is to search for ways to achieve short-term successes. The lack of coherence in American policy making yields unintended and undesired results, and the confusion makes it difficult for managers to plan and to take a long view.

While the policies of other nations' governments have tended to play a more positive role in their economic performance, the policies of the U.S. government have partially accounted for weak U.S. performance. Although competitiveness is hard to assess, by most measures—standard of living, balance of payments, investment, R&D spending, and trade—the United States is falling behind. Federal borrowing and corporate and personal debt can maintain existing living standards for only so long. If productivity does not keep pace, future generations will be left with large amounts of money to pay back without having the capability to do so.

Government's Responsibility for Declining Competitiveness

According to the critics, the government's responsibility lies in two main areas.[24]

1. Contradictory, Stop-and-Go Macroeconomic Policies. President Lyndon Johnson's "guns and butter" spending policies were not matched by tax increases. He conducted the war on poverty at the same time that the United States was engaged in the war in Southeast Asia. Thus, strong inflationary pressures already were present at the time of the 1973 Arab oil embargo. The transfer of huge amounts of money to oil exporting nations weakened the economy still more.

The efforts by presidents Nixon, Ford, and Carter to deal simultaneously with high inflation and unemployment were largely ineffective. Existing macroeconomic theory was not designed to cope with these conditions. It had good remedies for one problem at a time—either a high rate of inflation or a high rate of unemployment. With both problems on the scene, successive administrations waffled between stimulatory policies to end the recessionary conditions and deflationary policies to put a brake on the high prices.

President Reagan took new initiatives. He cut taxes to spur consumer spending and increased government spending on defense. Meanwhile, the Federal Reserve Bank, under the leadership of Paul Volcker, tightly controlled the money supply. While the rapidly accelerating inflation of the late 1970s was brought to a halt, at the cost of a massive recession, the immediate result was weak economic growth, which depleted government revenues.

The combined effects of these policies yielded a rapidly growing federal deficit, which went up from a total of $715 billion in 1980 to $1,312 billion in 1985. The annual interest payments on the debt accelerated from $52 billion in 1980 to $129 billion in 1985. Government demand for money to finance the deficit "crowded out" private investment, which hurt lagging U.S. competitiveness.

With the demand for money high, U.S. interest rates were greater than those in other nations. Foreign money was attracted to the United States, raising the value of the dollar. With the dollar highly valued, American manufacturers had difficulty selling their goods abroad and foreign producers found it easy to sell their goods in the United States.

2. Inconsistent Industrial and Ineffective Trade Policies.   At the same time that macroeconomic difficulties were taking place, the government did not develop consistent industrial policies or effective trade policies. To many people in the business community, federal tax, credit, spending, and trade policies were inefficient, random, and confusing. The tax system, for instance, rewarded real estate investments but discriminated against manufacturing investments. The assistance provided to industries such as chemicals and aerospace was greater than that given to paper products and pharmaceuticals.

The reasons for these differences were not apparent. Federal policies neither created an even playing field nor marshalled resources in an effective manner to assist targeted growth industries.

Trade policies also were ineffective. The United States failed to recognize that other nations did not adhere to free trade in the same way it did. They used a variety of unfair trade practices, from discrimination against foreign producers to dumping. The U.S. response of selective prosecution of countries for unfair trade practices and the threat of retaliation did not adequately deal with the problem.

Business Responsibility for Declining Competitiveness

Arguments about government's responsibility for lagging American competitiveness were matched by arguments about why business was responsible.[25]

- American managers had a short-term time horizon (see Exhibit 10–5).
- They did not pay sufficient attention to product quality and costs.
- They were bureaucratic and indecisive and slow in introducing new technologies, manufacturing processes, and products.
- They were more interested in financial manipulation and short-term cost reduction than in achieving long-term competitiveness and market share.
- They set high ROI targets so that many potentially worthy projects were not undertaken.
- Their preoccupation with selling and buying assets kept them from focusing on production; it also caused unnecessary labor-management friction.
- Their investments in real estate and commerce, speculative activity, and interest in takeovers sacrificed long-term competitiveness and markets for short-term results.

Critics maintained that foreign managers had different goals and time frames. The goals and timetables of the foreign managers matched the different goals and time frames of their governments. Rather than short-term profitability and shareholder wealth maximization, foreign managers pursued long-term growth, competitive viability, and stable employment. These goals—not those pursued by American managers—were needed for sustained success in international markets.

EXHIBIT 10–5   Corporate Objectives: U.S. and Japanese Managers

U.S. Managers	*Japanese Managers*
1. Return on Investment	1. Market Share
2. Share Price Increase	2. Return on Investment
3. Market Share	3. New Products
4. Product Portfolio	4. Rationalize Production & Distribution

SOURCE: Adapted from G. C. Lodge, *Comparative Business Government Relations* (Englewood Cliffs, N.J.: Prentice Hall, 1990), p. 26.

On Free Trade

Given that the United States was falling behind in international commerce, some argued that it should move away from its traditional commitment to free trade. To what extent should the American government remain committed to free trade? Adam Smith argued in favor of the benefits of free trade because it stimulated competition and provided opportunities for countries to specialize and to achieve economies of scale. Countries would be able to produce what they were best at making and trade for the rest.

However, what if a country's economy was weak. What if it was not good at making anything and it had an absolute disadvantage in all areas? To understand this situation, David Ricardo formulated the principle of comparative advantage, perhaps one of the most powerful in economics.[26]

If in Greece it takes 10 hours of labor to make a gallon of wine and 20 hours to make a pound of cheese and in Poland it takes 60 hours of labor to make a gallon of wine and 30 hours to make a pound of cheese, then Greece is more productive than Poland with respect to both commodities. It has the absolute advantage in wine and cheese, but its comparative advantage is in wine while Poland's comparative advantage is in cheese. It makes sense for Greece to specialize in wine production and for Poland to specialize in cheese production, and for the two countries to trade with each other. By doing so, both are better off; however, since Greece's workers are more efficient than Polish workers, they will earn more income.

Trade does not make earning across countries equal when productivity differs; it just makes both countries better off than they otherwise would be. Tariffs and quotas, on the other hand, reward inefficient domestic producers and make goods more expensive (and less plentiful) for domestic consumers. The economy has less reason to be innovative. Consumers in economies that are insulated from international competition have to pay higher prices for lower quality goods and services.

The GATT

Since 1947, the world has benefited from the General Agreement on Tariffs and Trade (GATT), which has promoted free trade.[27] Its secretariat monitors the trade policies of its almost 100 members. Originally composed of 23 nations, the GATT has fought against a legacy of protectionism that severely hurt the world in the period between World War I and World War II and made the Great Depression worse.

GATT works on the basis of three principles.[28] The first is *reciprocity*. If a country lowers its tariffs against another country's exports, the other country is expected to lower its tariffs in turn. The second principle is *nondiscrimination*. Countries should not grant favorable trade treatment to other countries or groups of countries. The third principle is *transparency*. Countries are supposed to replace nontariff barriers, such as import quotas, with tariffs and then they are supposed to bind these tariffs by promising not to raise them.

In the period between 1948 and 1973, the GATT was extremely successful.[29] The growth rate in international commerce went up 7 percent per year after 1948 after having only grown at a rate of 0.5 percent per year between 1913 and 1948. From 1950 to 1980, the sum of imports and exports rose from 8.4 percent of U.S. GNP to 21.1 percent. For West Germany, the increase was from 25.4 percent to 57.3 percent and for Japan from 20.1 percent to 31.2 percent.

The largest increases in world trade followed the so-called Kennedy round of negotiations, which lasted from 1963 to 1967.[30] Cuts of 50 percent and more were made on more than two thirds of the industrial countries' products. Between 1969 and 1973, world exports more than doubled.

Unfortunately, the result was a call for protectionism as specific sectors had trouble adjusting to the new competition. Under the GATT, however, countries were restricted in what they could do. Only developing countries and advanced nations with severe balance-of-trade problems could use quotas. Also, a country had to consult with other GATT nations before raising a tariff, and it had to provide affected nations with compensation. Countervailing duties in a home country were allowed only if an exporter subsidized its goods; special duties were sanctioned only if an importer could prove dumping, that is, the exporter was selling in the importer's country at below-cost prices.

Because of these restrictions, countries resorted to more subtle forms of trade protection: voluntary export restraints (bilaterally negotiated quotas), public subsidies, and nationalistic procurement policies. The Tokyo round of GATT talks, which lasted from 1973 to 1979, was successful in lowering tariffs (the weighted-average tariff rate went down from 7 percent to 4.67 percent) but was unsuccessful in eliminating ambiguities in the treatment of nontariff barriers.[31]

Against Free Trade

During this period, the arguments against free trade continued to gain momentum. In brief, these arguments consisted of the following:[32]

1. There are national security reasons for violating free-trade principles; a country needs certain vital industries in case of war.
2. Violating free-trade principles for the sake of job protection is justified. Low wages in underdeveloped countries provide an unfair trade advantage that rob the developed countries of jobs.

Much of international trade is in the form of intrafirm transactions wherein a company exports manufacturing to low-wage countries.

3. Some countries create unfair trade advantages. They do so via tax incentives and selected subsidies such as government-sponsored R&D, preferential loans, and allowing companies the freedom to collude. Companies in countries that cannot compete with the subsidized companies can violate free-trade principles to allow them to compete.

4. During the infancy of an industry, special subsidies are appropriate provided they are removed when the industry gains strength and matures. Protection of infant industries has long been accepted in international trade theory. To build comparative advantage in particular industries, a country may have to protect them when they are young.

5. It might be justifiable to violate free-trade principles to obtain more favorable terms of trade. If threatened with a cut in sales by a tariff, an exporter is likely to lower the price.

However, trade wars, in which countries retaliate against the protectionism practiced by one another, can be extremely damaging to the world economy, and a severe decline in world trade would hurt everyone. The only group that would be helped would be special interests, for example, a domestic industry unfit to compete internationally that was aided by protectionist measures.

The 1988 Trade Act

Under the 1988 Omnibus Trade and Competitiveness Act, the U.S. government became more vigilant in trying to remove nontariff barriers.[33] The act strengthened U.S. trade negotiators' leverage and gave the government negotiating authority for the Uruguay round of trade talks. The 1988 act also required notification of plant closings. It expanded assistance to workers who lost their jobs. The U.S. agenda in international trade negotiations is to lower agricultural trade barriers and to deal with questions of intellectual property and services.

Under the "Super 301" provision of the act, the U.S. government has the right to name "priority" unfair trading practices and "priority" unfair trading countries. Doing so starts a 12-to-18 month negotiation period to remove the cited nation's trade barriers. In 1989, Japan was cited for exclusionary government procurement practices with regard to supercomputers and satellites and for technical barriers preventing forest product imports. Brazil was cited for quantitative import restrictions and India for trade-related investment barriers and for closure of its

The Mechanics of Exporting

Exporting is far more complicated than producing and selling domestically.[1] The U.S. Department of Commerce, which has 47 local offices, provides information about trade and investment opportunities abroad, foreign markets, financing and insurance, tax advantages, trade exhibitions, documentation, licensing, and import requirements. Most of its offices have a business library, and they have lists of people who are experienced in exporting.

The Business Counseling Section of the International Trade Administration provides advice to exporters. Programs in the Export-Import Bank and Overseas Private Investment Corporation offer information about political conditions in various countries. Large commercial banks in the United States have international departments with expertise about different countries. The State Department and industry trade associations are additional sources of information.

In selecting a foreign market, a prospective exporter can use the *Foreign Trade Report*, which is published by the Bureau of the Census. It includes statistical records of the merchandise shipped from the United States to foreign countries. *Overseas Business Reports* provides details on marketing strategies for individual countries. U.S. embassies and consulates prepare *Foreign Economic Trends* with country-by-country data on business conditions. International economic indicators, demographic data, and market-share information can be obtained from other government reports. For a nominal annual subscription fee, TOPS (the Trade Opportunities Program) will make matches between individual firms and particular business opportunities.

Developing an export marketing strategy involves deciding what is unique about the product and how it will stand up to foreign competition. For example, the product may have to be modified for the foreign market. Also, the perception of quality is important because American products have slipped in this area. Questions about production capacity, promotion and advertising, training and translation, distribution, and customer service should be also considered. For instance, to what extent will the product have to be disassembled for ease of shipping. All of these questions will bear on the final price of the product.

The U.S. producer can sell goods directly overseas or rely on a sales intermediary for sales and shipping. There are many different types of intermediaries. Foreign firms often use commission agents to find foreign products they need; country-controlled buying agents fulfill the same function. Export management companies, on the other hand, purchase U.S. goods for sales abroad, with the manufacturer usually bearing the risk. To enhance the practicality of exports by small and medium-sized companies, joint exporting trading companies may be established. It is also possible to rely upon conventional sales representatives, wholesale outlets, and government purchasing agents.

---

[1]M. L. Whicker and R. A. More, *Policies to Build a More Competitive America*, paper presented at the American Political Science Association annual meetings, 1987.

insurance market to foreign firms. (see the feature on page 285, "The Mechanics of Exporting").

Comparing National Strengths and Weaknesses

Trade theory holds that each economy in the world builds up unique advantages and disadvantages, and by means of mutually beneficial deals, all benefit. Thus, for the whole world to prosper there should be a division of labor among the world's major trading partners. In what follows, the advantages and disadvantages of the major industrial nations—West Germany (prior to unification), Japan, Great Britain, and the United States—are compared.[34]

West Germany.   The particular strengths of the West German economy have been in chemicals, plastics, machinery, printing, and optics-related products (see Exhibit 10–6). The economy is adept at complex production processes that require a high degree of precision. There is strong domestic rivalry for prestige in science and technology. A pragmatic, technical management aims to master and dominate sophisticated market segments. It puts a stress on quality, premium-high-performance products that command high prices. The West Germans compete based on quality and differentiation, not on cost.

West Germany has a large domestic market, sophisticated buyers, and an international orientation among its companies. Banks hold shares in companies and bank executives serve on company boards. To a greater extent than in the United States or Great Britain, ownership is in private hands. The firms tend to be small, hierarchical, well-disciplined, and owner-managed. For all these reasons, West German

EXHIBIT 10–6   Strengths of National Economies

West Germany	Japan	Great Britain	United States
Chemicals	Electronics	Services	Computers
Plastics	equipment	Consumer goods	Software
Machinery	Steel	Publishing	Biotech
Printing	Transportation	Advertising	Consumer goods
Optics	Office computing	Luxury	Forest Products
	Cameras	Leisure	Agriculture
		Consulting	Defense
			Aerospace
			Health care
			Entertainment
			Leisure

firms have a long-term perspective; they are not preoccupied with quarterly profits.

These advantages have not prevented major declines in the steel, coal, shipbuilding, and apparel industries. West Germany has relatively few natural resources, with the exception of coal and coke, and domestic markets are saturated in many areas. The government imposes tough product standards and has demanding environmental laws. Consumers are sophisticated, but also cautious and conservative and not easily swayed by image marketing. In any event, television and radio advertising on the publicly run media in West Germany is limited. A product does not make rapid headway if intangible brand name and mass communication is critical to its success.

West German businesses have not been strong in consumer products; in the business services area, they have been held back by high wages. Public ownership and regulation have inhibited innovation in telecommunications, transportation, and electric power. Management education is weak; electronics and computer industries have failed to flourish, and the pace of small-business formation has been slow. Finally, group decision making has retarded innovation, and a creeping financial orientation plus poorly developed risk-capital markets have prevented further progress.

Japan.   Japanese strengths are in electronics products, heavy equipment, steel and transportation related industries, office machines, computing equipment, and cameras. Although it has strong in-company R&D programs, it does a lot of technology sourcing from abroad. Project teams are able to bring new products into production very quickly. The emphasis on product quality is great to overcome the previous image of cheap Japanese goods.

The dynamism of the Japanese economy has been promoted by intense domestic rivalry, demanding buyers, cooperative suppliers, rapid upgrading of technology, and an international orientation. Savings and investment are high and capital investment strong (see prior discussions of the Japanese economy). Investment has been aimed at creating large, efficient facilities that have the latest technology. Rather than making incremental adjustments, the Japanese approach, adopted in the post–World War Two II period, has been to scrap old production facilities and to build new ones.

The large, homogenous home market offers a wide range of climatic and geological conditions. Sophisticated domestic buyers—especially interested in cars, consumer electronics, and cameras—insist upon the latest model with the most up-to-date features, and expect frequent model changes. Japanese companies have been aware that presentation and packaging is an important part of sales, and the mass media as well as advertising are well developed.

Japanese companies expect a great deal from their suppliers. World-class suppliers have developed cooperative, long-term relationships with Japanese companies, in which information flow is very important. Company groupings (the *zaibatsu*) also facilitate the exchange of information among companies. Trading companies help exporters penetrate foreign markets. Distribution channels, however, are dominated by diverse and highly fragmented outlets, not the uniform mass-marketing channels such as supermarkets and discount chains that dominate in the United States.

The goals of Japanese business are usually defined in terms of market share. Companies try to maintain employment, achieve economies of scale, and outdo rivals. Considerable publicly available information on the economy is available, and production and market-share information is readily obtainable.

Still, the Japanese economy has weaknesses in some areas, such as forest products, chemicals, plastics, food and beverages, and personal consumer products; these sectors are far behind world competition. Also, Japan has few raw materials, and its work force is not known for being creative. Labor is in short supply and very expensive, women have been excluded from the work force, and domestic markets are saturated. Japan has been less successful in businesses that require individual achievement and interorganizational competition.

Great Britain. The strengths are in service industries, consumer goods, and trading. Businesses in Britain have available to them a large pool of capital and a favorable geographic location. The British economy has a cost advantage in advanced human resources, which provide it with an important edge in consultancy, publishing, and advertising. Facility in the English language helps because English remains the international language of business. Great Britain is also a leading market for luxury and leisure goods, for entertainment, and for wealth. British companies possess many internationally known and recognized brand names (e.g., Schweppes "bitter lemon"), and Great Britain's businesses have competed well in many areas, including consumer packaged goods, alcoholic beverages, food, confectionery products, personal products, cigarettes, cosmetics, perfume, household furniture, insurance, auctioneering, money management, international legal services, petrochemicals, pharmaceuticals, entertainment, and leisure. Great Britain, incidentally, has the highest per capita consumption of sugar in the world. Gains in petroleum and petroleum-related products were made with the discovery of North Sea oil and coal (see Chapter 12).

British disadvantages are a lack of domestic rivalry and a long slide in living standards that has eroded domestic demand conditions. The average consumer is not particularly quality-conscious because of the falling standard of living. Also, many exports are to former colonies that are underdeveloped countries with undemanding and unsophisticated buyers. While many parts of the economy have been successful, the core manufacturing areas have been declining for a relatively long period and have showed few signs of revival. Great Britain has had to rely heavily on foreign inputs and machinery for its industry. Losses have been greater than gains, and few positions exist where industry is unusually strong. R&D and investment in new capital are behind other countries and are not likely to catch up soon.

Investors often are short-term institutional buyers whose major concern is share price appreciation and dividends. Banks do not hold equity in companies and there has been an explosion of acquisitions and takeovers. Along with an attitude of gentlemanly rivalry, which encourages satisfactory, not outstanding, performance, managers lack strong profit motivation or market-share orientation. British companies appear to be merging rather than competing. For many, competition remains vulgar and distasteful.

Great Britain seems to have fallen into a comfortable pattern of slow decay. Entrepreneurs tend to be outsiders who adopt upper-class norms once they succeed and then distance themselves from commerce. Widespread state ownership and regulation have retarded dynamism and innovation and have contributed to the stodgy attitude in companies, the dependency on protocol, form, and bureaucracy. Government-directed intervention in the forms of subsidy, consolidation, and protection has not worked. There were notable failures after the government encouraged mergers to create world-class companies in steel, autos, machine tools, and computers. The government's choices of promising technologies have led to few commercial successes. Moreover, the accession of new governments has been followed by sharp policy reversals. Great Britain is in a vicious cycle where it has become very hard to turn around its economy now that it has turned downward. No shock or jolt seems to be able to reverse the cycle.

The United States.   The economy is strong in computers, packaged software, biotechnology, consumer goods, and services; however, 15 of the top 25 industries are natural resource–based, such as forest products and agriculture, which reflects the relative abundance of natural factors of production that the United States still possesses. It has a commanding position in defense, aerospace, and related fields that are affected by government spending and remains strong in health care, entertainment and leisure, and consumer and business services.

The United States has many remaining advantages: strong scientific research, especially in the fundamental disciplines; its media, chain stores, and modern marketing; and its strong financial services and money management capabilities. It remains a good place to start new businesses. The average productivity of the work force is still as high as any other nation, and real wages are declining.

However, broad segments of U.S. industry (e.g., autos, machine tools, semiconductors, consumer electronics) have been losing competitive advantage. The United States has large trade deficits, anemic productivity growth, and low rates of investment in industry. It has been slow to adopt new process technologies, upgrade its facilities, and introduce new products and features. Further, its lead in innovation has been dwindling. It has developed great science and technology, but it has lagged in converting these assets into competitive industries. Moreover, relatively low wages and high employee availability actually have been lowering the pressure to automate.

Manufacturers have been making mass-produced, standardized, disposable goods for a large domestic market where consumers have had an insatiable demand for credit. Goods have been made with compromises in product design, quality, and service. The relationship between producers and suppliers has been opportunistic and at arms length. Managers have not been technically sophisticated. Institutional stock ownership has yielded a short-term profit orientation with an emphasis on quarterly appreciation. Also, management has been heading off takeovers by boosting short-term earnings and restructuring in a way that has not been in the long-term interests of the company.

U.S. companies have applied the world's highest rate-of-return targets to screen investment opportunities. Mergers and alliances have been carried out to create stock market excitement, but relatively little capital has gone into new plants, products, and technology. In addition, unrelated diversification, downsizing, and paring back excess capacity have undermined competitiveness. Companies have sought government protection to deal with competition, claiming that foreign competitors engage in such uncompetitive acts as dumping. As a result, the government has cut regulatory programs (antitrust, environmental health, and safety), which should force companies to compete at world levels.

U.S. Decline?

Compared to other nations, to what extent is the United States in serious irreversible decline? Is it appropriate to apply the British analogy? Are Western Europe and Japan overtaking the United States as an economic and world power?

The argument about decline probably has been overstated because the world has been moving toward an era of complex interdependence where no nation can dominate as the United States did in the period immediately after World War II.[35] In addition, the United States has certain advantages other countries do not have. For example, it remains a country of immigrants that is constantly being revitalized by the entrepreneurial talents and energies of newcomers (see Exhibit 10–7). Its military prowess can be matched by no other country.

The U.S.-British analogy, while appropriate in some ways, misses an essential element. Britain was a colonial power that lost its empire because of the rise of nationalism. The United States has been primarily a continental power with no empire to lose. It attracts capital from the rest of the world, while Britain exported it.

Europe's resources are impressive—twice those of Japan's. It plays a larger role in world trade than Japan, and its armed forces—if combined—outnumber those of the United States. However, the issue of political cohesiveness remains a stumbling point. With national sovereignty still strong, a truly united Europe may be a long way off. Moreover, the European economy is showing no greater dynamism than the U.S. economy. Unemployment is higher in most European countries than it is in the United States. There are also special problems; for example, West Germany will be preoccupied with unification with East Germany during the near term.

Japan's per capita GNP surpassed U.S. per capita GNP in 1988 before being corrected for purchasing power. Also, Japan is the world's largest creditor nation, has the second largest economy, is the second largest exporter of manufactured goods, and has the world's 10 largest banks. However, the Japanese economy is very tied to the U.S. economy. Its major markets are in the United States. Thus, if the U.S. economy falters, it is sure to affect the Japanese economy.

The future success of the Japanese economy is not guaranteed. Inefficiencies remain in its agriculture and consumer services. Japan also has weaknesses in higher education, demographics (an aging population), exclusion of women from the work force, and exporting of jobs and industries abroad.

EXHIBIT 10–7   Immigrant Skills Compared with Those of U.S. Population: 1988

	Immigrants Entering United States (Percentage)	*U.S. Population (Percentage)*
College education	22.7%	19.9%
Engineers	2.9	1.5
Teachers	3.4	3.8
Doctors	0.6	0.5
Skilled blue collar	10.2	12.1

SOURCE: Adapted from Council on Competitiveness. Based on Immigration and Naturalization Service, Labor Department, and Census Bureau data.

The Japanese economy remains closely tied to that of the United States. The United States is the largest foreign market for Japanese goods and services. The United States is heavily indebted to Japan. Further, Japan is militarily weak and has few domestic natural resources. It needs a viable and successful U.S. economy as much as the United States needs a viable and successful Japan. Clearly, the world is entering a new era in which complex patterns of interdependence are likely to be dominant.

An Agenda for Restoring U.S. Competitiveness

There are obvious things the United States can do to help restore its competitiveness.[36] First, increase savings and investment while keeping consumption at a fixed share of GNP. Second, try to lower military expenditures by eliminating the causes of war. As with Great Britain before it, the United States will have difficulty combining high domestic consumption with substantial military commitments.

There are other things that the United States can do:[37]

1. *Open foreign markets to U.S. exports.* U.S. strengths often are in industries, such as agriculture or aerospace, that other countries protect for special reasons. The United States must try to get those countries to open their markets to imports in these areas.

2. *Provide managers with the incentive to take a long-term perspective.* The United States must align managerial interests with owners' interests. Many mechanisms are available, for instance, allowing bank ownership of equities, providing managerial bonuses that are tied to performance, granting incentives for stable, concentrated ownership patterns, and removing firms from publicly traded securities markets when necessary.

3. *Elevate technically sophisticated individuals to top management positions.* Engineers and scientists who understand technology have to play a greater role in managing American businesses (see Chapter 15). Also, M.B.A.'s need to obtain a rudimentary knowledge of complex technological processes and not simply manage based on accounting numbers.

4. *Take away the incentive for financial manipulation and paper profits.* We must eliminate rampant asset shuffling in which companies are bought and sold for no other purpose than to make a quick profit for those who carry out the deals. The United States should remove the various governmental incentives that encourage unrelated mergers and acquisitions (e.g., tax credits for corporate debt).

5. *Raise the educational standards in U.S. schools.* A multipronged effort is desperately needed to get at the root of why so many students and schools fail. The core problems of unstable families, poverty, and prejudice have to be addressed, along with inadequate mathematical scores, poor ability in foreign languages, and lack of technical skills.

6. *Increase the level of U.S. savings and investment.* Tax deductions for mortgages and for other activities cause debt. They need to be removed so that American saving rates can be increased. Also, the budget deficit needs to be gotten under control—if for no other reason than to release funds for private investment.

7. *Educate consumers to be more sophisticated and demanding.* Ultimately, business will benefit if it has to serve domestic markets where the standards are higher. Consumers have to be taught that they no longer have to tolerate shoddy, throwaway goods that have been poorly designed and manufactured.

8. *Put greater emphasis on innovation in process technologies.* The United States remains the world leader in invention and in the development of new products. It needs to put equal emphasis on manufacturing and on getting new products to the market.

9. *Encourage private industry to sponsor more research and development.* The key to productivity improvement in the future will be in developing new products and new ways to make them and bring them to the market. The United States cannot afford to lag behind other nations in commercial R&D spending.

10. *Strengthen the incentives for environmental protection and energy conservation.* The best way to promote the environment and reduce reliance on foreign energy is through full social costing, not through regulation. The government can figure out how much damage energy consumption and pollution causes, and impose a tax to compensate. The tax provides a healthy incentive for innovation and at the same time lowers pollution and energy use (see Part IV of this book).

11. *Achieve greater consistency in federal policy.* The government should not give in to every industry that demands trade protection. It should draft policies carefully for determining the circumstances that warrant trade protection. In most cases, protection would not be provided. It would also make sure that it does not act arbitrarily in changing or interpreting its policies, which makes it more difficult for business managers to plan.

12. *Reform the system of product liability.* The strict liability system is beneficial as a disciplining device for industry. However, if the United States moves to extremes in comparison to other nations, then product innovation will be stifled (see Chapters 17 and 18).

Summary and Conclusions

This chapter considered arguments that the U.S. economy is in serious decline. It examined how well the U.S. economy is doing in comparison to its major international rivals. The decline in U.S. manufacturing has been related to weak investment and high capital costs. Weaknesses in high-tech areas such as supercomputers and semiconductors have also been noted. Reasons for the success of the Japanese economy have been examined, and the role of government in the United States and Japan has been compared. We reviewed the arguments for free trade and the institutions built up in the post–World War II period to promote free trade. We closed with a comparison of the strengths and weaknesses of four national economies—West Germany, Japan, the United Kingdom, and the United States—and we provided proposals about what the United States can do to enhance its international competitiveness.

Discussion Questions

1. What are some of the charges made against the U.S. economy? How true are these charges?
2. Would it be all bad if other countries caught up with the United States?
3. In what ways is the U.S. economy performing well? In what ways is it performing poorly?
4. What are some of the reasons for the decline of the U.S. economy?
5. Compare the role of government in the Japanese and the American economy. What can be done to change the role that government plays in the United States?
6. To what degree is the U.S. government responsible for declining U.S. competitiveness?
7. To what extent is business responsible for declining U.S. competitiveness?
8. Why is free trade good for the international economy?
9. What is GATT? Why was it created? What does it do? What role has it played in promoting free trade?
10. What are some of the arguments against free trade? Are they valid?
11. What are some of the major provisions of the 1988 trade act? To what extent does this act further free trade? To what extent does it usher in protectionism?
12. What role does the domestic market play in the economies of Germany, Japan, Great Britain, and the United States? What role do suppliers play? What role does industry structure play? What role do management style, talents, and competencies play? What role do natural resources play? What role do advertising and mass mar-

keting play? What role do distribution channels play? What role does R&D play?

13. Interdependence is used to describe the evolving world economy. What does this word imply? Is it a good descriptor of where things are moving?

14. What can the United States do to enhance its competitiveness? What policies should a major business group like the Business Roundtable propose to the U.S. government?

Endnotes

1. P. Kennedy, "The (Relative) Decline of America," *The Atlantic Monthly*, August 1987, pp. 29–38; P. Kennedy, *The Rise and Fall of the Great Powers* (New York: Vintage Books, 1987).

2. L. C. Thurow, "How to Get Out of the Economic Rut," *New York Review of Books*, February 14, 1985, pp. 9–10; U.S. Competitiveness in Manufacturing. case from the Harvard Business School, 9–386–133, 1986.

3. *U.S. Competitiveness in Manufacturing.* See also I. M. Destler, *American Trade Politics: System under Stress* (Washington, D.C.: Institute for International Economics, 1986).

4. R. Z. Lawrence, *Can America Compete?* (Washington, D.C.: The Brookings Institution, 1984); J. S. Nye, *Bound to Lead* (New York: Basic Books, 1990); J. E. Schwartz, *America's Hidden Success: A Reassessment of Public Policy from Kennedy to Reagan* (New York: W. W. Norton & Co., 1988); J. E. Schwartz and T. J. Volgy, "The Myth of America's Economic Decline," *Harvard Business Review*, September–October, 1985, p. 101.

5. D. B. Yoffie, *Note on Free Trade and Protectionism*, working paper 383–174, Harvard Business School, 1983.

6. President's Commission on Industrial Competitiveness, *Global Competition: The New Reality*, vol. 1 (Washington, D.C.: Government Printing Office, 1985).

7. Ibid.

8. *U.S. Competitiveness in Manufacturing*, case 9–386–133, Harvard Business School, 1986; *U.S. International Competitiveness: Perception and Reality*, New York Stock Exchange, Office of Economic Research, August 1984.

9. Directorate of Intelligence, Central Intelligence Agency, *Handbook of Economic Statistics* (Washington, D.C.: Government Printing Office, 1991).

10. E. F. Denison, *Trends in American Economic Growth, 1929–1982* (Washington, D.C.: The Brookings Institution, 1985); *U.S. Competitiveness in Manufacturing;* Council of Economic Advisers, *Economic Report of the President*, (Washington, D.C.: Government Printing Office: 1984).

11. Denison, *Trends in American Economic Growth, 1929–1982;* OECD Economic Outlook, *Historical Statistics 1960–1983* (Paris: OECD, 1985); "The Revival of Productivity," *Business Week*, February 13, 1984, pp. 154–58; *U.S. Competi-*

tiveness in Manufacturing; Council of Economic Advisers, *Economic Report of the President.*

12. *U.S. Competitiveness in Manufacturing.*

13. C. Rapoport, "Why Japan Keeps Winning," *Fortune,* 1991, pp. 76–88.

14. Ibid.

15. Commerce Department data.

16. Ibid.

17. W. Ouchi, *The M-Form Society: How American Teamwork Can Recapture the Competitive Edge* (Reading, Mass.: Addison-Wesley Publishing Co., 1984).

18. Rapoport, "Why Japan Keeps Winning."

19. R. Dore, *Flexible Rigidities: Industrial Policy and Structural Adjustment in the Japanese Economy, 1970–80* (London: The Athlone Press, 1986); N. Coates, "Determinants of Japan's Business Success: Some Japanese Executives' Views," *The Academy of Management Executive* 2, no. 1, 1988, pp. 69–72.

20. A. Etzioni, "The MITIzation of America," *Public Interest,* Summer 1983, pp. 44–51; G. Gilder, "A Supply-Side Economics of the Left," *Public Interest,* Summer 1983, pp. 29–43.

21. M. Sutherland, E. Liederman, and T. K. McCraw, "Japan in the Mid-1980s: Miracle at Risk?" case 383–177, Harvard Business School, 1983; G. L. Curtis, *The Japanese Way of Politics* (New York: Columbia University Press, 1988).

22. R. Reich, "An Industrial Policy of the Right," *Public Interest,* Fall 1983, pp. 3–17; R. B. Reich, *The Next American Frontier: A Provocative Program for Economic Renewal* (Harrisonburg, Va.: R. R. Donnelley & Sons Company, 1983).

23. A. A. Marcus, "Policy Uncertainty and Technological Innovation," *Academy of Management Review* 6, 1981, pp. 443–48.

24. U.S. House Committee on Banking, Finance and Urban Affairs, *Industrial Competitiveness Act,* April 1984; *U.S. Competitiveness in Manufacturing.*

25. Denison, *Trends in American Economic Growth, 1929–1982;* C. W. L. Hill, M. A. Hitt, and R. E. Hoskisson, "Declining U.S. Competitiveness: Reflections on a Crisis," *The Academy of Management Executive* 2, 1988, pp. 51–60; U.S. House Committee on Banking, Finance and Urban Affairs, *Industrial Competitiveness Act; U.S. Competitiveness in Manufacturing.*

26. J. D. Gwartney and R. L. Stroup, *Economics: Private and Public Choice* (Harcourt Brace Jovanovich, 1987); *The Steel Industry and Imports (A) 1977,* case 9–379–041, Harvard Business School, 1978; Yoffie, *Note on Free Trade and Protectionism;* Yoffie and J. W. Rosenblum, *Zenith and the Color Television Fight,* case 383–070, Harvard Business School, 1982; D. B. Yoffie and J. K. Austin, *Textiles and the Multi-fiber Arrangement,* case 383–164, Harvard Business School, 1983.

27. "Jousting for Advantage," *The Economist,* September 22, 1990; N. Vousden, *The Economics of Trade Protection* (New York: Cambridge University Press, 1990).

28. Ibid.

29. Yoffie, *Note on Free Trade and Protectionism.*

30. Ibid.

31. Ibid.

32. Ibid.

33. J. S. Lublin, "U.S. Food Firms Find Europe's Huge Market Hardly a Piece of Cake," *The Wall Street Journal*, May 15, 1990, p. A1; B. Stokes, "Off and Running," *National Journal*, June 17, 1989, pp. 1562–66.

34. M. Porter, *The Competitive Advantage of Nations* (New York: Free Press, 1990); J. Chipman, *On the Concept of International Competitiveness*, discussion paper 118, Strategic Management Research Center, University of Minnesota, 1989; R. T. Kudrle, *Business-Government Relations Abroad: What's Important for the U.S.?* discussion paper 81, Strategic Management Research Center, The University of Minnesota, 1987; S. A. Lenway, "Between War and Commerce: Economic Sanctions as a Tool of Statecraft," *International Organization* 42, 1988, pp. 397–426; J. A. Limprecht and R. H. Hayes, "Germany's World-Class Manufacturers," *Harvard Business Review*, November–December 1982, pp. 106–14; P. S. Nivola, *More Like Them? The Political Feasibility of Strategic Trade Policy*, paper prepared for delivery at the annual meeting of the American Political Science Association, San Francisco, August 30 to September 2, 1990; M. E. Porter, "The Competitive Advantage of Nations," *Harvard Business Review*, March–April 1990, pp. 73–93; "Two Germanys United Would Pose Challenge to Other Economies," *The Wall Street Journal*, November 13, 1989, p. A1.

35. J. S. Nye, *Bound to Lead* (New York: Basic Books, 1990); J. E. Schwarz, *America's Hidden Success: A Reassessment of Public Policy from Kennedy to Reagan* (New York: W. W. Norton & Co., 1988); J. E. Schwarz and T. J. Volgy, "The Myth of America's Economic Decline," *Harvard Business Review*, September–October 1985, p. 101.

36. R. Rosecrance, *America's Economic Resurgence: A Bold New Strategy* (New York: Harper & Row, Publishers, 1990).

37. cf. Porter, *The Competitive Advantage of Nations*.

11 | DECLINING WORLD ECONOMIC GROWTH

Since 1973, economic growth in Western countries has slowed in terms of all relevant measuring rods. The phenomenon has been strikingly general, persistent, and large.

Angus Maddison, "Growth and Slowdown in Advanced Capitalist Economies."

Introduction and Chapter Objectives

All nations in the world experienced economic decline after 1973, but in some countries the decline was greater than others. What accounts for the differences in national growth rates? Economic theory stresses the role of labor and capital. The role of consumers and markets, however, also is important, as the examples of the formerly centrally planned economies of the Soviet Union and Eastern Europe show. The capitalist economies of France and South Korea demonstrate the importance of international market exposure. The ability to incorporate the latest technology into high-quality, low-cost goods also plays a role. The United States, while still strong in product innovation, has lagged behind in production. Product innovation has to be matched by production strength. The Japanese have lagged behind in introducing new products but have excelled at making the products others originated.

This chapter again discusses the differences between the U.S. and Japanese economy. The British sociologist Ronald Dore argues that the U.S. economy is built on a contract model, while the Japanese economy is built on a community model that leads to a sense of fairness in

Japanese society. The continued success of Japan is questioned by some who see a "hollowing out," as Japan becomes more interested in investment abroad than manufacturing at home. This chapter explores these questions, focusing on the reasons for the varying rates of economic growth in different nations.

Worldwide Slowdown

The U.S. economy is not the only one in trouble: since the 1973 Arab oil embargo, the entire world economy has been slipping; that is, the world as a whole has experienced a slowdown in economic growth.[1] While some economies like Japan did better than others, some other economies floundered more than the United States. The U.S. average annual economic growth rate during the period from 1973 to 1985 was 2.3 percent, while the average annual growth rate in Great Britain was 1.1 percent, in the Netherlands 1.6 percent, in West Germany 1.7 percent, and in France 2.2 percent.[2] The economies of some of the newly industrializing Asian nations such as Taiwan and South Korea were flourishing, but the economies of the ex-Soviet Union and the countries of Eastern Europe had deep troubles in the late 1970s and early 1980s from which they have not emerged to this day.

As world economic growth leveled off from its strong 1945–73 showing, the economies of all nations had difficulties they had not experienced earlier. In major industrial countries, GDP growth fell from the 5.6 percent average annual increases in the 1950–1973 period to 2.1 percent from 1974 to 1984.[3] The U.S. average annual growth rate declined from 3.7 to 2.3 percent, but so did that of other countries.[4] Japan could not be happy with a mere 3.8 percent average annual growth rate after having enjoyed average annual growth rates of more than 10 percent during the 1960s.[5] In the 1970s, Japan's decline was the greatest among industrialized nations (see Exhibit 11–1).

Many factors contributed to the change: the 1973–74 and 1979–80 oil price shocks (see Chapter 12), the movement from a fixed to a floating monetary system, and major worldwide recessions in 1974–75 and 1980–81. Perhaps the rate of growth in the period after World War II was exceptional, and the world was simply regressing toward a growth rate that was more normal and sustainable.

The reasons for the slowdown are not readily apparent, nor is it clear why some countries and some regions of the world fared better than others. The extent to which government policies contributed to different country economic performance is not certain. In any case, with the slowdown came changes in relative competitive advantage. Among

EXHIBIT 11–1 **Average Annual Growth Rates in Major Industrial Nations**
Real Gross National Product per Capita

	1961–70	*1971–80*	*1981–85*	*1986–90*
Japan	9.4	3.4	3.2	5.1
France	4.4	3.0	1.0	2.4
West Germany	3.6	2.6	1.3	2.8
Canada	3.3	3.3	1.9	2.3
United States	2.5	1.7	1.8	2.0
United Kingdom	2.2	1.8	1.7	2.4

SOURCE: Adapted from Directorate of Intelligence, Central Intelligence Agency, *Handbook of Economic Statistics* (Washington, D.C.: Government Printing Office, 1991), p. 59.

developing nations, some performed better than others. Between 1965 and 1985, the average growth rate for a sample of 20 developing nations with populations of more than 5 million was 2.9 percent per year, but the seven best nations in this sample—Taiwan, South Korea, Brazil, Thailand, Portugal, Greece, and Yugoslavia—had average annual growth rates of more than 5.0 percent (see Exhibit 11–2).[6]

The gap between the United States and some of the other countries in the world was becoming smaller. The so-called follower nations were catching up with the leader. If the U.S. economy did not pick up, it would be left behind.

Labor and Capital

Economists use labor and capital productivity to account for differences in national growth rates (see Exhibit 11–3).[7] Labor input consists of weekly working hours, while capital input is increments in investment minus depreciation. Labor input can be augmented by improvements in educational quality and in work intensity that partially offset a decline in working hours.

The average Japanese, for instance, continues to work substantially more hours per year (2,149) than the average West German (1,676), American, (1,632), French (1,554) or British worker (1,518).[8] The main reason for the difference is that the Japanese work week is six days, while employees in other countries work five days. Other differences have to do with vacation and sick time and time lost due to occupational accidents, strikes, and other disturbances.

EXHIBIT 11-2   **Statistics on Selected Developing Nations: 1990**

	GDP (% Real Growth)	Per Capita Purchasing Power ($)	Population (Millions)
Thailand	10.0	1,410	56.6
South Korea	9.0	5,560	42.8
Singapore	8.3	12,810	2.7
Taiwan	5.2	7,390	20.4
Pakistan	5.0	380	114.6
India	4.5	300	852.7
Zimbabwe	4.2	550	10.4
Mexico	3.9	2,650	88.0
Columbia	3.7	1,300	33.1
Hong Kong	2.5	11,000	5.8
Philippines	2.5	700	64.4
Egypt	1.0	700	53.2
Zaire	−2.0	190	36.6
Argentina	−3.5	2,560	32.3
Brazil	−4.6	2,560	152.5

SOURCE: Adapted from Directorate of Intelligence, Central Intelligence Agency, *Handbook of Economic Statistics* (Washington, D.C.: Government Printing Office, 1991), p. 30.

Educational Quality and National Competitiveness

Differences in the educational quality of the work force can play a role in national competitiveness.[9] West Germany, for instance, is known for its highly skilled work force especially in scientific and technical areas and for its high-quality scientific and technical education and specialized training. It has distinctive industrial apprenticeship systems that few countries can match. These factors, along with its world-class research capabilities in science and technology and good management-labor relations, result in very high labor productivity.

Japanese workers also are known for their skills in subjects such as mathematics, and for their discipline, willingness to work hard, and group orientation. The pool of well-trained engineers is large in Japan, and the in-house company training programs are excellent. Japan's strengths in elementary and secondary education and in-house training more than compensate for weaknesses in its colleges and universities.

Great Britain has a truly outstanding upper tier of people who are noted for their creativity, inventiveness, and independent thinking and for their capabilities in areas such as pure scientific research. However, the overall work force is poorly skilled and motivated. The educational system lags behind those of other countries, with access to top-quality education available only to the elite. Also, technical colleges have very low status and there is no well-developed apprenticeship system.

EXHIBIT 11–3 The Contribution of Labor, Capital, and Technology to Economic Growth

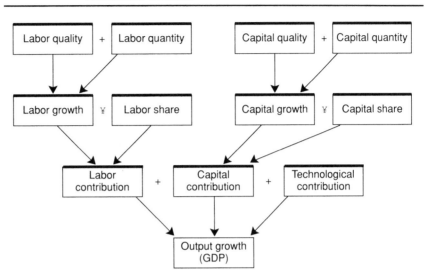

The English elite focused on the humanities and pure science instead of on practical pursuits like engineering. Working too hard and striving too much to earn a living have not been qualities that the elite classes have valued. Managers generally have their origins in lower middle-class families, and often they lack higher education. In-house company training, which is not particularly strong, has been unable to compensate for this weakness. A high degree of labor-management antagonism also exists. It tends to breed narrow definitions of responsibility and an unwillingness to change traditional practices.

The eroding quality of human resources in the United States has long been the topic of discussion.[10] The United States possesses very high quality schools at the top, but the standards of the average German university are higher than the standards of the average American university, and the percentage of students with technical majors in U.S. universities is lower. In comparison to their foreign counterparts, public elementary and high schools in the United States have low educational standards and weak discipline and provide poor training in the sciences, mathematics, and languages.

The weaknesses of American schools often are cited as a major reason for declining U.S. competitiveness (see Exhibit 11–4). Functional illiteracy is said to exist among a high proportion of the work force. Neither a significant apprenticeship system nor a well-developed vocational school system exists to compensate for this weakness.

EXHIBIT 11–4   **Education Expenditures in Industrialized Countries: 1985**
As a Percentage of Gross Domestic Product

	K-12	Higher Education	All Levels
Canada	4.0	1.8	6.3
France	3.9	.7	5.5
United States	3.8	2.5	6.2
Japan	3.1	1.0	4.8
United Kingdom	2.3	.9	4.8
West Germany	2.2	.9	4.1

SOURCE: Adapted from United Nations Educational, Scientific, and Cultural Organization, *Statistical Yearbook* (Paris: 1988).

Concerns about the U.S. educational system are deep-rooted and have received much national attention. Recommendations range from better teacher training to providing prenatal and preschool programs for disadvantaged youngsters. A key to improving American education is to reach children from low-income families. Educationally disadvantaged youth, who constitute more than a third of the country's young people, are more than three times as likely to drop out of school than students from more affluent families.[11] These young people have to be better trained if the United States is going to have an effective work force in the future.

Capital Augmentation

Capital, as well as labor, has to be improved. Capital can be augmented by the replacement of old-vintage buildings and equipment with new vintage.[12] New-vintage capital is supposed to embody the fruits of technical progress (investments in R&D); thus, investing in new capital should be the surest way to realize economic gains.

Some augmentation of capital also takes place from the experience and knowledge employees gain on the job, and from recombining and retrofitting existing capital rather than replacing it with new capital. With regard to capital, the following trends are worth noting.[13] First, in the long term in the major industrialized nations, increases in short-lived assets have been greater than those in durable assets. Second, government's share of total capital (in the form of roads, schools, public buildings, and government enterprises) varies in different countries. For instance, in Great Britain it is 42 percent, while in the United States and West Germany it is about 30 percent. Third, capital in all the major industrial countries grew older after 1973. After declining in age from 1950 to 1973, it went up from 1974 to 1984. Older vintage capital is likely to be an important reason for the slowdown in economic growth and the relative decline in productivity in some countries in comparison to others.

Beyond Capital: The Importance of Markets

Analyses done on developing countries show that the accumulation of capital (measured by investment to GDP) is the most significant predictor of economic development.[14] However, economists recognize that a theory that emphasizes capital without paying attention to markets the capital is supposed to serve is insufficient. For instance, Porter has noted that Japanese demand for compact, portable, quiet, light, multifunctional products comes from the crowded living conditions and small plants, offices, and warehouses that exist in that country.[15] These conditions have led to innovations in the use of materials, energy, and logistics. They have resulted in the production of compact and space-efficient goods and to innovations in short production lines, the avoidance of unnecessary storage space and inventory, and combined production operations. Pioneering in space-saving and just-in-time production has been necessary to meet the demands of sophisticated home buyers who have limited room.

Sophisticated and quality conscious home-country consumers can force a nation's firms to be more innovative and to produce to more exacting standards, generating competitive advantage when those firms face global markets. Japan's success has its roots in its sophisticated consumers. In contrast, American consumers often are willing to accept shoddy goods and merchandise, according to Porter.

Centrally Planned Economies

Centrally planned economies like the former Soviet Union have not been subject to this kind of market discipline (see Exhibit 11–5). Although the Soviet Union possessed attributes needed for economic growth, including a well-educated work force, technically trained with guaranteed lifetime employment, and a government bureaucracy, with a long-term planning horizon, a willingness to sacrifice today's consumption for tomorrow's growth, Soviet economic performance was dismal during the 1980s. It pushed that country into a massive crisis.

The Soviet Union was a closed economy, unexposed to world economic conditions. It built up its human and physical capital without responding to market forces. Its work force was skilled and capable; human resources were not a major problem in this large and diverse

EXHIBIT 11–5 **Average Annual Growth Rates of Formerly Centrally Planned Economies**
Real Gross National Product per Capita

	1961–70	1971–80	1981–85	1986–90	Population	Per Capita Purchasing Power (($)
Soviet Union	3.5	1.5	.9	.2	290.9	9,140
Czechoslovakia	2.4	2.3	1.0	.5	15.7	8,100
Hungary	3.1	2.5	.6	−.2	10.6	6,100
Poland	3.3	3.0	1.0	−1.8	37.8	4,400
Romania	4.2	3.5	−.6	−3.3	23.3	3,200

SOURCE: Adapted from Directorate of Intelligence, Central Intelligence Agency, *Handbook of Economic Statistics* (Washington, D.C.: Government Printing Office, 1991), pp. 29 and 38.

country. Historically, its leaders had been willing to make long-term capital commitments; indeed, they had sacrificed the present for the future and forced people to save by literally confiscating their possessions. But the lack of innovative activity and the tendency of the Soviet system to produce low-quality goods that fell far short of world standards severely hindered Soviet development.[16]

The Soviet Union was battered by its inability to compete successfully in increasingly competitive world markets. The quality problem with Soviet goods had a number of dimensions: an abundance of low-quality goods that consumers were forced to accept because there were no alternatives, goods that were several generations behind those available in the rest of the world, and low-quality services (e.g., in retailing and transportation) that both enterprises and consumers had to rely on.

In a centrally planned economy, the planners, not the producers or consumers, make the important decisions. The planners cannot always anticipate what producers or consumers want. Producers experience serious bottlenecks in making goods, and consumers endure shortages in the goods they value, while store shelves fill with the goods that consumers shun.

The socialist ideology also hinders development. Its dedication to income equality and job security takes away incentives people need to excel.[17] Since few opportunities are open and the options for advancement are limited, people have little reason to make great efforts to succeed. Thus, apathy reigned among Soviet workers, and dissatisfaction was high.

A final problem was the Soviet central planners' desire to maintain price stability.[18] Prices were not used to adjust the economy to changing competitive conditions. Market signals, needed to bring change into motion, were missing. The system, therefore, was static and rigid.

The Failure of Reform in Eastern Europe

Before the political revolutions that brought an end to communism in Eastern Europe and the Soviet Union, there were attempts to reform the socialist economies of these regions. They were largely unsuccessful.[19]

What convinced the leaders of the Eastern bloc that their economies were not working were the serious declines in economic growth that they experienced in the late 1970s and early 1980s. These declines took place despite the fact that investment was high (typically 30 to 45 percent of GDP) and consumption was being squeezed to release further resources for investment. The countries were heavily in debt, but the centrally planned economies of Eastern Europe were ill-suited for choosing appropriate targets for investment. Resources were being channeled to inefficient enterprises that were being protected from foreign and domestic competition.

Many Eastern-bloc leaders understood that a system in which central planners told people how much to produce and what to charge for it would not work. Supply, demand, and prices had to replace the commands issued to producers and consumers. Market signals were needed instead of fixing prices and quantities by central decree. Something had to be done, but introducing markets and market-like mechanisms into a centrally planned economy was far from an easy task.

The Soviet Union already had made various efforts to reform its economy.[20] Khrushchev in 1957 proposed devolution of economic decision making to regional councils. Kosygin retracted these changes but created a new system of bonuses for enterprises. Brezhnev at first again centralized, but when the economy stalled he was forced to reintroduce and expand the bonus mechanisms which, by 1979, were reestablished in the Soviet economy.

The Hungarians

The Hungarians under Janos Kadar went much further than the Soviets. The 1968 reform, which was called the new economic mechanism, took the state out of the planning business. Its role would be the same as that of the state in capitalist countries. It would manage the macroeconomy and allow enterprises to make decisions about inputs and outputs. Managers would make their own deals with suppliers and customers and would be given an incentive to maximize profits. Managers and workers could earn bonuses, and successful enterprises had the right to invest some of their financial surplus. Wage and price controls were modified but unfortunately they were not entirely abolished.

The Hungarian reforms got off to a very good start. By 1971, the proportion of consumer spending determined by market prices was 34 percent, but no significant increase occurred thereafter. To promote competition, a second wave of reforms was necessary in 1979. Competition was promoted by allowing small cooperative enterprises to operate and by lifting some of the controls on the private sector.

Poland too gave enterprises an element of flexibility in setting prices, partially eliminating the determination of output by central authorities. It gave bonuses and other incentives to managers and workers to enhance efficiency. The Polish reforms, though, were largely in response to political disturbances.

Why Reform Did Not Succeed

But none of these reforms seemed to work. All of the Eastern European economies, including the Soviet Union, continued to experience declining growth rates and worsening shortages. The question is why. The answer, to begin with, is that none of the reforms attempted to do away with socialism completely.[21] They were efforts to reform the system from within to make it work better, but state ownership of most of the economy was not abolished in any East European country or in the Soviet Union.

The Eastern European reforms gave managers and workers who had specialized knowledge the right to make decisions. Workers councils were set up in Poland and enterprise boards in Hungary. The councils and boards appointed the managers. They had the right to divide the enterprise's surplus between wages and investment after paying the government taxes and dividends on the cost of capital. Many new businesses did spring up in Hungary, but private and cooperative enterprises never employed more than a third of the work force. The bulk of the capital continued to be owned by the state.

The reforms made a difference, particularly in Hungary, but overall they failed dismally. The bureaucrats in the central planning agencies, who had the most to lose, resisted and attempted to sabotage the efforts. They permitted liberalization only partially and they continued to try to allocate supplies and to set targets for production.

In addition, managers in newly run enterprises were unsure of themselves. They felt that their freedom was incomplete. They had to make their own choices, but could not do so without continuing controls. Many preferred the old situation where they were told in advance what supplies to expect and how much they had to produce and for whom. They squandered the freedom they gained by raising wages, rather than investing in new capital, because they were not the true owners of production.

Soviet Attempts to Follow Hungary

The Soviet Union attempted to follow in the footsteps of Hungary, but its efforts to do so did not work.[22] In 1987, the Law on State Enterprises reduced the number of centrally determined targets and gave enterprises the right to engage in wholesale trade with each other. The 1988 Law on Cooperatives tried to foster the growth of a small business sector. The hope was that by 1990 orders from central ministries would decline from 100 percent of total output to 40 percent. The rest of trade would be conducted voluntarily among the enterprises. However, only 10 percent of trade was conducted in this manner in 1990.

The new small-business cooperatives had trouble obtaining supplies. They had to resort to semilegitimate means and charged exorbitant prices. Soviet citizens considered them to be disreputable. Still, the number of cooperatives in the Soviet Union more than doubled and the profits they made were large.

A key problem, as indicated, was that managers and workers were allowed to make decisions, but they did not own the enterprise. The incentive was to maximize current income and raise wages but not to improve the physical capital or hire new workers.[23] There was no reason to replace worn-out machinery, repair buildings, or attract skilled and talented new people if this took money away from existing managers and workers.

If the managers and workers could borrow money at will from state banks without fear of bankruptcy, there was nothing to prevent them from raising their salaries and wages without working harder or trying to make the enterprise more efficient. As long as the competition from other enterprises was limited, they would simply raise prices and rely on subsidies from the state to stay afloat.

Once the state caught on to what the worker-run enterprises were up to, it had to reintroduce controls on investments, wages, and recruitment of new workers. Thus, the attempt to decentralize decision making was defeated.

Needed: A "Big Bang"

The only cure for these economies was to allow massive unemployment and inflation to take hold for a period in the hope that the economy would correct itself.[24] Thus, the Solidarity-led government in Poland, under its deputy prime minister Leszek Balcerowicz, tried the "Big Bang" approach in January 1990: while market reforms are taking place, the price system will determine which economic enterprises are commercially viable. By contrast, the former Soviet Union had failed to heed the suggested reforms of Leonid Abalkin, its deputy prime minister for economic reform, who had called for property laws that would establish the legal framework for a market economy. Ultimately, these reforms did not succeed and communism failed throughout Eastern Europe and the Soviet Union.

International Market Exposure

In contrast to the formerly communist nations of the East, the economic success of France and South Korea has been built upon extensive exposure to international market forces. The experience of these two countries, however different, demonstrates the importance of international market exposure.

France

Contrary to the myth that French economic development is mainly a result of planning, carried out by an elite trained in France's best schools of public administration and policy, the underpinnings of French success are in its international market exposure.[25] The strategy France employed after World War I, political isolation and economic exploitation of its traditional adversary Germany, had failed.

France's goal after World War II was to integrate as much as possible with its European neighbors so as to make war impossible and to enhance its own prosperity and that of all of Europe. France became a charter member of the General Agreement on Tariffs and Trade (GATT) in 1947 (see Chapter 10 for a discussion of GATT). In 1948 it became a member of the Organization for European Economic Cooperation (OEEC). It was committed in principle, if not always in practice, to the doctrine of free trade. The OEEC had great trouble at first in liberalizing trade, and some of the earliest problems, such as the timing of compliance for the loosening of quotas, involved France.

Nonetheless, in 1950 France called for the creation of a European common market for coal and steel, and the Treaty of Paris established the European Coal and Steel Community (ECSC). Six of the ECSC members then agreed in 1957 to extend the scope of their agreement, and the Treaty of Paris created the European Economic Community (EEC). The EEC prohibited tariffs, quotas, and subsidies that restricted or distorted trade between member states.

Meanwhile, France was losing her colonies and its economy increasingly became focused on developed, as opposed to developing, nations. The share of exports that France's ex-colonies absorbed declined from 42 percent in 1952 to about 10 percent in 1962, when most of them had achieved independence.[26]

The French, like the rest of the EEC nations, became heavily exposed to foreign direct investment. It served to increase the competitive vigor of the markets in which French companies competed. Overall, it is probable that the salutary effects of international exposure rather than government planning largely explain French success in the post–World War II period.

Toward a Single European Market

In 1985 the European community made the decision to create a single market by 1992. Its reasons were that continuing European fragmentation harmed consumers and prevented European businesses from effectively competing against U.S. and Japanese concerns.[27]

The problems with fragmentation were numerous:

1. European companies had to have additional engineers on staff to design products for the different standards that prevailed in different European countries. Philips Industries, for instance, employed an additional 70 engineers to make the seven types of television sets needed for different European countries. The cost to Philips was over $20 million a year.

2. Long truck lines at European borders meant that truckers had to wait an average of 80 minutes before the paperwork was cleared. These delays cost the European economy an estimated $10 billion a year.

The all-European market was designed to:

· Harmonize regulations and standards.
· Liberalize the movement of capital, people, and services.

There would be baseline essential standards in such areas as health, safety, environmental protection, deregulation of the transportation and insurance industries, and mutual recognition of professional qualifications. However, some border controls to check for narcotics, terrorism, and illegal immigration would have to continue, and the goal of equalizing taxes would not be achieved. Differences in value-added and excise taxes would remain because high-tax countries would lose too much money and low-tax countries would have to raise taxes if tax rates were harmonized. Many high-tech businesses in the United States were concerned about the implications of a possible "fortresslike" Europe, which would impose specific conditions that U.S. firms would find hard to accept. Nonetheless, the Western European nations were committed to unification because they had learned that exposure to international market conditions (at least in Europe) was essential for their growth.

South Korea

South Korea's growth also has involved exposure to international markets stimulated by the government's strong proexport policies and by the economy's ability to take over Japanese markets as the yen appreciated.[28] Initially, South Korea tried to compete with Japan as a low-cost producer; it relied on its low labor rates to enter the world cotton textile market. However, it did not have certain Japanese advantages—group control over industry, large manufacturing units, shipping subsidies and low transportation costs, bulk purchases of raw materials, and efficient marketing of finished products. In addition, low wage rates imposed costs in the form of low domestic spending, purchasing power, and productivity.

Currency manipulation did not provide a way out of this dilemma. Devaluations, which were intended to make South Korean exports cheaper and increase sales abroad, made the raw materials and capital goods South Korea needed more expensive—which wiped out the gains that could be made from devaluation. Exchange rate fluctuations, other than accounting for increased volatility, appear to have little impact on real economic growth and national competitiveness (contrary to the views of the economist Martin Feldstein, who has advocated devaluation as a means to alleviate the U.S. trade deficit).[29] Dollar depreciation has adverse effects on the price of imports, including energy costs, which in turn increase the cost of a country's exports without any compensating increase in consumer income. The cure for the problem is productivity growth, not devaluation. Efforts to appreciate the currency have the opposite effect. Neither path can pull an economy out of backwardness.

The South Korean government imposed itself on the economy in other ways.[30] It assumed control over the private sector with the purpose of creating significant export-led growth. First, it used the Law for Dealing with Illicit Wealth Accumulation to confiscate assets from profiteers. Then it forged alliances with these profiteers and provided them with the incentives to become legitimate businesses so long as they were willing to lay the groundwork for this export-led growth.

The government tried to provide the newly formed firms with incentives to offset some of Japan's advantages. Barriers were imposed on imports and firms were allowed to inflate their returns on domestic sales. The government nationalized the banks, and it offered long-term capital at favorable rates to targeted firms and industries that were willing to invest heavily in foreign trade. A strong interventionist state made exports a compulsion rather than a choice for South Korean companies.

Other factors helped. Inflows of foreign credit came to South Korea from financial institutions like the World Bank and International

Monetary Fund. South Korea, which is on the borders of the Communist world, was considered a strategic asset. The loans allowed South Korea to purchase modern plant and equipment. Learning by doing aided in the rapid productivity enhancements. Synthetic fibers reduced the need for expensive foreign raw materials. When Japan's wage levels rose, South Korea was ready to take Japan's place as a low-cost producer of textiles.

The emphasis on export-led growth means that none of the other industrial powers, including Japan, now has such a high dependence on foreign trade as South Korea.[31] Only Hong Kong, Singapore, and Taiwan are comparable, and yet by world standards they are small countries, whereas South Korea, with a population of over 40 million people, is not.

The government-orchestrated strategy of export-led growth has helped make the South Korean economy strong in an extremely short period of time. The South Korean story illustrates how important an emphasis on export-led growth can be. Investments must be based on the existence of a market for the goods that have been made. A central effort by a relatively small nation like South Korea to enhance its economy in a neomercantilist fashion can have good results. The South Korean example goes against the argument that central planning can have little effect on strengthening a country's export potential.

A Comparison of Taiwan's and South Korea's Paths to Prosperity

Comparison between Taiwan and South Korea is in order. Both Taiwan and South Korea have made enormous strides in the post–World War II period. The progress they have achieved is instructive because it can be directly compared to the backwardness of its Communist neighbors, the Peoples Republic and North Korea, both of which started at similar levels but did not go nearly as far.[32] While Taiwanese per capita GNP in 1990 was close to $8,000, per capita GNP in the Peoples Republic was about $350. South Korea had a GNP per capita of about $5,000, while the North Korean per capita GNP was just above $1,000.[33]

Social welfare and equality in both Taiwan and South Korea are at all time highs. The unemployment rate in Taiwan is consistently below 2 percent. In South Korea it has not exceeded 4 percent in the last 20 years.[34] Taiwan is the most egalitarian society in the world, and South Korea's income distribution equals that of Japan or the United States. Both have made important advances toward democracy, but neither is where it should be.

Also, both countries have few resources, little arable land, and high population densities. And both have pursued export-led growth policies. However, they have done so differently.

Taiwan has been less aggressive in protecting domestic industry. The South Korean government has been more interventionist in rewarding companies for some activities and punishing them for others.

Taiwan has relied more on the free market and highly educated, technically trained (more than a third of Taiwanese students in higher education study engineering), and enterprising work force. It has let interest rates rise to their market level, encouraging savings and investment and creating a very atomized industrial structure. Taiwan's companies are financed through equity markets; they are lightly leveraged and small. In 1981 more than 80 percent of the firms had fewer than 20 employees.[35]

In comparison, South Korea's companies are highly concentrated and very heavily leveraged. They have been the recipients of low-interest loans from government planners who have used their control over bank credit to direct cheap money to companies they thought would be export-oriented. These firms grew into the South Korean giants known as the *chaebol*. In 1984, the sales of the top 10 *chaebol* came out to about two thirds of South Korea's GNP (see Exhibit 11–6).[36]

There is much controversy about which country's economy will be stronger in the future. While the South Korean *chaebol* have some admirable strengths, including people, persistence, agility, and financial clout, they also have notable weaknesses including bureaucracy, lack of focus, and lack of creativity.

Technology

As the discussion so far suggests, market opportunities are important, but by themselves they are not likely to be sufficient if the goods an economy produces do not incorporate the latest technological sophistication.

EXHIBIT 11–6   South Korea's Chaebol: 1990

	Sales (in billions)	Net Profit (in millions)
Samsung	$35.6	$348
Hyundai	31.8	445
Lucky-Goldstar	22.8	308
Daewoo	15.8	217
Sunkyong	10.6	90
Ssangyung	7.2	159
Kia	6.1	100
Lotte	4.9	142

SOURCE: Adapted from *The Economist*, June 8, 1991, p. 76.

The goods must have very high quality or sufficiently low price to be competitive in the world marketplace. To achieve high quality or low cost requires technical change and the ability to rapidly adopt new innovations.

The Austrian economist Joseph Schumpeter argued that new capital replaces old capital in waves ("creative destruction") as particular sectors (e.g., textiles, steel, railroads, automotive, chemicals, pharmaceuticals, telecommunications, computers, biotechnology) dominate the world economy at certain intervals. Thus, technical change and the ability to generate innovations are critical for economic growth (see Chapter 15).[37]

R&D spending by corporations is an important part of this process. U.S. companies have lost market share in 12 of 15 critical industries in the period from 1960 to 1986.[38] This drop in market share is connected to lower R&D spending by American firms. Corporate R&D, not government-sponsored R&D, spurs competitiveness, and U.S. firms fund R&D at a rate lower than firms in other countries. The large, diversified American company, organized into separate profit centers and dominated by professional managers rather than owners, is likely to be risk-averse and invest less heavily in R&D than focused firms that are functionally organized and operating to maximize returns to investors.[39]

U.S. firms also may not be as capable as Japanese firms of managing the R&D process.[40] The Japanese approach involves the deliberate creation of excess information, which is shared by different groups that are linked horizontally and vertically both inside and outside the firm. Project teams in Japan have cross-sectional diversity, which is supposed to produce ideas of higher quality and quantity. Every member involved in a project is given a part in creating or suggesting solutions to problems regardless of the position they hold in the organization. Vendors and subcontractors also are consulted about project needs. Different phases in project development are overlapped to speed entry into the market and gain rapid information from consumers. The Japanese aim is to gain insights from consumers about product improvements while at the same time maintaining their existing customer loyalty.

Product versus Process

When a group of Europeans rated the 50 best people in the world in nine technologies, U.S. scientists and engineers rated best in five instances, they were tied for first twice, and they were second twice.[41] However, Japan was number two in every case where the United States was number one, and it was number one in the two cases where the United States was number two. The gap between the United States and countries such as Japan has been narrowing. More U.S. patents were going to foreigners, especially the Japanese, than ever before.

While the United States was spending about the same on R&D as a percentage of GNP as Japan and West Germany—about 2.7 to 2.8 percent—only 1.7 to 1.8 percent of U.S. spending was for civilian research and development (see Exhibit 11–7).[42] Virtually all Japanese and West German spending was on civilian research and development. Military spin-offs to the commercial sector, once common (e.g., the jet aircraft), now were infrequent. Instead, the U.S. commercial sector often developed technologies which were "spun into" the military (e.g., the semiconductor).

The Japanese in particular excelled at process technologies (e.g., robotics). The U.S. decline in this area, according to Lester Thurow, dean of the Sloan School at MIT, was directly related to the slump in productivity growth.[43] Very smooth, consistent growth in productivity of about 3 percent per year existed prior to 1965. Since then, U.S. productivity growth has been increasing at about 1 percent per year, matching Great Britain's in the 20th century, a country that has not kept-up with the rest of the world in per capita living standards. Major U.S. competitors like Japan and West Germany continue to improve their productivity at a rate of about 3 percent per year, which means that they will ultimately pass the U.S. as other countries passed Great Britain.[44]

U.S. companies have thought that the highest returns on investment came from new products, not from building old products better. First-rate people went into new-product development. Process technologies were left for the second-rate people. However, the Japanese discovered that it was unnecessary to invent new products. By manufacturing existing products cheaper and better than the people who invented them, they could capture the profits.

Americans, for instance, invented the video recorder, but could manufacture them only at a unit cost of $100,000. The Japanese lowered the costs of manufacturing so that they could sell VCRs at unit cost of

---

EXHIBIT 11–7   Defense Expenditures of Major Industrialized Nations
As a Percentage of GNP

	1965	*1975*	*1985*	*1988*
United States	7.2	5.6	6.5	6.1
United Kingdom	5.9	4.9	5.2	4.3
France	5.2	3.8	4.0	3.9
Canada	3.0	1.9	2.2	2.1
West Germany	4.3	3.6	3.2	2.9
Japan	1.0	.9	1.0	1.0

SOURCE: Adapted from Directorate of Intelligence, Central Intelligence Agency, *Handbook of Economic Statistics* (Washington, D.C.: Government Printing Office, 1991), pp. 29 and 38.

$300. No VCRs are now manufactured in the United States. Instead, the Japanese have made enormous profits selling this product to Americans.

White-Collar Productivity

The decline in U.S. productivity is often attributed to a less highly skilled, trained, and motivated work force, but additional factors are at work.[45] Blue-collar employment was down by 1.5 million in the years 1980 to 1988, but private output was up 18 percent, which equals a 23 percent productivity gain. White-collar employment was up by 11.8 million people, a 23 percent increase, but white-collar productivity declined by 5 percent in this period.

There were about two white-collar workers for every blue-collar worker in the United States, 60 million persons who were employed in service jobs compared to 30 million who were employed in manufacturing.[46] Many service employees (the fastest growing segment, an additional 1 million between 1980 and 1988) were employed as office cleaners, janitors, and maintenance employees in the office towers that had sprung up in U.S. cities. Many white-collar workers worked in these offices. Their productivity should have been enhanced more by computer technology, but it was not. The office automation that exists in the United States does not exist in Japan. A usable word processor for the Japanese language, for instance, has not been built.[47] The Japanese do not have the "exploding information" that gives them instantaneous access to data that American managers routinely have at their disposal. The problem for American managers is to learn how to use this information to make operations more efficient. Americans have yet to figure out how to use it productively.

Technology and Internationalization

Thus, the technology problem in the United States has a number of dimensions: relatively poor management of the R&D process, an emphasis on product development rather than manufacturing, and an inability to use technology to increase white-collar worker efficiency. Japanese firms tend to emphasize investment in new technology and internationalization to increase productivity, while U.S. firms attempt to increase it by rationing (elimination of excess capacity) without investment in new technological processes.[48] The U.S. firms can carry out a strategy of downsizing because of a high degree of labor market mobility.

Most of the recent gains in U.S. productivity are the result of lower labor costs. From 1982 to 1987, unit labor costs in the United States fell 1.0 percent compared to a 1.1 weighted-average rise for 11 foreign countries.[49] The Japanese firms are constrained by job security from engaging in the strategy that the U.S. firms favor. However, they can invest in technology and internationalize because capital costs are low, business-government ties are close, and firms are willing to cooperate with one another for this purpose.

Fairness

Much has been said about Japanese success in this book and numerous factors have been mentioned that contribute to it. It might be useful to recapitulate and in so doing suggest a central theme that runs through the factors. According to Ronald Dore, the British sociologist, who has lived for long periods of time in Japan and written extensively about Japanese society, a sense of fairness contributes to Japanese success.[50]

Tying Together Ethics, Public Policy, and Global Competition

The concept of fairness combines key elements from this book—ethics, public policy, and global competition. Dore believes that Japanese capitalism is practiced according to a "community model," which distinguishes it from the "company law" model of the capitalism in the United States and Great Britain.[51] According to the community model, managers are senior members in the firm, and shareholders are one of many stakeholder groups that have to be satisfied (see Chapter 6). Japanese managers therefore are free from the short-term pressures imposed by stock market prices and quarterly profits. They are able to take a long-term approach. In contrast, the company law model is one in which the firm is the property of shareholders and managers act as their agents seeking to maximize shareholder wealth and to minimize expenses such as employee wages.

For the community model to flourish, the participants must feel that the system is fair. They must practice "restraint in the use of market power" out of consideration for the interests of their bargaining partners and adversaries. Dore suggests that this sense of fairness is fostered by many elements:[52]

1. Government:
   a. *The size of government in Japan is relatively small.* Both the United States and Britain absorb more of national income in taxes than does Japan. The U.S. tax code is more burdensome than Japan's.
   b. *The Japanese value and honor public service.* Government ministries are able to recruit some of Japan's most talented people into the civil service, which is considered a prestige career.

Ministries like MITI thus have the respect of the business community. The official economic White Papers and "Visions" that it issues are influential in mobilizing and unifying public opinion on economic issues.

c. *By contrast, the Japanese do not much honor politicians, whose role in running the economy is small.* This eliminates, for the most part, destabilizing swings in policy caused by changes in party control of government. The Liberal Democratic party has maintained power for over 30 years (see Chapter 10). Politicians have less economic influence than ministry officials.

2. Labor:

   a. *The Japanese work well, not only hard.* Although yearly working hours are greater than in the United States or Britain, Dore suggests that the crucial difference behind product quality and innovation in Japan is that the Japanese managers and engineers work well as much as hard.[53] Institutional and cultural characteristics account for their dedication to hard work.

   b. *The Japanese are well educated.* The educational quality of the work force is high: over 90 percent of each age group stays in school until the age of 18, 40 percent proceed to college and 50 percent of all master's degrees are in engineering.[54]

   c. *The Japanese work cooperatively in large corporations.* Decision-making processes emphasize widespread and slow consultation and diffusion of responsibility, yet swift execution of agreed decisions. Decisions may take longer to make, but implementation proceeds rapidly because of the commitment earned during the decision-making process. Specific features of the employment system—lifetime employment as the norm, representation of employee interests, and predictable tracks of promotion by merit with minimum-seniority thresholds—are thought to foster cooperation.

   d. *There is a constant emphasis on quality.* Since Japan became aware in the mid-1950s that the rest of the world perceived its goods as shoddy, the Japanese perspective has been that improving quality is a constant battle.[55] While American managers have blamed workers for quality gaps and have relied on end-of-the-line inspections to maintain quality, Japanese firms have stressed process improvements and the constant redesigning and upgrading of products as the way to enhance quality.

   e. *Japanese workers have a sense of ownership.* The Japanese payment system is based on bonuses to employees for profitability gains rather than straight salaries that have to be paid regardless of how well or poorly the firm has done. Japanese workers therefore feel that they are the owners of the businesses that employ them.

f. *Japan has an effective form of union-management relations.* All Japanese companies settle by individual enterprise bargaining with unions at the same time. Pay raises start at the same date (April 1).

3. Capital:

a. *Japan has a high savings rate and low interest rates and corporate investment is very high.* Culture has an influence here. Japanese culture values prudence and a willingness to defer gratification. Its weak natural-resource position may also contribute to the high savings rate.

b. *Japan has a managerial, production-oriented capitalism, not a shareholder-dominated capitalism.* A high proportion of corporate capital is in the form of back loans rather than equity (see Chapters 6 and 10). Equity is often held by the banks that finance the loans. By contrast, creditors and owners are separate in the United States. The close working relationships between Japanese banks and corporations are responsible for lower agency costs and expected bankruptcy costs. Managers are thus able to foster long-term developments that might cause a short-term drain on resources.

4. Industry:

a. *There are extremely close ties with subcontractors in manufacturing.* Loyalty to subcontractors limits cost reductions, yet facilitates quality, prompt delivery, and rapid response times to unique requests. Relationship stability may appear inefficient in an economic sense because it ignores the potential gains from switching vendors to gain the lowest prices, but it provides more rapid flow of information, reduced risk, better conflict resolution, and the creation of goodwill.

b. *Japanese corporations are good at forming semi-cartel-like arrangements with each other.* Japan, as has been discussed, has an impressive array of industry associations that foster cooperation between corporations.

Predictable Cycles of Decline?

Another view of the Japanese economy is that its form of capitalism is not so different from the capitalism practiced in other countries, that Japan too will pass through a predictable cycle wherein its rise inevitably will be followed by its decline.[56] This view attributes Japanese success to other matters than those cited by the community model.

The mercantile period in Japan lasted from 1945 to 1980.[57] During this period the government promoted exports, restricted imports, and manipulated incentives for the formation and use of capital. Japan initially focused on labor-intensive, low-technology industries like textiles. The dominance of heavy industry like steel was next, and then Japan focused on high-value-added products like electronics.

Japanese successes yielded very large current-account surpluses that provided Japan with the means to make the transition from being an industrial economy that concentrates on trade to being an investment-oriented economy. Even though the Japanese could afford to consume more, they did not do so, and they have maintained their frugal saving habits, which have provided them with even more funds for foreign investment.

Earlier Japanese investments were in low-tech industries and raw-material sources in Asia and elsewhere. Japanese foreign direct investment then moved up the product value chain. Foreign direct investment in raw materials declined from 60 percent in 1980 to 28 percent in 1985.[58] Total foreign investment was up from $0.4 billion in 1960 to $38.5 billion in 1985, paralleling the rise in Japan's trade surplus, with much of the new investment destined for manufacturing in the United States.[59]

With U.S. trade restrictions in place, Japan's only alternative for expanding market share in the United States was to expand its U.S.-based manufacturing. This investment in manufacturing abroad could lead to declines in domestic productivity growth, as it did in the United States and Great Britain when these countries took similar routes. The existence of any easy income source abroad may distract industrial producers from the dynamic and innovative pursuit of productivity in the domestic sector.[60]

Hollowing Out

The hollowing out of Japanese industry, according to Young Kwan Yoon, is already occurring. Lower production levels are adversely affecting the lifetime employment system, which may hurt quality and loyalty. Also, the relationships between suppliers and manufacturers are changing. Less growth is taking place in domestic investment, and the ratio of gross private capital formation to GNP is not increasing as rapidly as before. Most important, production experience is moving overseas. Organizational learning, which is often tacit, will not be easily transferred back to Japan. The Japan of the mid-1990s may be a miracle at risk.

Understanding Comparative Economic Performance

Finally, in understanding the comparative economic performance of nations the effects of the following factors are important to recognize:[61]

1. *The steady decline of the share of employment in industry and the growth in services.* Productivity in industry is considerably higher than productivity in agriculture and in services. As long as national economies are moving from agriculture to industries, their productivity rates accelerate. Japan experienced the most marked movement in this direction among advanced industrial nations in the post–World War II era. However, since 1973 all advanced industrial nations have seen a movement away from basic industries toward services, where productivity improvements are harder to achieve. These improvements are harder to achieve in service industries because the personal and individual nature of what is offered resists automation (e.g., to what extent is automated medical care possible?) and because of measurement problems.

2. *The catch-up phenomenon.* Over time, the relative advantage of the United States in such areas as natural resources, investment, education, and research has played less of a role. The nation depleted its natural resources, but international markets expanded and transportation costs declined so that having ample domestic resources was no longer as important. Other countries also caught up with U.S. investment, education, and research advantages. They copied U.S. technology and improved upon it without having to bear the large initial costs associated with its development. Thus, they enjoyed the opportunities of backwardness, which wither away as the economies of the United States and other economies converge.

3. *The foreign-trade bonus.* GATT removed trade barriers after the war, which facilitated international commerce. But the tariff reduction process since 1973 has been less pronounced. Loosening of foreign trade restrictions was important because it gave to the other nations in the world the advantages of a huge marketplace, which previously only the United States had enjoyed. Large markets meant economies of scale and efficiencies that could not otherwise be realized.

4. *Government policies.* These policies may be inwardly oriented and protective of domestic industries, however inefficient they may be; or they may be outwardly oriented and export-led, fully exposing economies to world economic competition. Government policies can be used to raise savings, lower interest rates, and increase investment. They can be employed, alternatively, to devalue and appreciate the domestic currency to make domestic goods cheaper on international markets or to make imported raw materials and capital cheaper. Political stability and the social solidarity that governments can create also is important. For

example, it is hard to imagine rapid economic development in the Middle East because of the civil discord and political tension that has prevailed.

What Managers Can Do

Economic growth and international competitiveness are complex phenomena composed of many elements, and only some factors are under direct managerial control? What can managers do to increase a nation's competitiveness?

For managers this broad question has to be focused on the kinds of issues that managers are best able to address. For example:

- Facilitating innovation through research and development.
- Aligning ownership patterns to take a long-term view.
- Forging alliances so as to combine different firms' strengths.
- Instilling an awareness of product quality and safety among employees.
- Changing organization structures to acknowledge different international conditions.[62]
- Diversifying with competitiveness in mind.[63]
- Generating employee commitment to improved productivity.[64]
- Effectively managing the business cycle.[65]
- Effectively managing political risk.[66]

The Many Paths to Development

This chapter has argued that when considering different rates of growth among countries in the world, examining only labor and capital is insufficient. A host of other factors are important: international market exposure, technological innovation, and a sense of fairness that is reinforced by other conditions in the economy. Specific country examples have shown how these elements play a role in economic development. A more inclusive list of some of the elements involved in enhancing a nation's economic performance is provided in the special feature "Elements Involved in Enhancing a Nation's Economic Performance."

Elements Involved in Enhancing a Nation's Economic Performance

1. Labor productivity:
   a. Value of leisure time.
   b. Work intensity.
   c. Educational quality.
   d. Experience and knowledge gained on the job (learning by doing).
   e. Employment contracts (short-term versus life-time).
   f. Payment schemes (straight salary versus salary + bonus).
   g. Unions and relative wages.
   h. The work ethic.
   i. Cultural factors (e.g., Confucianism/the Protestant ethic).

2. Capital accumulation and innovation:
   a. Extent of investment increments.
   b. Age of capital:
      (1) Replacement of old with new (modernization).
      (2) Investment in short-lived versus durable.
      (3) Recombination and retrofitting of existing capital.
   c. Ability to innovate in use of capital:
      (1) R&D spending in the firm.
      (2) R&D spending in society as a whole.
      (3) Extent of engineers in the population.
      (4) Technical education.
      (5) Ability to exploit scale economies from large-scale projects.
      (6) Development of an entrepreneurial/managerial class with the requisite motivations and skills to start projects and sustain economic development.

   d. Risk-taking propensities in population (e.g., availability of venture capital opportunities).
   e. Requisite flexibility in use of capital: capability of managers to shift resources to most profitable applications:
      (1) Skill development among managers.
      (2) Training and awareness.

3. The cost of capital:
   a. Ability of firms to generate retained earnings.
   b. Savings.
      (1) Government programs to expand savings.
      (2) Individual propensity in population to delay gratification.
   c. Debt:
      (1) Availability and use of domestic financing and government saving.
      (2) Availability and use of foreign financing, foreign aid, and assistance from the World Bank and IMF.
      (3) Conditions imposed by banks in financing and refinancing loans.
      (4) Types of financial institutions (bank/nonbank):
         (a) Expansion of these institutions.
         (b) Their soundness.
         (c) Government ownership and direction.
         (d) Legal climate for lending.
         (e) Acceptance of equity ownership by banks.

Elements Involved in Enhancing a
Nation's Economic Performance continued

    d. Equity market and bond market development: pressures exerted by these markets for short-term pay-offs.

    e. Return on investment (actual/expected) needed for loans and capital market investment.

4. Resource/sectoral factors:

    a. Energy intensity.

    b. Natural resource intensity.

    c. Sectoral elements (industrial versus service sector versus specialization in primary and secondary products).

    d. Emphasis on labor-intensive or capital-intensive industries.

5. Government factors:

    a. Industrial policies:

        (1) Inward orientation or export-led.

        (2) Aggressive/nonaggressive.

        (3) Sector-specific/neutral.

        (4) Responsiveness to market signals/nonresponsiveness.

        (5) Government control of financial sector (e.g., benefits offered exporters).

        (6) Government control of trade policy and other instruments.

            (a) Import barriers.

            (b) Import substitution targets.

    b. Extent and type of government regulation.

    c. Government commitment to private sector and extent of privatization.

    d. Extent and type of government ownership.

    e. Ratio of government expenditures to GDP.

    f. Extent of government deficits.

    g. Willingness to use deficits for countercyclical purposes.

    h. Political stability:

        (1) Social solidarity/political cohesion.

        (2) Distribution of income.

        (3) Extent of democratization.

    i. Skills of economic policymakers (e.g., existence of people with perception, artfulness, imagination, and skill in leadership class and bureaucracy).

6. World market orientation of firm and economy of which firm is a part:

    a. Closed/open character of economy.

    b. Government protection of infant industries/promotion of exports.

    c. Knowledge of foreign markets and language capabilities among managers needed to enter foreign markets.

    d. Extent of involvements in foreign markets:

        (1) Import intensive (raw materials).

        (2) Export intensive (finished products).

    e. Imitation capabilities:

        (1) Introduction of foreign technology.

        (2) Absorption of foreign know-how.

        (3) Abilities to take over markets opened by others.

    f. Exchange rate influences:

        (1) Availability of foreign exchange.

        (2) Competitive devaluations/inflation.

Summary and Conclusions

Since 1973 the world economy has been in general decline but some nations have performed better than others. This chapter has examined the factors that account for the varying economic performance of nations. Labor and capital are the classic factors economists consider to be important. However, they are insufficient to explain the comparative economic performance of nations. For example, the formerly socialist economies of the Soviet Union and Eastern Europe had a well-educated work force and government-sponsored capital investment, but their economies stalled.

To be truly successful in today's economy, international market exposure and orientation are needed. An example of international market exposure is France, via the European Economic Community, and of international market orientation is South Korea, via the policies of its state. The South Korean and Taiwanese economies are very different in this respect, for while both have international market orientation, Taiwan has relied on decentralized market forces to achieve its goals while South Korea has relied on centrally led state directives and large concentrated businesses.

Besides labor, capital, a market orientation, and international exposure, this chapter has argued that technological innovation is important to economic development. Innovation is needed in products *and* in processes. Lagging behind Japan in manufacturing, the United States has performed capably as an innovator of new products, but not as an innovator of new processes.

This chapter returned to the reasons for Japan's economic growth. It cited the community model, which emphasizes a sense of fairness, to distinguish the Japanese economy from the U.S. economy, which, according to sociologist Ronald Dore, relies on a contract model. The possible hollowing out of Japanese industry as it relies more on foreign investment and less on domestic manufacturing was also discussed.

Summary points were made about changes in the world economy after 1973 that have contributed to a slowdown in growth and to the rise of some economies in comparison to others. First, there is the continued decline of manufacturing and the rise of services. Second, there is the catch-up phenomenon of the formerly less developed nations. Third, there is the declining effect of foreign trade barrier reductions. And finally, there is the role governments have played (or failed to play) in the economic development of their nations.

Discussion Questions

1. What happened to the world economy after 1973?
2. What role do labor and capital play in economic development?
3. How can labor's input be augmented?
4. What role does educational quality play in national competitiveness?
5. Why aren't labor and capital sufficient to explain economic growth? What other factors have to be considered?
6. Why didn't the formerly socialist economies of Eastern Europe and the Soviet Union work?
7. What has to be done now to get these economies to work?
8. What explains the success of the French economy in the post–World War II period?
9. What explains the success of the South Korean economy?
10. Compare the South Korean economy with the economy of Taiwan?
11. What role does technology play in economic development?
12. What is the difference between product innovation and process innovation? Which country excels at product innovation? Which country excels at process innovation? Why do these differences exist?
13. What theme does sociologist Ronald Dore use to explain Japanese economic success? Do you agree with his analysis? Why or why not?
14. What is the future of Japan's economy? Is hollowing out going to have a negative effect? Why or why not?
15. What should managers do to make their companies more competitive? What are your recommendations?
16. What should they propose that their governments do to make the national economies in which they operate more competitive?

Endnotes

1. A. Maddison, "Growth and Slowdown in Advanced Capitalist Economies," *Journal of Economic Literature*, 1987, p. 649; R. L. Bartley, "The Great

International Growth Slowdown," *The Wall Street Journal*, July 10, 1990, p. A18; G. Bombach, *Postwar Economic Growth Revisited* (New York: North-Holland, 1985).

2. Maddison, "Growth and Slowdown in Advanced Capitalist Economies."
3. Ibid.
4. Ibid.
5. *World Development Report 1987* (New York: Oxford University Press, 1987); Maddison, "Growth and Slowdown in Advanced Capitalist Economies."
6. K. Dervis and P. Petri, "The Macroeconomics of Successful Development," *NBER Macroeconomics Annual*, 1987, pp. 211–62.
7. K. Choi, *Theories of Comparative Economic Growth* (Ames, Ia.: The Iowa State University Press, 1983); Maddison, "Growth and Slowdown in Advanced Capitalist Economies."
8. Ibid.
9. G. S. Becker, *Human Capital: A Theoretical and Empirical Analysis, with Special Reference to Education*, 2nd ed. (Chicago: The University of Chicago Press, 1975); M. Porter, *The Competitive Advantage of Nations* (New York: Free Press, 1990), pp. 69–131.
10. "Human Capital: The Decline of America's Work Force," *Business Week*, September 19, 1988; C. Kerr, *Education and the Decline of the American Economy: Guilty or Not?* The George Seltzer Distinguished Lecture, Industrial Relations Center, University of Minnesota, 1989.
11. "Human Capital."
12. Maddison, "Growth and Slowdown in Advanced Capitalist Economies."
13. Ibid.
14. Dervis and Petri, "The Macroeconomics of Successful Development"; Yuan-li Wu and Hung-chao Tai, "Economic Performance in Five East Asian Countries," in *Confucianism and Economic Development* (Washington Institute, 1989), pp. 38–55.
15. Porter, "Determinants of National Competitive Advantage."
16. P. Gumbel, "How Gorbachev's Plan Has Left Soviet Union without Much Soap," *The Wall Street Journal*, November 20, 1989, p. A1; E. A. Hewett, ed., *Reforming the Soviet Economy: Equality versus Efficiency* (Washington, D.C.: The Brookings Institution, 1988); E. A. Hewett, "Soviet Economic Performance: Strengths and Weaknesses," in *Reforming the Soviet Economy*, ed. E. A. Hewett (Washington, D.C.: The Brookings Institution, 1988), pp. 31–94.
17. Hewett, "Soviet Economic Performance."
18. Ibid.
19. P. Gumbel, "Soviet Leaders Split on Economic Goals," *The Wall Street Journal*, April 3, 1990, p. A21; Y. N. Maltsev, "The Politics of Perestroika: When Reform Collides with Ideology," *The American Enterprise*, March/April 1990, pp. 88–91; "Perestroika: And Now for the Hard Part," *The Economist*, April 28–May 4, 1990; "The Soviet Economy: The Hard Road from Capitalism to Capitalism," *The Economist*, November 18–24, 1989, pp. 21–24.
20. "Perestroika: And Now for the Hard Part."
21. Ibid.; "The Soviet Economy: The Hard Road from Capitalism to Capitalism."

22. "Perestroika: And Now for the Hard Part"; "The Soviet Economy: The Hard Road from Capitalism to Capitalism."

23. Ibid.

24. Ibid.

25. W. J. Adams, ed., *Restructuring the French Economy: Government and the Rise of Market Competition since World War II* (Washington, D.C.: The Brookings Institution, 1989); W. J. Adams, "A New International Environment," in *Restructuring the French Economy*, ed. W. J. Adams (Washington, D.C.: The Brookings Institution, 1989), pp. 120–206.

26. Adams, *Restructuring the French Economy.*

27. Commission of the European Communities, *The Competitiveness of the Community Industry* (Luxembourg: 1982); "The European Community: An Expanding Universe," *The Economist*, July 7, 1990.

28. A. H. Amsden, *Asia's Next Giant: South Korea and Late Industrialization* (New York: Oxford University Press, 1989), pp. 55–79.

29. M. Baxter and A. C. Stockman, "Business Cycles and the Exchange-Rate Regime," *Journal of Monetary Economics* 23, 1989, pp. 377–400; J. Chipman, *Trade Balance and Exchange Rates*, discussion paper 117, Strategic Management Research Center, University of Minnesota, 1989; R. Dornbusch, "Real Exchange Rates and Macroeconomics: A Selective Survey," *Scandinavian Journal of Economics* 2, 1989, pp. 401–32; J. A. Frenkel and M. Goldstein, "The International Monetary System: Developments and Prospects," *Cato Journal* 8, 1988, pp. 285–306; "South Korea: An Impromptu Performance," *The Economist*, August 18, 1990.

30. Amsden, *Asia's Next Giant*, "The ABCs of Japanese and Korean Accumulation."

31. Ibid.

32. "Taiwan and Korea: Two Paths to Prosperity," *The Economist*, July 14, 1990, pp. 22–29; E. Hartfield, "The Divergent Economic Development of China and Japan," in *Confucianism and Economic Development* (Washington, D.C.: Washington Institute, 1989), pp. 92–115.

33. "Taiwan and Korea: Two Paths to Prosperity."

34. Ibid.; Porter, "Determinants of National Competitive Advantage."

35. "Taiwan and Korea: Two Paths to Prosperity."

36. *The Economist*, June 8, 1991, p. 76.

37. Porter, "Determinants of National Competitive Advantage."

38. L. G. Franko, "Global Corporate Competition: Who's Winning, Who's Losing, and the R&D Factor as One Reason Why," *Strategic Management Journal* 10, 1989, pp. 449–74.

39. C. L. Hill and A. A. Snell, "External Control, Corporate Strategy, and Firm Performance in Research-Intensive Industries," *Strategic Management Journal* 9, 1988, pp. 577–90; R. E. Hoskisson and M. A. Hitt, "Strategic Control Systems and Relative R&D Investment in Large Multiproduct Firms," *Strategic Management Journal* 9, 1988, pp. 605–62.

40. I. Nonaka, "Redundant, Overlapping Organization: A Japanese Approach to Managing the Innovation Process," *California Management Review*, 1990, pp. 27–38.

41. R. H. Hayes and W. J. Abernathy, "Managing Our Way to Economic Decline," *Harvard Business Review*, July-August 1980; L. C. Thurow, *Technology*

Leadership and Industrial Competitiveness (The Center for the Development of Technological Leadership, University of Minnesota, Minneapolis, 1988).

42. Ibid.
43. Thurow, *Technology Leadership and Industrial Competitiveness.*
44. Ibid.
45. Ibid.
46. Ibid.
47. Ibid.; J. M. Schlesinger, "One High-Tech Race Where U.S. Leads: Personal Computers," *The Wall Street Journal*, October 31, 1989, p. A1.
48. P. Enderwick, "Multinational Corporate Restructuring and International Competitiveness," *California Management Review*, 1989, pp. 44–58.
49. J. Erceg and T. Bernard, "Productivity, Costs and International Competitiveness," *Federal Reserve Bank of Cleveland*, November 15, 1988.
50. R. Dore, *Taking Japan Seriously* (Stanford, Calif.: Stanford University Press, 1987).
51. Ibid.
52. Ibid.
53. Dore, *Taking Japan Seriously.*
54. Ibid.
55. R. E. Cole, "U.S. Quality Improvement in the Auto Industry: Close but No Cigar," *California Management Review*, 1989, pp. 71–85.
56. E. J. Lincoln, *Japan: Facing Economic Maturity* (Washington, D.C.: The Brookings Institution, 1988); Maddison, "Growth and Slowdown in Advanced Capitalist Economies."
57. Young Kwan Yoon, *The Irony of Plenty: Japanese Foreign Direct Investment and Productivity*, APSA paper, 1987, pp. 1–36; G. S. Hansen and B. Wernerfelt, "Determinants of Firm Performance: The Relative Importance of Economic and Organizational Factors," *Strategic Management Journal* 10, 1989, pp. 399–411; W. S. Kim and E. Lyn, "FDI Theories and the Performance of Foreign Multinationals Operating in the U.S.," *Journal of International Business*, 1990, pp. 41–54; K. Miller and P. Bromiley, "Strategic Risk and Corporate Performance," *Academy of Management Journal* 33, 1990, pp. 756–79.
58. Young Kwan Yoon, *The Iron of Plenty*; K. Gartrell, "Innovation, Industry Specialization, and Shareholder Wealth," *California Management Review*, 1990, pp. 87–101; J. E. Butler, "Theories of Technological Innovation as Useful Tools for Corporate Strategy," *Strategic Management Journal* 9, 1988, pp. 15–29.
59. Young, *The Irony of Plenty*; B. Mascarenhas, "Domains of State-owned, Privately Held, and Publicly Traded Firms in International Competition," *Administrative Science Quarterly* 34, 1989, pp. 582–97; R. Osborn and C. C. Baughn, "Forms of Interorganizational Governance for Multinational Alliances," *Academy of Management Journal* 33, 1990, pp. 503–19.
60. Young, *The Irony of Plenty.*
61. Maddison, "Growth and Slowdown in Advanced Capitalist Economies."
62. W. G. Egelhoff, "Strategy and Structure in Multinational Corporations," *Strategic Management Journal* 9, 1988, pp. 1–14; S. Ghoshal and N. Nohria, "Internal Differentiation within Multinational Organizations," *Strategic Management Journal* 10, 1989, pp. 323–37.

63. J. M. Geringer, P. W. Beamish, and R. C. deCosta, "Diversification Strategy and Internationalization: Implications for MNE Performance," *Strategic Management Journal* 10, 1989, pp. 109–19; W. C. Kim, P. Hwang, and W. P. Burgers, "Global Diversification Strategy and Corporate Profit Performance," *Strategic Management Journal* 10, 1989, pp. 45–57.
64. P. C. Earley, "Social Loafing and Collectivism," *Administrative Science Quarterly* 34, 1989, pp. 565–81; I. Harpaz, "The Importance of Work Goals: An International Perspective," *Journal of International Business*, 1990, pp. 75–93.
65. B. Mascarenhas and D. A. Aaker, "Strategy over the Business Cycle," *Strategic Management Journal* 10, 1989, pp. 199–210; C. Y. Kwok and L. D. Brooks, "Examining Event Study Methodologies in Foreign Exchange Markets," *Journal of International Business*, 1990, pp. 189–224.
66. R. Johnson, V. Srinivasan, and P. Bolster, "Sovereign Debt Ratings: A Judgmental Model Based on the Analytic Hierarchy Process," *Journal of International Business*, 1990, pp. 95–117.

CASE IIIA
ALLIANT TECHSYSTEMS INC.
Changing Government Priorities[1]

Alliant Techsystems Inc., a defense contractor and supplier of armaments and ordnance to the United States military, finds itself at an interesting crossroad in its brief life. Recently spun off from Honeywell Inc., Alliant is faced with the potential of declining sales and profits.

Economic and political events beyond its control are exacerbating an already severe federal budget deficit, resulting in demands for sizable cuts in Pentagon expenditures. As Alliant relies on the military for 85 percent of sales, the implications of this policy are significant. Alliant must choose a course of action: Should it remain in business as primarily a defense contractor? Or should it attempt to broaden its economic base by diversifying into other markets?

The Company

Alliant has been supplying defense products and systems to the United States and its allies for 50 years. Alliant was formerly Honeywell's Defense and Marine Systems Business (DMSB), Test Instruments Division and Signal Analysis, and it was launched as an independent company in September 1990.[2] As Exhibit IIIA–1 shows, Honeywell's sales for 1985–1990 were flat, with net income ranging between $13 million and $46 million.

Honeywell's progeny had a difficult birth. A casualty of corporate restructuring, DMSB was offered for sale in October of 1989. Despite initial interest, the sale proved difficult. Buyers were leery of projected declines in Defense Department expenditures. As one defense industry analyst put it, "The expectation of flat sales is the primary reason why Honeywell has been trying to sell. . . . Also why nobody bought."[3] Honeywell's board rejected the few offers submitted as being inconsistent with the subsidiary's true value.[4] Ultimately, DMSB was spun off as a separate entity, with Honeywell shareholders receiving one share of stock in the new company for every four shares they held in Honeywell. Although a somewhat unwanted child, Alliant Techsystems was born.

Alliant is a leader in each of its business areas: precision armament, ordnance (munitions), marine systems, and information storage. Its major programs include the design and manufacture of the 120 millimeter shells for the M-1 Tank, the Mark 48 torpedo, cluster bombs, mines, various "smart" weapons, antisubmarine missiles, and graphic recorder products. With a work force of 8,300 employees and 1990 sales of $1.4 billion, it is the 15th largest direct supplier to the U.S. Department of Defense.

Approximately 85 percent of Alliant's business is with the U.S. Defense Department. An additional 8 percent is with U.S.-allied governments. The balance, approximately 7 percent, represents commercial accounts.[5]

Exhibit IIIA–1   Selected Combined Historical Financial Data for Honeywell

			(dollars in thousands)				
	Six Months Ended		**Years Ended December 31**				
	July 1, 1990	July 2, 1989	1989	1988	1987	1986	1985
Income statement data:							
Sales......................	$565,458	$558,154	$1,258,927	$1,438,866	$1,252,216	$1,060,032	$946,184
Cost of goods sold	464,384	456,124	1,012,914	1,205,448	1,015,548	831,377	723,159
Gross margin..............	101,074	102,030	246,013	232,418	236,668	228,655	223,025
Operating expenses:							
Research and development	16,960	20,643	39,074	48,144	37,860	36,650	39,129
Selling...................	32,360	39,787	78,668	73,697	64,295	67,754	57,216
General and administrative	20,972	10,549	45,177	50,708	43,937	39,117	35,529
Restructuring and other unusual charges..........	6,987	—	14,873	10,405			
Total operating expenses....	77,279	70,979	177,792	182,954	146,092	143,521	131,874
Royalty income and other (expense) net	(1,621)	969	(136)	2,872	3,174	193	95
Income before interest and income taxes............	22,174	32,020	68,085	52,336	93,750	85,327	91,246
Interest expense	4,449	5,695	10,485	11,294	10,606	9,406	6,292
Income before income taxes	17,725	26,325	57,600	41,042	83,144	75,921	84,954
Provision for income taxes	3,863	7,031	15,306	27,621	35,708	36,599	38,856
Net income...................	$ 13,862	$ 19,294	$ 42,294	$ 13,421	$ 47,436	$ 39,322	$ 46,098
Balance Sheet Data (at end of period): EPS	1.49	2.07	4.54	1.44	5.10	4.23	4.95
Total assets...................	$440,836	$460,418	$479,197	$442,317	$413,380	$378,453	$316,933
Working capital...............	90,554	122,522	112,745	94,046	129,211	121,039	73,712
Long-term debt...............	104,906	139,742	111,381	126,663	136,725	122,261	60,538
Total equity	$148,011	$145,080	$164,158	$127,069	$143,660	$147,200	$154,520

Macroenvironment

A significant portion of Alliant's sales is associated with long-term contracts and programs for the U.S. government that have significant inherent risks. U.S. government contracts entered into by Alliant are, by their terms, subject to termination by the government either for the government's convenience or through default by Alliant. In addition, many government contracts are conditioned upon the continuing availability of Congressional appropriations. Because the U.S. government provides, directly and indirectly, approximately 85 percent of Alliant's revenue, the loss of a significant portion of this business would have a materially adverse effect on Alliant's operations and profitability.

Unfortunately (for Alliant), the economic reality of severe budgetary constraints is forcing Washington to reevaluate the wisdom of ever-increasing defense expenditures.

The 1980 federal "on-budget" deficit was $72.7 billion,[6] but it will be an estimated $374.4 billion in 1991 (see Exhibit IIIA–2). In an effort to control this soaring deficit spending, the Bush administration has proposed defense outlays of $295.2 billion for fiscal 1992.[7] This marks the first time in 10 years that the White House has proposed an actual year-to-year reduction in military expenditures (see Exhibit IIIA–3). Significantly, if adjusted for inflation, defense spending decreases 11.3 percent, the sixth real decline in a row.[8]

Political realities are propelling the administration into proposing even larger cuts for future defense budgets. For example, the Warsaw Pact has collapsed, and the former nations of the Soviet Union are refocusing their energies away from the West and towards their internal troubles.

In addition, the United States and the Russian federation are currently negotiating to reduce current levels of armaments. And in the wake of Operation Desert Storm, the United States finds itself uniquely secure in the world. Recognizing the changing political landscape, and responding to Congressional demands for a "peace dividend," Secretary of Defense Cheney has proposed slashing the Pentagon's budget to $283 billion by 1996. In real terms, this means a

---

Exhibit IIIA–2   Federal Deficit, on Budget, 1980–1992 (in billions of dollars)

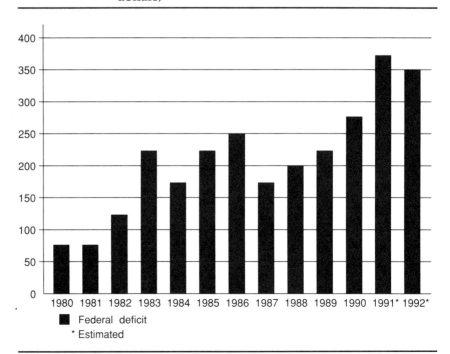

■ Federal deficit
* Estimated

Source: Council of Economic Advisers, *Economic Index—January 1991.*

EXHIBIT IIIA–3   Defense Budget, 1980–1992 (in billions of dollars)

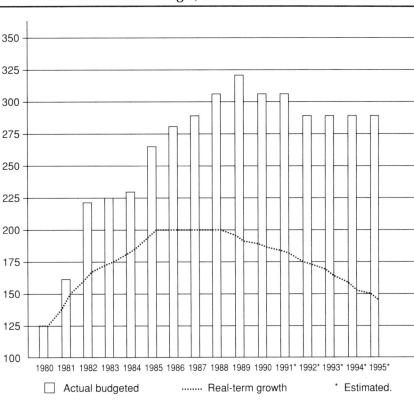

□ Actual budgeted   ······· Real-term growth   * Estimated.

SOURCE: Council of Economic Advisers, *Economic Index—January 1991.*

cumulative 34 percent decline in appropriations since 1985. At a projected 3.6 percent of GNP, military spending in 1996 would be at its lowest since 1939.[9]

In practical terms, the impact could be immense. The plan envisions cutting the size of the army by 25 percent, slashing the navy's fleet of combat ships nearly that much, and retiring more than 400 fighters and bombers in the air force. Nearly all military construction is proposed to be frozen in fiscal 1993, and nearly 100,000 employees, or 10 percent of the Pentagon's civilian work force, are slated to be off the payroll by the end of calendar 1996.[10]

Ramifications for Alliant

These proposals to reduce Pentagon spending have serious ramifications for Alliant. Specifically, by canceling existing programs and by changing government procurement policies through the reduction of "sole-source" contracting, the government is taking steps that threaten several of Alliant's major military contracts. As a result, the company's financial health and existence are challenged.

In an effort to control defense expenditures, the Bush administration has proposed to eliminate or curtail several programs that directly affect Alliant. Production of cluster bombs is scheduled for termination after 1992. As sole-source provider of this weapon, Alliant will lose $125 million in annual revenues.[11] In addition, Defense Secretary Cheney proposes to eliminate production of the M1 tank. As primary supplier of the tank's 120 millimeter shells, Alliant estimates a loss of up to 25 percent of the $250 million in annual revenue that this program generates.[12] Together these programs represent a potential yearly revenue loss of $190 million.

Curtailing sole-source contracting by the Defense Department will also harm Alliant. Under this form of contracting, a manufacturer agrees to develop a product for the military, with the right to be the only, or sole, source for that product.[13] The Defense Department now requests that contracts be "dual source," requiring a sharing of the technology among firms and competitive bidding for shares of the total contract amount. The idea is that "the guy that's got the best price gets the biggest share [of the contract]."[14] The burden, in the form of lower sales and profits and in the loss of proprietary rights, falls upon the military contractor.

This issue is of critical importance to Alliant. The company is currently the sole-source provider for the Navy's Mark 46 torpedo. At $300 million of yearly revenue, or almost 21.4 percent of sales, the Mark 46 is the largest of Alliant's defense contracts.[15] However, the Mark 46 program is scheduled for termination and will be superseded by a new torpedo, the Mark 50. Developed as a dual-source contract with Westinghouse, the Mark 50 contract will be awarded on a competitive-bid process.[16] Under a worst case scenario, Alliant could lose this entire contract. Typically, however, the contract is split. The company with the low bid receives the majority of the contract, with the balance going to the competitor. Significantly, the addition of competitive bidding into the contracting process will almost certainly reduce profit margins. As one defense industry analyst put it, the loss of the Mark 50 program would make Alliant's future "pretty grim."[17]

The loss, cancellation, or "dual-sourcing" of these contracts underscores the seriousness of Alliant's condition. In a worst-case analysis the company could lose $490 million of its major contract business, an almost 35 percent reduction in sales. And depending on how deeply the defense budget is cut, other contracts between the company and the Pentagon could also be canceled or reduced.

Opportunities

While political and economic realities have created significant challenges for Alliant, they have also created opportunities, the chief among them being expanding export markets and the projected explosion in so-called smart weaponry.

A direct result of Operation Desert Storm has been an increased demand for U.S. weaponry and defense technology. Defense analysts estimate that Egypt and the Mideast kingdoms will spend upwards of $25 billion over the next five years to rebuild their armies and upgrade their defense capabilities.[18] The U.S. defense industry, with weaponry fresh from victory over its Soviet counterparts in Iraq, is the beneficiary of this buildup. Thus, Alliant, as supplier of precision armament and ordnance, should directly benefit.

In addition, the success of the Gulf War of technologically sophisticated weaponry has refocused Congressional attention on smart weapons.[19] The trend of the future for the defense industry is development of ever more discriminating weapons, those that pinpoint and attack enemy targets while distancing combatants ever farther from the field of battle. The creator of the next Patriot missile, Stealth Fighter, or Tomahawk cruise missile will be in a position of demanding, and receiving, a larger slice of the shrinking Pentagon expenditures pie.

Alliant is attempting to shift its market to take advantage of these opportunities. Predicting growth markets in the Mideast, Alliant has set a goal to increase exports from 8 percent of sales in 1991 to 15 to 20 percent by 1995.[20] In addition, the company is continuing its research into third-generation smart weapons. Development of the Mark 50 torpedo, surface-ship torpedo defense systems, smart artillery–delivered anti-tank ordnance, and "autonomous underwater vehicles" demonstrates Alliant's continuing attempts to diversify through technology.[21]

The Brink

Despite these opportunities, Alliant appears to be a company poised on the brink of a precipice, balancing to keep from plunging into the abyss of declining sales and earnings. Toby Watson, chairman of Alliant, indirectly acknowledges this through his own conservative financial forecasts. His optimal projection is for a decline in defense spending of 2 percent per year, in real terms, through 1996; with a maximum real-term decline of 20 percent. Based on these numbers, he projects company sales to remain flat, at $350 million to $400 million a year. As a result, he expects that Alliant will continue its no-dividend policy for the foreseeable future.[22]

This analysis is far from optimistic. Projected sales and earnings are flat, despite the inclusion of expanding export markets and the introduction of new weaponry. In addition, the analysis underestimates projected real-term declines in Pentagon spending through 1996, 20 percent versus the administration's proposed 34 percent.

The financial markets also discount Alliant's opportunities. In fact, Honeywell's failure to sell DMSB had been a direct result of market pessimism towards the future profitability of the company, including both domestic and international sales. In its prospectus Alliant conceded that

> the impact of these various [political and economic] developments is likely to be a sizeable decrease in the defense spending, which despite being concentrated in particular program areas, may cause a contraction of the defense industry as a whole. . . . No assurance can be given that the general slowdown in the defense industry will not have a material adverse effect on the Company's business or that the Company will be profitable in future years.[23]

This was an acknowledgement that Alliant did not have a significantly broad base to weather downturns in defense spending. That is, with 85 percent of its sales currently by the Department of Defense and an additional 8 percent by foreign governments, Alliant finds itself a hostage to political and economic conditions outside its control. In a period of enormous federal deficits and uncertain political alliances, defense spending must suffer. So too will Alliant's sales and profits.

Employee morale has been very low. A survey of 231 nonunion personnel showed that most were bitter about management's performance.[24] More than 1,700 workers have been laid off. The remaining work force numbers just 7,200. A profit-conscious corporate culture has been imposed on staff via a series of consolidations and reorganizations of people and facilities. Employees also resent the fact that more than $1 million was spent to remodel corporate offices, while more than $7 million has been spent closing facilities and relocating workers.

Diversification

The difficulty of diversifying Alliant's product line into the consumer market is summed up in comments by Mr. Watson: "It's very difficult to imagine [our] machines making lipstick cases."[25] Indeed, it is problematic to find a consumer market in which Alliant can transfer its expertise in munitions and armaments, while at the same time generating a respectable profit.

However, one product that does lend itself to Alliant's unique abilities is that of small-caliber munitions. This industry manufactures, markets, and distributes cartridges for handguns, shotguns, and rifles to a broad range of users, including the police, sportsmen, and recreational shooters. This industry is compatible with its existing business, it is profitable, it is easy to enter, and there is a history of successful defense industry involvement.

A significant advantage of entering this market is the compatibility with Alliant's existing businesses. The only practical difference between manufacturing a 120 millimeter shell for the M-1 tank and a bullet for a 22-caliber hunting rifle is the diameter of the shell. Beyond that, their basic elements are similar: a casing, a primer, a charge, and a projectile. Alliant could utilize these similarities to achieve economies of scale, transferring production of small-caliber munitions to its existing ordnance plants. In effect, Alliant can gain an outlet to the consumer market without significantly altering its product mix.

The small-caliber munitions industry also has the sales volume and profitability to support Alliant. With over 9,000 employees, the industry reported combined 1989 sales of $910 million and net profits of slightly over $50 million.[26] This is up from 1988's figures of $800 million and $35 million, respectively. The market for consumer ordnance is expected to remain stable, with industry revenues and earnings expected to grow at 5 percent annually.[27]

In addition, the consumer ordnance market is an easy one to enter. With 77 manufacturers, it is still relatively segmented.[28] Many manufacturers serve one particular segment or one specific geographical region. Among all the manufacturers, only 17 are considered major players and have a national presence.[29] This degree of segmentation provides a number of candidates for acquisition, as well as offering an opportunity to subsequently increase market share through consolidation.

History has shown that a large defense contractor can successfully and profitably integrate a consumer ordnance manufacturer. Olin Corporation, a direct competitor with Alliant in the Government munitions market, is the parent corporation of Winchester, one of the largest munitions and armament manufacturers in the consumer market. With over $3 billion in sales, Olin does not break out the sales and earnings of Winchester into its munitions and armaments divisions. However, its annual report states that the consumer ordnance division made significant contributions to its 1990 earnings.[30] While not guaranteeing success for Alliant, it does indicate that the defense and consumer ordnance industries are compatible.

In addition, the inherent difficulties of consolidating a defense contractor with a consumer products firm do not seem insurmountable. For example, unfamiliarity with the consumer market, including marketing, distribution, and contracting, can be avoided by acquiring an existing, profitable concern. Ultimately, the two industries have more similarities than differences.

Other Strategic Thrusts

The corporation has also been making other strategic thrusts such as forming partnerships with former adversaries. If two defense contractors join forces, major defense programs are in less danger of being terminated. Combined technologies strengthen the program and two companies can better defend it than one.

An example is "sense and destroy armor" (SADRAM), a program Alliant used to compete for with Aerojet, a California company. But now the firms have joined forces to produce the system. SADRAM is no longer a winner-take-all project; the Defense Department awarded the contract to Aerojet, which is using Alliant as a subcontractor. The two companies thus will share the $4.5 billion award over the next decade through a joint-venture agreement.

Alliant has developed similar joint-venture agreements with four European weapons firms to develop weapon systems and to seek weapons contracts. Canada, the Netherlands, Turkey, and Japan all buy Alliant's MK46 Torpedo. The U.S. government will pay Alliant $150 million to replace cluster bombs used in the Gulf War, and there is potential to sell this weapons system internationally.

The question for Alliant is, What should it do? Should it diversify into consumer sectors, continue to cut back its operations, examine possible acquisition targets, continue to develop partnerships with other weapons' manufacturers, or look for markets overseas? How can it take advantage of its technological prowess, given new federal budget circumstances?

Discussion Questions

1. What factors threaten Alliant's future?
2. What can Alliant do to influence these factors?
3. What strengths does Alliant have?
4. How should Alliant realign itself to current market conditions? To what extent should it remain mainly a military company? To what extent should it explore other options?
5. If Alliant were to explore other options, how would it go about doing so?

6. What civilian markets have real potential? Could Alliant succeed in these markets?

Endnotes

1. This case was written by Jon Bogen, Paul Ness, Tom Rectenwald, and Paul Rutzen.
2. *Information Statement*, Minneapolis, Minn.: Alliant Techsystems Inc., October 1,1990, p. 9.
3. *Puget Sound Business Journal*, October 15, 1990, p. 3.
4. *Information Statement*, p. 9.
5. Ibid., p. 15.
6. The term *on budget* reflects actual deficit spending before any budgetary reserves are added. It is a truer reflection of deficit spending than the frequently quoted off-budget figures.
7. Council of Economic Advisers, *Economic Index—January 1991* (Washington, D.C.: Government Printing Office, 1991), pp. 32–34.
8. *The Wall Street Journal*, March 5, 1991, p. A14.
9. Ibid., p. A14.
10. *The Wall Street Journal*, February 11, 1991, p. A3.
11. *St. Paul Pioneer Press*, October 1, 1990, p. 7.
12. Ibid., p. A14.
13. *Washington Post*, February 12, 1989, p. 41.
14. *St. Paul Pioneer Press*, p. 6.
15. Ibid., p. 1 col. 4.
16. *Information Statement*, p. 33.
17. *St. Paul Pioneer Press*, p.1.
18. "NBC Nightly News with Tom Brokaw," March 5, 1991.
19. S. L. Kirsch, "How Defense Will Change," *Fortune* 123, no. 6, p. 58.
20. Dow Jones Wire Service, September 28, 1991, 5:21 P.M., p. 3.
21. *Minneapolis Star Tribune*, September 17, 1990, p. 7d.
22. Ibid.
23. *Information Statement*, p. 14.
24. S. Gross, "More Changes Lie Ahead for Alliant," *Star Tribune*, June 24, 1991, p. 10D.
25. *St. Paul Pioneer Press*, October 1, 1990, p. 5.
26. "Ordnance and Accessories," in *1990 Census of Manufacturers* (Washington, D.C.: Department of Commerce, 1990), p. 3.
27. *Value Line*, February 8, 1991, p. 1255.
28. *1990 Census of Manufacturers*, p. 1.
29. *Value Line*, p. 1256.
30. *1990 Annual Report*, Olin Corporation, p. 16.

CASE IIIB
WALTER WRISTON AND THE
CHRYSLER BAILOUT[1]

Walter Wriston was a firm believer in the benefits of a free market. As far as he was concerned, the market became less efficient whenever the government tried to influence it. In the long run, people were poorer on account of it. Wriston was fond of quoting Justice Hugo Black:

> The unrestrained interaction of competitive forces will yield the best allocation of our economic resources, the lowest prices, the highest quality, and the greatest material progress, while at the same time providing an environment conducive to the preservation of our democratic political and social institutions.[2]

Now Wriston had been asked to testify before the congressional banking committee that was holding hearings on the proposed bailout of the Chrysler Corporation. He had to decide what to say.

Citicorp's Stake in the Bailout

Walter Wriston was chairman of Citicorp, one of the largest banks in the world. Citicorp had the most capital funds of any privately owned bank holding company, with $5.9 billion, and had earned $541 million in 1979. The bank had both consumer loan services (serving 16 million individuals worldwide) and commercial loan services, and already held one of the largest shares of Chrysler's bank debt.

Under provisions of the proposed bailout, the banks, including Citicorp, would have to come up with an additional $680 million in new loans and debt forgiveness for Chrysler. Wriston didn't like the idea of loaning Chrysler more money. The automaker had lost more money in 1979 than any company in history. There was no doubt that better loans could be made to entrepreneurs with more promising business prospects.

Wriston had a fiduciary duty to invest funds wisely, and lending additional funds to Chrysler did not seem like a wise use of Citicorp's money. However, he was under intense pressure to make the loans to Chrysler. A great many jobs, apparently, were at stake, as well as the economic health of the communities where Chrysler had plants—and perhaps the economic health of the whole nation. Congress would only authorize the $1.5 billion in loan guarantees it was considering if Chrysler's stakeholders would grant the company $2.6 billion in loans, wage and benefit sacrifices, and other financing.[3]

No stakeholder was exempt from being asked to make sacrifices. Banks, employees, suppliers, dealers, and shareholders were expected to contribute to the $2.6 billion total. The authors of the bailout package were explicit that even those who had loaned Chrysler less than $100,000 had to participate. Legislators reasoned that if exceptions were allowed, each party would want to be excused from its obligations. Should Citicorp be part of this deal?

Government Bailouts

Wriston, who was philosophically opposed to government bailouts, did not know what to do. Federal efforts to save failing corporations were common. During the Great Depression the government's Reconstruction Finance Corporation (RFC) provided low-interest loans to failing businesses. The Small Business Administration continued the tradition of government assistance when the RFC ceased to exist. There had been several highly visible federal bailouts of large enterprises in recent years, including those of Penn Central and Lockheed.[4]

Penn Central.   By the late 1960s, railroads were not a profitable business in the United States, particularly in the Northeast. Unfavorable federal tariff regulations, inadequate investment in maintenance of the railroads' assets, and the movement away from transportation by rail in favor of highways, waterways, and air all contributed to the industry's sorry financial situation. The 1968 merger of two of the largest railroads, the Pennsylvania Railroad and the New York Central, at first seemed like a step toward recuperation for the ailing Northeast lines. It was not to be. By mid-1970 the Penn Central railroad was bankrupt. Shaky from the start, the giant corporation lost more than $1 million per day in 1970 and by the summer its liabilities were almost three times the size of its assets.

A great many people had a lot to lose if the company was liquidated via bankruptcy proceedings. The company's creditors numbered 100,000. There were nearly as many employees with jobs on the line. About 200 Penn Central subsidiaries were served by a multitude of suppliers who would be hurt if the railroad failed. Communities throughout the Northeast could lose rail service. The financial markets, already shaken by recession and the war in Vietnam, could be upset. They might panic if what was the sixth-largest firm in the country when it was formed in 1968 collapsed.

The federal government therefore stepped in to rescue the company. In 1971 Congress created the National Railroad Passenger Corporation (Amtrak) and took over the nation's intercity rail passenger service. Congress created the Consolidated Rail Corporation (Conrail) in 1976 to take over the unprofitable freight operations of six bankrupt eastern railroads, including Penn Central. The government paid Penn Central a total of $2.1 billion for its railroad operations, and invested an additional several billion dollars in repairing its assets and making good on its debts.

The new Penn Central Corporation, no longer in the railroad business, was solidly profitable by 1980 as a diversified firm involved in a variety of energy, real estate, and entertainment businesses. The majority of railroad employees kept their jobs until retirement. Communities continued to be served by rail operations now under quasi-governmental control. The successor to Penn Central in running the railroads, Conrail, however, was still losing money in 1979.

Lockheed.   Lockheed was one of the largest defense contractors during the 1960s, supplying the Pentagon with technologically sophisticated hardware like ballistic missiles for submarines. However, the company suffered a series of financially devastating setbacks late in the decade when it incurred large cost overruns on a number of defense contracts. It spent, for example, $3.7 billion to produce the C-5A military transport aircraft, which it had contracted to produce for $2.3 billion. Further, it only delivered 81 of the 115 planes called for in the contract.

Just as Lockheed's financial picture was worsening further due to cutbacks in the space program and defense contracts, serious problems with another contract developed. Rolls-Royce, the company that produced the engines for the L-1011 Tristar commercial aircraft Lockheed built, was in danger of imminent failure unless it received assistance from the British government. The British government agreed to rescue Rolls-Royce, but only if the U.S. government agreed to guarantee $250 million in loans that Lockheed needed to buy Rolls-Royce engines to complete the Tristar contract.

Debate on the Lockheed loan guarantee proceeded in the congressional banking committees through early 1971. Lockheed's supporters argued that over 50,000 jobs would be lost if the company folded. The already distressed aerospace industry would be threatened. All of the suppliers and subcontractors on the Tristar project, who had already advanced hundreds of millions of dollars, would be harmed, pushing many into bankruptcy. Moreover, national security would be hurt if a large defense contractor went out of business.

Over the objections of those who argued that such a bailout would set a bad precedent and was not really necessary (since Lockheed's missile and military aircraft divisions could have been reorganized and kept in business, or another defense contractor could buy the company), a loan guarantee bill was passed in August 1971. The bill contained provisions designed to ensure that the government had first claim on Lockheed's assets if the company went under, that no more than $250 million in guarantees would be outstanding at any time, and that the government would issue no loan guarantees if other sources of credit were available.

The guarantees reassured Lockheed's creditors, who restructured the company's debt and extended additional credit. Substantial foreign sales, a recovering economy, and more-lucrative government contracts all contributed to the company's improved financial condition, and Lockheed paid off the last of its government loans a few months before they were due in 1977.

Government Intervention in Germany and France

If the federal government were to help Chrysler, it wouldn't be the first time a nation had come to the aide of its auto manufacturers. The West German and French governments had both done so.[5]

West Germany.   By 1974, Volkswagen, the German automaker founded under the guidance of the Nazis in 1939, was in serious financial straits.[6] The company's sales depended on a single model (the Beetle), which, though very popular up through the 1960s, was suffering from increasing competition from Japanese makes. In 1971 the company initiated a program to develop new models, but the program was expensive and fraught with difficulties. Rising competition offered the firm no breathing room. U.S. demand for Volkswagens was hurt by the 1974 recession and Japanese competition; sales fell 11 percent that year. Overseas production plants in Brazil and elsewhere required large capital expenditures and were not providing much of a return. The company needed help.

Since World War II, the West German government had adopted a largely non-interventionist policy with respect to rescues of firms in trouble. Bankers and businessmen in general opposed government intervention, fearing that government control might result. Instead, bailouts were usually financed by the banks whose investments in the troubled company were at stake. If there was any government intervention, it was usually at the state, rather than the federal, level.

When all else failed, though, the federal government was willing to step in. In Volkswagen's case, the federal and state governments agreed to finance an assistance program for the 40,000 workers that would be laid off as a result of a cost-reduction agreement between the labor unions and the company. The agreement gave Volkswagen enough time to develop a successful new model (the Rabbit), and by 1976 the company was profitable again.

France.   The French government's attitude toward bailouts was significantly more interventionist than that of the German government.[7] The French government played an active role in shaping French industrial policy, using taxes and loans to encourage business to operate in ways conducive to achievement of the government's social goals. The government had nationalized a number of important industries. Renault, the leading French automaker, had been nationalized in 1945, and though day-to-day operations were directed by business professionals, the government's public-policy goals still strongly influenced the firm's strategic decision making.

In the wake of the 1973 oil crisis, which threatened Renault's financial future, the company assimilated a number of companies in related tools and parts industries in accordance with a government-sponsored rescue plan. Renault formulated its expansion plans to take into account the government's interest in spreading manufacturing plants, and thus jobs, around the country rather than concentrating them in a few areas, even though concentrating the plants might be more profitable. In another case involving France's other automaker, the government's $310 million direct loan made possible Peugeot's takeover of Citroen in 1974–75. The Ministry of Industry also sent one of its top officials to join the company. Because Renault was owned by the French government and Peugeot-Citroen was a major employer, they could count on assistance from the French government if they got into trouble like Chrysler.

The History of the Chrysler Corporation

The problems that brought Chrysler to the brink of bankruptcy were, in some respects, the kinds of problems that Walter Chrysler had made a name for himself solving.[8] An ambitious and confident man who had a talent for understanding engineering machinery, Chrysler enjoyed early success in the Buick division of General Motors by eliminating waste and inefficiency.

In the early 1920s Chrysler was persuaded to come out of retirement to manage a series of failing auto makers: the Willys-Overland Company, and soon afterward, the Maxwell Motor company. Commanding a $1 million salary, he initiated the development of a completely new automobile featuring a high-compression engine. The new car, the Chrysler, was a smashing success, generating $4 million in profit for the firm in the first year on sales of 32,000 cars. In 1925 the name of the Maxwell Motor Company was changed, and the Chrysler Corporation was born.

Demand for the firm's cars developed quickly, and Chrysler acquired new manufacturing facilities by buying the Dodge Corporation in 1928 in what was at the time the biggest acquisition ever. Chrysler's strategy of "shallow" integration, in which it relied heavily on suppliers for parts rather than building its own, gave it great flexibility in an era of rapid automotive technological change. By the time Walter Chrysler retired in 1937, the company was completely free of debt, having paid off the last of the bonds it issued to finance the Dodge acquisition.

Walter Chrysler's successors did not oversee the same untarnished string of achievements as the company founder. As the automobile market evolved, innovative technologies became less important than automotive good looks. The company began losing market share in the early 1950s under top management that refused to follow the trend toward sharp-looking design. The company yielded second place (never to be regained) to Ford in 1953, and went from a 22 percent share of the market in 1951 to less than 10 percent in 1962. The company lost money during the 1958 recession and again the next year.

The Successful 1960s. In 1961, Chrysler hired a new president, Lynn Townsend, who quickly developed a strategy for recovery based on tightening up operations and expanding into the international auto market as well as nonautomotive domestic businesses. Townsend introduced the industry's first five-year, 50,000 mile warranty and oversaw the development of a line of cars widely acknowledged as the best-designed products Chrysler had offered for years. The company expanded into other businesses: real estate, chemicals, outboard marine engines, air conditioners, space technologies. It also expanded overseas: into France, Britain, Peru, Colombia, Venezuela, Argentina. By the end of the decade, Chrysler had plants in 18 different countries.

The 1960s were a time of robust expansion in the American economy, and Townsend made sure Chrysler wasn't left behind. His 1963 $700 million, 10-year expansion plan expanded six-fold by 1965 as the company added large new manufacturing facilities and founded the Chrysler Financial Corporation to provide credit to dealers and customers. Townsend's plan seemed to work. The company's assets tripled between 1961 and 1968, while debt fell as a percentage of equity from 35 percent to less than 20 percent. Market share rose to 16 percent in 1968.

The Unfavorable 1970s. In 1970, however, began a decade-long string of unfavorable economic developments and just plain bad luck. The first of a series of oil price increases and a recession in 1970 hurt Chrysler's earnings. The company posted its first loss since 1961 in the last quarter of 1969. The expansion had depleted the firm's cash reserves and run up a long-term debt burden of $790 million, larger than that of General Motors. When profits softened, the company was forced to abandon plans both to automate its operations and to develop a line of subcompacts to compete with Volkswagen. The new company president, John Riccardo, initiated a two-year austerity program that cut overhead by several million dollars.

By 1973 auto sales had recovered sharply and so had Chrysler's earnings. Riccardo attributed Chrysler's renewed success largely to its strategy of focusing on the company's profitable compact cars rather than pursuing the subcompact market. Chrysler's Dodge Dart and Plymouth Valiant were doing well in the compact market, and it was picking up some profits from selected segments of the big-car market. The company earned record profits on its highest ever sales in the second quarter of 1973 and was well into a $450 million program to restyle its large cars.

By early 1974, however, large cars were not what customers wanted. The Arab oil embargo in late 1973 put fuel economy at the top of car buyers' lists, and small cars accounted for half of all car sales. As the country suffered through several years of high inflation and stagnant growth, Chrysler's situation grew more perilous. The company's inventories, already swollen by management policies that rewarded high production figures regardless of demand, expanded further. A *Business Week* cover photo featured some of the 360,000 new cars the company couldn't sell. A new austerity plan was implemented to further cut costs, and in the process the jobs of four out of five of the company's engineers were eliminated. Research and development budgets were cut 19 percent. Investment in tools and facilities decreased 39 percent in two years. The company was fighting to stay solvent and was sacrificing its ability to adapt to the future in the process.

The years 1976 and 1977 offered a brief respite to the beleaguered company. Profits rose again as auto sales recovered and customers turned to the company's Aspen and Volare lines for the only luxury compacts on the market. Disaster struck again, though, when numerous technical defects in the Aspen/Volare lines became evident. The cutbacks in engineering had taken their toll. By the end of 1977, Chrysler had spent more than a half million dollars just to mail the recall notices on the more than 90 percent of Aspens and Volares that had to be brought back for fixing. The Center for Auto Safety awarded the Aspen/Volare its "Lemon of the Year" award.

The Need to Increase Investment.   It was clear to Riccardo that the company needed to dramatically increase its investment in the development of new vehicles. Accordingly, he proposed a $7.5 billion plan to provide all-new products and modernize the manufacturing facilities. In order to finance the restructuring, the company began selling off its foreign subsidiaries. Peugeot-Citroen bought an 85 percent interest in Chrysler's French, British, and Spanish plants for $530 million in cash and Peugeot stock. Peugeot also bought Chrysler's European financial subsidiary for $80 million. Volkswagen bought two thirds of Chrysler's Brazilian operation for $50 million, and General Motors bought the company's Venezuelan and Colombian plants for $30 million. Chrysler stockholders also reluctantly approved a new stock issue that raised $200 million.

These funds were not enough. The company lost more than $200 million in 1978 and more than $1 billion in 1979.

New Leadership: Lee Iacocca at the Helm.　In late 1978 the company looked to new leadership to put the company back on its feet. This time it was Lee Iacocca, a thirty-year veteran of Ford who had a knack for developing profitable cars that the public wanted.

Iacocca had proven himself a tough, imaginative, and effective manager during his career with Ford. His greatest success had been the Ford Mustang, introduced in 1964, and still a money maker for Ford. As he moved through the company's ranks on the way to becoming president in 1970, he developed expertise in both product development (he joined the company as an engineer) and marketing, as well as a keen understanding of public relations: when the Mustang was introduced, he managed to get his and the car's picture on the front of both *Time* and *Newsweek*.

Fired in 1978 by Henry Ford II (who explained that he "just didn't like" him), Iacocca was quickly hired as the new president of Chrysler, with the understanding that he would become CEO when Riccardo retired. The move was applauded by most industry observers.

Revamping the Product Line.　Most observers believed that the company needed to substantially revamp its product line. The investment required to do so would be substantial. Retained earnings wouldn't be enough; Chrysler wasn't currently producing and selling enough of the kind of cars people wanted to generate any earnings. The company had already sold off most of its foreign subsidiaries and domestic nonautomotive businesses, so there weren't many suitable assets left to sell. The commercial paper market was largely closed to the company since ratings on its bonds had plummeted due to its recent history of financial trouble. It could not expect much further help from its lenders, which had already put together a last-ditch $567 million line of credit that Chrysler had largely exhausted. Most of the lenders already had lent the maximum that regulations or bank policy would allow to be risked on a single firm. Desperate to keep the company running until the development programs could bring the promising new line of fuel-efficient, luxury compacts (code named K-cars) to market, Iacocca went to the government to ask for help.

The Development of the Bailout Deal

Chrysler's best calculations suggested that the company needed at least $1.2 billion to make it through to 1982. They'd need $334 million in 1979, $1.2 billion in 1980, and $600 million in 1981, for a cumulative total of $2.1 billion, of which $928 million could be covered by further asset sales, leaving a $1.2 billion gap. The company had discretely tested the federal waters in late 1978 when Riccardo suggested to President Carter's chief domestic policy adviser, Stuart Eizenstat, that the company be exempted for two years from certain pending federal fuel economy and auto emission standards. Riccardo said that compliance would cost Chrysler many millions of dollars. The idea was scrapped later as it became clear that even drastic regulatory relief would not be enough to keep Chrysler solvent.

Another early proposal was that the government grant Chrysler a $1 billion advance on the tax credits it had accrued through the enormous losses of recent years. Corporations are allowed to deduct past business losses from current income in order to reduce tax liability. Chrysler had huge losses to write off against future earnings, but no prospect of any earnings in the near future. The idea was to write Chrysler out a check for $1 billion in advance against the future tax benefits of the past losses. This proposal was also scrapped fairly quickly by Treasury Secretary William Miller, who disliked the precedent that such a special tax deal would set.

As late as 1978, Chrysler's management was against the idea of federally guaranteed loans, recognizing that news of such loans invariably shook public confidence in a business, something which would be disastrous for a car company's sales. But by late 1979, guaranteed loans were pretty clearly the only viable option. Bills to provide such loan guarantees to Chrysler had been introduced in the Senate and House Banking Committees, and the struggle over the final form of the guarantee began.

Complicating the discussions was the lack of solid information on Chrysler's present and likely future financial situation. Treasury Department officials who reviewed data submitted by the corporation were frustrated, calling it "completely inadequate," and characterizing the business plan the data was based on as "sophomoric."[9] To remedy the situation, bushels of Chrysler financial documents were transported to the Treasury Department, and a team of analysts began trying to develop a useful financial appraisal from scratch.

A number of legislators were skeptical of the plan to guarantee Chrysler loans and were determined to see that the federal government was not the only party with something at stake. William Proxmire, the Wisconsin senator who chaired the Senate Banking Committee, insisted that Chrysler stakeholders, who had much more to lose than the public at large, universally contribute to the bailout as well or there would be no legislation. Much of the discussion centered on just how much each of Chrysler's constituencies would be required to sacrifice and what form that sacrifice would take.

According to the proposed law, before the government issued any loan guarantees, Chrysler would have to get binding commitments from its constituents for financial aid totaling $2.6 billion. Each constituent's share was to be spelled out so that none of the parties could assume the government or another party would take up the slack. Chrysler union employees would give up wage increases, vacations, and other benefits worth $462.5 million, nonunion benefits would be reduced $125 million, and pension funds would be deferred to save $342 million. Another $628 million would be raised through further asset sales. State governments would have to loan another $187 million. Canada would have to contribute $170 million in loan guarantees after 1982. Chrysler dealers and suppliers would purchase $63 million in convertible debentures. Finally, Chrysler's lenders, domestic and foreign, including Citicorp, would be expected to come up with $642 million by extending the maturity dates on existing loans, forgiving some interest, and deferring other interest payments.

Chrysler owed $4.8 billion to banks all over the world. About a quarter ($1.6 billion) was in loans to the car company, and the other three quarters ($3.2 billion) was loaned to the Chrysler Financial Corporation, which was in relatively good shape. The $1.6 billion loaned to the car company broke down like this:

Consortium led by Manufacturers Hanover:	$567 million
Other U.S. lenders:	$72 million
Japanese lenders:	$400 million
Canadian lenders:	$290 million
European lenders:	$305 million
	$1.6 billion

Not a Good Risk.   Chrysler was not a good risk for further loans, to say the least. By late 1979, the company was already in blatant violation of many of the loans' covenants binding the company to minimum standards of fiscal soundness, and any one of the banks could have exercised its right to bring the automaker to court to demand payment, surely triggering a stampede of such requests.

If the Loan Guarantee Act was actually passed, and the banks were expected to make further loans to the company, bank officers would be presented with a tough decision. Every one of them, down to the smallest lender, would be required to ante up a share of the additional loans proportionate to their existing exposure.

There was some doubt over how the foreign lenders would respond. They were less vulnerable to patriotic appeals, and some of them, just like many U.S. lenders, had no idea that their small involvements with Chrysler would put them on the spot. A Spanish bank, for example, had issued a small 90-day loan to the company, and was incensed that it would be expected to be involved in the same long-term restructuring plans as the major lenders.

Philosophically, Walter Wriston was against the bailout plan. If it was put in effect, he would have to be involved with it whether he liked it or not. He thus reviewed the arguments for and against Citicorp's participation.

The Case for the Bailout

The most frequently repeated reason for putting together a loan guarantee package was the number of jobs at stake. If Chrysler failed, according to Lee Iacocca, 140,000 Chrysler employees would be out of work, and as many as two million other people—families of workers, dealers, and suppliers—would be "severely impacted.[10] The economies of auto-producing states like Michigan would be seriously threatened, and even the national economy would feel the reverberations of a failure.

A Chrysler failure would cost the federal government anywhere from $3 to $15 billion in lost tax revenues and increased unemployment benefits, welfare payments, and food stamp programs. It would also put a strain on the Pension Benefit Guarantee Corporation, the federal guarantor of pension benefit plans like Chrysler's.

Proponents of a bailout argued that there were well-established precedents for targeted government assistance: both the Penn Central and Lockheed bailouts had been successes. Others argued that a Chrysler failure would imperil the national balance of trade as the Japanese rushed to fill in the gap left by Chrysler. The nation would lose the fuel-efficient luxury K-cars the company was working on, and there would be less competition in the U.S. auto industry.

Iacocca argued that there were no alternatives to the guaranteed loan program that would save Chrysler. Declaring bankruptcy and going through a Chapter 11 reorganization might work for some firms, but it wouldn't for an automaker, he said. Customers would not know the difference between a reorganization and liquidation, and would cancel orders, cutting the company's cash flow. Suppliers would demand cash payment upon delivery. Dealers would lose their ability to finance purchases from the company. The company would go under. Bankruptcy simply wasn't a workable option.

The Case against the Bailout

Perhaps a bailout was the only way to save the company, but some, including Wriston, weren't convinced the company should be saved. Wriston felt that

> there [was] no avoiding the fact that a bailout was an attempt by the government to move economic resources to places where they would not otherwise go. Such distortions inevitably would lead to less, not more, productivity—and therefore to fewer jobs, less return of investment, and fewer bona fide lending opportunities for banks and everyone else.[11]

He sympathized with the view that the bailout would set a bad precedent, sending a message to large companies that they didn't need to be efficient because the government would be there to save them if they went bankrupt. It wasn't fair to small businesses that failed all the time. Those failures meant losses for investors, suppliers, employees, and banks, too. That was the price the market exacted for inefficiency. Why should big business be helped just because it could afford an army of lobbyists to capture Congress's attention?

Senator Adlai Stevenson III of Illinois argued that the real solution to the problem was to invest in a retraining and reallocation program for Chrysler workers who would lose jobs in a bankruptcy and not to prop up failing industries as did Great Britain, which had seen its economy gradually ruined as a result.

Wriston's Predicament

Wriston considered the arguments for and against the bailout. If a bailout plan was signed into law by the president, disbursements to Chrysler would be blocked if final commitments by every Chrysler constituent to contribute its share of additional funding were not forthcoming. If the bill were passed, and if Wriston decided not to join in, the whole deal would be scuttled, Chrysler would quickly fail, and fingers would be pointed at Citicorp and any other holdouts as the cause of failure.

Now, in late 1979, Chrysler was nearly out of cash and had been ignoring its suppliers' bills. If a bailout wasn't worked out soon, there might as well be none, for the company would fold. On the other hand, Citicorp had a responsibility to its depositors to invest their money wisely.

Wriston had a difficult decision to make. What should he say to Congress? And if a bailout plan were enacted, should he participate or should he take the heat as the bank president who prevented the plan from proceeding?

Discussion Questions

1. When—if at all—is it justified for the national government to try to help save a declining company?
2. What form should this help take?
3. What can be learned from past precedents?
4. Describe the plan to bail out Chrysler? What exactly did it involve? What was the likelihood that it would be successful?
5. What should Walter Wriston say to Congress about the bailout? Should his company participate, or should he try to stop the bailout?

Endnotes

1. This case was written by Mark Jankus, with the editorial guidance of Alfred Marcus.
2. Statement of Walter Wriston, Chairman, Citibank, Hearings before the Senate Committee on Banking, Housing, and Urban Affairs, Part 2, November 16, 19, 20, and 21, 1979; 96th Cong., 1st sess., *Chrysler Corporation Loan Guarantee Act of 1979* (Washington, D.C.: Government Printing Office, 1979), p. 1284.
3. G. Starling and O. Baskin, in *Issues in Business and Society: Capitalism and Public Purpose* (Boston, Mass.: Kent Publishing, 1985), pp. 29–51; R. B. Reich and J. D. Donahue, *New Deals: The Chrysler Revival and the American System* (New York: Times Books, 1985).
4. N. A. Bailey and C. Lord, "On Strategic Economics," *Comparative Strategy* 7, 1988, pp. 93–97.
5. Ibid.
6. J. A. Hart, "West German Industrial Policy," in *The Politics of Industrial Policy*, ed. C. E. Barfield and W. A. Schambra (Washington, D.C.: American Enterprise Institute, 1986).
7. Bailey and Lord, "On Strategic Economics."
8. Reich and Donahue, *New Deals*.
9. Ibid., p. 98.
10. Ibid., p. 120.
11. Statement of Walter Wriston, p. 1284; M. B. Fuller, *Note on Auto Sector Policies*, case 9–382–121, Harvard Business School, 1982.

CASE IIIC
CHRYSLER AND HONDA

Lee Iacocca, Chrysler's chairman, wanted to understand the success of his competitors in the automobile industry better. While his company again was in decline, some of the competitors had made major advances. Iacocca was most interested in understanding the success of Honda Motor Co. From 1976 to 1986 it grew more rapidly than any auto company. The Accord became the best-selling car in the United States, and Honda surprised everyone with its successful entry into the luxury car market.

Iacocca posed the following questions to his staff:

- Based on Honda's distinct history and culture, how can its strategy be understood?
- Based on the strategic moves it has made in the past, what are its tendencies? What initiatives is it likely to take in the future?
- What can Honda's U.S. competitors do to counter these moves?
- What can Chrysler learn from Honda's way of behaving? Which aspects of Honda can be imitated, and which cannot, by a U.S. company like Chrysler?

Chrysler's Position in 1990

As for Chrysler, Iacocca admitted that it was in serious trouble.[1] One of its biggest mistakes was to diversify. It became involved in aerospace and defense industries, which diverted management attention from making cars. It had made other mistakes, for instance, joining with Italy's Maserati in an aborted effort to produce a new luxury coupe.

An important issue was the effort to slash costs. Even though it had shut down a third of its assembly plants in three years (in the past 10 years Iacocca had shut down 20 plants and laid off over 100,000 people), Chrysler had too many levels of management. As the fifth largest car seller in the U.S., behind Honda and Toyota as well as General Motors and Ford, it could not afford to have a top-heavy structure based on a holding-company model.

To break even, Chrysler had to sell 1.9 million vehicles a year. This was up from a breakeven point of only 1.1 million vehicles just a few years ago. Chrysler had the capacity to make 2.3 million vehicles annually. Sales in 1990, however, plunged 17 percent, more than the overall industry decline of 5 percent. Chrysler's stock price dipped to $12 a share on September 14, 1990. The company could be bought for $2.8 billion. No other company in the United States with revenues and sales as high could be purchased so cheaply. Many expected a foreign automaker that needed a U.S. distribution network (perhaps Fiat) to make a bid for Chrysler.

The company needed new and attractive products, but the money for product development was not available. A project to create a small minivan was dropped because of a shortage of cash; the introduction of a new mid-sized family sedan was delayed; and a new jeep model, scheduled for introduction in 1992, might not be ready on time. Chrysler was having trouble finding new products to match the hits it achieved in the 1980s—the Dodge Caravan and Plymouth Voyager minivans and to a lesser extent the LeBaron convertible. It had to avoid the mistakes it had made with the Omni and Horizon lines, which had now been discontinued.

Costs had to be cut and vehicles brought online when some of the company's best talent was leaving. With bonuses and perks reduced, layoffs already happening, and more expected, some of the company's best managers sought employment elsewhere. Gerald Greenwald, second in command, left to become CEO at another company. A group of highly talented tailpipe engineers went to work for Ford. A marketing person took a job with an ad agency that did business with Ford, and another talented engineer went back to teaching.

The Acquisition of AMC.   Chrysler gained from acquiring American Motors (AMC); however, important mistakes had been made with the acquisition:

- The decision to move its Omni/Horizon assembly operations to a former AMC plant in Kenosha, Wisconsin, which Chrysler then shut down 15 months later.
- The agreement to produce a mid-sized sedan, AMC's Premia, because of an obligation to Renault.
- The inability to match Ford's price on the Explorer sport-utility vehicle, which competed directly with the Jeep Cherokee.

Chrysler could not successfully market the Premia, but was obligated to pay Renault more than $100 million because it was producing fewer Premias than the merger required. The purchase of the Jeep Cherokee was the main reason for the AMC deal since it was the best-selling four-door sport-utility vehicle. However, when Ford introduced the less-expensive Explorer, sales of the Cherokee plunged by 22 percent.

Employees also didn't like Iacocca's decision to build a new $1 billion technical center and possible headquarters 30 miles north of Detroit. They called the complex the "Taj Mahal." Iacocca had to hold a series of "town hall" meetings with them to discuss this and other moves the company had made.

Employees often asked Iacocca's opinion of Honda especially after a series of ads where he proclaimed that a survey suggested that Americans preferred buying Chryslers to Hondas. Douglas Fraser, retired president of the United Auto Workers, called Iacocca's ads ridiculous.[2] The facts were that one in four American buyers chose a Japanese-made car, while only one in 11 chose a Chrysler-made vehicle.

Honda's Rise

In contrast to Chrysler's demise, the ascendance of the Japanese manufacturer Honda was truly remarkable.[3] Honda only came into existence in 1948. Founded by an unschooled, feisty, and temperamental Japanese mechanic, Sochiro Honda, its first product was a motorcycle conversion kit for bicycles, which initially had many defects. Mr. Honda bought cheaply and retooled small engines the Japanese Army had used for communication purposes. They were in great demand during the postwar occupation as people often had to travel long distances to buy bread and other necessities.

Sochiro Honda was the son of blacksmith, who left the small village where he was born to find fortune in the big city in 1922. Always a maverick who spoke his mind, he had a razor-sharp temper and cultivated a "David versus Goliath" image throughout his life.[4]

Sochiro Honda was a brilliant mechanic who loved working with machines. He understood that he did not have the business sophistication to be successful. In 1949, he took on a partner—Takeo Fujisawa—to add needed financial and marketing expertise to his fledgling company. Honda described Fujisawa as someone who had "lofty ideas," but "translated thoughts into actions . . . If he had been a man who did nothing but chase dreams, I would not have been impressed."[5]

A Full-Scale Motorcycle Producer.   After Mr. Fujisawa had come aboard, Honda became a full-scale motorcycle producer, but it was a late entrant to the industry. Its manufacturing capabilities were limited, and it had no standardized drawings, procedures, or equipment. The best it could do was to keep abreast of recent technological developments, persuade distributors to carry it as a second line, and engage in direct advertising to consumers.

In the early 1950s the company was floundering. Therefore, to demonstrate the firm's technical prowess and enhance its reputation, Sochiro Honda concentrated on winning international motorcycle racing events like Great Britain's Isle of Man, the Olympics of motorcycle racing. His success came from developing a new combustion chamber configuration that doubled the horsepower of the engine and halved its weight.

Fujisawa set the company the challenge of designing a safe, inexpensive motorcycle that could be driven with one hand to make it easier to transport packages. Such a motorcycle was needed to facilitate the movement of goods and services among Japan's densely crowded commercial enterprises. Thus, the Honda 50cc Supercub was born. Soon, it constituted more than 60 percent of Honda's sales. The company set up an automated plant with a 30,000-unit-per-month capacity, and it distributed directly to retailers (mostly bicycle shops) on a cash-on-delivery basis.

The next challenge was to sell in the United States. Two Honda executives arrived in the United States in 1958 with no other strategy than to make some sales. According to Kihachiro Kawashami, one of the executives: "It was a new frontier, a new challenge, and it fit the 'success against all odds' culture that Mr. Honda cultivated."[6]

Kawashami did not see a large U.S. market. His first impression of the country was that everyone drove large, powerful, and luxurious cars. There were less than a half million motorcycle registrations in the United States and about 60,000 European imports in 1958. Kawashami's goal, simply, was to compete with the European imports; he would be satisfied with about 10 percent of the import market.

Kawashami started small in the Los Angeles market where there was year-round sunshine, a growing population, and a Japanese immigrant community. Early sales, however, were threatened when the cycles Honda manufactured started to leak oil and have clutch failures. In the United States they were driven faster and harder than they were in Japan, and Honda's test facility in Japan had to work 24 hours a day until it solved these problems.

Kawashami soon noticed that Honda's smaller cycles were being bought by normal Americans and not by "black leather jacket" motorcycle enthusiasts. Sporting goods stores wanted to sell them, not motorcycle dealers that catered to the enthusiasts. This observation presented a dilemma. If Honda focused on the Americans who bought its bikes, it risked alienating the enthusiasts, who would buy premium motorcycles at high prices. The company could not be a wimp in an industry where Harley Davidson set the standard and characters that Marlon Brando and Lee Marvin played in *The Wild Ones* were role models. That strategy defied all logic and common sense.

Nevertheless, as an outsider, Honda took the risk. Its advertising campaign stressed the kinder, gentler aspects of motorcycle riding. The theme it adopted was "You Meet the Nicest People on a Honda." The campaign theme originally came from an undergraduate during his course work at UCLA. Tapping a new cycle market that did not previously exist, Honda captured almost 50 percent of U.S. motorcycle sales by 1964.

Shifting Attention to Cars.　With the retirement of its founders, Honda was ready to shift its attention to cars. Its first lightweight truck and sports car had been introduced in 1962. These products were followed by the Honda Civic, with its revolutionary Compound Vortex Controlled Combustion (CVCC) engine that it brought to the market in 1971. The Civic was the first car to comply with the U.S. Clean Air Act. It also got EPA's highest rating for fuel economy; by 1983, 51 miles per gallon for highway driving.

Then, when the Japanese were considered to be the masters of the small, economical car, Honda came out with the mid-sized Accord. This car helped move the Japanese manufacturers beyond the image of producing only basic, no-frills transportation. It was not only larger than the typical Japanese car, but it was considered a milestone because it had quality features that rivalled those of Mercedes-Benz, BMW, and Porsche.

Honda started to manufacture Accords indistinguishable from those made in Japan in Marysville, Ohio, in 1982, thus becoming the first Japanese auto manufacturer to successfully set up a facility in the United States. It was actually exporting Accords made in Ohio to Japan. By 1989, the Accord was the top-selling car in the United States, and Honda was the fastest growing automaker in the world. It had made a phenomenal entry into the U.S. luxury car market with the Accura and was competing head-to-head with U.S. manufacturers in all segments of the market. According to the J. D. Power and Associates Customer Satisfaction Index, the Accura was the world's most satisfying car to own.[7]

In 1991, Honda announced a new Civic engine that would get 50 miles per gallon in the city and 65 on the highway, thus improving existing auto efficiency by 10 to 25 percent and creating additional challenges for U.S. automakers.[8] It also was adding a station wagon to its line of Honda Accords.[9]

Honda's Philosophy.   In marketing automobiles, Honda was guided by a philosophy that had certain basic principles.[10]

1. Honda was trying to *create new markets*. It was not interested in competing in industries where existing markets already had been created. To create new markets it had to think about styling and comfort, as well as technology. For instance, the Supercub motorbike's configuration made it easier for women to ride. However, it was also necessary to be on the leading edge technologically. Thus, Honda established an independent research and development center early in its existence and took seriously the ideas of the people who worked there. All of the presidents who followed Mr. Honda came from the research department.

2. Honda encouraged *employee participation in management*. Employees had to learn to trust management. They had to be instilled with a sense of common purpose. They had to believe that management and labor stand on common ground. Sochiro Honda insisted that the division of labor "not deprive people of their right to think."[11] Only if everyone thinks about improvements can the industry prosper. These principles are carried out in a number of ways.

- Honda does not have separate cafeterias for white- and blue-collar workers.
- Everybody wears the same white cotton shirt and green and white baseball cap.
- Workers have voluntarily banded together to create quality circles that consider topics like employee welfare and recreation, as well as production efficiency.
- Honda hires people not simply on the basis of their abilities and willingness to cooperate. It will, unlike other Japanese manufacturers, tolerate outspoken mavericks, like Mr. Honda, its founder. Its third president, Tadashi Kume fought a vigorous battle against Mr. Honda to have the CVCC engines be water-cooled rather than air-cooled.[12] Mr. Kume won despite Mr. Honda's opposition.
- Employees are asked to keep diaries of their ideas so that they, not their supervisors, gain full credit for their creative activities.
- There are two promotion systems: one for advancement in rank as a manager and one for advancement in rank as an expert.

Mr. Honda has stated that the workplace "is no battlefield."[13] It is not a place "where the winner smiles and the loser cries."[14] His emphasis is on cooperation and trust, the essential factor in a successful manufacturing strategy.

3. Honda's *international orientation* is matched by *close ties to the community where it locates new plants*. It recognizes that successful international operations depend on these ties. Honda was the first Japanese company to set up manufacturing facilities in the United States. Part of the reason was that its annual import quota (under the voluntary guidelines) to the United States of about 350,000 cars was less than the 500,000 for Toyota and 450,000 for Nissan. Thus, it could only expand U.S. sales by creating U.S. production facilities. However, it has never been reluctant to move its plants overseas. After World War II it was the first Japanese company to establish a manufacturing facility abroad, setting up a motorcycle plant in Belgium in 1962. Honda now had more than 50 plants in over 30

countries. It carried out this localization strategy to remain close to the customer.[15]

4. Honda used *unique approaches* to solving problems. It sought to distance itself and set itself apart from other companies. It wanted to be free from customs, routines, precedents, and conventional ways of doing things. It relished the role of being the maverick in the industry, since its competitors could not predict what it was likely to do. For instance, during the 1950s economic boom in Japan, rather than increasing production to boost profits, it reduced costs, improved production methods, and raised the technical level of employees. It did not build a larger, bulkier rod for a racing engine to avoid its collapse, but made the engine smaller, lighter, and sturdier, in accord with the Japanese saying that "a large tree cannot stand against powerful winds, while the slender and more flexible bamboo can."[16] Importantly, Honda decided against using catalytic converters to clean up auto pollutants; instead, it developed a new engine design the CVCC that did not need the converters. It thus anticipated the pollution prevention principle that only became popular much later in the United States.

Could Honda Sustain the Advances It Had Made?   The 1991 recession struck all the world's automakers hard, including Honda.[17] Its sales dropped, and for the first time it had to park 2,000 unsold Hondas on a storage lot outside its plant in Ohio. Its traditional no-discount policy had to be changed, and it offered dealer rebates of $900 per car. Its earnings plunged 26 percent in the first quarter of 1991, but Honda was still profitable while the other U.S. automakers reported record losses.

More troubling to Honda was its decline in the Japanese market. It went from a third place tie with Mitsubishi in 1989 to a fourth place finish barely staying ahead of Mazda in 1990. Honda executives believed that the reason for the decline in the Japanese market was that Honda had become too cautious and overly bureaucratic. It was choosing conservative styling that was more appropriate to the mass-market than the niche markets to which it appealed in Japan. Its cars were perceived as competent but dull. In Japan, the Accord sold only about 4,000 a month, as opposed to projected sales of 7,000 cars. Jazzier versions of the Accord, the Vigor and Inspire, were selling at a combined rate of 10,000 a month, about three times more than expected. The main difference was one of image, not performance, but in style-conscious Japan, image had become critically important. Whimsically styled cars with sporty names like Figaro and Diamante, manufactured by Nissan and Mitsubishi, gained ground on Honda's more conservative offerings.

To overcome these problems, Honda's president Nobuhiko Kawamoto was considering some major changes. He was thinking of moving Honda out of Formula One auto racing, where its engines dominated, and redirecting resources to environmental research and fuel economy. He was also considering dismantling some of the slow, collegial style decision making in the company and assigning more individual responsibility. Young engineers apparently were frustrated by the long meetings, the lack of agreement, and the slowness of the decision-making process.

Since the departure of Honda's founders, the company had been governed by what company officials called the republican system. All 30 senior executives spent most of their days gathered around conference tables at headquarters. They carried out their activities in a single unpartitioned office that was about the size of a small gym. The company's top executives sat so close to each other that if they wished to speak they could tap each other on the shoulder. Kawamato was considering eliminating some group decision making, setting up private offices, assigning individuals specific duties, and holding them accountable. These proposed changes were unprecedented for Honda.

Some Statistics on the Auto Industry

In 1989, Japanese companies captured a record 26 percent of U.S. auto sales.[18] Japanese transplants accounted for 22 percent of the cars built in the United States. The bulk of GM and Ford profits came from their operation in Europe, not the United States. The Japanese, however, were establishing assembly plants in Britain and on the Continent and promised to be a strong threat to the United States in Europe. Chrysler had already sold its European holdings.

With regard to productivity, GM needed 5 workers a day to build a car, Chrysler 4.4 workers a day, Ford 3.4 workers a day, and the typical Japanese manufacturer just less than 3. The Japanese were able to design, engineer, and launch new cars more than twice as fast as U.S. manufacturers.

With respect to quality, in 1980, the average Ford car had 6.7 defects, GM 7.4, and Chrysler 8.1 in comparison to a Japanese average of 2 defects per car. By 1990, Ford was down to 1.5 defects per car, GM to 1.7, and Chrysler to 1.8, but the Japanese had reduced their defects to 1.2 per car.

The Japanese cost advantage had been more than $2,000 per car a decade ago. In 1990, it was under $600 per car.

Iacocca's Choices

Lee Iacocca had some tough choices to make. After considering the Honda experience, he was wondering what, if anything, his company could do to catch up. What could it do to emulate Honda's success?

Iacocca wondered where Honda would move next. Could it continue to innovate now that it was getting so much bigger *and* more bureaucratic? Would it remain a dynamic force in the auto industry?

How could Chrysler counter competitive moves from Honda? Was there any way Chrysler could regain its position in the U.S. market or stake out a new position as a global competitor on the scale of Honda?

Chrysler was issuing $720 million in new equity to help ensure that it had the financial strength to launch new products in 1992. It had plans to spend $16.6 million on plant, equipment, and products through 1995.[19] What could Chrysler learn from the Honda experience to make sure that this money was well spent?

Discussion Questions

1. What mistakes did Chrysler make? Why did it make these mistakes?

2. Why was Honda successful?

3. What could Chrysler learn from Honda?

4. What challenges did Honda face? How was it likely to respond to these challenges?

5. What type of long-term competitor was Honda likely to be in the U.S. auto market?

6. What should Chrysler do? How should it restructure itself so that it could compete in the world auto market?

Endnotes

1. P. Ingrassia and B. A. Stertz, "With Chrysler Ailing, Lee Iacocca Concedes Mistakes in Managing," *The Wall Street Journal*, September 17, 1990, p. 1.

2. Ibid.

3. R. T. Pascale, Honda (B), Harvard Business School case, 1983.

4. D. E. Sanger, "Sochiro Honda, Auto Innovator, Is Dead at 84," *New York Times*, August 6, 1991, p. 1.

5. T. Sakiya, *Honda Motor* (Tokyo: Kodansha International Limited, 1982), p. 66.

6. Pascale, p. 4.

7. A. Taylor, "Who's Ahead in the World Auto War?" *Fortune*, November 9, 1987, p. 78.

8. "Honda, Mitsubishi Redesign Gas-Saver Engine for Compacts," *Star Tribune*, August 3, 1991, p. 1M.

9. J. Gilbert, "Honda Accord Adds Wagon Utility without Trading Off Sporty Manners," *Star Tribune*, August 3, 1991, p. 1M.

10. Sakiya, *Honda Motor*, pp. 20–21.

11. Ibid.

12. Taylor, "Who's Ahead in the World Auto War?" p. 88.

13. Sakiya, *Honda Motor*, p. 104.

14. Ibid.

15. H. S. Stokes, "Honda the Market Guzzler," *Fortune*, February 20, 1984, p. 106.

16. Sakiya, *Honda Motor*, p. 113.

17. C. Chandler and P. Ingrassia, "Just as U.S. Firms Try Japanese Management, Honda Is Centralizing," *The Wall Street Journal*, April 11, 1991, p. A1.

18. P. Ingrassia, "Auto Industry in U.S. Is Falling Relentlessly into Japanese Hands," *The Wall Street Journal*, February 16, 1990, p. A1.

19. B. Stertz, "Chrysler to Issue $720 Million in New Equity," *The Wall Street Journal*, August 18, 1991, p. A3.

Case IIID
General Motors
The Challenges of Global Competition[1]

The competitive situation of General Motors at the beginning of the 1990s was still uncertain, despite a decade of the most far-reaching strategic changes the company had ever made. The world's largest industrial company (1989 sales were $127 billion) still sold more cars than any other automaker in the world, but the company's market share was one-fourth lower than it had been at the beginning of the decade. It wasn't clear that the changes initiated by GM chairman Roger Smith in his decade-long tenure had positioned the company to regain its position as the industry's competitive leader.

Now, in the summer of 1990, Smith was preparing to retire from the chairmanship. His successor would be assuming control of the company at a challenging time for the auto industry. After a decade that saw periods of substantial growth in car sales, the economies of the United States and other major industrial nations seemed to be entering a sluggish, recessionary phase. Smith's changes at GM would be put to the test by an economic downturn. Among the company's major strategic efforts were a joint ventures with Toyota, the development of a completely new car (the Saturn), a major restructuring of GM's five divisions, and the acquisition of two high-tech subsidiaries, Electronic Data Systems (EDS) and Hughes Aircraft. Continued innovation by GM's domestic and foreign competitors ensured that the company would have little breathing room as it strove to work out the kinks of its restructuring efforts.

NUMMI: The Joint Venture with Toyota

In 1983 GM announced that it would participate in a 50–50 joint venture with Toyota to build 200,000 small cars per year at a plant in Fremont, California. GM hoped to learn the secrets of Japanese automaking methods, and Toyota would gain experience in operating facilities in the United States, something it had never done in the past and that was important in its long-term strategy to increase market share worldwide. The joint venture surprised and worried other automakers, who anticipated that cooperation between the number one and number three automakers would reduce competition in the small car market. These antitrust concerns prompted the Federal Trade Commission to undertake an exhaustive study of the proposed deal, and only after the two partners agreed to terminate the venture no later than 1996 were they given FTC permission to proceed.

The new company was called New United Motor Manufacturing, Inc. (NUMMI). The 1983–1996 time frame would give the company time to move through three complete car development cycles at the plant. The first car made would be a version of a car that Toyota already produced and sold in Japan, but would be marketed in the United States under the Chevrolet Nova nameplate. Toyota would produce the drive train and several other components in Japan and would ship them to the NUMMI plant where stamping and assembling operations would complete the vehicles.

Under the terms of the agreement, GM would contribute the Fremont plant (which had been closed the year before) and cash, for a total investment of $100 million. Toyota would contribute $100 million in cash and would manage the plant, choosing the venture's CEO and top management and implementing Japanese production and management techniques.

These techniques would be a major departure from previous practice for a GM operation. NUMMI would use a just-in-time inventory system to minimize inventory expense, save space, and increase quality by providing no parts stockpiles to cushion the effects of defective components. In another production innovation, production teams would be responsible for developing their own schemes for coordinating body movement, parts location, and the time required to do the job.[2]

These changes aside, GM executives were surprised at how little new technology was actually used at the plant. One executive noted, "I was amazed that they basically used 1950s technology, and they did a heck of a job with it. All the press lines were the same as the older types, except, of course, they were new presses. But it wasn't anything fancy."[3]

The real innovations at the NUMMI plant were in the way the work force was selected and managed. The number of job classifications was reduced to four from the nearly 200 used at some GM plants. Prospective employees underwent an intensive 35-hour screening process and, when hired, were guaranteed they wouldn't be laid off. New employees were extensively trained in the production philosophies of Toyota. Toyota based its work force management philosophy on the assumption that employees wanted to do a good job, and that they would do so if treated respectfully and given the responsibility to improve the quality and efficiency of their output. Workers were rewarded for learning how to do more of the jobs in the plant. A work team even had permission to stop the entire production line if a problem was spotted. Quality control would be ensured by attention to detail at each step of the production process rather than by an inspection when the car was completely assembled, the standard practice at other GM plants.

The idea of giving employees such a degree of control was something foreign to GM's traditional management philosophy, which assumed an adversarial relationship between management and labor and assumed that intimidation was required to make an employee work.[4] GM workers often had little or no idea of what their particular production job actually contributed to the assembly of a car. One GM manager who later had experience with the NUMMI project recalled how, at another GM plant, he brought two production workers to the defect repair area to show them how the repair personnel had to disassemble a significant portion of a car to weld in a part that the two workers had consistently failed to install. He recalled their response: "'You mean to tell me that bracket holds the sunshade?' [The worker] had been doing this job for two years and nobody had ever told her what part she was welding."[5]

By 1986 NUMMI was in operation and by 1987 it seemed to be a success. Worker productivity had increased enough that one study estimated it would cost $750 more and take 50 percent more employees using the same technology at the old Fremont plant to assemble the same car. GM ranked the Nova as one of its best-built vehicles.[6] Toyota was impressed enough to decide to begin assembling 15,000 Corolla FX16's at the plant.[7]

Employee morale was also high. Absenteeism had dropped from 22 percent (at the old Fremont plant) to 2.5 percent. Workers had positive things to say about the new management philosophy: "I learned a different meaning for the word respect—one that doesn't include fear," said one. "My responsibility now is to the team, which works together like a family to solve problems and do the job. And no one places blame when something goes wrong."[8]

Unfortunately, it seemed as though GM was ill-prepared or unwilling to seriously apply the lessons learned at NUMMI to its other operations. According to author Maryann Keller, this may have been because GM's top management had expected to learn primarily technological lessons from NUMMI and was unprepared to change the GM culture to adopt the management philosophy that was at the heart of NUMMI's success.[9] GM rotated teams of managers through NUMMI, prepared training tapes and other instructional materials on the NUMMI concepts, and took thousands of managers on tours through the plant, but it had no established plan for actually incorporating the new concepts at its other facilities. NUMMI-trained managers that moved to other GM divisions generally found that their new ideas received an unfriendly reception. Some left for jobs elsewhere.

Though NUMMI was profitable in its first two years of operation, it lost approximately $100 million in 1988. Sales of the Nova were weaker than expected and were expected to fall by 50,000 units to about 150,000 cars in 1988.[10] Analysts attributed the disappointing sales figures to a weak marketing effort by Chevrolet, competition with other subcompacts, and a nameplate (Nova) that had been associated with a less-respected car in the past.[11]

The 1996 cutoff date was rapidly approaching and GM had yet to decide what to do with the NUMMI work force when the operation was disbanded. By 1990 the facility had begun producing the Prizm, and Toyota had made plans to build trucks there as well.

By 1990, though, it also appeared that GM had learned some lessons from NUMMI after all. The 1987 contract with the United Auto Workers (UAW) inaugurated a new kind of management-labor relationship codified in an agreement known as The Quality Network. Committees composed of management and labor representatives would work together cooperatively in a program to improve efficiency that relied heavily on the teamwork and continuous-improvement concepts of the NUMMI operation. The UAW was guaranteed that no plants would be closed, and the plan made no distinction between hourly and salaried employees—all would be expected to contribute.[12] Whether the inertia of GM's corporate culture could be overcome remained to be seen.

The Saturn: GM Starts from Scratch

The same year that the NUMMI venture was announced, 1983, GM announced another innovative project: the Saturn car, named after the rockets that propelled astronauts to the moon. The Saturn would be the first new GM nameplate since 1918. The new company's mission would be to "market vehicles developed and manufactured in the United States that are world leaders in quality, cost, and customer satisfaction through the integration of people, technology and business systems and to transfer knowledge, technology, and experience throughout General Motors."[13]

The concept of designing a car company from the ground up sprang from Smith's belief that GM needed to develop a leading-edge product if it was to have a chance of remaining number one in the future. A whole new approach to a new-car development was needed because the old approach, as described by Keller, wasn't working anymore:

> Every competitive effort turned into a frightful reduction of the global reality. If customers wanted small cars, the company would chop a foot off big cars; if customers wanted economy, it would eliminate luxury features such as air conditioning; if customers loved the Honda, it would build a model that was its interpretation of what a Honda was.[14]

In the new company, as it was originally envisioned, the Saturn plant would be fully automated. The most advanced robotics and automation technologies would assemble more of the car than ever before. A highly computerized accounting and management system would make the whole operation paperless. An innovative labor/management agreement unlike anything seen before in the U.S. auto industry would be developed, as well as a separate franchise and dealer system.

As the planning phase progressed, the degree of automation and computerization was scaled back, but much remained that was new, especially in the way the work force was managed. Japanese management techniques like those used at NUMMI (which was not online when Saturn was conceptualized) would be utilized. Eighty percent of the work force would be guaranteed lifetime employment. There would be no hourly workers; instead, workers would be paid a salary based on 80 percent of the national average autoworker's wage, with additional pay based on an incentive plan which rewarded good worker performance. There would be no more than five job classifications (one for production workers) and all employees would share one cafeteria.[15]

The Saturn production workers would enjoy more autonomy than workers at any other automaker's plants, including the Japanese. They would participate in the hiring process and would approve new additions to their work team (the workers were organized into 165 teams of ten employees each). They would make most of the decisions concerning how to organize their work flow and would have authority to stop the entire line if a problem developed. They were responsible for the financial performance of their part of the operation, and had the power to veto or modify decisions concerning the purchase and installation of the equipment they used.[16]

The original plans called for a $5 billion investment in the project, which would begin producing 500,000 import-fighting cars at the new plant in Spring Hill, Tennessee, in 1990. As the years passed the plans were scaled back. Instead of 6,000 new hires, only 3,000 workers would be employed. The project's budget was cut back to $1.7 billion and its projected output halved to 250,000 cars. The cars would be more expensive and larger than originally envisioned, yet company analysts still expected the project to run in the red for 15 years before becoming profitable because of the huge fixed costs associated with the start-up.[17]

As the 1990 debut approached, it became clear that the car had to be a success. GM had announced new products before (like the X-cars and J-cars) that were supposed to beat the Japanese at their own game, and had fallen short. After the fanfare with which Saturn was announced and covered by the media, GM's credibility was at stake. It couldn't afford another well-publicized failure.

Customers aside, some analysts wondered what Saturn really had to offer the corporation. If the car was a money-loser before it ever hit the showroom floor, then its value had to be in the lessons the corporation would learn by producing the car. Unfortunately, by 1989 it seemed that the personnel management lessons learned through the NUMMI experience were making the most innovative aspect of the Saturn project seem redundant.[18]

Some industry observers questioned the wisdom of Saturn's marketing plan (which, among other things, called for the car's advertising to make no mention of the company's relationship to GM). The editor of a trade newsletter was skeptical: "They're not going to steal market share from the Japanese. It's more likely that they'll cannibalize other GM products, so for the company it will be a net wash in market share."[19]

The initial reviews upon the car's introduction in 1990 were generally lukewarm. *Autoweek*'s comments were typical: "We are neither over- nor underwhelmed. We are merely whelmed, at least by import standards."[20] Later reviews were quite favorable. Saturn was seen as a qualified success.

1984: GM Reorganizes

By the early 1980s it was becoming evident to GM's top management that the corporation's organization was an impediment to the kind of adaptability that was required to respond to the rapid changes in the global auto industry. Since 1916 GM had been composed of five separate divisions—Chevrolet, Pontiac, Buick, Oldsmobile, and Cadillac—that operated independently of one another. Two other major divisions, Fisher Body and General Motors Assembly Division (GMAD), were responsible for the engineering and tooling/assembly operations. According to the division of responsibilities that existed up until 1984, a car division would develop the design for a car completely independently of the engineering and assembly divisions. It would then pass the design on to Fisher Body, which would engineer the body to comply with design, and then pass that on to GMAD, again without consulting the other divisions. GMAD would then prepare the dies and stamping operations and assemble the car. All divisions reported in a strictly vertical fashion, with the top management resolving all problems and no interaction between lower-level people.[21]

As competition in the industry heated up, and costs and quick responses to market changes became more important, the flaws of the ossified management structure became impossible to ignore. It wasn't enough for a designer to find a solution to a technical flaw in some car part—implementing the solution could take years.

"You have to produce fifty thousand studies to show that it's a better solution," complained one employee. "Then you have to go through ten different committees to get it approved."[22]

A consulting firm, McKinsey and Company, was brought in to assess the situation. It concluded that Fisher Body and GMAD had become bureaucratic empires unto themselves and that a complete reorganization was in order.[23]

In January 1984, the reorganization was implemented in one quick organizational convulsion. The five car divisions were divided into two supergroups: BOC, composed of Buick, Oldsmobile, and Cadillac; and CPC, composed of Chevrolet, Pontiac, GM of Canada, NUMMI, and Saturn. The Fisher Body and GMAD divisions would be split in two and absorbed into both super groups. Henceforth, each supergroup would be responsible for all aspects of development for its own products, including design, engineering, manufacturing, assembly, and marketing. The old divisions would continue to serve as marketing arms.[24] Within each supergroup, product development teams composed of representatives from the design, engineering, and marketing functions, as well as representatives of suppliers, would take responsibility for one of the 50 to 60 major components of a new vehicle design. In this way, Smith hoped to facilitate the kind of rapid response to market demands that the company had lacked.

The reorganization did not proceed particularly smoothly, which was not surprising considering the extent to which old loyalties and old ways of doing business were ingrained in the company's culture. Many of the 10,000 Fisher Body employees affected were upset by the change, which they viewed as something akin to a hostile takeover.[25] Further compounding the problem was the fact that within Fisher Body were subdivisions which considered themselves to be largely independent of Fisher Body. Ternstedt, a trim manufacturer, was such a division:

> "Those Ternstedt guys were alive and well within Fisher," recalled an executive involved in planning the reorganization. "When they were absorbed by Fisher [in a 1970 buyout], they simply circled their wagons and did their own thing. The Ternstedt people were still *Ternstedt people* even though they were being paid by Fisher Body."[26]

Another complication arose when it became clear that the reorganization was severing the informal communications network that had developed over the years and that was largely the means by which things were accomplished in the overly bureaucratized behemoth. "It wasn't that the design engineering group did this or that," said one consultant. "It was *Joe Sampson* did this or that."[27]

Still, Smith expected that the company might require years to fully adjust to the changes. "We changed the structure in six months; moved all the boxes around. The systems will take three to five years. The style might take ten to fifteen years," he noted.[28]

By the late 1980s the reorganization seemed to have been at least partially successful. The quality of GM's cars was higher than it had been at the beginning of the decade, and the organization was more flexible for having gone through such a tremendous change. Still, corporate headquarters had not been subject to reorganization, and the company's culture had hardly changed. There was the possibility that the two supergroups could develop into smaller versions of the old GM, complete with bureaucratic logjams. The head of the CPC supergroup had already organized his group along functional lines with a strictly vertical chain of command, which meant that disputes had to be resolved at the highest levels of management, just as in the old structure.[29]

GM Acquires Electronic Data Systems (EDS)

In 1984, while GM was adapting to the changes wrought by the reorganization, the company made its biggest acquisition to date: a $2.55 billion buyout of Electronic Data Systems (EDS), a rapidly growing firm that designed and operated data processing systems. Founded by billionaire entrepreneur H. Ross Perot, the company was the third largest in its field and was flourishing: its earnings per share quadrupled between 1980 and 1983.[30]

Roger Smith thought EDS would be good for GM in a number of ways. The automaker had 200 IBM mainframe computers and 200,000 terminals, but no centralized data processing system to coordinate interdepartmental operations. At the time, the company's different departments frequently used different computer systems, making electronic communication between departments impossible. The system's inefficiency was estimated to cost GM $600 million per year.[31] Smith envisioned EDS developing a new data processing systems for GM that would coordinate the collection of financial and operations data from throughout the company, process health care claims (the company used 187 different health care carriers and its health care costs came to $450 per car in 1983), and link dealers to the company's financial subsidiary and car divisions, among other things.

Smith also felt that exposure to the highly competitive corporate culture of EDS would be good for GM. The company was known for its rigorous training and testing program, strict code of ethics, and emphasis on results. As an observer put it:

> Candidates for employment were rigorously screened, and would be rejected if even the smallest detail didn't line up correctly. . . . EDS could sometimes feel like a boot camp, with Perot playing the role of unbudgeable drill sergeant. . . . He pushed employees to their limits, expecting them to do the impossible. The important thing was the goal—to get the job done, no matter what.[32]

Where compensation at EDS was based largely on performance incentives, at GM it was based on seniority. Poor performance by a GM employee often went unaddressed for years. One former employee remembered a co-worker whose performance was rated as unsatisfactory or poor from the day he was hired until the day he was fired—16 years later. Only around 100 salaried employees were fired each year, out of a white-collar work force of nearly 150,000.[33]

The merger of the 8,000 GM computer employees with the 6,000 EDS employees did not go smoothly. There was no clear strategy for integrating the two companies. The vice president who was put in charge of the operation remembered:

> I drafted the announcement for Roger Smith to sign that went to the GM people. We *made up* the scope of EDS's authority and responsibility. It had never been negotiated and absolutely no plans were made. There was not a single piece of paper given to me that said, "Here's the plan."[34]

The news that they would be absorbed into the EDS organization hit the GM employees hard. Already distressed that they would lose their generous GM pensions and benefits (they would receive shares of a new class of GM stock instead), they were further alienated by the approach taken by EDS staffers assigned to the GM plants. Over the New Year holiday the EDS staff inventoried the GM computer equipment and left bright orange EDS stickers on it all. Some GM employees began to wear the stickers on their foreheads.[35] Hundreds of GM data processing employees quit and others were fired by the EDS management, which was still independent of GM under the terms of the buyout agreement.

Despite the difficulties, by 1986 EDS had modernized GM's health care claim processing system, saving the company $200 million annually. By 1987 it had nearly completed a private international satellite communications network that would allow GM to communicate among its branches and save hundreds of millions in telecommunications costs. By 1989 EDS was one of the corporation's most profitable businesses, contributing $423 million in earnings—which contrasted sharply with the nearly $1 billion the company's North American car operations lost that year.[36]

Another High-Tech Acquisition: Hughes Aircraft Co.

A year after buying EDS, GM outbid Ford and Boeing to acquire the Hughes Aircraft Company, a major defense contractor and think tank. The $5 billion price tag was almost double the cost of EDS and made the sale the largest acquisition outside the oil business in history.[37]

Hughes developed a wide range of electronic defense systems that were used in everything from aircraft and weapons guidance systems to surveillance satellites. The company employed 26,000 engineers and more than 1,450 Ph.D.'s who were developing more than 100 different technologies for use in 12,000 products and services. Among other things, the company developed computer systems and software, a capacity Smith hoped to utilize by having Hughes help automate GM's computer-integrated manufacturing systems.[38] Hughes was grouped together with GM's Delco Electronics and Delco Systems Operations subsidiaries and the instrument-and-systems-display subgroup of the AC Spark plug division to form GM Hughes Electronics Corporation (GMHE).

Smith believed that high-tech acquisitions like Hughes and EDS would make GM the world leader in automotive technologies well into the 21st century. Hughes would provide GM with a pool of elite technical experts to develop futuristic automotive technologies like night vision systems, a satellite-based vehicle identification and location system, automotive collision-avoidance and near-obstacle-detection systems, and others. The acquisition would also further diversify GM into the defense, electronics, and aerospace industry, providing a hedge against declines in the auto business.

Others thought less of the deal. Hughes had recently been penalized by the military for missing deadlines, inflating costs, and practicing poor workmanship. "We've poured billions and billions into Hughes for the past forty years and they've never built a successful missile," said a Pentagon official at the time.[39] Recurring problems with the company's Maverick missile program had led Congress to attempt to find a more reliable supplier. Critics also doubted whether a developer of one-of-a-kind big-ticket defense systems would have much to offer the auto industry, which relies on mass-produced components with low unit costs. GM board member H. Ross Perot argued strongly against making the purchase: "We can become so preoccupied with using capital to solve our problems that the front-end investment will be so large that it alone will make it difficult for GM to be competitive."[40] In a letter to Smith he noted that "the Japanese are not beating us with technology or money. They use old equipment, and build better, less expensive cars by better management, both in Japan and with UAW workers in the U.S."[41] (Perot's share in GM was later bought back by the company for $700 million.)

The Challenge Ahead

By 1990, GM had spent $77 billion in its decade-long effort to modernize its plants, automate its equipment, and develop new car models. Its truck and foreign car operations were doing well, earning more than $3.5 billion in 1989, but the North American car business continued to lose money. Despite the huge investment, car and truck assembly efficiency had only improved 5 percent since 1980, compared with a 31 percent improvement at Ford.[42] The company operated the 11 least-efficient plants in the country.[43] GM's cars cost an average of $250 more to build than Ford's, and $750 more than Japanese models made in the United States, making it the industry's high-cost producer.[44] Profitability per vehicle fell from $588 per vehicle in 1984 to $12 per vehicle in 1989. All told, the company sold a third fewer cars than it had a decade before, and its market share had fallen almost 12 percentage points to 34.7 percent. During the same period the Japanese manufacturers' combined market share had increased 10.4 percent.[45] Further clouding the future of the company's domestic sales was the fact that, according to a survey of 35,000 U.S. car owners, customers under age 45 preferred Japanese cars by a two-to-one margin over GM's.[46]

Compounding GM's problems was the fact that growth in the domestic motor vehicle market had leveled off during the 1980s, and showed little promise of improving in the 1990s. Total U.S. auto and truck sales grew at a 4.6 percent annual average rate during the 1950s and 1960s, but had only grown at a 0.5 percent rate since 1973.[47] Because of a deceleration in the growth of the driving-age population and number of households in the 1980s, the market wasn't growing as fast as it had in the past. Further, owners were holding on to their old vehicles longer—an average of 7.6 years in 1985, compared to 6.4 years in 1979—because of a decline in household savings and because the vehicles were better made than in the past and didn't wear out as fast.[48]

Much of the increased market share of the foreign manufacturers was due to the success of their "transplants"—manufacturing facilities built in the United States. The voluntary import quotas that had restricted the number of cars Japan could export to the United States had prompted the Japanese manufacturers to look for new ways to penetrate the U.S. market. Establishing production facilities in the United States became economically attractive to Japanese manufacturers in the 1980s as the value of the dollar fell relative to the yen (more than 40 percent between 1985 and 1989), and Japanese cars produced in the United States would be unlikely to be affected by any protectionist legislation that Congress might pass. Honda opened the first transplant operation in 1982, and by 1990 seven more Japanese-owned plants had been built in the United States with a combined production capacity of 1.6 million vehicles annually, about 12 percent of the total U.S. new car/light truck capacity.[49] The transplants helped the Japanese manufacturers continue to expand their share of the market: for every percentage point increase in the market share of transplant vehicles, U.S.

producers' market share dropped two thirds of a point, and the imports' market share dropped one third of a point.[50] GM was the domestic producer whose market share was suffering the most at the hands of the transplants.

But not all of the news was bad. GM had made dramatic progress in its effort to improve the quality of its cars. The number of defects per 100 vehicles had dropped 77 percent to 168, nearly as good as the Japanese average of 121.

Roger Smith's Retirement

In August 1990, after nine years as GM's CEO, Roger Smith retired and was succeeded by the company's president, Robert Stempel. Stempel had worked at GM for 32 years, beginning as a transmission design engineer, and was the first engineer to run the company, which had traditionally been led by people with finance backgrounds. GM's workers and dealers were enthusiastic about the prospect of a "car guy" leading the company, but it wasn't clear that Stempel's approach would be much different from Smith's. "We made our decision to go with the long-term view, and it's paying off overseas, in trucks, and in our acquisitions," he told an interviewer. "We just have to stay the course in North America."[51]

Discussion Questions

1. Evaluate the actions taken by Roger Smith during the 1980s. Were they the right actions to take? Was General Motors in a better position at the end of the decade than it had been when the decade started?
2. What should Roger Smith's successors do?
3. Will General Motors be able to survive in the world auto industry?

Endnotes

1. This case was written by Mark C. Jankus under the editorial guidance of Alfred Marcus.
2. M. Keller, *Rude Awakening: The Rise, Fall, and Struggle for Recovery of General Motors* (New York: William Morrow and Company, 1989), p. 132.
3. Ibid., p. 137.
4. Ibid., p. 129.
5. Ibid., p. 127.
6. Ibid., p. 131.
7. J. L. Badaracco, *The 'New' General Motors*, case 9–387–171, revised February 1988, Harvard Business School, p. 5.
8. Keller, *Rude Awakening*, p. 142.
9. Ibid., pp. 135–42.
10. J. L. Badaracco Jr., *General Motors in 1988*, case 9–388–118, revised April 1988, Harvard Business School, p. 6.
11. J. L. Badaracco, Jr., *General Motors' Asian Alliances*, case 9–388–094, revised May 1988, Harvard Business School, p. 5.
12. Keller, *Rude Awakening*, p. 242, 249–50.
13. Ibid., p. 248.
14. Ibid., p. 93.
15. Badaracco, *The New General Motors*, p. 7.

16. J. Szczesny, "The Right Stuff," *Time*, October 29, 1990, p. 76.
17. Keller, *Rude Awakening*, p. 163.
18. Ibid., p. 249.
19. Szczesny, "The Right Stuff," p. 78.
20. "To Saturn and Beyond," *Fortune*, November 5, 1990, p. 12.
21. Keller, *Rude Awakening*, p. 100.
22. Ibid., p. 106.
23. Ibid., p. 109.
24. Badaracco, *The 'New' General Motors*, p. 8.
25. Keller, *Rude Awakening*, p. 114.
26. Ibid., p. 113.
27. Ibid., p. 118.
28. Badaracco, *The 'New' General Motors*, p. 15.
29. Keller, *Rude Awakening*, p. 120.
30. Badaracco, *General Motors in 1988*, p. 7.
31. Keller, *Rude Awakening*, p. 147.
32. Ibid., p. 149.
33. Ibid., p. 31.
34. Ibid., p. 152.
35. Badaracco, *General Motors in 1988*, p. 8.
36. A. Taylor, "The New Drive to Revive GM," *Fortune*, April 9, 1990, p. 53.
37. Badaracco, *The 'New' General Motors*, p. 13.
38. Ibid., p. 15.
39. Keller, *Rude Awakening*, p. 168.
40. Cited in Ibid., p. 173.
41. Ibid., p. 172.
42. Taylor, "The New Drive to Revive GM," p. 60.
43. C. P. Work, "Detroit's Drive for the Fast Lane," *U.S. News & World Report*, January 11, 1990, p. 41.
44. Taylor, "The New Drive to Revive GM," p. 53.
45. Ibid., p. 53.
46. Ibid., p. 57.
47. M. F. Bryan and J. B. Martin, *Realignment in the U.S. Motor Vehicle Industry*, a publication of the Federal Reserve Bank of Cleveland, June 1, 1991.
48. Ibid.
49. Ibid.
50. Ibid.
51. Ibid., p. 55.

PART

IV

ENERGY AND THE ENVIRONMENT

12

FROM NATURE

Energy Policies

If it is very easy to substitute other factors for natural resources, then there is in principle no (energy) 'problem.' The world can, in effect, get along without natural resources, so exhaustion is just an event, not a catastrophe.

Robert Solow, "The Economics of Resources or the Resources of Economics."

Introduction and Chapter Objectives

Resources need to be available for businesses to make the goods and provide the services that people need. The availability of resources depends on market forces (the laws of supply, demand, and price), technical capabilities, and government policies.[1] In the long run smooth transitions from the use of one set of resources to another should take place if markets function without unnecessary government interference and if technological change takes place in response to market signals. In the short run, however, there can be unexpected price hikes and resource scarcity. Severe economic problems and adjustment difficulties accompany these conditions. Governments make the situation worse when they try to cushion people from the effects of higher prices, since doing so leads to inappropriate long-run decisions that prolong the crisis (e.g., decisions to purchase energy-inefficient capital equipment).

Energy issues are very political in nature, with advocates of free-market solutions opposing advocates of planning. Different segments of the energy industry—coal, oil, and electric utilities—are affected by the policy changes governments introduce. To understand the policy changes, it is necessary to become familiar with major international as well as U.S. participants. This chapter therefore analyzes the actions taken by international energy producers (the Organization of Petroleum Exporting Countries, or OPEC), and consumers (Japan, France, and Great Britain) following 1973 when OPEC members embargoed oil to the West.

Resource Availability

You find the following headline in your morning newspaper: "Iraq Takes Control in Kuwait: Bush Embargoes Trade."[2] Your heart sinks as you wonder what this development will mean (see Exhibit 12–1). Between them Iraq and Kuwait control nearly 20 percent of the world's proven oil reserves (see Exhibit 12–2).

Managers rely on the classic components of the production function—labor, capital, and raw materials—to make the goods and provide the services that consumers demand and to make the economy grow.[3] Without resources taken from nature and converted into usable goods, businesses could not function. The resources they need to operate, however, come from highly unstable areas of the globe, with leaders prone to rash action that have unpredictable consequences. In an interdependent world, no nation is self-sufficient.

Some analysts have always forecast catastrophe because of resource scarcity (see Exhibit 12–2).[4] The United States, however, is a very richly endowed country. Until the mid-20th century there was little reason to be concerned about the adequacy of raw materials to sustain continued economic growth. Resource scarcity was not a problem.[5] As high-grade resources became scarce, prices would rise, providing the incentive for

---

EXHIBIT 12–1   Evolution of the Gulf Crisis 1991

July 17	President Saddam Hussein of Iraq accuses Persian Gulf countries that exceed their oil production quotas of "stabbing his country in the back."
July 18	Tareq Aziz, Iraqi foreign minister, denounces Kuwait to Arab League nations claiming that it has "stolen" $2.4 billion worth of Iraqi oil.
July 24	Iraq, maintaining that oil prices should rise to $25 a barrel, deploys thousands of troops on the Kuwaiti border.
July 25	Iraq, refusing to give assurances that it will not attack Kuwait, demands payment of $2.4 billion in compensation from Kuwait.
July 27	While Iraq continues to demand that Kuwait meet its "legitimate rights," the Organization of Petroleum Exporting Countries (OPEC) agrees to increase oil prices to $21 a barrel.
August 2	Iraq, unsatisfied, sends its troops and tanks into Kuwait, launching an attack on that country.

EXHIBIT 12–2   Proven Oil Reserves and Production: 1990

	Proven Reserves (Billions of Barrels)	Production (Millions of Barrels per Day)
Saudi Arabia	255.0	4.9
Iraq	100.0	2.8
Kuwait	94.5	1.6
Iran	91.5	2.9
Soviet Union	58.4	11.6
United States	34.1	7.6
Rest of Middle East	117.9	4.1
All others	259.0	28.1
World total	1,012.0	63.6

SOURCE: Adapted from *BP Statistical Review of World Energy, 1990.*

---

conservation of the high-grade reserves (via such means as efficient use and recycling), extraction of low-grade reserves, and development of inexpensive means for extracting the low-grade reserves. Lower grade resources simply would replace the higher grade ones.[6]

The oil embargo of 1973, however, rekindled the controversy about supply adequacy. At current usage rates, reserves for energy-producing minerals such as coal extend hundreds of years or more into the future.[7] However, there are questions about whether their impurities will affect the extent to which low-grade stocks can be extracted and used. Knowledge of the physical composition of the earth's crust is limited as is knowledge of the location, amount, and the quality of the various deposits.[8] As rich grades of resources are exploited, it is uncertain whether low-grade resources can be easily extracted. Technological progress to lower extraction costs may be needed to replace old high-grade energy sources as an input to production and GNP.

Substitution of one grade of resource for another is an economic process that depends not only on supply but on the economic feasibility of extraction; this in turn depends on the kinds of technology available and the anticipated prices for low-grade resources once they have been extracted. Neither technological innovation, future prices, nor the existence of the additional reserves can be predicted with great precision.

To predict the future, people extrapolate from the past, but success depends on choosing an appropriate extrapolation method. More than one theory may be equally consistent with past observations, and each theory may have different implications for action. Also, the underlying structure of the economy can change, making it erroneous to test alternative theories by using past data. However, the alternative to using past data, to rely on engineering judgment, also has its limitations since judgment is just that—no matter how informed, it cannot provide certainty about the future.

Substitution of Capital and Labor

Many economists argue that the world needs few or no natural resources because capital and labor can substitute for natural resources.[9] This claim has been challenged with the argument that "natural resources are the very sap of the economic process. They are *not* just like any other production factor."[10] The extensive adjustments implied by factor substitutions (see the quotation at the beginning of this chapter) may violate physical laws.

Many economists admit that the substitution of capital and labor for natural resources cannot take place smoothly or indefinitely.[11] Without some input of natural resources, even if only an "infinitesimal amount, production is impossible; however, a small input may be all that is needed if it can be compensated for with a sufficiently large input of capital."[12] These economists argue that if the present generation gives the future fewer resources (which is inevitable given that natural resources are exhaustible), future generations will have a higher level of technology and more capital. Therefore, future generations will be better off. But others question this "dogma . . . that technology can always substitute new resources for old, without limit."[13]

The Role of Markets and Government

Market imperfections (see Chapter 8) challenge economic assumptions about smooth transitions. Advances in the ability to extract resources may be made at the expense of clean air and water and recreational amenities. As dependence on natural resources decreases, materials that take their place may be synthetic compounds that bear "only the remotest relation to materials occurring in nature."[14] They may be the sources of additional new pollution. To treat resource scarcity separately from environmental quality is impossible. Unless the government intervenes to offset the imperfections of markets, there may be no smooth and efficient transition to new economic circumstances.

An examination of U.S. government policy following the 1973 and 1979 energy shortages reveals that it is not only market imperfections that mean less-than-perfect adjustment.[15] The U.S. government inappropriately intervened in energy markets, keeping prices of natural gas and petroleum artificially low when it would have been better to allow them to rise. Artificially low prices fail to provide producers with an incentive to explore for new supplies and consumers with an incentive to conserve. They led to demand greater than supply and contributed to shortages such as the long lines at gas stations that existed during the 1970s.

The history of inappropriate government intervention is an old one.[16] The Eisenhower administration introduced quotas on foreign imports of petroleum products in order to maintain domestic supplies and assure national security, but exactly the opposite was achieved. Because of an inability to import, domestic supplies were rapidly depleted and the United States became dependent on foreign imports.

Structural Change

Despite market and government imperfections, the economies of America and other industrialized nations have been undergoing a transformation toward less-intensive resource use. The shift has been from the processing of basic materials toward the production of refined and complex goods.[17] If these trends continue, then future industrial energy requirements may decline.

Energy- and resource-intensive sectors such as petroleum refineries, primary metals, paper, chemicals, and stone, clay, and glass are not the rapidly growing sectors in the economy. The decline of these sectors corresponds to a reduction in industrial energy use in the economy.

As nations become wealthier, natural resources play a less-important role in the economy. In national economies with high levels of income there is a saturation point in natural resource use, beyond which it starts to fall. From 1947 to 1958 in the United States natural resources inputs to the economy declined, while other types of inputs rose. Intensity of resource use increases with greater per capita income, plateaus, and eventually goes down. The lack of a connection between resource use and economic growth at high income levels started before the energy price increases of the 1970s, suggesting that the movement away from intensive resource use is not simply a result of the price changes.

Unexpected Price Surges

In the long run, resource availability is assured if lower grade resources exist, labor and capital substitutions take place, and market imperfections and inappropriate government interventions do not prevent adjustment. In the long run, there has been change in the U.S. and world economy from more-intensive to less-intensive resource use. In the long run, resource scarcity may not be an important problem.

Even in the short term, as long as major wars or other events do not cause widespread disruption of energy shipments, shortages are unlikely to occur.[18] If a country has inadequate domestic supplies, it should be able to import the resources it needs by offering a high enough price. The real problem in the short term is unexpected price shocks, caused by large-scale, unanticipated curtailments in supply, that increase prices.

To understand such supply shocks, the effects of past examples can be examined. Oil prices almost quadrupled following the Arab-Israeli War, from $3.50 a barrel in 1973 to $13.50 a barrel in 1974, and oil prices nearly tripled following the Iran-Iraq War, from $13.50 a barrel in 1979 to $34.50 a barrel in 1980.

After the 1973 price jolt, inflation rates rose from an already high point of 8 percent in 1973 to double-digit levels in all the world's major industrialized countries except for Switzerland.[19] Economic growth in the industrialized countries slumped from an average annual rate of 4.9 percent from 1965 to 1973 to 2.7 percent from 1973 to 1979. The direct effects, that more domestic resources had to be traded for each unit of energy, signified a substantial loss in consumer purchasing power.

The 1974 increase in oil prices resulted in the transfer of about 2 percent of gross domestic product (GDP) from the developed countries to the oil exporting countries.[20] The deterioration in terms of trade meant that less real total national income was available for domestic consumption and investment.

No economic policy can offset these declines. The extent of the effect depends on energy's share in a nation's economy and the degree to which consumers make adjustments in energy use. The adjustments in energy use, however, are not instantaneous. Behavioral change is immediate, but long-term changes in the capital stock also are necessary. The time it takes to make these adjustments makes the crisis worse.

Inflation

The impetus to inflation comes directly from higher energy prices and indirectly from demands made by workers for higher wages to offset higher energy prices. The main effect during the period of the energy shock is an increase in the average percentage of household expenditures devoted to energy purchases.

After the 1973 and 1979 price shocks, household expenditures for energy expenditures went up about 5 percent.[21] Wage increases lagged, taking place after the shock. Economic models attribute a 2 percent increase in inflation to the 1973–74 energy shock and a 1 to 3 percent increase in inflation to the 1979–80 energy shock. The oil price shocks of 1973–74 and 1979–80 produced immediate short-term bursts of inflation that receded by the third year. Energy price shocks should not further affect the underlying inflation rates unless government fiscal and monetary policies exacerbate the situation.

Declining Productivity

Since 1965, the growth rates in labor productivity in the United States have been declining. Following the first energy price spike, the average annual labor productivity growth rate held about steady. However, in the period of the second price hike, 1978 to 1981, it fell.[22] After the first energy price spike, measures of technical productivity declined substantially. They recovered in the 1975–78 period, but then declined again between 1978 and 1981, corresponding to the second energy price hike.[23]

With declining productivity, stagnation ensued. The energy price shocks of 1973 and 1979 were major contributors to the high inflation and low growth the world economy experienced in the 1970s and early 1980s. Real disposable income and consumer wealth declined, which depressed consumption expenditure and aggregate demand.

Over time the economy adjusts to these conditions through shifts in capital stock and technology. Plant and equipment become obsolete, and producers replace them with energy-efficient stock. In the process producers become less energy dependent. The challenge to management is to help to facilitate these changes. Behavior change (e.g., turning down thermostats) has to be followed by retrofitting (e.g., insulation and computer controls) and replacement of capital (e.g., the design and construction of new buildings).

U.S. Government Policies

During past energy price surges, U.S. government policies worked at cross purposes, simultaneously stimulating and suppressing demand thereby diluting the net effect of the adjustment to higher energy prices.[24] U.S. motor vehicles consumed nearly nine tenths of the world's oil in the early 1970s. Policy makers considered, but failed to adopt, large increases in gas prices that would have made U.S. prices more equivalent to those in other nations. To reduce consumption, the increase in gasoline prices would have had to be hefty, but policy makers considered the political and economic costs of large gasoline tax increases to be too great.[25] The most serious economic problem confronted by ordinary citizens was inflation, and politicians did not want to be identified with policies that would appear to make this situation worse.

Instead of relying on market solutions, politicians turned to regulation, imposing the 55 MPH speed limit and Corporate Average Fuel Efficiency (CAFE) standards. The speed limit reduced traffic fatalities but did not save much oil.[26] The CAFE standard aimed to achieve a fleet fuel efficiency of 27.5 MPG by 1985, which it eventually did. Some 15 million households made energy conservation investments of some kind in 1978, and six million took advantage of government tax credits. However, higher prices and concerns about energy availability played as significant a role as government policy in bringing about these changes.[27]

Some government policies had no clear effect. The purpose of the Power Plant and Industrial Fuel Use Act (PPIFUA) of 1978 was to prohibit new plants from using oil or natural gas. However, coal had a clear price advantage over oil and natural gas, and there were escape clauses for the utilities to evade the government's restrictions.

Federal conservation policies were mostly symbolic. Price controls and entitlement policies had the real effect. The price controls were designed to keep producers from earning "unjust profits."[28] They prevented domestic oil from becoming as expensive as OPEC oil and thus maintained prices at levels lower than they otherwise would have been. Lower prices had many undesirable effects. They encouraged consumption, discouraged exploration and production, and took away some of the incentive for conservation.[29] Entitlement policies also acted to lower oil prices. Refiners received compensatory payment in the form of lower priced domestic oil. The impact of the price controls and the entitlement transfers dwarfed that of the conservation measures.

The Redistributional Effects

If they were so counterproductive, why were these U.S. policies carried out? In retrospect, it seems clear. Their real purpose was not to save energy, but to shift the burden of the sudden rise in oil prices from consumers to producers.[30] With the quadrupling of oil prices in 1973, the value of domestic American reserves held by producers skyrocketed from $100 billion to over 1 trillion dollars. The burden of the price increases, on the other hand, fell hardest on the poor, on those who lived in regions with the coldest winters and hottest summers, and on those who dwelled in areas that had no indigenous energy. The poor did not have as many choices as the rich about what they would consume, and they did not have the money for new energy-efficient cars and appliances.

The embargo was considered a hostile act by the legislators who represented those who suffered. The main purpose of the regulations they enacted, therefore, was to protect consumers from paying and to stop the owners of domestic petroleum from capturing the windfall profits.

Price controls and entitlements, however, yielded a substantial loss in economic efficiency.[31] People did not accomplish anything productive by sitting in gas lines. They made poor investment decisions because of the distorting effects of the incorrect price signals, which led them to purchase the wrong energy-using equipment. The net impact was to create a small and temporary price cushion for consumers that partially protected them from the OPEC action, but at an overall cost to the economy.

The Mobilization of Political Interests

The 1973 oil embargo resulted in an extraordinary mobilization of political interests. Advocates of strong government action called for decisive activity to alter consumption habits and reduce the nation's vulnerability. They were opposed by proponents of free markets, who considered the government itself to be responsible for the crisis. Few issues were subject to such intensive scrutiny and fundamental value conflict.

The executive branch accepted responsibility for the energy system as a whole, gathering together the government's programs and creating the Department of Energy. In addition, Congress centralized decision making. In the House, the Commerce Committee became the central energy policy–making body. In the Senate, the Committee on Energy and Natural Resources, created in 1977, became the most influential policy-making body. These changes signified an end to the old method of energy policy making, where decisions had been made sector by sector in different policy-making arenas.

The White House tended to side with producers. It viewed price increases as part of the solution because they had the potential to reduce consumption and lessen dependency on foreign sources. Consumers, backed by a majority in the House and Senate, insisted that price increases were the problem and controls the only means of protecting average citizens.

Outside the Government

Outside the government, interest groups and lobbyists mobilized, representing diverse causes from renewable energy and conservation to nuclear power.

An influential advocate of the period was Amory Lovins, a catalyst for the renewable-energy movement. In *Soft Energy Paths: Toward a Durable Peace* he argued that energy problems came about because large corporations and government bureaucracies had imposed expensive centralized technologies like nuclear power on people.[32] The real solution was in small-scale, dispersed, technologies. The "hard path" imposed by corporations and the government lead to an authoritarian, militaristic society. The "soft path" of small-scale dispersed technologies would result in a diverse, peaceful, self-reliant society (additional discussion of Lovins' views is found in Chapter 13).

Business interests also expanded their lobbying. The main business sectors affected were coal, petroleum, and electric utilities (see Exhibit 12–3).

Coal

Coal, because it was so abundant, appeared to have a good future, but this expectation proved to be mistaken. The union-management alliance that controlled the industry in the 1960s succeeded in increasing productivity by means of mechanization. However, this alliance disintegrated

EXHIBIT 12–3   **Primary Energy Production by Type: The United States**
Thousands of Barrels per Day Oil Equivalent

	1970	*1980*	*1990*
Coal	7,359	9,785	11,989
Crude oil	11,380	10,170	8,825
Natural gas	10,686	9,838	8,814
Hydro/nuclear	1,394	2,774	4,525

SOURCE: Adapted from Central Intelligence Agency, Directorate of Intelligence, *Handbook of Economic Statistics, 1991* (Washington, D.C.: Government Printing Office, 1991), p. 84.

in the 1970s. Wildcat strikes hurt productivity, which also declined because other problems had to be addressed: safety problems following passage of the 1969 Coal Mine Health and Safety Act, and environmental problems following passage of the National Environmental Policy Act of 1969, the Clean Air Act of 1970, the Federal Water Pollution Control Act of 1972, and the 1977 Surface Mining Control and Reclamation Act. Worker productivity in the mines dropped sharply, from 19 tons per worker to 14, which decreased coal's price advantage over other fuels.

The 1974 Energy Supply and Environmental Coordination Act and the 1978 Fuel Use Act, which required utilities to switch to coal, had little effect because few new plants were built. Western coal did grow in importance. From 15 percent of production in 1973, it increased to 36 percent in 1983. Utilities used 85 percent of the nation's coal, up from 69 percent in 1973, and oil companies and steel companies continued to acquire coal interests.[33]

The Major Petroleum Companies

The integrated petroleum companies had lost direct control of their reserves to the producer governments. They became buyers of offshore oil and increased their investments in other energy sources (see the ARCO Solar case), nonenergy minerals, and unrelated economic activities. By the early 1980s, they owned about 40 percent of nongovernment coal reserves and from one third to one half of proven uranium reserves.[34] Nearly 75 percent of domestic copper was in the hands of oil companies after the acquisition of Anaconda by ARCO.[35]

The oil companies diversified out of the energy business. Mobil bought Montgomery Ward, and Exxon purchased Reliance Electric. Mergers and concentration were the rule in the industry. By early 1985, Texaco had acquired Getty, Mobil had acquired Superior, and Socal had acquired Gulf Oil. These acquisitions often were prompted by the need to dispose of the large sums of cash the oil companies had earned.

The ties the companies forged with other energy sources, different natural resources, and alternative lines of business meant that the objectives of the industry as whole became more diverse and complex. Industry cleavages impeded efforts to counter critics who wanted to dismantle or radically restructure the industry. The industry's credibility was hurt by scandal, the disclosure of the bribing of politicians in the United States and abroad, and accusations of improperly using and interpreting oil price regulations.

The petroleum companies were major holders of natural gas, and this industry also underwent substantial transformations during the period. As demand for natural gas grew, supply did not keep pace, and shortages resulted. Producers achieved phased deregulation and significant price increases. The decision to unify the market and to end the special deregulated status of intrastate gas, however, hurt the interests of many holders of gas reserves.

Electric Utilities

Electric utilities probably experienced the greatest turbulence.[36] Managers in this industry were used to operating in a stable environment where they could routinely pass on price increases to consumers. Now they faced hostile regulatory commissions suspicious of their requests for higher prices. Utility executives no longer could depend on steady, predictable increases in demand, nor could they produce less-expensive electricity because fuel costs were rising, technological improvements were lagging, and scale economies did not yield expected savings.

With higher prices, consumers were beginning to cut back on demand. In 1974, average use per customer declined for the first time in nearly 30 years.[37] Even though larger plants no longer succeeded in producing economies of scale, the habit of investing in large plants, often based on unrealistic projections, persisted. High inflation rates, interest rate increases, and unexpected delays yielded huge cost overruns.

The Three Mile Island accident altered public attitudes toward nuclear power and demonstrated to utility executives that the uninsured costs of accidents could be devastating.[38] Although many new nuclear power plants were brought online, plans to construct more than 100 additional nuclear power plants were abandoned. The earnings of the utilities deteriorated, their stock values and bond ratings dropped, and indebtedness increased (see Exhibit 12–4). (More discussion of this important industry can be found in the special feature, "The Electric Utility Industry Faces the Future.")[39]

The Electric Utility Industry Faces the Future

Neither a producer of energy like the oil companies nor a consumer like households, utilities convert energy from one form to another.[1] The electricity created is attractive because it is clean, versatile in its uses, and can be moved great distances nearly instantaneously. Demand for electricity has grown even as demand for energy as a whole has contracted. Consumption of electricity grew from one quarter of total energy consumption in 1973 to about a third in 1990.

The major participants in the electric power industry are about 200 investor-owned utilities that generate 78 percent of the power and supply 76 percent of the customers. The industry is very capital-intensive, heavily regulated, and has a large impact on other industries, including aluminum, steel, electronics, computers, and robotics. The largest consumer of primary energy in the United States, the electric power industry by itself consumes over one third of total U.S. energy demand. At the same time it supplies one tenth of that demand, and in the process loses from 65 to 76 percent of the energy in conversion, transmission, and distribution losses.[2]

The pressures and uncertainties to which this industry has been subject have had a profound impact on its economic viability. They have forced it to reexamine numerous assumptions that had previously governed its behavior. The main strategy the industry followed in the post–World War II period was to "grow and build."[3] During this period demand increased rapidly at a rate of over 7 percent per year, and new construction was needed to meet the growing demand. Conditions in the industry were mainly positive. New construction yielded economies of scale, greater efficiencies, and declining marginal costs. Public utility commissions lowered prices, which stimulated additional demand.

The utilities were required by law to meet customer demand. As a regulated natural monopoly, they had an obligation to serve. As long as prices were falling, demand continued to rise and additional construction was necessary. New construction also occurred for another reason. If the industry was earning its allowed rate of return, the only way to increase profits was to expand the rate base by building new plants and equipment.

The idyllic period of industry growth came to an end in the 1970s. Numerous forces came together to force a reevaluation of the prior strategy. In briefest form the effect of these forces can be seen in the industry's deteriorating financial condition:[4]

1. Fuel prices escalated, including the weighted-average costs of all fossil fuels (oil, coal, and natural gas) and the spot market price of uranium oxide.

2. Economic growth rates slowed.

3. Operating and maintenance costs, including the costs of labor, supplies and material, and administrative expenses, went up, leading to higher costs per unit of capacity (higher costs per kwh).

4. The price of electricity went up.

---

[1]S. Fenn, *America's Electric Utilities under Siege and in Transition* (Washington, D.C.: Investor Responsibility Research Center, 1983).

[2]Ibid.

[3]Ibid.

---

[4]P. Navarro, *The Dimming of America* (Cambridge, Mass.: Ballinger, 1985).

5. Sales growth rates declined.

6. Interest rates escalated, and inflation rates accelerated.

7. The cost of capital and the yield on bonds grew.

8. Construction costs rose.

9. Nuclear power plant and coal power plant capital costs increased.

10. The average cost of new generating capacity and installed capacity per kwh went up.

11. Net earnings, earnings per share, and revenues per kwh were down, and long term debt escalated.

12. New long-term bonds and stock had to be issued and short-term bank loans made.

13. Interest coverage ratios and credit ratings declined.

14. Surplus generating capacity increased.

15. Major generating units were canceled and capital appropriations cut back.

Many people came to believe that coal and nuclear power plants were a threat to the environment, that new options had to be developed, and that conservation was important.[5] Environmental and safety regula-

tions increased utility costs. The federal government affected utility operations in other ways. For example, in 1978 it deregulated interstate power sales.[6] Thus, the utilities would have to purchase alternative power (solar, geothermal, etc.) from qualifying facilities at fully avoided costs.

Perhaps the greatest change took place in the electric power companies' relationship to the public utility commissions.[7] This once friendly relationship deteriorated under the onslaught of the other changes taking place. The number of requests for rate increases grew as did the dollar amounts requested, but the percentage of rate increase requests granted actually went down.

In response to these changes, the grow-and-build strategy no longer was tenable. Different segments in the industry followed different courses based on divergent perceptions of where these trends would lead and what the future would bring:[8]

Marketing Differentiation. Creative rate designs promoted use when excess capacity was available and discouraged use when it was not available. Multiple rate structures for different classes of customers also might accomplish this purpose.

Cost Reduction. Almost all the utilities tried to negotiate long-term contracts that lowered their fuel procurement costs.

[5]*Three Mile Island: A Report to the Commissioners and to the Public*, vol. I and II, Parts 1, 2, and 3, NUREG/CR 1250, U.S. Nuclear Regulatory Commission, 1980, M. Rogovin, Director, Nuclear Regulatory Commission Special Inquiry Group; *Three Mile Island: The Most Studied Nuclear Accident in History*, EMD-80–109, General Accounting Office, 1980; *TMI-2 Lessons Learned Task Force Final Report*, NUREG-0585, U.S. Nuclear Regulatory Commission, Office of Nuclear Reactor Regulation, 1979.

[6]"Competition in the Production of Electricity," in *Electric Power*, ed. J. Moorhouse (San Francisco: Pacific Research Institute, 1986), pp. 63–97.

[7]D. Anderson, *Regulatory Politics and Electric Utilities* (Cambridge, Mass.: Auburn House, 1981); Navarro, *The Dimming of America*.

[8]Fenn, *America's Electric Utilities under Siege and in Transition*.

The Electric Utility Industry Faces the Future continued

Attempts also were made to limit construction, maintenance, and administrative costs.

Modified Grow and Build.   A number of utilities (Commonwealth Edison, Long Island Lighting, Carolina Power and Light, the TVA) pursued a modified grow-and-build strategy based on the perception that economic growth would recover and that conservation and renewable energy would not be able to handle the increased demand.

Capital Minimization.   Some utilities (Consolidated Edison, Duke Power, General Public Utilities, Potomac Electric Power) pursued an option of capital minimization. They were located in areas of the country that were not growing and where the demand for power was decreasing.

Renewable Energy Supply.   In areas of rapidly growing energy demand where the

regulatory climate discouraged nuclear and coal plant construction, utilities (Southern California Edison and Pacific Gas and Electric) might have no option but to rely on their strong internal R&D capabilities and progressive leadership to explore alternative energy options. They became energy brokers buying alternative power from third-party producers.

Diversification.   The main attraction of diversification for some utilities (Texas Utilities, Pacific Power and Light, American Electric Power, Montana Power, New England Electric System) was that it freed them from the profit limitations imposed by the public utility commissions. Outside the utility business (in real estate, banking, and energy-related services), there was more risk but no limits on making money from profitable ventures (see table).

The energy crisis dramatically transformed this once stodgy industry.

Electric Utility Diversification

	Number of Active Subsidiaries		
	1966	*1976*	*1986*
Mining and construction	19	65	101
Manufacturing	2	4	18
Transportation, communication, electric, gas, and sanitary services	14	18	45
Wholesale and retail trade	3	2	14
Finance, insurance, and real estate	9	13	94
Services	1	7	66

SOURCE: Michael Russo, *Generating Strategy,* dissertation (Berkeley, Calif.: University of California, School of Business, 1989) based on a sample of 54 utilities.

EXHIBIT 12–4   Declining Utility Financial Condition: 1965–80

	Average % Return on Newly Issued A-Rated Utility Bonds	*Percentage of Companies with Bond Ratings above Baa*	*Common Stock Market-to-Book Ratio*	*Common Stock Dividend Yield (%)*
1965	4.7%	89%	2.3	3.3%
1970	9.2	78	1.3	5.9
1975	10.3	50	.8	9.7
1980	13.4	37	.7	12.0

SOURCE: Adapted from P. Navarro, *The Dimming of America.* (Cambridge, Mass.: Ballinger, 1985).

Cartel Theory and OPEC

To understand the role of energy in the international economy, it is important to examine the actions taken by the major producing and consuming nations outside the United States (see Exhibit 12–5). The major producers belong to the world oil cartel, OPEC, which came into existence in 1960 following decisions by the multinational oil companies to reduce the price of oil.[40] From 1970 to 1973, the already dominant position of OPEC in terms of world oil production and reserves (three fourths of the world's oil discoveries between 1945 and 1973 had been in OPEC countries) grew. From 1970 to 1973, world oil demand increased, while non-OPEC supply went up by only 0.7 millions of barrels per day (mbpd). The demand for OPEC oil expanded by nearly 7.5 mbpd in three years. OPEC's production in 1973 was 31 mbpd, almost all of which it exported. OPEC was supplying over 80 percent of the free world's exports. The five founding members (Saudi Arabia, Iran, Iraq, Venezuela, and Kuwait) were operating close to maximum sustainable capacity.

Massive Price Increases

The first massive price increase followed the outbreak of the Arab-Israeli War in October 1973. The Organization of Arab Petroleum Exporting Countries (OAPEC), consisting of Saudi Arabia, Abu Dhabi, Libya, Algeria, Kuwait, Bahrain, Qatar, and Dubai, curtailed production by 10 percent and did not permit oil shipments to the United States. This move was initially successful because supply and demand did not respond to the price changes. However, after 1977 there were substantial increases in production from Mexico, the North Sea, and Alaska. Increases in non-OPEC production alleviated the pressure on oil prices.

EXHIBIT 12–5   Selected Statistics of OPEC Nations: 1990

	Crude Oil Production (Thousands of Barrels per Day)	Share of Oil in GNP (%)	Population (Millions)	Per Capita Purchasing Power ($)	Trade Balance (Billions)
Saudi Arabia	6,436	54	14.1	6,430	6.6
Iran	3,076	20	57.0	1,400	1.8
Venezuela	2,103	22	19.7	2,150	10.1
United Arab Emirates (UAE)	2,062	40	2.3	11,870	2.1
Iraq	1,948	50	18.8	1,940	4.0
Nigeria	1,779	42	118.8	310	1.7
Libya	1,350	45	4.2	5,860	−0.1
Indonesia	1,249	9	190.1	490	5.7
Kuwait	1,222	31	2.1	9,700	5.2
Algeria	765	25	25.4	2,130	1.3
Qatar	385	30	.5	13,200	0.9
Ecuador	285	15	10.5	920	0.9
Gabon	280	40	1.1	3,1000.5	

SOURCE: Adapted from Directorate of Intelligence, Central Intelligence Agency, *Handbook of Economic Statistics, 1991* (Washington, D.C.: Government Printing Office, 1991), p. 32.

As markets became weaker, OPEC's share of world crude production went down.

At the time of the Iranian revolution real oil prices actually had started to fall. Between 1979 and 1980, however, petroleum prices again doubled. Iranian oil production dropped off because of the revolution. Various countries, led by Japan, tried to take precautions against a possible decline in the flow of oil out of Gulf, and additional pressure on prices came from a buildup in stocks by these countries in 1979 and 1980.

Decline in Demand

World oil demand reached a peak in 1979. Demand fell thereafter because of energy savings and interfuel substitution, non-OPEC supplies, including natural gas liquids from the Soviet Union, and the deep worldwide recession of 1980–82.[41] In response to these changes, mistrust among the OPEC nations grew. They were unable to meet in November 1980 in Baghdad because of differences about the Iran-Iraq War. OPEC's radical camp—consisting of Iran, Algeria, and Libya—vehemently opposed the United States and favored short-run OPEC revenue maximization. The Gulf Cooperation Council, led by Saudi Arabia, was a moderate faction (see Exhibit 12–6). It sought a less-restrictive pricing policy

---

EXHIBIT 12–6   Members of the Gulf Cooperation Council: 1989

	Oil Reserves (Billions of Barrels)	Population (Millions)	GDP per Capita ($)	Armed Forces
Saudi Arabia	255.0	14.1	6,400	65,700
UAE	97.7	1.6	15,200	43,000
Kuwait	94.5	2.1	11,250	20,300
Qatar	4.5	0.4	14,700	7,000
Oman	4.3	1.5	5,900	25,500
Bahrain	0.1	0.5	7,200	3,350

SOURCE: *Oil and Gas Journal,* Institute for Strategic Studies.

---

leading to long-run revenue maximization. An independent group, consisting of the remaining six members including Iraq, altered its position quite often. In this group were Indonesia, Nigeria, Venezuela, Ecuador, and Gabon.

The first price reduction in the 23-year history of OPEC occurred at the March 1983 London meeting when prices were reduced from $34 to $29 a barrel.[42] Individual OPEC countries resorted to separate deals with consuming nations to maintain their market shares. The cartel began to unravel. It lost control of the oil market in 1985–86 because its members could not enforce an acceptable market-sharing scheme. OPEC production declined from a peak of 31 mbpd in 1979 to 16.5 mbpd in 1985. By the end of 1985 it reached a low of 15.5 mbpd, a level below OPEC's agreed-upon ceiling and no more than 40 percent of the non-Communist world's oil output.[43]

Under these circumstances, the Saudis decided that they had to increase their share of the world oil market, as did some of their Gulf neighbors, to maintain revenues. The Saudis were able to sell at low prices without suffering substantial revenue losses because price declines were offset by production increases. In taking the actions it did, Saudi Arabia risked hostile retaliation from the OPEC radicals—Iran, Iraq, and Libya (see Exhibit 12–7).

Why Most Cartels Fail

Like OPEC, numerous other cartels, formed to control the price and supply of a commodity, have existed on international markets, but most ultimately failed.[44] Of the 51 studied by Eckbo, only 19 were able to maintain prices for significant periods at levels substantially greater than would have occurred without the cartel.[45]

EXHIBIT 12-7   **Major Oil Exporters, 1970 to 1990**
Hundreds of Thousands of Barrels per Day

	1970	*1975*	*1980*	*1985*	*1990*
OPEC					
Saudi Arabia	3.6	6.8	9.3	2.6	6.1
Iran	3.5	4.9	.9	1.7	2.2
Venezuela	3.4	2.0	1.8	1.2	2.0
UAE	.8	1.7	1.7	1.0	2.2
Iraq	1.5	2.1	2.5	1.2	1.7
Nigeria	1.1	2.7	2.0	1.3	1.2
Libya	3.3	1.5	1.8	1.0	1.3
Indonesia	.7	1.1	1.2	.7	.9
Kuwait	2.8	2.0	1.6	.9	1.2
Algeria	1.0	.9	.9	.5	1.0
Non-OPEC					
USSR	1.9	2.6	3.2	3.3	3.2
Mexico	0	.1	.8	1.6	1.3

SOURCE: Adapted from Directorate of Intelligence, Central Intelligence Agency, *Handbook of Economic Statistics, 1991* (Washington, D.C.: Government Printing Office, 1991), p. 87.

In theory, cartels have within them the seeds of their own destruction because in response to higher prices, people search for alternative suppliers, reduce their use, and try to locate substitutes. When the market for a cartel's product diminishes, the problems it faces in continuing collusion grow. Under the best of circumstances, collusion is not easy to maintain. Once a price is established, the cartel faces the problem of how to distribute total sales and profits. The strategy it chooses is likely to yield divergent benefits for cartel members.

One possibility is to establish quotas relying on the relative sales of members in the precartel period. Another possibility is to rely on the productive capacity of cartel members. However, the choice of a base period and the measure of capacity are likely to be matters of dispute. Quota determination is a matter of bargaining and negotiation that breeds mistrust and suspicion. Also, political views exacerbate tensions stemming from economic interests.

When the market for the cartel's product declines, the mistrust and suspicion increase.[46] With less output and smaller profits, the conflict among cartel members for a fair share of output grows. Under these circumstances, the temptation for the individual cartel member is to produce beyond its quota and to sell additional amounts of the commodity at discount rates without revealing to other cartel members what it has done. If everyone in the cartel sells at a discount, the cartel rapidly disintegrates. When the cheating becomes rampant, cartel members abandon further cooperation.[47]

OPEC Survives

In the first half of 1986, crude oil prices were at about $12 a barrel. When adjusted for changes in the general price level, they were as low as they had been in 1973 prior to the first embargo. OPEC revenues drastically declined, and yet OPEC survived (see Exhibit 12–8). Low prices led to a recovery in world oil demand and OPEC output increased. In December 1986, a new OPEC accord set prices at $18 per barrel.

Non-OPEC producers showed no desire to break the cartel because they benefited.[48] Banks that had loaned billions of dollars to oil producers like Mexico, Venezuela, and Nigeria counted on the cartel to prop up oil prices so that they could secure their loans. The cartel also had support from many industrial nations that believed that it served a useful role in stabilizing oil prices.

Comparative Energy Policies

Major consuming nations responded to the energy crises of 1973–74 and 1979–80 differently (see Exhibit 12–9). Japan and France, although via different routes, made substantial progress in decreasing their

EXHIBIT 12–8 Oil Revenues of OPEC Nations and the USSR: 1975–90
Billions of U.S. Dollars

	1975	1980	1985	1989	1990
Saudi Arabia	27	99	26	24	45
Iran	19	13	15	11	16
Venezuela	8	18	13	9	14
UAE	7	19	12	11	17
Iraq	8	25	11	15	9
Nigeria	7	24	12	9	14
Libya	6	23	10	6	10
Indonesia	4	13	12	6	8
Kuwait	8	19	9	9	6
Algeria	4	15	13	6	9
Qatar	2	6	3	2	3
Ecuador	1	2	2	1	1
USSR	8	28	34	30	27

SOURCE: Directorate of Intelligence, Central Intelligence Agency, *Handbook of Economic Statistics, 1991* (Washington, D.C.: Government Printing Office, 1991), p. 32.

EXHIBIT 12–9   **Major Consuming Nations: 1960–90**
Hundreds of Thousands of Barrels per Day

	United States	Japan	West Germany	France	United Kingdom	Canada
1960	9.8	.6	.7	.6	1.0	.8
1970	14.7	4.0	2.6	2.0	2.0	1.5
1980	17.1	5.0	2.6	2.3	1.6	1.8
1985	15.7	4.3	2.3	1.8	1.6	1.4
1990	16.9	5.3	2.4	1.8	1.8	1.7

SOURCE: Directorate of Intelligence, Central Intelligence Agency, *Handbook of Economic Statistics, 1991* (Washington, D.C.: Government Printing Office), pp. 85, 87.

dependence on Mideast oil in the period following 1973. Great Britain was the only major industrialized nation to become almost completely self-sufficient in energy production, but this fact did not greatly aid its ailing economy. Moreover, when energy prices declined and then stabilized in the 1980s, many consuming nations eliminated the conservation incentives they had put in place.

Japan

Japan is a great trading nation, but it produces only 0.2 percent of its total energy requirements. Next to the United States it is the largest consumer and importer of energy in the world.[49] The price of energy and other raw materials are extremely important to its economy. After 1973, energy policy was probably its highest domestic political priority.[50] The aim was to reduce demand and diversify energy sources.

Japan is the most heavily petroleum dependent industrialized nation.[51] In 1983 it imported 65 percent of its oil from the Mideast. In that year, its imports comprised 25 percent of the total exports from Arabian/Persian Gulf nations. Japan had cooperative technical and economic agreements with most of the OPEC producers, as well as with many non-OPEC producers. It made numerous investments in the development of industry and infrastructure in the Gulf, and the Gulf states had purchased large amounts of Japanese securities. Japan had a major interest in seeing political stability prevail in the region.

Paying for a High Level of Energy Imports via Exports.   To pay for a high level of energy and raw material imports, Japan had to export goods it produced (see Exhibit 12–10).[52] To finance the energy price increases that occurred in 1973, it had to expand exports. With the exception of the first two years after 1973, it was generally successful in maintaining trade surpluses and controlling inflationary pressures following

EXHIBIT 12–10   The Costs of Oil Imports: 1980–90
Billions of Dollars

	United States	Japan	West Germany	France	United Kingdom
1980	76.9	58.9	35.1	30.7	14.0
1985	51.4	40.6	24.1	18.8	10.5
1990	64.5	33.4	19.0	14.8	15.1

SOURCE: Directorate of Intelligence, Central Intelligence Agency, *Handbook of Economic Statistics, 1991* (Washington, D.C.: Government Printing Office, 1991), p. 89.

the energy price shock. Indeed, it was so successful that its trade surpluses became major irritants in its relationship with the United States. In 1983 Japan exported nearly twice the dollar value of goods to the United States as it imported.[53]

Economic Growth and Energy Consumption in Japan.   The rate of economic growth in Japan declined after 1973. Annual GNP growth averaged nearly 10 percent from 1963 to 1973; from 1973 to 1983 average annual growth was just under 4 percent. The association between economic growth and energy consumption, however, also weakened.[54] Growth in primary energy consumption was small and consumption of oil fell by 20 percent from 5.1 mbpd in 1973 to 4.2 mbpd in 1985.[55]

These changes occurred for many reasons. Production in the basic materials industry, particularly aluminum and petrochemicals, was stagnant because world economic growth was weak, and the competitiveness of these parts of Japanese industry, given higher energy prices, declined. Japanese economic growth took place in processing and assembly industries and in the expanding service sector, which were less energy-intensive. Energy conservation became more common in transportation and in household and commercial heating. Improved production equipment was installed. Finally, two severe recessions played a role in the movement away from petroleum. Consumption grew in 1976, 1979, and 1983–84, but stagnated in 1977–78 and fell in 1980–82.[56]

The Energy Rationalization Law of 1979 was the basis for Japan's energy conservation efforts. It provided for the financing of conservation projects and for a system of tax incentives. It has been estimated that over 5 percent of total Japanese national investment in 1980 was for energy-saving equipment.[57] In the cement, steel, and chemical industries over 60 percent of total investment was for energy conservation.

Nuclear Power and Liquified Natural Gas in Japan.   Japanese society shifted from petroleum to a reliance on other forms of energy, including nuclear power and liquefied natural gas (LNG). Between 1982 and 1983, the Japanese Ministry of International Trade and Industry (MITI) revised its forecast of Japanese petroleum consumption downward.[58] Moreover, expected economic growth also was revised downward from 5 to 4 percent.

The use of all energy forms was expected to be less in the year 2000, but no reduction in the use of nuclear power was expected. By 1995 oil was expected to provide only about 50 percent of Japan's energy needs, down from 62 percent in 1982. Nuclear would provide 14 percent and LNG would provide 12 percent, both up from 7 percent in 1982.

Oil prices started to decline in constant dollars in 1982 and in terms of the yen in 1983. The decline continued through 1986 when they reached levels below $13 a barrel in Japan. Lower prices created additional demand for imported oil.[59] In particular, the demand for transportation fuels went up. Gasoline demand increased by 2.5 percent in 1986 from 1985 levels, because more cars were on the road, they were bigger, and they were being driven more miles. Demand for jet fuel also increased as did demand for other petroleum products. At the same time the Japanese were not spending substantially more for energy because of the appreciation of the yen.

France

France's energy resources were extremely limited.[60] It possessed some natural gas, coal, and hydropower, but together these energy sources constituted only 0.7 percent of the world's total production. By 1973, oil made up 67 percent of the total energy used in France, up from 25 percent in 1960. French dependence on foreign energy had grown to 76.2 percent.

Since World War I France had been aware of its dependence on foreign energy and had taken steps to overcome it. It owned stock in the Iraq Petroleum Company, which discovered oil in that country in 1927, and French national oil companies helped develop the oil resources of the former French colonies in North Africa.

Political instability in the Mideast and North Africa led France to take a leading role in the development of civilian nuclear power after World War II. In 1945 de Gaulle set up the French Atomic Energy Commission (Commissariat a l'Energie Atomique, or CEA) to develop the military and peaceful uses of nuclear power. By the end of the 1960s, however, civilian nuclear power had made few advances in France. The nuclear program was proceeding at a very slow pace of around one reactor per year at the time of the 1973 energy shock. However, after the 1973 energy embargo there was rapid growth in France's reliance on nuclear power and there also were largely successful efforts at conservation.

French Nuclear Power.   The French nuclear program took off after the embargo (see Exhibit 12–11). The French government became committed to the construction of six 900 Mwe reactors per year, the rationale being that nuclear energy was the only form of power that could be developed with French resources (France had 120,000 tons of uranium reserves) at a reasonable cost. The French developed capabilities in all areas of the nuclear power cycle, from reactor design and construction to fuel supplies and waste treatment. French commitment to nuclear power extended to commercialization of the fast-breeder reactor (the Phoenix and Superphoenix facilities), a reactor type that the U.S. abandoned in the mid-1970s.

By 1990, over 70 percent of French power came from nuclear. More than 50 reactors had been constructed. The average construction time was a little under 6 years, while in the United States the average construction time was nearly 12 years. France was exporting electricity to nearly all its neighbors. Its electricity rates meanwhile were about the lowest in Europe. French success can be attributed to a variety of factors, including standardization in design and construction of its nuclear plants, greater sensitivity to the consequences of oil dependence, the competence and sophistication to run a technology with high-risk potential, and the political will to carry out the nuclear program.

Conservation in France.   From 1973 to 1980 the French economy grew by 22 percent, the number of cars increased by 20 percent, and the number of homes equipped for heating grew by 50 percent; yet energy and oil consumption only grew by 7 percent. Between 1975 and 1986 GDP grew by 27 percent but energy demand increased by just 13 percent. Substantial conservation gains were made in manufacturing and to a lesser extent in the residential and commercial sectors and transportation.[61]

EXHIBIT 12–11   Installed Nuclear Generating Capacity: 1970–90
Thousands of Megawatts

	United States	Japan	West Germany	France	United Kingdom	Canada
1970	6.0	.8	.3	1.7	4.1	.2
1980	51.7	14.5	8.6	12.9	8.0	5.1
1985	79.4	26.3	16.1	33.8	11.1	9.6
1989	96.0	28.1	22.4	51.4	13.7	11.8

SOURCE: Directorate of Intelligence, Central Intelligence Agency, *Handbook of Economic Statistics, 1991* (Washington, D.C.: Government Printing Office, 1991), pp. 85, 96.

In manufacturing, producers responded to price signals by reorienting output toward less energy-intensive activities. Starting in 1976 the government subsidized through the Energy Conservation Agency (AEE) 3,100 projects at a cost of more than 8.4 billion francs.[62] These subsidies were particularly effective in getting companies that might not otherwise invest in energy conservation to do so. They came to an end in 1980 when they were replaced by tax deductions meant to last until 1985. Manufacturing conservation generally focused on new heat pumps, energy exchangers, processes to recover waste heat or waste by-products, technologies to control energy flows, new manufacturing processes, and better insulation. The manufacturing sector moved toward greater use of electricity, which saved energy.

In the residential and commercial sector, the government mandated that temperatures in public buildings be lowered. Higher energy prices, government incentives, regulations and standards for new buildings, and forecasts about long-term energy prices resulted in retrofitting of existing dwellings, construction of new homes with more insulation, and the replacement of boilers by more energy-efficient models.

The goal in transportation was to increase average gasoline mileage from 26.7 MPG in 1979 to 39.2 MPG in 1990.[63] Experimental vehicles achieved 60 MPG and 80 MPG, and a media campaign urged people to drive less and to drive more efficiently. New speed limits also were placed on all the major highways. However, the number of vehicles grew from more than 15 million in 1975 to 21 million in 1986. The average distance driven per year went down slightly from 13,200 km per vehicle per year in 1975 to 12,800 km per vehicle per year in 1986, and the number of vehicles using diesel fuels went up from 300,000 in 1975 to 2.1 million in 1987.

The result of all these changes was that by 1986 France was 46.2 percent dependent on national sources of energy.[64] This accomplishment was very close to its goal of being 50 percent energy self-sufficient by 1990. How much of this change, however, was permanent? As oil prices declined, behavior could revert to old patterns, but existing technical progress would remain even if investments in new energy-saving technology would become more unusual as the French government took away its extensive program of incentives and subsidies.

Great Britain

In the 16th century England adjusted to deforestation by becoming the world's largest coal producer.[65] By the 19th century, its coal production was six times the rest of the world's combined production. Along with such innovations as James Watt's steam engine, coal became the catalyst of the industrial revolution. Other innovations in energy use came from natural gas for lighting and Michael Farady's invention of the modern dynamo which made possible the generation of electric power. During World War I, Britain was vulnerable to interruptions in petroleum supply. After the War, the British companies, British Petroleum and Shell, took the lead in the international search for oil. With the discovery of natural gas in the North Sea in the 1960s, the building of a national pipeline, and the signing of long-term contracts for natural gas at relatively low prices, the United Kingdom became heavily dependent on natural gas. It consumes one quarter of this fuel used in Western Europe. Gas constituted about 40 percent of total energy use in Britain, with electricity, coal, and oil sharing the rest of the market about equally.

After the 1973 energy price shock, oil was reserved for premium uses, and coal made something of a comeback after having been in decline for a considerable period. In the middle of the 1970s there were major discoveries of oil reserves in the North Sea, and Britain just about regained energy self-sufficiency.

Energy Self-Sufficiency in Britain.   What have been the consequences of this accomplishment? The United Kingdom and Norway, the countries which made the North Sea finds, have enjoyed low annual growth rates for energy prices.[66] From 1978 to 1984, the average in the United Kingdom was 3.9 percent and the average in Norway was 4.1 percent. These figures compared with price increases in the United States of 4.8 percent, in Germany of 5.5 percent, in France of 5.6 percent, in Japan of 6.6 percent, and in Italy of 6.8 percent. The tax revenues from energy in the United Kingdom also have been large, amounting to 131 billion pounds in 1985.

However, in comparison to other nations, the United Kingdom had old capital stock, low industrial investment, and low labor productivity, which were driving down its international competitiveness (see Chapter 10), even as the country achieved greater energy self-sufficiency. The United Kingdom could not escape from the vicious cycle of low investment, low productivity, and low economic growth, which contributed to continued low investment.

During the world recession of the late 1970s and early 1980s, it retired much outdated capital stock, reducing output and increasing unemployment, and in this way productivity went up. But it had to give up on much of its basic manufacturing base because developments in the energy sector absorbed capital that might otherwise have gone into manufacturing.

While the development of new energy reserves in some ways contributed to Great Britain's economic growth, it also discouraged economic revitalization by competing with other industry for capital and by having exchange rates effects that hurt the country's international competitiveness.

Great Britain's Nationalized Energy Industries.   As a consequence of the precarious supply situation during World War I, the British government took a majority interest in British Petroleum and tried to play a leading role in the search for new oil.[67] After World War II, the government nationalized the coal, gas, and electricity industries. Partly for ideological reasons and partly for the purposes of postwar reconstruction, it created the National Coal Board (NCB), the British Gas Corporation (BCG), and the Central Electricity Generating Board (CEGB). In the 1970s, after the discovery of oil reserves in the North Sea, the British National Oil Company, a government corporation, was established. It produced about 7 percent of North Sea oil and ultimately handled about 60 percent of the oil produced there.[68] Thus, all the energy sectors in the United Kingdom—oil, coal, gas, and electricity—had been either partially (oil) or completely (all the other sectors) nationalized.

Government relations with the nationalized industries were often difficult. The state's interests were different from those of the nationalized industries. It intervened to pursue macroeconomic objectives such as price restraint or attempted to stimulate investment at times of unemployment. Decision making was highly politicized. The electric and gas industries had substantial operating profits and they could finance their capital requirements from their revenues, but profits in the coal industry were poor, the work force was unionized, and opposition to the closure of uneconomic mines was great. It was estimated that 90 percent of mining losses came from 30 of the 190 pits in Great Britain, but only since 1984–85 has there been rapid mine closure and enhanced productivity.[69] New power plant construction was poorly managed. Comparable coal-fired power stations costs were twice as much in Great Britain as they were in France or Italy.

The Conservative party proposed that the United Kingdom's nationalized energy industries be privatized. However, with the exception of coal, the energy industries had natural monopoly characteristics—economies of scale and the need to prevent duplicate investment in fixed infrastructure. The Conservative party platform called for regulation to deal with the natural monopoly characteristics of these industries. It took many steps toward privatization but in only one area carried out its program to completion. The British National Oil Company was abolished and its assets were transferred to Britoil and Enterprise Oil, private companies.

Sustaining the Gains in Energy Efficiency.   Since 1973 all the countries in the European Economic Community (EEC) except the industrializing nations of Greece and Portugal have seen their energy intensity ratios (total primary energy used/GDP) decline.[70] The steady decline in energy intensity was much steeper after 1979, as the response to the 1979 crisis was more marked than the response to the 1973 crisis.[71] West Germany was an exception in that its steepest decline in energy intensity occurred after 1973, not 1979. Its response to higher energy prices was immediate, as opposed to the delayed response that occurred elsewhere. The United Kingdom response to the first oil crisis, in contrast, was less vigorous than in other West European countries. Electricity intensity, as opposed to overall energy intensity, increased over the entire period, but the increase slowed somewhat after 1979.

Electricity intensity increased more in France than in other West European countries, reflecting the policy preferences of that nation for nuclear power. In the EEC countries, programs to boost energy conservation were introduced in the 1979–82 period, the period of sharply rising energy prices, but many of these programs were terminated or reduced after 1982–83. Since then, because of budgetary reasons, most government energy conservation policies have been operating at a low level.

Energy Supply and Demand in the Future

Thus, as this chapter has shown, upward fluctuations in energy prices, especially if they are sudden and unexpected, have a dampening effect on the world economy. The need for conservation is great. It is said to be 2 to 10 times cheaper to take this route than to create new supply.[72] Market forces, however, are essential to induce the needed conservation, and price is the principal driver. When prices are high people tend to use less energy. They tend to search for more abundant sources and to substitute other inputs, such as insulation, for fuel. They feel the need to develop technologies for more efficient use and to shift consumption purchases in the direction of less energy intensive goods and services.

Two Scenarios

In the long run, at least, two scenarios are possible. The first sees prices rising substantially over the next two decades. The 1980–86 price declines tempered the demand-reducing effects of prior price increases. Eventually, economic growth, when it gains momentum, will act to further weaken the demand-reducing effects of the price increases.

Oil resources remain heavily concentrated in the Persian Gulf and no alternative exists that is cheap, clean, and plentiful. Prospects for continuing expansion of non-OPEC production are limited. U.S. production is around 7 percent below its 1970 peak despite higher prices. Without Alaska, U.S. output would be 25 percent less than it was in 1985.

The only substantial non-OPEC discoveries in the post-1973 period, despite heavy exploration, have been in Mexico, and Mexico's share of world reserves is only about 10 percent. U.S., Canadian, and North Sea oil would be depleted after three decades of production at current levels, while Persian Gulf producers can sustain current output levels for more than a century.

A different scenario sees energy prices, like all resource prices, falling over time. According to this view, the premise of a fixed stock is mistaken. All natural resources should be viewed as inexhaustible or at least as nonbinding constraints on production. Although humans tend to exploit the cheapest stock of natural resources first, diminishing returns are more than offset by increasing knowledge about how to obtain new stock and how to utilize the existing stock more efficiently.

In 1945 in the United States it appeared as if no more oil could be discovered. The United States was more "drilled up" than any other country, it was claimed, and remaining reserves were thought to be only 20 billion barrels of oil. Yet over the next 40 years, the United States produced over 100 billion barrels of oil, excluding Alaska.

Any effort by any nation or group of nations to withhold production is not likely to work in the long run because the interests of the nations holding petroleum reserves vary. This too puts downward pressures on long-term oil prices.

Can the Connection between Energy Consumption and Economic Growth Be Broken?

To reduce the impact of price shocks, the key long-term challenge is to break the dependence on energy consumption.[73] The feedback effects between energy and the economy, however, are extremely complicated.[74] Consumption of energy is both necessary for economic growth and a consequence of it. Inseparability means that the connection between energy consumption and growth cannot be broken. According to this view, cutting back on energy consumption would mean an end to economic progress. The opposing view is that reduced energy use is feasible without creating damaging effects on economic activity. That is, the energy consumption needed to support a given level of economic growth can be changed.

The competing view is based on the following arguments. Different nations have different energy-to-GNP elasticities, that is, different percentage growth rates in energy consumption compared to percentage growth rates of GNP. Sweden and Canada have similar living standards and climate, but energy consumption in Canada is about twice what it is in Sweden. There is a substantially higher energy consumption pattern in the Eastern bloc countries than in Western Europe. Per capita consumption of energy in the United States is substantially higher than in other industrialized nations; the U.S. energy/output ratio far exceeds the level in countries such as France, Germany, and Sweden, whose per capita income and output are not that different.

The explanations for the different ratios among different countries are complex. They include different pricing policies, the extent to which the countries are import-dependent, their product mix, and the state of technology. The composition of GNP, exchange rates, climate, and geography play a role, as do environmental, demographic, and sociological factors. The people in countries with lower energy/output ratios than in the United States have displayed traits not commonly found in the U.S. population, including an abhorrence for waste and a willingness to change life-styles and to substitute other economic goods for energy.

The stages of economic development also appear to be significant. Underdeveloped countries typically have low energy-to-GNP ratios. As they become more developed, the energy-to-GNP ratio rises, becoming greater than that of the already developed countries. When economic growth slackens in already developed nations, the energy-to-GNP ratio tends to fall.

In the United States, growth rates in energy usage closely paralleled growth rates in GNP.[75] Analysis indicates that in the 20th century, U.S. growth rates for energy consumption and GNP were nearly identical, 3.2 percent and 3.3 percent, respectively. For OECD countries as a whole, the 1960–73 period saw a 1 percent annual increase in energy usage associated with a 1 percent annual increase in gross domestic product (GDP). However, between 1973 and 1981, when GDP grew at average annual rate of 2.3 percent, consumption of total primary energy grew by a mere 0.2 percent per year. This dramatic decline in energy intensity reflects structural changes in the use of energy, responses to policies and prices, and cyclical effects.

In the past, when there was no conscious effort to conserve energy, energy intensity and the economy grew in tandem. The implications of the 1973–81 experience, however, appear to be that if high energy prices exist and conservation is encouraged, it is possible to reduce demand. A substantial dent in the link between economic growth and energy consumption can be made.[76]

Summary and Conclusions

This chapter has examined the question of whether resources are exhaustible. Is the world really likely to run out of a major economic resource like energy? Does the availability of resources put a limit on economic growth? This chapter has developed the economic argument that resources are not exhaustible in the long run. It has provided background on why the 1973–74 and 1979–80 energy price increases occurred, and on the immediate and long-term consequences of these price increases. How the U.S. government responded to the price hikes and the effects of the U.S. government responses have been discussed. The impacts of the price increases on various segments of the energy economy (i.e., coal interests, petroleum companies, and the electric utilities) have been addressed.

We also analyzed the role of major producing (OPEC) and consuming (Japan, France, and Great Britain) nations. OPEC's near collapse in the mid-1980s was discussed and the factors that permitted it to continue to exist were examined. We also considered why most cartels fail in the long run. We assessed the long-term prospects for energy supply and demand in the world, as well as the question of whether the connection between energy consumption and economic growth can be broken.

Discussion Questions

1. Are resources exhaustible? Is the world likely to run out of major resources? Does resource availability put a limit on economic growth? What do economists argue? What do you believe?

2. What happens to economies as they mature? Do they use less or more resources? Why?

3. Why did the 1973–74 and 1979–80 energy price increases occur? What were the immediate and long-term consequences of these price hikes?

4. How did the U.S. government respond to the 1973–74 energy price hike? What were the effects of the U.S. government response?

5. What do you think of price controls as a response to energy price hikes? Do you think they are a good policy? Why or why not?

6. What were some of the structural changes in the way the federal government is organized that occurred after the 1973–74 price increases?

7. Describe some of the political forces that mobilized after the price increases.

8. What were the impacts of the price increases on various segments of the energy economy (e.g., coal interests, petroleum companies, and the electric utilities)?

9. How did the electric utility industry respond to the turbulence in energy markets that set in after 1973?

10. What is OPEC? What role did it play in the 1973–74 price increases? What role did it play in the 1979–80 price increases?

11. Why did OPEC almost collapse in the mid-1980s? What permitted it to continue to exist?

12. Why do most cartels fail in the long run?

13. Describe the energy policies of Japan, France, and the United Kingdom. In what ways were these energy policies different? In what ways were they similar? How did they compare to the energy policies of the United States?

14. Which nation (or nations) had the most effective energy policies? Which nation (or nations) had the least effective policies? Why?

15. What are the long-term prospects for energy supply and demand in the world?

16. Can the connection between energy consumption and economic growth be broken? Why or why not?

Endnotes

1. V. K. Smith, ed., *Scarcity and Growth Reconsidered* (Baltimore: The Johns Hopkins University Press, 1979). Many of the arguments made in this chapter are developed more fully in A. Marcus, *Controversies in Energy Policy* (Beverly Hills, Calif.: Sage Press, 1992).

2. G. Brooks and T. Horwitz, "Gulf Crisis Underscores Historical Divisions in the Arab 'Family,'" *The Wall Street Journal*, August 13, 1990, A1; G. H. Anderson, M. F. Bryan, and C. J. Pike, "Oil, the Economy, and Monetary Policy," *Economic Commentary*, Federal Reserve Bank of Cleveland, November 1, 1990; "Iraqi Invasion Raises Oil Prices, Threatens U.S., Other Economies," *The Wall Street Journal*, August 3, 1990, A1: A. Murray and D. Wessel, "Iraqi Invasion Boosts Chances of Recession in the U.S. This Year," *The Wall Street Journal*, August 6, 1990, A1; "Oil's Economic Threat Is Less Than in '70s," *The Wall Street Journal*, August 20, 1990, A1; "Rising Oil-Import Bill Will Slow Trade Gains," *The Wall Street Journal*, March 5, 1990, A1; C. Solomon and R. Gutfeld, "Petroleum Reserve Has Lots of Oil, but Using It Could Be a Challenge," *The Wall Street Journal*, September 5, 1990, A1; C. Solomon, "Sudden Impact: Prices at U.S. Gas Pumps Soar," *The Wall Street Journal,* August 6, 1990, B1; A. Sullivan, "Gasoline Exports Rise Despite Concern over Supplies," *The Wall Street Journal*, September 17, 1990, B1; A. Sullivan, "It Wouldn't Be Easy, but U.S. Could Ease Reliance on Arab Oil," *The Wall Street Journal,* August 17, 1990, p. A1; A. Sullivan, "OPEC May Face Long Wait to See Higher Oil Prices," *The Wall Street Journal*, July 30, 1990, A4; J. Tanner, A. Murray, and B. Rosewicz, "Crude-Oil Prices Fall as Saudis and Others Plan to Boost Output to Offset Shortages," *The Wall Street Journal*, August 9, 1990, A3; J. Tanner, "Crude-Oil Prices Register Sharp Drop on Worries of Possible Glut in Supply," *The Wall Street Journal*, April 6, 1990, C6; J. Tanner, "Petroleum Use Starting to Fall, Agency Reports," *The Wall Street Journal*, October 5, 1990, A3; J. Tanner, "OPEC Adds Capacity, Easing Risk that Cost of Oil Will Soar in '90s," *The Wall Street Journal*, November 22, 1990, A1; J. Tanner, "Supplies of Oil Start to Shrink,

Firming Prices," *The Wall Street Journal*, September 6, 1990, A3; J. Tanner, "Surge in Oil Output Could Lead to a Glut Even if Persian Gulf Standoff Drags On," *The Wall Street Journal*, November 12, 1990, A3; J. Taylor, A. Q. Nomani, and S. W. Angrist, "Hedgers Enjoy an Edge as Oil Prices Swing," *The Wall Street Journal*, August 29, 1990, B1; "How Big an Oil Shock?" *The Economist*, August 11, 1990, pp. 12–13; M. Wald, "America Is Still Demanding a Full Tank," *The New York Times*, August 12, 1990, E3; M. L. Wald, "Effect of Fall in Soviet Oil Output," *The New York Times*, September 6, 1990, D1; A. Murray and D. Wessel, "Iraqi Invasion Boosts Chances of Recession in the U.S. This Year," *The Wall Street Journal*, August 6, 1990, A1.

3. V. K. Smith and J. Krutilla, "The Economics of Natural Resource Scarcity: An Interpretive Introduction," in *Scarcity and Growth Reconsidered*, ed. V. K. Smith (Baltimore: The Johns Hopkins University Press, 1979), pp. 1–36; J. E. Stiglitz, "A Neoclassical Analysis of the Economics of Natural Resources," in *Scarcity and Growth Reconsidered*, ed. V. K. Smith (Baltimore: The Johns Hopkins University Press, 1979), pp. 36–67.

4. H. Daly, "Entropy, Growth, and the Political Economy of Scarcity," in *Scarcity and Growth Reconsidered*, ed. V. K. Smith (Baltimore: The Johns Hopkins University Press, 1979), pp. 67–95; D. H. Meadows, D. L. Meadows, J. Randers, and W. W. Behrens, *The Limits to Growth* (New York: Universe Books, 1972).

5. Smith and Krutilla, "The Economics of Natural Resource Scarcity."

6. Ibid.

7. Ibid.

8. Ibid.

9. Stiglitz, "A Neoclassical Analysis of the Economics of Natural Resources."

10. N. Georgescu-Roegen, *Energy and Economic Myths* (New York: Pergamon Press, 1976), p. 98; see also Daly, "Entropy, Growth, and the Political Economy of Scarcity."

11. Stiglitz, "A Neoclassical Analysis of the Economics of Natural Resources."

12. Ibid. See also P. Nulty, "We Can Wring More Out of the Oil Patch," *Fortune*, December 31, 1979, pp. 58–63.

13. Daly, "Entropy, Growth, and the Political Economy of Scarcity," p. 71.

14. Smith, ed., *Scarcity and Growth Reconsidered*.

15. R. A. Solo, "Developing an Energy Alternative," in *Energy Resources Development: Politics and Policies*, ed. R. L. Ender and J. C. Kim (New York: Quorum Books, 1987).

16. Ibid.

17. R. H. Williams and E. D. Larson, "Materials, Affluence, and Industrial Energy Use," *Annual Review of Energy* 12, 1987, pp. 99–144.

18. R. Pindyck and J. Rotemberg, "Energy Shocks and the Marcroeconomy," in *Oil Shock*, ed. Alm and Weiner (Cambridge, Mass.: Ballinger, 1984), pp. 97–121; R. S. Pindyck, eds., *Advances in the Economics of Energy and Resources* (Greenwich, Conn.: JAI Press, 1979).

19. Hui-Liang Tsai, *The Energy Illusion and Economic Stability: Quantum Causality* (New York: Praeger, 1989).

20. Ibid.

21. H. G. Huntington, "Oil Prices and Inflation," *Annual Review of Energy* 10, 1985, pp. 317–39.

22. E. R. Berndt and D. O. Wood, "Energy Price Shocks and Productivity Growth: A Survey," in *Energy*, ed. R. L. Gordon, H. D. Jacoby, and M. B. Zimmerman (Cambridge, Mass.: The MIT Press, 1987), pp. 305–43; S. Schurr, "Energy Use, Technological Change, and Productive Efficiency," *Annual Review of Energy* 9, 1987, pp. 409–25.

23. Berndt and Wood, "Energy Price Shocks and Productivity Growth"; Schurr, "Energy Use, Technological Change, and Productive Efficiency."

24. U. Erol and E. Yu, "On the Causal Relationship between Energy and Income for Industrialized Countries," *Journal of Energy and Development* 13, no. 1, 1988, pp. 113–39; H. Geller, "The Role of Federal Research and Development in Advancing Energy Efficiency: A $50 Billion Contribution to the U.S. Economy," *Annual Review of Energy* 12, 1987, pp. 357–95; M. Levine, "A Decade of United States Energy Policy," *Annual Review of Energy* 10, 1985, pp. 557–87; P. W. MacAvoy, *Energy Policy* (New York: W. W. Norton and Company, 1983); J. McKie, "Federal Energy Regulation," *Annual Review of Energy* 9, 1984, pp. 321–49; Tsai, *The Energy Illusion and Economic Stability*; S. Tugwell, *The Energy Crisis and American Political Economy* (Stanford, Calif.: Stanford University Press, 1988); Yu and Choi, "The Causal Relationship between Energy and GNP"; Y. Wang and W. Latham, "Energy and State Economic Growth: Some New Evidence," *Journal of Energy and Development* 14, 1989, pp. 197–221.

25. "Energy Taxes for America," *The Economist*, July 21, 1990, p. 11; J. J. McConnell and C. J. Muscarella, "Corporate Capital Expenditure Decisions and the Market Value of the Firm," *Journal of Financial Economics* 14, 1985, pp. 399–422.

26. Tugwell, *The Energy Crisis and American Political Economy.*

27. Ibid.

28. Ibid.

29. Ibid.

30. Ibid.

31. J. McKie, "Federal Energy Regulation."

32. A. B. Lovins, *Soft Energy Paths: Toward a Durable Peace* (New York: Friends of the Earth International, 1977).

33. Levin, "A Decade of United States Energy Policy."

34. Ibid.

35. Ibid.

36. D. Anderson, *Regulatory Politics and Electric Utilities* (Cambridge, Mass.: Auburn House, 1981); S. Fenn, *America's Electric Utilities under Siege and in Transition* (Washington, D.C.: Investor Responsibility Research Center, 1983); P. Navarro, *The Dimming of America* (Cambridge, Mass.: Ballinger, 1985); M. Russo, *Generating Strategy: A Dynamic Analysis of Regulation and Diversification in the Electric Utility Industry*, unpublished Ph.D. dissertation, the University of California, Berkeley, Haas School of Management, 1989, pp. 90–116; A. Zardkoohi, "Competition in the Production of Electricity," in *Electric Power*, ed. J. Moorhouse (San Francisco: Pacific Research Institute, 1986), pp. 63–97.

37. Fenn, *America's Electric Utilities under Siege and in Transition.*

38. S. D. Thomas, *The Realities of Nuclear Power* (New York: Cambridge University Press, 1988).

39. Navarro, *The Dimming of America.*

40. M. V. Samii, "The Organization of the Petroleum Exporting Countries and the Oil Market: Different Views," *Journal of Energy and Development* 10, 1985, pp. 159–73.

41. D. Gately, "The Prospects for Oil Prices Revisited," *Annual Review of Energy* 11, 1986, pp. 513–88; D. Gately, "Lessons from the 1986 Oil Price Collapse," in *Economic Activity 2*, ed. W. C. Brainard and G. L. Perry, (Washington, D.C.: The Bookings Institution), pp. 237–87.

42. W. Lowinger, G. Wihlborg, and A. Willman, "An Empirical Analysis of OPEC and Non-OPEC Behavior," *Journal of Energy and Development* 11, no. 2, 1986, pp. 119–41.

43. Gately, "The Prospects for Oil Prices Revisited"; Gately, "Lessons from the 1986 Oil Price Collapse"; Lowinger, Wihlborg, and Willman, "An Empirical Analysis of OPEC and Non-OPEC Behavior."

44. D. J. Teece, "Assessing OPEC's Pricing Policies," *California Management Review* 26, 1983, pp. 69–87; Tsai, *The Energy Illusion and Economic Stability.*

45. Tsai, *The Energy Illusion and Economic Stability.*

46. W. M. Brown, "Can OPEC Survive the Glut?" *Fortune*, November 30, 1981, pp. 89–96; W. Mead, "The OPEC Cartel Thesis Reexamined: Price Constraints from Oil Substitutes," *Journal of Energy and Development* 11, no. 2, 1986, pp. 213–42; M. V. Samii, "The Organization of the Petroleum Exporting Countries and the Oil Market: Different Views," *Journal of Energy and Development* 10, 1985, pp. 159–73; M. Shaaf, "Strong Dollar, Low Inflation, and OPEC's Terms of Trade," *Journal of Energy and Development* 10, no. 1, 1985, pp. 121–28.

47. Gately, "The Prospects for Oil Prices Revisited"; Gately, "Lessons from the 1986 Oil Price Collapse"; Lowinger, Wihlborg, and Willman, "An Empirical Analysis of OPEC and Non-OPEC Behavior"; Tanner, "OPEC Adds Capacity, Easing Risk that Cost of Oil Will Soar in '90s."

48. Lowinger, Wihlborg, and Willman, "An Empirical Analysis of OPEC and Non-OPEC Behavior."

49. B. Mossavar-Rahmani, "Japan's Oil Sector Outlook," *Annual Review of Energy* 13, 1988, pp. 185–213; R. J. Samuels, *The Business of the Japanese State* (Ithaca, NY: Cornell University Press, 1987).

50. E. Ramstetter, "Interaction between Japanese Policy Priorities: Energy and Trade in the 1980s," *Journal of Energy and Development* 11, no. 2, 1986, pp. 285–301.

51. M. Sakisaka, "Japan's Energy Supply/Demand Structure and Its Trade Relationship with the United States and the Middle East," *Journal of Energy and Development* 10, no. 1, 1985, pp. 1–11; B. Chandler and M. W. Brauchli, "How Japan Became So Energy-Efficient: It Leaned on Industry," *The Wall Street Journal*, September 10, 1990, p. A1.

52. Ramstetter, "Interaction between Japanese Policy Priorities."

53. Sakisaka, "Japan's Energy Supply/Demand Structure."

54. Ibid.

55. Mossavar-Rahmani, "Japan's Oil Sector Outlook."

56. Ramstetter, "Interaction between Japanese Policy Priorities."

57. Mossavar-Rahmani, "Japan's Oil Sector Outlook."

58. Sakisaka, "Japan's Energy Supply/Demand Structure."

59. Mossavar-Rahmani, "Japan's Oil Sector Outlook."
60. A. Giraud, "Energy in France," *Annual Review of Energy* 8, 1983, pp. 165–91.
61. N. Jestin-Fleury, "Energy Conservation in France," *Annual Review of Energy* 13, 1988, pp. 159–83.
62. Ibid.
63. Ibid.
64. Giraud, "Energy in France."
65. S. Carter, "The Changing Structure of Energy Industries in the United Kingdom," *Annual Review of Energy* 11, 1986, pp. 451–69.
66. R. Bending, R. Cattell, and R. Eden, "Energy and Structural Change in the United Kingdom and Western Europe," *Annual Review of Energy* 12, 1987, pp. 185–222.
67. Carter, "The Changing Structure of Energy Industries in the United Kingdom."
68. Bending, Cattell, and Eden, "Energy and Structural Change in the United Kingdom and Western Europe."
69. Carter, "The Changing Structure of Energy Industries in the United Kingdom."
70. E. Jochem and T. Morovic, "Energy Use Patterns in Common Market Countries since 1979," *Annual Review of Energy* 13, 1988, pp. 131–57; M. Lonnroth, "The European Transition from Oil," *Annual Review of Energy* 8, 1983, pp. 1–25.
71. Bending, Cattell, and Eden, "Energy and Structural Change in the United Kingdom and Western Europe"; Gately, "The Prospects for Oil Prices Revisited"; Gately, "Lessons from the 1986 Oil Price Collapse."
72. Schurr, "Energy Use, Technological Change, and Productive Efficiency."
73. Ibid.
74. Erol and Yu, "On the Causal Relationship between Energy and Income for Industrialized Countries"; Tsai, *The Energy Illusion and Economic Stability*; Yu and Choi, "The Causal Relationship between Energy and GNP"; Wang and Latham, "Energy and State Economic Growth."
75. J. Darmstadter, J. H. Landsberg, H. C. Morton, and M. J. Coda, *Energy, Today and Tomorrow: Living with Uncertainty* (Englewood Cliffs, N.J.: Prentice Hall, Inc., 1983); E. Kanovsky, "The Coming Oil Glut," *The Wall Street Journal*, November 30, 1990, A14; Schurr, "Energy Use, Technological Change, and Productive Efficiency"; S. H. Schurr, ed., *Energy in America's Future: The Choices before Us* (Baltimore: The Johns Hopkins University Press, 1979).
76. Tsai, *The Energy Illusion and Economic Stability.*

13 | TO NATURE
Environmental Philosophy and Economics[1]

The Second Law of Thermodynamics states that there is always a waste byproduct of any process. It is the Law of Entropy, of irrevocable dissipation, not only of energy but of matter. The ultimate fate of the universe is chaos. All kinds of energy are gradually transformed into heat and heat becomes so dissipated that humans cannot use it.

Adapted from Nicholas Georgescu-Roegen, "Energy and Economic Myths."

Introduction and Chapter Objectives

Environmental and pollution problems are transforming the world economy. They not only drive technological innovation, but they also help shape the legal and economic context of management in the United States and abroad. This chapter introduces environmental issues and discusses the challenges that they pose to managers.

Three environmental challenges are addressed. The first is a philosophical challenge emanating from the ethical viewpoint of environmentalists, which is increasingly understood and appreciated by broad segments of the public but which is at odds with some of the tenets of business philosophy. The second challenge is in the area of public policy, where economic approaches have been developed and applied to pollution problems. They attempt to balance the costs and benefits of environmental protection; their strengths and weaknesses need to be better understood by managers. The third challenge relates to the adequacy of scientific information for resolving thorny environmental issues. Ultimately, the adequacy of this information determines how capable public officials are to resolve environmental disputes.

Waste Production as a By-Product of Business Activity

In the process of extracting raw materials from nature, transforming the raw materials into useful products and transporting the finished products to markets, businesses produce waste. These essential business activities yield by-products with undesirable qualities that have to be absorbed by nature. Thus, the physical environment not only provides goods and materials to the economy (Chapter 12), but goods and materials flow back again to the environment as wastes or residuals.[2]

In making business decisions, managers need to keep the costs and risks associated with waste generation in mind. They also need to be aware that preventing and managing wastes provide opportunities for business gain. Managers are in a position to profit from creatively handling society's wastes.

People have long recognized that nature is of critical importance as a source of material inputs to economic activity, but they have been less aware that the environment also plays an essential role as a receptacle for society's unwanted by-products. A simple materials balance model illustrates the relationship between the economy and the environment (see Exhibit 13–1).[3] The production sector, which consists of mines and factories, extracts materials from nature and processes them into goods and services. Transportation and distribution networks move and store the finished products before they reach the point of consumption. The environment provides the material inputs needed to sustain economic activity and carries away the wastes generated by it.

Energy conversion supports materials processing by providing electricity, heating, and cooling services. It also aids in transportation and

EXHIBIT 13–1   From Nature to Nature—The Flow of Materials

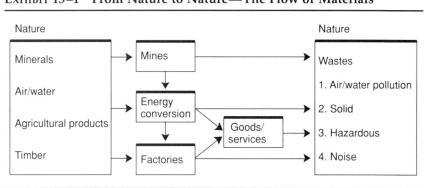

distribution. The environment provides essential elements for materials processing, including air and water, fossil fuels, agricultural products and timber, and minerals. The by-products of these processes, however, are numerous, and they must be absorbed or assimilated by the environment. The by-products include air pollutants, such as hydrocarbons, carbon monoxide, sulfur dioxide, and particulate matter; solid wastes, such as bottom and fly ash from combustion; radioactive wastes; and noise.

The useful energy from energy conversion helps make food, forest products, chemicals, petroleum products, metals, and structural materials such as stone, steel, and cement. The processes by which these materials are made, however, produce wastes: chemicals dissipated in processing, other processing losses, noise, and rubbish. Some of these materials are recovered by recycling, but most are absorbed by the environment. They are dumped in landfills, treated in incinerators, and disposed of as ash. They end up in the air, water, or soil.

Through this process, households have useful products to consume, but households too generate waste that has to be disposed of somehow. A large portion of this waste is discarded as garbage, which also finds its way back to nature.

The law of the conservation of energy dictates that the material inputs and energy that enter the economy cannot be destroyed.[4] Rather, they change form, finding their way back to nature in a disorganized state as unwanted and perhaps dangerous by-products. The ultimate limits to economic growth, to the splendid affluence achieved in developed countries, does not come simply from the availability of raw materials in nature. Nature's limited capacities to absorb wastes set a limit on an economy's ability to produce.

Environmental Philosophy and the Environmental Movement

The environmental movement has brought the spoilage of nature caused by production to the attention of people. The movement, worldwide in character, is showing strength and vitality that it has not seen since the 1970s.[5] One of its primary attractions is that it provides a political alternative to traditional ideologies, both laissez-faire capitalism and socialism. People of different political persuasions (see Chapter 8) have been able to unite behind environmental causes. A *New York Times*/CBS poll in 1989 found that 79 percent of the American population agreed that "environmental improvements must be made regardless of cost."[6] In 1981, when the same question was asked, only 45 percent accepted this statement (see Exhibit 13–2).

EXHIBIT 13–2   Emerging Public Consensus on the Environment

- Americans believe the condition of the environment is worsening and consider the environment a top priority.
- Most believe that business, government, and consumers have not done enough to protect the environment.
- Most believe that creating a cleaner environment can actually create jobs and help the economy.
- Despite the recession, nearly three fourths of the public favor protecting the environment even at the risk of slower economic growth.
- Most have taken some personal action to improve the environment and consider themselves environmentalists.
- Trend-setting environmental consumers have changed their personal economic behavior to protect the environment.

SOURCE: Environment Opinion Study; also see *The Environment: Public Attitudes and Individual Behavior,* a study conducted by the Roper Organization, July 1990, New York.

The 1990s have been labelled the Earth Decade, meaning they are supposed to spawn a "new environmentalism" with features different from the "old."[7] The new environmentalism also has gained expression in the request made of companies to subscribe to the Valdez Principles. Companies have been asked to reduce their wastes, use resources prudently, market safe products, and take responsibility for past harm (see Exhibit 13–3).

The philosophy out of which the new environmentalism springs is an amalgam of diverse sources and ideas that combines numerous points of view. Some of the key aspects of this philosophy are noted in a sketch of the history of the movement as reflected in the ideas of some of its influential thinkers.[8]

Conservation versus Environmentalism

The conservation movement, which predates the environmental movement, has been anthropocentric (human- as opposed to nature-centered), technologically optimistic, and chiefly concerned with the efficient use of resources. It adheres to the tenets of scientific management; that is, it seeks to avoid waste by promoting the rational and efficient use of nature's riches and maximizing long-term yields, especially of renewable resources. Moreover, the leaders of the conservation movement as a whole have not questioned the system of political authority or the character of the economic system.

The environmental movement, in contrast, has shown that the unintended negative effects of human economic activities on the environment are often greater than the positive effects. There are links, for example, between forest cutting and soil erosion and between the draining

---

Exhibit 13–3 Valdez Principles

Protection of the biosphere: Minimize the release of pollutants that may cause environmental damage.

Sustainable use of natural resources: Conserve nonrenewable resources through efficient use and careful planning.

Reduction and disposal of waste: Minimize the creation of waste, especiallly hazardous waste, and dispose of such materials in a safe, responsible manner.

Wise use of energy: Make every effort to use environmentally safe and sustainable energy sources to meet operating requirements.

Risk reduction: Diminish environmental, health, and safety risks to employees.

Marketing of safe products and services: Sell products that minimize adverse environmental impact and are safe for consumers.

Damage compensation: Accept responsibility for any harm the company causes the environment; conduct bioremediation and compensate affected parties.

Disclosure of environmental incidents: Public dissemination of accidents relating to operations that harm the environment or pose health or safety risks.

Environmental directors: Appoint at least one board member who is qualified to represent environmental interests; create a position for vice president for environmental affairs.

Assessment and annual audit: Produce and publicize each year a self-evalation of progress toward implementing the principles and meeting all applicable laws and regulations worldwide. Environmental audits will also be produced annually and distributed to the public.

---

of marshes and lakes and the decline of animal life. Early environmentalists such as John Muir (1838–1914) and Aldo Leopold (1886–1948) argued that humans are not above nature but a part of it. Also, nature is to be revered for the spiritual experience it provides. It is not for humans to subdue but is sacred and should be preserved not simply for economic use but for its own sake, that is, for what humans can learn from it.

The environmental movement has stressed technological limitations. Humans should neither control nor dictate to nature. The political and ideological dimensions of the anti-technological attitude have led to a questioning of the logic of private investment decisions, production, expansion, and economic growth. It is ascetic in its orientation: human beings should live simply, without display, excess, or ostentation.

Science and the Environment

Rachel Carson's best-selling book *Silent Spring* helped ignite the modern environmental movement by alerting the public to the dangers of unrestricted pesticide use.[9] She discussed the accumulation of insecticide residues in the fatty tissues of fish and birds that eat fish, the resistance insects develop to the toxins, the dispersion of the toxins far from their source, and the interaction of the toxins in the human body. Carson brought together the findings of toxicology, ecology, and epidemiology in a form accessible to the public. Melding together scientific, moral, and political arguments, she made the connection between environmental politics and values and scientific knowledge.

Barry Commoner's *Science and Survival* continued in this vein.[10] But in addition, he explicitly expanded the scope of ecology to include everything in the physical, chemical, biological, social, political, economic, and philosophical worlds.[11] All these elements fit together, and they had to be understood as a whole. The symptoms of environmental problems are in the biological world, but their source is in economic and political organizations, and the solutions are political.

This combination of science and environmental politics has not been an easy one.[12] Many in the scientific community have opposed it, and many in the environmental community have been hostile to what science has had to offer. Scientists generally feel that they are obligated to improve the material condition of humanity. Environmentalists, on the other hand, often question whether additional material progress is necessary. Some environmentalists interpret the ecological perspective to mean that nature establishes immutable limits to human progress. Today, this debate seems closer to being resolved by a general agreement that additional growth should be sustainable within nature's limits. The concept of sustainable development has been adopted by many environmental activists and even by many in the business community who are ordinarily outside the environmental movement. The exact meaning of sustainable development is still a matter of debate, however.

Within the scientific community, the distinction between engineering and the physical sciences, on the one hand, and biology and the life sciences, on the other, is important. Engineers and physicists generally have had greater faith in technology than biologists and life scientists, who are more sensitive to nature's limitations. Environmentalists generally criticize the "linear, non-integrated, hyper-specialized" character of engineering and the physical sciences as being responsible for many environmental problems.[13] They hold that the narrowness of these disciplines means that environmental consequences and costs are not considered when human interference with natural processes takes place.

Economics and the Environment

Environmentalists also tend to criticize conventional economics for its notions of efficiency and its emphasis on economic growth.[14] For example, environmentalists argue that economists do not adequately consider the unintended side-effects of growth. Economists need to supplement estimates of the economic costs and benefits of growth with estimates of effects that cannot be measured in economic terms. According to environmentalists, the burden of proof should rest with proponents of the new technologies. The new technologies should not be implemented simply because they advance material progress. In affluent societies, mere economic expansion is insufficient.

E. J. Mishan, an economist who contributed to the development of cost-benefit analysis, has criticized society's obsession with growth.[15] Growth is promoted for many reasons—to restore the balance of payments, to make the nation more competitive, to create jobs, to reduce the deficit, to provide for the old and sick, and to lessen poverty. The public is encouraged to focus on statistics of productivity, balance of payments, and growth, while ignoring the obvious costs. The goal of many environmentalists is a steady-state economy, where population and per capita resource consumption stabilize. Herman Daly defines a steady-state economy as one in which "constant stocks of people and artifacts [are] maintained at some desired level . . . by the lowest feasible flows of matter and energy" (see Exhibit 13–4)[16]

Paul Hawken foresees "the next economy" as being based on products that last longer because they have been better designed.[17] These products should be lighter, stronger, and easier to repair; they also should consume less energy; and they will be traded again and again.

Human services do not require much energy or material throughput and yet contribute to economic growth. Environmental cleanup and

---

EXHIBIT 13–4   Business and Environmental Viewpoints Compared

	Business	*Environmentalists*
Imperative	Preservation of the organization	Preservation of natural systems
Key stakeholders	Shareholders, employees, customers	Natural systems, future generations
Basis for decisions	Short- to moderate-term return on investment	Long-term preservation of natural systems
View of natural resources	Means to achieve ends Use efficiently based on cost	Ends unto themselves Use only if needed and with proper safeguards in place
Regulating mechanisms	The market	Natural systems Government
View of economic growth	Desirable, depends on increased resource consumption	Not desirable when it requires resource consumption or pollution above sustainable limits

energy conservation also contribute to economic growth while having a positive effect on the environment. Growth can continue, according to environmentalists, but only if the forms of growth are carefully chosen. As Paehlke writes: "What is manufactured will be less of an object than an idea, or proportionately less an object and more an idea."[18]

Free time would have to be a larger component of an environmentally acceptable future economy. Free time removes people from potentially harmful production. It also provides them with the time needed to make alternative production processes and techniques work, including organic gardening, recycling, public transportation, and home and appliance maintenance for the purposes of energy conservation.

The problem with reducing the rate of economic growth, as many environmentalists admit, is what it might do to the aspirations of the poor for economic mobility. Rising output satisfies the demands of the poor and middle class for better living conditions without challenging the privileges of the wealthy. Without economic expansion, the struggle for economic advancement might lead to social disorder.

Another requirement of an environmentally acceptable economy, then, is that people accept a "new frugality," a concept that also has been labeled "joyous austerity," "voluntary simplicity," and "conspicuous frugality," to contrast it with the conspicuous consumption which Thorsten Veblen described as being prevalent in an earlier stage of capitalism.[19] (On how environmentalists deal with trade-offs between energy and environmental requirements, see the special feature on page 418, "Amory Lovins: The Soft Energy Path").

Radical Environmentalism

In Bill McKibben's best-selling book *The End of Nature* the reverence for nature and resentment of intrusions from human technologies is absolute.[20] His concern is that technology and businesses have made everything on earth "manmade and artificial." Nature is being completely "crowded out" by human interference.[21]

McKibben expresses a sense of sadness and loss because "nature's independence" has been destroyed.[22] Humility toward nature is what he offers because nature is spiritually superior to human beings. McKibben believes that nature has rights over which human beings have no intrinsic authority. Humans should be prevented from doing whatever they want to nature. They should be stopped from exercising their dominion over nature for the sake of material progress.

What is surprising about McKibben is the extremism of his ideas, his willingness to sympathize with the notion that "individual suffering—animal or human—might be less important than the suffering of species, ecosystems, the planet."[23] For much of history, most humans have not experienced nature as kind and gentle but as harsh and dangerous, and therefore human beings have felt compelled to subordinate nature in order to protect themselves.

McKibben's extremism is partially a consequence of his desperation. As he sees it, there can no longer be "personal solutions." A person cannot escape from industrial society by "moving to the woods" because the woods are no longer inviolate. The solutions McKibben believes are necessary could entail infringements on individual rights that differ from the market-based solutions proposed by some environmentalists.

The Warnings of Environmentalists

Environmentalists believe that the earth is in great danger. They see a catastrophe coming as early as the late 20th century. The earth cannot tolerate the additional contaminants of industrial civilization. Environmentalists project current resource use and environmental degradation into the future to demonstrate that civilization is running out of critical resources.[24] Human intervention, in the form of technological innovation and capital investment complemented by substantial human ingenuity and creativity, is insufficient to prevent this outcome unless drastic steps are taken soon. Numerous civilizations have been destroyed because they abused the environment.

Environmentalists use the laws of physics (the notion of entropy) to show how society systematically dissipates low-entropy, high-concentration forms of energy by converting them to high-entropy, low-concentration waste that cannot be used again except at very high cost. They also rely upon the laws of biology (the notion of carrying capacity) to show that the earth has a limited ability to tolerate the disposal of contaminants. They draw on engineering and management concepts to argue that exceedingly complex and dangerous technologies cannot be managed by humans without disastrous consequences for humanity and the environment.

Their philosophy does not blend in easily with the optimistic tenets of management theory and the materialistic beliefs of businesses. Environmentalists point out that nearly every economic benefit has an environmental cost, and that the sum total of the costs in an affluent society often exceed the benefits.

Public Policy and Economic Approaches

Public policy and economic approaches to environmental issues counter claims made by the environmentalists.[25] They argue that limits to growth can be overcome by human ingenuity, that benefits afforded by

Amory Lovins: The Soft Energy Path

For some environmentalists, the energy price shocks of 1973 and 1979 necessitated a reformulation of environmental values. This reformulation was accomplished by Amory Lovins, a physicist whose books and writings on the "soft energy path" (SEP) were highly influential in the 1970s.[1]

After the 1973 oil embargo environmentalists were on shaky ground. They opposed offshore oil drilling, the Alaskan pipeline, and additional coal burning, and favored auto emission reductions that had the potential to decrease automotive fuel efficiency. Their programs appeared to increase U.S. vulnerability to OPEC. Lovins answered the criticism by proposing policies for an alternative energy future based on renewable resources and energy efficiency. His program promised to reduce pollution and at the same time increase economic growth.

Lovins argued that environmental problems were mainly problems of energy. Human beings were at a crossroads. They had a choice between two paths—the so-called hard energy path (HEP) of the past and the soft energy path (SEP) of the future. HEP involved nonrenewable energy sources that were capital intensive and threatened the environment. In contrast, SEP was based on the efficient use of energy in housing design and other areas. It also was based on obtaining increasing amounts of energy from renewable sources such as sunlight, geothermal energy, wood stoves, wind, water, waves, and tides, plants, alcohol, and solar photovoltaics, which promised to be the ul-

timate soft technology. Lovins struggled against the presumption that the more energy people used, the better off they were. Another part of his analysis concerned the diseconomies of scale in distributing energy from central sites to dispersed consumers. Thus, the social aspect of SEP was a society that was more decentralized in character.

Lovins was a major critic of nuclear power, which he opposed because of potential malfunctions, accidents on a scale no other industry could have, radioactivity, and problems associated with reprocessing, terrorism, sabotage, and theft. Safety in the nuclear industry required a corps of highly trained, dedicated personnel. Alvin Weinberg, one of the founders of the nuclear power program in the United States, referred to this group as a "technological priesthood."[2] The managers of nuclear production in the U.S. had to be a group of experts who stood apart from the rest of society. They had to maintain rigorous standards to prevent accidents. To recruit this group, extensive psychological testing might be required. To control it, the monitoring of the personal, psychological, and financial affairs of nuclear personnel might be necessary. Capital punishment for crimes involving nuclear personnel might be imposed. Lovins therefore believed that nuclear power could only succeed in centrally planned economies like the Soviet Union and France where personal control over individuals was greater and where bureaucratic power could override economic limitations. His description is

[1]A. B. Lovins, *Soft Energy Paths: Toward a Durable Peace* (New York: Friends of the Earth International, 1977).

[2] R. Paehlke, *Environmentalism and the Future of Progressive Politics* (New Haven, Conn.: Yale University Press, 1989).

Amory Lovins: The Soft Energy Path continued

only partially true as nuclear power did see its greatest failure, Chernobyl, take place in the ex-Soviet Union, but its greatest success was in France.

Ultimately, though, it was the economic weaknesses of nuclear power that Lovins stressed. In his opinion, nuclear power simply was not competitive in the free market. The basic premise of his position was that conservation and renewable resources would win in the marketplace if only the competition were fair.[3] Fair competition meant that the full social and environmental costs of a technology had to be included in the price consumers paid for energy. Lovins advocated what economists had proposed for the electric utilities, that is, marginal cost pricing that would charge users the full cost of new supplies. He also advocated flat or inverted rate structures, which would mean that large users would have to pay as much or more per unit of energy as small users. His economic arguments about the long-term unfeasibility of nuclear power have proved to be more true than his arguments about the social requirements of the technology.

His approach, moreover, was in harmony with economic values. Price signals emanating from the marketplace would provide people with the incentives they needed to adapt and conserve. Environmentally benign alternatives to fossil fuel would be introduced in the context of a free market. The role of the government was to remove economic and political barriers and allow creative individuals to find solutions.

The noninterventionist approach of Lovins to economic policy was in contrast to that

taken by most environmentalists. It was more in line with a theory of business management in which the market, not government, was sovereign. Lovins, however, provided managers with a major challenge. Implementing SEP meant replacing or substantially modifying virtually the whole capital stock of society—appliances, autos, housing, and highways. OPEC and SEP provided an impetus for environmentalists to accept new technologies and emerging industries, such as telecommunications, computers, and information processing that appeared environmentally benign. It also freed them from a politics of negativism and confrontation with the organized forces of society.

Not all environmentalists, however, were happy with this approach.[4] They had technical disagreements. For instance, they pointed out that there would be competition between using biomass (plant material) for fuel and using it for food under the soft path. Further, even if the entire U.S. corn crop were converted to alcohol, it could provide only about 7.5 percent of the nation's need for motor fuel and only a little more than 1 percent of the total energy needed.[5] Environmentalists also pointed out that U.S. coastlines and mountain tops would have to be cluttered with windmills, and that endless acres of land would have to be devoted to biomass-derived fuels. Indeed, some environmentalists even argued that Lovins was wrong, and that the use of some nuclear power was benign because it produces large amounts of energy in a relatively harmless (when compared to the alternatives) way.

---

[3] Ibid.

[4] J. R. Emshwiller, "Energy-Efficient Guru Sees Fertile Field for Start-Ups," *The Wall Street Journal*, October 30, 1990, p. B2.

[5] Paehlke, *Environmentalism and the Future of Progressive Politics*.

environmental protection have a cost, and that government programs to clean up the environment are as likely to fail as the market forces that produce pollution.

Overcoming the Limits to Growth

The traditional economic view is that production is a function of labor and capital, and in theory, that resources are not necessary since labor and/or capital are infinitely substitutable for resources (see Chapter 12).[26] Impending resource scarcity results in price increases that lead to technological substitution of capital, labor, or other resources for those in scarce supply. Price increases also create pressures for efficiency in use, leading to reduced consumption.

Thus, resource scarcity is reflected in the price of a given commodity. As resources become scarce, their prices rise accordingly, and price increases induce substitution and technological innovation.

People turn to less-scarce resources that fulfill the same basic technological and economic needs provided by the resources no longer available in large quantities. To a large extent, the energy crises of the 1970s (the 1973 price shock induced by the Arab oil embargo and 1979 price shock following the Iranian Revolution) were alleviated by these very processes: higher prices leading to the discovery of additional supplies and to conservation. By 1985, energy prices in real terms were lower than they were in 1973 (see Chapter 12).

People respond to signals about scarcity and degradation. But they respond not only to price signals and not only in economic terms; their response is also political, sociological, and psychological.[27] Governments express people's collective sentiments and start programs to counter the impending scarcity and degradation. Social movements begin to affect people's expectations and life-styles. People's attitudes and values change. These feedback loops, which are expressive of human change in the face of information about natural resource scarcity and environmental degradation, are inadequately factored into the simple deterministic models.

Extrapolating past consumption patterns into the future without considering the human response is likely to be a futile exercise. As far back as the end of the 18th century, thinkers such as Thomas Malthus have made predictions about the limits to growth, but the lesson of modern history is one of technological innovation and substitution in response to price and other societal signals, not one of calamity brought about by resource exhaustion. In general, the prices of natural resources have been declining despite increased production and demand.[28] Prices have fallen because of discoveries of new resources and because of innovations in the extraction and refinement process.

Policy analysts and economists also question the motives and intentions of environmentalists. For example, the interests of already affluent sectors are served by arguing that the prospects for additional growth are limited, thus closing channels for those who are less well off. This was a main issue between developed and undeveloped nations at the 1992 Rio Conference on economics and development sponsored by the United Nations. The argument that growth is limited is also in the interests of those whose professional occupation means that they are going to manage humankind toward sustainability. According to some economists, a triad of the affluent "members of the leisure class, intellectuals, and professionals"—may increase social tension and decrease the prospects for peaceful and democratic settlement of national and international conflicts because of their antigrowth pronouncements.[29]

Balancing the Costs and Benefits

Another point of contention between environmentalists and economists/policy analysts is that environmentalists might believe that total elimination of risk is possible and even desirable, but economists and policy analysts argue that the benefits of risk elimination have to be balanced against the costs.

Measuring risk is itself very complicated (see Chapter 16). It involves determining the conditions of exposure, the adverse effects, the levels of exposure, the level of the effects, and the overall contamination.[30] Further, long latency periods, assessing the implications for human populations of laboratory studies of nonhuman animal species, and the impact of background contamination complicate these efforts. Simple cause-and-effect statements are out of the question.

The most usually that can be said is that exposure to a particular contaminant *is likely* to have caused a particular disease. Risk has to be stated in terms of probabilities, not certainties, and it has to be distinguished from safety, which is a societal judgment about how much risk society is willing to bear. When comparing technological systems, different types of risks (e.g., from mining, radiation, industrial accidents, and climate impacts) have to be compared.[31] This type of comparison further complicates the judgments that have to be made.

Reducing risk involves asking the extent to which the proposed methods of reductions are likely to be effective, and how much these proposed methods will cost. In theory, decision making could be left to the individual. Society could provide people with information (e.g., warning labels) and each person would then decide what to do—whether to purchase a product or service depending upon the environmental and resource consequences. However, relying upon individual judgments in the market may not adequately reflect society's preference for an amenity such as air quality if that amenity is a public good with no owner and no price attached to it. Thus, social and political judgments are needed.

However much science reduces uncertainty, in making social and political judgments, gaps in knowledge remain.[32] Scientific limitations open the door for political and bureaucratic biases that may be nonrational. In some instances, politicians have framed legislation in ways that seriously hinder, if not entirely prohibit, the consideration of costs (e.g., the Delaney Amendment and the Clean Air Act). In other instances (e.g., the Presidents' Regulatory Review Council), they have explicitly forced cost factors to be considered. Moreover, cost factors can be considered in various ways. Analysts can carry out cost-effectiveness analysis in which they attempt to figure out how to achieve a given goal with limited resources, or they can carry out more formal risk/benefit and cost/benefit analyses in which they have to quantify both the benefits and the costs of risk reduction.[33]

Qualitative Judgment in Cost-Benefit Analysis

Economists and policy analysts would be the first to admit that formal, quantitative approaches to balancing costs and benefits do not eliminate the need for qualitative judgments. Cost-benefit analysis was initially developed for water projects where the issues, while complicated, were not the same as society now faces.[34] For example, today we must determine: what is the value of a magnificent vista obscured by air pollution? What is the loss to society if a given genetic strain of plant or animal species becomes extinct? What are the opportunity costs of spending vast sums on air pollution that could have been invested in productivity enhancement and global competitiveness?

Equity issues, both interpersonal and intergenerational, cannot be ignored when doing cost-benefit analysis.[35] The costs of air pollution reduction may have to be borne disproportionately by the poor in the form of higher gasoline and automobile prices. The costs of water pollution reduction, on the other hand, may be borne to a greater extent by the rich because these costs are financed through public spending. Regions dependent on dirty coal may find it in their interests to unite with environmentalists in seeking pollution control technology. The pollution control technology saves coal-mining jobs in West Virginia and the Midwest where the coal is dirty but impedes the development of the coal-mining industry in the West where large quantities of clean-burning coal are located.

Intergenerational equity also plays a role.[36] Future generations have no current representatives in the market system or political process. How their interests are taken into account ultimately amounts to a philosophical discussion about altruism: To what extent should current generations hold back on their own consumption for the sake of posterity? Should Bentham's "achieving the greatest good of the greatest number" be modified to read "sufficient per capita product for the greatest number over time?"[37]

These questions are particularly poignant given the fact that most people living on earth today do not have "sufficient per capita product." Achieving moral consensus is extremely difficult in a worldwide community when there are many differences between cultures and cultural values. We must consider the extent to which it is appropriate for political coercion to play a role in achieving global standards on such matters as consumption and procreation. These are issues for which economics and policy analysis has no simple answers. They are ethical issues that require choosing some appropriate ethical rule.

Economists offer the Pareto optimum—"a situation where no one can be better off without making someone worse off."[38] Political philosophers (see Chapter 4) propose alternative standards. John Rawls formulates a contemporary liberal philosophy around this maxim: "Each person is to have an equal right to the most extensive basic liberty compatible to similar liberty for others [and] social and economic inequalities are to be arranged so that they are both (*a*) reasonably expected to be to everyone's advantage and (*b*) attached to offices and positions open to all."[39] Robert Nozick formulates the contemporary libertarian position as "any act that improves an individual's [or several individuals'] well-being and harms no one is the moral or 'right.' "[40] However, none of these principles applies directly to environmental matters. How to apply them and how to decide which is appropriate are themselves important issues. Too often cost-benefit analysis revolves around technical matters when what is needed is greater sensitivity to the ethical issues.

Market and Government Failures

Most policy analysts and economists accept that markets ordinarily are the superior means for fulfilling human wants (see Chapter 8). In a market deals are struck between consenting adults only when the parties to the deals feel they are likely to benefit. Society as a whole gains from the aggregation of individual deals that take place because of the calculations individuals make about their own welfare. The wealth of a society grows by means of the invisible hand that offers spontaneous coordination with a minimum of coercion and explicit central direction. The intervention of government may be justified only under special circumstance, if, for instance, markets are not perfectly competitive; market participants are not fully informed; or property rights are not appropriately assigned.

The fact that property rights are not appropriately assigned is a major justification for government intervention for the sake of natural resource and environmental protection. Since nature lacks a discrete owner, its rights may be violated by market exchanges between consenting parties. As a "common property resource," it is subject to overuse and degradation. Lacking a discrete owner, it is inadequately protected from deals affecting it unless there is some form of government protection.

Policy analysts and economists view the degradation of nature that comes about because of the lack of specific property rights as a type of externality, that is, the imposition on society of costs that have not been incorporated within the price system. The costs to society are to be understood as costs to nonconsenting third parties whose interests in nature have been violated by a deal. The consenting parties inflict damage without compensating the other parties because without clear property rights, no entity stands up for the rights of violated nature in which the other parties have a stake.

Nature's owners are a collectivity that is hard to organize. They are a large and diverse group that cannot easily pursue remedies in the legal system. In attempting to gain compensation for the damage done, they suffer from the "free-rider" problem, which makes collective action difficult. This problem can be understood as, "Let someone else take care of it:" it is not sufficiently in the interest of any member of the group to pursue. Each only has a small amount to gain. Thus, government intervention is needed to protect the interests of the collectivity, which has ownership rights in the natural world, which would otherwise be harmed.

Policy analysts and economists, however, point out that although collective action problems provide a rationale for government involvement, government involvement will not necessarily be effective in addressing the problem. Just as there can be market failures, there can be government failures as well.

With respect to politicians, citizens may send them inadequate signals.[41] Voters may not understand the issues well enough to formulate coherent options to present to politicians. Political decision making also may be dominated by interest groups and biased information, by partisanship, ideology, personal deals and arrangements, and financial constraints. In addition, the laws are carried out by civil servants, who may not succeed because the goals in the legislation may be too diverse or other problems may exist that prove intractable: resources are insufficient, political opposition is too great, other issues gain higher priority, and bureaucratic infighting sabotages the effort.

Economists and policy analysts speak of the "deadweight costs" of any government program that must be balanced against the proposed benefits. The term *internalities* is used to describe the inefficiencies in public decision making (see Chapter 8).[42] Both the government and the corporate bureaucracies that implement environmental policies are less than perfect instruments for the task.

The Burden on Scientific Information

A problem policymakers face is the burden placed on them of insufficient or inadequate scientific information. The political process puts an immense burden on science to give definitive answers to such questions as the potential for generating energy from exotic technologies like fusion and solar power and the risks to exposed populations from various chemicals. But science rarely completely stands up to this challenge.

Society needs all kinds of knowledge. It needs to know the true extent of resource limitations, and it needs to estimate the risks from environmental contaminants and the expense of cleaning up these contaminants. It also requires knowledge about the strengths and weaknesses of government- and non-government-based solutions to environmental problems. Unfortunately, many uncertainties persist.

The Catalytic Converter Controversy

An interesting example of the burden that scientific information puts on the political process is the catalytic converter controversy. To understand this controversy it is necessary to go back to the period prior to the birth of the Environmental Protection Agency (EPA). In President Nixon's 1970 statement about the EPA, he stressed the need to merge pollution control programs so as to manage the environment "comprehensively." He argued that energy and environmental issues should be considered together, but his plan for comprehensive environmental management was never realized.

At the time EPA was created, Senator Edmund Muskie, Democrat from Maine and head of the powerful Senate Subcommittee on Air and Water Pollution, was searching for "handles" that would force the automobile industry to achieve air quality goals by a specific date. He addressed a problem of regulatory administration that scholars have called "vague delegation of authority."[43] According to this doctrine, the typical regulatory statute has indefinite provisions. In effect, Congress says to the bureaucracy, "Here is the problem—deal with it." The regulatory agency lacks the binding authority needed to coerce industry into complying with statutory requirements. The remedy for problems attributable to vague and ill-formed legislation is to draft statutes that have clear goals and explicit means of implementation. The 1970 Clean Air Act, passed into law on December 31, 1970, mandated that auto manufacturers achieve a 90 percent reduction in hydrocarbon and carbon monoxide emissions by 1975, and a 90 percent reduction in nitrogen oxide emissions by 1976. Similar legislation passed by the state of California in 1992 required that 2 percent of a car company's sales in that state have "zero emissions" by 1998 and that 10 percent have "zero emissions" by 2003.

The air quality goals in the 1970 Clean Air Act, however, were "based on incomplete data and large margins of safety."[44] The required 90 percent reductions were taken from calculations of the highest levels of carbon monoxide emissions ever recorded in Chicago, the highest levels of nitrogen oxide emissions ever recorded in New York, and the highest level of hydrocarbon emissions ever recorded in Los Angeles.

Meanwhile, President Nixon warned the American people about the possibility of energy shortages. In a 1973 speech he said that the United States had only 6 percent of the world's population, but it used one third of the world's energy. Then, the Syrian and Egyptian armies launched their surprise attack on the state of Israel, and the Arab oil-producing nations imposed an oil embargo. U.S. consumers experienced hour-long waits in line for gasoline, truck drivers blockaded highways to protest fuel shortages and price increases, and the National Guard in some states had to be called out to maintain order (see Chapter 12).[45]

President Nixon urged Congress to modify the Clean Air Act, saying that the interim 1976–77 auto emission standards should be extended so that manufacturers could concentrate on fuel economy. The automobile emission deadlines already had been extended once in 1973 after the United States Court of Appeals for the District of Columbia found that the EPA should take into account the economic burden on the auto manufacturers. Congress passed a law calling for the extension Nixon proposed in 1974. Emission deadlines were extended another year, and the auto manufacturers were given the right to ask for still another one-year extension.[46]

To meet the emissions standards then in effect, auto makers had retuned existing engines. The problem was that the retuning reduced fuel economy by about 10 percent.[47] EPA officials believed that if auto companies used catalytic converters, there would be no fuel penalty. The National Academy of Sciences backed up the EPA. Its studies showed that 90 percent reductions were possible in cars equipped with catalytic converters with no fuel penalty.[48]

Acid Emissions

The Ford Motor Company then asked for another extension, because sulfuric acid emissions had been discovered in catalytic converter discharges. John Moran, an EPA research scientist, held an unauthorized press conference in the fall of 1973 that alerted the public to the danger. Moran, a health effects researcher located at Research Triangle Park—

EPA's scientific complex near Durham, North Carolina—made public a study showing that although catalytic converters reduced hydrocarbons and carbon monoxide, they emitted significant amounts of sulfuric acid with probable adverse effects on public health. Moran's study pointed out that the converter, which was supposed to eliminate the health hazards caused by air pollution, caused a health problem. The acid emissions were minute, but in regions of high traffic density, they could be dangerous.

Moran's statements were attacked by EPA staff. They held their own unauthorized press conference and accused Moran of leaking information about health risks because he wanted EPA headquarters to continue funding his emissions-testing program. They claimed that only under special circumstances were the emissions of sulfuric acid significant; otherwise, sulfuric acid emissions were too small to make a difference. Only at sufficiently high concentrations were adverse health effects associated with sulfuric acid, but these concentrations were unlikely to occur.

In 1975, Congress held hearings on amendments to the Clean Air Act.[49] All the participants in the debate—environmentalists, industry, representatives of the administration, and experts—used the language and rhetoric of science to advance their positions. They buttressed their arguments with some form of scientific study.[50] Ultimately, catalytic converters were allowed, but not without substantial delay in implementing the Clean Air Act. Predictably, environmentalists were disappointed, but surprisingly, General Motors also was upset. It had spent hundreds of millions of dollars on catalyst research, built an expensive plant for fabricating catalytic converters, and signed long-term contracts to obtain the precious metals used in the converters—all steps that its U.S. competitors, Ford and Chrysler, had not taken.

How Scientific Knowledge Is Generated and Used

Environmental issues compel consideration of how scientific knowledge is generated and used in public policy debates. Most important choices are made under conditions of "residual risk": complete knowledge is unavailable, nor are the decisions made thoroughly at random, a result of mere guesswork.[51] Some knowledge, as with the catalytic converter, exists but it is imperfect. Even if total knowledge were available, the appropriate actions based on this knowledge would not be apparent. Moreover, existing knowledge changes, and as it changes over time, uncertainties may grow making it more difficult to know what to do.

Choices about policy and implementation are made and remade in response to a process of sorting out what is known and unknown. This process depends on the imperfect capabilities of individuals, groups, and organizations to perceive risk and to act on the basis of their perceptions. Implicit in the process is an evaluation of "societal negligence." Derived from the classic formulation of Judge Learned Hand, this concept postulates that in evaluating risk, a "reasonable" person considers (*a*) the probability of injury, (*b*) the gravity of the injury should it occur, and (*c*) the burden of taking adequate precaution. Judge Hand argued that if the expected injury (probability × gravity) exceeds the costs of precaution and the defendant takes no action, then the defendant is negligent.[52]

Extended to society at large, the costs of precaution (in the prior example, from introducing the catalytic converter and exposing the public to the sulfuric acid) should be balanced against the probability of harm from automotive air pollution times the costs of harm (impaired health). Environmentalists are likely to emphasize the probability and costs of harm while downplaying the burdens of precaution. When the expected danger is great, the movement's prevailing philosophy of more government involvement, slower growth, and simpler living can be implemented. By contrast, corporations are likely to focus on the burdens of precaution, since these burdens fall disproportionately on them and have far-reaching implications for their products and how these products are made.

The government should be guided by rational and scientific judgments, but because the uncertainties are great, both elected officials and bureaucrats are swayed by the viewpoints of environmentalists and business. Environmentalists and business groups contribute information to the debate, and they sponsor studies and interpret existing studies in accord with their point of view. Also, neutral experts contribute information to the debate. In the end, public officials are caught in the middle, having to make binding decisions based on the uncertain information.

Summary and Conclusions

Waste products are made when businesses produce any good or service. These waste products have to be disposed of properly. The capacities of natural systems to absorb this waste are an ultimate limit on the economic expansion a society can achieve.

This chapter has described different approaches to environmental problems. Environmentalists emphasize the limits of nature's capacity to absorb waste. Public policy analysts/economists show how these limits can be overcome by the price system and government; they admit that regulation is needed in some instances but warn that the value of regulation has to be balanced against the costs. Cost-benefit analysis is the way policy analysts/economists prefer to deal with environmental issues, but cost-benefit analysis, as public policy analysts/economists will admit, has qualitative components. It does not get around important normative considerations, and these normative considerations play a critical role.

Important too is public officials' knowledge about environmental issues. This chapter has concluded with a discussion of the uncertainties encountered in implementing environmental policies.

Discussion Questions

1. Describe the flow of materials from nature to nature. What effect does this flow have on economic growth?
2. Describe the major tenets of the conservation movement. Compare its tenets with those of environmentalism.
3. What contributions did Rachel Carson and Barry Commoner make to the environmental movement?
4. How do environmentalists view economic growth? How are their views on this topic different from the views of economists?
5. What is the soft energy path? How does it differ from the hard energy path?
6. What if the price system was fixed as Lovins advocated? Would energy choices made by society be different? Why or why not?
7. How do you view the environmentalism of Bill McKibben? Does nature deserve absolute respect?
8. According to policy analysts/economists, how are limits to growth to be overcome?
9. What are some of the arguments for and against cost-benefit analysis? What are the appropriate uses for cost-benefit analysis?
10. What do the deadweight costs of any government action have to do with solving environmental problems?
11. What does the regulatory problem "vague delegation of authority" refer to? How does the 1970 Clean Air Act approach this problem?
12. In 1975, when Congress held hearings on the Clean Air Act, what should General Motors have done? What kind of arguments should it have made? What types of analysis should it have used to support its arguments?
13. What does the term *residual risk* suggest? How important is it in describing environmental issues?
14. What is Judge Learned Hand's rule? To what extent is it helpful in determining if society has been negligent?

Endnotes

1. I would like to acknowledge the assistance of the following students in my course on business and the environment who contributed to parts of Chapters 13 and 14. Dan Batterman, Jose Blando, Therese Bodine, Chris De Vanes, Franz Hofmeister, Rob Hogg, Pat Keran, Debora Knops, Brent Korengold, Carin Peterson, Gregory Steininger, Mark Van Wie, Rosemary Ward, and Warren Winkelman. My teaching assistant for courses in this area has been Gordon Rands, and he too has made a substantial contribution to the ideas expressed here. Many of the ideas in this chapter and the next can be found in R. Buchholz, A. Marcus, and J. Post, *Managing Environmental Issues: A Case Book* (Englewood Cliffs, N.J.: Prentice Hall, 1992).

2. A. Freeman, R. Myrick, H. Haveman, and A. V. Kneese. *The Economics of Environmental Policy* (New York: John Wiley & Sons, 1973); A. V. Kneese, *Economics and the Environment* (New York: Penguin Books, 1977).

3. Freeman, Myrick, Haveman, and Kneese, *The Economics of Environmental Policy*; Kneese, *Economics and the Environment*.

4. N. Georgescu-Roegen, *Energy and Economic Myths* (New York: Pergamon, 1976).

5. D. Kirkpatrick, "Environmentalism: The New Crusade," *Fortune*, February 12, 1990, pp. 44–55; R. Irwin, "Clean and Green," *Sierra*, November/December 1985, pp. 50–56; J. Crudele, "Environmental Issues Could Be Hot Item of '90s," *Minneapolis Star and Tribune*, March 18, 1990, p. 2D; R. Buchholz, A. Marcus, and J. Post, *Managing Environmental Issues: A Case Book* (Englewood Cliffs, N.J.: Prentice Hall, 1990).

6. Kirkpatrick, "Environmentalism: The New Crusade."

7. Ibid.

8. R. Carson, *Silent Spring* (Cambridge, Mass.: Houghton-Mifflin, 1962); R. Paehlke, *Environmentalism and the Future of Progressive Politics* (New Haven, Conn.: Yale University Press, 1989), pp. 13–41, 76–143; R. Nash, ed., *The American Environment* (Reading, Mass.: Addison-Wesley, 1968); R. Revelle and H. Landsberg, ed., *America's Changing Environment* (Boston: Beacon Press, 1970); L. Caldwell, *Environment: A Challenge to Modern Society* (Garden City, N.Y.: Anchor Books, 1971); J. M. Petulla, *Environmental Protection in the United States* (San Francisco: San Francisco Study Center, 1987).

9. Carson, *Silent Spring*.

10. B. Commoner, *Science and Survival* (New York: Viking Press, 1963).

11. B. Commoner, *The Closing Circle: Nature, Man and Technology* (New York: Bantam Books, 1971).

12. R. Paehlke, *Environmentalism and the Future of Progressive Politics* (New Haven, Conn.: Yale University Press, 1989), pp. 13–41, 76–143.

13. Ibid.

14. Ibid.

15. Cited in Paehlke, *Environmentalism and the Future of Progressive Politics*.

16. Cited in Paehlke, *Environmentalism and the Future of Progressive Politics*, p. 130.

17. P. Hawken, J. Ogilvy, and P. Schwartz, *Seven Tomorrows: Toward a Voluntary History* (New York: Bantam Books, 1982); Paehlke, *Environmentalism and the Future of Progressive Politics.*
18. Paehlke, *Environmentalism and the Future of Progressive Politics,* p. 136.
19. Ibid.
20. B. McKibben, *The End of Nature* (New York: Random House, 1989).
21. D. Kevies, "Paradise Lost," *New York Review of Books,* December 21, 1989, pp. 32–38.
22. Ibid.
23. Cited in Kevies, "Paradise Lost," p. 35.
24. D. Mann and H. Ingram, "Policy Issues in the Natural Environment," in *Public Policy and the Natural Environment,* ed. H. Ingram and R. K. Goodwin (Greenwich, Conn.: JAI Press, 1985), pp. 15–47.
25. A. Nichols and R. Zeckhauser, "The Perils of Prudence," *Regulation,* November/December 1986, pp. 13–25; J. F. Morrall, "A Review of the Record," *Regulation,* November/December 1986, pp. 25–35; Buchholz, Marcus, and Post, *Managing Environmental Issues: A Case Book*
26. A. Kneese, "The Economics of Natural Resources," in *Population and Resources in Western Intellectual Traditions,* ed. M. Teitelbaum and J. Winter (Washington, D.C.: The Population Council, 1989), pp. 281–309.
27. Mann and Ingram, "Policy Issues in the Natural Environment."
28. Kneese, "The Economics of Natural Resources."
29. W. Rostow cited in Mann and Ingram, "Policy Issues in the Natural Environment," pp. 146–48.
30. W. Lowrance, "Choosing Our Pleasures and Our Poisons: Risk Assessment for the 1980s, in *Technology and the Future,* ed. A. Teich (New York: St. Martins Press, 1990), pp. 180–207.
31. Mann and Ingram, "Policy Issues in the Natural Environment."
32. A. A. Marcus, "Risk, Uncertainty, and Scientific Judgment," *Minerva* 2, 1988, pp. 138–152.
33. L. Lave, *The Strategy of Social Regulation* (Washington, D.C.: The Brookings Institution, 1981).
34. Kneese, "The Economics of Natural Resources."
35. Mann and Ingram, "Policy Issues in the Natural Environment."
36. Ibid.
37. Ibid.
38. Ibid.
39. Ibid.
40. Ibid.
41. A. Marcus, *Controversies in Energy Policy* (Beverly Hills, Calif.: Sage Press, 1992).
42. Mann and Ingram, "Policy Issues in the Natural Environment," p. 41; J. Q. Wilson, *American Government: Institutions and Policies* (Lexington, Mass.: D. C. Heath and Co., 1980).
43. See R. Noll, *Reforming Regulation: An Evaluation of the Ash Council Proposals* (Washington, D.C.: The Brookings Institution, 1971); and T. Lowi, *The End of Liberalism* (New York: W. W. Norton, 1969).
44. Ibid., p. 30.

45. Ibid., p. 91.

46. *Energy Supply and Environmental Coordination Act of 1974*, Public Law 93–319 (88 Stat. 248) 1974.

47. *Report on Automotive Fuel Efficiency* (Washington, D.C.: EPA, February, 1974).

48. J. Quarles, *Cleaning Up America* (Boston: Houghton Mifflin, 1976), p. 194; and Committee on Motor Vehicle Emissions, *Semi-Annual Report* (Washington, D.C.: National Academy of Sciences, February 12, 1973).

49. Public Law 91–604 (84 Stat. 1676), December 31, 1970.

50. See S. Hays, "Clean Air: From the 1970 Act to the 1977 Amendments," *Duquesne Law Review* 17, no. 1, 1978–79, p. 40.

51. Marcus, "Risk, Uncertainty, and Scientific Judgment."

52. R. Cooter, and T. Ulen, *Law and Economics* (Glenview, Ill.: Scott, Foresman and Company, 1988).

CHAPTER

14

WORLDWIDE ENVIRONMENTAL ISSUES

*The . . . principle of ecology is holism. . . . The biosphere is a unity. . . .
Following immediately from this . . . principle is the fact of interdependence.
Everything within any ecosystem . . . can be shown to be related to everything
else; . . . there are no linear relationships; every effect is also a cause in the
web of natural interdependence; . . . ecologists . . . convey this sense of
pervasive community and interrelationship [with] . . . "You can never do just
one thing."*

William Ophuls, *Ecology and the Politics of Scarcity.*[1]

Introduction and Chapter Objectives

Environmental problems are worldwide in character and so are corporate activities. To compete on a global level, U.S. managers need to understand how pollution problems manifest themselves outside the country. This chapter therefore discusses the environmental movement in Western Europe, one of the major areas where U.S. firms do business. It examines two key issues: solid wastes and atmospheric pollution. These are among the most pressing issues that will confront businesses worldwide in the 1990s. We discuss some of the practical steps managers can take to constructively cope with environmental problems in the final section of this chapter.

The Greening of Western Europe

Environmental problems present themselves differently in different countries and regions of the world. Managers must be savvy about the nuances of these problems if they are to be successful.[2] This section focuses on Western Europe.

The European Economic Community (EC) was created in 1957 by the Treaty of Rome. From 6 original members, it has grown to 12: Luxembourg, West Germany, France, Belgium, Netherlands, Denmark, the United Kingdom, Italy, Ireland, Greece, Spain, and Portugal. Originally, environmental policies did not play much of a role in the EC. However, since 1972, the EC has embarked on a series of environmental action plans, each more serious than the last one.

The West European environmental movement started somewhat later than the American movement, but in important respects (e.g., the sale of environmentally safe products and electoral politics) it has gone farther than its American counterpart. For U.S. firms doing business in Western Europe in the 1990s, environmental concerns are increasingly important (see Exhibit 14-1).

Consequences of EC Activism

In 1985 the EC amended its governing legislation to give it specific authority in the area of environmental protection. Member states were required to create or amend their own legislation in accord with commission directives. The purpose was to standardize environmental policies in the EC and prevent the creation of pollution havens in the poorer countries.

The EC has taken major environmental initiatives in a number of areas.[3] Many of these actions (e.g., strict limits on emissions from new power plants) necessitate increases in capital investment and production

---

EXHIBIT 14–1   Pollution Control Expenditures in EC and Non-EC Countries: 1990
U.S. 1980 Dollars per Capita

European Community Nations		Non-European Community Nations	
Netherlands	$117	Japan	$126
West Germany	111	Canada	126
France	74	United States	80
United Kingdom	65		
Italy	12		

Source: Adapted from Directorate of Intelligence, Central Intelligence Agency, *Handbook of Economic Statistics, 1991* (Washington, D.C.: Government Printing Office, 1991), p. 28.

costs for business. Regulations are also expected for the release of toxic substances by chemical plants into waterways.

The EC's activism has had some interesting consequences. For example, it has put limits on the British government's program of privatization. Great Britain's Water Authorities have been unable to meet the EC's water quality standard. The government has to comply with the standards before it can sell $11 billion in shares of the Water Authorities to the public.[4]

Another consequence comes from the 1985 EC law affecting automotive emissions. Initially the EC applied U.S.-style standards that called for expensive three-way catalytic converters only on large cars. Small cars could meet the requirement by having lean-burn engines. The West German government, however, provided tax breaks to customers who bought cars with the converters, and the EC decided to move toward the U.S. standard by 1993, when all cars will have to have catalytic converters. This decision provides competitive advantage to GM, which had been anticipating the change in the standard, and was a blow to companies like Fiat, Renault, Peugeot, and Ford, which had been specializing in the lean-burn engines.[5]

The EC decision on auto emission standards also provided a boost to manufacturers of auto emissions equipment. A subsidiary of Allied Signal, an American company that supplies catalysts, expanded production capacity in northern France to meet anticipated demand. Cars with catalytic converters require special injection systems that feed the engine precisely mixed doses of fuel, and Robert Bosch of West Germany, the world's largest producer of fuel injection systems, planned to spend $500 million to expand its plants in Germany, France, and Belgium.[6]

EC activism has also affected Coke and Pepsi, the large American beverage companies, that see Europe as a huge growth market because the average European drinks less than a third the volume of soft drinks consumed by the average American. American companies now rely almost exclusively on aluminum cans and plastic bottles, which are less expensive, lighter, and more transportable than glass bottles. In Britain, France, Spain, and Italy, cans and plastic have gained acceptance, but West Germany, Denmark, Switzerland (which is outside the EC), and the Netherlands rely mostly on reusable bottles. Denmark has actually banned cans and plastic bottles. West Germany is considering a quota system to limit them to 20 percent of the soft drink market and 10 percent of the beer market. In these countries, environmentalists have allied themselves with local bottlers to prevent the introduction of alternative packaging. According to the European Court of Justice, these countries have the right to do so. They can even block free trade if it is done for environmental reasons.[7]

American companies need to understand that there is a large growth market in Western Europe for environmentally friendly products, but that winning this market poses substantial challenges. The West German government, for instance, stamps these products with a Blue Angel insignia. So far over 3,000 products have received environmental approval. In Great Britain, John Elkington's *Green Consumer Guide*, a review of ecologically safe products, was on the best seller list for nine months. It spent one week as number one. Procter & Gamble is already adapting to the situation in Britain by marketing diapers that have been pulp bleached without toxic chlorine gas.

Characteristics of the West European Environmental Movement

The West European environmental movement is rather different from its U.S. counterpart. First, the West European environmental movement started in a different way.[8] The first major party, the West German Greens, began as an explosive mixture of pacifists, antinuclear activists, environmentalists, feminists, and proponents of alternative life-styles. It struggled against the presence of U.S. missiles in Europe and had among its ranks militant Communists. The fight against nuclear power in Western Europe involved pitched battles with police with many people injured and some killed.

Second, the Greens in Europe have been very interested in achieving political power. The movement decided that it had to win elective office to influence political decision making. In 1980 the West German Greens started their own party. In 1983 they won 28 seats in the Bundestag. In 1987 they won 8.3 percent of the popular vote and had 44 deputies in the Bundestag.[9] Nearly all West European nations now have Green political parties.

Third, the European Parliament, a quasi-legislative advisory body, plays a special role. The European Greens aim to use the European Parliament to forge greater cohesiveness and discipline among different national movements. In earlier European Parliament elections, the West German, Belgium, and Dutch Green parties made the best showing. In the 1984 elections the West German party captured 8.2 percent of the popular vote as did the Belgium party, and the Dutch party captured 6.9 percent of the popular vote.

But in the 1989 elections surprisingly big gains were made in the European Parliament by the English and French parties. The English Greens captured 15 percent of the popular vote (up from 2.7 percent of the vote in 1984), and the French Greens captured nearly 12 percent of the popular vote (up from about 3.5 percent in 1984). Overall, the Greens increased their representation in the European Parliament from 11 in 1984 to 27 in 1989.[10] The French had the most seats, 9, followed by the West Germans with 8. The English Greens did not win representation in the European Parliament because of the direct rather than proportional election scheme that prevails in Great Britain's elections (see the special feature on page 438, "The Strong Showing of the Greens in Britain").

Fourth, conflict exists between moderates and militants in the West European environmental movement. As the movement has switched to the electoral arena the conflict between its moderate and extreme wings has intensified.[11] In West Germany, the Hamburg Greens are the most radical, and they refused to participate in a power-sharing arrangement with the Social Democrats. The Frankfort Greens have participated in such power-sharing arrangements. Currently, they have three positions on the municipal government.[12] The French Greens have elected numerous municipal counsellors, of whom about a dozen are mayoral assistants in important cities. Most of the elected officials are moderates.

Local Issues

American managers need to understand local issues. Besides opposition to nuclear power, which has been a Europewide phenomenon, each country has had issues of particular interest to its Green movement. For example, in West Germany it has been the declining forests, in Belgium a campaign against plans to expand France's super-fast railways, in Italy opposition to hunters, and in Greece and Ireland efforts to preserve historically important sites from the ravishes of pollution.

Environmentalists in Europe have been successful in halting many projects.[13] In the wake of Chernobyl, the Greens played an important role in halting the further expansion of nuclear power. They also have had local successes in stopping industrial development. It is now impossible to plan a large-scale project in Western Europe without considering the reaction of the Greens.

A Threat to Business?

To what extent are the European Greens a threat to business? As indicated, their origin is on the Left in the antimilitary and antinuclear campaigns of the 1970s and 1980s. They have a strong moralistic tone and although they may be anticapitalist they borrow economic ideas and doctrines from all shades of the political spectrum. Indeed, many of the followers of the Greens are apolitical and hostile to the traditional Left.

The main breech is over the question of growth, which remains a core value of worker parties in Europe.[14] The Greens favor sustainable development and the quality of life that leave less room for improvement in the plight of the lower classes. Some Greens would argue that it is not possible to separate the social struggle from the struggle for an ecologically sound existence, but they cannot deny that their views do not fit easily into conventional working-class politics.

The Strong Showing of the Greens in Britain

The English Greens did extraordinarily well in 1989 Europewide elections. The elections were the first that Thatcher's Conservative party lost since she became Prime Minister. The defeat was due as much to the Greens's strength as it was to the moderate tone adopted by Neil Kinnock of Labor.

The Greens's 15 percent plurality was the biggest Green party share of the popular vote in a national election. Their strength was particularly noteworthy in the more affluent southern part of Britain, a traditional Conservative stronghold.

Mrs. Thatcher took note of the strength of the Greens in a variety of ways in the period following the election. She replaced the unpopular Nicholas Ridley as her environment secretary with Chris Patten. Also, the environment figured prominently in her October speech to the Conservative Party Conference in which she said that we do not have a "freehold on this earth"; rather, we have a "life-tenancy—with a full repairing lease."[1] What she meant by a "full repairing lease" was that we have to return nature to its original condition.[2] Within the Conservative party, the Tory Green Initiative was formed to promote an environmental agenda. In her public statement on the environment Mrs. Thatcher stressed global issues like the ozone layer, the greenhouse effect, and the need to promote sustainable development. She did not mention more local issues such as water pollution, toxic wastes, endangered species, pesticides residues, or land-use conflicts.

The environmental movement always had support from the English population. A 1982 Gallup poll found that 50 percent of the population supported environmental protection even if it meant a rise in inflation. By 1988, support for this proposition had increased to 74 percent.[3] A quarter of those polled in May of 1989 identified the environment as a very important issue, and a 1987 poll showed that over 60 percent of the English people considered environmental policies to be either "fairly important" or "very important" in determining their vote.[4] However, it was only in the spring 1989 elections to the European Parliament that these concerns began to have a discernable effect on election outcomes.

Environmental organizations in Britain have been growing, and many people are willing to buy environmentally safe products if price and performance with other products are comparable. The rise of the environmental movement reflects a feeling of disgust with the decay and squalor of ordinary life and a longing for spiritual as well as material goals in life. The question is whether the environmentalists can translate their new electoral gains into political influence, for traditionally in England environmentalists have had little real political clout.[5] For example, the 1974 Control of Pollution

---

[1]T. Burke, "The Year of the Greens," *Environment*, November 1989, p. 18.
[2]Ibid.

[3]Ibid.
[4]Ibid.
[5]T. O'Riordan, "The Politics of Environmental Regulation in Great Britain," *Environment*, October 1988; pp. 6–9, 39–44.

The Strong Showing of the Greens in Britain continued

Act had been formulated through a consensual process that gave established interests disproportionate influence and ignored the demands of environmental organizations.

The British regulatory tradition is less adversarial than that of the U.S., and English environmentalists have been less confrontational than environmentalists in other countries.[6] They have been hindered by official secrecy, which keeps them from obtaining the government information necessary to document their case. Also, under the British system of government (direct rather than proportional representation), they cannot win seats in Parliament based on the number of votes they obtain in national elections. Thus, they have been able to elect only local councillors.

The question is to what extent the Conservative party's vision of an "enterprise culture" is compatible with increased environmental protection.[7] An enterprise culture implies privatization, an emphasis on individual responsibility, self-reliance, and entrepreneurial behavior. The British government now realizes that the privatization of its water authorities, for example, can be accomplished only if there is increased regulation, and it has set up a new public agency,

the National Rivers Authority, to carry out water protection functions. However, in other areas, regulatory bodies such as the local environmental health departments have been stripped of their funding and are demoralized. The proposal that has been made is for these regulatory bodies to charge fees for services such as preparing and executing a license. This way they can be largely self-sufficient. The "polluter pays" principle, however, has not generally caught on in Britain, and polluters are not being assessed charges on the basis of the damage they cause the environment.

The Conservative party's enterprise culture, though, has spawned green capitalism in Britain on a scale that previously did not exist. It has stimulated the pollution abatement industry, innovations in the use of materials and energy by manufacturers, private investment in restoring degraded areas, and private investment in wildlife parks, exhibitions, and charitable trusts.

Changes in U.K. practices might also come about because of growing pressure from the EC. The EC's directives will force the United Kingdom to move from add-on-device type of pollution control to process redesign, maintenance and management, and recycling. The nation will also have to clean up the sewage and industrial effluent that is being discharged into rivers that drain into the North Sea. Finally, for the first time, developers will have to submit Environmental Impact Assessments (EIAs) before proceeding with certain types of projects. All of these chances provide opportunities for experienced foreign firms to aid the British in cleaning their environment.

---

[6]D. Vogel, *Evaluating British and American Environmental Regulation: Effectiveness, Efficiency and the Politics of Compliance*, paper prepared for the 1984 annual meeting of the American Political Science Association.

[7]O'Riordan, "The Politics of Environmental Regulation in Great Britain."

Indeed, extreme right-wing parties, which are also seeing a resurgence in Europe, are beginning to borrow themes and slogans from the Greens, including romanticism about nature and nostalgia about simpler times in the past.[15] The notion that there are ideals greater than material progress for which a person must sacrifice fits in with the conservative tradition about virtue and honor being purer goals that transcend such mundane matters as raising the standard of living.

No party in Europe can ignore the Greens. Conventional conservative and social democratic parties also have borrowed their ideas and incorporated them into their programs. In Denmark, for example, the Greens have never received more than 1.3 percent of the popular vote because the other parties argue that they are green and that they have an ecological perspective.[16]

In summary, environmental activism in Western Europe is strong primarily because of the initiatives of the EC, the strength of the environmental movement, and electoral successes. Companies selling products in this part of the world must consider growing consumer consciousness about environmental protection. Industries that pollute or make polluting products have to think about how they are going to adjust to the new reality. The problems in Western Europe are much less likely solved than in some other parts of the world because of the density of the population, the age of the manufacturing base, and the relative affluence of the people. Needless to say, the environmental problems of the bordering nations of Eastern Europe, so recently liberated from Communism, add immensely to the challenges, and opportunities, that lie ahead.

Two Important Issues: Solid Wastes and Atmospheric Pollution

Now we turn to two important environmental issues. They illustrate the slogan "Think Globally and Act Locally." Solid wastes are primarily a local issue but they have global implications. Atmospheric pollution is a global issue but its origins, like many environmental problems, are in personal consumption decisions made at the local level. These issues have taken on great urgency in the 1990s.

Solid Wastes: Overview of a Complex Issue

One hundred sixty million tons of trash are generated by Americans each year, which is approximately 3.5 pounds of solid waste per person per day (see Exhibit 14–2).[17] This volume is 80 percent greater than it was in 1960, and by the year 2000 it is expected to be up by an additional

---

EXHIBIT 14–2   Estimates of the Annual Waste Generated in the United States and Other Countries in the Late 1980s

	Municipal Waste (Thousands of Metric Tons)	*Industrial Waste (Thousands of Metric Tons)*	*Nuclear Waste (Heavy Metal in Metric Tons)*
United States	208,800	760,000	1,900
Japan	48,300	312,300	770
W. Germany	20,230	61,400	360
United Kingdom	17,700	50,000	900
France	17,000	50,000	950

SOURCE: Directorate of Intelligence, Central Intelligence Agency, *Handbook of Economic Statistics, 1991* (Washington, D.C.: Government Printing Office, 1991), p. 174.

---

20 percent.[18] There is no sign that this volume of waste will decrease. Currently, it would take 1,000 football fields 30 stories high to store the waste generated annually by Americans.[19]

The news that brings the issue to the attention of the public is alarming. For example, Philadelphia citizens sued to have the city remove mounds of toxic ash stored near its incinerators. When local landfills refused to accept the ash (as did also landfills in neighboring states) it was piled in a barge that traversed the world for more than a year until it came to its resting place in a secret location, presumably the Indian Ocean.

Landfills

The three main methods of disposing of municipal solid waste are landfills, incinerators, and recycling. Eighty percent of the solid waste in the United States goes into landfills. Although they are the primary waste disposal option, they have a finite life span; landfills are designated to last for only 10 years. More than two thirds of the nation's landfills have closed since the 1970s.[20]

While modern sanitary techniques and lined landfills greatly reduce the risk of environmental contamination, many existing landfills were built without these precautions. Thus, they are little more than holes in the ground. Moreover, many were built on or near wetlands; it was believed that the water would wash away and purify the wastes. However, now it is generally recognized that the waste material contains inks, paints, dyes, and a host of chemicals that can leach into the groundwater and cause serious drinking-water contamination.[21]

Advances in sanitary landfilling are meant to mummify the wastes to prevent leaching. However mummification has its own set of problems. For example, biodegradable plastics are meant to break down and may be harmful because of the complexity of their construction. They simply degrade to smaller pieces without reducing the amount of space in the landfill that they occupy.[22] In fact, nondegradable plastics may be better landfill material because they are inert and compactable. In any event, plastics constitute less than 10 percent of the total volume of material finding its way into landfills.[23] Nearly 50 percent of what goes into modern landfills is paper, and yard waste contributes another 20 percent (see Exhibit 14–3).[24]

Finding new landfill space is difficult because of the NIMBY ("Not in my backyard") syndrome. In the Northeast it is virtually impossible to site a new landfill. Alternatives to operating landfills have to be found.

Incineration

An alternative is incineration, which can reduce the volume of waste by 90 percent.[25] Other alternatives are recycling and source reduction, which prevent wastes from permanently entering the waste stream. In West Germany and Japan, about 50 percent of the waste is recycled, and almost all of the rest is burnt in incinerators.[26] However, the United States has had trouble moving from a system that relies on landfilling to one that relies on incineration and recycling.

EXHIBIT 14–3   Materials Discarded into the Municipal Solid Waste Stream
(Tons in Millions)

Materials	1970		1984		2000	
	Tons	*Percent*	*Tons*	*Percent*	*Tons*	*Percent*
Paper and paperboard	36.5	33.1%	49.4	37.1%	65.1	41.0%
Glass	12.5	11.3	12.9	9.7	12.1	7.6
Metals	13.5	12.2	12.8	9.6	14.3	9.0
Plastics	3.0	2.7	9.6	7.2	15.5	9.8
Rubber and leather	3.0	2.7	3.3	2.5	3.8	2.4
Textiles	2.2	2.0	2.8	2.1	3.5	2.2
Wood	4.0	3.6	5.1	3.8	6.1	3.8
Other	—	0.1	0.1	0.1	0.1	0.1
Food wastes	12.7	11.5	10.8	8.1	10.8	6.8
Yard wastes	21.0	19.0	23.8	17.9	24.4	15.3
Miscellaneous inorganics	1.8	1.6	2.4	1.8	3.1	2.0
Totals	110.3	100.0	133.0	100.0	158.8	100.0

SOURCE: Adapted from Franklin Associates, EPA, Office of Solid Waste, *Characterization of Municipal Solid Waste in the United States, 1960–2000*, PB-178323, 1986.

To what extent is incineration a viable option in the United States? Originally billed as a panacea for landfill overcrowding, groundwater contamination, and alternative energy generation, it has met with many obstacles. During the 1970s incineration became synonymous with such terms as "resource recovery" and "waste to energy." Energy prices rose throughout this period, making previously uneconomical power sources appear reasonably priced. Thus, energy-generated revenues associated with incineration played a major role in justifying construction. Incinerator developers and their financial supporters estimated that the energy generated and sold eventually would amount to over half of the revenue needed to cover the costs of incineration. The Public Utilities Regulatory Policies Act (PURPA) of 1978 offered a guaranteed market for the energy produced.

However, in the 1980s energy prices plummeted, ending hopes that the energy produced would make a major difference in covering the costs of incineration. Also helping to justify construction were investment tax credits, which financed up to 10 percent of construction costs, accelerated depreciation allowances, and favorable industrial revenue bonds financing policies. But these incentives also ended with the passage of the Tax Reform Act of 1986.[27] Thus, incineration in the late 1980s was faced with decreasing economic justification as well as growing public opposition.

Public opposition was based, first and foremost, on environmental and health considerations. Incinerators emit many pollutants, both toxic and nontoxic, including, among the toxins, dioxins, DDT, lead, mercury, arsenic, and benzene.[28] People in the vicinity of incinerators absorb these chemicals through breathing, eating, and drinking the contaminated substances.

Public opposition to incineration in the United States also was based on reports of operational problems, mechanical failures and shutdowns, and cost overruns in construction. Hidden costs of construction included water sewer lines and surface roads that had to be constructed to accommodate the increased traffic to and from incinerators. Another concern was the ash left after combustion. If it was categorized as hazardous, disposal costs would increase from 5 to 10 times.[29]

In addition, opponents of incineration claim that municipality guarantees to provide the needed waste for incineration are a deterrent to starting effective recycling and waste reduction programs. After the huge financial commitment to incineration has been made, it is asserted, local officials will be loath to do anything to threaten incineration's success. If insufficient waste is available, an incinerator would be likely to be a failure financially.

Proponents of recycling also claim that while incineration generates a small amount of energy, recycling saves much more. For instance, recycling aluminum saves about 90 percent of the energy needed to make aluminum from virgin materials.[30] Recycling paper saves about half the energy needed to make new paper.

Recycling

Recycling programs in the United States, however, have met with only moderate success. The passage of the Resource Recovery Act in 1970 gave symbolic recognition to the public's interest in recycling, but recycling rates in the United States in the 1970s never exceeded 5 to 7 percent of the waste generated, and by the end of the 1980s only amounted to about 10 percent of the nation's total waste stream.[31]

Some solid waste professionals claim that up to 80 percent of the nation's wastes can be recycled; however, the exact amount is difficult to determine due to lack of precise information about the composition of the waste stream.[32] Recycling rates vary from material to material; up to 80 percent of the nation's aluminum is recycled but virtually none of the wet garbage (organic material like table wastes) is recycled.

Recycling requires a high degree of coordination among consumers, business, and government, which is often difficult to achieve. Consumers need to provide waste material and to separate it. They then need to buy products made from recycled (secondary) materials. Although consumers express a willingness to buy recycled products, even when they are more expensive, this willingness has not yet been reflected in increased product sales. Also, consumer disdain for less than bright white paper, and other materials rendered less attractive when made from secondary materials, has limited the amount of recycling that is done.

For recycling to succeed in a major way, businesses too would have to choose secondary materials over virgin materials. They would also have to develop products for secondary materials and processes for handling these materials. However, recyclable materials can be highly dispersed, and the cost of collecting them can be labor-intensive and very expensive. Moreover, they often are of low grade and contain impurities, factors that raise the costs of preparation for remanufacture.

Most manufacturing facilities are set up to use virgin materials; they cannot use secondary ones. Thus, companies would have to make expensive new capital investments if they were to use recycled materials. These investments would have to compete with other business opportunities for corporate funds.

As long as current markets for secondary materials are limited, recycling programs will have difficulty gaining ground. There is only so much demand for such items as cereal boxes made from recycled newsprint. The capital investment to develop equipment and processes for recycled materials is high. Also, volatility of the secondary-materials market discourages many companies from entering it; the flow of materials is often unpredictable and price can be greater than that for virgin materials.

Recycling will take off only if manufacturers believe that it is profitable. For example, many companies recycle high-grade computer paper because it fetches high prices and it saves the tipping fees of landfill disposal.[33] Recycling even low-grade office waste, which contains multiple materials, yields a decent price and avoids tipping fees.

Government can promote community recycling efforts, fund R&D, and buy recycled products. It also can promote recycling by removing the tax advantage that virgin materials have. Mining, timber, and energy companies are given depletion allowances of between 5 to 22 percent of the value of the minerals produced.[34] They also have capital gain advantages that lead to overinvestment in virgin materials production. The social costs of depleting nonrenewable resources, on the other hand, are not included in the price of the virgin materials.

The national government's role in recycling is largely symbolic. EPA, for instance, is committed to a 25 percent recycling goal, but spends only 1 to 2 percent of its budget on recycling programs.[35]

Source Reduction

Source reduction is unique in that it is not an "end of the pipe" solution. Its purpose is to eliminate waste before it is generated. The actual potential for source reduction is unknown. Businesses can modify their production processes to be less wasteful, and many have done so when it appears profitable. 3M for example has a highly successful "Pollution Prevention Pays" program.[36]

Businesses can modify their products to use less material and packaging. Consumers can change their life-styles in many small but meaningful ways. They can shop for goods that contain less packaging and use nondisposable alternatives whenever feasible. Since recycling brings with it environmental problems (processing already used materials, transporting them to markets, and reusing them), source reduction is a better solution to the waste problem (see Exhibit 14–4). But source reduction is very threatening to an acquisitive society that thrives on convenience.

Special problems are posed by beverage bottles and diapers.[37] They were once reused, but now are commonly thrown out. Wholesalers and retailers do not want the bother of handling reusable bottles. Many working mothers as well as hospitals and day-care centers would find it unthinkable to give up plastic diapers.

Manufacturers have created whole systems around throw-away products and packaging, and Americans have become accustomed to the convenience they offer. Certainly, by reducing garbage at the source, we would have to process less of it at landfills and incinerators. The

EXHIBIT 14-4   **Waste Management Hierarchy**

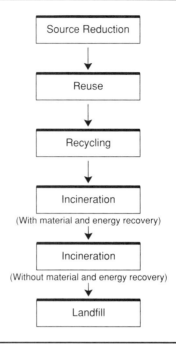

SOURCE: L. Blumberg and R. Gottlieb, *War on Waste* (Washington D.C.: Island Press, 1989).

American people, however, have chosen a life-style that may make this aspiration difficult to achieve.[38]

Atmospheric Pollution

The pollutants historically regulated by the government are hydrocarbons, nitrous oxides, carbon monoxide, sulfur dioxide, and particulate matter. Emitted from automobiles and smokestack industries like steel, chemical, and petroleum refining, these pollutants mainly threaten human health. Sensitive individuals are likely to suffer increased incidence of cardio-pulmonary diseases such as asthma under conditions of high exposure. However, the threats to the atmosphere from ozone depletion and carbon dioxide buildup are somewhat different and more serious.

Ozone Depletion

Scientific evidence strongly supports the theory that chlorofluorocarbons (CFCs) are destroying stratospheric ozone (see Exhibit 14–5).[39] Other naturally occurring and manufactured agents such as carbon

---
EXHIBIT 14-5   How CFCs Contribute to Ozone Depletion

Application	*Percentage*
Aerosol propellants and other miscellaneous uses	5%
Solvent cleaning of metal and electronic parts	12%
Sterilization of medical equipment and instruments	4%
Production of plastic foam insulation products	28%
Mobile air conditioners	19%
Refrigeration and space air conditioning	9%
Unallocated production	22%

SOURCE: Adapted from U.S. EPA, 1986; see Daniel Dudek et al., "Business Responses to Environmental Policy: Lessons from CFC Regulation," (Washington, D.C.: Environmental Defense Fund, 1989).

dioxide produced by decaying vegetation and nitrogen-based fertilizers also contribute to the phenomenon. Still other agents and natural processes counteract ozone depletion, increasing the complexity of the issue. The methods used to validate the theory and to measure the amount of ozone being depleted by CFCs suggest that a multitude of relevant agents are responsible, but primarily implicate CFCs.

Invented by Thomas Midgley Jr. in 1930 to be used as cooling agents for the Frigidaire division of General Motors, CFCs are chemically stable, low in toxicity, and nonflammable. For many years they were believed to be completely safe and hundreds of applications for them were found. Sold under trademarks such as Freon (made by Du Pont), CFCs are used as aerosol propellants, coolants in refrigerators and air conditioners, cleaning solvents for electronic components, and foaming agents in the manufacture of furniture and mattresses, styrofoam, and building insulation. Despite the fact that the United States has banned CFCs for use in aerosol propellants, about one third of all CFCs in global use are produced and consumed in the United States (see Exhibit 14–6).

Substantial evidence indicates that CFCs are harming the ozone layer of the stratosphere, the upper atmosphere between 15 and 30 miles above the Earth. Stratospheric ozone, which acts as a shield by absorbing radiation from the sun, allows only safe levels of ultraviolet (UV) rays to reach the earth's surface. Although estimates of ozone depletion caused by CFCs vary, even conservative estimates raise serious concerns about increased levels of surface radiation as the earth's protective shield is reduced.

Even though there has been complex computer simulation of the problem, taking into account a large number of factors and variables, the actual percentage of ozone depletion is still a matter of debate. Estimates vary according to the factor included and the assumptions made using a given model; they range from a low of about 4 percent to a high of over

EXHIBIT 14–6   **Economic Scope of CFC Application in the United States**

Use	Value (Billions of Dollars)	Employment (Thousands)
Refrigeration	$ 6.0	52
Air-conditioning	10.9	125
Mobile air-conditioning	2.0	25
Cooling servicing	5.5	472
Plastic foam	2.0	40
Food freezing	0.4	<1
Sterilants	0.1	<1
Totals	$26.9	715

SOURCE: Adapted from Alliance for a Responsible CFC Policy, 1986. See Daniel Dudek, et al. "Business Responses to Environmental Policy: Lessons from CFC Regulation," (Washington, D.C.: Environmental Defense Fund, 1989).

31 percent.[40] A five- to sevenfold increase in skin cancer is expected for every percentage point decrease in ozone.[41] Other potential harmful effects from the destruction of the ozone layer include increased incidence of cataract formation, reduction in crop yields, elimination of marine life, and the weakening of materials, including plastics.

Significant actions are underway in the United States and internationally to reduce the risks of CFC-related ozone depletion (see Case IVC, "Dupont and the 1990 Clean Air Act"). They include EPA regulations and international agreements, such as the Montreal Protocol, to reduce and monitor CFC production, use, and disposal and to develop safe substitutes for CFCs.[42] The Montreal Protocol on Substances That Deplete the Ozone Layer is an international treaty that calls for a freeze at 1986 levels of the five most harmful types of CFCs. Additionally, CFC production would be reduced by 20 percent by 1994 and another 30 percent by 1999, for a total planned reduction of 50 percent in 10 years (see Exhibit 14–7).

Carbon Dioxide Buildup

Human activities of the past hundred years also are altering the composition of the atmosphere, threatening a global warming trend.[43] Many scientists already are convinced that warming has started and that it will get only worse through the next century. Since 1900, scientists estimate a warming trend of between 0.5 and 2 degrees centigrade.

Warming is caused by the greenhouse effect, that is, trapping of infrared energy, or heat, in the stratosphere. Heat is trapped by carbon dioxide and other greenhouse gases. These gases are transparent to sunlight, thus letting the energy penetrate the earth. Absorbing most of the

---

EXHIBIT 14–7   **CFC Alternatives and Consequences of Their Use**

Application	*Substitute*	*Trade-Offs*
Refrigeration and	Ammonia	Toxic, explosive
air conditioning	Sulphur dioxide	Combustible, less efficient
Plastic foams	Pentane	Flammable, smog precursor
	Methylene chloride	Suspected carcinogen
Food freezing	Cryogenic systems	Less energy efficient

SOURCE: Adapted from Alliance for a Responsible CFC Policy, 1986. See Daniel Dudek, et al. "Business Responses to Environmental Policy: Lessons from CFC Regulation," (Washington, D.C.: Environmental Defense Fund, 1989).

---

sunlight, the earth converts the light energy into heat. Unabsorbed light is reflected back into space as heat. As it rises from the earth, it strikes the carbon dioxide and other greenhouse gases. Some heat is reflected back towards the earth, causing the warming effect. (The effect is the same as that of a greenhouse where the panes of glass allow higher energy light waves to enter easily, but do not allow the heat of lower energy waves to escape through the glass.)

Major emphasis is placed on carbon dioxide because it is 50 percent of the problem. Carbon dioxide is measured in the atmosphere at approximately 344 parts per million (ppm). This amount is large considering that only 100 years ago the concentration was only 293 ppm. Thus, an increase of about 15 percent has occurred in the last 100 years.

The major reason for the increase in carbon dioxide is the burning of fossil fuels—oil, coal, and gasoline. Scientists tend to be pessimistic about reducing the use of fossil fuels, thus estimating an increase in carbon dioxide emissions of between 0.5 and 2 percent per year for the next several decades (see Exhibit 14–8).

The other gases contributing to the greenhouse effect are methane, CFCs, nitrous oxides, and ozone. The atmosphere contains 100 percent more methane than it did during glacier periods. This increase is caused by the harvesting of rice paddies, the use of landfills, and the flaring of natural gas wells. Methane causes about 20 percent of the greenhouse effect. CFCs emitted from the earth are found in the atmosphere at one part per billion. They cause about 15 percent of the greenhouse gases. Nitrous oxides in minute traces are found in the atmosphere because of the use of fertilizers, natural processes (the emittances of soil microbes), and the burning of fossil fuels. Nitrous oxide emissions account for about 10 percent of the greenhouse effect. The last major gas that contributes to the greenhouse effect is ozone. Even though the ozone layer provides ultraviolet protection at high levels in the atmosphere, it is dangerous at lower levels, where it is more commonly known as smog.

EXHIBIT 14–8   **CO2 Emissions, Auto Registrations, and Energy Consumption: Major Industrial Nations**

	United States	Canada	West Germany	United Kingdom	Japan	France
CO2 emissions (metric tons per capita)	5.34	4.58	3.00	2.67	2.20	1.56
Auto registrations (units per thousand persons)	571	448	462	353	241	395
Energy consumption (barrels of oil equivalent per capita)	57	61	32	27	24	29

SOURCE: Adapted from Directorate of Intelligence, Central Intelligence Agency, *Handbook of Economic Statistics, 1991* (Washington, D.C.: Government Printing Office, 1991), p. 28.

Ozone accounts for about 5 percent of the greenhouse effect. The activities contributing to the greenhouse effect are energy use and production (57 percent), use of CFCs (17 percent), agricultural practices (14 percent), deforestation (9 percent), and other industrial practices (3 percent).

In addition, there are natural processes that counteract the greenhouse effect. For instance, carbon dioxide is absorbed by the oceans and by tropical rain forests and other forms of vegetation, and it is reflected back into space by the clouds. The oceans are considered to be the major sink for carbon dioxide. It is readily dissolved into sea water where aquatic plants absorb it and hold on to it. The quantity of carbon dioxide absorbed by the oceans, however, is unknown. Because of the oceans' vastness, scientists find it difficult to estimate the exact quantities of carbon dioxide plants absorb and oxygen they produce through photosynthesis.

The rate of absorption by terrestrial plants is estimated to be 500 billion tons of carbon dioxide annually worldwide, but this estimate is also uncertain. Because of deforestation, it could be decreasing rapidly.

Unlike the oceans and the rain forests, clouds naturally counteract heat retention not by absorbing carbon dioxide but by reflecting sunlight back into outer space. If the infrared light from the sun does not reach the earth, heat cannot be created, and if the heat on the earth's surface does not go up, the greenhouse effect cannot occur. However, when infrared light does reach the earth, clouds reflect the heat back towards the earth, thus warming it.

Major uncertainty exists about the role of clouds in counteracting the greenhouse effect. Ultimately, this matter is extremely complicated because it depends on subtle distinctions about cloud thickness.

Impacts

The greenhouse effect can have many impacts on the world. Some of the major predicted consequences are listed below. These predictions assume that the levels of carbon dioxide and the other greenhouse gases will be emitted at the present rate:[44]

- In Greenland and the North Pole, some of the permafrost and ice will melt, causing the oceans to rise and threatening flooding along coastal areas.
- The midwestern United States will be hit hard by drought conditions; the warmer weather will increase evaporation and cause drier soils.
- With the increased evaporation, river levels will decrease, thus causing a shortage in water supplies, lower generation of power, and a disruption in agricultural irrigation.
- Eastern Europe and the Russian Federation will gain approximately 40 days in their growing season, which could make them net exporters of grain to the rest of the world.
- The increased temperatures will cause a wider area of rain forest growth, moving the African rain forests north and bringing rain to Chad, Sudan, and Ethiopia, breaking their prolonged dry spell.

Canada and the United States have the highest emission levels of greenhouse gases per capita among the developed western democracies. The highest level of greenhouse gas emissions per capita in the world, however, is found in what was formerly East Germany. Brazil and the Ivory Coast have the highest levels of emissions per capita among developing countries. Per unit of GNP, Brazil's and India's emissions of greenhouse gases surpass the levels found in the United States. The U.S. contribution to the greenhouse effect is 21 percent, that of the former Soviet Union is 14 percent, and that of the EEC is 14 percent. China contributes 7 percent, Brazil 4 percent, and India 4 percent. All other countries contribute 36 percent.

Limiting Carbon Dioxide Buildup

A first approach to limiting carbon dioxide buildup would be making energy supply and use more efficient.[45] Examples of available technology for conservation are efficient light bulbs in commercial buildings, better insulated buildings, and vehicles that obtain more miles per gallon. Prototype vehicles have got up to 70 MPG.

U.S. fuel standards for new vehicles have been 27 MPG. As the vehicle stock turns over, the entire fleet average is increased. A fleet average of 40 MPG, with no increase in miles driven, would cut U.S. auto-related carbon emissions in half.

Another option to reduce the use of fossil fuels is to use different sources of energy. Alternatives such as nuclear power, hydropower, solar technologies, and natural gas produce far less carbon dioxide. The Bush administration has proposed that methanol be given serious consideration as an alternative motor vehicle fuel. Methanol made from biomass (primarily wood, organic wastes, or agricultural produce) would not contribute to greenhouse emissions as long as the biomass feedstock was replaced. Alternative fuel vehicles will be a necessity when California's strict new motor vehicle emission guidelines start to go into effect in 1998 (see Chapter 13). The European Community is considering a carbon tax, which should also stimulate the market for alternative fuel vehicles.

Hydrogen appears to be a good long-term alternative if technical difficulties can be overcome. A hydrogen-based fuel would emit only water vapor and nitrous oxides, the latter at significantly lower levels than those produced by fossil fuels. Estimates of hydrogen's costs place it between $2 and $4 for a gallon equivalent shortly after 2000, which would make it competitive with gasoline if gas taxes were increased to reflect gasoline's true social cost. A big problem is fuel tank storage. Improvements are needed so that smaller tanks can be used without sacrificing the range of hydrogen cars. Another problem with the fuel tank is safety. There is also the matter of the energy used to generate the hydrogen. The process to separate hydrogen from oxygen in water can be energy intensive and polluting.

A final method of reducing carbon dioxide buildup is to reduce the deforestation of the world's rain forests.[46] The burning of the rain forests emits an estimated 1 billion tons of carbon dioxide a year, and at the same time the earth loses one of its major sinks to absorb carbon dioxide. Encouraging the reforestation of areas of the globe that have been denuded of their natural tree cover is a gesture of important symbolic significance. Unfortunately, it cannot make an important dent in carbon dioxide buildup.

An International Treaty

We may need an international treaty on global greenhouse gases, modeled on the Montreal accord with respect to CFCs. The delegates to the U.N. conference on the environment in Rio worked on such a treaty in 1992, but what they produced was far short of the Montreal accord. The circumstances that produced the Montreal accord are much different from those surrounding the buildup of greenhouse gases. First, the Montreal accord was reached amid growing international acceptance of the scientific basis for the ozone depletion theory. Negotiations gathered momentum when scientists directly observed the rapidly growing ozone hole over the Antarctic.

While a scientific consensus seems to be emerging about global warming, the uncertainties are still great. Firm evidence that the world is rapidly warming may be needed to convince nations to take climate change seriously. Of course, by then it might be too late. As the adage has it, throw a frog into a cauldron of boiling water and it will jump out to save its life, but boil it gradually and it will stay put until it dies.

The second difference between ozone depletion and carbon buildup is that many companies favored a worldwide agreement to limit CFC production. They did so not simply because of their sense of corporate social responsibility. As manufacturers of expensive CFC substitutes, these companies stood to gain from a movement toward new substances.[47] If regulation was going to be inevitable, they preferred that it be uniform in coverage and enforceable so that no companies could cheat and offer cheap CFCs as competition to the higher priced alternatives. With the forced adoption of CFC alternatives, companies with alternatives could gain ground on the companies that were incapable of manufacturing them. This argument in no way negates the formidable difficulties that any company, even a giant like Du Pont, with its strong research and scientific capabilities, would face in developing CFC substitutes. Companies with the potential to manufacture substitutes preferred that regulation be orderly and predictable so that they could plan for a transition to the new era.

Carbon dioxide buildup, however, is unlikely to see a convergence between scientific recognition and industry support.[48] The industry situation is very different. CFCs are produced by a relatively small number of companies and have a relatively narrow range of uses. In comparison, fossil fuel producers are very numerous and its uses are legion. Moreover, fossil fuels are very hard to replace. In comparison to agreements on CFCs, an international agreement on climate change that calls for limits on the use of fossil fuels will be very hard to reach. And once reached, it will be even more difficult to enforce.

What Companies Can Do

Thus, pollution and environmental problems pose substantial challenges for companies.[49] These challenges occur at the highest levels in the firm, the levels of business strategy and organization, and they affect corporate staff, in the public affairs and legal areas, as well as line people in traditional functional areas such as operations, marketing, accounting, and finance. It is the comprehensiveness of the challenges that make them so interesting.

Companies have to make environmental considerations part of decision making from the beginning, not simply something they consider at the end. They may have to engage in long-term thinking even if profits suffer in the short term. To meet these expectations, top management support is essential. Changes of the magnitude that these issues call for cannot be accomplished without top management support.

Various companies such as Du Pont, 3M, and Pacific Gas and Electric (PG&E) have made creative responses to environmental challenges in the past.[50] Their responses may have relevance for other companies as they face new challenges from environmental and pollution problems. Using the actions of these companies, we have provided a list of actions companies can take.

Strategy and Organization.   Companies can take the following actions:

1. *Cutback on environmentally unsafe operations.* Du Pont, the leading producer of CFCs (chlorofluorocarbons), has announced that it will voluntarily pull out of this $750 million business by the year 2000, if not sooner.[51]

2. *Carry out R&D on environmentally safe activities.* Du Pont has announced that it is spending up to $1 billion on the best replacements for CFCs.

3. *Develop and expand environmental cleanup services.* Building on the expertise gained in cleaning up its own plants, Du Pont is forming a safety and environmental resources division to help industrial customers clean up their toxic wastes. The projected future revenues are $1 billion by 2000.[52]

4. *Compensate for environmentally risky endeavors.* Applied Energy Services, a power plant management firm, donated $2 million in 1988 for tree planting in Guatemala to compensate for a coal-fired plant it was building in Connecticut. The trees were meant to offset emissions that might lead to global warming.

5. *Make structural changes.* The Valdez Principles call on companies to appoint an environmentalist to the corporate board and to conduct an annual public audit of the company's environmental progress.[53] The environmental auditing movement has taken off, and many companies now routinely, if for no other reason than to prevent liability, conduct audits.

Public Affairs.   Companies can take the following actions:

1. *Try to avoid losses caused by appearing insensitive to environmental issues.* A cost to Exxon of appearing to be unconcerned about the Valdez incident was that 41 percent of Americans said that they would consider boycotting the company.[54]

2. *Attempt to gain environmental legitimacy and credibility.* Edgar Woolard, the CEO of Du Pont, has been very vocal about his support for

environmental protection in his company He regularly delivers speeches on corporate environmentalism. The cosponsors of Earth Day 1990 included Apple Computer, Hewlett-Packard, Shaklee, and the Chemical Manufacturers Association. McDonald's has made efforts to show that it is a proponent of recycling. It has tried to become a corporate environmental "educator."

3. *Collaborate with environmentalists.* Woolard of Du Pont also regularly meets with environmentalists. PG&E's executives claim that they seek discussions and joint projects with any willing environmental group. They have teamed up with environmental groups to study energy efficiency, and the company is now renting a computer model from the Environmental Defense Fund (EDF) that shows the relationship between conservation and electricity costs.

The Legal Area   Companies can take the following actions:

1. *Try to prevent confrontation with state or federal pollution control agencies.* W. R. Grace faces expensive and time-consuming lawsuits from its toxic dumps, and Browning-Ferris, Waste Management, and Louisiana-Pacific confront violations that have damaged their reputations.

2. *Comply early.* Since compliance costs only increase over time, the first companies to act will have lower costs. This enables them to increase their market share and profit and win competitive advantage. Thus, 3M's goal is to meet government requirements to replace or improve underground storage tanks by 1993 instead of 1998.

3. *Take advantage of innovative compliance programs.* Instead of source-by-source reduction, EPA's bubble policy allows a factory to reduce pollution at different sources by different amounts provided that the overall result is equivalent. 3M therefore has installed equipment on some production lines and not on others at its tape manufacturing facility in Pennsylvania, thereby lowering its compliance costs.[55]

Operations.   A company can take the following actions:

1. *Promote new manufacturing technologies.* Louisville Gas and Electric has taken the lead in installing smokestack scrubbers, Consolidated Natural Gas has taken the lead in using clean-burning technologies, and Nucor has taken the lead in developing state-of-the-art steel mills. PG&E has agreed to rely on a combination of smaller scale generating facilities like windmills or cogeneration plants, along with aggressive conservation efforts. It has canceled plans to build large coal and nuclear power plants.

2. *Encourage technological advances that reduce pollution from products and manufacturing processes.* 3M's "Pollution Prevention Pays" program is based on the premise that it is too costly for companies to employ add-on technology and they should attempt instead to eliminate pollution at the source.[56] Add-on technology is expensive because it takes resources

to remove the pollution, the pollution removal then generates new wastes, and more resources are needed to remove the additional waste.

3. *Develop new product-formulations.* One way to accomplish source reduction is by developing new product-formulations. For example, 3M's rapid fire-extinguishing agent for petroleum fires did not meet EPA requirements. Thus, the company had to develop a new formulation. The new formulation was one-fortieth as toxic but equally effective and less expensive to produce.

4. *Modify production equipment and change manufacturing operations to achieve source reduction.* Another way to accomplish source reduction is to modify equipment and change operations. For example, 3M's new Kenlevel metal-plating process does not require the use of cyanide. It is up to 50 percent more energy efficient and creates a competitive advantage.

5. *Eliminate manufacturing wastes.* With fewer wastes, add-on equipment becomes less necessary. 3M's philosophy is to invest in reducing the number of materials that can trigger regulation. For example, it has replaced volatile solvents with water-based compounds, thereby eliminating the need for costly air pollution equipment. AMOCO and Polaroid have similar pollution reduction programs.

6. *Try to find alternative uses for wastes.* When Du Pont halted ocean dumping of acid iron salts it discovered that the salts could be sold to water treatment plants at a profit.

7. *Recycle wastes.* 3M is recycling and reusing solvents it once emitted to the atmosphere. Other firms with active recycling programs are Safety-Kleen (solvents and motor oil), Wellman (plastic), Jefferson Smurfit (paper), and Nucor (steel).

Marketing.   A company can take various actions in this area:

1. *Try to cast products in an environmentally friendly light.* A 1989 Michael Peters Group survey found that 77 percent of Americans say that a company's environmental reputation influences what they buy.[57] Companies such as Proctor & Gamble (P&G), Arco, Colgate-Palmolive, Lever Brothers, 3M, and Sunoco have tried to act on the basis of this finding. Wal-Mart has made efforts to provide customers with recycled or recyclable products. The Body Shop is a London-based chain of skin and hair care stores that provides literature on ozone depletion and global warming to its customers and has collected signatures on a petition asking the Brazilian president to save the rain forests. The number of new green products that have been introduced in the United States increased from 24 in 1985 to 308 in 1990.[58] Nearly 10 percent of all new product introductions in 1990 were green products.

2. *Avoid being attacked by environmentalists for unsubstantiated or inappropriate claims.* British Petroleum claimed that a new brand of unleaded gasoline caused no pollution, a claim that it had to withdraw after

suffering much embarrassment. The degradable-plastics controversy should provide producers with another warning about the perils of unsubstantiated or inappropriate claims. Companies have to be honest with their customers and have to educate them incessantly.

Accounting.   A company can take the following actions:

1. *Make sure to demonstrate that antipollution programs pay.* 3M's "Pollution Prevention Pays" program is based on the premise that only if the program pays will there be the necessary motivation to successfully carry it out. Because of environmental pressures, American companies have had to spend large sums of money that could otherwise have been used for capital formation, new product research and development, and process improvements that could raise productivity. Thus, every company owes it not only to itself but also to the nation to use a minimum of resources in trying to achieve pollution reduction. Companies should develop approaches that not only reduce pollution but encourage innovation at the same time.

2. *Show the overall impact of the pollution reduction program.* Companies have an obligation to account for the costs and benefits of their pollution reduction programs. 3M's 1980 status report listed 394 projects in 3M operations worldwide that have generated savings of $56.5 million in five years: $13 million for pollution control equipment and facilities that were delayed or eliminated, $16.8 million for pollution control costs, $1.8 million for energy savings, and $9.7 million for sales of products that might otherwise have been removed from the market.[59] By 1989 3M reported that it had reduced wastes by 50 percent and had saved the company over $400 million. In 1989, 3M's pollution prevention program added almost 6 cents a share, or $13 million, to the company's profits. This figure does not include the value of reused material or savings coming from reduced disposal costs (see Exhibit 14–9).

Finance.   A company can take the following actions:

1. *Gain the respect of the socially responsible investment community.* Socially responsible rating services and investment funds try to help people invest with a clean conscience.[60] Their motto is that people should be able to "do well" while they are "doing good." The theory is that socially responsible investments are likely to be profitable because if the companies can deal creatively with pollution, safety, and employment problems, they will tend to be innovative in other areas as well. The growth of socially responsible investment in the United States in the 1980s was substantial. From $40 billion in assets in 1984, it grew to $62.5 billion in 1991.[61]

Franklin Research and Development of Boston, a socially responsible investment firm, evaluates corporate environmental activities. The Dreyfus Third Century Fund ranks companies on the basis of social

---

EXHIBIT 14–9   3M's Pollution Prevention Programs: 1975–91

Pollutant Prevented 1975–1989	United States (First-Year Reductions)
Air pollutants	112,000 tons
Water pollutants	15,300 tons
Sludge/solid waste	397,000 tons
Wastewater	1 billion gallons

Savings from pollution prevention: $426 million.

   Goal: Reducing pollution at the source through:
   - Product reformulation.
   - Process modification.
   - Equipment redesign.
   - Recycling and reuse of waste material.

   Goal: By the year 2000, achieve global leadership as a "Sustainable Development" corporation, whose products, facilities, and operations have minimal environmental impact so that its business can continue to grow without adverse effect on the earth.

---

criteria and then selects the most profitable ones for its investments. The Calvert Managed Growth Portfolio assesses companies' financial performance first and then compares them against others in the industry on social issues. The New Alternatives Fund focuses on natural resource investments in solar and alternative energy companies.

The problem, of course, is that there is no consensus on what constitutes socially responsible investing. Definitions may be more or less restrictive. Comparisons may be made within an industry or between industries. The socially responsible funds only have government enforcement data and interviews with corporate officials upon which to rely. They may have trouble reconciling inconsistent company behavior. For example, Fort Howard Paper Company has played a leading role in recycling paper, but it also has played hardball politics regarding the Wisconsin Clean Air Act and used "job blackmail," the threat that it may lay off workers, to get its way.[62] It is also the largest paper mill source of PCBs. Some of the funds emphasize "positives"—demonstrated commitment to the environment or efforts to go beyond legal requirements. They also tend to include corporations that sell systems to analyze, clean up, or protect the environment. Other funds emphasize "negatives." They exclude companies whose records should discourage investors.

2. Recognize true liability. Smith Barney, Kidder Peabody and Co., and other investment houses have environmental analysts who search for a company's true environmental liability in evaluating their potential performance. They looked closely at ITT Corporation's $30 million charge against earnings for a plant in Georgia that made creosote-soaked railroad ties and telephone poles. The land on the plant site had been damaged and would have to be cleaned up.

3. *Recognize business opportunities.* Smith Barney's index of stocks in the solid-waste business rose 59 percent in 1989, and its index of hazardous-waste stocks rose more than 42 percent, while the overall stock market rose just 27 percent. The prospects for solid-waste companies (e.g., Waste Management, Laidlaw Industries, and Browning Ferris) are supposed to be very good because of a scarcity of landfill in parts of the country, and because cities like New York have no alternative ways to get rid of their garbage. The prospects of hazardous-waste companies may be good because the Departments of Defense and Energy will have to clean up toxic wastes they have created in various parts of country. Of course, the prospects for these companies depend on a host of other factors, not just market demand.

In summary, a firm can take numerous steps, covering all aspects of its business, to meet the challenge posed by pollution and environmental problems.

Summary and Conclusions

This chapter has tried to make the following points:

1. Pollution problems are worldwide, and businesses operate in settings throughout the world where environmental conditions, environmental movements, and environmental laws vary. It is important for managers to be aware of the differences, for such awareness may provide them with opportunities for gain and the potential to avoid liabilities.

2. Two of the most pressing pollution problems affecting the globe are solid-waste disposal and atmospheric pollution. Solid-waste disposal is a local problem. By creating programs to reduce and recycle wastes, companies can do something about it now. Atmospheric pollution is a global problem with long-term consequences. International treaties are needed to deal with problems like the ozone hole and global warming. Companies require long-term plans for these uncertain contingencies.

3. The actions companies can take to cope with environmental problems are numerous and extend from strategy making and organization to marketing, finance, accounting, and operations. Efforts to reduce pollution are in accord with various other

efforts to enhance quality, lower costs, and introduce new products and technologies.

Discussion Questions

1. Discuss environmental policies in the European Community. What have been some of the consequences of these policies for business?
2. In what ways is the West European environmental movement different from the environmental movement in North America? What are the consequences of these differences for business?
3. To what extent does Great Britain provide fertile ground for the expansion of U.S. firms experienced in the technologies and know-how of environmental protection?
4. What other countries in Western Europe might provide fertile ground for the expansion of experienced U.S. firms.
5. What are the three main methods of disposing of solid wastes? What are the advantages and disadvantages of these methods of waste disposal?
6. What business interests are represented by the different methods of waste disposal? What public policies would these different business interests tend to favor? What challenges do they face in building their business?
7. Why hasn't recycling been more successful?
8. What are the prospects for source reduction? What special problems and opportunities does source reduction offer business?
9. What are the public risks posed by ozone depletion? What are the challenges to business? Will business be able to meet these challenges?
10. What risks are posed to the world by carbon dioxide buildup? What do businesses have to do to confront this issue? What should government officials do?
11. Environmental issues pose numerous challenges to business. Discuss actions that companies can take in different functional areas.
12. Which potential company actions listed in this chapter are most important? Which are the easiest to take? Which are companies least likely to take? Why? Can you identify any examples of actions that companies can take that have been left out of this chapter?
13. As a practicing manager, what kind of environmental policy would you draft for your company? How would you make sure that the company carried out this policy?

Endnotes

1. W. Ophuls, *Ecology and the Politics of Scarcity* (San Francisco: W. H. Freeman and Company, 1977), pp. 21–22.
2. R. Buchholz, A. Marcus, and J. Post, (1992). *Managing Environmental Issues: A Case Book* (Englewood Cliffs, N.J.: Prentice Hall).
3. S. Tully, "What the 'Greens' Mean For Business," *Fortune*, October 23, 1989, pp. 159–64.
4. Ibid.
5. Ibid.
6. Ibid.; S. McMurray, "Chemical Firms Find that It Pays to Reduce Pollution at Source," *The Wall Street Journal*, June 11, 1991, p. A1.
7. Tully, "What the 'Greens' Mean for Business."
8. R. Cans, "Les Saga des Verts Europeans," *Le Monde*, June 1, 1989, p. 1; H. de Bresson, "La Tentation du Pouvoir," *Le Monde*, June 1, 1989, p. 9.
9. Ibid.
10. Ibid.
11. Ibid.
12. Ibid.
13. Ibid.
14. Cans, "Les Saga des Verts Europeans"; de Bresson, "La Tentation du Pouvoir."
15. Ibid.
16. Ibid.
17. "Buried Alive," *Newsweek*, November 27, 1989, pp. 66–76.
18. L. Blumberg and R. Gottlieb, "The Growth of the Waste Stream," in *War on Waste*, ed. L. Blumberg and R. Gottlieb (Washington, D.C.: Island Press, 1989), pp. 3–26.
19. "Buried Alive."
20. Directorate of Intelligence, Central Intelligence Agency, *Handbook of Economic Statistics, 1991* (Washington, D.C.: Government Printing Office, 1991), p. 174.
21. Blumberg and Gottlieb, "The Growth of the Waste Stream."
22. W. Rathje, "Rubbish!" *The Atlantic Monthly*, December 1989; pp. 99–109.
23. Blumberg and Gottlieb, "The Growth of the Waste Stream."
24. Ibid.
25. L. Blumberg and R. Gottlieb, "The Resurrection of Incineration" and "The Economic Factors," in *War on Waste*, ed. L. Blumberg and R. Gottlieb (Washington, D.C.: Island Press, 1989), pp. 26–58 and pp. 123–155.
26. Ibid.
27. Ibid.
28. J. Stevens, "Assessing the Health Risks of Incinerating Garbage," *EURA Reporter*, October 1989: pp. 6–10.
29. Ibid.
30. Blumberg and Gottlieb, "The Resurrection of Incinceration" and "The Economic Factors."
31. L. Blumberg and R. Gottlieb, "Recycling's Unrealized Promise," in *War on Waste*, ed. L. Blumberg and R. Gottlieb, (Island Press, 1989), pp. 191–226.

32. Ibid.
33. Ibid.
34. Ibid.
35. Ibid.
36. D. Brunner, W. Miller, and N. Stockholm, "3M Company: Creating Incentives Within the Individual Firm," in *Corporations and the Environment: How Should Decisions Be Made,* ed. D. Brunner et al. (Stanford, Calif.: Stanford Business School, 1981), pp. 97–110.
37. L. Blumberg and R. Gottlieb, "The Squeeze on Reuse Strategies," in *War on Waste,* ed. L. Blumberg and R. Gottlieb (Washington, D.C.: Island Press, 1989), pp. 226–58; C. Lehrburger, "The Disposable Diaper Myth," *Whole Earth Review,* Fall 1988, pp. 60–66; F. Lyman, "Diaper Hype," *Garbage,* January/February 1990, pp. 36–40.
38. K. Oldenburg and J. Hirschhorn, "Waste Reduction," *Environment,* March 1987, pp. 16–20, 39–45; A. Yazdani, "Waste Reduction," *Environment,* November 1989, pp. 2–4.
39. F. S. Rowland, "Chlorofluorocarbons and the Depletion of Stratospheric Ozone," *American Scientist,* January–February 1989, pp. 36–45.
40. S. F. Singer, "My Adventures in the Ozone Layer," *National Review,* June 30, 1989, pp. 34–38.
41. J. Morone and E. Woodhouse, "Threats to the Ozone Layer," in *Averting Catastrophe,* ed. J. Morone and E. Woodhouse, (Berkeley, Calif.: University of California Press, 1986), pp. 76–96.
42. F. Reinhardt, "Du Pont Freon Products Division," in R. Buchholz, A. Marcus, and J. Post, *Managing Environmental Issues: A Casebook* (Englewood Cliffs, N.J.: Prentice Hall, 1992), pp. 261–86; D. Dudek et. al., "Business Response to Environmental Policy: Lessons from CFC Regulation" (Washington, D.C.: Environmental Defense Fund); S. Gannes, "A Down to Earth Job: Saving the Sky," *Fortune,* March 14, 1988, pp. 137–41.
43. A. Ramirez, "A Warming World," *Fortune,* July 4, 1988, pp. 102–7.
44. "A Cool Look at Hot Air," *The Economist,* June 16, 1990, pp. 17–20; G. MacDonald, "Scientific Basis for the Greenhouse Effect," *Journal of Policy Analysis and Management* 3, 1988, pp. 425–44; I. Mintzer, "Living in a Warmer World: Challenges for Policy Analysis and Management," *Journal of Policy Analysis and Management* 3, 1988, pp. 445–59; L. Lave, "The Greenhouse Effect: What Government Actions Are Needed?" *Journal of Policy Analysis and Management* 3, 1988, pp. 460–70; P. Brown "Policy Analysis, Welfare Economics and the Greenhouse Effect," *Journal of Policy Analysis and Management* 3, 1988, pp. 471–75.
45. W. Chandler, H. Geller, and M. Ledbetter, *Energy Efficiency: A New Agenda,* American Council for an Energy Efficient Economy, 1988, pp. 19–65; J. Godemberg et. al., "An End-Use Oriented Global Energy Strategy," *Annual Review of Energy,* 1985, pp. 613–88; J. Marinelli, "Cars—The Technology Already Exists to Make Cars that Get 50+ MPG," *Garbage,* November/December 1989, pp. 28–37; S. Plotkin, "The Road to Fuel Efficiency in the Passenger Vehicle Fleet," *Environment,* July/August 1989, pp. 19–20, 36–42; R. Whitford, "Fuel Efficient Autos: Progress and Prognosis," *Annual Review of Energy,* 1984, pp. 375–408.
46. R. Sedjo, "Forests Might be Able to Moderate or Postpone the Buildup of

Atmospheric Carbon," *Environment,* January/February 1989, pp. 15–20; R. Repetto, *The Forest for the Trees? Government Policies and the Misuse of Forest Resources,* (Washington, D.C.: World Resources Institute, 1988), pp. 1–43; R. Buchholz, A. Marcus and J. Post, *Managing Environmental Issues: A Case Book* (Englewood Cliffs, N.J.: Prentice Hall, 1992).

47. F. Reinhardt, "Du Pont Freon Products Division."

48. "A Cool Look at Hot Air."

49. F. Friedman, "Implementing Strong Environmental Management Programs," in *Practical Guide to Environmental Management,* ed. F. Friedman (Washington, D.C.: Environmental Law Institute, 1988), pp. 27–57; W. Petak, "Environmental Management: A System Approach," *Environmental Management* 3, 1981, pp. 213–24; C. Priesing, "A Framework for the Environmental Professional in the Chemical Industry," *The Environmental Professional* 4, 1982, pp. 299–315; Buchholz, Marcus, and Post, *Managing Environmental Issues: A Casebook.*

50. D. Kirkpatrick, "Environmentalism: The New Crusade," *Fortune,* February 12, 1990, pp. 45–55.

51. Reinhardt, "Du Pont Freon Products Division."

52. D. Kirkpatrick, "Environmentalism: The New Crusade."

53. "Olin Corporation's Regulatory Audit Program," in *Current Practices in Environmental Auditing* (Cambridge, Mass.: Arthur D. Little, 1984), pp. 13–33; Report to U.S. Environmental Protection Agency, "Allied Corporation's Health, Safety, and Environmental Surveillance Program" in *Current Practices in Environmental Auditing* (Cambridge, Mass.: Arthur D. Little, 1984), pp. 33–53; C. Duerksen, *Environmental Regulation of Industrial Plant Siting* (Washington, D.C.: The Conservation Foundation, 1983), pp. 17–49, 79–109; F. Friedman, *Practical Guide to Environmental Management,* pp. 85–97 and pp. 133–43.

54. Kirkpatrick, "Environmentalism: The New Crusade."

55. D. Brunner, W. Miller, and N. Stockholm, "3M Company: Creating Incentives Within the Individual Firm," in *Corporations and the Environment: How Should Decisions Be Made,* ed. D. Brunner et al. (Stanford, Calif.: Stanford Business School, 1981), pp. 97–110; A. Mazur, "Controlling Technology," in *Technology and the Future,* ed. A. Teich (New York: St. Martins Press, 1990), pp. 207–220; M. Greenberg et al., "Network Television News Coverage of Environmental Risks," *Environment,* March 1989, pp. 16–43; D. Stone, "Casual Stories and the Formation of Policy Agendas," *Political Science Quarterly,* Summer 1989, pp. 281–301.

56. Brunner, Miller, and Stockholm, "3M Company: Creating Incentives Within the Individual Firm."

57. Kirkpatrick, "Environmentalism: The New Crusade."

58. Marketing Intelligence Service.

59. Ibid; R. Irwin, "Clean and Green," *Sierra,* November/December 1985, pp. 50–56.

60. Irwin, "Clean and Green."

61. Social Investment Forum, May 1991.

62. Ibid.

CASE IVA
ARCO SOLAR INC.[1]

In early 1988, top management at Atlantic Richfield (ARCO) had an important decision to make concerning the future of the company's solar energy division (see Exhibit IVA–1). The wholly owned subsidiary, ARCO Solar Inc., was a world leader in photovoltaic cell production (photovoltaics are semiconductors that produce electricity directly from sunlight), yet in the 11 years since ARCO had purchased the company, it had never turned a profit.[2] ARCO instituted a restructuring plan in 1985 that called for the company to divest itself of operations unrelated to its core oil, gas, chemicals, and coal businesses; yet, the solar technologies being developed by ARCO Solar seemed within a few years of profitability. At the same time, ARCO enjoyed a reputation as a model of good corporate citizenship for continuing to support photovoltaic research and development for so long.

ARCO

Atlantic Richfield was originally incorporated in 1870 as the Atlantic Refining Company and, until the 1960s, was exclusively an oil and gas business. The company was renamed when it merged with the Richfield Oil Corporation in 1966. In 1961, ARCO expanded into the chemicals and plastics business, and by 1977 was well established in the coal business. By 1988, ARCO was one of the largest integrated petroleum enterprises in the industry. ARCO subsidiaries conducted oil and gas exploration, production, refining, transportation, and marketing. The chemicals, plastics, and coal operations along with the oil and gas businesses constituted the core of ARCO's business.[3]

ARCO expanded into nonpetroleum businesses with limited success. In 1967, ARCO bought the Nuclear Materials & Equipment Company, a producer of uranium- and plutonium-bearing fuels, which it sold in 1971. ARCO also, at one time or another, owned a newspaper, an air-conditioning company, a plant cell research institute, and a building products operation. All were eventually sold.

The 1970s were a turbulent time for the petroleum industry. The energy crises of 1973–74 and 1979 precipitated a national search for energy alternatives to petroleum. One of the most attractive alternatives was solar energy—supply was not controlled by foreign countries and it was a clean source of energy. It was also abundant: the sunlight striking the earth in a year contains approximately 1,000 times the energy in the fossil fuels extracted in the same time period.[4] With gasoline and heating-oil prices rising beyond anything the public had experienced, there was a great deal of enthusiasm for solar power.

The enthusiasm seemed justified. Photovoltaic (PV) cells, which produce electricity directly from sunlight, were invented in 1954, and were first used to power U.S. satellites at a cost of over $1,000 per peak watt (a measure of a cell's output at maximum sunlight). By 1974, the price had dropped to $50 per peak

EXHIBIT IVA–1 **Atlantic Richfield: Consolidated Balance Sheet**
In Millions of Dollars

	December 31	
	1987	*1986*
Assets		
Current assets:		
Cash	$ 174	$ 122
Short-term investments	3,761	2,275
Marketable equity securities	758	0
Accounts receivable	709	348
Notes receivable	57	246
Refundable income taxes	0	764
Inventories	801	779
Prepaid expenses and other current assets	204	209
Total current assets	6,464	4,743
Investments and long-term receivables:		
Affiliated companies accounted for on the equity method	898	920
Other investments and long-term receivables	289	338
	1,187	1,258
Fixed assets:		
Property, plant, and equipment, including capitalized leases	26,663	26,175
Less accumulated depreciation, depletion, and amortization	12,258	11,325
	14,405	14,850
Deferred charges and other assets	614	753
Total assets	$22,670	$21,604
Liabilities and Stockholders' Equity		
Current liabilities:		
Notes payable	$ 1,373	$ 872
Amounts payable for securities purchased	626	0
Accounts payable	1,147	957
Taxes payable, including excise taxes	243	225
Long-term debt and other obligations due within one year	422	874
Accrued interest	229	356
Other	427	466
Total current liabilities	4,467	3,750
Long-term debt	6,028	6,661
Capital lease obligations	286	307
Deferred income taxes	3,641	3,562
Other deferred liabilities and credits	2,154	2,065
Minority interest	216	0

EXHIBIT IVA–1   Atlantic Richfield: Consolidated Balance Sheet
(continued)

	December 31	
	1987	*1986*
Liabilities and Stockholders' Equity		
Stockholders' equity:		
Preference stocks	2	2
Common stock ($2.50 par value:	544	543
shares issued—1987, 217, 484, 404; 1986, 217, 279, 037		
shares outstanding—1987, 177, 686, 928; 1986, 177, 510, 339)		
Capital in excess of par value of stock	1,034	1,073
Retained earnings	6,683	6,173
Treasury stock, at cost	(2,438)	(2,445)
Foreign currency translation	53	(87)
Total stockholders' equity	5,878	5,259
Total Liabilities and stockholders' equity	$22,670	$21,604

watt; by 1977 it was $17 and was continuing to decline as the cells were improved.[5]

ARCO initiated a study of the potential of the solar energy field in 1972. By 1976, with oil apparently on the way out and solar power a promising energy source for the future, the company's studies culminated in a decision to enter the solar field. ARCO did so in 1977 with the purchase of Solar Technology International, Inc., a tiny Chatsworth, California, operation with eight employees. Solar Technology was renamed ARCO Solar Inc.

ARCO Solar Inc.

Solar Technology International was founded in 1975 by an engineer, J. W. (Bill) Yerkes, with $80,000 he pulled together by mortgaging his home and obtaining loans from relatives.[6] The company produced PV panels that powered microwave repeater stations, corrosion-prevention systems in pipelines, navigational aids, irrigation pumps, electrified livestock fences, and trickle chargers for batteries on boats and recreational vehicles. When Yerkes sold the company to ARCO in 1977 for $300,000, he stayed on as ARCO Solar's first president.[7]

In 1979, the company bought a 90,000-square-foot building in Camarillo, California, and built the world's first fully automated production line for PV cells and panels. By 1980, the company was the first to produce panels generating more than a megawatt of power in a year. Sales had more than doubled from the previous year.

In order to interest electric utilities in photoelectric power generation, the company constructed demonstration projects where PV's potential for supplying large amounts of energy could be proven. In 1981, the company installed a prototype power generation facility on the Navajo reservation in Arizona and New Mexico that was large enough to power 200 homes. The project was judged a

---

EXHIBIT IVA–1 **Atlantic Richfield: Consolidated Statement of Income and Retained Earnings (*concluded*)**

In Millions of Dollars except per Share Amounts

	1987	1986	1985
Revenues:			
Sales and other operating revenues, including excise taxes	16,829	14,993	22,492
Interest	308	283	176
Other revenues	471	498	412
Total revenues	17,608	15,774	23,080
Expenses:			
Costs and other operating expenses	10,760	9,495	14,770
Selling, general, and administrative expenses	1,107	1,223	1,295
Taxes other than excise and income taxes	702	629	1,114
Excise taxes	547	506	769
Depreciation, depletion, and amortization	1,661	1,646	1,762
Interest	985	972	622
Unusual items	0	0	2,303
Total expenses	15,762	14,471	22,635
Income from continuing operations before gain in issuance of stock by subsidiary	1,846	1,303	445
Gain from issuance of stock by subsidiary	322	0	0
Income before income taxes, minority interest and discontinued operations	2,168	1,303	445
Provision for taxes on income	932	688	112
Minority interest in earnings of subsidiary	0	0	0
Income from continuing operations	1,224	615	333
Discontinued operations—net of income taxes:			
Loss from operations	0	0	(21)
Loss on disposal	0	0	(514)
Net income (loss)	$1,224	$ 615	$ (202)
Earned per share:			
Continuing operations	$6.68	$3.38	$1.55
Net income (loss)	$6.68	$3.38	$(0.97)
Retained earnings:			
Balance, January 1	$6,173	$6,264	$8,782
Net income (loss)	1,224	615	(202)
Cash dividends:			
Preference stocks	(4)	(5)	(8)
Common stock	(710)	(701)	(766)
Cancellation of treasury stock	0	0	(1,542)
Balance, December 31	$6,683	$6,173	$6,264

success, and the company moved from a largely research mode into a marketing stage.

An even larger demonstration project was conceived, and by the end of 1982, the company had constructed a PV power facility three times larger than the biggest such plant then in existence. The $15 million, one-megawatt plant near Hesperia, California—large enough to power 400 homes—was constructed on 200 acres of Southern California high desert, an area with no strong winds that might blow sand on the panels, thereby blocking sunlight and wearing down the mechanisms.[8]

The power at Hesperia was generated by 108 "trackers," double-axis computer-controlled structures that turn to follow the sun. Each tracker had 265 one-by-four-foot 40-watt PV modules, each of which were made of 35 individual single-crystal silicon cells. The trackers' ability to follow the sun boosted their power output by 40 percent over what a stationary panel could generate.[9] The electricity generated by the plant fed into the Southern California Edison grid and was purchased by the utility.

The plant was constructed in six months from construction start-up to completion in December 1982, a record for a power plant. Even more impressive, the plant was completed under budget, an uncommon occurrence for a new power-generating facility.

Encouraged by the success of the Hesperia project, the company began construction of a 16-megawatt plant on the Carissa Plain, near Bakersfield, California. The six-megawatt first phase of the project, completed in early 1984, occupied 640 acres. The project utilized several technical improvements in the PV module and tracker construction, which increased each tracker's peak power output by 50 percent, reducing the number of trackers needed.[10] As in Hesperia, a utility bought the power generated by the plant at the avoided cost of generating power from its most expensive fuel, gas or oil. This rate (around 6 cents/kwh) was less than what it cost ARCO Solar to generate the power, but a 37 percent federal and state tax credit for the solar installation brought the cost down enough to justify it as a demonstration of PV's potential (see Exhibit IVA–2).[11]

Meanwhile, in 1983, ARCO Solar took the industry by surprise by announcing it would begin selling thin-film amorphous silicon products the next year, much earlier than industry analysts had thought possible. "Genesis," a one-square-foot amorphous silicon cell, was the first use of thin-film technology beyond the tiny cells used in calculators and watches. Developed by a 100-person ARCO Solar research team whose existence had been kept secret, the five-watt module had a 6 percent conversion efficiency, a 20-year design life, and sold to distributors for about $45.[12] It generated enough electricity to maintain batteries in recreational vehicles, cars and boats, or to power security systems or other low-power remote applications.

Genesis made ARCO Solar the world leader in the race to commercialize thin-film technology.[13] The company's sales doubled again in 1984, and its international network of distributors continued to expand. By 1986, the company was selling 400 Genesis modules per month.[14]

ARCO Solar increasingly turned its attention to thin-film technology. The efficiencies of the thin-film cells steadily improved: by 1985 the company's researchers had a thin-film cell with a record 13.1 percent efficiency, and were

EXHIBIT IVA–2 **Estimates of PV Module Selling Prices Required to Meet Different Levelized Costs of Electricity for Central Station PV Plants***

Levelized Cost of Electricity (Cents/kwh)	*PV Module Efficiency*	*Required Selling Price of Modules (Dollar/peak watt)*†
6	10	0
6	15	0.30
6	20	0.39
9	10	0.51
9	15	0.69
9	20	0.81
12	10	0.90
12	15	1.09
12	20	1.29

*Based on a fixed, flat-plate PV array.

†This represents the price for a PV module at which a generator of electricity would be indifferent between PV-generated electricity and other sources of electricity. For example, at a levelized cost of electricity of 6 cents per kwh, an electric utility would not be interested in 10% efficient PV modules at any price. However, assuming the same levelized price of electricity, the utility would be willing to pay up to 30 cents per peak watt for 15% efficient panels.

SOURCE: D. E. Carlson, "Low Cost Power from Thin-Film Photovoltaics," in *Electricity: Efficient End-Use and New Generation Technologies, and Their Planning Implications.* ed. T. B. Johansson (Washington, D.C.: American Council for an Energy Efficient Economy, 1989).

predicting 20 percent efficiencies by 1990. Sales volume continued to climb due to the success of the Genesis modules.

In 1986, the company entered into joint ventures with a Japanese company (Showa Shell Sekiyu K.K.) and a German firm (Siemens A.G.) to manufacture and market ARCO Solar products in the Pacific and Europe. ARCO Solar was now the largest manufacturer of PV products in the world.[15]

But even though sales continued to climb, the company still remained unprofitable. Research and development continued to require a large commitment (35 to 40 percent of sales revenues), and though ARCO Solar's products had improved greatly, the market for PVs, due to the oil glut, was not growing as the company had hoped.

The PV Industry

When ARCO entered the industry in 1977, it was only one of a number of oil industry giants investing in the infant industry. Exxon had become involved in 1969, Shell in 1973, Mobil in 1974, and Amoco in 1979. Chevron, Union Oil of California, Occidental Petroleum, Phillips, Sohio, Gulf, Sun, and Texaco were also funding PV research.

These oil companies, flush with profits from the rising price of oil, were interested in expanding into new businesses that showed promise. In the late 1970s, solar energy seemed to be the energy source of the future.

As an energy source, PVs competed directly with fossil fuels. With oil prices rising and the equivalent price of PV electricity falling, the new technology's future looked promising. Worldwide sales of PV products rose rapidly, from around $11 million in 1978 to an estimated $150 million in 1983.[16] Industry analysts forecasted a billion-dollar PV industry by 1990 and PV electricity at half the equivalent price of oil. The government's 1976 "Project Independence" goal of PV electricity at 50 cents per peak watt seemed achievable in the not-too-distant future.

However, things began to sour for the industry in the early 1980s. By 1982, the price of oil began to fall (see Exhibit IVA–3). As the nation learned to conserve energy, the demand for electricity fell below projections in many areas, and utilities, not needing new capacity, lost interest in PV demonstration projects. The oil glut that developed as the 1980s wore on made fossil fuels plentiful again, and it made renewables like PVs appear unnecessary. The utilities that needed to expand wanted an established, uninterruptable source of power, and were unwilling to invest in an unproven technology.

Another threat to PVs arose in the early 1980s: a severe cutback in the federal government's commitment to solar energy research and development (see Exhibit IVA–4). President Ronald Reagan, elected to the White House by a landslide and committed to slashing federal nonmilitary spending, cut heavily into the funding that facilitated much of the progress in PV technologies. Federal funding for solar energy (including research, business and residential tax credits, guaranteed loans for solar installations, energy conservation programs, and demonstration programs), which rose from $2 million in 1972 to $2 billion in 1978, was cut by more than half in 1982 from its 1981 level. With two exceptions,

EXHIBIT IVA–3 World Crude Oil Prices, 1977–1987

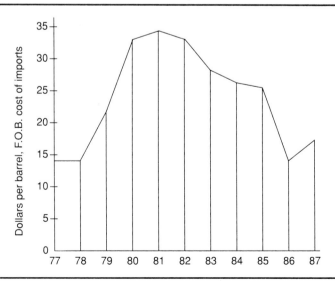

SOURCE: Solar Energy Industries Association.

EXHIBIT IVA–4 **Federal Appropriations for Photovoltaic Research and Development, 1977–1987**

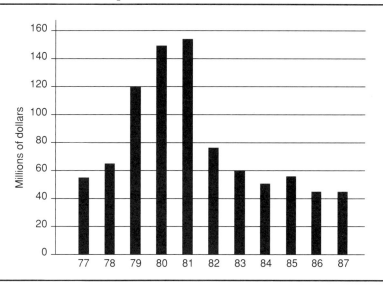

SOURCE: Solar Energy Industries Association.

federal funding continued to drop every year for the rest of the decade.[17] In 1987, the imposition of the Gramm-Rudman-Hollings federal deficit reduction budget cuts reduced the PV research budget to the lowest level ever. The burden of financing solar energy research, of which the government had shouldered 75 percent in 1980, fell increasingly on industry alone.

Besides cuts in research funding, the federal tax credits that encouraged consumers and business to invest in solar technologies expired in 1985. The 40 percent residential tax credit and 15 percent tax credit for industrial, commercial, and agricultural installations, had helped the solar industry's sales to rise rapidly. While the commercial tax credits were extended in 1986 after an intensive lobbying effort by the solar energy industry, the residential credits were not renewed when they expired in 1985.[18]

By the mid-1980s, the decline in crude oil prices was forcing the oil industry to slash capital spending and lay off employees. Various oil companies, particularly those that were forced to sell service stations and refineries, took a hard look at their portfolios, and some decided to get out of the solar energy business. Exxon's Solar Power Company ceased operations in 1983; Standard Oil wrote off the $85 million it invested in a solar energy joint partnership and quit in 1986. By 1988, ARCO and Amoco were the only major U.S. oil companies that still played a significant role in the PV industry.[19]

In addition, foreign competition grew tougher throughout the decade. While U.S. government R&D funding fell throughout the 1980s, this was not true of the funding commitment of some foreign governments. By 1985, the Japanese government was spending 19 percent more on PV R&D than the U.S.

government. In 1988, for the first time, both the West German and Japanese governments spent more on PV research than the United States.[20] And their investments were paying off; the U.S. companies' share of the world PV market fell from 80 percent in 1981 to 60 percent in 1983 to about 35 percent in 1987.[21] In 1985, only five of the top 20 PV firms in the world were located in the United States, though ARCO Solar was number one worldwide.[22] At the same time, the market itself seemed to be stagnant. After growing rapidly in the late 1970s and early 1980s, world PV sales stalled at the $125 million to $150 million level in the mid-1980s.[23] With all its promise, solar power still accounted for only 0.1 percent of the electricity generated each year.[24]

Competition in the PV Market

As they had in other industries, the Japanese showed their expertise in taking an existing technology and commercializing it. In the late 1970s, most attention in the PV industry was directed toward developing cheaper, more efficient single-crystal cells. These cells had the highest conversion efficiencies of any of the PV technologies, but they were also very expensive.

The Japanese, however, used a new type of cell (amorphous silicon), which was much less efficient than the single-crystal cells (3–5 percent efficiency versus 15–20 + percent efficiency) but much cheaper to produce. They used amorphous silicon cells to power small consumer electronic products like calculators. By 1985, the Japanese were selling 100 million amorphous-silicon-powered calculators and other small electronic products per year. Their experience in amorphous silicon cell production gave them the early lead in PV manufacturing technology, along with economies of scale and lower production costs. In 1985, the Japanese manufacturers shipped seven megawatts of amorphous silicon, almost all of it in consumer products, compared to 0.5 megawatts by U.S. producers.[25]

The most lucrative markets for PVs, though, was utility or grid power generation. In 1987, PVs were economical in grid systems only for what is known in the utility industry as "peaking power": more costly power sources that are used only during peak load periods.

The other major potential market was in providing power for areas without grid systems. Three quarters of the world's population are without grid electricity, yet many people live in areas where sunlight is abundant and intense. Thousands of small, solar energy systems were already operating in these areas and the potential market seemed huge. The Department of Energy estimated that the potential market was 10 to 20 times the current sales level.[26]

Most of the U.S. producers' attention was directed toward developing a cell that could generate electricity at a price competitive with fossil fuels. The price of PV electricity was falling, but whereas electricity from coal cost about 4 to 8 cents per kilowatt-hour (kwh) and oil or natural gas 5 to 10 cents/kwh, PV electricity cost about 25 to 30 cents/kwh (see Exhibit IVA–5).[27]

By the mid-1980s, thin-film technologies, like amorphous silicon, seemed to hold the most promise. These technologies, which used a fraction of the material required to produce single-crystal cells and less labor, were continually being refined to yield more efficient cells. By 1986, thin-film technologies had been developed to the point where they seemed to be within a few years of reaching 7

EXHIBIT IVA–5 Cost of a Solar Cell per Peak Watt of Electricity Generated

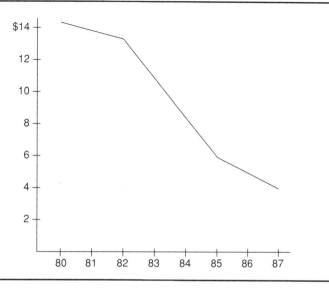

SOURCE: SEIA.

---

to 8 cents/kwh, which would make PVs competitive with fossil fuels and nuclear power (see Exhibit IVA–6).

Besides the emergence of thin-film technologies, there was another reason for optimism. By 1988, the search for new energy sources began to regain the momentum it had in the 1970s, though for a different reason. The threat posed by global warming had begun to draw attention. Experts warned that consumption of fossil fuels had to be reduced significantly to address the problem. Also, the Three Mile Island and Chernobyl nuclear accidents severely damaged the nuclear power industry's credibility and chances for a large role in the future of electricity generation appeared unlikely. Hydroelectric power, while clean and safe, had limited expansion potential. Solar energy's potential was once again becoming apparent.

ARCO Solar Inc. in 1988

By 1988, ARCO Solar was the undisputed world leader in the PV industry, with 20 percent of the $150 million market (see Exhibit IVA–7). The company was leaner than it had been, with 350 employees, half the number in 1983, and sales forecasts were optimistic; the company had a growing backlog of orders. The company's research labs had made advances in a new type of thin-film material, copper indium diselenide (CIS), which promised nondegradability and had even better efficiencies than amorphous silicon. The company was four to five years ahead of the competition in CIS technology, and a line of CIS cells was planned.[28]

EXHIBIT IVA–6   Efficiencies of Experimental Amorphous Silicon Cells

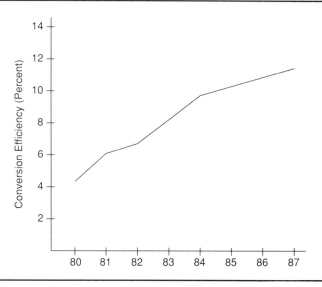

SOURCE: National Photovoltaics Program 1987 Review, U.S. Dept. of Energy.

EXHIBIT IVA–7   U.S. Photovoltaic Shipments, in Megawatts

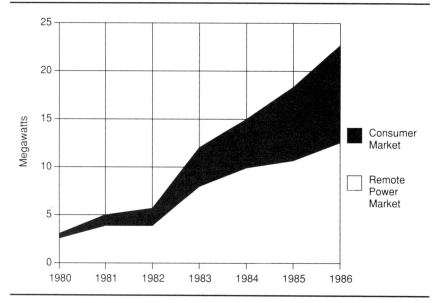

SOURCE: Department of Energy, "National Photovoltaic Program: 1987 Program Review."

Though ARCO Solar was the world's leading producer of PV cells, it still had never made a profit. Its $30 million in revenue was matched every 15 hours by its parent company.[29] Though ARCO Solar's president was confident the company could stand on its own feet within two or three years, some analysts believed that the $200 million ARCO had invested in its solar subsidiary had hurt the parent company's standing.

Other criticisms began to surface in the press. Bill Yerkes, the founder and first president of the company, told the *Los Angeles Times* that "the company was screwed up two years after [ARCO] bought it. We went from making cells for $10 a watt and selling them for $15 to making cells for $32 a watt and selling them for $5."[30] Other former employees cited additional examples of instability: the company's headquarters had shifted five times, and six men had been president in 12 years (three presidents in the first 3 years alone). One former employee recalled how a colleague had more than a dozen different job titles during this tenure.

What Should ARCO Do?

Meanwhile, in 1985, ARCO had undergone a restructuring that signaled a shift in corporate strategy. Anticipating continued low oil prices, the company cut costs by $500 million, repurchased 24 percent of its outstanding common stock, and wrote off $1.5 billion for losses on the sale of assets and expenses due to personnel reductions. The chairman of the board retired and the CEO stepped down.

The new CIS thin-film technology showed promise of being the basis of a line of PV cells that would be truly competitive with fossil fuels for utility-scale power generation in the next few years. Given the rising concern over global warming, an economically competitive PV cell for large-scale power generation could be a bonanza.

ARCO also enjoyed its reputation as a socially responsible corporation for continuing to support its solar subsidiary when so many oil companies had dropped out of the solar energy field. Although critics had claimed in the late 1970s that the oil companies were buying up the solar technology in order to suppress it, "Big Oil," with its deep pockets, was now generally acknowledged as being good for the PV industry. ARCO was a hero of sorts in the renewable-energy community.

Should ARCO sell ARCO Solar? Top management had a difficult decision to make.

APPENDIX
How Photovoltaic Cells Work

A photovoltaic cell produces electricity directly from sunlight. When the sunlight strikes the surface of the semiconductor material of which the cell is made, it energizes some of the semiconductor's electrons enough to break them loose. The loose electrons are channeled through a metallic grid on the cell's surface to junctions where they are combined with electrons from other cells to form an electric current.

Different semiconductor materials' electrons are broken loose by different wavelengths of light, and some wavelengths of sunlight reach the earth's surface with more intensity than others. Consequently, much of the effort of photovoltaic research has been to find semiconductor materials that are energized by the light wavelengths that are most intense and have the potential to provide the most energy.

Single-crystal silicon cells were the first type widely used, powering satellite radios as early as 1958. These cells are energized by some of the most intense sunlight wavelengths, and have achieved conversion efficiencies (percentage of light energy converted to electricity) over 20 percent. Nonsilicon single-crystal cells have achieved efficiencies over 27 percent.[31]

While efficient, these single-crystal cells are also expensive to produce and the crystals are difficult to grow. Much of the crystal is wasted when it is sawed into pieces for individual photovoltaic cells. Because they cost so much, their use has been limited mainly to applications where electricity is necessary and there are no other alternatives, such as in the space program.

In order to reduce production costs, researchers began to search for ways to fabricate silicon into cells that did not require the expensive and wasteful single-crystal techniques. One result of their efforts is *polycrystalline silicon cells*, which sacrifice some efficiency in return for cheaper manufacturing methods. The most efficient polycrystalline cells to date achieve better than 15 percent efficiencies. Together, single-crystal and polycrystalline cells account for two thirds of those sold.[32]

Perhaps the most promising PV technologies are the thin-film techniques, in which cells as large as four square feet—as opposed to crystalline cells, which are in the neighborhood of one-quarter inch in diameter—are produced by depositing a film of PV material less than a hundredth the thickness of a crystalline cell on a suitable base, or substrate. These cells are only about half as efficient as single-crystal cells, but because they can be produced for about one fourth the cost or less, they offer the greatest potential for large-scale use.

Thin-film silicon cells (called *amorphous silicon*) accounted for 37 percent of the world market for photovoltaics in 1987. One drawback to amorphous silicon cells, however, is that they typically lose about one sixth of their power output in the first few months of use. However, other thin-film materials do not suffer from this light-induced degradation. Two of the most promising are copper indium deselenid (CIS) and cadmium telluride (CdTe).

The world leader in CIS technology is ARCO Solar Inc. The company has developed a four-square-foot CIS cell with 9 percent conversion efficiency, demonstrating that large-scale applications of thin-film technology are feasible. A Texas company, Photon Energy, Inc., has developed an inexpensive, simple process for applying CdTe to panels as large as ARCO's, achieving 7 percent efficiency. The company has managed better than 12 percent efficiencies in the laboratory and expects to do even better in the near future.

Besides improving conversion efficiencies by developing new photovoltaic compounds, researchers have been breaking efficiency records by "stacking" cells. These "mechanically stacked multijunction" (MSMJ) cells are actually two cells pasted together. The top cell extracts the energy from one part of the light spectrum, and the lower cell uses the energy from a different part. A MSMJ cell composed of a single-crystal gallium arsenide cell and a single-crystal silicon cell has achieved over 30 percent efficiency, and researchers believe that a three-layer cell with a 38 percent efficiency is possible.[33] Efficiency improvements via stacking of more-economical thin-film cells are also being investigated.

The continuing improvements in conversion efficiencies are especially remarkable considering that as recently as 1982, theoretical physicists believed that the maximum achievable efficiency of a solar cell was 22 percent. The highest efficiency achieved at that point was 16 percent. Now, theoreticians estimate that 38 to 40 percent is the limit, although the physics of thin-film technology is not completely understood.

Other Sun-Powered Energy Sources

Photovoltaics are not the only way of utilizing the sun's energy.[34] In fact, PVs are not even the major producer of electricity from sunlight. That distinction belongs to solar thermal technologies. Solar thermal systems work by using the heating rays of the sun to warm air, water, or oil for space heating or thermal power generation. Luz International has been the world's largest producer of solar thermal electric plants. The company's seven plants in California's Mojave Desert produce 90 percent of all solar-generated power in the world. Company officials estimate that solar thermal plants occupying just 1 percent of the Mojave could supply all of Southern California Edison's peak power requirements. Solar thermal facilities, which on sunny days can achieve conversion efficiencies twice that of some PVs, generate power at a cost equal to late-generation nuclear plants, and the cost is dropping.

Biomass technologies focus on developing quick-growing plants that can be burned to extract the solar energy the plants store. A promising biomass technique involves growing certain types of algae in shallow ponds located in the desert. The algae produce an oil which can be extracted and used as fuel.

Ninety percent of the wind-generated electricity in the United States is produced by wind turbines located in three mountain passes in California. These three passes have been credited with having 80 percent of the world's usable wind supply, though experts estimate that under the right conditions, wind power could generate up to five percent of the nation's electricity. The California turbines accounted for one percent of California's electrical production in 1989. Production of new wind-powered facilities has been sluggish since tax credits for such construction ended in 1985, and also because at current prices, wind power is not quite competitive with fossil fuels.

Hydro power, which is the cheapest power source, is the largest generator of electricity among the renewables. It has limited potential for further expansion, though, since all the most convenient rivers have already been dammed.

Altogether, renewables (hydro, wind, solar, biomass, and geothermal) account for about 9 percent of the electric power generated in the United States.

Discussion Questions

1. In deciding what to do about ARCO Solar, what factors should the company consider?
2. What potential do the products that ARCO Solar is developing have?
3. Even if the products were very promising, should ARCO sell its solar division? Why or why not?
4. What role should long-term energy price factors play? What role should social responsibility play?

Endnotes

1. This case was written by Mark C. Jankus with the editorial guidance of Alfred Marcus and Gordon Rands, both of the Curtis L. Carlson School of Management, University of Minnesota; see R. Buchholz, A. Marcus, and J. Post, *Managing Environmental Issues: A Casebook* (Englewood Cliffs, N.J.: Prentice Hall, 1992).
2. D. Woutat, "Atlantic Richfield Plans to Sell ARCO Solar Unit, Cites Poor Prospects for Growth," *Los Angeles Times,* February 25, 1989, p. IV-1.
3. ARCO Annual Reports, 1977–1989.
4. "Waiting for the Sunrise," *The Economist*, May 19, 1990, p. 95.
5. Solar Energy Industries Association, *15 Years in Business with the Sun* (Washington, D.C.: 1989).
6. B. A. Jacobs, "Bill Yerkes—The Sunshine King," *Industry Week*, July 8, 1985, p. 66.
7. J. Bates, "Sale of ARCO Unit Casts Shadow on Future of Solar Energy Venture," *Los Angeles Times,* March 7, 1989, p. IV-1.
8. "1-MW Solar Facility Planned in California," *Electrical World*, May 1982, p. 25.
9. D. Best, "PV Power Goes On-Line in Hesperia," *Solar Age*, April 1983, p. 37.
10. "Solar Plant Is Largest," *Engineering News-Record*, April 7, 1983, p. 16.
11. A. A. Lappen, "Solar Lives!" *Forbes*, August 15, 1983, p. 104.
12. D. Best, "ARCO Goes Amorphous," *Solar Age*, November 1983, p. 15.
13. K. Berney, "Why the Outlook Is Dimming for U.S.-Made Solar Cells," *Electronics*, September 23, 1985, p. 32.
14. B. Yerkes, "Big Oil's Future in Photovoltaics,"*Solar Age*, June 1986, p. 14.
15. D. Best, "ARCO Solar Enters Joint Venture with Japanese Firm," *Solar Age*, May 1986, p. 20.
16. K. R. Sheets, "Solar Power Still the Hottest Thing in Energy," *U.S. News & World Report*, May 2, 1983, p. 45.
17. *15 Years in Business with the Sun*, informational pamphlet, Solar Energy Industries Association (Washington, D.C.: 1989).
18. Berney, "Why the Outlook is Dimming for U.S.-Made Solar Cells," p. 32.

19. M. L. Wald, "U.S. Companies Losing Interest in Solar Energy," *New York Times*, March 7, 1989, p. 1.
20. Ibid.
21. B. Rosewicz, "ARCO is Trying to Sell Solar-Panel Unit, Reversing Move into Alternative Energy," *The Wall Street Journal*, February 27, 1989, p. B3.
22. Best, "ARCO Solar Enters Joint Venture with Japanese Firm," p. 20.
23. L. Kuzela, "Days are Sunny for Jim Caldwell," *Industry Week*, October 13, 1986, p. 75.
24. "Waiting for the Sunrise," p. 95.
25. Berney, "Why the Outlook Is Dimming for U.S.-Made Solar Cells," p. 32.
26. Department of Energy, National Photovoltaics Program: 1987 Program Review, April 1988.
27. D. E. Carlson, "Low-Cost Power from Thin-Film Photovoltaics," in *Electricity: Efficient End-Use and New Generation Technologies, and Their Planning Implications*, ed. T. B. Johansson (Washington, D.C.: American Council for an Energy Efficient Economy, 1989).
28. M. Crawford, "ARCO Solar Sale Raises Concerns Over Potential Technology Export," *Science*, May 26, 1989, p. 918.
29. J. Bates, "Sale of ARCO Unit Casts Shadow on Future of Solar Energy Ventures."
30. *Los Angeles Times*, March 7, 1989, p. IV-11.
31. N. G. Dhere, "Present Status of the Development of Thin-Film Solar Cells," *Vacuum* 39, nos. 7–8, p. 743.
32. "Waiting for the Sunrise," p. 95.
33. D. Gardner, "Solar Cells Reach Efficiency Highs," *Design News*, April 24, 1989, p. 38.
34. Information in this section is adapted from J. R. Chiles, "Tomorrow's Energy Today," *Audobon*, January 1990, p. 58.

CASE IVB
THE FUTURE OF NUCLEAR
POWER[1]

As a planner for the Florida Power and Light Company (FPL), Gary Armstrong had to figure out where nuclear power fit into the utility's future (see Exhibit IVB–1). FPL had four operating reactors. The two at its Fort Pierce, Florida, site (St. Lucie 1 and 2) were Combustion Engineer pressurized water reactors, which had come online (i.e., first started to produce power) in 1976 and 1983. The two at its Miami, Florida, site (Turkey Point 3 and 4) were Westinghouse pressurized water reactors, which first started to produce power in 1972 and 1973.

FPL supplied electricity to an area that included five of the six fastest growing metropolitan regions in the United States. The utility served a population base that was expected to grow 34 percent in the next 10 years. Energy sales were up

EXHIBIT IVB–1   **Florida Power and Light and Subsidiaries**
                Financial Highlights

	(Dollars and Shares in Thousands)		
For the Years Ended December 31	*1989*	*1988*	*Percent Change*
Operating revenues	$6,179,796	$5,853,513	5.6
Operating income	$913,918	$921,913	(0.9)
Net income	$410,416	$447,787	(8.3)
Average number of common shares outstanding	131,639	131,106	0.4
Earnings per share	$3.12	$3.42	(8.8)
Dividends paid per share	$2.26	$2.18	3.7
Book value per share—year-end	$25.89	$24.90	4.0
Market price per share (high/low)	$36–29	$32–27	
Return on equity	12.2%	14.1%	(13.5)
Total assets	$12,325,309	$11,793,337	4.5
Employees—year-end	18,900	19,000	(0.5)
Construction expenditures	$783,309	$667,631	17.3
Average number of utility customers	3,064,446	2,953,681	3.8
Energy sales (thousand kwh)	64,146,204	59,892,036	7.1

7.1 percent from the previous year and had been growing at a compound annual rate of 4 percent for the past decade.

Though the utility projected demand to grow at a slightly lower rate in the near future, at least 5,000 megawatts of additional capacity were going to be needed. Buying Canadian hydro was simply out of the question for a utility located as far south as FPL.

FPL generated almost all of its power from its 10 fossil-fuel plants and 4 nuclear power plants (see Exhibit IVB–2). The St. Lucie plants had the capacity to generate 1,664 megawatts of power. The Turkey Point plants had the capacity to generate 1,322 megawatts of power. They were an important part of the utility, supplying more than 25 percent of its power output.

The St. Lucie plants had one of the highest rankings, in a listing of the top 30 reactors in the world, based on historic capacity factors. In contrast, the Turkey Point plants continually were in trouble. Only recently were they taken off a Nuclear Regulatory Commission list of reactors requiring additional surveillance (the "Watch List").

FPL had tried to make significant improvements in the Turkey Point plants' management and operations and was hoping that its added expenditures in these areas would result in better performance. A comparison of FPL's nuclear power plants is provided in Exhibit IVB–3.

The History of Nuclear Power

In preparation for his presentation to the board, Gary Armstrong reviewed the history of nuclear power in the United States.[2]

EXHIBIT IVB–2 Florida Power and Light Energy by Fuel Type (Percent)

	1985	1986	1987	1988	1989
Nuclear	35%	32%	23%	30%	25%
Oil	13	27	21	26	23
Gas	19	20	21	17	18
Coal	0	0	1	2	2
Additional resources	33	21	34	25	32

SOURCE: 1989 annual report of Florida Power and Light.

EXHIBIT IVB–3 Comparison of FPL's Nuclear Power Plants

	Emergency Shutdowns		NRC Violations		Safety System Failures		Capacity Factors		Operations and Maintenance Budget (Dollars in Thousands)	
	1989	1990	1989	1990	1989	1990	1989	1990	1989	1990
St. Lucie 1	2	0	6	12	0	0	95%	62%	42	41
St. Lucie 2	2	1	5	12	0	0	75%	73%	42	41
Turkey Point 3	1	2	17	16	3	4	59%	55%	78	80
Turkey Point 4	2	2	16	16	4	5	34%	72%	78	80

In 1988, there were 108 reactors in the United States with 14 more under construction. The United States obtained 20 percent of its electricity from nuclear power. By comparison, France obtained more than 75 percent, Belgium more than 65 percent, and South Korea more than 50 percent. None of the reactors in the non-Communist world were like the Chernobyl reactor in the Soviet Union, where a blast destroyed the nonconcrete roof and immediately killed 32 people, the worst nuclear power accident in history.

Safety Philosophy.   The philosophy used to assure safety in the U.S. nuclear industry was known as "defense-in-depth." This meant that four different mechanisms assured reactor safety: dense ceramic pellets around the nuclear fuel, a steel pressure vessel covering the core, a concrete shield building around the pressure vessel, and an emergency core cooling system that would spray the core with thousands of gallons of water in case of an emergency. Sensors shut down the reactor automatically if predetermined safety levels were exceeded.

In the Three Mile Island accident, while other barriers had been breached, the concrete containment building, the last and most formidable barrier, maintained itself throughout the accident.[3] No immediate deaths took place. However, the uranium core was uncovered by coolant for nearly 40 minutes and General Public Utilities, the owner of the Three Mile Island (TMI) unit, lost its entire investment, nearly $1 billion.

The likelihood of a far worse accident at a U.S. reactor was low, but still possible.[4] At full power the temperature inside the core was over 3,300 degrees fahrenheit, which if not covered by water, would melt the fuel cladding and do very serious damage. The fear in the nuclear industry was always of a massive pipe break that would uncover the core and allow such an accident to take place.

Nuclear Power's Initial Attraction.   The initial attraction of the nuclear technology was the incentive to maximize the rate base. So long as the rate of return allowed by public utility commissions was fixed, the only way to increase profits was to expand the rate base (i.e., the cost of capital, which was the basis for profits allowed by public utility commissions).

The need for capital expansion existed in the 1960s when demand for power grew at a pace of 7.3 percent per year. In a decade's time, this growth translated into a need to double the existing generating capacity. The accepted wisdom in the industry was that cheap power came from economies of scale. Nuclear power, being the most capital intensive form of power generation, was the technology of choice.

The Oil Embargo.   With the rise of fossil fuel prices following the 1973 oil embargo, the attraction of nuclear power only grew. In comparison to coal, the fuel costs associated were relatively low, about a third of the total costs of production as opposed to two thirds with coal. Nuclear power involved the substitution of capital, which amounted to two thirds of its generating costs, for a nonrenewable resource, coal, whose price was tied to oil.

Moreover, with the ascendance of the environmental movement, nuclear power appeared to have an additional advantage: it was less polluting. It involved virtually no emissions of sulfur dioxide, carbon dioxide, or other pollutants into the atmosphere.

Between 1972 and 1974, the utilities ordered 79 new nuclear power plants (see Exhibit IVB–4). Thirteen of these orders came from utilities that had no previous experience with nuclear power. Major construction problems, however, developed, which were traceable to the financial pressures the utilities confronted in the postembargo period and to institutional relationships that prevailed in the industry.

Financial Pressures

Achieving the financial advantage of nuclear power over coal depended on the ability to control nuclear power capital costs. With nuclear, the initial costs of construction were great, but they yielded substantial operating benefits. Unfortunately, however, there was a tail of waste disposal costs strung out indefinitely into the future. With coal, in contrast, the initial construction costs were modest, but the operating costs were relatively high primarily because of the dearness of the fuel.

Moreover, the environmental damage with coal, unlike that with nuclear, was immediate. It involved the mining of the coal and the air pollution associated with its burning. This air pollution not only caused acid rain but also was a main contributor to the greenhouse effect.

EXHIBIT IVB–4 Orders for New Electric Generating Capacity: 1962–79

	Generating Capacity Ordered (Megawatts)			Nuclear as a Percent of Total Capacity Ordered
Year	Total	Nuclear	Fossil	
1962	8,971	628	8,343	7.0%
1963	16,633	2,495	14,138	15.0
1964	na	0	na	0.0
1965	28,466	4,490	21,676	15.7
1966	37,204	16,367	20,837	44.0
1967	50,669	25,522	25,147	50.4
1968	36.066	12,895	23,171	35.8
1969	34,278	7,203	27,075	21.0
1970	44,613	14,266	30,347	32.0
1971	36,244	19,931	16,313	55.0
1972	52,678	35,843	16,835	68.0
1973	64,581	38,687	25,894	60.0
1974	72,476	38,978	33,498	53.8
1975	14,924	4,100	10,824	27.5
1976	9,712	3,400	6,312	35.0
1977	14,353	2,300	19,053	43.3
1978	21,353	2,300	19,053	10.7
1979	5,436	0	5,436	0.0

SOURCE: Adapted from S. D. Thomas, *The Realities of Nuclear Power* (New York: Cambridge University Press, 1988).

As long as public utility commissions gave utilities an incentive to maximize the dollar value of capital, nuclear was more attractive than coal. When the oil embargo took place and fuel costs skyrocketed, the choice seemed clear. Nuclear had a distinct advantage. However, if the main advantage of nuclear was in substituting capital costs for fuel costs, then it was essential that capital costs be controlled.

High Capital Costs. The capital costs of nuclear, however, got out of hand. With high energy prices after 1973, demand for power decreased to about half of what it was in the 1960s. Construction work continued, but while in progress this construction work was not part of the rate base. Only when it was completed and actually producing power could it achieve this status. In the meantime, utility earnings were not sufficient to cover the cost of capital. Utilities also could not use retained earnings to finance new nuclear power construction, because the retained earnings were subject to public utility commission controls on prices and profits. Retained earnings could not be large if public utility commissions carried out their mandate of regulating in the public interest.

During the 1970s only about 60 percent of the rate increase requests utilities made were granted (see Exhibit IVB–5).[5] The utilities appealed to the public utility commissions to allow investments for construction work in progress to be

---

EXHIBIT IVB–5   Utility Requests for Rate Increases: 1965–80

Year	Amount of Increase Requested	Amount Approved	Percent Approved
1963	na*	0.0	—
1966	na	33.0	—
1967	na	0.7	—
1968	na	20.0	—
1969	na	145.0	—
1970	790	533.0	67
1971	1,368	836.0	60
1972	1,205	853.0	71
1973	2,135	1,089.0	51
1974	4,555	2,229.0	49
1975	3,973	3,094.0	78
1976	3,747	2,275.0	61
1977	3,953	2,311.0	58
1978	4,494	2,419.0	54
1979	5,736	2,853.0	50
1980	10,871	5,932.0	55

*NA = not available.

SOURCE: Adapted from P. Navarro, *The Dimming of America*, (Cambridge, Mass.: Ballinger, 1985).

included in the rate base, but consumers opposed this request and the public utility commissions often denied it.

With the cost of capital rising, the utilities' need for capital grew. To finance nuclear power construction, they had to tap the external capital markets.[6] Inflation during this period was going up at unprecedented rates, and therefore the utilities had to offer lucrative interest rates on bonds to attract investors. As a consequence, their interest on outstanding debt increased. The interest coverage ratios (the relationship between annual earnings and annual interest payments on debt) rose, and their bond ratings declined.

Utilities sold new shares of their stock at low prices and raised dividend yields to attract investors. Their market-to-book ratios (the stock's current selling price over total assets) declined, and their price-earnings ratios slipped. They were having trouble raising new capital and financing their nuclear power projects and started to cancel the projects.

Technological Infancy.   Another weakness of nuclear power in comparison to coal is that while coal had a long history, nuclear power was in its technological infancy. In 1979, the Three Mile Island (TMI) nuclear accident shook the industry. It was followed by the second oil price shock, which was associated with the Iranian Revolution. The world plunged into the worst recession since the Great Depression, and demand for power slipped as conservation took hold in response to higher energy prices and weakening economic conditions. After 1979, the utilities ordered no new nuclear power plants and canceled construction even at sites where significant progress had been made (see Exhibit IVB–6).

EXHIBIT IVB–6   **Cancellation of New Electric Generating Capacity Orders: 1974–82**

| Year | Generating Capacity Cancelled (Megawatts) | | | Nuclear as a Percent of Total |
	Total	Nuclear	Fossil	
1974	18,216	7,216	11,000	39.6
1975	16,596	14,699	1,897	88.6
1976	4,446	1,150	4,406	20.7
1977	12,510	10,814	1,696	86.4
1978	15,670	14,487	1,183	92.5
1979	11,674	9,552	2,122	81.8
1980	21,350	18,001	3,349	84.3
1981	6,706	5,781	925	86.2
1982	na	21,937	na	na
1974–81	108,278	81,700	26,578	75.0

SOURCE: Adapted from S. D. Thomas, *The Realities of Nuclear Power* (New York: Cambridge University Press, 1988).

Institutional Influences

The decline in nuclear power did not take place only because of financial pressures. Institutional influences played a role. In comparison with France, where nuclear power gained momentum in this period, three differences were important.

1. In the United States, private competitive markets allocate most capital; in France, the state has greater control. Debt is not such a great burden on the French utility.
2. In the United States, the state has control over profit rates via public regulation; in France, the utility is publicly owned. Government regulation of safety plays a much greater role in the United States than it does in France.
3. In France, standardization of plants exists, which has many benefits; the nuclear power program has greater capacity to learn from experience. In the United States, the complexity of institutional arrangements leads to many problems.

Learning from Experience

Learning from experience is critical to the success of a nuclear power program. Feedback of design, production, and operational experience is one of the most important ways for progress to take place with respect to any technology, but especially with regard to nuclear, which at the time was relatively untried and untested.

The nuclear design was difficult to test. Production costs were high, there were few operating units, and the safety implications of failure were great. The whole system could not be subjected to destructive testing. Subsystems could be tested, but the effects on the whole system would be known only through computer simulation. Since subsystems were highly interdependent, simulation might miss the full consequences of failure.

With a small number of plants operating and little standardization, it was difficult to accumulate meaningful statistical analyses of plant performance. When design changes were understood to be necessary, they might not be carried out because of regulatory delays and the expense of making unique changes on custom-built systems.

In France standardization reduced construction costs, prevented delays, and simplified repairs and maintenance.[7] Efficiencies were achieved in the recognition and correction of error. When an error was discovered, it had uniform applicability. Design improvements had to be incorporated into all plants. Corrections had to be made universally.

Spare-parts inventories also could be maintained. Spare parts can be produced via batch and mass production; they did not have to be produced one-at-a-time. There were also some costs to this standardization. For example, errors were embodied in all plants—if there were severe problems, all plants have to be shut down.

Complexity.   Learning requires communication. The key to success in nuclear is effective communication of information among all those involved in the power program—vendors, architect engineers, construction companies, utilities, and regulators. When an incident occurs, for example, an equipment failure, it is critical that this information be disseminated among all the parties for whom it will have consequences. They all must have the chance to recognize the implications of the failure for their segment and to alter their practices in light of experience.

Because of the complexity of the nuclear power programs in the United States, the communication process has not been smooth. In France, because of standardization, the process has worked much better. U.S. nuclear power programs require coordinating the work of four vendors, 12 architect-engineers, over 50 utilities, an almost equal number of public utility commissions, and the Nuclear Regulatory Commission (NRC).

Vendors.   The four vendors are Westinghouse, General Electric, Babcock and Wilson, and Combustion Engineering. General Electric produces boiling water reactors (BWRs); the other three vendors produce pressurized water reactors (PWRs). The vendors compete against each other. They do not have the incentive to share information. Westinghouse and General Electric manufacture turbine generators, and Babcock and Wilcox and Combustion Engineering provide steam supply systems. All four companies are large and diversified. They rely on about 200 subcontractors.

Westinghouse and General Electric have the longest history in the nuclear power program. They participated in the power demonstration program established by the AEC in the 1950s. The reactors ordered in the precommercial stage of development were their creations. They were awarded the first 12 fixed-price, turnkey orders for commercial nuclear power plants and have produced most of the reactors made since.

Babcock and Wilcox and Combustion Engineering won their first orders only in 1966 after 20 reactor orders already had been placed. Their first reactors were large ones. Thus, they never had the chance to learn from experience by scaling up their operations. Not surprisingly, Babcock and Wilcox reactors have had performance difficulties. But Westinghouse and General Electric reactors have not been trouble-free. Westinghouse reactors have had problems with steam generator corrosion, and GE reactors have had difficulties with cracks in the pipe work.

Architect-Engineers. Architect-engineers like Bechtel, Stone and Webster, and Sargent and Lundy are responsible for station design and component specification and procurement (see Exhibit IVB–7). They also are likely to be the construction company in charge of supervising and scheduling construction, but it is not uncommon in the U.S. industry for there to be a different architect-engineer and construction company. Some utilities (Duke Power and the Tennessee Valley Authority, or TVA) have performed these functions themselves; in this respect they are more like the giant, government-owned and operated French utility Electricite de France (EDF), which carries out all of these functions.

Delays and failures mean that replacement power has to be purchased and there is a reduction in the present value of future project benefits (see Exhibit IVB–8). Many times, though, the architect-engineer or construction company is not responsible for the delays or failures; rather, regulatory disruptions,

---

EXHIBIT IVB–7 Nuclear Architect-Engineers

Architect-Engineer	No. of Orders	No. Cancelled or Work Suspended	Date of First Order
Bechtel	61	26	1965
Stone and Webster	28	16	1966
Sargent and Lundy	21	7	1965
Ebasco	15	8	1965
United Engineers and Constructors	13	8	1965
Gilbert	7	1	1965
Southern Services	6	4	1969
Burns and Roe	5	1	1967
Gibbs and Hill	4	1	1966
Offfshore Power Systems	4	4	1974
Fluor	3	0	1967
Black and Veatch	2	2	1973
Brown and Root	2	0	1973
Unassigned	18	18	—
Utility as architect-engineer	37	14	—
TVA	17	8	1966
Duke	13	6	1966
Others	7	0	—

SOURCE: Adapted from S. D. Thomas, *The Realities of Nuclear Power* (New York: Cambridge University Press, 1988).

EXHIBIT IVB–8   **Average Construction Times**

Year of Construction Permit Issue	Average Length of Construction Time (Months)	No. of Units
1964	53	2
1965	—	—
1966	66	5
1967	69	14
1968	84	21
1969	82	8
1970	98	9
1971	89	4
1972	86	3
1973	124	9
1974	148	9
1975	132	5
1976	125	5
1977	100	4
1978	(116)	(1)

SOURCE: Adapted from S. D. Thomas, *The Realities of Nuclear Power* (New York: Cambridge University Press, 1988).

financial difficulties, and low demand for power have often led utilities to make the choice to stretch out construction schedules.

Utility Diversity.   The utilities that own and operate nuclear power plants in the United States are very diverse organizations (see Exhibit IVB–9). Some are very large and have strong technical leadership and engineering capability (Commonwealth Edison, Duke Power, Pacific Gas and Electric). Some are equally large but are not known for their technical leadership and engineering capability (AEP, Middle South Utilities, and GPU). These utilities are holding companies that are only loosely held together. They may have nuclear power plants in many different parts of the country (e.g., AEP).

Some utilities that own and operate nuclear power plants in the United States are vertically integrated. They are involved in nearly all stages in the production of power from mining to marketing and waste management. A few utilities (e.g., Duke Power) have been their own architect-engineers and construction companies. Some utilities have decided to take the route of unrelated diversification to protect themselves against short-term market perturbations, to avoid financial losses, and to be in a position where they can redeploy valuable staff when adversity strikes. A movement toward diversification has affected almost all utilities as they search for ways to escape from the profit restrictions imposed by public utility commissions.

Most American utilities that own and operate nuclear power plants are investor-owned. The exception is the TVA, which is the biggest owner and operator of nuclear power plants in the United States. Public ownership should give TVA some unique advantages, for example, an ability to escape the vicissitudes of market changes, to absorb short-term setbacks, and to draw on the

---
EXHIBIT IVB–9 Major U.S. Utilities Owning Nuclear Power Plants

---

Owner	*Ownership*
1. U.S. government	Federal
2. Tennessee Valley Authority	Federal
3. The Southern Company	Private
4. American Electric Power	Private
5. Commonwealth Edison	Private
6. Texas Utilities Electric	Private
7. Middle South Utilities	Private
8. Florida Power and Light	Private
9. Southern California Edison	Private
10. Duke Power	Private
11. Houston Lighting and Power	Private
12. Central and South West	Private
13. General Public Utilities	Private
14. Pacific Gas and Electric	Private
15. Virginia Electric Power	Private

SOURCE: Adapted from S. D. Thomas, *The Realities of Nuclear Power* (New York: Cambridge University Press, 1988).

government's pool of skilled employees. However, TVA has been among the worst performing among U.S. utilities with nuclear power plants.

Some utilities that own and operate nuclear power plants are in rapidly growing areas of the country (Southern California Edison, Florida Power and Light, and Houston Lighting and Power). The demand for the power sold by these utilities is growing much more rapidly than the demand for other utilities' power. Also, some utilities played a pioneering role in the nuclear power industry (Duquesne Light, Con Ed, Commonwealth Edison, Yankee Atomic Energy), ordering reactors in the precommercial stage and gaining valuable experience before constructing and operating reactors for commercial use, whereas others put off ordering their first reactors until 1973–74 when the large bulk of orders for reactors were made.

The worst performing nuclear power plant in the United States in terms of its construction experience was the Washington Public Power Supply System (WPSS). Underwritten by many local municipalities and co-ops, the utility aimed to construct five different reactors with three different vendors and three different architect-engineers. Numerous small suppliers and subcontractors also were involved. The whole project got out of managerial control and only one unit reached the final licensing and commercial operation stage. All the other units were canceled. The WPSS project ultimately defaulted on its bonds.

Self-Regulation.   Only after the unfortunate TMI incident did the U.S. utilities band together for the purposes of self-regulation in a utilitywide association, the Institute for Nuclear Power Operations (INPO). INPO inspects operating plants, reviews and analyzes abnormal events, and helps the utilities with training and emergency planning. A consortium of insurance companies that bears the risk of nuclear power operations that is above $500,000 (a federal government insurance scheme under the Price-Anderson Act bears the risk of operations up to $500,000) relies on INPO reports to assess nuclear power plants. This arrangement adds some weight to INPO recommendations. Earlier industrywide bodies, the Electric Power Research Institute (EPRI) and the Edison Electric Institute (EEI), acted as research and lobbying arms of the industry and had no supervisory functions.

Government Regulation.   The Nuclear Regulatory Commission (NRC) carries out safety regulation in the United States at the national level. The burden of owning and operating a nuclear power plant is different from the burden of owning and operating other types of technology, because safety has to be a critical consideration, not simply efficiency or technical improvements. Also, safety has to be viewed broadly in terms of the general public, not just the safety of operators and users.

The early research in light water-reactor technology was carried out by the federal government as part of the Atoms for Peace Program inaugurated by President Eisenhower. In its inception the program, which was housed in the Atomic Energy Commission (AEC), was closely tied to the military. The prototype for the commercial PWR was the submarine model designed by Admiral Hyman Rickover for use by the Navy. The early work in scaling up the nuclear Navy submarine version of the PWR to commercial size was done in government labs with little communication with the ultimate commercial users, the electric utilities. Electric utilities had little impact on the choice of technology or on the direction that technological development would take.

In 1971 the environmental movement took on nuclear power in the United States. The first of many battles was decided in the environmentalists' favor. Under the Calverts Cliff decision, the Supreme Court required utilities to file environmental impact statements under the National Environmental Policy Act (NEPA) before proceeding with the construction of nuclear power plants. The estimated delay time that this requirement added to licensing was 18 months, a substantial amount in a period when utilities were beginning to feel the pressure of inflation and the high costs of capital.

It was not until 1974 that the AEC was split up into a regulatory body, the NRC, and a research arm that continued with its prior mission of promoting nuclear power. The research arm took with it the military programs of the AEC into the Energy Research and Development Administration (ERDA) and ultimately into the Department of Energy. The two major tasks that the NRC had to deal with early in its existence were to issue construction permits to the vast number of nuclear power plants ordered at this time, and to set standards for emergency core cooling systems (ECCS), a necessary part of those reactors.

Lack of Standardization.   Each of the newly ordered plants was somewhat different. There was no standardization in the U.S. program at that time, no real efforts to promote standardization, and no real understanding of the costs of the extensive customization that was taking place. With four vendors, more than 12 architect-engineers, and over 50 different utilities, it was not surprising that every reactor was unique and that each plant required its own separate safety analysis. The requirement to deal with this diversity imposed a mighty burden on the newly created NRC.

The emergency core cooling system controversy also was draining of time and energy. The issue was contentious and dragged on with sophisticated technical challenges to the NRC's policies. The rule-making hearing lasted nearly 18 months. In the meantime utilities that had started constructing new plants were unsure about how they should proceed with a vital safety component.

Post-TMI Safety Requirements. After TMI, public expectations again increased about what the NRC should do. The NRC imposed new requirements on the control room, training, communications between utilities and vendor, and emergency planning. Emphasis was given to minor failures that could develop into major accidents with widescale consequences. The NRC was supposed to pay greater attention to human factors. Merely concentrating on the technical aspects of nuclear power was insufficient.

The NRC multiplied the number of backfits it required utilities to make. Each of these requirements may have made sense in isolation, but they were so numerous that they overburdened the utilities with more than they felt they could capably handle. The utilities complained that there was no system to the NRC requirements, that they were not well coordinated, and that no consideration was given to cost-effectiveness or to the potential deleterious unintended consequences.

Clearly, nuclear power plant capacity factors sunk after TMI, while prior to the incident they had been improving (see Exhibit IVB–10). Also, in the 1980s, nuclear power plant safety performance started to get better (see Exhibit IVB–11).

EXHIBIT IVB–10 U.S. Nuclear Power Plant Performance

	Capacity Factor (Percent)	Net Capacity (MW)	No. of Units
1972	68.7%	1,270	2
1973	68.7	3,031	5
1974	53.3	6,558	10
1975	57.6	10,507	16
1976	62.7	16,023	23
1977	64.7	26,895	36
1978	68.7	34,616	45
1979	60.9	38,363	49
1980	57.3	43,838	55
1981	57.4	47,657	59
1982	55.9	48,441	60
1983	55.1	50,260	62
1984	55.7	54,532	66
1985	59.0	55,680	67
1986	56.3	58,674	70

SOURCE: Adapted from S. D. Thomas, *The Realities of Nuclear Power* (New York: Cambridge University Press, 1988).

EXHIBIT IVB–11   Safety Improvements in Nuclear Power Operations

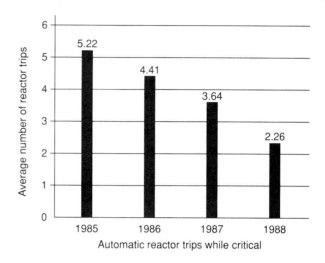

Automatic reactor trips while critical

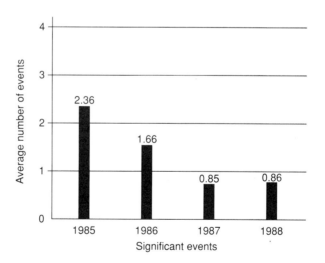

Significant events

EXHIBIT IVB–11   **Safety Improvements in Nuclear Power Operations (concluded)**

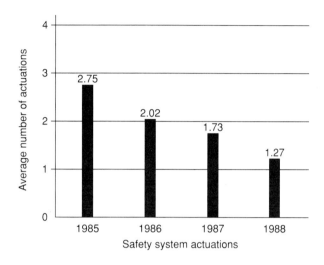

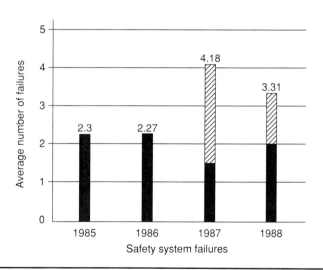

NOTE: The hatched area represents the additional data resulting from reclassifying safety system failures.

SOURCE: Adapted from the Nuclear Regulatory Commission, AEOD Annual Report, 1988, NUREG 1272.

New Developments

Growing recognition of the importance of the greenhouse effect seemed to be making the nuclear option attractive to the utility industry again. New fossil-fuel plants emitted greenhouse gases. The risk of having regulations passed that would curtail their use was great. Utilities might have no choice but to build new nuclear stations.

"Inherently Safe" Designs.   As a consequence, there was much discussion in the industry about efforts to commercialize "inherently safe" designs.[8] For instance, the integral fast reactor (IFR) was an advanced concept that had become one of the focuses of the Department of Energy's research and development program. The IFR was cooled by liquid sodium at low pressure and fueled by a new metal alloy fuel. Liquid sodium had a far higher boiling point than water and was better capable of absorbing unexpected heat surges. While a water reactor's coolant had to be kept at high pressure—up to 150 times atmospheric pressure—to prevent it from turning to steam, liquid sodium did not require pressurization. If the pumps circulating the coolant ruptured, the liquid sodium plus air naturally circulating outside the reactor would indefinitely prevent core damage. The problem was that liquid sodium reacts violently to the presence of air or water and extraordinary steps such as double walling the reactor vessel would have to be taken to prevent exposure.

Improved assurance of reactor safety was a main objective of this design. Compared to existing reactors, IFR safety relied more on passive characteristics of the system and less on proper functioning of complex engineering systems and on operators taking correct actions. In tests of the concept, conditions were created that would be expected to lead to rapid meltdown in most types of reactors. The IFR prototype simply shut itself down without operator intervention and without damage of any kind.

Improved nuclear waste management was another goal of IFR. The fuel in a liquid sodium reactor could be reprocessed with a new technology, called pyroprocessing, and refabricated into new metal fuel rods for use in the reactor. The pyroprocess was supposed to keep all the very long-lived carcinogenic materials together with the fuel for recycle back to the reactor. The nuclear wastes would be harmful for hundreds of years, not millions. If nuclear power was to substitute for conventional means of power generation, such as coal and oil, that produce vast amounts of carbon dioxide, then new reactors based on different designs would be needed. Rival proposals to develop commercial models of a liquid sodium-cooled reactor had been developed by General Electric and Rockwell International, but a full-scale prototype never had been built.

Process-Inherent Ultimate Safety.   Another concept—process-inherent, ultimate safety (PIUS)—was being promoted by the Swedish company Asea Brown Boveri. Here the conventional water-cooled reactor was surrounded by cold, heavy water containing boron. The sheer pressure of the regulatory coolant would keep the boron, which halted nuclear operations by absorbing neutrons, away from the core during normal operations, but in case of an accident the loss of pressure would flood the core with the boron automatically, without direct human intervention. Operators would have at least a week to figure out what to do next while the boron cooled the core. In contrast, with conventional reactors operators might have only 20 minutes to make critical decisions.

Advanced Water-Cooled Reactors.   Defenders of conventional water-cooled reactors claimed that the new designs were untried and untested and that small modifications could be made on the conventional reactors that could greatly increase their safety. GE and Westinghouse were working with Japanese companies on advanced models with evolutionary refinements in controls, pumps, and other equipments, but a real jump in safety could be achieved if new small reactors that these companies, along with Combustion Engineering and Babcock and Wilcox, were developing came to fruition.

Westinghouse, for example, was planning to create a 600 megawatt reactor with advanced passive features. It was called the AP600. Fuel and water temperatures would be lower, and there would be no need for externally powered emergency core cooling systems to protect the reactor in case of an emergency. Instead, valves would open automatically and pour 400,000 gallons of emergency coolant on top of the reactor core. The water would sit on top of the reactor and flow to the core by means of gravity. The reactor would be cool enough for operators to have at least three days, rather than 20 minutes, to identify and fix the problem.

Projected costs of the AP600 were $2,000 per kw at current prices, less than half of the costs of old-fashioned reactors. Clearly, the AP600 was competitive with coal. Orders placed in the early 1990s could be producing before the end of the decade. The advocates of the AP600 believed that scale economies did not pay off in the nuclear industry. The smaller reactor required less than half the pumps, valves, and control cables of the larger reactor. Its design was simpler, construction costs were lower, and operations would be safer.

Gas-Cooled Reactors.   A more exotic notion was to develop gas-cooled reactors. In the United States, General Atomics Corporation was an advocate of this concept. Internationally, the West German companies Siemens and HRB were involved, as well as the Swedish company Asea Brown Boveri. The basic idea was to coat tiny uranium fuel spheres with multiple layers of ceramic material. The most heatproof and radiation-resistant of these materials was silicon carbide. The coatings would perform the same basic function as the multiple containment barriers in a conventional plant, but at a fraction of the size. They did not melt, and they vaporized only at temperatures above 3,300 degrees fahrenheit, a temperature much higher than the level reached when a reactor lost all coolant.

The problem was not the inherent safety of these reactors. It was their efficiency. They only converted about 28 percent of the heat created to electricity. In contrast, a water cooled reactor transforms about 34 percent of the heat to electricity. Britain and France, which had built many of these reactors in the 1950s and 1960s, abandoned the concept in favor of the conventional water-cooled reactor.

Helium-Cooled Gas Reactors.   Here was another option that had been explored by the United States, West Germany, and Great Britain in the 1960s. U.S. utilities had ordered 10 reactors from General Atomics, but all but one of the orders ultimately was canceled because of reduced power demand. The only operational helium-cooled gas reactor in the United States was the Fort St. Vrain plant near Denver. It had been plagued with difficulties related to the use of water as opposed to oil as a lubricant for the circulators that keep the helium moving through the reactor. None of these operational difficulties challenged the basic promise of a technology that involved very low radiation levels.

The West Germans built a new 300-megawatt (MW) plant near Hamm, northeast of the Ruhr area. The plant was expensive—$2 billion—but for its first 19 months it ran two thirds of the time and converted heat to electricity at a level of 41 percent. In the case of a worst case accident, authorities would have at least eight hours before the fuel heated to 3,600 degrees fahrenheit. The radiation release would be small and no one would have to be evacuated. The West Germans planned to build another 550-MW plant at a lower cost so that the power produced would be less expensive.

Modular Reactors.   General Atomics believed that the reactor of the future would be a helium-cooled gas reactor. Built in modular form of 135-MW units in factories, it would be placed in silos underground so that four separate units placed next to each other would equal a total of 540 MW.

The ground would absorb sufficient heat to avoid an accident. Fuel temperature never would rise about 2,900 degrees fahrenheit. Even in the event of an accident, people near the plant would be exposed to no more radiation than they obtained in a short airplane ride. Projected costs of a four-unit model were between $1.5 billion and $1.7 billion, but additional development work was needed. General Atomics was seeking assistance from the Department of Energy to help defray the development costs.

Gary Armstrong reviewed the advantages and disadvantages of these different forms of nuclear power and started to formulate some recommendations that he would make to FPL's board. To what extent should FPL continue to rely on nuclear power, and what form should the nuclear technology that FPL used take in the future?

Discussion Questions

1. How much more generating capacity will Florida Power need in the next 10 years? How much will it need in the next 25 years?
2. Why initially was nuclear power so attractive to U.S. utilities?
3. What happened? Why have no new nuclear power plants been ordered since 1979? What went wrong?
4. To what extent will conventional nuclear power plants figure in Florida Power's future?
5. To what extent will new forms of nuclear generation figure in Florida Power's future?
6. Compare the advantages and disadvantages of different ways to provide people with power. Toward what mix of power provision should Florida Power aim?

7. What can Florida Power learn from the history of nuclear power? How can the mistakes of the past be avoided in the future?

8. What should Gary Armstrong say to Florida Power and Light's board?

Endnotes

1. This case was prepared by Alfred Marcus.
2. A. Marcus, *Controversies in Energy Policy* (Beverly Hills, Calif.: Sage Press, 1992).
3. M. Rogovin, Director, Nuclear Regulatory Commission Special Inquiry Group; *Three Mile Island: A Report to the Commissioners and to the Public,* vol. I and II, Parts 1, 2, and 3, 1980, NUREG/CR 1250, U.S. Nuclear Regulatory Commission; *Three Mile Island: The Most Studied Nuclear Accident in History* EMD-80–109, General Accounting Office, 1980.
4. E. Faltermayer, "Taking Fear Out of Nuclear Power," *Fortune,* August 1, 1988, pp. 105–14.
5. P. Navarro, *The Dimming of America,* (Cambridge, Mass.: Ballinger, 1985).
6. J. Campbell, *Collapse of an Industry* (Ithica, N.Y.: Cornell University Press, 1988).
7. S. D. Thomas, *The Realities of Nuclear Power* (New York: Cambridge University Press, 1988), pp. 1–117.
8. J. Beyea, "Is There Any Role for Nuclear Power in Preventing Climate Disrup20i" hearing before the House Subcommittee on Energy and Power of the Committee on Energy and Commerce, *Advanced Reactor Technologies,* March 15, 1989, pp. 97–110; Faltermayer, "Taking Fear Out of Nuclear Power"; M. W. Golay, "Advanced Light-Water Reactors," *Scientific American,* April 1990, pp. 82–89; L. M. Lidsky, "Safe Nuclear Power," *The New Republic,* December 28, 1987, pp. 20–23; L. M. Lidsky, "Nuclear Power: Levels of Safety," *Radiation Research,* February 1988; J. Sillin, "Nuclear Medicine for Energy Ills," *The Wall Street Journal,* September 21, 1988, p. 24.

CASE IVC
DU PONT AND THE 1990 CLEAN AIR ACT[1]

By the time Congress recessed for the 1990 Memorial Day holiday, it was clear that new clean air legislation would soon be passed, legislation that would have a greater impact on Du Pont than any legislation ever had.[2] Both the House and Senate had passed amendments to the nation's Clean Air Act, and after the holiday lawmakers would reconvene in a conference committee to reconcile the two versions, as well as to accommodate the Bush administration's concerns. That would be Du Pont's last chance to influence the legislation, if it chose to do so.

As one of the 10 largest companies in the United States and, according to government reports, the nation's fifth-largest polluter, E. I. du Pont de Nemours & Co. had more at stake than perhaps any other company (see Exhibit IVC–1). Nearly every type of atmospheric pollution identified in the proposed legislation was generated by a Du Pont subsidiary. Du Pont's main substitute for chlorofluorocarbons (CFCs) would be banned under the new legislation a decade sooner than the company had hoped. Provisions designed to address the acid rain problem would threaten parts of Du Pont's coal operations. Operating costs for the company's chemical division would rise significantly if the law's new requirements concerning toxic air emissions survived the conference committee in their strictest form. And Conoco, Du Pont's gasoline subsidiary, would be affected by provisions mandating cleaner-burning gasoline.

The question now facing Du Pont was how to respond to the legislation.

The Clean Air Act

The Clean Air Act (CAA), enacted in 1970, was intended to protect people and property from the ill effects of air pollution.[3] The three titles of the law dealt with pollution from both stationary (industrial plants, buildings, and factories) and

EXHIBIT IVC–1 Du Pont's Financial Performance: 1987–89

Industry Segments	Sales			After-Tax Operating Income		
(in millions)	*1989*	*1988*	*1987*	*1989*	*1988*	*1987*
Industrial products	$ 3,702	$ 3,082	$ 2,636	$ 629	$ 355	$ 319
Fibers	5,966	5,465	5,012	729	676	601
Polymers	5,581	5,423	4,783	455	531	475
Petroleum	12,314	10,995	10,560	538	391	277
Coal	1,818	1,757	1,770	223	226	157
Diversified business	6,153	5,638	5,170	307	275	271
Total company	$35,534	$32,360	$29,931	2,881	2,454	2,100
Interest and other corporpate expenses:						
Net of tax				(401)	(264)	(314)
Net income				$2,480	$2,190	$1,786

(dollars in millions except per share amounts)	*1989*	*1988*	*1987*
Sales	$35,534	$32,360	$29,931
Net income	2,480	2,190	1,786
Earnings per share	3.53	3.04	2.46
Dividends per share	1.45	1.23⅓	1.10
Net return	15.7%	14.6%	12.9%

SOURCE: Adapted from Du Pont's 1989 annual report.

mobile sources (cars, trucks, buses, and airplanes). The CAA originally required the nation's air to be clean by 1975. However, this proved impossible, and the law was amended both in 1975 and 1977 to allow more time for industry either to comply or to deal with newly discovered pollutants and ambiguities in the law. By 1982, most of the nation's air quality control regions had met the established limits for four of the six major pollutants: lead, nitrogen oxides, particulates, and sulfur oxides. Ozone and carbon monoxide proved more intractable, and some parts of the country had failed to attain the standards set for these pollutants by the end of the decade. However, progress had been made overall. The EPA reported that between 1978 and 1987, the level of carbon monoxide dropped 32 percent, lead by 88 percent, nitrogen dioxide by 12 percent, ozone by 16 percent, particulate matter by 21 percent, and sulfur dioxide by 35 percent.

Environmentalists, however, were dissatisfied with this progress, citing the threats that airborne pollutants posed to forests, waterways, and wildlife when precipitated out of the atmosphere in the form of so-called acid rain. But their efforts to amend the CAA in the 1980s failed, largely because of the deregulation ideology of the Reagan administration. By 1990, however, the political situation had changed. The Senate finally passed a clean air bill in April 1990 and the House completed voting on its version in late May.

The administration estimated that the bill would cost U.S. industry—already spending $33 billion a year on air pollution control—at least another $21.5 billion annually, more than General Motors, General Electric, Ford Motor, IBM, and Exxon collectively earned in 1989.[4] The amendments designed to combat acid rain could mean double-digit electricity rate increases for the heavily industrialized midwest. The nation's coal miners could expect to lose thousands of jobs. Antipollution equipment could raise the price of a new car by $600. On the other hand, the estimated expected benefits were also significant: air pollution was contributing to the premature deaths of over 50,000 people per year and costing the nation $10 billion to $25 billion annually in health care.[5]

In the ranks of industry there certainly would be winners and losers. For each company that would have to spend some of the upwards of $20 billion that the air act was supposed to cost, there would be several other companies that would win substantial dividends as the recipients of that spending.[6]

Du Pont and the New Clean Air Act

The new legislation, which experts called economically more significant than any other environmental law ever passed, would have profound consequences for Du Pont. The corporate giant, founded in the early 19th century as an explosives manufacturer, had $35.5 billion in sales in 1989, 10 percent higher than in 1988. The company had made a name for itself by harnessing science for commercial purposes. Du Pont's laboratories were the birthplace of nylon, Teflon, Orlon, Dacron, Lycra, and Kevlar. Du Pont helped General Motors develop Freon and became the first producer of the ubiquitous chemical. The company produced a wide range of products, from pesticides to biomedical equipment.

The new CAA had economic implications for most of Du Pont's businesses, but the chlorofluorocarbon, chemical, coal, and gasoline businesses were particularly affected.

Chlorofluorocarbons

Chlorofluorocarbons (CFCs) are a group of chemical compounds prized by industry for their wide range of uses, stability, economy, and nontoxicity. Once used in the United States as an aerosol propellant, CFCs are still widely employed as coolant in refrigerators and air conditioners, foaming agents in many types of insulation, solvents for cleaning electronic equipment, and for hundreds of other purposes.

Du Pont's Freon Products division is the largest producer of CFCs in the world, supplying half the U.S. demand and 25 percent of demand worldwide. Though CFC sales are significant (Du Pont's sales are about $750 million), their future is limited because of the threat they pose to the earth's stratospheric ozone layer, which protects the planet from harmful ultraviolet radiation. In 1974, a wave of concern following the discovery of this threat led to a 1978 ban on the use of CFCs as aerosol propellants in the United States, Canada, and several Scandinavian countries. But concern waned until 1985 when the "ozone hole" over Antarctica was discovered. When stratospheric ozone measurements showed that the ozone layer was being depleted faster than the best models had predicted, political leaders from around the world agreed to a phaseout of CFCs, an agreement codified in the Montreal Protocol in 1987. The Protocol calls for a cap on the production of CFCs at 1986 levels by the year 1989, and a 50 percent reduction in production by 1998.

In 1988, Du Pont—acting on its pledge to stop their production if CFCs proved harmful—vowed to completely end production of CFCs in the year 2000. The company shifted its attention to developing a marketable substitute, spending $5 million in 1985, more than $30 million in 1988, and planning to spend more than $1 billion on the effort by 2000. Known substitutes like propane, carbon dioxide, or pentane were dangerous, inferior, or more expensive. A promising possible substitute that Du Pont called 132b had to be scrapped when it was discovered the compound caused sterility in male rats.

By early 1990, the company rested its greatest hopes on a class of chemicals called HFCs and HCFCs. These chemicals performed many of the same tasks as CFCs, but because their molecular composition allowed them to break down before they reached the upper atmosphere, they had either zero (HFCs) or only 2 to 10 percent (HCFCs) of the ozone-depleting capacity of CFCs. In 1987, Du Pont estimated that these compounds could be produced at two to five times the cost of CFCs. Though more expensive, they were not prohibited under the Montreal Protocol and appeared to be the most viable alternative. But while the Montreal Protocol did not restrict HCFC use, the new House and Senate bills would. The bills would freeze production of most HCFCs in 2015 and ban nearly all production in 2030. Both dates were decades earlier than the 2030–2050 timeframe Du Pont had determined reasonable.

This posed a serious obstacle to Du Pont's plans for the substitute chemical. Customers would be hesitant to adapt to a substitute that would itself be phased out. For example, HCFC-22 could be used in automobile air conditioning systems, but only if the systems were substantially redesigned to handle the higher operating pressures necessary to use HCFC-22. General Motors executives estimated the necessary retooling would cost their company $600 million.

Up until 1986, Du Pont disputed the scientific basis for the ozone threat and led the effort to oppose restrictions on CFC production. The company was instrumental in forming the Alliance for Responsible CFC Policy, an industry trade group that lobbied for an approach to CFC regulation that took into account the economics and usefulness of the compounds. But when new scientific information on the ozone hole appeared in 1986, Du Pont changed its strategy and came out in favor of an international approach to the ozone problem. The company was concerned that the United States might undertake unilateral limitations on CFC production, giving a competitive advantage to foreign CFC producers.

The new CAA bills again raised the threat of unilateral action, but this time with respect to HCFCs. In March 1990, citing competitive issues, the company sent a letter to its Freon customers urging them to contact their congressmen to protest the legislation for an earlier-than-planned phaseout of HCFCs. Nonetheless, both House and Senate bills mandated the early phaseout. Publicly, Du Pont executives were silent on how the company would respond. But even before debate on the issue began, Du Pont had designed its first new commercial-size HCFC plant to initially produce only small quantities of the chemical, in case a market did not develop.

Du Pont managers were now faced with hard decisions about where to focus the CFC and CFC-substitute division's energies. How hard should it lobby Congress to end the early ban on HCFCs? To what extent should it redirect its research and development efforts to other possible substitutes?

If Du Pont was going to redirect its corporate development strategy, it needed an assessment of the scientific and technical issues that was clear, understandable, and definitive. However, the state of scientific and technical knowledge was in such a state of flux that reaching such an understanding would not be easy.

Chemicals

Two major provisions of the proposed CAA legislation had substantial implications for Du Pont's chemical operations. Du Pont was the largest U.S. chemical company and had 80 or more plants around the country that could be affected.

First, the Senate bill would require chemical plants to stop production unless they reduce toxic emissions to the point where people living near the plant face no more than a 1-in-10,000 risk of getting cancer from these emissions. Several Du Pont plants in Texas and Louisiana, which emitted carcinogens like carbon tetrachloride (which is used to produce synthetic rubber), had been cited by the EPA for posing an unacceptable cancer risk to nearby residents. Some of these cited plants already controlled their toxic emissions through state-of-the-art technology; additional safety measures to further reduce emission levels would be very expensive.

Achieving the Senate mandated 1-in-10,000 risk level would be very difficult. But even more difficult would be proving that it was achieved, as risk analysis itself is a tricky business. Different groups of experts practicing it use different assumptions, which can be contested not only in the legal system but in the court of public opinion, where estimates of risk raise emotions and arouse both public concern and controversy.

Unlike the Senate bill, the House bill did not specify an acceptable level of risk, relying instead on the EPA to conduct further risk-assessment studies and make recommendations to Congress. These studies could take years to complete and digest, time that Du Pont could use to plan for the needed changes. Du Pont favored the House bill, but was unsure what, if anything, it should do to pressure Congress. Becoming too identified with the House's position might backfire; environmentalists would use industry backing as a tactic to obtain more stringency from Congress.

The second major provision affecting chemical operations was contained in both versions of the bill, and it required that every production line nationwide install the best available emission control technology. The measure was designed to reduce toxic fumes by 90 percent. If companies on their own could not meet the 90 percent reduction, EPA would set standards for the companies, defining the best available control technology and requiring the companies to install it.

Toxic fumes are blamed for 2,700 potential cancer cases annually (0.2 percent of all reported cases) as well as other health problems. The cost to industry of the best-technology requirement was pegged at $5 billion per year. However Du Pont, acting on its own initiative, had already begun spending hundreds of millions of dollars to reduce its emissions voluntarily by 60 percent from their 1987 levels by 1993. This effort was in addition to the company's ongoing reductions in air pollutants, which it had tracked since the early 1970s. If Du Pont were to continue with its own plan, it might be able to meet the 90 percent reduction guideline that would exempt it from EPA-specified emission control measures. On the other hand, if the company failed to satisfy the reduction requirement, it would have spent millions of dollars on control equipment only to find that the EPA might require different equipment. Whether to continue with its own plan or wait for the EPA regulations to be clarified was a key issue for the chemicals division.

Coal

After a decade of debate, Congress and the administration were ready in 1990 to combat acid rain. Formed when sulfur and nitrogen oxides precipitate out of the atmosphere, acid rain damages forests and lakes, particularly those in the nation's northeast region. A major culprit in the formation of acid rain is the high-sulfur coal used by some coal-burning energy utilities and industrial plants. Du Pont's Consolidated Coal subsidiary is one of the two biggest high-sulfur coal producers in the country, with high-sulfur coal accounting for 60 percent of its production.

Congress and the administration were largely in agreement on the provisions that would address the acid rain problem. Under the plan, utilities would be forced to cut sulfur dioxide emissions by 10 million tons annually by the year 2000, at a cost of about $4.1 billion per year. The president's proposal included an innovative pollution-trading system, which would allow utility companies that cut their emissions by more than the required amount to sell their unused pollution "rights" to utilities that could not meet the standards.

Because many utilities would find it cheaper to buy low-sulfur coal than to invest in costly emission-control technology, Consolidated executives estimated that from $40 million to $50 million in annual revenue would be lost, between

750 and 800 company coal miners would lose their jobs, and perhaps two of the company's four high-sulfur coal mines would be forced to close starting in 1995. Again, it was unclear what Du Pont should do. Protesting to Congress at this late date was likely to be futile. There seemed to be little opportunity for creative adjustment to this change in government policy.

Gasoline

The proposed CAA amendments that dealt with gasoline seemed to offer the most opportunity to Du Pont's Conoco subsidiary. The opportunity for Conoco stemmed from the fact that a gasoline meeting the standards proposed for the mid-1990s had not yet been developed. Both the Senate and House versions of the legislation would require that cleaner burning gasoline be sold in nine of the nation's smoggiest locations: Los Angeles, New York City, Houston, Chicago, Milwaukee, Baltimore, San Diego, Philadelphia, and much of Connecticut.[7] Together, these areas comprise 25 percent of the U.S. gasoline market, but a very small portion of Conoco's market. The Senate version specified what the reformulated gasoline should contain, while the House version allowed refineries more leeway as long as they met the minimum performance standards.

If the oil industry failed to persuade lawmakers to change the reformulation requirement, there would be a large market for any company that came up with an acceptable, working formulation. Conoco researchers started working on the problem shortly after President Bush unveiled his clean air proposal requiring cleaner fuels.

After being caught off-guard when the Senate passed the reformulation amendment, industry trade groups and companies undertook an unprecedented, multi-million-dollar lobbying effort to defeat a similar amendment in the House.[8] Conoco neither contributed to this lobbying effort nor initiated its own effort. A $1 million newspaper ad campaign attacked both the gasohol lobby, which was pushing for the reformulation provision, and Congressman Bill Richardson (New Mexico) who sponsored the provision. Several oil companies set up 800 numbers, encouraging their shareholders to call or to send prepaid mailgrams to Congress protesting the amendment. The oil companies also urged their employees and dealers to deluge Congress with mail on the subject. The American Petroleum Institute (API), an industry trade group, circulated API-financed research that discounted the benefits of reformulated gasoline.

The lobbying blitz backfired. According to an environmental lobbyist involved with the legislation, not only did the oil industry lack credibility, but House members were irritated by its heavy-handed tactics. Consequently, the barrage of mail and attention on the issue confirmed the belief of many lawmakers that Congress needed to define exactly how gasoline should be reformulated rather than leave it to the oil industry to decide.

What Next?

The CAA amendments in their final form would substantially determine how Du Pont would spend its environmental-equipment budget, which was slated to be $500 million by 1991. But other costs would also increase as a result of the legislation (e.g., the company's electric bill). By some calculations, Du Pont—

which uses about 0.5 percent of all the electricity generated in the U.S.—could expect to spend up to $40 million more per year in energy costs alone. Of course, there were opportunities as well. Du Pont's fledgling environmental-services business was projected to expand 10-fold during the 1990s, up to $1 billion per year.

Not only did management have to consider how to approach the legislation in the short term, but how to prepare for its implementation in the long term.

APPENDIX: MAJOR PROVISIONS OF THE 1990 CLEAN AIR ACT

Smog

Some 96 areas missed the deadline for meeting health standards for ozone, a main ingredient of smog. The new bill requires that all but nine areas comply by November 1999, all but Los Angeles, Baltimore, and New York by 2005, Baltimore and the NYC area by 2007, and Los Angeles by November 2020.

Areas that are moderately polluted or worse must cut smog 15 percent within six years. After that, areas that are seriously polluted or worse must make 9 percent improvements every three years until they meet the standards.

Tougher tailpipe standards are phased in starting with 1994 models to cut nitrogen oxides by 30 percent and hydrocarbons by 40 percent. Even deeper cuts are required for 2003 models if the EPA finds they are cost-effective and needed. These standards have to be maintained for 10 years or 100,000 miles.

Warranties on pollution control equipment must last eight years or 80,000 miles for catalytic converters and electronic diagnostic equipment and two years or 24,000 miles for other pollution gear.

Special nozzles are required on gasoline pumps in almost 60 smoggy areas. Also, fume-catching canisters are to be phased in on all new cars, starting in the mid-1990s. Gauges are also required on cars to alert drivers to problems with pollution-control equipment.

Industrial polluters that emit as little as 10 or 25 tons of smog-forming chemicals a year may have to make cuts, depending on the severity of smog in their areas. The present law sets the limit at 100 tons a year. Forty-three other categories of smaller pollution sources, including printing plants, are also regulated.

Alternative Fuels

Beginning in 1995 all gasoline sold in the nine smoggiest cities must be cleaner burning, reformulated gasoline that cuts emissions of hydrocarbons and toxic pollutants by 15 percent. By the year 2000 the reductions must equal 20 percent.

Starting with 1998 models, fleets of 10 or more cars in the two dozen smoggiest cities must run 80 percent cleaner than today's autos. Trucks must be 50 percent cleaner. Requirements could be delayed three years if clean vehicles are not available.

By the model year 1996, car makers must begin producing at least 150,000 superclean cars and light trucks annually under a California pilot program designed to launch vehicles that can run on nongasoline fuels, such as natural gas and methanol. By the year 2001, even cleaner models must be produced.

Toxic Emissions

Only seven chemicals have been regulated since 1970, but over the next 10 years the majority of polluting plants must use the best technology available to reduce their emissions of 189 toxic chemicals by 90 percent.

For any remaining cancer risks, the EPA is required to set health-based standards that produce ample margins of safety—a cancer risk of not more than about 1 in 10,000—for people living near factories. Coke ovens are eligible for extensions until 2020 if they make extrastringent reductions in the first round.

The alternative fuels program should significantly reduce toxic emissions from vehicles. Additional cuts from cars or fuel are required after an EPA study. Benzene and formaldehyde must be controlled.

Acid Rain

In the first phase, the 111 dirtiest power plants in 21 states must cut sulfur dioxide emissions by 1995 for a total cut nationwide of 5 million tons. Two-year extensions can be given to plants that commit to buy scrubbing devices that allow continued use of high-sulfur coal.

In the second phase, more than 200 additional power plants must make sulfur dioxide cuts by 2000, for a total nationwide cut of 10 million tons. This deadline can be extended until 2004 for plants that use new clean-coal technology.

An innovative trading system is created in which utilities that make extradeep pollution reductions get credits they can sell or swap to utilities that want to increase their emissions. Bonus pollution credits are awarded to dirty utilities that install scrubbers and to power plants in high-growth and extremely low-polluting states plus the hard-hit Midwest.

A nationwide cap on utility sulfur dioxide emissions is imposed after the year 2000.

Utilities must cut nitrogen oxide emissions by 2 million tons a year, or about 25 percent, beginning in 1995.

No help is provided for ratepayers beyond changes in the trading system. Coal miners and others put out of work because of clean air rules may qualify for extra weeks of unemployment pay under a $250 million five-year job assistance program.

Source: *Adapted from R. Buchholz, A. Marcus, and J. Post.* Managing Environmental Issues: A Casebook *(Englewood Cliffs, N.J.: Prentice Hall 1991), pp 96–97.*

Discussion Questions

1. What should Du Pont's strategy be vis-a-vis the proposed legislation?
2. What types of changes in Du Pont's business strategy will the Clean Air Act signify?
3. What opportunities are there for Du Pont with the passage of this bill?
4. How will the passage of the bill affect Du Pont's position vis-a-vis its competitors?

Endnotes

1. This case was written by Mark C. Jankus under the editorial guidance of Alfred A. Marcus, Curtis L. Carlson School of Management, University of Minnesota. See R. Buchholz, A. Marcus, J. Post, *Managing Environmental Issues: A Casebook* (Englewood Cliffs, N.J.: Prentice Hall, 1992).
2. B. Rosewicz and R. Koenig, "How Clean Air Bill Will Force Du Pont into Costly Moves," *The Wall Street Journal*, May 25, 1990, p. A1.
3. *The Clean Air Act: A Primer & Glossary,* pamphlet, Clean Air Working Group.
4. B. Rosewicz and R. Gutfeld, "Clean Air Legislation Will Cost Americans $21.5 Billion a Year," *The Wall Street Journal*, March 28, 1990, p. A11.
5. D. Wessel, "Air Bill's Cost-Benefit Data Look Very Foggy Close Up," *The Wall Street Journal*, May 25, 1990, p. A7.
6. R. Gutfeld, "Firms, Environmentalists Gear Up for Crucial Round," *The Wall Street Journal*, May 25, 1990, p. A7.
7. A. Sullivan and R. Gutfeld, "Bill Would Require Oil Companies to Sell Advanced Fuel," *The Wall Street Journal*, May 25, 1990, p. A7.
8. J. Abramson, "Big Oil May Have Misfired in Heavy Lobbying Drive," *The Wall Street Journal*, May 25, 1990, p. A6.

V

TECHNOLOGY AND THE LAW

CHAPTER

15

THE PROMISE OF TECHNOLOGY

Our decisions to do something positive, the full consequences of which will be drawn out over many days to come, can only be taken as a result of animal spirits—of a spontaneous urge to action rather than inaction, and not as the outcome of a weighted average of quantitative benefits multiplied by quantitative probabilities. . . . Thus, if the animal spirits are dimmed and the spontaneous optimism falters, leaving us to depend on nothing but a mathematical expectation, enterprise will fade and die . . . [and] individual initiative will only be adequate when reasonable calculation is supplemented and supported by animal spirits, so that the thought of ultimate loss, which often overtakes pioneers, . . . is put aside as a healthy man puts aside the expectation of death.

John Maynard Keynes[1], *General Theory of Interest, Employment, and Money.*

Introduction and Chapter Objectives

This chapter is about the contributions technology can make to economic growth and prosperity. Forecasting technology change is important for managers. We discuss some of the key technologies that are likely to play a role in the future. We ask, why do some technologies succeed, while others fail? In addition, we will review technological developments in Japan. The chapter concludes with a description of the innovation process, emphasizing the important social role of technology.

509

The Importance of Technology

Economic growth—the capacity of a nation to produce the goods and services its people desire—is dependent on an array of factors, including the quantity and quality of labor and natural resources; capital, machines, and equipment, which are increased by savings and investment; and values that encourage hard work, diligence, and thrift (see Chapter 11). Other factors needed for economic growth include: a high level of technology and the knowledge to convert the factors of production into goods and services. Technology leads to increasing mechanization and gives rise to an efficient division of labor, which improves productivity and permits the accumulation of capital.

All the classical economists of the late 18th and early 19th centuries, including Adam Smith, David Ricardo, and John Stuart Mill, stressed technology as a critical component of economic development.[2] Technology is both the cause of many of the world's worst environmental problems and the best hope for their cure. Thomas Malthus's pessimism that runaway population would lead to increasing misery as the world's population expanded more rapidly than the food supply was based on the premise that technological developments would fall behind population growth.

Technological pioneers often are stubborn dreamers who stick tenaciously to their vision despite the odds against their succeeding (see the special feature, "A Technological Leader: Bill Gates"). Since few new ideas bear fruit, it sometimes takes foolhardy optimism to overcome a natural inclination toward caution.

Waves of Innovation

The Russian economist Kondratiev expounded a theory that economic progress was not linear.[3] It took place in long waves, each of them lasting about half a century. Each wave had periods of prosperity, recession, depression, and recovery. Joseph Schumpeter, the Austrian economist, connected these waves of growth to technological innovations.[4] The first period (1782–1845) saw major innovations in steam power and textiles; the second (1845–1892) in railroads, iron, coal, and construction; and the third (1892–1948) in electrical power, automobiles, chemicals, and steel.

Technological change is not gentle. According to Schumpeter, it is like a "series of explosions." Innovations concentrate in specific sectors, in leading-edge industries that provide the momentum for growth. These leading sectors propel the economy forward; without them, economic growth is not possible.

Entrepreneurs, seeing the opportunities for profit, vigorously

A Technological Leader, Bill Gates

Bill Gates is the founder of Microsoft Corporation in Redmond, Washington, just outside Seattle.[1] Microsoft created MS-DOS, the operating system that runs IBM and IBM-compatible personal computers and that set the standard for the industry. It allows IBM and other computers to use the same word processing, spreadsheet, and other systems.

Gates combines qualities not often found in a business leader: a grand technological vision and sophistication, a ruthless drive to succeed, and a shrewd ability to make deals.[2] He has been characterized as a person who hates to lose and who is a nonstop worrier and workaholic who has been plagued by periods of doubt and depression despite his meteoric rise to the top. Feared by his rivals for his fierce competitive drive, he believes that in the rapidly changing computer software business, opportunities missed are irretrievably gone; there are no second chances to catch up with a new technical wave.

Gates has pursued his ambitions in a single-minded fashion. Consumed with achieving stunning business success in an industry created by technical hackers who showed little concern for business matters, he now wants Microsoft to dominate in all areas of emerging computer software technology. This would include putting its software into fax machines and electronic notepads and supplying data bases and networking and home-entertainment software. He regrets the company's inability to develop software that ties PC's together and its inability to develop a distinctive data management product.

A recent Microsoft product is a new program, Windows 3.0, which has been designed to make it easier for personal computer users to run their machines. Microsoft's last major project, a new operating system called OS/2, did not live up to the firm's expectations. Windows 3.0 is designed to operate like Apple Computer's easy-to-use operating system Apple has sued Microsoft because the similarity, in its view, is so great.

IBM and Apple have grown in their resentment of Microsoft. They now have united against it to develop their own software. As the computer industry matures, future competition is likely to be intense. Technological leadership will be the key to success in this highly competitive environment.

Bill Gates is an intensely competitive individual who knows the technical specifications of his competitors' products and the claims they make in their advertisements and who tells his product managers to constantly think of the competition.

---

[1]G. P. Zachary, "Opening of 'Windows' Shows How Bill Gates Succeeds in Software," *The Wall Street Journal*, 1990, May 21, p. A1.

[2]Ibid.

exploit new technologies. The pioneers are followed by a swarm of imitators. The combined activity of the pioneers and followers generates boom conditions. Soon, however, there are so many imitators that prices fall and bust follows. This process is one of "creative destruction" in which lagging sectors fall behind. Their time passes; they wither and die or are kept afloat by government subsidy and bailout. To spur a revival, new innovation is needed.

Alternative Futures

The prosperity of the post–World War II period has been built on innovations in semiconductors, consumer electronics, aerospace, pharmaceuticals, petrochemicals, and synthetic and composite materials (see Exhibit 15–1).[5] A dynamic growth phase existed from 1945 to 1964, with the mid to late 1960s being a period of consolidation. By the end of the 1960s, many markets were saturated. The technologies of the postwar period were reaching a state of maturity.

As markets stagnated, manufacturing unemployment grew. Many companies lowered production costs by making incremental manufacturing improvements. They exported jobs to foreign countries where labor costs were lower. After 1973, growth rates throughout the world declined (see Chapter 11). The post-World War II boom lost its momentum.

The Limits to Growth

A report produced by the Club of Rome in 1972 ignited a controversy about the viability of continued growth.[6] Pessimists claimed that the human race was in imminent danger. On the other hand, the late Herman Kahn, who, with others (H. Brown, O. Helmer, W. Harman, B. Fuller, etc.), was among the first to develop modern forecasting, contended that technological innovations and rational policies could push back apparent limits bringing about huge increases in global living standards.[7]

Methodological differences existed between these camps. The Club of Rome relied on computerized global modeling, whereas Kahn depended on qualified trend extrapolation. The forecasters' methodologies and beliefs influenced their predictions.

EXHIBIT 15–1   Waves of Innovation

1782–1845	Steam power, textiles
1845–1892	Railroads, iron, coal, construction
1892–1948	Electrical power, automobiles, chemicals, steel
1948–present	Semiconductors, consumer electronics, aerospace, pharmaceuticals, petrochemicals, synthetic and composite materials

Technological Pessimists

The systems approach of the Club of Rome considered interrelated features of world growth simultaneously, rather than studying each facet in isolation.[8] J. W. Forrester of the Sloan School of Management at MIT had used this approach to describe the functioning of industrial concerns. Using the same methodology, he developed a world model. The work carried out for the Club of Rome was an extension of Forrester's models. It extrapolated worldwide values for population, available resources, pollution, and agricultural and industrial output to the end of the next century. Feedback mechanisms charted how a change in one parameter affected others. The results indicated a crisis sometime in the next century, with rapid decline in per capita consumption. According to the Club of Rome authors, the crisis could be averted only if very Draconian measures, the most important of which was a zero increase in population, were taken in the very near future.

Technical criticisms of the Club of Rome report included:[9]

1. Data bases were not well developed enough for such far-reaching conclusions.
2. Assumptions of estimated levels of available nonrenewable resources were pessimistic.
3. Insufficient account had been taken of likely technological improvements.
4. Sociological, political, and psychological considerations were ignored.
5. The world was treated as a whole rather than as a system of different political and economic entities.

The authors admitted that the data required for a fully satisfactory world model were unavailable. However, they held that their model was more satisfactory than alternative ones, and that the concepts and ideas incorporated into it were clearly exposed for discussion and debate.

Technological Optimists

The late Herman Kahn's forecasts were based on trend extrapolation, scenario writing, and simple intuition. Long-term trends were the most basic device, but inasmuch as trends did not always move in straight lines, qualified extrapolation was added to develop exploratory forecasts. *The Year 2000* was appropriately subtitled *A Framework for Speculation on the Next Thirty-Three Years* because of the conjectural nature of the forecasts.[10] Acknowledging that new crises or unexpected events might divert current trends and alter expectations, the authors maintained that the following trends were likely to occur:

- High growth rates in GNP per capita.
- Increased emphasis on life's meaning and purpose.
- Extreme turmoil in the developing nations.
- Possibility for nativist, messianic, or other mass movements in the United States.
- Reemergence of Japan as a major world power.
- The further rise of Europe and China.
- The relative decline of the United States and the Russian Federation.

Kahn et al. projected a continuation of the marked economic growth that began with the Industrial Revolution and accelerated during the 1950s and 1960s. It would be accompanied by rapid technological innovations in the use of robots and machines; home education by video; computerized and programmed learning; cheap, convenient, and reliable birth control; extensive use of artificial limbs; and commercial extraction of oil from shale. To allow for surprises, Kahn et al. included variations from the standard projections. Variations could be brought about by invasion, war, civil strife and revolution, famine, pestilence, despotism, natural disaster, depression or economic stagnation, and new religious philosophies.

Nonetheless, the United States would have an economy in which service-oriented activities were dominant, and by the year 2020, the standard of living would be three to six times as high as it was in 1965. Leisure time would increase and political processes remain democratic. Politically, economically, and militarily, the United States would be relatively secure.

This version of the future assumed that key trends from the past would continue to operate in similar ways in the future, though with some variation. However, critics of *The Year 2000* maintained that it took insufficient notice of countervailing trends that would yield outcomes vastly different from what was predicted.

The Postindustrial Society

Daniel Bell offered an ideal concept of postindustrial society—an analytical construct of diverse changes in society and a logical construction of what *could* be.[11] A postindustrial society differed from an industrial society in five ways:

1. In the economic sector, there was change from a *goods*-producing to a *service*-producing economy.
2. Occupational distribution was affected by the preeminence of *a professional and technical class.*

3. *Theoretical knowledge* became the central source of innovation for society.

4. An orientation to the future would exist, with the control of technology and *technological assessment* becoming primary activities.

5. Decision making would be influenced by *new intellectual technologies* such as modeling, simulation, cybernetics, decision theory, systems analysis, and other techniques.

A primary source of problems in postindustrial society would be the widening of so-called disjunctions between the social structure, the polity, and the culture. These realms, according to Bell, were governed by called conflicting axial principles. The principle of "meritocratic economizing," which governs the social structure, was incompatible with both the principle of participation, which governs the polity, and the principle of fulfillment and enhancement of self, which governs the culture. According to Bell, postindustrial society would see an increased clash of different realms. This clash, arising from each individual's following "his own whim" would lead necessarily "to a greater need for collective regulation . . . [with a reduction of personal freedom]." [12]

Bell combatted the "apocalyptic hysteria" of the Club of Rome forecasts, on the one hand, and the "technological euphoria" of Kahn's forecasts, on the other. [13] He felt that Kahn's notion of a postindustrial society was too narrow. Kahn saw it merely in terms of mass consumption with the only problem being how to respond to abundance. Bell believed that rising costs and limited resources would generate continued scarcity, and that technological innovation would be needed to deal with these challenges.

The "Powers of the Mind"

George Gilder extended Bell's vision of postindustrial society. He argued that "wealth in the form of physical resources" was "steadily declining in value and significance," and that "the powers of the mind" were "everywhere ascendant over the brute force of things." [14] Prior economic activity involved the manipulation and movement of "massive objects against friction and gravity." [15] The Industrial Revolution was built upon physical labor, natural resources, and capital. However, ascendant nations and corporations today were not masters of "material resources but of ideas and technologies." [16]

Electronics, computer software, and telecommunications relied upon human creativity. They were the emancipators of human beings from their dependence upon the physical world. The microchip, according to Gilder, symbolized this "worldwide shift of the worth of goods from materials to ideas" as the material costs of the product constituted only about 2 percent of the total costs of production.[17] The most valuable part of the microchip was the idea for its design. The rise of the mind as a source of wealth spanned industries. It would be among the most important forces in the 21st century.

Technological Forecasting

Managers have to forecast technological change to anticipate breakthroughs early when the response times are long and they are in a better position to respond to them.[18] Technology is dynamic and has important implications for business expansion and contraction. Estimates are that as much as 25 percent of existing technology is replaced every year.

The means managers have for coping with these changes include simple trend analysis, monitoring expert opinion and other sources of information for indications of changes, and constructing alternative scenarios.[19]

Trends.   Trends in one area are important because they often forecast trends in another (e.g., military jet speeds foretell commercial jet speeds). Managers can extrapolate, for example, the number of components needed to manufacture one product to estimate the number to manufacture a similar product. But trends have to be analyzed with caution. Simple extrapolation can be deceiving if it discounts the impact one trend has on another, ignores how the human response to trends can change their direction, and has no room for surprises. Economic forecasts are good at predicting the future based on the past so long as the future resembles the past in most important ways. However, radical breaks take place (e.g., the 1973 Arab oil embargo), which no economist can predict.

Experts.   Expert opinion can be used, but experts, too, make mistakes. The British Parliament established a committee of experts at the end of the 19th century to investigate the potential of Thomas Edison's incandescent lamp. It found the idea unworthy of attention.[20] During World War II, a panel of experts selected by the federal government did not believe that an intercontinental ballistic missile could accurately deliver its payload 3,000 miles away.[21] The Rand Corporation, a think-tank in Southern California, has devised the "Delphi method" to aggregate the beliefs of experts about particular issues.[22] Each expert is asked to predict important events and to clarify the reasons why he or she believes the event is likely to occur. Successive requestioning in light of the answers provided sharpens the results obtained.

Alternative Scenarios.   Often when the future is uncertain, the best coping method is to construct alternative scenarios.[23] Managers create a series of possible sequences of future events that take the uncertainty into account. Shell Oil Company, for instance, forecast three different energy scenarios in 1972. It assessed immediate (2 years), middle-range (10 years), and long-range (25 years) implications based on the scenarios. This exercise forced Shell's managers to think through what they would do if unfavorable circumstances should arise and provided them with the opportunity to better manage future contingencies when they came.

Managers need to monitor the environment for signals that may be the forerunners of significant changes. To do so, they have to clarify their ideas about which indicators to follow. Then they have to understand how to put the information together and interpret it for the purposes of decision making. In a free society, the amount of information produced is immense. Professional conferences, technical papers, and the media yield data that vie for a manager's attention. What to focus on and what to ignore—distinguishing the true signal from the noise—is a perpetual problem.

The Next Wave of Innovation

For economic growth to take off, a new wave of innovation is needed. But from where is it likely to come? The following technologies may play an important role.[24]

1. *Artificial intelligence.* Computer use will continue to expand to areas where human intelligence formerly was applied. The computers will be able to carry out such activities as learning, adapting, recognizing, and self-correction.

2. *Genetic engineering.* The genetic code of living organisms will be mapped, restructured, and remodeled to enhance or eliminate certain traits. This potential will allow scientists to predict and correct genetic diseases. It will give them the ability to create new drugs such as Interluekin-2 to fight diseases such as cancer. It should allow them to create crops that are pest-resistant and drought-proof.

3. *Advanced computers.* Evolving chip technologies open up the promise of the development of faster and more powerful computers. Sarnoff chips, that contain 100 or more tiny lasers, have been used to create the first functional optoelectric integrated circuit. They will be used in powerful new desktop computers in the future.

4. *Bioelectricity.* Damaged or dysfunctioning nerves, muscles, and glands can be stimulated to promote their repair and restore their healthy functioning. Currently, this technique can be used in humans with severed bones and defective hearts and lungs. It speeds the healing rates of wounds and is an alternative to addictive pain killers.

5. *Multisensory robotics.* Robots can be made that will be able to do more than simple, repetitive tasks. Useful service robots such as smart shopping-carts are in the works, as are mobile helpers in factories and for personal use.

6. *Parallel processing.* This technique permits many computers to be used simultaneously in dealing with a problem. It greatly enhances computer power and performance and thereby increases the complexity of the scientific and technical tasks that can be handled.

7. *Digital electronics.* Information from audio, video, and film can be digitized so that it can be retrieved more quickly. The use of optical memory systems such as optical disks, film, and bar-code readers is likely to be expanded.

8. *Lasers.* Lasers are light amplified by the stimulated emission of radiation. They permit holography (3-D imagery), which may become common in advertising. Also, microwave scalpels equipped with lasers are likely to replace the metal scalpels now used in surgery.

9. *Fiber optics.* Fiber optics carry up to four signals at once (television, telephone, radio, and computer). They promise to greatly improve and expand communications.

10. *Microwaves.* New applications are being developed beyond sending wireless digital information on satellite dishes and using heating devices such as the microwave oven. Possibilities include microwave clothes dryers and cancer treatment systems.

11. *Advanced satellites.* As more countries send satellites into orbit, satellites will be used for new purposes. Possible new uses include oil and mineral exploration and pinpoint surveillance and mapping.

12. *Solar energy.* Photovoltaic cells convert sunlight to energy (see Case IVA, "ARCO Solar Inc."). New uses should develop beyond pocket calculators and remote power applications. Solar technologies can be used for rural electrification projects in third world countries and as alternatives to auto and jet fuel.

13. *Microtransistors.* A quantum transistor 100 times smaller and 1,000 times faster than current transistors has been developed. If mass-produced, it would revolutionize the electronics industry.

14. *Molecular design.* New materials can be constructed molecule by molecule and atom by atom by using supercomputers in their design. Tailor-made enzymes for industrial use have been developed. Similar products promise to move out of the lab.

15. *New polymers.* Lighter, stronger, more resistant to heat, and able to conduct electricity, these new polymers can be used in many products. The products range from garbage bags to Army tanks, ball bearings, moldable batteries, and running shoes.

16. *High-tech ceramics.* These materials promise to be resistant to corrosion, wear, and high temperatures. They will be used in autos and elsewhere to create cleaner-running engines. They open up the

possibility of a new engine design, such as the gas turbine, that would be more efficient and less polluting.

17. *Fiber-reinforced composites.* These composite materials, lightweight and noncorrosive, often are stronger than steel. They can be used in buildings, bridges, and aircraft.

18. *Superconductors.* These materials carry electricity without loss of energy. They make possible less-expensive but more-advanced magnetic imaging machines for hospitals. They can be used in TV antennas and faster computer circuits. Ultimately, developments would permit the construction of magnetically levitated trains.

These technologies involve many fields, from telecommunications to computers, health, transportation, and energy. They rely on new materials and manufacturing processes for their realization. They promise to extend human sensory capabilities and intellectual processes.

Obstacles to Adopting Promising Technologies

In theory, these technologies are very promising, but formidable obstacles stand in the way of their widescale adoption and use. A promising idea, commonly referred to as an invention, is not the same as an innovation.[25] An invention is merely the creation of the idea in the laboratory. It is the test of a certain principle, an act of technical creativity wherein a concept that may be suitable for patenting is described. By contrast, innovation is putting this idea into widespread use; it is the effort to commercially exploit the idea, to assure its broad application. The following sections describe some of the obstacles that have been encountered in commercializing two of the technologies previously listed.

Artificial Intelligence

So far, the marketplace applications of artificial intelligence have been very disappointing.[26] Many companies established in the mid-1980s have ceased to exist, and others have shrunk in size and cut back their work forces. Sales that were supposed to be in the billions of dollars did not exceed $600 million in 1990.[27] Much of the venture capital funding and many of the talented technical people who were attracted to the field abandoned it.

Artificial intelligence (AI) allows computers to mimic ordinary human intelligence. It includes systems that help machines in factories "see," that enable computers to analyze aerial photographs, and that permit language recognition for translation or dictation. Security applications for guarding warehouses have been developed, but AI's greatest promise is in expert systems—software packages that can imitate the reasoning and decision processes of specialists in various fields using their rules of thumb and available data.

A successful application of AI was its use by American Express Company in its credit authorization department. A program was developed to review cardholders' requests for credit to make big purchases. The customer's credit history was reviewed in an instant, and if problems existed, they were identified immediately for employees to investigate.

Despite the promise of these and other applications, the developers of AI have not shown a good understanding of potential markets. For instance, Applied Expert Systems tried to sell a $50,000 software package to professional financial planners, claiming that the computer could produce a better financial plan than the planners.[28] Understandably, the professional planners felt threatened by this claim, and they refused to buy the package. Applied Expert Systems then had to find an alternative market for the product, and it tried to sell it to banks and insurance companies, which were less threatened.

Another artificial intelligence program, called LISP, was simply too expensive. LISP Machine Inc., Xerox, and Texas Instruments all had workstations that used LISP, but the program cost as much as $100,000, which was more than most customers were willing to pay.[29]

The problems in the AI industry may have been due to the fact that many of its founders were researchers who lacked a good sense of market forces. Initially, they were very well funded and spent money freely, but without a sense of the limits of either time or budgets, which are essential in making a venture a commercial success.

Genetic Engineering

Genetic engineering companies have fared somewhat better than the artificial intelligence companies.[30] Sales in 1990 were about $1 billion and were projected to be much higher in the mid-1990s.[31] Again, venture capitalists had invested hundreds of millions of dollars in the industry, but as of 1990, only nine new biotechnology drugs had come to the market and only eight were waiting regulatory approval. Seventy-five percent of the 1,000 or so companies involved in the industry were unprofitable; most were still developing products in the labs.

The technology was very seductive, and entrepreneurs and scientists hyped the chances of its success. However, researchers had trouble focusing on the specific products they would make and often misjudged the time it would take to test the products and obtain regulatory approval. For example, Liposome Co. believed that fatty, water-filled membranes could be used to deliver drugs more effectively. To identify the five diseases that would be addressed, it had to screen more than a million possibilities. Then, it had to develop a method by which the drugs could be delivered through the membranes. Finally, it required large-scale manufacturing methods.

Five federal agencies have some jurisdiction over biotechnology products; guidelines are very unclear, so regulators have been an obstacle to commercialization. Many companies have had to maintain manufacturing facilities at below full capacity and sales forces that cannot market a product because they are awaiting regulatory acceptance. To get around the regulatory process, companies have looked for applications that minimize the need for regulatory approval. They also have allied themselves with large drug and chemical companies that are experienced at obtaining approval. The large manufacturers help them shoulder the risks, and they benefit from the marketing capabilities of the manufacturers.

The large manufacturers that have entered the biotechnology business on their own have also not been particularly successful. Monsanto, for instance, made a huge investment in biotechnology research.[32] A bovine growth hormone (BGH) that it developed to boost cows' milk production was banned by the governor of Wisconsin after opposition from dairy farmers who were supposed to be the product's main customers. BGH is a protein similar to the one cows make naturally; it is injected into the cows twice a month and increases yields by 10 to 20 percent. Farmers, however, feared that a milk glut would lower prices. Consumer anxieties about artificial foods and the fears voiced by big grocery chains like Krogers that people would not buy milk from cows injected with BGH have prevented the product from being widely used.

Environmentalists have criticized another type of genetically engineered product Monsanto is developing—new strains of cotton and soybean that can withstand spraying from Monsanto's herbicide Roundup. Pesticides can kill crops as well as weeds and are useful only early in the growing season, before crops break through the soil. But pesticide-resistant crops could withstand herbicides application later, as the crops mature. However, environmentalists see Monsanto's effort to develop pesticide-resistant crops as a means to get farmers more hooked on pesticides, especially Monsanto's, and they wonder why Monsanto cannot work on pest-resistant crops rather than crops that resist pesticides.

Biotechnology, too, may make it possible to use plant cells to make large quantities of valuable substances that plants make in small quantities.[33] And genetically manufactured products such as melanin would offer protection from skin cancer. Other genetically manufactured products would modify or enhance the flavor of fruits and vegetables, help in the petroleum-refining process, and protect people from inadvertent exposure to radiation. Commercialization depends on whether these products can overcome the regulatory hurdles and gain public acceptance.

Why Technologies Fail

However promising, many ideas fail to come to find widescale application (see Exhibit 15–2). According to some estimates, only 1 to 10 percent of all projects succeed depending on the industry and the circumstances.[34] After a commercial launch has occurred and less-attractive R&D projects and proposals have been weeded out, the success rate is higher. Still, failure is common, and the reasons for it are difficult for managers to control: it is hard to pick winners.

Economists distinguish between conditions where the odds of success are known with certainty (e.g., flipping a coin), which they call risk, and conditions where the odds of success are unknown, which they call uncertainty.[35] Classification is a question of degree. The art of assigning statistical probabilities is just that—an art. When the odds are known with certainty, the situation is insurable, but technical innovation is an uninsurable phenomenon. Before the fact, the odds of success cannot be stated with precision.[36] Moreover, better management does not easily reduce the failure rate. Managers cannot always manipulate the situation to their liking or produce the results they desire. After the fact, it may be easy to say why success or failure occurs, but it is not easy to know what to do beforehand. What can be recognized after the fact cannot always be controlled while the situation is evolving.

Technical and Commercial Feasibility

Most managers have powerful reasons to keep risk to a minimum. In deliberating about whether to undertake a particular project, they have to consider technical and commercial feasibility. They have to estimate:[37]

1. Probable development, production, and marketing costs.
2. The approximate timing of these costs.
3. Probable future income streams.
4. When the income streams are likely to develop.

All of these calculations are fraught with uncertainty. The only way to reduce uncertainty is to undertake safe projects.[38] Thus, managers tend

---

EXHIBIT 15–2   **Obstacles to the Commercialization of Technologies**

Artificial intelligence:	Failure to understand potential markets
Genetic engineering:	Unclear regulatory responsibilities
	Consumer anxieties
	Environmental criticism

to concentrate on innovations where success is easy. The bias is toward simple, well-tread areas, since fundamental research and invention involve greater uncertainties.

Managers establish new generations of existing products, introduce new models, and differentiate a product further rather than creating different products and new product lines. They reduce uncertainty by licensing other people's inventions, imitating other people's product introductions, modifying existing processes, and making minor technical improvements. An automobile with a new type of engine, for instance, is less likely to be introduced than an auto with simple modifications of an existing engine.

For a new product to be launched, managers must have an optimistic bias.[39] Without it, the contemplation of failure overwhelms the inclination to proceed. An optimistic bias affects all types of investment decisions; innovations are no different. Entirely sober and realistic assessments of the actual chances of success would lead to less innovation than occurs. Engineers, for instance, are known to make optimistic estimates of development costs.[40] Actual development costs and probabilities of technical success, even in the best of circumstances, are hard to determine.

Moreover, it is difficult to predict market success. Market launch and growth in sales are distant in time, and future conditions vary. Reactions of competitors to the threat of new products are unknown. Achieving an advance understanding of the costs, given changing economic circumstances, is difficult. Also, it is hard to know in advance how long a product will be on the market and how dominant it will be, given the threat of technical obsolescence.

The empirical evidence appears to confirm that "early estimates of future markets have been wildly inaccurate."[41] Even with successful products, the developers did not recognize the extent to which they would be successful. For instance, the developers of computers thought that less than 4,000 would be sold in the United States by 1965, and that the market would be confined to a few specialized government bureaus and scientific applications. They did not dream that over 20,000 units would be sold in the United States by 1965 and that the potential market was unlimited.

Even with sophisticated techniques for estimating project success, companies make egregious errors. For instance, no firm was more experienced than Du Pont with new product introductions, and none spared less expense in estimating costs and likely results, yet Du Pont has lost large sums with some products before it withdrew them from the market. Three types of uncertainty that affect new product development—technical, business conditions and the market, and government—have to be considered.

Technical Uncertainty

Even after prototype testing, pilot plant work, trial production, and test marketing, technical uncertainty is likely to exist in the early stages of introducing products (see Exhibit 15–3). The question typically is not whether a product will work but one of degree—of standards of performance under different operating conditions and of the costs of improving performance under these conditions. Unexpected problems can arise before a product reaches the market, in the early stages of a promising commercial launch, and after product introduction, as the examples below illustrate.

Before a product reaches the market: Unexpected problems affected the pharmaceutical company Syntex even before it got a new product, called Enprostil, on the market.[42] Syntex needed a new product because the patent on its major money-maker, Naprosyn, an antiinflammatory drug, was about to expire. It thought it had come up with a new ulcer drug, called Enprostil, which not only eased the pain of ulcers but also lowered cholesterol. With about 23 million people worldwide suffering from ulcers, drugs that treat the problem, like SmithKline Beecham's Tagamet and Glaxo Holdings PLC's Zantac, yielded substantial profits. However, the principal researcher who pioneered Enprostil's development spotted evidence of dangerous blood clots that might produce new ulcers, and test-tube clotting suggested that it might pose a risk of heart attack or stroke. Enprostil had trouble winning FDA approval and was not a commercial success.

The early stages of production: Serious setbacks can also occur in the early stages of a promising commercial launch. For instance, Weyerhaeuser Company sought to become an important player in the disposable diaper market with its Ultrasofts product.[43] Ultrasofts had superior features—a cloth-like cover and superabsorbent pulp material woven into the pad designed to keep babies super dry. Consumer tests showed that parents favored it two to one over competing brands. The advertising and promotion campaign offered coupons saving parents $1 per package to try the product. Procter & Gamble and Kimberly-Clark Co., which together controlled 85 percent of the $3.8 billion baby diaper

---

EXHIBIT 15–3   **Technical Uncertainty**

- Whether product will work
- Performance under different operating conditions:
    Before product reaches market
    In early stages of promising commercial launch
    After product introduction

market, came back with aggressive cost cutting and promotion campaigns to keep customers loyal. Meanwhile, manufacturing problems occurred in Weyerhaeuser's Bowling Green, Kentucky, plant. The system that sprayed the superabsorbent material into the diapers started to break down and a fire broke out. Weyerhaeuser had to raise prices to retailers by 22 percent to cover the unexpected expenses. The retailers refused the product shelf space, and Weyerhaeuser had to withdraw the product from the marketplace.

After a product is on the market: Serious setbacks also take place when a product is on the market.[44] At GE, the appliance division's market share and profits had been falling. It relied on a cumbersome 1950s technology to make compressors in triple the time it took Japanese and Italian manufacturers. The compressor, a pump that creates cold air in a refrigerator, is as crucial to it as an engine is to a car. GE committed $120 million to building a factory to make a newly designed compressor that worked with rotary technology the company had invented for use in air conditioners.[45] The new compressor was lighter and more energy-efficient than the old model. It was identical to the one GE used in air conditioners except for two parts made of powdered metal as opposed to hardened steel. Powdered metal was more easily fabricated to the extreme tolerances that were needed and it was cheaper than steel. Evaluation engineers, however, told the designers that powdered metal had not worked in air conditioners. The designers discounted their views. The test data senior executives saw showed no failures, and a technician's report of having observed excessive heat was ignored. Field testing was limited to about nine months, instead of the usual two years, because managers wanted the product on the market immediately. GE scrapped its old compressors and proudly declared that an American company could still take the lead in world manufacturing. Consumers bought the refrigerators with the new compressor in record numbers, with GE increasing its market share by 2 percentage points, its best showing in years. However, after about a year on the market, some compressors began to fail, and GE, which had sold the refrigerators with five-year warranties, decided to recall and replace them.[46]

General Business Uncertainty

General business uncertainty also affects the introduction of new products. It had a negative effect on General Motors efforts in bringing Saturn to the market.[47] Saturn's introduction at a time of poor economic conditions and overcapacity in the industry meant disappointing sales. When the car was introduced, consumer demand for high-quality small cars with good gasoline mileage was faltering. Dealers had been hand-picked to offer exceptional customer service, but they had been given near-monopoly status, which took away their incentive to offer deep discounts to stimulate sales in case of an economic downturn.[48] GM's labor-management relations at the Saturn facility were different from what was practiced elsewhere (see Case IV–D). Workers, basically, accepted less pay for more control over the production process. Managers and workers in other GM divisions complained that the company's commitment to Saturn drained resources from projects that might have had a greater payback.[49] The expansion at the Saturn facility was occurring at the same time GM was cutting back elsewhere. Touted as a top-quality U.S. small car, the Saturn did not incorporate technology that was more advanced than Japanese technology, nor were the costs of production lower—the expense of building a new production facility had been very high.[50] The promised automation in the production process ("a totally computerized, paperless operation") failed to be realized completely. For about the same amount GM spent setting up the Saturn facility ($2 billion), Honda had established a plant in Ohio that produced twice the number of cars yearly (half a million as opposed to about 250,000 Saturns).[51] Honda expanded in stages, adding capacity as demand required it and more sophisticated production techniques as workers were capable of dealing with them. GM, with its all-or-nothing approach, was devastated by the changing business conditions of the early 1990s when Saturn was introduced.

The Role of Customers.   Pioneering new technologies carries great uncertainties in knowing what consumers want and providing it to them in a timely fashion. Having a good idea is not enough. Models of innovation that start with scientific and technological advances miss the important role that customers play both in the adoption decision and in subsequent refinements.[52]

For example, Motorola's excellence as an engineering company is widely recognized.[53] It won the prestigious Malcolm Baldrige National Quality Award in the United States and the Nikkei Prize in manufacturing in Japan. However, it has been unable to keep its customers from defecting to such rivals as Intel, Sun Microsystems Inc., and Mips Computer Systems Inc. The obsession with technological excellence—its engineers had to create the best-designed, fastest, and highest quality product possible—prevented it from meeting market needs in a timely fashion. It delayed in introducing new products. While competitors were already shipping products to customers, it was still making revisions, refusing to put products on the market before all the problems had been worked out. IBM chose Intel's chip to be the standard in personal computers, not because Motorola's was technically inferior, but because Intel was more responsive to its needs. Motorola did capture nearly 80 percent of the market for microprocessors used in workstations, but the market was much smaller than the personal computer market. Transferring technology from the laboratory to the market is not easily accomplished when technically oriented managers dominate.

Uncertain Government Support

New products also can be hurt by uncertain government support. For instance, high definition television (HDTV) was once a favorite among politicians and business lobbyists in Washington, D.C.[54] Sharp images, perfect sound, and the convenience of large, thin screens had great appeal. The consumer market was considered to be worth over $100 billion. Government and business officials met together to map out a strategy to compete with Japan and other foreign nations. The idea was to have collaboration in developing a new technology in the United States. However, the Bush administration would not cooperate. Its belief was that the government should support only basic research projects. Support for research that had commercial potential should come from the private sector, not government. Thus, the administration cut government support for HDTV. The only American firm willing to take on the risks by itself was Zenith. All other companies exited because the high costs of development were not subsidized.

Striving for Constant Innovation

These examples illustrate the lesson that an innovator cannot afford to rest on its laurels. GM could not assume that since it was the dominant automobile manufacturer in the world, it would remain so. Motorola could not assume that since its engineering was technically superior, customers would continue to reward it by purchasing its products. U.S. television manufacturers could not assume that they would be subsidized to the same extent as their foreign competitors. Firms needs to strive for constant innovation in product introduction, marketing, and financing. Past success does not guarantee success in the future.

For instance, a company that had scored an initial success but was unable to follow up on it was SmithKline Beckman.[55] Tagamet, the ulcer medicine it introduced in 1976, was for a time a huge success. For years the biggest problem the company faced was meeting demand. However, Glaxo Holdings PLC, a British company, developed a competing drug, Zantac, with fewer side effects. SmithKline, meanwhile, was unable to come up with new blockbuster drugs despite spending vast sums on research. In retrospect, it was easy to say that SmithKline did not act quickly enough to build up a world-class research capability, but in the pharmaceutical industry, luck may play as much of a role as talent and organization. There was only so much that SmithKline's management could do to develop new pharmaceuticals. Still, the lesson is this: to maintain its technical and market leadership, a firm has to strive for constant innovation. To remain ahead, it cannot be satisfied with an initial triumph.

Technology-Push and Market-Pull

The "technology-push" model of innovation starts with discoveries in basic science and engineering. From these discoveries new goods and services come to the marketplace. However, numerous empirical studies and descriptions of innovation demonstrate the importance of a clear perception of market needs.[56] Successful innovations need both scientific/technical advances and market appeal (see Exhibit 15–4).

Shumpeter posited that science and technology drove technological change.[57] In his view, exceptionally creative entrepreneurs and researchers in large corporations harnessed the ideas of science and technology and found useful applications. But Schmookler contested this claim, arguing that market factors were more important, and that market growth and potential (i.e., "market-pull") were the main determinants of innovation.[58] Recently, however, researchers have concluded that the linking of these two components, the one deriving from technology and the other from the market, over the product life cycle, is important.

Studies by von Hippel show that about equal amounts of innovation come from scientific/technical people and from manufacturers and users. Frequent interactions between these groups are important.[59] Users have to be sophisticated enough to make technically relevant recommendations, and they have to have the ability to purchase and use the products that incorporate their suggestions.

The challenge innovators face is to match technological opportunity with market need. For managers, this means bringing together the different in-house functions (such as marketing, R&D, and manufacturing) that have a knowledge of consumer needs and scientific and technical developments. The essence of successful innovation, then, is that it fuses technological possibility together with market demand. Exclusively, technology-push or market-pull models are now viewed as

---

EXHIBIT 15–4   Evaluating New Products: The Commercial and Technical Screen

		Technical Potential	
		High	*Low*
Commercial	High	Sure success	Need technical breakthrough
Promise	Low	Need market acceptance	Sure failure

atypical examples of a more general process in which constant interaction takes place between market requirements and scientific achievement.[60]

Although more R&D does not necessarily result in more innovation, market need alone may yield such simple, incremental innovations that they do not add up to much in the long run.[61] In the end, different types of innovation, science and technology–based or market-driven, are necessitated by differing stages in the product life cycle.

Japanese Innovation

Japanese innovation has been more of the market-pull variety.[62] It has relied on imitation, purchase, and copy of foreign technology. Its improvements have been incremental and involve modest, but commercially extremely important, refinements of inventions made elsewhere, most often in the United States.

Buying Western Technology

From 1950 to 1980 Japan bought western technology through more than 30,000 licensing and technology importing agreements for which it paid more than $10 billion.[63] The videotape recorder, for instance, was an American invention, created by Ampex Corporation for television productions. Sony made the changes necessary in video recording to appeal to a mass consumer market. For instance, it introduced the technique called azimuth helical scanning, which allowed a vast amount of viewing material to be put into a very small tape.

Japan has excelled in this type of applied research. However, it has been trying in recent years to go beyond applied research and the adaptation of western technologies and to make original breakthroughs of its own. The nation's leaders realize that it needs to be able to achieve the kinds of scientific and technical breakthroughs that can create new industries and transform an entire economy. Spurred by a desire for self-reliance and national pride, the leaders have been trying to shift Japanese research priorities toward basic science and research.[64] Symbolic of this shift was the 1983 decision by the Japanese Parliament to create 19 new mammoth research and industrial complexes by the year 1990.

Obstacles to Ascendance in Basic Research

The obstacles to Japanese ascendance in basic research are great. Creativity is necessary for success in basic research. The emphasis in Japanese education, however, has been on rote learning and brute memorization, which are designed to give students the skills to pass rigorous standardized tests. The Japanese have succeeded in lifting their average student above what is generally found in the United States. Thus, the average Japanese blue-collar and salaried worker is better educated and more disciplined than the average blue-collar or salaried worker in the United States. However, U.S. elites are probably more skilled than those in Japanese. Japan has had few Nobel Prize winners in the sciences. West Germany has had 4 times as many, Great Britain 10 times as many, and the U.S. 30 times as many.[65]

Since Japanese culture stresses consensus and conformance to group norms, intellectual dialogue and confrontation are not as common. The individual genius who shows disdain for what others do and succeeds despite breaking all the rules is not accepted in Japanese society. In areas where creativity is called for, such as computer software, Japan is lagging behind the United States and other western nations.

The population of graduate students in Japan is much smaller than in the U.S.—only about 3 percent of the total student population, compared with about 12 percent in the United States.[66] Most Japanese research is carried out in corporations, not universities. The corporations do not emphasize doing basic research, but rather finding practical, commercial applications and solving real-world problems.

The Japanese, however, understand that to maintain economic leadership they will have to extend their technical competence beyond the incremental innovations in which they have excelled. They will have to emphasize basic discoveries. The Japanese realize that the time when they could simply live off western technology is passing, that to succeed in the long run they will have to export original ideas. In such areas as automobile manufacture, cameras, memory chips, video equipment, robots, fiber optics, video equipment, quality steels, and composite materials, the Japanese are making great strides. About half the patents filed worldwide come from Japanese corporations.[67] Japanese technology promises to produce flat television sets with very high quality pictures, telephones that automatically translate between English and Japanese, and high-speed trains suspended magnetically a few inches above the ground. These advances are mostly in hardware areas. They continue to show the Japanese genius for manufacturing. But they do not indicate that the Japanese have caught up with the United States and other western nations in the creative software types of industries such as movies, records, and pharmaceuticals.

Product Focused

Japan has more technical and scientific workers per capita than any nation in the world (5,000 per million of population in comparison to 3,500 in the United States, and 2,500 in Germany), and it spends as much on research and development as a percentage of GNP as the United States and more than any European nation.[68] Japan's research, moreover, is not directed toward military needs. Inasmuch as it is conducted in corporations and not in universities or specialized research institutions and it is not military oriented, it has more of a product focus than research in the United States. And Japan has the capital (from a high rate of savings) to spend on new factories to exploit the new products it brings to markets. It is able to create the new products and to export much of the manufacturing technology to other countries in the Pacific Rim where the labor costs are cheap.

The successes Japan has enjoyed have been based on many factors (see Exhibit 15–5).[69]

· First is the fusion factor—the ability to blend incremental improvements from sometimes alien fields to create a product with entirely new features. The fact that Japanese industrial groups (the keiretsu) have companies that are so heavily invested in each other facilitates this process.

· Second is the recognition in Japan that making a fundamental breakthrough is insufficient, that to be really successful at innovation it is necessary to devise a better way to manufacture and market the product. For instance, Corning Glass, an American Company, first developed fiber optics, but Japanese companies solved the practical problems that prevented customers from using this product; for instance, fiber optic cables fell apart too easily and the messages sent often were lost during transmission. Also, robots with various forms of "soft automation" have given the Japanese great advantages in easily redesigning their production facilities in response to changing consumer preferences. Japanese engineers tend to take cost factors and manufacturability into consideration from the beginning, while American engineers tend, simply, to want to see if a project can be carried out from a technical point of view regardless of the cost.

· Third, Japanese managers do not rigidly adhere to rate-of-return criteria in assessing new projects since they believe that one successful innovation is likely to breed another, and that these waves of innovation

---

EXHIBIT 15–5   Characteristics of Japanese Innovation

· Fusion—a blend of incremental improvements from different fields.
· A recognition that marketing and manufacturing innovation have to go hand in hand with product innovation.
· Less reliance on conventional rate-of-return criteria and belief in waves of innovation.
· Insistence on speed in getting a product to market in effort to obtain feedback from customers.
· Persistence and refusal to accept failure.

cannot be predicted by conventional rate-of-return techniques. For instance, a new optical chip fashioned from gallium arsenide could both promote new tools for chip manufacture and solve remaining problems in developing high-definition television (HDTV), thereby speeding innovations in both areas.

· Fourth, the Japanese typically believe that speed in getting a product to the market is critical. Even if the product is not perfect, it is better for customers to buy the product and get used to it. In doing so, companies developing the product can earn needed income while receiving invaluable feedback about what the next generation of the product should be like. This feedback cannot be obtained from conventional marketing studies. For instance, U.S. scientists at MIT developed a machine capable of recognizing over 400 words, but had no plans for immediately bringing this machine to the market, while the Japanese telecommunications giant Nippon Telegraph and Telephone had a machine that recognized only 32 words but it already was working on a commercial application.

· Fifth, Japanese engineers apparently do not know the meaning of failure. They push on to success regardless of the obstacles. Studies of the working habits of Japanese and American engineers show that after a hard day of work American engineers go home to their families. Japanese engineers are more willing to stay on the job and continue what they are doing. The so-called samurai spirit is built into a culture that believes that only attack is acceptable, that retreat or surrender cannot be tolerated because they would be accompanied by great shame.

As U.S. scientists become reluctant to share their technology with the Japanese, the Japanese will have to build their success on an indigenous capability for invention.[70] Nonetheless, they have developed many important and unique qualities that have led to technological successes, and these qualities are likely to persist.

The Innovation Process

What should be remembered is that new ideas rarely are carried out as expected, product gestation periods are often longer than anticipated, and R&D costs are often underestimated while markets are overestimated. After analyzing numerous innovations, Van de Ven et al. conclude that the innovation process typically consists of the following types of stages:[71]

1. The gestation period of an invention, which lasts for many years, after which seemingly coincidental events occur that set the stage for the innovation to be initiated.

2. Often it is internal or external shocks to an organization that get things going because without them the level of apathy is great.

3. Dissatisfaction is needed to move people from the status quo.

4. The plans submitted by the developers of an invention to the "resource controllers" are in the form of "sales pitches," not realistic assessments of the costs and the obstacles as the innovation unfolds.

5. Once development begins, those involved usually discover that there is disagreement and lack of clarity about what the innovation is supposed to entail.

6. The ideas about what should be done proliferate, which makes the challenge of managing the innovation very difficult.

7. Continuity among innovation personnel is broken as people come and go for many reasons, including frustration with the process as well as additional career opportunities.

8. Emotions run high and frustration levels build as normal setbacks are encountered, mistakes made, and blame apportioned.

9. At first, schedules are adjusted and additional resources are provided to compensate for the unanticipated problems, but as the problems snowball, the patience of the resource providers weakens.

10. The goals of the resource providers and innovation managers begin to diverge, and a struggle for power emerges about project goals and how the project should be evaluated.

11. Resources tend to get tight and run out before the dreams of the developers are fulfilled.

Innovations often are terminated because new resources are not forthcoming. The ideas continue to show promise, but the resource providers lose patience. The ability to see a project to the end, which the Japanese have displayed to a greater extent than Americans, is critical to the successful completion of an innovation.

No project evaluation technique has been developed that would make this process smoother or that would resolve the difficulties inherent in it. Advanced portfolio methods, which have been created by statisticians and management consultants, typically are not used.[72] Critical success factors often are the enthusiasm and commitment of a project leader, the skills and abilities of the people involved, unanticipated spin-offs from and to other projects, relationships the innovators forge with customers and resource providers, and intangibles that cannot be assessed with certainty beforehand.

Hunches and Persistence

Thus, hunches, persistence, and "animal spirits," the very factors that are most feared by cautious investors, are also the factors needed for innovations to succeed. The acceptance of a high degree of uncertainty associated with an innovation usually is confined to special cases: small entrepreneurs willing to take a big gamble, large firms with a portfolio of innovations where one major success or many small ones can compensate for inevitable failures, large firms with lots of resources and few constraints on their use, large and small firms persuaded by the enthusiasm of inventors and product champions to overlook the sober assessments of financial analysts, and government-subsidized research that is allowed to proceed despite the financial risks because of some pressing national need such as national security.[73]

The social importance of technology, even with all the problems in its development, remains high. Technology promises to aid the visually impaired with products like a closed circuit television device that enlarges print up to 60 times its normal size, to produce a safe and effective birth control pill that can terminate an unhealthy pregnancy up to seven weeks after the last onset of menstruation, to make plastics more recyclable, to help doctors predict who will get cancer, to unleash the stagnant economies of Eastern Europe, and to do much more.[74]

Summary and Conclusions

This chapter has shown that economic progress occurs in stages that are driven by new technologies. The world has reached an impasse with regard to the next group of technologies that will drive economic growth. It is unclear which technologies will prevail in the future. Many technologies have promise and are contending for leadership.

We have discussed the obstacles that stand in the way of the development of new technologies. Technical, economic, and political in nature, the obstacles have an effect at all stages in the development process, from before a product is on the market, to when it is introduced, to after it has been sold. Evaluating the promise of a technology requires careful assessment of both the technology's maturity and the market potential. Both factors work together in the successful launching of new technologies.

Japanese innovation has been more market oriented than U.S. innovation. Other characteristics that distinguish Japanese innovation are the ability to fuse incremental improvements from many fields, the attention paid to manufacturing and marketing as well as new product development, the disregard for strict rate-of-return assessments, the rush to put products on the market so as to obtain feedback from customers, and the drive to succeed at all costs. The chapter stressed the many disappointments that exist in developing new technologies, the social importance of technology, and the need for creative entrepreneurs to play their hunches and be persistent despite the odds against success.

Discussion Questions

1. Why is technology important?
2. Forecast the future evolution of the computer industry. What role will Bill Gates play in it?
3. Describe Schumpeter's theory. What current relevance does it have?
4. What are the arguments of the technological pessimists? What are the arguments of the optimists? What does Daniel Bell say? What do you believe?
5. What are the differences between simple extrapolation, expert advice, and scenario building in forecasting the future?
6. Select a technology that has promise (e.g., biotechnology). Chart what has been accomplished in bringing the fruits of this technology to market and what still has to be accomplished. Give your estimate of the technology's potential.
7. What kind of estimates do developers of technology have to make? Why are these estimates inherently uncertain? What kind of system would you set up in a company so that better estimates could be made?
8. What problems did Enprostil encounter? What problems did Ultrasoft encounter? What problems did GE encounter with its new refrigerator compressor? What could have been done to avoid these problems?
9. Why didn't the Saturn succeed at first?
10. Analyze Motorola's problems in the chip market.
11. Will the United States be competitive in the market for HDTV? Why or why not?
12. Why do firms have to strive for constant innovation?
13. Which is dominant in innovation—the technology-push or market-pull models? Why?
14. As an innovator, what are Japan's strengths and weaknesses?
15. What role do hunches and persistence play in innovation?

Endnotes

1. Cited in C. Freeman, *The Economics of Industrial Innovation*, 2nd ed., (Cambridge, Mass.: MIT Press, 1982), p. 156; J. M. Keynes, *General Theory of Employment, Interest, and Money* (New York: Macmillan, 1936).

2. J. D. Gwartney and R. L. Stroup, *Economics: Private and Public Choice* (New York: Harcourt Brace Jovanovich, 1987).

3. N. Kondratiev, "The Major Economic Cycles," *Voprosy Konjunktury* 1, 1925, pp. 28–79; English translation reprinted in *Lloyd's Bank Review,* no. 129, 1978.

4. I. M. Kirzner, *Perception, Opportunity, and Profit: Studies in the Theory of Entrepreneurship* (Chicago: University of Chicago Press, 1979); J. A. Schumpeter, *Business Cycles: A Theoretical, Historical and Statistical Analysis of the Capitalist Process* (New York: McGraw-Hill, 1939).

5. R. Rothwell and W. Zegveld, *Reindustrialization and Technology* (Armonk, N.Y.: M. E. Sharpe, Inc., 1985).

6. D. H. Meadows, D. L. Meadows, J. Randers, and W. W. Behrens, *The Limits to Growth* (New York: Universe Books, 1972).

7. H. Kahn, W. Brown, and L. Martel. *The Next 200 Years: A Scenario for America and the World* (New York: William Morrow and Company, 1976).

8. Meadows, et al., *The Limits to Growth.*

9. Ibid.; B. Mitnick, "The Limits to Prediction," *Orbis* 2, 1973, pp. 1073–79.

10. Kahn, Brown, and Martel, *The Next 200 Years.*

11. D. Bell, *The Coming of Postindustrial Society: A Venture in Social Forecasting* (New York: Basic Books, 1973).

12. Ibid.

13. Ibid.

14. G. Gilder, "The World's Next Source of Wealth," *Fortune,* August 28, p. 116.

15. Ibid.

16. Ibid.

17. Ibid.

18. G. Starling, *The Changing Environment of Business*, 3rd ed. (Boston: PWS-Kent Publishing Company, 1988).

19. Ibid.

20. Ibid.

21. Ibid.

22. Ibid.

23. R. E. Willis, *A Guide to Forecasting for Planners and Managers* (Englewood Cliffs, NJ: Prentice Hall, 1987); P. Wack, "Scenarios: Uncharted Waters Ahead," *Harvard Business Review,* September–October 1985, pp. 89–99; M. Magnet, "Who Needs a Trend-Spotter?" *Fortune,* December 9, 1985, pp. 51–56; Willis, *A Guide to Forecasting for Planners and Managers.*

24. D. A. Burrus, "A Glimpse of the Future: Twenty New Technologies That Will Alter the Career Paths of the Class of '91," *National Business Employment Weekly,* Spring 1991, p. 6.

25. W. M. Bulkeley, "Bright Outlook for Artificial Intelligence Yields to Slow Growth and Big Cutbacks," *The Wall Street Journal,* July 5, 1990, p. B1.

26. Ibid.

27. Ibid.

28. Ibid.

29. Ibid.

30. U. Gupta, "Watching and Waiting: Biotechnology Holds Great Promise, but Investors are Still Waiting for the Payoff," *The Wall Street Journal*, November 13, 1989, p. R32.

31. R. Koenig and R. Smith, "Drop in Tagamet Sales Is Putting SmithKline in Danger of Takeover," *The Wall Street Journal*, January 13, 1989, p. A1.

32. Koenig and Smith, "Drop in Tagamet Sales"; A. Newman, "Biotech Shares May Soon Fulfill Profit Promise," *The Wall Street Journal*, October 8, 1990, p. C1.

33. Bylinsky, 1988; C. Freeman, *The Economics of Industrial Innovation* 2nd ed. (Cambridge, Mass.: MIT Press, 1982).

34. F. Knight, *Risk, Uncertainty, and Profit* (New York: Houghton Mifflin, 1921).

35. Knight, *Risk, Uncertainty, and Profit*; Freeman, *The Economics of Industrial Innovation*.c

36. Freeman, *The Economics of Industrial Innovation*.

37. Ibid.

38. Ibid.

39. Ibid.

40. Ibid.

41. Ibid., p. 155.

42. M. Chase, "Did Syntex Withhold Data on Side Effects of a Promising Drug?" *The Wall Street Journal*, January 8, 1991, p. A1.

43. A. Swasy, "Diaper's Failure Shows How Poor Plans, Unexpected Woes Can Kill New Products," *The Wall Street Journal*, October 9, 1990, p. B1.

44. T. F. O'Boyle, "GE Refrigerator Woes Illustrate the Hazards in Changing a Product," *The Wall Street Journal*, May 7, 1990, p. A1.

45. Ibid.

46. Ibid.

47. J. B. White and M. G. Guiles, "GM's Plan for Saturn, to Beat Small Imports, Trails Original Goals," *The Wall Street Journal*, July 9, 1990, p. A1.

48. Ibid.

49. Ibid.

50. Ibid.

51. Ibid.

52. Rothwell and Zegveld, *Reindustrialization and Technology*.

53. S. K. Yoder, "Motorola Loses Edge in Microprocessors by Delaying New Chips," *The Wall Street Journal*, March 4, 1990, p. A1.

54. B. Davis, "High-Definition TV, Once a Capital Idea, Wanes in Washington," *The Wall Street Journal*, June 1, 1990, p. A1.

55. Koenig and Smith, "Drop in Tagamet Sales"; R. Koenig, "Rich in New Products, Monsanto Must Only Get Them on Market," *The Wall Street Journal*, May 18, 1990, p. A1.

56. Rothwell and Zegveld, *Reindustrialization and Technology*.

57. J. A. Schumpeter, *Business Cycles: A Theoretical, Historical and Statistical Analysis of the Capitalist Process* (New York: McGraw-Hill, 1939).

58. J. Schmookler, *Invention and Economic Growth* (Cambridge, Mass.: Harvard University Press, 1966).

59. M. Betz, *Managing Technology: Competing through New Ventures, Innovation, and Corporate Research;* E. Von Hippel, *Appropriability of Innovation Benefit as a Predictor of the Functional Locus of Innovation,* working Paper 1084–79, Sloan School of Management, MIT, Cambridge, Mass., 1979; E. Von Hippel, "The Dominant Role of Users in the Scientific Instrument Innovation Process," *Research Policy* 5, 1976; E. Von Hippel, "Users as Innovators," *Technology Review* 80, 1978.

60. D. C. Mowery and N. Rosenberg, "The Influence of Market Demand upon Innovation: A Critical Review of Some Recent Empirical Studies," *Research Policy* 8, 1978.

61. R. H. Hayes and W. J. Abernathy, "Managing Our Way to Economic Decline," *Harvard Business Review,* July-August 1980.

62. E. Mansfield, "Industrial R&D in Japan and the United States: A Comparative Study," *Innovation and Change in Japan and the United States* 2, 1988, pp. 223–28; S. Lehr, "The Japanese Challenge: Can They Achieve Technological Supremacy?" *New York Times Magazine,* July 8, 1984, pp. 18–23; "Thinking Ahead," *The Economist,* December 2–8, 1989.

63. "Thinking Ahead."

64. Lehr, "The Japanese Challenge."

65. Ibid.

66. "Thinking Ahead."

67. Ibid.

68. Ibid.

69. Ibid.

70. A. Murray and U. C. Lehner, "What U.S. Scientists Discover, the Japanese Convert—Into Profit," *The Wall Street Journal,* June 25, 1990, p. A1.

71. A. H. Van de Ven, H. L. Angle, and M. S. Poole (eds.), *Research of the Management of Innovation* (N.Y.: Harper and Row, 1989).

72. Freeman, *The Economics of Industrial Innovation.*

73. Gupta, "Watching and Waiting"; Freeman, *The Economics of Industrial Innovation.*

74. S. C. Bakos, "Abortion Pill Ready for Use in Five Countries," *Star Tribune,* October 2, 1988, p. 1E; Chase, "Did Syntex Withhold Data on Side Effects of a Promising Drug?"; A. K. Naj, "GE Pushes to Develop Recyclable Plastic," *The Wall Street Journal,* August 13, 1990, p. B5; A. K. Naj, "GE's Latest Invention: A Way to Move Ideas from Lab to Market," *The Wall Street Journal,* June 14, 1990, p. A1; E. J. Tracy, "An Air Bag That Could Crash the Cost Barrier," *Fortune,* October 29, 1984, p. 88; R. Brenner, *Betting on Ideas: Wars, Inventions, Inflation* (Chicago: University of Chicago Press, 1985); M. Waldholz, "A Genetic Discovery Helps Doctors Predict Who Will Get Cancer," *The Wall Street Journal,* October 31, 1989, p. A1; R. Ricklefs, "Firms Introduce Products Aimed at Visually Impaired," *The Wall Street Journal,* September 28, 1988, p. B25.

16

THE IMPACT OF TECHNOLOGY

Time and time again warnings are ignored, unnecessary risks taken, sloppy work done, deception and downright lying practiced. . . . Better organization will always help any endeavor. But the best is not good enough for some technologies that we have decided to pursue. . . . There is no technological imperative that says we must have power or weapons from nuclear fission or fusion, or that we must create and loose upon the earth organisms that will devour our oil spills.

Charles Perrow, *Normal Accidents.*[1]

Introduction and Chapter Objectives

Some technologies are inherently dangerous—they have catastrophic potential and may be disaster-prone. Even under the best conditions, they are difficult to manage. This chapter considers how society can best manage these inherently dangerous technologies. It looks at the risks in everyday life, at rational risk assessment, and the question of, how safe is safe? Risk and uncertainty in economics are compared with risk and uncertainty in science and engineering. We consider the fact that managers must make judgments with imperfect knowledge and that psychological misperceptions and organizational biases affect these judgments. The chapter also considers the critical question of how much a human life is worth.

Normal Accidents

Technologies like nuclear power plants, chemical plants, aircraft and air traffic control, ships, dams, nuclear weapons, space missions, and genetic engineering may be inherently dangerous. They pose potentially catastrophic risks to operators, passengers, innocent bystanders, and even future generations. They have the capacity to take the lives of many people at once, as well as to do irreparable harm to the population and the environment.

Perrow maintains that no matter how effective management practices are, these technologies are likely to fail.[2] Better operator training, safer designs, more quality control, and more effective regulation cannot eliminate the risk. These technologies suffer from complexity and tight coupling.

Complexity means that they have many components (parts, procedures, and operators) that interact in unexpected ways. Failure can take place in more than one component simultaneously (a fire will start and the fire alarm will be silent). Given the interaction of multiple failures, the causes of the failure will be incomprehensible to operators for a critical period of time. During this critical period the operators will not be able to figure out what has gone wrong and what to do.

The problem of not knowing what to do can be overcome if slack is available. Slack is the time and resources needed to figure out what has happened and how to fix it (see the discussion in Case IVB of "inherently safe reactors"). However, the systems do not have sufficient slack. They are very *tightly coupled*. They work very fast, their parts cannot be isolated from each other, and they cannot be quickly or easily shut off. In addition, many of the interactions that take place are not directly observable by operators, so that it is very hard for them to know what is really going on.

EXHIBIT 16–1   Problems in Managing Dangerous Technologies

	Catastrophic Potential	*Inconsistent Management Principles*
	Many components:	Prepare for unexpected:
Complexity	Unexpected interactions. Causes of failure incomprehensible for critical period.	Operators have to be prepared to take independent, creative initiative.
	Systems interconnected:	Can't afford mistakes:
Tight coupling	Work fast Parts canot be isolated. Systems cannot be easily or quickly shut off.	Operators have to be carefully monitored and controlled.

Because of complexity and tight coupling, management of these technologies is difficult (see Exhibit 16–1). The two features are contradictory. Complexity means preparation for unexpected contingencies. Therefore, the operators have to be able to take independent, creative action. Tight coupling means the actions of operators have to be carefully monitored and controlled. The operators cannot afford to make mistakes. They cannot be given the freedom to take independent action.

These organizational contradictions make it hard to manage high risk technologies. According to Perrow: "The systems cannot be both decentralized and centralized at the same time; they are organizational Pushmepullyous, straight out of Dr. Doolittle stories, trying to go in opposite directions at once."[3]

Does Risk Taking Enhance Safety?

Aaron Wildavsky expresses the opposite view from Perrow in his book *Searching for Safety.*[4] He believes that risk taking has enhanced the safety, health, and well-being of society. A society's welfare is a function of how wealthy it is, and the wealth of a society increases in proportion to its willingness to take risks.

The risk taking of entrepreneurs in capitalist societies is reflected in a willingness to court technological dangers. For example, when first introduced, bridges, natural gas lines, and commercial air travel appeared to be very dangerous. Today, these technologies are accepted and commonplace. By recognizing and dealing with the problems, society has learned how to cope with the residual danger.

Trial-and-error learning increases the welfare of society. It consists of hypothesis testing, feedback, the discovery of error, and the incremental correction of error. Thus, dangers to humans and the environment are gradually decreased. In capitalist societies entrepreneurs pursuing economic gain engage in this activity in a decentralized, flexible way that is unimpeded by government interference, which slows the discovery of danger and impedes its correction. Risk-averse government officials, according to Wildavsky, prevent error correction. The centralized, slow, planned, simulated trial-and-error learning carried out by government makes for a rigid system. It sets limits on what can be tested. It puts constraints on innovation, learning, and the correction of error.

The goal should be to increase total safety so that more people are better off over a period of time. Markets, not government, advance this goal. They do so by giving people the right to experiment by trial and error and risk taking. According to Wildavsky, "Encouraging trial and error promotes resilience—learning from adversity how to do better—while avoiding restrictions that encourage the continuation of existing hazards."[5]

Perrow, in contrast, believes that learning from events such as nuclear power accidents or chemical plant explosions, is neither tolerable nor possible: "In the past, designers could learn from the collapse of a medieval cathedral under construction, or the explosion of boilers or steamboats, or the collision of railroad trains on a single track. But we seem to be unable to learn from chemical plant explosions or nuclear plant accidents."[6] Perrow believes that learning about the operation of high-risk technologies quickly reaches a plateau, that the learning curve is likely to be flat. Wildavsky, however, vigorously disputes that conducting trials that involve error is too risky and that the only alternative is trial without error. He maintains that "increasing the pool of general resources, such as wealth and knowledge, secures safety for more people than using up resources in a vain effort to protect against unperceivable, hypothetical dangers."[7]

The Risks of Everyday Life

Everyday life is risky. Each year about 2 million Americans die.[8] This means that the average person in the United States faces about a 9-in-1,000 risk of dying each year. The major causes of death are heart disease, cancer, stroke, accident, suicide, and homicide in that order. Nearly 750,000 Americans die each year from heart disease and about 400,000 from cancer, while 27,000 are suicide victims and 22,000 are homicide victims (see Exhibit 16–2).

As people age, their risk of dying goes up. At age 80 the risk of dying goes up to 83 in 1,000. A 5-year-old's annual risk of death from all causes is 0.3 in 1,000, and at age 40, the annual risk of death from all causes increases to about 2 in 1,000.

Sports such as air shows/air racing, mountaineering, boxing, and hang gliding are very risky, but smoking is more risky than any of these except air shows/air racing. Over 300,000 Americans die annually from this activity. The risks of dying from smoking are greater than the risks of active duty in Vietnam. Moreover, the risk to a pilot who participates in air shows decreases with frequency, since the pilot's skill level and experience go up, while the risks of smoking go up with continued smoking. A heavy smoker who smokes 10 times as many cigarettes as an occasional smoker faces more than 10 times the risk.

The risks of dying from cancer are 2 in 1,000 and from dying in an accident 0.5 in 1,000. Most federal regulations are designed to reduce the risk of dying from cancer and accidents. The extent to which cancer deaths can be reduced is difficult to ascertain. Scientists have only a partial understanding of the disease. There are controversies in the scientific community as to where to look for causes and cures. Different types

---

EXHIBIT 16–2   The Risks of Dying

• At age 80—83 in 1,000
• From participating in air shows/air racing—5 in 1,000
• From smoking—3 in 1,000
• From heart disease—3 in 1,000
• From cancer—2 in 1,000
• At age 40—2 in 1,000
• From active duty in Vietnam—2 in 1,000
• From a mountaineering accident—0.6 in 1,000
• From accidents—0.5 in 1,000
• From working in mines—0.5 in 1,000
• From a boxing accident—0.5 in 1,000
• From working in construction—0.4 in 1,000
• From a hang-gliding accident—0.4 in 1,000
• At age five—0.3 in 1,000
• From suicides and homicides—0.1 in 1,000
• From all occupations—0.1 in 1,000
• From being struck by a lightning bolt—.00005 in 1,000

SOURCE: Adapted from J. F. Morrall, "The Perils of Prudence," *Regulation,* November/December 1986, pp. 25–39.

of cancer exist and each appears to have a different origin. The disease mainly affects people in old age and appears to be related to a person's genetic endowment. A study by the Congressional Office of Technology Assessment traced 35 percent of all cancers to diet, 30 percent to smoking, and 6 percent to occupational and environmental exposures. The ability of the government to affect these factors may be limited.

Similarly, the ability of the government to reduce accidents may not be great as many accidents are caused by factors (e.g., reckless driving) that are beyond the government's control (see Exhibit 16–3). Accidents take around 100,000 American lives annually; the main type of accident is motor vehicle accidents, which result in almost 50,000 deaths annually.

Some occupations are riskier than others. The annual risk of a work-related death in all occupations is 0.1 in 1,000. The risk of driving to work is greater than the chances of dying on the job. Those who work in mines face five times the average risk in all occupations, and those who work in construction face four times the average risk.

Rational Risk Assessment

Rational risk assessment calls for a more rational ordering of risks.[9] The funds for risk reduction are not limitless and the costs keep mounting. Estimates are that by the year 2000, 3 percent of GNP will go for

EXHIBIT 16–3 Motor Vehicle Death Rates in Different Countries
Deaths per 100,000 Population

	Year	*Rate*	*Number*
United States	1987	19.4	47,297
France	1988	18.2	10,165
Italy	1986	16.3	9,329
Canada	1987	16.3	4,180
West Germany	1988	12.9	7,905
Japan	1988	11.0	13,420

SOURCE: Adapted from World Health Organization, Geneva, Switzerland, unpublished data, and *Motor Vehicle Facts and Figures* (Detroit: Motor Vehicle Manufacturers Association of the United States, Inc.).

environmental cleanup alone.[10] Rather than allowing risk management to be influenced by fearful citizens, self-promoting politicians, and outraged columnists, we should view risks in a more detached and analytical way.

Polls suggest that Americans worry most about such dangers as oil spills, acid rain, pesticides, nuclear power, and hazardous wastes, but scientific risk assessments show that these are only low- or medium-level dangers.[11] Greater hazards come from radon, lead, indoor air pollution, and fumes from chemicals such as benzene and formaldehyde. Radon, the odorless gas that naturally seeps up from the ground and is found in people's homes, causes as many as 20,000 lung cancer deaths per year, but hazardous waste dumps cause, at most, 500 cancer deaths. Yet the Environmental Protection Agency (EPA) spends over $6 billion a year to clean up hazardous waste sites while it spends only $100 million a year for radon protection.[12] To test a home for radon costs about $25 and to clean it up if it is contaminated costs $1,000. To make the entire national housing stock free from radon would cost a few billion dollars. In contrast, projected spending for cleaning up hazardous waste sites is likely to exceed $500 billion despite the fact that only about 11 percent of such sites pose a measurable risk to human health.

Greater rationality would mean that less attention would be paid to some risks and more attention to others. For instance, scientific risk assessment suggests that sizable new investments will be needed to address the dangers of ozone depletion and greenhouse warming (see Chapter 14).[13] Ozone depletion is likely to result in 100,000 more cases of skin cancer by the year 2050. Global warming has the potential to cause massive catastrophe.

For businesses, rational risk assessment provides a way to allocate costs efficiently, and they are increasingly using it as a management tool.

For instance, to avoid another accident like Bhopal, Union Carbide has set up a system by which it rates its plants "safe," "made safer," or "shut down."[14]

Environmentalists, on the other hand, generally see risk assessment as a tactic powerful interests use to prevent regulation of known dangers or permit building of facilities where there will be known fatalities. Even if the chances of someone contracting cancer and dying are only one in a million, still someone will indeed perish, which the studies by risk assessors document. Society, according to the environmentalists, should be concerned about the fate of these individuals. Moreover, among particularly vulnerable groups of the population (e.g., allergy sufferers, who are seriously threatened by benzene), the risks are likely to be much greater, perhaps as high as one fatality for every 100 persons.[15] Thus, the environmentalists argue, the way risk assessors present their findings is too conservative; by treating everyone alike, they overlook the real danger to particularly vulnerable people. Therefore, environmentalists argue that risk assessment should not be used as an excuse for inaction.

How Safe Is Safe?

Efforts to define, identify, and reduce risks to the public are impeded by a dearth of scientific data, a lack of resources, and the intrusion of political and ideological considerations into the legislative and regulatory processes. Regulators have trouble answering the basic question of how safe is safe.[16] Since absolute safety is impossible and some degree of risk is inevitable and is with people every day in every part of their lives, it is hard to decide what constitutes acceptable risk. To do so, regulators and business managers have to balance competing social and financial considerations, as well as health and safety factors (see Exhibit 16–4).

The first step in analyzing risk is an assessment of its magnitude. This means analyzing information about the nature, potency, and

---

EXHIBIT 16–4   Analyzing Risk

Its magnitude:
  Nature, potency, distribution of hazard.
  Number of people exposed.
  Means by which exposed.
  Adverse health effects at different exposure levels.
Its management:
  Action based on public health requirements, environmental goals, legislation, legal precedent, values, and financial and social considerations.

distribution of hazardous substances, the number of people exposed, the means by which they are exposed, and the adverse health effects at various levels of exposure. The second step is managing the risk. This means taking action based on the goals of public health and environmental protection, relevant legislation, legal precedent, and the application of social, economic, and political values.

Uncertainties are associated with both steps. Risk assessment, for instance, is plagued by the problem of extrapolating results from animal studies to humans, while the principles that apply to risk management are often contradictory or unclear. The clean air and water acts require that pollution be reduced to the lowest achievable level consistent with an adequate margin of safety, while the pesticide and consumer protection laws require that the costs of regulation be balanced against the benefits. Also, courts can intervene after the fact to overturn agency decisions. The Supreme Court demanded a cost benefit analysis from OSHA with respect to a benzene standard it had established, and OSHA had to change an earlier decision to make it more lenient.

Judgment is critical to this process. Regulators usually consider risks greater than one in a million to be significant, but mitigating circumstances may present themselves in a particular situation. For instance, the risk of lung cancer to the residents near an Idaho nuclear processing plant operated by the Department of Energy may be 1 in 1,000; however, few people live near the plant. Only one additional cancer case may occur every 13 years, and the costs of lowering this figure may be as high as $78 million for each cancer death averted. In a case such as this, the EPA may decide not to promulgate a regulation.

The responsibility that government officials and business managers have is great. While an individual may be willing to take a risk where the likelihood of death is high (1 in 20,000), regulators and managers decide for large populations, who have no real choice as to whether they would voluntarily accept such a risk. As a consequence, they have to live up to very high decision standards.

Risk, Uncertainty, and Managerial Judgment

Managers face troubling dilemmas with regard to the risks of the technologies they control. The decisions they make often depend on "answers to questions which can be asked of science and yet which cannot be answered by science."[17] An example is the introduction of new pesticides, where the conflict between increased agricultural productivity and health and environmental damage is difficult for science to resolve.[18]

In the case of the pesticides, for scientists to reach a confidence level of 95 percent about safety requires the testing of huge numbers of experimental animals, but even with the large numbers of animals the scientists can only say that no effect is probable. In the case of many technologies, to identify every failure mode is impossible, and it is extremely costly and utterly impracticable to build full-scale prototypes and to test them under every conceivable circumstance.

Limitations of time and money and incomplete knowledge mean that some scientific and technological questions cannot be definitely resolved. In these cases, both individual and collective judgments play a role. While confrontation between individuals of opposing positions is desirable, it is senseless to believe that adversary procedures can resolve, with scientific certainty, issues that are on or beyond the boundaries of what is scientifically known.

Human beings behave rationally in simplified situations where they have full knowledge. But these are not the characteristic conditions in the real world.[19] The German sociologist Max Weber's conception of organizations as reliable means for achieving desired ends depends on having knowledge available that is adequate to the organizations' tasks.[20] However, this conception is too simple; it ignores conditions where knowledge is partial, limited, and contested (see Chapter 12).

Insufficient knowledge is, however, not the only source of organizational failure. Negligence or failure to attend to what is known is also a source of failure. For example, negligence brings about breakdowns such as those at Three Mile Island, Bhopal, Chernobyl, Valdez, and the Challenger. Investigations into these accidents started with the search for technological deficiencies and ended with an emphasis on individual negligence and organizational insufficiency. In each of these cases, early warnings had been issued but had gone unheeded. After the fact there was evidence that people in the organization knew what was likely, but took no action.

Risk and Uncertainty in Economics

In economics, decision making under uncertainty has been reserved for a particular class of people, entrepreneurs (see Chapter 15). The distinction made is between risk, where the "distribution of the outcome of a group of instances is known," and uncertainty, where "it is impossible to form a group of instances" because the situation "is in a high degree unique."[21] When probabilities are known (flipping a coin), the situation is considered to be an example of risk. To the extent that knowledge of probabilities is certain, probabilities may be based on deduction from assumed principles, scientific knowledge, empirical observations, and individual judgments.

All economic activity involves choice between rewards, some of which are small and can be anticipated with confidence, and some of which are large and cannot be anticipated with confidence. The larger the expected reward, the greater the uncertainty that the entrepreneur faces and the greater the expected reward. The prospect of the reward induces the entrepreneur to take the risk. For society, the issue of economic uncertainty is resolved by placing the burden on entrepreneurs, a specialized group of persons who willingly bear the burden because of the expected payback. They perform the valuable function of being the risk-bearers for society. They estimate future demand and the results of proposed activities in meeting this demand; however, estimations of this demand are inherently uncertain. Although entrepreneurs strive to reduce the uncertainty, when they are in a detached mood, they may admit that this objective is unattainable (see Chapter 15).

Involuntary Risks

Uncertainty about the impact of technologies cannot be resolved by allocating the costs to a specific group. Only some risks (e.g., those ascribable to motorcycling and smoking) are voluntarily undertaken; that is, the individuals involved have chosen to accept these risks. Many risks are involuntary ones that individuals have not agreed to accept, such as those connected with proximity to nuclear power plants or inhaling smoke that has been emitted by people in public places or by factories owned by others.

The risk that a technology will harm a person is a statistical likelihood. Ranging from local phenomena to global hazards, the risks people face are usually not reliably known by those exposed to them or by those who bring about the exposure. When the risks are unknown, those exposed are in no position to make a rational decision about what to do. Ultimately, it depends on the benefits, but people cannot rationally weigh the benefits versus the costs if they do not have a complete rendering of the risks.[22] In some instances, groups in the population that bear a particular risk are unknown in advance. Moreover, some hazards involve irreversibility and intergenerational effects; the affected but unborn generations cannot make a choice. In these cases, the individuals who must bear a large portion of the burden have no choice. They have not consciously chosen to be subjected to the risks.

Gaining knowledge that will reduce risk may be too costly. For example, although engineering usually advances by trial and error, in the case of reactor safety it may be unacceptable to learn in this manner because of the incalculability of widespread human casualties and environmental damage that would result from a major mishap.[23] Entrepreneurial failures, by contrast, mainly affect individuals who have voluntarily accepted the possibility that their ventures might not succeed. Unlike the failures of complex, dangerous technologies, entrepreneurial failures do not have broad-based, catastrophic potential for many people in society.

Risk and Uncertainty in Science and Engineering

When engineers assess the risks of a new technology, they are not concerned about scientific principles. Instead, their concern is technical: Will the system function as designed? Scientific uncertainty reflects a lack of fundamental knowledge about the behavior of the physical and biological world. Technical uncertainty reflects uncertainty about whether a backup safety system, for instance, will work under conditions of stress when it has to do so to prevent loss of life. To the engineer, it does not really matter what theories are used to explain the behavior of the backup system; what matters is that the system works. On the basis of engineering principles and informed conjecture, the engineer tries to calculate the likelihood that the backup system will fail and how many fatalities and injuries will occur. The engineer analyzes potential accidents, for example, those arising from the explosion of a chemical plant, with this in mind. The engineer estimates the consequences should an accident occur, and represents the results as a probability, which then becomes the measure used to describe the risks of the technological installation.

If this probability could be reliably determined (i.e., adequately estimated on the basis of assumed principles and actual experience), then understanding of the risk would be complete. There would be no residual uncertainty. However, because tacit assessments and informed judgment play a role in constructing the model, it is incomplete and the probability itself is uncertain.

This kind of uncertainty is reduced by more testing and better understanding of principles, but it cannot be eliminated. As Haefele has written, because "it is impossible to measure initial and boundary conditions with the completeness and accuracy necessary for a fully deterministic prediction of the performance of a technical component or device," there always remains an element of "residual risk: . . . We can always improve our knowledge about contingent conditions, but we can never make it complete. . . . The risk can be made smaller than any small but predetermined number which is larger than zero. The remaining risk . . . opens the door . . . to . . . hypotheticality."[24] Of course, better knowledge can reduce residual risk, but it takes time and money to generate a more complete understanding and both time and money are scarce.

Furthermore, even if knowledge of the risks improves, that alone does not solve the problem of weighing the anticipated benefits against the costs. Estimating benefits and comparing them with costs are not scientific problems; they require value judgments by society at large or its representatives. Society must decide how far it wishes to remain committed to a product or technology in light of the balance of costs and benefits.

Judgment with Imperfect Knowledge

Under conditions of perfect ignorance (i.e., complete uncertainty), choices about risks necessarily would be random. Those who make decisions under conditions of complete ignorance cannot reliably link consequences to alternatives because any outcome is equally probable. If the results conform with expectations, that is merely a matter of chance. On the other hand, conditions of perfect knowledge would permit decisions to be fully rational. Between the extremes of perfect knowledge and perfect ignorance lie virtually all relevant problems of risk and uncertainty that affect society.

When some evidence is available, but uncertainty—despite good efforts to dispel it—still exists, subjective estimation of probabilities plays an important role. Consider the process of evaluating the risk of a particular chemical substance.[25] The process of the assessment of risk starts with the identification of the hazard. This aims to characterize the potential adverse effects on health of exposure to the chemical substance—whether the substance can cause an increase in the occurrence of, for example, cancer and birth defects.

However, the knowledge available is wholly reliable in only very few cases. Risk assessment often requires extrapolation from animals to human beings; the aim is to prevent inadvertently developing human data because of some catastrophe, as with thalidomide. Determinations, therefore, are made on the basis of the effects of the chemical on experimental animals.

Animal Study Inferences

Inference from animal studies to human beings is necessary, but there are cases where these inferences are ambiguous or uncertain. For instance, the best evidence of oncogenic effects is consistently positive results in two sexes and in several strains and species and higher incidence at higher doses. However, more often than not such consistent observations are not available. Often, experimental data leading to a positive finding barely reach a threshold of statistical significance. Also, the experimental data frequently involve types of diseases of uncertain relation to human diseases.

Moreover, interpretation of animal data may be difficult. Typically, a given percentage of test animals have the disease, a smaller percentage in the control group have the disease, and it is up to the analyst to decide if the difference is statistically significant or attributable to chance. One group of animals is usually given the highest dose that can be tolerated, a second group may be exposed at half that dose, and a control group may be unexposed. The highest dose that can be tolerated is used for a number of reasons. First, if a small dose is used, it might not induce a sufficient quantity of disease in a small group of experimental animals to be statistically significant. Tests on 10 animals, for example, might actually fail to detect tumors affecting 37 percent of the population, and tests on 100 animals might fail to detect tumors affecting 4.5 percent of the population. In a population of over two hundred million human beings, that is equivalent to nearly 10 million cases of cancer. Second, individuals are not exposed to a single pathogen under experimental conditions, but to numerous pathogens which may act concurrently with each other.

However, the testing of animals at very high doses has been challenged by scientists who argue that the high doses may overwhelm normal defense mechanisms, that this method is unrealistic given the lower doses to which individuals are actually exposed, and that people differ in important ways from laboratory animals.[26] In fact, the acceptance of data from laboratory animal studies by the legal and regulatory system still is regarded as relatively controversial; it gained greater legitimacy only in the mid-1970s.

Psychological Misperceptions

Psychologists have taught that when confronted with decisions under uncertainty, human beings are prone to make fundamental mistakes.[27] For example, some individuals tend to consider themselves personally immune from hazards—such as those arising from the use of automobiles, motorcycles, power mowers, and toxic substances—that other individuals would readily acknowledge. Some individuals also have difficulty imagining events of low probability with severe consequences—such as airplane crashes, tornadoes, earthquakes, and nuclear power accidents—happening to themselves.

Another common finding is that the risks of involuntary activities, such as exposure to nuclear energy, are more unacceptable than the risks arising from voluntary activities, such as motorcycle driving. Most individuals find motorcycles less unacceptable than nuclear power plants no matter what the actual risks may be; they fear events of low probability with severe consequence, like nuclear power accidents, more than they fear events of high probability with small consequence, like motorcycle accidents.

People also tend to underestimate the error and unreliability that are inherent in small samples of data. They have unreasonable expectations about the replicability of early results and undue confidence in these results. In addition, they judge the probability or frequency of events on the basis of the ease of the retrievability of information about similar events from memory, and they rely on the saliency, as well as the recentness, of events in their evaluations.

Judgment is biased, furthermore, by direct experience with a lethal event and exposure to reporting about the event on television and in the press. No matter what the implications of further evidence, natural starting points, or "anchors," act as aids in judgment, and there is a tendency to believe that past performance is a valid indicator of future occurrences. Human beings also tend to be overconfident about their estimates.[28]

Most people rely on vague impressions in making judgments on subjects on which they are inexpert. Experts, however, are trained to rely on computational tools, theories, specific observations, and their experience to estimate risk. These methods, however, also have limitations. For example, experts assign the same weights to hazards that take many lives at once as they do to hazards that take many lives one at a time. Also, they tend to lump voluntary and involuntary hazards together and to underestimate possible pathways to disaster.

In recent years, there have been a number of cases where experts failed to consider adequately how human deficiency or negligence affects technological systems. Among the most prominent of these cases was the Three Mile Island nuclear power accident, but this phenomenon has recurred in other major accidents, such as Chernobyl, the Challenger, and Bhopal. Experts also tend to be insensitive to how systems function as wholes; for example, they ignored the fact that decompression of the DC-10 cargo compartment could destroy the plane's control system. And they have been known to be slow to detect chronic, cumulative environmental effects, such as acid rain and the gradual accumulation of carbon dioxide in the environment.

Collective Risk Decisions

Collectively shared attitudes and conceptions of risk are of considerable importance as most risk decisions are made by groups of people, not by individuals. However, there may develop in groups working on these problems an illusion of invulnerability and the suppression of doubts.[29] Such attitudes are affected by the consensus within the group, the insulation of the group from external criticism, and the active promotion of a dominant individual to the exclusion of the views of others.

On the other hand, shared information in groups can lead to greater realism in the perceptions of risk.[30] New information and rationally persuasive arguments can be introduced into discussions within a group, and better use can be made of existing information. Thus, rational discussions in a group can increase the prospects for realistic judgment, depending on such factors as the size of the group, its composition, and its values.

Three Models

Graham Allison has proposed the use of three models in analyzing the influence of organizational factors on decisions (see Exhibit 16–5).[31] Model I is the "rational actor model," and outcomes are the result of rational choices by individuals, but he believes that this model has the least explanatory power. Model II is the "bureaucratic model," and outcomes are the result of the parochial preferences, perceptions, and procedures of managers. Lower level managers, for example, present facts in a distorting manner and report only facts that support their position.[32] Organizational objectives, capacities, and interests have a limiting effect on rational decision making. Model III is the "political model"; outcomes are the result of conflict among formal institutional participants with conflicting interests and accounts of the situation. For example, in the government, temporarily appointed heads of agencies, outside experts, and permanent civil servants have different motivations, knowledge, and outlooks. Yet they all participate in decisions about risk in the federal government, and each is likely to develop different positions.[33]

Probabilistic knowledge is not likely to satisfy the needs of organizational decision makers who require precise and unequivocal knowledge.[34] They confront many sources of information that compete for their attention. Some of this information is more complete, some of it is more pertinent, and some of it has greater reliability. To understand and to use the information is difficult, especially for individuals whose experience may be in practical affairs and who cannot ordinarily aggregate or organize diverse bits or probabilistic technical information according to clear principles, and recall it without error.[35] Under these conditions, critical information might be ignored or suppressed and only congenial information might be recalled and emphasized.

EHIBIT 16–5   **Models for Analyzing Organizational Factors**

Outcomes are the result of:
  1. Rational decisions by individuals.
  2. Organizational procedures, routines, and standard operating procedures.
  3. Bargaining and negotiation among institutional leaders.

The Manipulative Use of Information

Scientific information in organizations is often used for other purposes than establishing the truth. It has manipulative or propagandistic value in promoting group interests. The manipulative use of information is well-known. For example, environmental partisans often take positions on issues because of the problems that voluntary associations have in attracting and maintaining membership. Without exaggerating dangers and expressing their arguments aggressively, the environmentalists would be unable to obtain the monetary support their organizations need.[36]

In industry, the tendency is to underestimate risks.[37] For example, after the Corvair was on the market for a few months it was clear to motor car experts and General Motors managers that the car was difficult to control; indeed, it would go out of control without warning. The crucial question is why these managers waited so long before making the necessary changes. One answer is economic: the redesign and production of a new suspension system would have cost too much money. Another answer is the disregard of relevant information by the managers. They believed that their car's record for safety was not unusual in comparison with other small cars of the time. The Volkswagen Beetle, for example, had a far worse record. Consequently, managers disregarded the rapid changes in public expectations and the legislative situation that were taking place.

The question is why managers of the Ford Motor Company waited so long with respect to the Pinto situation when they had the Corvair as a precedent. Public opinion had changed, and stiff new laws governing safety had been enacted. One reason for the wait was the demands of the production schedule—the car had one of the shortest production schedules in the history of the automobile industry. The Pinto rapidly became a success in the market. Demands for its recall were heard and heeded only years after the car had been introduced and the product and design managers who had participated in its development had been rewarded for meeting manufacturing schedules at a low cost. At their level, broader concerns about the company's reputation and its liability for suits seemed unimportant. The motivation to take into account these longer-term concerns was not particularly strong (see Case VC, "Auto Safety Policy at Ford: Revisiting the Pinto").

Government Agencies

Government agencies are another institution with an important role to play in risk decision making. They display many styles in making decisions about risk.[38] For example, different agencies using the same evidence can come to very different conclusions with regard to the same chemical.[39] After a report from the Chemical Industry Institute of Toxicology, issued in 1979, that showed that formaldehyde causes cancer in rats, the Consumer Product Safety Commission decided to ban the substance, while the Environmental Protection Agency and the Occupational Safety and Health Administration took no action.

These different results come about because agencies are authorized and governed by different statutes, they have different standards, and they use different procedures. There is no single or uniform federal cancer policy, for example, and at least 10 different laws and four different agencies regulate cancer-causing substances, including the Food and Drug Administration, the Occupational Safety and Health Administration (OSHA), the Environmental Protection Administration (EPA), and the Consumer Product Safety Commission. Moreover, the EPA has developed somewhat different policies regarding cancer under each of its separate statues that deal with air, water, drinking water, solid waste, hazardous waste, toxic substances, and pesticides.

Different agencies also have different procedures for dealing with risk. Some rely more on outside contractors and experts. Some rely less on these outside parties. Some agencies are more careful about separating the function of hazard identification from the function of policy making, and some are less careful about making this distinction. Some use outside scientific review panels, and some do not have these bodies or any formal or informal arrangements for peer review. Moreover, each agency has somewhat different principles for making inferences about risk to human beings from animal studies, and the agencies' guiding principles differ with respect to their comprehensiveness, detail, completeness, and flexibility.

The differences in how federal agencies view risk can be seen in the differing values they assign to human life. The federal government, under Executive Orders 12044 (promulgated by the Carter administration) and 12291 (promulgated by the Reagan administration), has mandated that cost-benefit analyses be carried out on all major regulatory initiatives. The analyses are reviewed by the Office of Management and Budget (OMB) in the White House, and they show that different agencies have been making different estimates of the value of a human life. OSHA has valued it between $2 million and $5 million, EPA's range of valuations has been between $1 million and $7.5 million, and the Federal Aviation Administration (FAA) has valued a human life at $650,000.[40] The agencies justify the differences by claiming that their regulations protect different types of people with different risk preferences. The agencies have opposed efforts to impose a single figure (see the special feature, "How Much Is a Life Worth?").

How Much Is a Life Worth?

The question of how much a life is worth may appear repellent and absurd since human worth cannot be truly captured in monetary terms; nonetheless, it is important to determine the benefits for risk reduction purposes. The costs of reducing a risk often are immediate and apparent, while the benefits are far off and hard to determine. Thus, it is important to try to develop an approximate value of these benefits which often involve the saving of human life.

A humanitarian would spend money on all worthy endeavors to eliminate risk, but resources are limited and choices must be made about where to maximize return. Rational assessments of how much to spend on a new medical technology, highway design, or air pollution policy require estimating the value of human life. It is necessary to know the dollar value of human suffering that would be avoided.

Until the late 1960s society had a simple answer to the problem of how much a human life was worth.[1] A person was valued according to the net present value of his or her expected lifetime earnings. Calculations in 1986 dollars showed that an American man in his late 20s was worth about $500,000 and a woman about $350,000. Clearly, this approach had problems. Not only were women valued less than men; minorities had less value than the majority, old people had less value than the young, and people without employment and without the prospect of working had no worth at all.

An alternative was to use a "willingness to pay" criteria. People were asked questions on surveys; for instance, how much would they be willing to pay to have an ambulance in their neighborhood, which would reduce the number of heart attack deaths by a certain percentage. Or how much they

---

[1]M. Geyelin, "Dollar Valuation of Life Pleasures Set Back," *The Wall Street Journal*, March 27, 1991, p. B6; L. Dyer, "Environmental Policy and the Economic Value of Human Life," *Journal of Environmental Management*, 1986, pp. 229–43; J. Leape, "Quantitative Risk Assessment in the Regulation of Environmental Carcinogens," *Harvard Environmental Law Review*, 1980, pp. 86–117; D. Seligman, "How Much Money Is Your Life Worth?" *Fortune*, March 3, 1986, pp. 26–27.

Informal Rules of Choice

Informal rules of choice play an important role when people are confronted with complex technologies where the degree of risk is highly uncertain.[40] As the tasks people face call for judgments that are too complicated to be entirely reduced to formulae, they have a large zone of discretion in which their individual skills and professional traditions can play a very significant role.

Most people cope with indeterminateness of their knowledge by attempting to simplify their tasks: they narrow the range of data they will take into account, putting limits on the amount of information they receive and analyze. They confine themselves to a small range of responses.

How Much Is a Life Worth? continued

would have to be paid to join a group of 10,000 persons, one of whom would be chosen at random for execution. Or how much they would pay to buy back various numbers of bullets in a Russian roulette game they were playing. The problem was that, given the artificiality of the questions, the answers were not entirely believable. Depending upon the types of questions asked, the range of estimates for the value of a human life was from a low of $75,000 to a high of $2 million in 1986 dollars.

In response to these limitations, economists tried to derive the value of a human life on a more objective basis. A 1981 study examined people's willingness to pay extra for homes in areas with little pollution and came up with a $600,000 to $900,000 price tag for a human life in 1986 dollars. A study of risk-time trade-offs among seat belt users and nonusers calculated the worth of a human life at about $625,000 in 1986 dollars. Labor market studies of the interaction of job safety and pay among workers concluded that the value of a human life was between $650,000 and $3 million in 1986 dollars, de-

pending on the risk preferences of the people involved (people in high-risk occupations tended to have a higher tolerance for risk).

A major point of contention has been the issue of what to do about slow-developing diseases that are likely to kill people only in the future. Should a future life be discounted so that money is available to save a life now? Also, it is conceivable that some breakthrough will take place over the next 30 years so the person's life is no longer threatened.

Another issue is the discrepancies in the value of a human life in different cultures. U.S. juries often award sums in excess of $10 million for wrongful death. In India, the typical award would be no more than a few hundred dollars. It is not surprising that the relatives of victims involved in the Bhopal disaster wanted the case tried in the United States, while Union Carbide wanted it tried in India (see Case VB, "The Bhopal Disaster"). The National Council of Churches and other groups have expressed their indignation about this legal double standard for the valuation of a human life, which they find morally unacceptable.

An example of informal rules of decision that government officials use is offered by toxicologists in the pesticide division of the Environmental Protection Agency. Demands on their time grew at a rapid pace during the 1970s. A program of reregistering the more than 50,000 substances that were already in use had been initiated. The number of new applications from industry increased, as did the required data submitted in support of these applications.

Expectations about the level of sophistication of the reviews done by the scientists were also raised. The pressure to deal with a mounting backlog increased during the Reagan administration, but the additional demands were not met by additional resources for the appointment of more scientists for the work. Rather, appropriations for the pesticide program declined in 1981, 1982, and 1983.[42] The budget for dealing with pesticides fell from $70.5 million in 1980 to $50.7 million in 1983. The number of persons employed went down from 829 to 537, and the number of registrations handled by each employee increased.

Some of the government reviewers coped with this situation by routinely copying verbatim the summary statements accompanying safety and health studies submitted to the agency by industry. They accepted without question the accuracy and completeness of interpretations made by industry of the experimental results. This was not a consequence of their having insufficient scientific knowledge. Rather, it was a matter of accepting unaccredited statements as valid or being negligent in judging the information needed—and perhaps available without great difficulty. Of 578 randomly selected applications reviewed by the scientific staff, one third contained some evidence of "cut and paste."[43] Twenty-nine reached scientifically challengeable conclusions, and five reviews actually failed to report major health effects because they relied on descriptions contained in the data submitted by the company.

On the other hand, some of the government officials coped with the demand for rapid decision making under conditions of uncertainty by using a number of shortcuts or rules of thumb. These officials also tended to rely on summaries, but only to flag positive results. But they would also use past actions taken by members of their agency, reviews of the literature, or their general knowledge and feeling for the substance, or they would contract out pieces of the work they did not feel competent to do. They relied on the general reputation of particular laboratories or toxicologists who did the studies, or looked for common and easily detectable shortcomings to enable them to discover abuses. They tried to find missing information and were alerted by numbers that did not quite add up or by data that looked too good. They tried to rely on their scientific knowledge and experience to put in perspective what they saw and to make conservative judgments to establish a position from which to bargain with the applicants.

Both the officials who copied verbatim the summaries submitted by particular firms and those who relied on rules of thumb were trying to cope given the limitations with which they had to work. Some officials were conscientious and constructive, responding with scientific, technical, organizational, and other solutions. They were loyal members of their agency, even though they worked under considerable strain.

In contrast, one prominent official became a whistle-blower. He tipped off the media to the cut-and-paste activities in the agency. Principle, not politics, is often thought to motivate whistle-blowers (see Chapter 3). But what is missing in such accounts is the extent to which whistle-blowers are guided not only by the dictates of moral conscience but more specifically by professional standards. Whistle-blowers may have greater commitment to professional ethics than they do toward the organization for which they work.

Officials who failed to exert themselves to use their best knowledge were neither loyal to their organization nor committed to professional standards. They lacked a desire to meet the obligations of their tasks. As the pressure intensified, they fell short of their responsibility to use their knowledge in the assessment of risks. In the face of great stress, they became demoralized. Also, in a government bureaucracy it was difficult to dismiss or otherwise penalize or discipline these individuals when their work was perfunctory.

New Skills

Many scientists and engineers believe that their education and training are inadequate for making decisions about policies that might contain considerable risks and uncertainties. They were trained in experimental methods in disciplines where one can find a definitive solution to a problem. Under experimental conditions, there are frequently simple yes and no answers.

In making assessments of risk for society, however, when almost everything seems grey and ambiguous, discretionary judgment is required. Under these circumstances, conventional scientific and engineering training, even if vigorous, might be of little assistance.

Scientists and engineers who are appointed to deal with problems involving risk cannot always rely on their expert knowledge. Traditional disciplinary training may be too narrow; risk assessment often requires scientific knowledge that goes beyond disciplinary boundaries. The scientists and engineers must have an understanding of a wide variety of disciplines and the ability to employ advanced statistical techniques that require subtle and discriminating, as well as broad, knowledge.

To function effectively in this setting, accomplished scientists and engineers often need to acquire new skills, especially those that facilitate clinical judgment. In most cases the acquisition of such skills is a slow and laborious process, and governmental agencies and private firms have not developed such elaborate training programs for the scientists and engineers whom they employ, nor do they provide other opportunities for the acquisition of such skills.

Error Correction

But it is not simply a matter of insufficient knowledge. Scientific assessors of risk for corporations and governmental programs often do not make sound use of the knowledge they already possess. Because of the pressures of time, they may be constrained to select solutions before all the information has been considered.[44] Even if they used all the information they had, it might be difficult to decide among the alternatives.

Since overlap and duplication sometimes compensate for error, it might be desirable to maintain or create organizational redundancies when assessing risk under conditions of uncertainty.[45] While the establishment of special units for monitoring and review might be useful, a potential shortcoming is that special units separate their members from the problems that front-line managers have to address. Such separation can breed resentment and uncooperativeness between the managers and those who assess what the managers do.[46]

In fact, those who work in special monitoring units often face considerable hostility and resentment.[47] For example, an analysis of safety review groups created at nuclear power plants after the Three Mile Island accident found that at plants where the authority for the identification of risk had been separated from the authority for taking action to correct deficiencies, there were considerable problems.[48] The nuclear power plant personnel responsible for the identification of risk were not in a position to change the situation, even after they had identified the risks. While members of safety review groups perceived many problems and made numerous recommendations for change, the officials responsible for production tended to ignore these recommendations and to consider them irrelevant because they interfered with production.

Prompt error correction is not easily accomplished even when errors and remedies have been discovered by the most reliable methods. As investigations of the Three Mile Island, Bhopal, Challenger, and Chernobyl accidents show, warnings from various sources might be ignored because of difficulties in distinguishing "true signals" from the "noise."[49] Scientists may recognize error slowly, because their training leads them to discard prevailing knowledge only when it clearly has been shown to be defective. Early measurements of ozone depletion were disregarded because they did not fit into prevailing theory. Civil servants may be reluctant to admit error because of fear of blame. The warnings of public interest groups may be dismissed because the crudity of their accusations makes it easy to refute their assertions.

Evidence about mistakes is rarely unambiguous and it is often difficult to cite it persuasively; it is likely, therefore, that at least some of the evidence will be discarded. The correction of error depends not only on its recognition. Someone must have enough power to take action based on the assessment. In this sense, a strategy of embracing error and rewarding those who admit to their mistakes cannot be readily carried out. As in all practical activities, it requires power and not merely knowledge to correct errors arising from risk assessments.

Decisions with Incomplete Knowledge

There are probably no technologies about which there is complete knowledge and hence complete certainty about the risks involved. In these instances where the knowledge is incomplete, the assessments of technological risks by managers are critically important. Managers have to make decisions about the implications of technologies for present and future generations; however, the norms for making these decisions, in organizational and social settings where the decisions often are highly controversial and the scientific information is ambiguous, are not very well established. Many approaches may be taken, but only reflective and conscientious self-examination by the managers is sufficient to guide them in actions that have critical consequences for society.[50]

In their role as decision makers, managers must claim no more for their knowledge than is defensible. Inevitably, the issues they face will be drawn into the adversary process.[51] The tendency will be for them to suppress awkward aspects of the evidence and to state a case more strongly than the evidence can support. However, it is important to admit where uncertainty exists and to acknowledge limitations arising from the current state of knowledge. However profound the achievements of science and technology, a great deal about its impacts is unknown. Managers do a disservice when they claim to know more about ultimate impacts than is actually the case.

Summary and Conclusions

This chapter has discussed the controversy about normal accidents. Some believe that they cannot be avoided, and therefore certain technologies have to abandoned; others maintain that trial-and-error learning applies to risky as well as nonrisky technologies, and that society over time improves its capabilities to handle dangerous technologies.

We reviewed the major causes of death in the United States and the extent to which government can affect these causes. We discussed the concept of rational risk assessment and analyzed the actual decision-making situation faced by managers. Managers often face situations of insufficient knowledge and situations where they are unable to take advantage of the knowledge that they have. Tragedies such as Bhopal are ones in which managers had the knowledge, but did not use it.

This chapter distinguished between risk and uncertainty in economics and in science and technology. It introduced the concept of residual risk to describe scientific and engineering risk. It discussed society's needs for making risk assessments based on inferences from animal studies.

This chapter also considered psychological, group, and organizational limits on decision making. It looked at the ways environmentalists, business people, and government officials view technological risk, the criteria society applies in evaluating the value of a human life, and some of the steps society can take to improve risk decision making.

Discussion Questions

1. Why do normal accidents occur? Can they be avoided?
2. To what extent can trial-and-error learning apply to risky technologies? Who is right about learning in risky situations—Perrow or Wildavsky? Why?
3. What are the major causes of death in the United States? To what extent can government regulatory agencies help reduce the cause of death?
4. What does the term *rational risk assessment* mean? To what extent would society be better off if risks were assessed more rationally?
5. What difficult dilemmas do managers face when introducing a new pesticide?
6. To what extent do you agree with the statement that insufficient knowledge is the main source of organizational failure with respect to risky technologies?
7. Distinguish between risk and uncertainty in economics. Who bears the burden of uncertainty in economic theory? How does this differ from who bears the burden with respect to risky technologies?
8. What does Haefele mean by the term *residual risk?*
9. In assessing risk, what is wrong with making inferences from animal studies? Why does society have little choice but to rely on animal studies?
10. What are some psychological misperceptions that bias people's risk perceptions? How significant are these biases?
11. To what extent do groups improve risk decision making?
12. In what ways do organizations bias risk decision making?
13. Why do businesses underestimate risk? Why do environmentalists overestimate risk?
14. What affects how government agencies view risk?
15. What are some of the different criteria society has used for evaluating the worth of a human life? How good are these criteria? Can you think of better criteria?
16. What is meant by an informal decision rule, a shortcut, or a rule of thumb as a means for evaluating risk?

17. What difference would it make if managers obtained clinical skills, as well as scientific skills, in evaluating risk?

18. What can society do to improve its risk assessment capacities?

Endnotes

1. C. Perrow, *Normal Accidents* (New York: Basic Books, 1984), pp. 10–11.
2. Ibid.
3. Perrow, *Normal Accidents.*
4. A. Wildavsky, *Searching for Safety* (New Brunswick, N.J.: Transaction Press, 1988), pp. 125–47.
5. Ibid.
6. Perrow, *Normal Accidents,* p. 12.
7. Wildavsky, *Searching for Safety.*
8. Discussion in this section is based on J. F. Morrall, "The Perils of Prudence," *Regulation,* November/December 1986, pp. 25–39.
9. J. Main, "The Big Cleanup Gets It Wrong," *Fortune,* May 20, 1991, pp. 95–101.
10. Ibid.
11. Ibid.; R. Morgenstern and S. Session, "Which Are the Largest Problems EPA Might Tackle? Which are the Smallest?" *Environment,* July/August 1988, pp. 15–17, 35–39.
12. Ibid.
13. Ibid.
14. Ibid.
15. Ibid.; P. Shabecoff, "Tangled Rules on Toxic Hazards Hamper Efforts to Protect Public," *The New York Times,* November 27, 1985, p. A1.
16. L. B. Lave, *How Safe Is Safe Enough? Setting Safety Goals,* formal publication no. 96, Center for the Study of American Business, Washington University, January 1990; Shabecoff, "Tangled Rules on Toxic Hazards Hamper Efforts to Protect Public."
17. A. Marcus, "Risk, Uncertainty, and Scientific Judgment," *Minerva* 2, 1988, pp. 138–52; A. Weinberg, "Science and Trans-Science," *Minerva,* April 1972, pp. 209–22.
18. D. Whiteside, "Note on the Export of Pesticides from the United States to Developing Countries," in *Ethics in Management* (Boston: Harvard Business School, 1984), pp. 121–36.
19. See P. Slovic and B. Fischoff, "Cognitive Processes and Societal Risk-Taking," in *Cognitive Social Behavior* (Hillsdale, N.J.: Lawrence Elbaum Associates, 1976); V. Covello, "The Perception of Technological Risks: A Literature Review," *Technological Forecasting and Social Change* 23, 4, 1983, pp. 285–98; and M. Weinstein and R. Quinn, "Psychological Considerations in Valuing Health Risk Reductions," *Natural Resources Journal,* June 1983, pp. 659–73.

20. M. Weber, *The Theory of Social and Economic Organization* (New York: Free Press, 1947).

21. F. Knight, *Risk, Uncertainty, and Profit* (New York: Houghton Mifflin, 1921).

22. Knight, *Risk, Uncertainty and Profit*, p. 233; also see S. Lippman and R. Rumelt, "Uncertain Imitability," *Bell Journal of Economics* 13, 1982, pp. 418–38.

23. A. Sage and E. White, "Methodologies for Risk and Hazard Assessment: A Survey and Status Report," *IEEE Transactions on Systems, Man, and Cybernetics,* August 1980, pp. 425–41.

24. W. Haefele, "Hypotheticality and the New Challenges: The Pathfinder Role of Nuclear Energy," *Minerva,* July, 1974, p. 313.

25. See W. Lowrance, *Of Acceptable Risk* (Los Altos, Calif.: William Kaufmann, Inc., 1976); and National Research Council, *Risk Assessment in the Federal Government: Managing the Process* (Washington, D.C.: MAS, 1983).

26. W. Havender, "Ruminations on a Rat: Saccharin and Human Risk," *Regulation,* March/April 1979, pp. 17–24.

27. B. Fischoff, S. Lichtenstein, P. Slovic, S. Derby, and R. Keeney, *Acceptable Risk* (Cambridge, England: Cambridge University Press, 1983); also see P. Slovic, B. Fischoff, and S. Lictenstein, *Perceived Risk,* paper presented at General Motors Symposium, Warren, Michigan, October 9, 1979.

28. See Covello, "The Perception of Technological Risks," p. 30.

29. I. Janis, *Groupthink: Psychological Studies of Policy Decisions and Fiascoes* 2nd ed. (Boston: Houghton Mifflin Co., 1982).

30. A. Vinokur, "Review and Theoretical Analysis of the Effects of Group Processes upon Individuals and Group Decisions Involving Risk," *Psychological Bulletin,* October 1971, pp. 231–41.

31. G. Allison, *Essence of Decision: Explaining the Cuban Missile Crisis* (Boston: Little, Brown, and Co., 1971).

32. See, for example, M. Halperin, *Bureaucratic Politics and Foreign Policy* (Washington, D.C.: The Brookings Institution, 1974).

33. J. Q. Wilson, *The Politics of Regulation* (New York: Basic Books, 1980); and A. Marcus, *Promise and Performance: Choosing and Implementing an Environmental Policy* (Westport, Conn.: Greenwood Press, 1980).

34. P. Shrivastava and I. Mitroff, "Enhancing Organizational Research Utilization: The Role of Decision-Makers' Assumptions," *Academy of Management Review* 9, 1984, pp. 18–26.

35. K. Hammond et al., "Fundamental Obstacles to the Use of Scientific Information in Public Policymaking," *Technological Forecasting and Social Change* 24, 1983, pp. 287–97.

36. M. Douglas and A. Wildavsky, *Risk and Culture* (Berkeley, Calif.: University of California Press, 1982). Douglas and Wildavsky say that they "survive only through attack."

37. See A. Marcus, *The Adversary Economy: Business Responses to Changing Government Requirements* (Westport, Conn.: Greenwood Press, 1984).

38. B. Keller, "Federal Agencies Set Varying Cash Value on Workers' Lives," *Minneapolis Star and Tribune,* October 27, 1984, p. 12A.

39. N. Ashford, W. Ryan, and C. Caldart, "Law and Science Policy in Federal Regulation of Formaldehyde," *Science,* November 25, 1983, pp. 894–900; also see H. Sapolsky, ed., *Consuming Fears: The Politics of Product Risks* (New York: Basic Books, 1986).

40. Lave, *How safe Is safe enough?*
41. See A. Marcus, "Professional Autonomy as a Basis of Conflict in an Organization," *Human Resources Management,* Fall, 1985.
42. House Committee on Agriculture, Subcommittee on Department Operations, Research, and Foreign Agriculture, *Regulations of Pesticides, Volume III: Appendix to Hearings* (Washington, D.C.: Government Printing Office, 1983).
43. E. Marshall, "EPA Ends Cut and Paste Toxicology," *Science,* January 27, 1984, pp. 379–80.
44. See J. Steinbruner, *The Cybernetic Theory of Decision* (Princeton, N.J.: Princeton University Press, 1974).
45. M. Landau, "On the Concept of a Self-Correcting Organization," *Public Administration Review,* November/December 1973, pp. 532–42.
46. D. Metaly, *Error Correction in Bureaucracies,* doctoral dissertation in political science, University of California, Berkeley, 1978.
47. A. Wildavsky, "The Self-Evaluating Organizational," *Public Administration Review,* September/October 1972, p. 519.
48. A. Marcus and R. Osborn, *Safety Review at Nuclear Power Plants: A Review Assessment* (Seattle, Wash.: Battelle Human Affairs Research Centers, 1984). Prepared for U.S. Nuclear Regulatory Commission.
49. See D. Faust, *The Limits of Scientific Reasoning* (Minneapolis: University of Minnesota, 1984).
50. E. Shils, "Science and Scientists in the Public Arena," *The American Scholar,* Spring 1987, pp. 185–202.
51. See R. V. Jones, "Temptations and Risks of the Scientific Adviser," *Minerva,* July 1972, pp. 441–52; and R. V. Jones, "The Obligations of Scientists as Counsellors," *Minerva,* January 1972, pp. 107–58.

17 PRODUCT LIABILITY

The Reasonable Man invariably looks where he is going and is careful to examine the immediate foreground before he executes a leap or bound; who neither stargazes nor is lost in meditation when approaching trap doors or the margin of a dock; . . . who never mounts a moving omnibus, and does not alight from any car while the train is in motion.

Lord Herbert[1]

Introduction and Chapter Objectives

Businesses invariably cause harm to innocent bystanders. How careful must they be? According to classic legal doctrine, they have to act as a so-called reasonable person would under the circumstances. If they do not conform to this standard, they are at fault and have to compensate the victims. Under modern legal theory, there is no need to prove fault in product liability cases; businesses are held strictly liable. Strict liability, however, does not mean that businesses are without a defense. They have to be able to show that there was no defect in the design and manufacture of a product. They have to demonstrate that they provided adequate warnings and that users have voluntarily assumed some of the risk. This chapter begins by comparing litigation in different countries, and then summarizes the classic legal doctrine of harm and shows how it has evolved from a fault-based system to one that is based on the doctrine of strict liability.

Litigation in Different Countries

There are vast differences in the number of judges, lawyers, and civil litigation in different countries.[2] In the United States more than 2,000 lawyers exist for every million persons. No country in the world is close to this figure. In Japan, there are fewer than 100 attorneys for every million persons (see Exhibit 17–1).

Some attribute differences in economic vitality to these differences.[3] U.S. competitiveness, according to this view, is diminished when lawyers engage in expensive and time-consuming litigation that results in the redistribution of existing resources rather than the creation of new ones.

Others point out that although the United States has more attorneys per capita, the number of civil cases brought in the United States is similar to the number brought in other Anglo-Saxon countries.[4] The Anglo-Saxon countries as a whole are more litigious than other countries. The U.S. estimate is about 44 civil cases per 1,000 persons. In Australia, more than 62 civil cases are brought for every 1,000 persons, whereas in Canada the number is about the same as in the United States. America's major international competitors, Japan and West Germany, however, have far fewer suits—in Japan about 12 cases per 1000 persons and in West Germany about 23 cases.

Reasons for the Differences: Japan

What accounts for these differences? With respect to Japan, the opportunity for conflict certainly exists. It is a small island nation with a large population. Its industrial output has grown rapidly since the end of World War II. The amount of industrial activity per square kilometer of inhabitable space is the greatest in the world.[5]

Real conflict among Japanese may not be reflected in the official statistics. When Japanese are involved in traffic accidents, police give them a minor violation. They are expected to apologize and visit the victim every week for up to a year. The obligation is enforced by local custom and by members of the community. No suit is brought, and the courts are not involved.

When a Japanese Airlines plane crashed killing over 200 people, the CEO personally approached all the families saying he was sorry for what had happened. Notables in the Japanese community, particularly the police and bankers, are available for conflict resolution. Insurance companies offer dispute resolution services that promise fast and cheap settlements. The full burden of dispute resolution does not fall on the judicial system. Conflicts are dealt with through many informal mechanisms.

EXHIBIT 17–1   **Number of Lawyers, Civil Cases, and Judges: Selected Countries**

	Lawyers (per Million Population)	Civil Cases (per Thousand Population)	Judges (per Million Population)
United States	2,348.7	44	94.9
	(1980)	(1975)	(1980)
Australia	911.6	62.1	41.6
	(1975)	(1975)	(1977)
Canada	890.1	46.6	59.3
	(1972)	(1970)	(1981–2)
West Germany	417.2	23.4	213.4
	(1973)	(1977)	(1973)
France	206.4	30.7	84
	(1973)	(1975)	(1973)
Japan	91.2	11.7	22.7
	(1973)	(1978)	(1974)

SOURCE: Adapted from M. Galanter, "Reading the Landscape of Disputes: What We Know and Don't Know. . ." UCLA Law Review 4, 1983.

Also, Japan is a more homogeneous society than the United States. Its traditions stress the group's obligations to society rather than the rights of the individual. The constitutional reforms adopted by Japan after the end of World War II, however, gave individuals comparable legal rights to those possessed by people in the United States. Nonetheless, conflict may not advance to the stage of formal legal proceeding because of Japan's longstanding tradition of informal dispute resolution.[6]

Informal Dispute Resolution

Japan institutionalized many of these techniques and applied them to pollution damages in 1970 when it passed a law for the Resolution of Pollution Disputes. The intent of the law was to anticipate controversy and defuse grievances at the outset. A Citizen's Complaint Referral Service gives authority to prefectural complaint counselors who operate under local ordinances. There are more than 3,000 such counselors in Japan serving more than 400 prefectural and local governments.[7] The law also created Local Pollution Review Boards and a Central Dispute Coordination Committee. All of these groups operate outside the formal legal process. They are supposed to encourage mediation (where the parties reach agreement by themselves), conciliation (where committees formulate nonbinding draft agreements for the parties), and arbitration (where arbitrators bind the parties to an agreement). A similar movement to have environmental disputes resolved outside the court system has arisen in the United States, but it has not gone as far as the movement in Japan.[8]

A Reluctance to Sue

The Japanese reluctance to sue is based on a number of factors.[9] When asked, most Japanese respond that they think suing is un-Japanese and that lawyers are to be despised. The reputation of a person who sues suffers. Other people shun doing business with the person.

The costs of litigation also are great, and suing ordinarily does not pay in Japan. If the court costs are 1,200 yen, it makes no sense to sue to recover 1,000 yen. Suing is unprofitable not only because of the reputational damage it can do to someone who initiates a suit. It is unprofitable because of a shortage of judges and attorneys; this makes suing expensive because it leads to court delays, expensive bond-posting requirements, and a lack of appropriate remedies.

Thus, the reasons for the Japanese reluctance to sue are complex and are based on a mixed set of motives best summed up by the idea that "suing is both wrong and unprofitable."[10] When it is wrong and unprofitable to sue, there are fewer lawsuits.

Legal Predictability

The predictability of Japanese law also may be a reason that the Japanese are less prone to sue than Americans.[11] Japanese courts do not have juries; judges determine outcomes. The parties to a conflict appear in front of the judge in intervals over a long period of time during which the judge can suggest what the likely outcome is going to be. When the parties have a good indication of how the judge is going to decide, they have strong reason to settle informally without pressing their case any further.

Another difference between the United States and Japan is that Japanese judges have been more willing to codify portions of the law (see Chapter 18). They have established well-accepted formulas for resolving difficult cases that involve damage awards. Again, the parties know in advance what the likely outcome will be so there is less reason to sue.

Litigation in the United States

In contrast to Japan, the amount of litigation has been growing in the United States. Most observers have pointed to an increase in the number of product liability cases filed and to the average and median awards that have been made (see Exhibit 17–2).[12] The question is whether these in-creases are disproportionate to the growth in population and if they are concentrated only in the product liability area. Legal scholar Marc Gal-anter holds that in proportion to population growth, the increase in the number of suits is not out of line; moreover, most of the increase in fed-eral court filings has been in areas other than product liability law. Still, there have been numerous well-publicized liability cases involving very large settlements.[13]

Legal scholar George Priest argues that there is no objective reason for the increase in suits. The suit system seems to be operating independently of the actual need for litigation, for if there were a greater need for litigation, it would show up in higher death and accident rates and in higher work-related and disability rates. Instead, the data show declines in both rates in the post–World War II era (see Exhibit 17–3).

However, in the 1974–1981 period many product-related injury totals in the United States did move upward.[14] They only started to decline again after 1981, as the examples in Exhibit 17–4 show. These data suggest that the greater number of injuries may have been the reason for the increase in product liability suits and that the increased number of claims then had a deterrent effect; they lowered the injury rates in the subsequent period. The data suggest a connection between litigation and the underlying causes and consequences of that litigation.

EXHIBIT 17–2   Cases Filed and Jury Awards in Both Average and Well-Publicized Product Liability Cases

Number of Federal Product Liability Cases Filed		Average Product Liability Jury Awards (1984 Dollars)		
Year	*Cases Filed*	*Years*	*Cook County*	*San Francisco County*
1975	2,886	1975–79	$597,000	$308,000
1980	7,755	1980–84	$828,000	$1,105,000
1985	13,554			

Well-Publicized Cases Involving Large Settlements: 1983–86

Case	*Jury Award*	*Plaintiff*
Agent orange	$180 million	2.4 million veterans
Three Mile Island	$25 million	280 residents
Love Canal	$20 million	1300 residents

SOURCE: Adapted from R. E. Litan, ed., *Liability: Perspectives and Policy* (Washington, D.C.: Brookings Institution, 1988).

EHIBIT 17–3   **Accident and Work-Related Death Rates**
Per 100,000 Persons

	Accident Death Rates	*Work-Related Death Rates*
1950	60.6	27
1960	52.3	21
1970	56.4	18
1980	46.7	13

SOURCE: Adapted from R. E. Litan, ed., *Liability: Perspectives and Policy* (Washington, D.C.: Brookings Institution, 1988).

EHIBIT 17–4   **Product-Related Injuries: Chain Saws and Power Saws**

	1974	*1981*	*1986*
Chain saws	23	64	41
Power saws	41	79	62

SOURCE: Adapted from R. E. Litan, ed., *Liability: Perspectives and Policy* (Washington, D.C.: Brookings Institution, 1988).

Business Executive Opinion

When surveyed in 1987, business executives reported a positive impact from the increased litigation (see Exhibit 17–5).[15] Forty-seven percent said that it had resulted in improved product usage and warnings, 35 percent claimed that it had improved the safety of their products, and 33 percent reported that their companies had redesigned product lines.

However, the same business executives also held that there had been adverse impacts, including discontinued product lines, the decision not to introduce new products, a decline in product research, and lost market share. The decision not to introduce new products, they argued, had hurt the global competitiveness of U.S. business.

The general public views the increasing number of suits with mixed feelings.[16] Fifty-one percent of the people surveyed in 1987 held that awards had been excessive, and 63 percent blamed attorneys who were looking for big fees. However, most people felt that there should be no limit on the size of damage awards, and that juries, not judges, should continue to set the amount of the damages.

Reforming U.S. Liability Laws

The type of reform executives most favored was to replace the strict liability system with a fault-based one.[17] However, most executives

EXHIBIT 17–5   Executive Opinion of Increased Litigation: 1987

Positive Impact		Negative Impact	
Improved product usage warnings	47%	Discontinued product lines	47%
Improved safety	35%	Decision not to introduce new products	39%
Redesigned products	33%	Decline in product research	25%
		Lost market share	22%

SOURCE: Adapted from *The Polling Report* 21, 1987.

believed that the type of reform most likely to occur was the imposition of caps on punitive damages.

Indeed, many states, including Alaska, Colorado, Minnesota, and Utah, have introduced some type of cap on damages, but no federal damage cap has been passed (see Exhibit 17–6).[18] One of the main reasons Congress failed to pass a bill was that the proposed reforms were so diverse. There was little agreement in the business community and in the general public about what type of reform would be best.

Among the many reform proposals that have been made are the following:[19]

1. A cap, or upper limit, on the amount that victims can recover. A cap can come in many forms—on pain and suffering damages, on punitive damages, on lawyer's contingency fees, and so on.
2. Allowing judges, not juries, to award punitive damages.
3. Limiting the principle of joint and several liability principle (in which each contributor to the damage—no matter how small its role—can be held fully liable for all the costs).

Later in this chapter and in Chapter 18, additional reform proposals will be examined, and further comparison will be made with Japan.

The Evolution of U.S. Liability Laws

Before discussing reform in more detail, it is necessary to understand how the law of damages has evolved in the United States.[20] In legal terminology, this branch of the law is called torts. Derived from French and Latin roots and meaning "to twist," it deals with private harm or injury. When a person is harmed by another person, the plaintiff (the person claiming to have been harmed) may bring an action against the defendant (the person alleged to have caused the harm). The purpose is to restore the situation to the condition before the harm was caused, and

EXHIBIT 17–6   **States with Caps on Damages: 1987**

State	Cap on Noneconomic Damages
Alaska	$500,000
Colorado	$500,000
Florida	$450,000
Maryland	$350,000
Minnesota	$400,000
New Hampshire	$875,000
Virginia	$350,000
Washington	$493,000
Wisconsin	$1 million

SOURCE: Adapted from National Conference of State Legislatures, *Liability Insurance,* May 1987.

inasmuch as possible, to compensate the plaintiff for the damage that was done.

Tort law is restorative in its intent, but it also has a deterrent effect. If a person knows that a victim must be compensated, then the person will be less likely to commit an act that causes harm. Insofar as tort law aims to restore a situation to its prior condition, its purpose is to promote a sense of justice in society.

The Classic Theory

According to the classic theory, the plaintiff has to prove three things.

1. *Breech of duty:* Even if harm is unintentional, the defendant owes the plaintiff the duty of care as would be shown by a reasonable person under the circumstances. The defendant, or *tortfeasor* as this person is known by the courts, is held liable, that is, negligent and at fault, for the breech of this standard.

There is, however, no precise statutory definition of the standard of reasonable care. Instead, the courts rely on custom, practice, and tradition to decide if it is exercised in a particular case. Because of the admirable flexibility of the standard, it has been subject to parody and ridicule. For example, a reasonable person is always supposed to be thinking of others. Prudence is supposed to be the person's guide, and "safety-first" the rule to which the reasonable person steadfastly clings (see the quotation at the beginning of this chapter).[21] Difficulties in defining the reasonable person's behavior have resulted in much legal disputation.

2. *Actual damages:* An additional element in the classic theory is that the plaintiff must show real damages. Carelessness or breech of duty without harm is called "negligence in the air." In this respect, the

requirements of the law and ethics diverge. Although ethically the tort-feasor is worthy of blame for carrying out actions that might result in harm, legally, if no actual harm results, the defendant is not responsible and does not have to compensate the plaintiff.

The harms for which a plaintiff can be compensated are broad, including relatively concrete matters like medical bills and lost wages, and less-tangible harms such as emotional distress and loss of companionship. For wrongful death, the victim's heirs are entitled to the present value of future wages that the victim would have earned minus the amount that would have been spent on personal consumption. How to value a human life has been strenuously debated, as noted in Chapter 16. The use of the present value of future wages as a standard does not take into account the emotional loss of the heirs (see Chapter 16).

The intent of tort law is compensation, not punishment, but there are exceptions to this rule. When the defendant means to inflict harm or acts in reckless disregard of the safety of others, punitive damages may be awarded. Punitive awards have been large, and companies like Johns Manville have been threatened with bankruptcy (see the special feature, "The Threat of Bankruptcy").[22] The trials where punitive damages are awarded are long and complex and more than half of the awards are usually consumed by attorneys' fees.[23]

3. *Causation:* The third element that the plaintiff must demonstrate is causation.[24] If the defendant has acted in a careless manner and there is damage but the defendant is not directly responsible for this damage, then the defendant has no legal obligation to compensate the plaintiff. The actions of the defendant must be the immediate and proximate cause of the harms suffered by the plaintiff.

For example, arguments by a theologian that the unmoved mover (God) caused the damage or by a psychologist that childhood experiences are the cause of the damages would have no legal bearing. The courts accept a limited concept of causation. They seek clear evidence of a direct cause and effect relationship, for example, a car that strikes another car or a bullet that is fired within view of reliable witnesses.

A case familiar to most law students is the 1928 Supreme Court decision in *Palsgraf* v. *Long Island Railway Co.*[25] The relevant facts are these. The plaintiff, Mrs. Palsgraf, was standing on a railroad platform. The guard for Long Island Railway helped a man board a train after it had started to move and jarred loose a package that the man had been carrying. Covered in newspapers and filled with fireworks, the package fell on the track and exploded. The explosion upset a set of scales at the other end of the platform where Mrs. Palsgraf was standing, causing injuries for which she sued. The Court decided against Mrs. Palsgraf. In the majority decision Justice Cardozo held that the railroad's actions were too far removed in the chain of causes to result in Mrs. Palsgraf's injuries.

The Threat of Bankruptcy

In recent years, filings of Chapter 11 bankruptcy petitions have become a common practice for large American corporations.[1] Economic theory assumes that if a firm goes bankrupt, its assets will be liquidated and the firm no longer will exist. The process of exiting from the market is an integral part of the discipline imposed upon firms by the capitalist system. Investors have to accept risk; if the companies in which they invest do not succeed, they will lose large portions of their investment. Then new investors will have the chance to purchase the liquidated assets at favorable terms; they can form new firms and enter the market. Because of some combination of lower costs, better management, and greater productivity, the new firm should be able to succeed, whereas the old one could not. In this way, capitalism is a dynamic system that perpetually revitalizes itself. It increases the growth and productivity of society at large by weeding out losing ownership teams and rewarding winning ones.

The discipline of the market, however, has been eroded by changes in the bankruptcy laws that make it harder for firms to fail. Until 1893, the United States did not have a permanent bankruptcy law. Under common law, debtors were sent to prison. Efforts to create a permanent bankruptcy law (in 1800, 1841, and 1867) came to naught because of disputes between Jeffersonians, Jacksonians, and Southern and Western Democrats who favored liberal bankruptcy laws, and Tories, High Federalists, Whigs, and Republicans who opposed them. The first enduring national bankruptcy act called

for strict liquidation of failing firms. It was not until 1938, in the midst of the depression, that an alternative to strict liquidation was made part of law. The 1938 bankruptcy act is the predecessor to current laws. Passed in a period when many people were debtors and comparatively few were solvent, it allows for corporate reorganization rather than liquidation.

The 1938 Bankruptcy Act was amended in 1977 when a new bankruptcy code took effect. Under the new code, liquidation takes place under Chapter 7 proceedings. However, there remains an alternative to liquidation—reorganization under Chapter 11. The 1977 amendments to the bankruptcy laws eliminate the need to be insolvent when filing for Chapter 11 status. As soon as a petition for bankruptcy is filed, the stay of creditors claims is automatic. Creditors do not have to be paid. Troubled firms then start a process of negotiations with creditors' committees. They can negotiate with employees about collective bargaining agreements and with executives about their compensation contracts.

These negotiations are designed to establish the conditions under which the distressed companies can remain going concerns. The bankruptcy judge acts as a mediator or arbitrator in this process. Legal fees must be paid first. The unsecured creditors get next preference. Employees, customers, and the government (taxes) have claim to the company's assets. The secured creditors obtain what is left. First in line for obtaining what is left are bondholders and preferred stockholders. The last group to be paid back is the common shareholders. They are referred to as the "residual claimants." They have claim to all remaining profit when the firm is doing well, and take the risk of

---

[1]W. F. Todd, "Aggressive Uses of Chapter 11 of the Federal Bankruptcy Code," *Economic Review*, Quarter 3, 1986, pp. 20–26.

losing everything when the firm does poorly.

Under 1984 amendments to the Bankruptcy Act, standards were established for judging the reasonableness of an employer's use of Chapter 11 to reject collective bargaining agreements.[2] These amendments were passed after Bildisco and Bildisco, Inc., used a Chapter 11 filing to unilaterally abrogate its collective bargaining agreements. Other celebrated cases involving the use of Chapter 11 filings to modify collective bargaining agreements were Continental Airlines in 1983 and Frontier Airlines in 1986.

The most significant uses of the Chapter 11 filing to modify claims, however, have been in the product liability area. The cases involving Johns-Manville in 1982 and A. H. Robins in 1986 (more details on the A. H. Robins bankruptcy are in the special feature in Chapter 18) attracted substantial attention.[3] Johns-Manville faced an unpredictable number of claims relating to the damage caused by asbestos. At the time of its filing for bankruptcy, it had 16,500 existing asbestos claims against it, which were being settled at an average of $40,000 per suit. Five large punitive damage awards, however, had averaged over $600,000 since 1982. With 500 new claims being made every month, the total number of estimated claims against

Johns-Manville were more than 50,000 and the total liability was estimated to be at least $2 billion. The lawyers were receiving $1.71 for every dollar that went to the victims and Johns-Manville's long-term legal costs could have been very large. Its insurers refused to pay, arguing that the damage had been inflicted upon the victims years ago. Long latencies with respect to the onset of the disease meant that different insurers had been around when the victims first suffered exposure. Present-day insurers argued that they could not be held accountable. Johns-Manville's out-of-court settlement with the insurers netted the company only $730 million.

The company's filing for Chapter 11 reorganization was a surprise and was the first time a company had used the bankruptcy laws to stay the claims of a group of creditors who were the victims of the company's past actions. Under the bankruptcy filing, Johns-Manville created a separate fund under which all present and future asbestos claims would be reimbursed. Meanwhile, the company could continue normal business operations. The fund for the reimbursement of victims was to receive $2.5 billion over 25 years and it had the right to at least 50 percent of the common voting shares of the corporation. The company had to pay up to 20 percent of its operating profits into the fund over 20 years. It would divest itself of its asbestos divisions, which were its most profitable. But Johns-Manville no longer could be sued by victims. With the stay of suits came an end to punitive damage awards.

Many felt that this use of the bankruptcy laws to evade punitive damage awards was unjustified—Johns-Manville deserved to be punished. The company defended itself by claiming that asbestos brought many advantages to society (e.g., fireproofing and insulation and better brake linings, which added to automotive safety). The company in-

---

[2]Todd, "Aggressive Uses of Chapter 11 of the Federal Bankruptcy Code."

[3]S. Labaton, "Manville Trust for Asbestos Victims Is Running Short of Funds," *The New York Times*, October 24, 1989, p. A18; W. Lambert and P. M. Barrett, "Nationwide Plan Set for Asbestos Cases," *The Wall Street Journal*, August 13, 1990, p. B3; R. Buchholz, W. Evans, and R. Wayley, *Management Response to Public Issues* (Englewood Cliffs, N.J.: Prentice-Hall, 1985), pp. 322–37.

[4]P. Brodeur, *Outrageous Misconduct: The Asbestos Industry on Trial* (New York: Pantheon, 1985).

The Threat of Bankruptcy continued

tended to do no wrong. Its position was that it knew definitely only in 1964, after a major study showed illness among asbestos workers, that exposure was dangerous. It relied on a state-of-the-art defense, which is typical in tort cases of this kind: at the time of production, the company was conforming to what it believed to be the best practice in the industry.

However, attorneys for the plaintiffs held that the company had to have known that asbestos caused health related problems.[4] One of its founders, Henry W. Johns, had died of chronic lung disease that was suspected to have come from his exposure to the substance. And medical studies going back 50 years showed that people who had been exposed to asbestos were likely to have severe pulmonary problems; their lungs would be damaged and breathing would be difficult. Also, in 1918 insurers refused to sell health insurance to asbestos workers because they understood the health problems.

Moreover, in 1933 top officials of asbestos manufacturers, including Johns-Manville, met together to discuss the health risks to asbestos workers. These risks had been revealed in a report by the Metropolitan Life Insurance Company commissioned by the industry. Extensive notes were taken during this meeting, and they were locked away in a safe in one of the companies. Lawyers for the victims referred to these notes whenever attorneys for the asbestos companies maintained that the companies had no early knowledge of asbestos dangers. The notes were used to show that the asbestos companies acted in reckless disregard of the health of their workers and deserved to be assessed punitive damages. Also, it was alleged that punitive damages were necessary in this case as a deterrent to other companies.

The plaintiffs' attorneys had additional evidence that showed the asbestos manufacturers knew of the health risk (e.g., a former doctor for Johns-Manville said that he had informed top company officials in the 1940s that only 4 of the 708 asbestos workers that he had X-rayed had healthy lungs, but the company officials refused to do anything about it). The lawyers had won large awards by showing that company officials knew of the risks but failed to do anything about them. With the Chapter 11 filing, the victims would no longer be able to collect punitive damages.

Many questioned, therefore, whether the Johns-Manville filing was done in good faith. The company in all other ways was financially sound. But representatives for Johns-Manville justified the use of Chapter 11, saying that the procedure was set up for companies that were not currently insolvent but might become so. Still, Johns-Manville was probably the healthiest company ever to declare itself bankrupt.

---

[4]P. Brodeur, *Outrageous Misconduct: The Asbestos Industry on Trial* (New York: Pantheon, 1985).

Long Latencies

In cases of long latencies between the time a person is exposed and the onset of a disease, the courts have difficulty assigning responsibility. A unique response to this problem was fashioned by the California Supreme Court in the case of *Sindell* v. *Abbott Laboratories* in 1980.[26] Several drug companies manufactured and sold diethylstilbestrol (DES), which was used to prevent miscarriages. The Food and Drug Administration (FDA) banned DES in 1971 when it was found to cause vaginal and cervical cancer in women whose mothers had taken the drug. The drug companies were sued. Over 200 companies had made DES and it was impossible to determine which one sold the drug which harmed a particular woman. The California Supreme Court allowed the plaintiffs to recover by apportioning responsibility based on market share at the time the plaintiff's mother took the drug.

The Case against Smoking

Problems in determining causation affect many tort cases. One reason that smokers have not recovered from cigarette manufacturers is that the evidence that shows a link between smoking and lung cancer, no matter how conclusive it may be to scientists, does not stand up in the courts. The scientific argument is a statistical one. It shows that there is greater tendency among smokers to contact cancer. However, scientists cannot say with complete assurance that a particular cancer is a result of a person's smoking. Unlike asbestos, which is associated with one type of cancer, many types of cancer are associated with smoking, and many factors, including genetic and environmental circumstances, can intervene.

Assume that the person smoked two packs of cigarettes a day for 20 years and contacted a form of lung cancer. What if the same type of cancer was found in the person's family among nonsmokers? What if the person lived in an area of high concentration of sulfur dioxide and other air pollutants? It would be hard for the victim's lawyers to prove that cigarette smoking was the immediate and proximate cause of the person's illness. The "but-for" test is the criterion the courts apply—but for A, the courts ask, would B have occurred?[27] Even without smoking, such a person might have contacted cancer. In the courts, probabilistic evidence usually is insufficient; there has to be a preponderance of evidence on the side of the plaintiff.

The Cipolione Case

The landmark 1988 case of Antonio Cipolione, whose wife died of cancer in 1964, was the first to be won by plaintiffs against a cigarette company.[28] In this case a federal jury in Newark, N.J., awarded $400,000 in damages to Mr. Cipolione. The reason for the large award was the finding that the Ligget Group, Inc., implied wrongly that cigarettes were safe in its advertising prior to 1966. The jury found that Ligget should have warned customers about the dangers of cigarette smoking prior to 1966, the year in which Congress required that warning labels be put on cigarette packages.

Lawyers for the plaintiff spent about $3 million and five years gathering evidence. Their aim was to bring to light thousands of pages of internal documents showing that the manufacturers knew of the dangers of cigarette smoking prior to the congressional action and that they sold cigarettes to the public without a warning even though they had this knowledge. The plaintiff's lawyers hoped that exposing these documents would make it easier for other attorneys for the plaintiffs to win awards in future cases.

The lawyers showed that the cigarette manufacturers made many implied promises in their advertising about the safety of their products. For instance, in the 1940s R. J. Reynolds claimed that "more doctors smoke Camels," and in the 1950s Lorillard said that the micronite filter in Kent Cigarettes was "so safe, so effective, it has been selected to help filter the air in hospital operating rooms." The lawyers alleged that these claims by the cigarette manufacturers had established an explicit warranty with their customers about the safety of the product.

Landmark Cases

Cases like Cipolione are needed to start a flood of lawsuits, and only after such landmark cases, against products, for example, like asbestos and intrauterine devices, are large jury awards won. Of course, these products have a number of characteristics that distinguish them from cigarettes, so it is easier to argue that victims have been unwittingly exposed to hazards. By contrast, many juries believe that smokers voluntarily engage in the behavior and know the danger of what they are doing.

Lawyers for the cigarette manufacturers have adhered to traditional defenses: (1) smokers have a sense that tobacco involves risks and that they must take some responsibility for their conduct, and (2) the evidence linking smoking to any particular type of cancer is ambiguous at best. Significantly, in the Cipolione case the jury found that smoking was at least partially responsible for Mrs. Cipolione's death. But the jury did not find that the defendants conspired against Mrs. Cipolione to suppress evidence that smoking was unsafe. Future cases will have to try to press forward with the conspiracy argument.

Arguments for the Defense

The classic theory of torts provides defendants with a number of arguments for refuting the claims against them (see Exhibit 17–7).[29] They may argue, for example, that their actions were responsible under the circumstances, that the plaintiff suffered no actual harm, or that their actions were not the direct causes of the plaintiff's injuries. Defendants also can claim contributory negligence and assumption of risk. These two claims will be addressed.

Contributory Negligence

Contributory negligence is based on the principle that both defendant and plaintiff must act according to the standard of reasonable care. For example, if the plaintiff is suing the defendant for failure to properly remove snow from a sidewalk but the plaintiff approached the sidewalk in a stupor after having imbibed a few too many Bloody Marys, then the defendant can claim that the plaintiff did not exercise reasonable care.

However, when fault can be found with the actions of both parties, the courts are not faced with an either/or situation. The courts have the right to apportion blame on a percentage basis (this is true in most states).[30] This reduces the plaintiff's burden to prove that the defendant is at fault. By applying a standard of comparative negligence, the states can reduce the award the defendant owes the plaintiff by the percentage the plaintiff is responsible. Some states will grant recovery only if the defendant is 50 percent or more responsible; any percentage above 50 percent is paid by the defendant. Other states will allow awards to the plaintiff at percentages below 50 percent responsibility.

Exact apportioning of responsibility between defendant and plaintiff is extremely difficult and is one of the most controversial aspects of tort law. Tough cases, for example, arise in deciding who is responsible for automobile accidents. Some form of no-fault insurance, therefore, has been adopted in many states. It simplifies the process by eliminating

---

EXHIBIT 17–7   Classic Tort Law

Plaintiff has to prove:
1. Breech of duty.
2. Actual damages.
3. Causation.

Defendant can argue:
1. Contributory negligence.
2. Assumption of risk.

costly and lengthy court procedures designed to determine who is at fault and by what percentage. It also guarantees that regardless of who is at fault, the victim will receive some form of compensation.

Assumption of Risk

Another claim that a defendant can make is that the plaintiff was aware of the risks but nevertheless decided to pursue the activity. As our society becomes more litigious, the protection offered by this claim has grown in importance. The plaintiff's awareness of risk need not be conscious and explicit, but the defendant's argument is strengthened if a consciousness of the risks involved is specific. Therefore, people are commonly required to sign papers admitting awareness of risks before medical procedures are performed. It is also common for ski lodges, baseball franchises, and transportation companies to put disclaimers on the back of tickets saying that in the event of harm the ticketholder was aware of the dangers. Because of the customers' implied assumption of risk, cigarette manufacturers and diet pop makers are not as unhappy as they might be about warning labels that must appear on packages.

When the plaintiff has been warned, the courts are unlikely to take punitive action against the tortfeasor. A plaintiff can recover even after admitting awareness of risk, but the awards will be limited to compensation for tangible medical costs and lost earnings rather than intangible emotional distress or pain and suffering, which means that awards will be substantially lower.

Strict Liability

The classic theory of torts puts the burden of proof on the plaintiff to prove that the defendant is at fault. However, modern tort theory has moved toward a theory of strict liability where the plaintiff no longer has to prove fault. The strict liability theory derives from the treatment the courts give to inherently dangerous activities. For example, if a person owns wild animals, such as snakes or leopards, that injure someone, the animals' owner is responsible regardless of the care exercised. Also, a company that uses explosives is responsible for harm even if it observes safety rules. According to strict liability, responsibility exists without the sense of moral opprobrium that applies under the classic theory (see Exhibit 17–8).

What is the justification for strict liability? Why should a defendant have to pay when the harm inflicted is unintentional and the defendant's actions are reasonable and appropriate under the circumstances? The answer to this question is complicated. First, it is necessary to recognize that the costs of damages have to be borne by someone. Either the

---
EXHIBIT 17–8   **Strict Liability**

Plaintiff does not have to prove:
  • Breech of duty.
Why?
  • Someone has to pay.
  • Buyer doesn't expect to be injured.
  • Manufacturer knows more about the product than the buyer.

---

victim, the injurer, or society at large, through its governmental institutions, has to pay for all or part of the damages. Modern tort law has decided to make the tortfeasor or the tortfeasor's insurance company mainly responsible.

Strict liability has seen its most complete development in the area of consumer injuries. The manufacturer of a defective product is held strictly liable regardless of whether the manufacturer is at fault. One of the justifications for this doctrine is the buyer's expectations. The buyer does not expect to be injured by the product.

Evolution of the Doctrine of Strict Liability

It is worth tracing the evolution of the doctrine of strict liability (see Exhibit 17–9). The issues have claimed national attention because of the large awards, the increases in liability insurance, and the withdrawal of companies from making products such as infant vaccines.[31]

The evolution of product liability doctrine consists of roughly three periods.[32] In the first period, which lasted until the beginning of World War I, recovery was mainly governed under contract law. During the second period, which lasted from World War I to the mid-1960s, the classic theory of torts developed. The third period, in effect since the mid 1960s, has seen the emergence of a strict liability standard.

Contract Law

Under contract law, if the manufacturer causes the product defect, the consumer has no right to recovery because the consumer's transaction is with the retailer, not the manufacturer. The most important case illustrating this principle, *Winterbottom* v. *Wright*, was decided in England in 1842.[33] It held that a person thrown from an imperfectly constructed wagon had no right to recovery against the wagon manufacturer because the wagon had been purchased from the retailer, not the manufacturer. According to this decision, the "privity" of contract exists between the consumer and the retailer, not between the consumer and the manufacturer.

EXHIBIT 17–9   Evolution of Tort Law

Contract law—A Classic tort law—Strict liability

The privity requirement, however, was seen by subsequent legal analysts as prejudicial against customers, who lacked the knowledge, expertise, and power of the manufacturers. Today, the courts do not allow human risk to be allocated contractually. In product defect cases, contractually based warranties apply only to the repair of the product and to property damage, not to human injury. Warranties remain in effect when they cover such characteristics as product durability, responsibility for labor and parts repairs, and the uses to which a product may and may not be put.

Warranties.   Two types of warranties exist—express and implicit.[34] Express warranties are a written part of the contract and the bargain for sale. Implied warranties are read into the contract by court cases and statute. For example, the Uniform Commercial Code holds that there is an implied warranty of merchantability, which requires that goods be fit for their intended use.

Express warranties serve two purposes. First, they are a way for the seller to support its contention that the product has superior qualities. If the product has these qualities, the seller shows a concrete willingness to back them up with a warranty. Second, express warranties are a way to efficiently divide the risks between the manufacturer and the purchaser. A manufacturer, for example, may be better able to fix refrigerator compressors and therefore takes on this responsibility; the purchaser is in a better position to take precautions against damage to the refrigerator door and therefore takes on this responsibility.

Standard warranties usually contain disclaimers against implied warranties. They also stipulate that the warranted good is free from defects in material and workmanship, and limit the time within which warranty claims can be made and the seller is obliged to repair or replace defective parts. Time limitations are established to assure that claims are due to the seller's defective workmanship or materials, not to the buyer's reckless or irresponsible use of the good in question.

Express warranties usually try to exempt the seller from liability for consequential damage. The reason is that buyers are supposed to be in a better position than sellers to cease from activities that will cause this type of damage. The insurance cost to the seller, therefore, would be greater than the insurance cost to the buyer. By placing the responsibility on the buyer, overall costs to society should be reduced.

Critics of express warranties maintain that the seller has greater bargaining power than the buyer and that the seller will impose its terms. Defenders hold that if the product market is competitive, the seller will not have the power to impose its terms. Even so, critics respond, buyers are incapable of reading or understanding the "fine print" in warranties and thus are still at a disadvantage. Moreover, buyers will not draft warranties that are advantageous to them because they are unaware of low-probability events and are unwilling to take precautions to protect themselves against them.

Magnuson-Moss Act. In the mid-1960s, Congress passed the Magnuson-Moss Warranty Act to protect buyers from unscrupulous warranty terms in contracts and bills of sale. This act restricts a seller's ability to disclaim implied warranties and imposes labeling and disclosure requirements on the seller. A seller must say if a warranty is "full" or "limited." If full, the warranty cannot exclude consequential damages and the manufacturer has to repair defects promptly without charge. If repair is impossible, the manufacturer must replace the item or give a refund within a specific time period.

Classic Tort Law

Contract law is designed to assist individuals in ordering their private relations. Classic tort law applies when it is too costly for individuals to foresee all contingencies and to devise detailed rules to cover cases of potential damage. For example, it is impractical for drivers to enter into contractual relations with all other drivers in case of potential accidents. Likewise, it is impractical for drivers to make contracts with all pedestrians. Tort law supplements contract law by devising rules for apportioning losses in these instances.

The *MacPherson* v. *Buick Motor Co.* decision of 1916 ended the privity, or traditional contract, requirement in product liability cases.[35] Irrespective of any contractual obligations, the court held the manufacturer responsible for injuries caused by its products. After this decision, product liability became a subset of tort law rather than contract law. This meant, as already discussed, that a buyer had to prove fault. *Fault* typically was defined to mean that reasonable safety features or adequate warnings had not been provided.

Hand's Rule. *Reasonable precaution* was defined in economic terms in a famous decision handed down in 1947 by Judge Learned Hand (see discussion of the Hand rule in Chapter 13). In *United States* v. *Carroll Towing Co.*, Judge Hand postulated that if the expected injury exceeds the costs of precaution and the defendant failed to take the precaution, then the defendant is negligent:

Since there are occasions when every vessel will break away from her moorings, and since, if she does, she becomes a menace to those about her; the owner's duty, as in other similar situations, to provide against resulting injuries is a function of three variables: (1) the probability that she will break away; (2) the gravity of the resulting injury, if she does; and (3) the burden of adequate precautions. Possibly it serves to bring this notion into relief to state it in algebraic terms: if the probability be called P; the injury, L; and the burden, B; liability depends upon whether B is less than L multiplied by P.[36]

Final Blow to Warranties.   The final blow to the use of warranties in product safety cases came in *Henningsen* v. *Bloomfield Motors*.[37] Decided by the New Jersey Supreme Court in 1960, this case held that warranty terms for exclusion of liability for consequential damages did not have bearing. Mrs. Henningsen was driving, but the warranty contained an express limitation of liability to the original purchaser, Mr. Henningsen. In addition, the manufacturer only accepted liability for defective parts for 90 days and 4,000 miles, but the accident occurred after this time-and-mileage stipulation had elapsed. The manufacturer waived any liability for consequential damage, but when the steering mechanism failed and Mrs. Henningsen was injured, the court decided to allow her to sue the manufacturer for her injuries. Its decision signified that tort law was dominant and that warranty provisions in contracts had no bearing when human injury occurred.

Judge Traynor's Decision.   The movement toward strict liability took place gradually over the years. The first major breakthrough was a case against Coca Cola Bottling Co., decided by Justice Traynor of the California Supreme Court in 1944. In this case a Coca Cola bottle exploded in the hands of a waitress. Judge Traynor wrote:[38]

A manufacturer incurs an absolute liability when an article that he has placed on the market, knowing that it is to be used without inspection, proves to have a defect that causes injury to human beings. . . .

Even if there is no negligence . . . public policy demands that responsibility be fixed wherever it will most effectively reduce the hazards. . . .

It is evident that the manufacturer can anticipate some hazards and guard against the recurrence of others, as the public cannot. Those who suffer injury from defective products are unprepared to meet its consequences. The cost of an injury and the loss of time or health may be an overwhelming misfortune to the person injured and a needless one, for the risk of injury can be insured by the manufacturer and distributed among the public as a cost of doing business. . . .

The liability of the manufacturer to an immediate buyer injured by a defective product follows without proof of negligence from the implied warranty of safety attending the sale. . . .

As handicrafts have been replaced by mass production with its great markets and transportation facilities, the close relationship between the producer and consumer of a product has been altered. Manufacturing processes, frequently valuable secrets, are ordinarily either inaccessible to or beyond the ken of the general public. The consumer no longer has means or skill enough to investigate for himself the soundness of a product, even when it is not contained in a sealed package, and his erstwhile vigilance has been lulled by the steady efforts of manufacturers to build up confidence by advertising and marketing devices such as trademarks. . . .

Consumers no longer approach products warily but accept them on faith, relying on the reputation of the manufacturer or the trademark. . . . Manufacturers have sought to justify that faith by increasingly high standards of inspection and a readiness to make good on defective products by way of replacements and refunds. . . . The manufacturer's obligation to the consumer must keep pace with the changing relationship between them. . . .

The manufacturer's liability should, of course, be defined in terms of the safety of the product in normal and proper use, and should not extend to injuries that cannot be traced to the product as it reaches the market.

Note three points implicit in Justice Traynor's decision, which have become part of the standard rationale for strict liability. First, it is cheaper for society to move toward a strict liability standard. A plaintiff has to prove only damage and causation, not fault; the burden of proof is reduced. Therefore, the time and expense of legal proceedings should be lower. While there may be more trials, the ease of their execution should reduce the total costs to society.

Second, as long as someone must bear the costs of the damage, it might as well be the manufacturer because it is less expensive for the manufacturer to bear the cost than it is for the victim. For the victim, who is often uninsured and unprepared, the cost of a single accident can be devastating. For the manufacturer, which should have the foresight to acquire insurance, the costs of an accident may be trivial. Also, accident costs can be passed onto consumers in the form of higher prices; this may amount to a few pennies for each product sold. The option of thus spreading the risk, available to the manufacturer, is unavailable to the customer.

The third rationale implicit in Justice Traynor's decision is that the manufacturer's intimate knowledge of the product and what can go wrong and its power to correct any defect dwarfs any knowledge or capability to change the situation that the consumer may have. The consumer buys mass-produced, technically sophisticated goods that pass through a long and complex chain from factory to retailer. The consumer lacks the time and the capability to adequately judge the product's potential. He or she is unlikely to know where in the chain of design, production, and distribution a defect is likely to occur. Therefore, if the consumer is seriously injured, the manufacturer is responsible.

The Second Restatement of Torts: Strict Liability

The three points from Justice Traynor's decision were incorporated into the 1965 Second Restatement of Torts by the American Law Institute.[39] Thus, strict liability became the norm. In effect, strict liability has replaced the slogan Let the Buyer Beware (caveat emptor). Seller beware! A seller is held strictly liable even if it exercises "all possible care in the preparation and sale."

A Movement toward Absolute Liability?

In the years since it has been drafted, the Second Restatement of Torts has undergone a number of refinements, which have made it more like the classic law of torts. Nonetheless, a counter trend also has been at work that has pushed legal doctrine in the direction of absolute liability. These two forces, which have moved strict liability both away from and toward absolute liability, will be briefly examined (see Exhibit 17–10).

First, pushing it toward classic tort law is the need to show product defect in order that a manufacturer be held liable. A defect can occur in the design or manufacture of the product or by virtue of a failure to warn. Determining whether a defect has occurred, especially in product design, is quite similar to determining whether fault has taken place under the classic theory. The concept of reasonable behavior under the circumstances, often formulated as a state-of-the art defense, plays an important role.

A second element pushing strict liability toward classic tort law is the fact that contributory negligence remains a consideration. Most courts would hold that a manufacturer cannot be held liable if the consumer blatantly misuses the product. If a consumer uses a lawnmower to trim hedges, for example, no liability would attach to the manufacturer because the product is not being used in its intended fashion. The consumer assumes the risk.

EXHIBIT 17–10   Absolute Liability?

The movement away from strict liability:
- Need to show product defect.
- Contributory negligence defense.
- Assumption of risk defense.

The movement toward strict liability:
- Manufacturer needs to find out about unknown dangers.
- State-of-the-art defense unacceptable.
- Curtailments of product misuse and assumption of risk defense.

A third way in which strict liability is similar to the classic doctrine is that it retains the concept of assumption of risk. Thus, warning labels and disclaimers are common, for the reasons discussed earlier.

Beshada *v.* Johns-Manville

These refinements of the Second Restatement have been challenged in some cases. For example, pushing the law towards absolute liability is the case of *Beshada* v. *Johns-Manville Prods. Corp.* which was decided by the New Jersey Supreme Court in 1982.[40] In this case, the defendant claimed that the dangers of asbestos were unknown to science at the time. The court said that even if this claim were true, the manufacturer would be responsible. The implication is that the manufacturer has a responsibility to find out about unknown dangers and that a state-of-the-art defense is unacceptable. The manufacturer may have to conduct its own product tests and warn workers if a problem exists even if scientists are not yet aware of the problem. Failure to do so may be grounds for liability.

In addition, some states have curtailed the application of product-misuse and assumption-of-risk defenses. Courts may expect manufacturers to foresee product misuse (such as driving under the influence of alcohol) and to design products so that damage cannot result even under these extreme conditions.

Reasons for Greater Liability

An interesting controversy has arisen as to why the movement toward greater manufacturer liability has taken place. This controversy is interesting because all of the legal scholars involved are conservatives, who would be appropriate nominees for President Bush's Supreme Court. On the one hand, G. L. Priest of Yale University maintains that manufacturer liability has gained acceptance not because it is the right doctrine but because its proponents have been skilled in propagating it.[41] Their arguments—that manufacturers have unfair bargaining power over consumers, that they can absorb the losses better, and that they are in a better position to invest in precaution and in research in superior technology—are powerful. But Priest believes these arguments are mistaken because they take away the incentives consumers have for precaution and provide a sense of entitlement without a concomitant sense of responsibility.

A contrary view proposed, by W. M. Landes and R. A. Posner of the University of Chicago, is that the movement toward manufacturer liability promotes general economic efficiency.[42] Their argument is that the expense for consumers of learning about product defects is greater than the expense for manufacturers when mechanization and the complexity of goods bought and sold are great. They assert that mass markets, which separate manufacturers from consumers, make the bargaining costs of allocating risks through contractual mechanisms prohibitively high. Thus, social welfare is served in most cases by a strict liability standard. As support for their argument, Landes and Posner have found that the movement away from a contractual standard toward strict liability is correlated with measures of urbanization.

Assessing Existing Reform Proposals

As indicated, in recent years, a number of interesting proposals have been made to reform product liability law. Many states have decided to put a cap, or upper limit, on the amount that victims can recover. For example, in medical malpractice suits in Missouri, victims can recover up to $350,000. In New Mexico, there is a recovery limit of $50,000 from tavern owners in cases of drunken driving. The federal government also has passed the Risk Retention Act in 1981, which allowed firms in the same industry to form insurance pools as an alternative to the high cost of commercially available products liability insurance.

Additional reform proposals have been made:

1. *Returning to the classic negligence theory.* The system of strict liability would be replaced with a fault-based system. Strict liability would be restricted to cases of inherently dangerous activities (like keeping wild animals or using explosives) and not extended to all products.

2. *Maintaining the strict liability principle, but clarifying that the system has not evolved toward absolute liability.* This can be done by strengthening the state-of-the-art defense. Defendants would be able to defend against a design defect if they did not know in advance about the product's dangers, or if there was no practical or feasible alternative way of designing or manufacturing the product.

3. *Establishing a reasonable-prudence standard.* A product would be held to be unreasonably dangerous if the manufacturer knew, or through the exercise of reasonable prudence should have known, about the dangers, and if a reasonably prudent person in the same or similar circumstances would not have manufactured the product or used the design or formulation that the manufacturer used.

4. *Strengthening assumption-of-risk and contributory-negligence defenses.* This implies a return to contractlike principles wherein warnings are seen as implicit contracts agreed to by consumers, who are presumed to understand that the products they use

have certain risks. The consumers then would have to take more responsibility for their actions.

Although there have been many proposals for a comprehensive national tort law reform act, Congress has failed to pass any of them. Robert Cooter from the University of California, Berkeley, and Thomas Ulen from the University of Illinois argue that putting a ceiling on recovery awards is similar to a ceiling on any price, and like rent control or other rate regulations, these limits are economically inefficient: if potential tortfeasors are aware of the cap, they will not take sufficient precaution.[43] However, Cooter and Ulen admit that the intellectual underpinnings of the product liability system have gone awry:

> The most efficient liability standard for this area is strict liability with the defenses of product misuse and assumption of risk. Briefly put, this standard would duplicate the sort of standard that would have been achieved by the consent of the manufacturer and consumer through voluntary exchange if the costs of bargaining were low. The current system has evolved beyond this standard and toward absolute manufacturer liability. It is this extension beyond strict liability with the usual defenses that is at the root of the current crisis.[44]

They support a uniform federal liability statute that would require:[45]

- Corroborating objective evidence (not just the testimony of experts) to prove defect in construction, design, or manufacture.
- A rejection of market share liability (the *Sindell* case).
- The awarding by judges, not juries, of punitive damages.
- The awarding of punitive damages only in cases of proven reckless disregard of consumer safety.
- The deduction of workers' compensation and other insurance benefits from damage awards.

Companies support a number of different types of laws, but none has passed.

In Chapter 18, another type of reform, which has been adopted in Japan for compensating the victims of pollution and other hazardous substances, will be discussed. This type of proposal has two main features:

1. *Granting injured persons the right to receive administrative relief.* Rather than relying on the court system and litigation, a person can make a claim to an administrative body. Based on proof of exposure, existence of the disease or injury, and compensable damages, the person can collect without having to show fault. The injured person would receive medical costs plus a portion of lost earnings but would not have the right to receive punitive damage awards.

2. *Assessing damages according to the principle of proportional liability.* If the person chooses to sue, the courts can establish liability and distribute compensation based on the principle of probable causation. The courts can rely on epidemiological evidence, which they currently refrain from using in the United States.

Summary and Conclusions

The litigation rate in the United States is high especially in comparison to other countries like Japan. In Japan, suing is considered to be both wrong and unprofitable. In addition, the Japanese legal system is more predictable, which takes away the incentive to sue. The U.S. litigation rate has been rising, and scholars disagree about whether this growth is inconsistent with population growth and with changing rates of death and injury. Also, business executives admit that their products are safer, but complain about discontinued product lines, decisions not to introduce new products, and lost market share. Most Americans think that lawyers have been earning excessive fees, but they do not favor limiting the size of damage awards. This chapter has reviewed the evolution of legal doctrine with respect to the harms caused by corporations. It has examined the many proposals made to reform product liability laws. None of these proposals has passed at the national level, though many states have capped the amount of awards for intangible damages.

This chapter has shown how U.S. tort law has evolved from an emphasis on contracts and warranties, to the classic tort doctrine, and now to strict liability. Under the classic doctrine, a plaintiff must show breech of duty, actual damages, and causation. Strict liability eliminates the need to show fault, but even under strict liability companies can use the defense of contributory negligence and assumption of risk. Plaintiffs, moreover, have to prove product defect for manufacturers to be held liable. The *Beshada* case questioned whether companies can use a state-of-the-art defense and suggests a movement toward absolute liability. Without a state-of-the-art defense, companies are forced to try to discover unknown dangers and to analyze the future effects of their products.

Because of large liability awards in cases such as asbestos, some companies have used the bankruptcy laws to avoid paying creditors when facing large liability settlements, even though they are technically solvent. The use of the bankruptcy laws to avoid paying victims is an unprecedented legal development brought on by the liability crisis in the United States.

Discussion Questions

1. Explain why there is less litigation in Japan than in the United States.
2. Why has the litigation rate in the United States been growing?
3. How do business executives feel about the growth of litigation? How does the public feel about it?
4. What are some of the proposals that have been made to reform product liability laws? Is reform needed? Which proposals do you think are the best?
5. Explain what tort law means. What is the intent of tort law?
6. Under the classic doctrine, what must the plaintiff prove?
7. What is the relevance of the *Palsgraf* case?
8. What is the relevance of the *Sindell* case?
9. Why haven't plaintiffs been able to win large awards in cigarette cases? To what extent was *Cipolione* a breakthrough?
10. What defenses does a company have if it is sued under classic tort law? What defenses does it have if it is sued under strict liability?
11. What is the difference between strict liability and the classic doctrine?
12. Why did tort law move from contract law to the classic doctrine? What were some of the significant cases that brought about this movement? What was decided in these cases?
13. Why was Judge Traynor's decision important? What argument was he making? Do you agree with this argument? Why or why not?
14. What does the Second Restatement of Torts say?
15. What court cases suggest a movement toward absolute liability? Why might this movement be taking place?
16. What is the difference between Chapter 11 and Chapter 7 bankruptcy? In what sense does Chapter 11 erode the foundations of a capitalist society? Do you agree with the argument that it does? Why or why not?
17. Do you think it was right for Johns-Manville to seek protection under Chapter 11? Why or why not?

Endnotes

1. Cited in R. Cooter and T. Ulen, *Law and Economics* (Glenview, Ill.: Scott, Foresman and Company, 1988), p. 329.

2. M. Galanter, "Reading the Landscape of Disputes: What We Know and Don't Know (and Think We Know) about Our Allegedly Contentious and Litigious Society," *UCLA Law Review* 4, 1983; M. Galanter, "Beyond the Litigation Panic, in the *Proceedings of the Academy of Political Science* (New York: The Academy of Political Science, 1988), pp. 18–30.

3. N. Glazer, "Towards an Imperial Judiciary," *The Public Interest* 104, 1975; Silberman, "Will Lawyering Strangle Democratic Capitalism?" *Regulation* 15, 1978, pp. 15–22; D. Oberdorfer, "The Tangled Saga of the Dalkon Shield," *Minneapolis Star and Tribune,* September 15, 1985, p. 1A.

4. Galanter, "Reading the Landscape of Disputes."

5. S. Reed, *Environmental Pollution Policies in Japan,* paper presented at the annual meeting of the American Political Science Association, Washington, D.C., 1979; M. R. Reich, "Environmental Policy and Japanese Society," *International Journal of Environmental Studies* 20, 1983 (Part I, pp. 191–98, and Part II, pp. 199–207.)

6. J. Gresser et al., *Environmental Law in Japan* (Cambridge, Mass.: MIT Press, 1981); A. A. Marcus, "Japan," In *International Public Policy Sourcebook: Education and Environment,* vol. 2, ed. F. N. Bolotin (New York: Greenwood Press, 1989), pp. 275–292.

7. Ibid.

8. D. Amy, "Environmental Mediation: An Alternative Approach to Policy Stalemates," *Policy Sciences* 15, 1983, pp. 345–52; A. Sarat, "Alternative Dispute Resolution: Wrong Solution, Wrong Problem," in the *Proceedings of the Academy of Political Science* (New York: The Academy of Political Science, 1988), pp. 162–173; A. Marcus, M. V. Nadel, and K. Merrikin, "The Applicability of Regulatory Negotiation to Disputes Involving the Nuclear Regulatory Commission," *Administrative Law Review* 36, 1984, pp. 213–38.

9. J. M. Ramseyer, "Reluctant Litigant Revisited: Rationality and Disputes in Japan," *Journal of Japanese Studies* 1987, pp. 111–23.

10. Ramseyer, "Reluctant Litigant Revisited," p. 112.

11. Ibid.

12. P. W. Huber, *Liability: The Legal Revolution and Its Consequences* (New York: Basic Books, 1988); R. E. Litan, P. Swire, and C. Winston. "The U.S. Liability System: Background and Trends" in *Liability: Perspectives and Policy,* ed. R. E. Litan (Washington, D.C.: The Brookings Institution, 1988), pp. 1–15; W. Olson, "The Liability Revolution," in the *Proceedings of the Academy of Political Science* (New York: The Academy of Political Science, 1988), pp. 1–3; W. K. Viscusi, "The Dimensions of the Product Liability Crisis," *The Journal of Legal Studies* 1, 1991, pp. 147–78.

13. Galanter, "Beyond the Litigation Panic"; Litan, Swin, and Winston, "The U.S. Liability System."

14. R. L. Abel, "The Crisis Is Injuries, Not Liability," In the *Proceedings of the Academy of Political Science* (New York: The Academy of Political Science, 1988), pp. 31–41; S. P. Croley and J. D. Hanson, "What Liability Crisis? An Alternative Explanation for Recent Events in Product Liability," *The Yale Journal on Regulation* 1, 1990, pp. 1–111.

15. "Lawsuits and Liability," *The Polling Report* 21, 1987, p. 1; E. P. McGuire, *The Impact of Product Liability,* research report no. 908, The Conference

Board, 1988; W. K. Viscusi, "Structuring an Effective Occupational Disease Policy: Victim Compensation and Risk Regulation," *Yale Journal on Regulation* 2, 1984, pp. 53–81.

16. Media General/Associated Press Poll, August 7–17, 1987, 1,223 adults nationwide.

17. McGuire, *The Impact of Product Liability.*

18. C. L. Allen, "The Angry Retort against Tort Law," *Insight on the News*, October 31, 1988, pp. 8–14; P. M. Barrett, "Tort Reform Fight Shifts to State Courts," *The Wall Street Journal*, September 19, 1988, p. 27.

19. C. L. Allen, "Reformers Gather Steam," *Insight on the News*, October 31, 1988, pp. 17–19; P. M. Barrett, "Courts May Have to Lead Product Liability Reform," *The Wall Street Journal*, October 7, 1988, p. B1; P. Huber, "The Legal Revolution in Product Liability," *Contemporary Issues Series 33*, Center for the Study of American Business, Washington University, July 1989; M. E. Kriz, "Liability Lobbying," *National Journal*, January 23, 1988, pp. 191–93; R. Neely, *The Product Liability Mess: How Business Can Be Rescued from the Politics of State Courts* (New York: The Free Press, 1988); J. O'Connell, "Neo-No-Fault: A Fair-Exchange Proposal for Tort Reform," in the *Proceedings of the Academy of Political Science* (New York: The Academy of Political Science, 1988), pp. 186–95; W. K. Viscusi, "Toward a Diminished Role for Tort Liability: Social Insurance, Government Regulation, and Contemporary Risks to Health and Safety," *Yale Journal on Regulation* 1, 1989, pp. 65–108; S. Wermeil, "High Court Urged to Rule on Punitive-Damages Issue," *The Wall Street Journal*, October 21, 1988; S. Wermeil, "High Court Will Get Chance to Put Limits on Punitive Damages," *The Wall Street Journal*, September 28, 1990, p. A1; D. Rosenberg, "The Causal Connection in Mass Exposure Cases: A 'Public Law' Vision of the Tort System," *Harvard Law Review* 97, 1984, pp. 851–929.

20. Cooter and Ulen, *Law and Economics.*

21. Ibid.

22. "Chronology of Chapter 11 Events," *Manville News Background Information*, October 1987; P. Brodeur, "The Asbestos Industry on Trial," *New Yorker*, June 10, 1985, pp. 49–101, June 17, 1985, pp. 45–111, June 24, 1985, pp. 37–77, August 1, 1985, pp. 36–80; A. Cifeli, "Asbestos Defendants Try a New Approach," *Fortune*, November 12, 1984, pp. 110, 165; W. Glaberson, "Of Manville, Morals and Mortality," *The New York Times*, October 9, 1989, p. F1; "Manville Chapter 11 Plan of Reorganization," *Manville News Background Information*, October 1987; "Note: The Manville Bankruptcy: Treating Mass Tort Claims in Chapter 11 Proceedings," *Harvard Law Review* 96, 1984, pp. 1121–42; Trauberman, "Statutory Reform of 'Toxic Torts.'"

23. S. Shavell, "Uncertainty over Causation and the Determination of Civil Liability," *Journal of Law and Economics* 28, 1985, pp. 587–611; L. Tribe, "Trial by Mathematics: Precision and Ritual in the Legal Process," *Harvard Law Review* 84, 1971, pp. 1329–93.

24. Ibid.; M. Rizzo and F. Arnold, "Causal Apportionment in the Law of Torts: An Economic Theory," *Columbia Law Review* 80, 1980, pp. 1399–1429; Rosenberg, "The Causal Connection in Mass Exposure Cases."

25. Cooter and Ulen, *Law and Economics.*

26. G. Robinson, "Multiple Causation in Tort Law: Reflections on the DES Cases," *Virginia Law Review* 68, 1982, pp. 713–69; Shavell, "Uncertainty over Causation and the Determination of Civil Liability."

27. Cooter and Ulen, *Law and Economics.*

28. D. Marcus and W. Lambert, "Tobacco Liability Case Nears High Court," *The Wall Street Journal,* March 4, 1991, p. B8.

29. Cooter and Ulen, *Law and Economics.*

30. Ibid.

31. E. Kitch, "Vaccines and Product Liability: A Case of Contagious Litigation," *Regulation,* May/June, 1985, pp. 11–18.

32. Cooter and Ulen, *Law and Economics.*

33. Ibid.

34. Ibid.

35. Ibid.

36. Ibid., p. 361.

37. Cooter and Ulen, *Law and Economics.*

38. Ibid., pp. 431–32.

39. Cooter and Ulen, *Law and Economics.*

40. Ibid.

41. G. L. Priest, "Understanding the Liability Crisis," in the *Proceedings of the Academy of Political Science* (New York: The Academy of Political Science, 1988), pp. 196–211; G. Priest, "Products Liability Law and the Accident Rate," in *Liability: Perspectives and Policy,* ed. R. E. Litan (Washington, D.C.: The Brookings Institution, 1988), pp. 184–222.

42. W. M. Landes and R. A. Posner, *The Economic Structure of Tort Law* (Cambridge, Mass.: Harvard University Press, 1987), pp. 438–39.

43. Cooter and Ulen, *Law and Economics.*

44. Ibid., p. 462.

45. Cooter and Ulen, *Law and Economics; Asbestos in the Courts: The Challenge of Mass Toxic Torts,* report, Rand Corporation Institute for Civil Justice, Santa Monica, California, 1985.

18

COMPENSATING VICTIMS: JAPAN AND THE UNITED STATES

We don't want your money. We want you to drink the mercury-filled water.
Japanese protest against mercury and cadmium poisoning that was caused by industry.[1]

Introduction and Chapter Objectives

In the last dozen years, many proposals have been made to reform the system for compensating victims of pollution and hazardous substances in the United States, but little concrete progress has taken place. Nothing new has emerged in spite of repeated problems arising from, for example, Kepone, Agent Orange, Love Canal, DES, the Dalkon Shield (see the special feature, "The Law Firm of Robins, Kaplan, Miller, and Ciresi"), and the bankruptcies of Manville, other asbestos manufacturers, and A. H. Robins.[2] In this final chapter, U.S. proposals for dealing with the problem of tort reform will be compared with the reforms that have been put in place in Japan.

U.S. proposals for reforming victims' compensation fall into three general categories: a balanced approach that combines administrative relief with tort reform, proposals that would provide administrative relief but eliminate tort remedies, and proposals to reform tort law that have nothing to say about administrative relief. While American policy-makers are still groping for a solution, in Japan changes in the law have provided a rationale for a system of administrative relief that preserves the victims' right to sue. The relevance of the Japanese case is that it shows the intimate connection between changes in tort law and the creation of an administrative compensation system, a connection that some proposals made in the United States would sunder.

The Law Firm of Robins, Kaplan, Miller, & Ciresi

A 200-member law firm in the Twin Cities, Robins, Kaplan, Miller & Ciresi achieved distinction when Solly Robins, one of its attorneys, won a case that established the principle of strict liability in Minnesota.[1] The case, *Andrea McCormack* v. *Hankscraft,* involved a girl who had been scalded by hot water spilling out of a vaporizer. The court decided that it was unnecessary to prove negligence in the manufacture of the product. Product defect was enough to establish liability.

Michael Ciresi, another attorney for the firm, successfully challenged A. H. Robins Co., the manufacturer of the Dalkon Shield.[2] His case was the first to win a major award against A. H. Robins. Eventually Ciresi won over $37 million in settlements in 198 Dalkon Shield cases, and A. H. Robins paid over $375 million before it filed for bankruptcy. Recently, Ciresi won an $8.75 million award from Searle Company in the Esther Kociemba Copper-7 intrauterine device case.

A. H. Robins was a successful multinational enterprise with more than $700 million in sales and 6,100 employees in 1985. Its strong product lines—Chapstick, Robitussin, and Sergeant's flea and tick collars—were well known to consumers. It had purchased the rights to market an intrauterine device called the Dalkon Shield.[3] Invented by Dr. Hugh Davis, a professor at Johns Hopkins University, Davis did the first clinical trials of the Dalkon Shield, which he published in the *American Journal of Obstetrics and Gynecology.* He followed 640 users of the Shield for five and a half months, not long enough to discover if the low pregnancy rates he was observing, 1.1 percent, were accurate or to see if these women developed pelvic infections. A. H. Robins did not have to do any premarket testing because it was not required to do so at the time by the Food and Drug Administration. Ultimately, it sold 2.9 million Dalkon Shields in the United States and controlled 40 percent of the market for intrauterine devices (IUDs), selling the Dalkon Shield for $4.35 when it cost 25 cents to manufacture.

With more customers came additional reports that the Dalkon Shield was ineffective

[1]G. Warchol, "Hit 'Em and Hit 'Em Hard," *Twin City Reader,* August 24–30, 1988, pp. 10–12.

[2]B. J. Feder, "What A. H. Robins Has Wrought," *The Wall Street Journal,* December 13, 1987, p. F2; R. Koenig and S. Wermeil, "Supreme Court Refuses to Hear Challenges in A. H. Robins Case," *The Wall Street Journal,* November 7, 1989, p. A3.

[3]G. A. Steiner and J. F. Steiner, *Business, Government, and Society: A Managerial Perspective* (New York: McGraw-Hill, 1991).

Proposals for Reforming Victims' Compensation

Pending claims in the Love Canal case exceeded $2.5 billion.[3] It was estimated that more than 230,000 additional cases of asbestos disease were likely by the end of the century. They would have resulted in over 50,000 new lawsuits had not Manville and other companies filed for bankruptcy

The Law Firm of Robins, Kaplan, Miller, and Ciresi continued

in preventing pregnancy. Worse still, it caused serious infections of the reproductive system and abdominal area. Many of these infections resulted in miscarriages and many women were left sterile. The cause of the infections often was a string on the Shield that was used as a safety device so that doctors could see if the Shield had been properly placed. If not properly placed, the Shield could perforate a woman's uterus and enter the abdomen. The problem was that the string, unlike those on competitors' IUDs, was made of interwoven fibers that acted like a wick that drew bacteria into a woman's body.

Roughly 4 percent of the women who used the Dalkon Shield suffered some type of injury. In the trials brought against the company, it was shown that the dangers of the Shield had been known by top company officials, who ordered that documents on the product's wicking tendencies be destroyed. Before it filed for bankruptcy, A. H. Robins estimated that payouts to Dalkon Shield victims would exceed $1 billion by the year 2002.

Michael Ciresi subsequently filed suit against G. D. Searle and Company for its Copper-7 IUD.[4] Ten million women are users of the Copper-7, and Ciresi claimed that the Copper-7 caused the same kind of problems as were discovered with the Dalkon Shield. In preparing for the Kociemba case, Robins, Kaplan, Miller, and Ciresi attorneys reviewed more than 600,000 pages of Searle documents. They found evidence that Searle officials knew of potential problems but decided not to warn the women who were users. Deleted from the label in the IUD package were phrases about the potential higher risks of infection and the increased risks to women who had never had children and recommendations that young women, women who had never been pregnant and women who had multiple sex partners seek another birth control device.

Opponents of Ciresi accuse him of histrionics, combativeness in the courtroom, and overaggressiveness.[5] They also argue that his campaign against the drug companies is making them too cautious. Important innovations that can help people are not coming on to the market in a timely fashion because the manufacturers are afraid of litigation. For women who want wider birth control options, this is a real problem.

Victims, however, know that they will find a forceful advocate in Robins, Kaplan, Miller & Ciresi. The Indian government, for instance, chose the firm to represent it in the suit it brought against the Union Carbide Company for Bhopal.

[4]Warchol, "Hit 'Em and Hit 'Em Hard."

[5]Ibid.

under Chapter 11. But the bankruptcy code may not be the way to deal with these issues, because it is questionable whether corporations that are apparently healthy in other respects should be allowed to use bankruptcy to seek refuge from tort liability (see special feature in Chapter 17).[4]

Some type of statutory solution, is needed, preferably at the national level. While the Japanese approach is imperfect, the early development of a policy has reduced legal and political uncertainties and provided a stable environment for economic growth. The Japanese development is remarkable, not because it shows harmony in Japanese society, central direction, or a rational and comprehensive effort, but because in Japan a policy was formulated and implemented relatively early on (starting in 1974).[5] In the United States, policymakers are still groping for an adequate solution despite the fact that the development of a policy tends to reduce legal and political uncertainties and to provide a more stable environment for economic growth.

On the one hand, some U.S. proposals would reduce or nearly eliminate the role of the tort system; victims' compensation would be an administrative rather than a judicial matter, as it is under workers' compensation. Other proposals have called for shifting the rules of evidence in tort cases because causation is so difficult for the victim to prove. However, all proposals have to be examined in light of a balanced approach that calls for both administrative compensation and traditional tort remedies. Long before it was proposed for the United States, a version of this plan had been implemented in Japan.

The Balanced Approach

The balanced approach came from a study group consisting of 12 attorneys designated by the American Bar Association, American Trial Lawyer's Association, the Association of State Attorneys General, and the American Law Institute. In 1980, Congress asked it to consider the hazardous substance personal injury problem in conjunction with the Superfund law (a bill to provide for the cleanup of hazardous dumps). The study group recommended a two-tier approach. The first tier, which would be the primary remedy for injured persons, would consist of administrative relief. This part of the system would operate in a manner similar to workmen's compensation. Within three years after the discovery of an injury or disease, an applicant would have to make a claim based on proof of exposure, existence of the disease or injury, and compensable damages. The applicant, without having to show fault, would receive medical costs and two thirds of earnings minus the amounts that could be obtained from other government programs. The money for the fund would come from industry sources through a tax on hazardous activities or some other means of eliciting contributions.

The majority of claims would be dealt with through the administrative system and without resort to the courts; however, the second tier in the program would keep intact existing tort law. Plaintiffs who chose this option would have to put up with the costs and delays of legal proceedings. However, a plaintiff able to win in the courts would have the right to collect unlimited damages, including full loss of earnings and compensation for pain and suffering.

Another proposal combines administrative relief with traditional tort remedies. Jeffrey Trauberman proposed a "Model Statute."[6] The approach was different from the attorneys' study group because it emphasized common law tort reform as the primary remedy, with the victims' compensation fund serving merely as "a residual or secondary source of compensation" in instances, for example, when the responsible party could not be identified, had become insolvent, or had gone out of business.

The major common law problem that Trauberman addressed was that of causation. Traditionally, the courts have been reluctant to accept probabilistic evidence as proof of causation. Trauberman, however, argued that evidence from epidemiology, animal and human toxicology, and other sources on the "frontiers of scientific knowledge" should be admitted. When a plaintiff was unable to demonstrate a substantial case of harm, Trauberman would permit *fractional recovery*, by which he meant that if a hazardous waste dump increased the total number of cancers in an area from 8 to 10 percent, then the increased incidence of cancer brought on by the dump was 25 percent; in these cases, victims should be able to recover 25 percent of their costs. Recovery for pain and suffering, which was unavailable to fund claimants, would be available through litigation.

Administrative Relief without Tort Justice

These balanced proposals are to be distinguished from bills introduced into Congress that would create an administrative compensation system but preclude tort remedies. Brodeur argues that under the guise of arguments (*a*) that costly pretrial discovery can consume years of time and (*b*) that after legal fees have been paid, plaintiffs take home less than half the awards, "sweeping efforts to weaken the tort system and in effect grant immunity to manufacturers of toxic substances" have been gathering force in the United States.[7] Under prodding from asbestos manufacturers, Congresswoman Millicent Fenwick, Republican of New Jersey, in 1977, and Senator Gary Hart, Democrat of Colorado, in 1980 introduced legislation that would bar victims from bringing product liability or common law tort actions and instead compensate them only from a federally or state-administered fund.[8] Known as Manville bailout legislation, the Fenwick and Hart bills were criticized for taking away from diseased and disabled workers the right to sue companies for negligence, to win punitive damages for outrageous and reckless conduct, and to obtain compensation for pain and suffering. Under the Fenwick bill, the U.S. Treasury would pay all claims filed before 1980; subsequent claims would be financed from mandatory contributions from industry.

Under the Hart bill, diseased workers or their survivors would have to prove their claims in proceedings that could be contested by employers and their insurance carriers.

In 1983, Congressman George Miller, Democrat of California, introduced an asbestos compensation bill that, like the Fenwick and Hart bills, would prevent victims from using the courts to pursue their rights.[9] The administrative system would be their sole remedy. However, like the 1969 Black Lung Benefits Act, Miller's bill would ease the claimant's burden of proof by incorporating numerous rebuttable presumptions in the claimant's favor. Under the act, billed originally as a limited plan that would cost no more than $40 million annually, awards mushroomed to nearly $2 billion a year by the late 1970s.[10] Benefits apparently had been distributed without adequate evidence of disability, and in 1981, Congress severely cut back on the presumptions in the act to aid sufferers of black lung disease. Viscusi argued that a similar bill for asbestos' sufferers would be more expensive than tort justice.[11]

Tort Reform without Administrative Relief

The next group of proposals to be discussed strengthens the role of tort law rather than weakens it. These proposals would ease the burden of proof for the plaintiffs and make it easier for them to win damages by means of litigation. Currently, under common law, if a company engages in "unduly hazardous" or "abnormal" activity, it can be held strictly liable regardless of the care it has exercised to prevent harm (see Chapter 17).[12] Starting in the late 1960s, many states began to extend strict liability to defective products. This principle was pivotal in allowing victims to recover damage against asbestos manufacturers.[13] Minnesota explicitly endorsed this principle to apply to hazardous wastes and other toxic substances. The 1983 Environmental Response and Liability Act (ERLA) imposed liability without regard to fault and without proof of negligence.[14] Minnesota also endorsed the principle of "joint and several liability." This meant that two or more persons could be joined as defendants when their actions produced a single injury. It also meant that each defendant could be sued individually and held wholly liable for the injury it helped cause even though others contributed to the harm. Minnesota also considered adding an administrative dimension to the changes it made in tort law, but did not take action because of concerns about the potential costs and the number of possible claimants.

A different type of proposal, developed by Rosenberg, which raised some of the same issues dealt with by Trauberman, has been under consideration in the state of Massachusetts.[15] The courts have been reluctant to accept probabilistic evidence as proof of causation.[16] Under the preponderance-of-evidence rule, which has prevailed in most courts, plaintiffs have found it difficult to win their cases. The legal system has been designed to deal with the obvious damages caused by bullets or cars. Cases involving subtle damages, which are affected by processes that may take decades to manifest injury, as is the case with disease generated from exposure to toxic chemicals, have been hard to prove. Developing scientific evidence has been extremely expensive, and the animal tests and epidemiological studies might have no bearing if the courts hold that statistical correlations which indicate probability of causation are an insufficient basis for liability and that some particularistic proof of causation is needed.

Rosenberg argued for a proportional liability rule rather than preponderance of evidence.[17] Under proportional liability, the courts would establish liability and distribute compensation in proportion to the probability of causation assigned to the excess disease risk in the exposed population regardless of individualized proof of causal connection. This proposal was basically equivalent to Trauberman's argument about fractional recovery; however, Trauberman believed that it should be applied only in exceptional cases, while Rosenberg proposed that proportional liability be the norm.[18] Shavell has demonstrated the theoretical superiority of proportional liability on the grounds that it "eliminates all problems due to uncertainty over causation . . . [and] . . . results in parties' facing expected liability equal to the expected losses they impose, and thus leads to socially desirable behavior."[19] However, Shavell asserted that legal costs (the number of suits brought, the likelihood that a suit once brought will result in litigation rather than settlement, and the expense per trial) would be greater under proportional liability. But Rosenberg refuted this contention, arguing that trials would be shorter because it would no longer be necessary to prove a specific causal connection, and lawyers' fees would be smaller because the awards would not be as great.

Thus, proposals to reform the toxic torts system in the United States have fallen into these three broad categories (see Exhibit 18–1). With the exception of the Fenwick and Hart bills, none of the approaches has had the support of industry, no mass political movement has organized around them, and none has been promoted by an agency of the federal government. In an era of retrenchment from federal regulatory goals, Congress has been reluctant to act on these proposals.

The Origins and Development of Japanese Policies

In contrast to the United States, Japan has some of the most noteworthy victims' compensation policies in the world.[20] It has adopted the

---

EXHIBIT 18–1   U.S. Proposals to Reform Victims' Compensation Laws

	Administrative Relief	*Tort System*
1. American Bar Association	Tier 1 (no fault)	Tier 2 (right to sue)
Environmental Law Institute	Secondary (no responsible party found)	Primary (fractional recovery)
2. Fenwick-Hart	Hearings (must prove claims)	No suits
Miller	Hearings (rebuttable presumption)	No suits
3. Minnesota	No mention	Strict liability/joint and several liability
Rosenberg (Massachusetts proposal)	No mention	Proportional liability (probabilistic evidence)

---

balanced approach that combines administrative relief with tort justice. The 1973 Law for the Compensation of Pollution-Related Health Injury, which replaced a simpler 1969 law, established an administrative system to oversee compensation payments.[21] Victims of designated diseases, upon certification by a council of medical, legal, and other experts, have been eligible for medical expenses, lost earnings, and other expenses, but they have received no allowance for noneconomic losses such as pain and suffering. Companies pay the entire cost. There has been an administrative review system, but in no case does this system prohibit recourse to the courts.

It is worth tracing the story of how changes in tort law provided the rationale for the system of administrative relief that was adopted by Japan. Japan has looked to U.S. jurisprudence for models and many of its laws (antitrust and securities exchange) are patterned after American examples. Not surprisingly, the first efforts to pass a national environmental control law in Japan in the 1950s met with a resounding failure. The first national environmental statutes of any significance were not passed in the United States until the 1960s. In Japan, opposition from business, government agencies, and the ruling Liberal Democratic Party blocked early efforts to deal with emerging environmental problems.[22] The postwar consensus was that the government should emphasize growth at the expense of other objectives. In the 1950s and early 1960s, the national government and industry ignored the growing concentration of noxious fumes in major cities and the early outbreaks of pollution-related diseases.[23] As a consequence, Japan has some of the world's worst pollution and industrial chemical problems.

Extraordinary Diseases

Starting in the mid-1950s, extraordinary diseases that had not been encountered before began appearing: mercury poisoning, or Minamata disease; cadmium poisoning, or Itai-Itai ("it hurts-hurts") disease; and severe pulmonary disorders. Scientists attributed the causes to pollutants that were released by nearby factories. A literature developed that depicted the victims' plight—the splintering of bone tissue, disfigurement, excruciating pain, paralysis, and death. This literature was journalistic, scholarly, pictorial, and literary. Its depiction of the victims' suffering "traumatized" Japanese society.[24] A protest movement began at the local level and grew into a national movement. Protest was often highly symbolic. For example, during pilgrimage festivals, victims in traditional white garments marched to shareholder meetings and chanted.[25] There were clashes between police and demonstrators.

As mediation, the time-honored method of settling pollution-related and other disputes, broke down, litigation became a group effort of the victims' movement. The movement became closely aligned with the organized bar. Some lawyers became emotionally involved, and some were ideologically motivated and used the pollution issue to attack the capitalist system. Altogether, there were four major cases. Again, symbolism played a role in the resolution of these cases. After a case, the victims would demand that executives from the "offending" companies bow in supplication and seek forgiveness.[26] These trials were moral victories in which companies often waived their right to appeal. The most important impact of the four cases was the introduction of an extremely flexible standard of proof that changed attitudes toward the handling of scientific data. These cases were the foundation upon which the 1973 administrative compensation system was built.

Itai-Itai Disease.   The first case dealt with Itai-Itai disease. It afflicted poor farmers who, at first, were thought to be suffering from undernourishment and overwork. Research by a local physician and the Ministry of Health and Welfare, however, proved that the disease's primary cause was cadmium poisoning. In 1968, victims brought suit against a company thought to be responsible for emitting the substance. The high court's 1972 decision in this case affirmed that epidemiological evidence could be used in establishing legal proof. Plaintiffs had to show that (1) pollution occurred before the outbreak of a disease, (2) increased exposure could lead to an increase in the disease, (3) clinical and experimental evidence did not contradict statistical inference of causality, and (4) in areas of low pollution, incidence of the disease was diminished.

Minamata Disease.   The next two cases had to do with Minamata disease. In these instances the district court ruled that "causation may be proved by an accumulation of circumstantial evidence if that explanation is consistent with the relevant scientific disciplines."[27] A high statistical correlation between the defendant's activity and the occurrence of the disease was sufficient if the plaintiffs could show that they had the disease and could show the mechanism by which the agent that caused the disease had entered their body. The court found that the defendants knew that their activities might be hazardous, but suppressed information and therefore were negligent. It ruled that companies had to be on the lookout for even remote risks to human health. They were "to take the strictest safety precautions to prevent even the slightest danger to humans and other living things."[28]

Yokkaichi City.   The final case involved air pollution from an industrial complex in Yokkaichi City. Two major innovations in tort law emerged from this case. The first was that the district court ruled that the harmfulness of high concentrations of sulfur dioxides was "generally known" and accepted. Second, the Court affirmed the principle of joint and several liability. Each defendant by itself need not have been capable of causing the full damage. If the defendants were in proximity to each other, knew of the others' existence, and were aware that discharges from their factories might combine with discharges from other factories, then they could be held liable singly and in combination.

In these cases, the attitudes the courts adopted toward scientific uncertainty was quite novel (see Exhibit 18–2). They integrated statistical, clinical, and experimental data in a common framework and applied it to a variety of diseases, many of which were chronic and attributable to multiple factors and sources. These cases were influential in moving Japan toward a national compensation system. Industry and the ruling Liberal Democratic party concluded that a compensation system would undercut victims' incentive to litigate. It would also spread the risk throughout the industrial community. The parallel with the develop-

---

EXHIBIT 18–2 Japanese Victims' Compensation Suits: Landmark Cases

Itai-Itai Disease:	Epidemiological evidence could be used in establishing legal proof.
Minamata:	Companies had to be on lookout for remote risks; had to take strictest precautions.
Yokkaichi City:	Acceptance of sulfur dioxides as harmful; affirmation of joint and several liability.

ment of workmen's compensation in the United States is striking. When the courts began to weaken the arguments employers used when workers sued, employers began the search for alternative ways to deal with the problem.

Local Funds

In Japan, funds to compensate victims had been established at the local level as far back as 1959. In 1965, Yokkaichi City set up a fund to pay the medical expenses of air pollution victims that became a model for other cities. In 1969, a national relief law based on the Yokkaichi model was passed. The 1973 law was novel because it used a statistical approach to victims' compensation that codified the legal principles developed in the four major cases. The courts' awarding of damages encouraged the government to take action even though there were unanswered scientific questions.

A National System

The prime mover behind the 1973 law was Osanori Koyama, director general of Japan's Environment Agency. In September 1972, he announced that the government would present a bill establishing a national compensation system to the Diet (Japan's Parliament). The role the Environment Agency played was significant. While in the United States legislation is often initiated by Senators and Congressmen, in Japan the federal bureaucracy rather than the Diet dominates the bill-drafting process.[29] The Environment Agency's advisory group, the Central Council on Environmental Pollution Control, developed the reasoning behind the Compensation Law. It met twice a month between September and December of 1972 and published in December an interim report that was circulated to concerned groups, including the victims, the industrial community, and local governments.

Under the 1973 act, victims did not have to prove disease causation. The basic approach to causation developed in the landmark pollution trials was applied. Causation was viewed as a statistical question. A significant correlation between a particular disease and a substance or a type of pollution was sufficient for inferring causation. Epidemiological analysis, clinical and experimental data, and mortality and morbidity statistics could play a role. When the likelihood that a person would contact a given disease was much higher when exposed to a substance (e.g., one chance in a hundred as opposed to one chance in a million), then causality was presumed.

Diseases were covered because administrators had extensive data on their origins and effects that were developed prior to and during the four major trials. Respiratory diseases associated with air pollution were covered in designated areas called Class 1 regions. Diseases caused by specific pollutants such as Minamata, Itai-Itai, and chronic arsenic poisoning were covered in designated areas called Class 2 regions. Broad discretionary powers in the act permitted compensation for other diseases if the scientific evidence needed to infer causality could be developed. Local councils made up of medical, legal, and other experts certified victims and disbursed benefits. The funds were collected by a quasi-governmental body whose principal officers and daily affairs were managed by industry under guidance of the government. For air pollution diseases, there was a levy on emissions of sulfur dioxides that was set linearly in direct proportion to the amount of discharge. Another 20 percent of the budget for compensating victims of these diseases came from an automobile weight tax. The responsible companies bore the full burden for victims of Itai-Itai, Minamata, and arsenic poisoning, with the exception of administrative costs and costs of rehabilitation, which were shared with federal and local governments.

Critics of the System

The administration of victims' compensation in Japan has been attacked both by the victims and by industry (see Exhibit 18–3). Charges made by industry are similar to those brought against America's Black Lung Act (i.e., that benefits have been granted too liberally). Industry has argued that the availability of compensation has brought out many persons who otherwise would have remained silent. Nearly 98 percent of the certified victims have been sufferers of various respiratory disorders, not of poisoning from mercury, cadmium, and arsenic.

Victims of pulmonary disease have not been excluded from compensation for respiratory ailments even if they have allergies or are smokers. The number or victims for this category of disease has increased, while concentrations of sulfur dioxides in most regions actually have declined.[30]

While the certification of sufferers from respiratory diseases may be too liberal, the certification of sufferers from mercury, cadmium, and arsenic poisoning may be too strict. A leader of the victims' movement has

EXHIBIT 18–3   Criticisms of Victims' Compensation in Japan

1. Benefits granted too liberally to sufferers of respiratory disease.
2. Benefits not granted liberally enough to sufferers of industrial poisonings.
3. Compensation not extended to other industrial diseases.

estimated that of the more than 200,000 Minamata victims, only 7,000 have applied for certification and only about 1,000 have received any form of assistance. Victims of Minamata disease have to display all the classical symptoms that were presented in the original pollution trials. Sufferers of Minamata disease have charged that the criteria for certification are arbitrary, unreasonably restrictive, and designed to exclude the majority of those afflicted.

Remaining Trials

Although pollution-related litigation declined after passage of the 1973 act, remaining noteworthy trials have had to do with the issue of certifying Minamata victims. For example, 372 victims brought suit against the governor of Kumamoto prefecture for procrastinating in processing certification applications. In 1976, the district court decided in their favor, and the governor made a public apology. A second group of plaintiffs had their claims recognized by the district court even though they had been denied certification. In 1979, they won a court damage award of 150 million yen.[31] Another trial, brought in 1980, joined together 85 plaintiffs and the Chisso Corporation, a major polluter. The plaintiffs claimed 1.4 billion yen in damages from the government for failure to regulate the polluter's discharges. A group of rejected Minamata applicants also brought suit against the government as well as against industry. These latter cases were part of a broader movement focusing on the liability of both government and industry for damages.

Liability for toxic damages has had a devastating effect on Chisso, a Japanese company that has been the defendant in many of the Minamata cases. Like Manville and A. H. Robins, Chisso is technically bankrupt. Its compensation payments created a gross deficit that was estimated to be greater than 365 billion yen in 1977. The Tokyo Stock Exchange removed it from the list of trading securities because it failed to pay dividends for five consecutive years and accumulated deficits exceeding the company's total assets for three consecutive years. The government tried to ease the company's debt burden by enacting special legislation that would permit the Environment Agency to screen and certify victims through a special council. It also permitted the prefecture government to issue special bonds and extend low-interest loans to the company so that it would be able to meet its compensation responsibilities. Victims of Minamata disease, however, have been very suspicious of the government's efforts. They believe that it signifies further restrictions on certification and compensation, subverts the "polluter pays" principle, and encourages companies to declare bankruptcy because they know that they can rely on the government's support.

Relevance for the United States

Does the Japanese case have any relevance for American policy? Two issues need to be considered. First, there is a substantive issue. What are the strengths and weaknesses of Japanese policy? Second, there is the issue of policy development. Given what is known about the differences between the Japanese and American political and legal systems, what accounts for early action in Japan and stalemate in the United States?

Substantive Issues

With respect to substance, the positive features of Japanese policy stand out. What is perhaps most important is the close connection between developments in tort law and the operation of administrative relief. The resolution of the landmark pollution cases led the way to a balanced approach to administrative compensation. Common law developments forced industry and the government to set up an administrative system so as to avoid the threat of further liability, as well as to prevent the courts from being tied up with numerous and potentially costly cases. Without the major cases, administrative reform would have been impossible. They provided a rationale for the system. The theories of causation and responsibility developed in the major cases were codified in the 1973 act. The burden of proving causation shifted from victims to administrators, who had the record of the major trials upon which to rely.

An important strength of the Japanese approach has been its ability to stem the tide of litigation without taking away the victim's right to sue. Even though victims in Japan still have the right to pursue litigation, most suits have been about certification under the administrative system. No major cases have been brought involving claims for full loss of earnings and pain and suffering, and victims have not tried to win punitive damages for outrageous and reckless conduct.

In Japan, unlike the United States, the problem of awarding damages to victims of pollution and hazardous substance, if not solved, has been controlled. In the United States, framers of proposals to establish an administrative system have been less successful in drawing upon tort law. In Japan the diseases covered by administrative relief are specifically those that were issues of contention in the major cases, but in the United States, proposals like that of the attorneys' study group, which in other respects is similar to Japanese policy, do not specify the diseases or substances that would be covered. This open-endedness leaves such proposals vulnerable to industry concerns about the number of potential victims and the amount of liability.

Problems.   The arguments in favor of the balanced approach should not lead one to lose sight of the problems; however, even the problems

encountered by the Japanese are instructive and may be useful in formulating U.S. policy. The first problem has been the designation of new
diseases. Although the 1973 act theoretically allows new diseases to be
covered, the Japanese government has been reluctant to recognize them.
Cancer, for example, has not been considered a candidate for becoming
a compensatible disease under the 1973 act. As in the United States, it
seems that a truly major court action or pollution incident is needed to
influence the Japanese government, and even then these events may not
be sufficient. The mood of the time as reflected by increased concern
with energy availability and economic conditions brought to a halt significant new changes in environmental policy in Japan as well as in the
United States. As a consequence, a more routine way to assess scientific
and tort law changes so that diseases can be added and subtracted more
rapidly from the compensation list would be an important improvement
if adopted in the United States.

A second problem with the Japanese approach has been the liberal
provisions for certifying victims of pulmonary and respiratory disease
in comparison to the conservative way that victims of Minamata disease
and other forms of metallic poisoning have been certified. As Namekata
observes, while the heavy metal poisoning cases have a fairly clear
exposure-effect relationship, the relationship between air pollution and
respiratory disease is obfuscated because factors such as heredity, smoking, and allergies affect causation. Measuring exposure in these air pollution cases also is extremely difficult.[32] Gresser, Fujikura, and Mori-
shima suggest that a major criterion for making diseases part of an
administrative compensation system is if natural incidence is low (as it
is with Minamata disease).[33] In these cases, the system should err on the
side of the victims. Where natural incidence of a disease is high (as is the
case with asthma and other respiratory ailments), and other potential
contributing causes (smoking and allergies) exist, the system should be
cautious in creating entitlements. At the very least, victims in cases
where natural forces or their own actions contribute to disease should
receive less compensation, or their compensation should be proportional to how much of the harm can be attributed to emissions from a
specific company or group of companies, as opposed to how much harm
has been caused by background factors and their own actions.

Policy Development

Even though Japanese policy is imperfect, the fact is that Japan has a
policy, while the United States does not. Japanese industry has outper-
formed American industry in recent years. One reason is the alleged
cooperative nature of Japanese society, so different from the adversary
character of American society.[34] American industrialists have maintained
that they are at a competitive disadvantage internationally because

Japanese environmental policies make it easier to do business in that country.[35] However, what is easier about doing business in Japan is not necessarily the leniency of Japanese policies but rather their stability. The existence of policies developed relatively early and maintained with little revision provides a more predictable climate for business growth.

Why has Japan had a relatively steady approach to victims' compensation, while the United States has yet to create a viable national policy? Contrary to what might be assumed, there are many similarities in the role that social institutions have played in the development of environmental policies in Japan and the United States. But emphasis has been different. Some factors that have been significant in Japan have been unimportant in the United States. In the remainder of this chapter, we compare the role played by various institutions in the development of victims' compensation policies in the United States and Japan (see Exhibit 18–4).

Environmental Movements

Unlike the United States, the environmental movement in Japan has been oriented toward health issues, and it is also tied to working-class parties. The victims of pollution, as portrayed in the Japanese press and other media, are common people—fishermen, workers, farmers.[36] The issue has been depicted in terms as big business versus the person in the street. Also, it may be that the collective trauma of having been the victims of atomic weapons during World War II and having had to create laws to compensate the victims of that catastrophe has played a role.[37] In contrast, the U.S. environmental movement has had an elitist image.[38] It has been viewed as attempting to slow development and has been regarded with suspicion by some labor unions. It has focused on protecting nature and preserving aesthetic values and has dealt with

---

Exhibit 18–4   A Comparison of Institutions
Policy Development for the Protection of Victims in Japan and the United States

	Japan	*United States*
Environmental movements:	Health	Harm to nature
The courts:	Landmark cases codified	No new legal ground broken
Local government:	Precedent setting	No precedents set
Organized interests:	Unified business community	Divided business community
The bureaucracy and legislature:	Initiative with the bureaucracy	Initiative with congressional committees

health issues more peripherally. Victims' compensation never has been at the top of the agenda of the American environmental movement. In the late 1960s and early 1970s, the basic thrust of environmental legislation in the United States, such as the National Environmental Policy Act (NEPA), was to prevent future harms to the environment, not to compensate the victims.[39] Meanwhile, Japan debated a law similar to NEPA, but it was not passed because of opposition from business and ministries like MITI that share in the national obsession of maintaining growth no matter what the costs.

The Courts

The courts have been significant in both the United States and Japan, but in the United States no group of landmark cases has been decided that has had the effect of changing legal doctrine. Instead, U.S. plaintiffs have won large awards against specific companies such as A. H. Robins and Manville in a series of separate cases that have broken no new legal ground. But no fundamental breakthrough has occurred in the way U.S. judges regard evidence about causality and responsibility. As a consequence, U.S. court cases have not played the role of being the precedents for an administrative compensation system, as occurred in Japan. Instead, U.S. proposals for administrative compensation have used ad hoc definitions of certain key principles and have left open major issues that in Japan were decided judicially. It is noteworthy that the Japanese Federation of Bar Associations has been a vigorous advocate for victims, and has been instrumental in carrying out the major pollution cases, in lobbying for an administrative compensation system, and in defending this system when it has been attacked by industry.

Local Governments

The role of local governments has been important in both countries. Before a national policy emerged in Japan, innovative approaches were developed at the city and prefecture level. Local relief to Minamata victims began in Kumamoto prefecture in 1958. The same program became policy in Niigata prefecture in 1960. A similar program to help Itai-Itai victims was set up by Toyoma prefecture in 1968. Yokkaichi City's medical payment allowances for air pollution victims have already been mentioned; they were copied by many Japanese towns. In the United States, three state governments have played a leading role, but they developed or considered policies much later than the Japanese. As noted previously, a 1983 Minnesota act incorporated the principles of strict liability and joint and several responsibility. Along with the proportionality rule proposed by Rosenberg, Massachusetts considered but did not accept the use of statistical and animal tests in court trials.[40] California adopted a victims' compensation program that provided up to $2 million per year when a responsible party could not otherwise be identified or no judgment obtained. The actions of these states, however, were exceptions as most states feared loss of industry if they innovated in this area.

Organized Interests

Another factor is the different way industry is organized in the two countries. In Japan, it is more centrally organized. Japan's peak business association, the Keidnaren, is highly encompassing and much more dominant than any in the United States.[41] There is no U.S. counterpart— not the Business Roundtable, Committee on Economic Development, Chamber of Commerce, National Association of Manufacturers, nor the American Business Conference. According to Mancur Olson, the proliferation and density of interest-group organizations in the United States have produced an inefficient pattern of economic growth.[42] In contrast, the high growth rate in Japan can be explained in part by the dominance of its peak association, the Keidnaren. Thus, no coordinated U.S. industry position has emerged with regard to victims' compensation. Instead, different industries have developed different positions according to their different interests. When faced with huge tort liabilities, for example the asbestos manufacturers helped draft bills that would impose an administrative compensation system, but would take away the plaintiff's right to sue. They had no major allies among other businesses and their proposal died. The chemical and petroleum manufacturers stood firm against any attempt by Congress to consider administrative compensation for victims of hazardous waste on the grounds that certification criteria would be too loose and a new type of welfare would be created. In contrast, the Keidnaren has helped maintain a tradition of industry self-regulation. As a representative of all of Japanese business, it was active in commenting on drafts of victims' compensation bills, played a role in the administration of the victims' compensation program once it was adopted, and criticized aspects of the program with which it was not satisfied.

The Bureaucracy and the Legislature

Another difference between Japanese and American institutions is in the role played by the bureaucracy and the legislature in developing new legislation. In Japan, the bureaucracy leads. The Diet actually has placed restrictions upon its own authority to develop new policy. Almost all new bills are drafted by the bureaucracy. The method by which the bureaucracy develops new legislation is quite unique. It is known as the "ringi" system, with draft legislation being circulated throughout the bureaucracy and a high degree of cooperation being achieved before a draft comes to a minister's attention. At all stages of the policy development process, formal procedures exist for the ministries to coordinate their activities both internally and with outside parties. The role of the Environment Agency in drafting victims' compensation legislation, as was seen, was very critical. In contrast, U.S. policy-making is fragmented (see Chapter 9); legislative initiatives can come from Congress or the bureaucracy. With the demise of the committee system and the disappearance of strong chairpersons, methods for coordinating the policy-making process within Congress are markedly absent. Extraordinary crises and issues may be needed to get Congress to act, and even these may not be enough if the mood of the times is antiregulation—indeed, any number of things may prevent individual members from endorsing a proposal for something as apparently novel as victims' compensation.

Thus, many bills to reform the victims' compensation system have come before Congress, but none has been passed. Unlike the Japanese case, victims' compensation has had no champion from within the bureaucracy. In recent years, in fact, the EPA and other regulatory agencies have opposed new initiatives. As a result, it is not surprising that Japan has developed a workable, if imperfect, victims' compensation policy, while the United States is still groping for a solution.

The Need for Reform

Reform is needed lest future litigation undermine the ability of the U.S. tort system to deliver justice. A Rand Corporation report makes the oft-repeated observation that the American tort system has been designed to handle ordinary injuries to individuals and is inadequate to deal with "thousands of claims involving complex medical questions, events, and decisions that occurred many years ago."[43] Consequently, justice for victims has been inconsistent, inequitable, and slow. Insolvency has jeopardized compensation in many cases. A torrent of litigation has forced companies to file for bankruptcy, with remaining claims to be decided through bankruptcy courts, which are not the most appropriate place to deal with this issue.

The lesson from Japan is that the connection between tort law and administrative relief is important. Policymakers cannot and should not sever this linkage. Changes in tort law should provide the rationale for the administrative system, and the administrative system should permit tort justice to be achieved. If the issue were merely a matter of efficiency and social welfare, then perhaps the administrative system alone would suffice. It is, however, also a matter of justice and rights where costs and benefits are unknown and cannot be known in advance, and bargaining between equally informed individuals is impossible.[44] Consequently, traditional tort remedies are needed in conjunction with administrative reform, not merely because such a balanced approach is more orderly and efficient, but also because it maintains the right of victims to have a hearing. Moreover, the discovery process in adversary proceedings can be a source of dynamism and innovation in legal doctrine that ultimately may have important administrative implications.

It is unpopular to argue in favor of the tort system, but a defense of its merits can come from an understanding of tort law's role in the development of victims' compensation policy in Japan.

Summary and Conclusions

This chapter has compared U.S. and Japanese approaches to victims' compensation policies. Japan has a policy in place, but the United States is still groping for a solution. U.S. proposals divide on whether they combine administrative relief with tort reform or whether they treat these categories separately. Japanese policies, which combine these elements, have evolved through a series of major court cases, which involved people suffering from unprecedented diseases. The results of the court cases have been codified into law. The Japanese system is imperfect and there have been abuses, but it has created a fairly straightforward way to compensate victims. Such a system does not exist in the United States, where the institutions responsible for developing victims' compensation policy have not as yet forged a coherent and satisfactory policy. It is the importance of consistent, stable, and workable public policies as a context for business growth that have been emphasized in this chapter. The lack of such workable public policies in the United States has been emphasized in this chapter and throughout this book.

Discussion Questions

1. Given what they knew about the *Dalkon Shield* case, should Searle executives have handled the Copper-7 IUD any differently? How could they have averted the expensive, time-consuming, and embarrassing encounter with Michael Ciresi?
2. What is the balanced approach for reforming victims' compensation? How does it differ from other approaches?
3. What is proportional liability? To what extent is it a reasonable approach? What are its strengths and weaknesses?

4. Explain Japanese victims' compensation policies. How did they evolve? What were the important breakthroughs in Japanese legal doctrine?

5. Explain the Japanese approach to epidemiological evidence. Compare it with the U.S. approach.

6. What do critics of the Japanese system argue? Are these criticisms justified? What could be done to improve the Japanese system?

7. Have Japanese firms gone bankrupt because of their liabilities? What has been the Japanese approach to these firms?

8. What are the strengths and weaknesses of victims' compensation in Japan? Should the United States imitate the Japanese approach? All or in part? Why or why not?

9. Are there institutional differences between Japan and the United States in developing policies like victims' compensation? Compare environmental movements, courts, local governments, organized interests, and the bureaucracy and the legislature in the two countries.

Endnotes

1. J. Gresser et al., *Environmental Law in Japan* (Cambridge, Mass.: MIT Press, 1981).

2. A. Marcus, "Compensating Victims for Harms Caused by Pollution and Other Hazardous Substances," *Law and Policy* 8, 1986, pp. 189–213; J. A. Worthley, and R. Torkelson, "Managing the Toxic Waste Problem: Lessons from Love Canal," *Administration and Society* 13, 1981, pp. 145–60; F. Schwadel, "Robins and Plaintiffs Face Uncertain Future," *The Wall Street Journal*, August 23, 1985.

3. R. Hinds, "Liability under Federal Law for Hazardous Waste Injuries," *Harvard Environmental Law Review* 6, 1982, p. 1–33.

4. *Projections of Asbestos-related Disease, 1980–2009,* Epidemiology Resources Inc., Cambridge, Mass., 1982; "Note. The Manville Bankruptcy: Treating Mass Tort Claims in Chapter 11 Proceedings," *Harvard Law Review* 96, 1984, pp. 1121–42.

5. R. Reich, "An Industrial Policy of the Right," *Public Interest*, Fall 1983, pp. 3–17.

6. J. Trauberman, "Statutory Reform of 'Toxic Torts': Relieving Legal, Scientific, and Economic Burdens on the Chemical Victim," *Harvard Environmental Law Review* 7, 1979, pp. 177–296.

7. P. Brodeur, "The Asbestos Industry on Trial," *New Yorker,* four part series, June 10, 1985, pp. 49–101; June 17, 1985, pp. 45–111; June 24, 1985, pp. 37–77; August 1, 1985, pp. 36–80.

8. Ibid.

9. House Committee on Education and Labor, *Hearings on H.R. 3175—The Occupational Disease Compensation Act of 1983 before the Subcommittee on Labor*

10. General Accounting Office, *Legislation Allows Black Lung Benefits to Be Awarded without Adequate Evidence of Disability* (Washington, D.C.: Government Printing Office, July 28, 1980).

11. W. K. Viscusi, "Structuring an Effective Occupational Disease Policy: Victim Compensation and Risk Regulation," *Yale Journal on Regulation* 2, 1984, pp. 53–81.

12. Hinds, "Liability under Federal Law for Hazardous Waste Injuries."

13. Brodeur, "The Asbestos Industry on Trial."

14. Minnesota Legislation Commission on Waste Management, *A Study of Compensation for Victims of Hazardous Substances* (St. Paul: Applied Research Center, William Mitchell College of Law, 1984).

15. D. Rosenberg, "The Causal Connection in Mass Exposure Cases: A 'Public Law' Vision of the Tort System," *Harvard Law Review* 97, 1984, pp. 851–929.

16. M. Dore, "A Commentary on the Use of Epidemiological Evidence for Demonstrating Cause-in-Fact," *Harvard Environmental Law Review* 7, 1983, pp. 429–40; K. Hall and E. Silbergeld, "Reappraising Epidemiology: A Response to 'Mr. Dove,'" *Harvard Environmental Law Review* 7, 1983, pp. 411–49.

17. Rosenberg, "The Causal Connection in Mass Exposure Cases"; S. Estep, "Radiation Injuries and Statistics: The Need for a New Approach to Injury Litigation," *Michigan Law Review* 67, 1960, pp. 50–82; M. Rizzo and F. Arnold, "Causal Apportionment in the Law of Torts: An Economic Theory," *Columbia Law Review* 80, 1980, pp. 1399–1429; G. Robinson, "Multiple Causation in Tort Law: Reflections on the DES Cases," *Virginia Law Review* 68, 1982, pp. 713–69.

18. Rosenberg, "The Causal Connection in Mass Exposure Cases."

19. S. Shavell, "Uncertainty over Causation and the Determination of Civil Liability," *Journal of Law and Economics* 28, 1985, pp. 587–611; D. Kaye, "The Limits of the Preponderance of Evidence Standard: Justifiably Naked Statistical Evidence and Multiple Causation," *American Bar Foundation Research Journal* 2, 1982, pp. 287–316; W. Landes and R. Posner, "Causation in Tort Law: An Economic Approach," *Journal of Legal Studies* 12, 1983, pp. 109–24; L. Tribe, "Trial by Mathematics: Precision and Ritual in the Legal Process," *Harvard Law Review* 84, 1971, pp. 1329–93.

20. S. Reed, *Environmental Pollution Policies in Japan,* paper presented at the annual meeting of the American Political Science Association, Washington, D.C., 1979.

21. Gresser, Fujikura, and Morishma, *Environmental Law in Japan.*

22. R. Reich, "An Industrial Policy of the Right."

23. Gresser, Fujikura, and Morishma, *Environmental Law in Japan.*

24. Ibid.

25. Ibid.

26. A. Meyerson, "Japan: Environmentalism with Growth," *The Wall Street Journal,* September 4, 1980, p. 14.

27. Gresser, Fujikura, and Morishma, *Environmental Law in Japan.*

28. Ibid., p. 126.

29. B. E. Aronson, "Environmental Law in Japan," *Harvard Environmental Law Review* 7, 1983, pp. 135–72.

30. T. Namekata, *Epidemiological Issues on Air Pollution in the Japanese Pollution-related Health Damage Compensation Law,* paper presented at the Workshop on Current Issues in Air Pollution Epidemiology during the 10th Scientific Meeting of the International Epidemiological Association in Vancouver, British Columbia, Canada, August 19–25.

31. Aronson," Environmental Law in Japan."

32. Namekata, *Epidemiological Issues on Air Pollution.*

33. Gresser, Fujikura, and Morishma, *Environmental Law in Japan.*

34. A. Marcus, *The Adversary Economy: Business Responses to Changing Government Requirements* (Westport, Conn.: Quorum Books, 1984); E. Vogel, *Japan as Number One: Lessons for America* (Cambridge, Mass.: Harvard University Press, 1980).

35. Meyerson, "Japan: Environmentalism with Growth."

36. Reed, *Environmental Pollution Policies in Japan.*

38. P. Weaver, "Regulation, Social Policy, and Class Conflict," *The Public Interest,* Winter 1978, pp. 45–64.

39. F. K. Upham, "After Minamata: Current Prospects and Problems in Japanese Environmental Litigation," *Ecology Law Quarterly* 8, 1979, pp. 213–68.

40. Rosenberg, "The Causal Connection in Mass Exposure Cases"; S. Lewis, *MASSPIRG Briefing Paper on the Interim Report of the Special Legislative Commission on Hazardous Materials Liability,* Boston, Mass., September 5, 1984.

41. I. Maitland and D. S. Park. The Political Economy of Japanese Economic Growth," paper presented at the second Pan-Pacific Conference, Seoul, Korea, May 14, 1985.

42. M. Olson, *The Rise and Decline of Nations: Economic Growth, Stagflation, and Social Rigidities* (New Haven: Yale University Press, 1982).

43. *Asbestos in the Courts: The Challenge of Mass Toxic Torts,* report, Rand Corporation Institute for Civil Justice, Santa Monica, Calif., 1985.

44. R. H. Coase, "The Problem of Social Costs," *Journal of Law and Economics* 3, 1960, pp. 1–40.

CASE VA
COCHLEAR IMPLANTS
Hearing for the Profoundly Deaf [1]

In granting approval for the commercial sale of one of 3M (Minnesota Mining & Manufacturing Co.) Company's cochlear devices in the United States in November 1984, the U.S. Food and Drug Administration (FDA) announced that this was the first time one of the five human senses had been replaced by an electronic device. Cochlear implant (CI) technology appeared to be an extraordinary innovation that would transform the traditional hearing aid industry, which had served only individuals with residual hearing, not the profoundly deaf.

Cochlear implants are biomedical devices that allow profoundly deaf people to discriminate sound through the electrical stimulation of the cochlea in the inner ear (see Exhibit VA–1). The concept of using electricity to bring hearing to the deaf goes back nearly 200 years to the experiments of the Italian scientist Volta, who first studied the effects of electrical stimulation of the ear. Research in the field since the mid-1970s had led by 1985 to a proliferation of different cochlear implant technologies that had commercial potential.

However, by late 1985, it was apparent that sales of the 3M cochlear implant device were not reaching projected levels. When 3M recalled it because of technical defects, the whole industry seemed in danger of being permanently derailed. The management of 3M had to decide whether it should go ahead with its plans to develop and market the new technology, or whether it was too late to salvage this promising innovation.

Cochlear Implant Technology

An implant could be extracochlear (i.e., the device's electrodes did not enter the cochlea, or inner ear) or intracochlear; it could be a percutaneous plug (the inner ear was reached by a direct channel through the cranium) or intracutaneus (access to the inner ear was made by means of magnetic couplings). Single-channel devices were available, and multiple channel devices in four, eight, or 22 channels were in various stages of development. 3M's approval for sale of a cochlear implant device from the FDA had been for a single-channel device. Surgery was necessary to install the device; some danger to the patient's inner ear was possible both during the surgery and after the device had been installed.

Implanting a device was not cheap; the average cost exceeded $20,000. Also, diagnosing if a patient would benefit was not easy. People had many different hearing defects. Doctors at the University of California at San Francisco had developed a measuring instrument for the evaluation of profound deafness, the "minimum auditory capability" battery. However, the criteria being used for cochlear implant patient selection and evaluation continued to vary. The

---

EHIBIT VA–1 Illustration of a Cochlear Implant Device

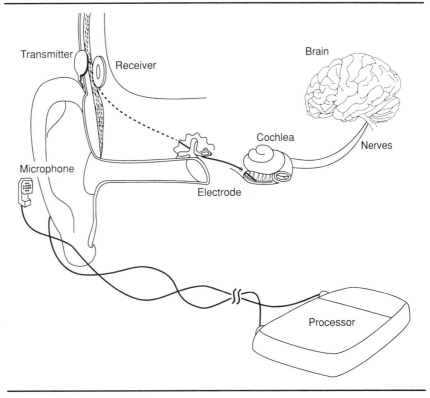

existence of the nerve fiber needed for stimulation could not be guaranteed regardless of the method of diagnosis used.

Even after a device was implanted, patients required substantial rehabilitation. Formerly deaf people who had the capacity to be helped by cochlear implants simply did not hear in the same manner as other people did. Audiologists, speech/language pathologists, psychologists, and otologists had to work with patients to get them to recognize and interpret the sounds that they heard.

Many deaf people, moreover, had adapted quite well to living in a world without sound. They relied on sign language, and through extensive involvement in schools, social activities, and other institutions they grew accustomed to their deafness. Firms in the industry had to think about creating both the diagnostic capabilities to identify people who would benefit and the rehabilitation services needed to get them to take full advantage of the opportunity.

The 3M Company

Starting with a relatively small sandpaper business, 3M had evolved into a major provider of goods and services to businesses worldwide. It had more than 60,000 products and over 40 product lines. Best known for making and distributing tapes, it had manufacturing plants in more than 30 states and did business in more than 63 countries. Twenty six of its manufacturing facilities were international and more than 50 percent of its revenues came from its international operations.

3M was growing at a rate of 10 percent per year based mostly on the introduction of new products and the penetration of markets throughout the world. While in the United States its growth rate had stalled, its growth rate outside the United States continued to rapidly rise. 3M was prepared to take advantage of coming European unity and had established joint ventures with Japanese companies so as to be well positioned in Asian markets.

While 3M had ROI and dividend objectives, its main goal was to reap 25 percent of its sales from products not in the market five years ago. It was known worldwide as a technological innovator with a heavy research emphasis. Its new products included familiar items such as Post-It notes. It also had created new uses for and modifications of existing products.

Indeed, 3M was one of the most successful companies in introducing new products in the United States. More than 6 percent of its total sales went into R&D, most of which was related to products that had commercial applications. 3M was working on new products in areas such as digital image processing, retroflection, optical recording, and supergravity. Its corporate culture was unique to the degree to which it fostered creativity and provided employees opportunities to realize their ideas.

3M's existing product lines included its core businesses based on abrasives and on adhesive-manufacturing technologies. 3M extended basic coating methods used in making sandpaper to such items as audio-visual tapes. Another 3M product line was coating fabrics with chemicals to provide them with stain-resistant or dust-free qualities, for example, Scotchguard. Still another product area was nonwoven material used in medical masks, tapes, and floormats.

3M had a medical products area that had developed pharmaceuticals as well as medical devices. It was in this group that the cochlear implants device was being reviewed.

The Development of Cochlear Implants

The basic research in cochlear implant technology had been carried out by physicians and researchers from around the world, who were associated with universities and teaching clinics, not companies. None of the researchers had been working exclusively on cochlear implants. Most of their work had been carried out with the intention of furthering basic knowledge on the science of hearing. Breakthroughs in many different disciplines had to take place before a workable cochlear implant device was possible.

In 1935, researchers reported that for the first time electrical stimulation of the auditory nerve had led to hearing. Experiments involving such stimulations were conducted by French researchers in the late 1950s. The first cochlear implant surgery in the United States was not performed until 1961 by a clinical physician, William House, who was founder of the House Ear Institute in Los Angeles.

Dr. House's energy and dedication as a champion of the cochlear implant technology was needed to bring different ideas together and overcome the obstacles that existed to creating a workable device. The extended gestation period for the technology lasted about 40 years (1935–76) during which time the basic thrust was to do the basic research to develop the technology. Research financing came mainly from universities and the government. No private company engaged in or funded the basic research.

Cochlear implant technology was first recognized as having commercial promise at a 1973 international conference on the electrical stimulation of the acoustic nerve. However, it was not until 1983 that the American Medical Association gave the technology its official endorsement. The American Speech Language and Hearing Association then created a special ad hoc committee on cochlear implants, and in 1985 the American Academy of Otolaryngology–Head and Neck Surgery endorsed cochlear implants, an important first step for the granting of Medicare coverage.

Private-Firm Involvement

Private firms did not become actively involved in cochlear implant development until the late 1970s when corporations such as 3M, Storz, Symbion, Nucleus, and Biostem initiated proprietary R&D activities to develop new businesses in cochlear implants. Efforts to establish cooperative relations among these firms did not work out. Each of the firms had ties with different academic institutions and teaching clinics. These ties provided access to the basic scientific knowledge needed to carry out an applied R&D program. However, each firm followed a different technological path and became a rival of the others.

3M's cochlear implant program progressed in stages, beginning with an initial exploration of the technology's business potential and eventually leading to the formal creation of a separate cochlear implant program in 1980. The 3M cochlear implant program generated the resources needed to develop proprietary products and competencies solely from within the company. In contrast, Nucleus, 3M's major competitor in the industry, raised resources both internally and from outside sources, including private investors.

In 1977, 3M was approached by the University of Melbourne, Australia, which was interested in commercializing the cochlear implant technology (see Exhibit VA–2). The relationship between the University of Melbourne and 3M, however, was terminated after only a brief period of negotiations. The University of Melbourne later entered into an agreement with Nucleus, at the time a new firm, which later became 3M's main competitor.

Between 1978 and 1982, 3M collaborated with Dr. Robin Michelson of the University of California, San Francisco (UCSF), to develop a multiple-channel implant. The 3M-UCSF relationship produced a cochlear device that was subsequently implanted in several individuals during 1980 and 1981. When 3M ended the partnership in 1982, UCSF went on to license its technology to another new business startup, Storz, in 1983.

3M entered into licensing agreements with the House Ear Institute and with researchers in Austria in 1981. Symbion and Biostem, two other firms in the fledgling cochlear implant industry, entered into relationships with cochlear

---

EXHIBIT VA–2   Key Events in the Development of 3M's Cochlear Implant (CI) Technologies

---

1977	University of Melbourne approaches 3M for joint venture; 3M decides to pursue CI program by itself.
1978	3M collaborates with UCSF.
1979	3M and House begin cooperative R&D; 3M takes up initial research of the House device.
1980	Separate CI program set up at 3M.
1981	Agreement between 3M and Austrian researchers.
	3M begins R&D work on Austrian device.
	Clinical trials initiated for House device.
	3M has to initially educate FDA about CI.
1982	3M initiates training program for physicians.
	UCSF-3M relationship terminated.
	Marketing activities initiated for House device.
1983	3M convinces third-party payers to cover House device.
	3M promotes Austrian device at a training program.
	3M submits first PMA for House device.
1984	3M establishes pilot plant at St. Paul and manufacturing facilities.
	3M receives PMA approval for House device.
	3M commences clinical trials for Austrian device.
1985	Six training programs initiated by 3M.
	3M starts servicing the House device.
	FDA grants IDE approval for Austrian device.
	3M recalls its House device from the market.
	FDA does not accept 3M's PMA application for children.
	Formation of industry council consisting of 3M, Cochlear Corporation, Storz, and Symbion.

---

implant research programs underway at the University of Utah and at Stanford University, respectively, both in 1983.

FDA Approval

All medical products, including cochlear devices, are subject to review and approval by the FDA. Before clinical tests can be conducted on human subjects, an investigational device exemption (IDE) must be obtained from the FDA based on clinical tests on animals. Next, each of the clinical sites must obtain an institutional review board clearance to certify its capability to conduct clinical tests on humans. After test results indicate that a minimum level of safety and effectiveness has been achieved, the device has to be submitted to an FDA panel for a premarket approval (PMA). If the FDA determines that the device is safe and effective, it approves commercial sale after having established that the company engages in "good manufacturing practices." The whole FDA approval procedure can take anywhere from three to five years.

In 1981, when 3M applied for IDE status for its first cochlear implant device, the FDA personnel responsible for ruling on the application did not know enough about the technology to evaluate the application. As a result, the FDA requested that 3M prepare additional documents and information in order to educate FDA's personnel and scientific review panels about cochlear implants and related safety issues. The FDA subsequently granted a number of approvals for clinical investigation and commercial marketing.

In November 1984 the FDA approved the 3M-House device for commercial sale, the first cochlear device to win FDA approval. The 3M-House device was a single-channel implant. 3M trumpeted the achievement in its 1984 annual report, estimating the market for the device at more than 400,000 persons and several billion dollars worldwide. In October 1985 the FDA granted its approval to Nucleus to commercially market its multichannel device in the United States. The multichannel device was considered by many otologists to be superior to House's single-channel device. They believed that once a single-channel device was implanted, the ear would not be suitable for a multiple-channel system. Thus, they opposed using the single-channel system because it would foreclose the use of further options. However, technological and scientific uncertainties, as well as an absence of common comparison criteria, made it difficult to compare the efficacy and safety of the different technologies. Whether single- or multiple-channel systems were better in the short term was not sufficiently clear, as well as which had more promise in the long term.

A major challenge to 3M's device took place in 1985 when the U.S. Office of Health Technology Assessment (OHTA) claimed that its implantation in children could result in inner ear damage. OHTA stated its concerns about limited research on cochlear implants for children and the potential for damaging a child's cochlea "thereby eliminating the patient from consideration for future cochlear implants with improved technology."[2]

More Problems

Although the FDA's approval of the 3M and Nucleus devices meant that cochlear implants could be sold commercially in the United States, the market for the devices did not develop as quickly as the manufacturers had hoped. Potential beneficiaries were reluctant to believe cochlear implants had anything to offer them. Many were accustomed to living in a world of deafness and feared entering a world of sound where additional and new demands might be put upon them. They did not feel ready to cope with these demands.

Hearing aids (which work on the principle of sound amplification) had not been able to help profoundly deaf people in the past. Vibrotactile devices, which transmitted pressure pulses through the skin and were poor substitutes for the real sensation of sound, offered only limited benefits. There was little, if any, marketing infrastructure in place to help the deaf understand the potential benefits of cochlear implants. To compensate, 3M encouraged physicians to promote cochlear implants.

However, marketing cochlear implants was further complicated by the high degree of technological uncertainty concerning their safety and efficacy. Unlike hearing aids and vibrotactile devices, cochlear implants had a significant risk factor; the surgery to implant the device could result in damage to the inner ear. Moreover, once implanted, the device's electrodes could not be replaced easily without adding further significant risk of damaging the cochlea. This meant that patients who had received cochlear implants might not be able to take advantage of improved electrode technologies. Consequently, the FDA decided to limit further research on children and many physicians felt reluctant to promote cochlear implant technologies.

These safety and efficacy considerations posed a marketing dilemma for 3M and the other firms. On the one hand, a company needs to present its products in as favorable a light as possible; on the other, researchers were still in the early stages of understanding. It was important to project a realistic picture and not make exaggerated claims. However, inasmuch as the authentication of claims was difficult, the perception of exaggeration was hard to remove. The technology had not yet reached a stage where cochlear implants permitted true speech discrimination. Exaggerated claims to the extent they were made, hurt the credibility of the product and made marketing difficult.

Another problem for the industry was that Medicare did not cover cochlear implantation and the cost of the device. Third-party reimbursement, unique to the biomedical industry, was essential for the success of any new product. The $20,000-plus-per-patient costs were too much for the average deaf person to bear without some kind of third-party reimbursement (Medicare or private medical insurance). An industry analyst reported that "third-party payers were capricious in their coverage of implant costs, with payment policies varying from state to state and from patient to patient."[3] Thus, many patients simply could not afford the devices despite FDA's approval for commercial sale.

Symbion initiated efforts to convince third-party insurance payers to extend coverage to cochlear implants in 1983. Other firms sought insurance coverage for their cochlear devices soon thereafter. In 1983, 3M was successful in obtaining coverage for its first single-channel cochlear device from some third-party insurers, but wider coverage by private insurance companies and by Medicare was still not a reality at the end of 1985.

A Struggling New Technology

Because of these problems, the commercial viability of the cochlear implant industry was uncertain. Symbion and Storz announced that they would reduce their commitments to their cochlear implant programs because they did not perceive the market to be growing rapidly enough. In late 1985 the industry was struck another blow when 3M, following FDA product recall guidelines, voluntarily withdrew its 3M-House device from the market because of technical difficulties. Realizing that the recall had the potential to irreparably tarnish the image of the new technology, 3M initiated discussions with other firms in the industry to devise a strategy to minimize the negative impact of the recall.

The 3M managers who had worked on development of the technology were not ready to give up. They still believed that there was promise: to extend the House device to be implanted in children, to create an advanced single-channel device in collaboration with the Australian researchers, and to carry out a program inside 3M that would lead to the development of an advanced multichannel device. But the company needed to rethink its strategy for making the device a success. It needed to come up with new ideas, perhaps in collaboration with other members of the industry.

Discussion Questions

1. What had gone wrong in the development of the cochlear implant technology?
2. Was there anything 3M could do to salvage its investment in this technology? Develop a plan of action.
3. How can this action plan be sold to 3M management?
4. How will Japanese innovations differ from American in the case of Cochlea implants?

Endnotes

1. This case was adapted by Mark Jankus and Alfred Marcus from R. Garud and A. H. Van de Ven, "Technological Innovation and Industry Emergence: The Case of Cochlear Implants," in *Research on the Management of Innovation*, ed. A. H. Van de Ven, H. L. Angle, and M. S. Poole (NY: Harper & Row, 1989), p. 489–532.
2. Garud and Van de Ven, "Technological Innovation and Industry Emergence," p. 497.
3. Ibid., p. 498.

Case VB
The Bhopal Disaster
Implications for Investments in Less-Developed Countries[1]

John Brown asked his secretary to hold his calls and settled back in his chair to begin preparing for the conference he would be attending next week on investing in less-developed countries (LDCs). In order to compete in the increasingly global economy, corporations had to be prepared to take advantage of expansion opportunities in foreign countries. The risks of such expansion, however, had been highlighted for all business people by the industrial accident that had occurred in Bhopal, India, the year before. The accident had killed more than 2,000 people and injured hundreds of thousands.

No industry was more concerned with the implications of the accident for foreign operations than the chemical manufacturers. The worst industrial accident in history had drawn critical attention to the industry. Congress and administrative agencies had proposed tougher laws and regulations governing how the industry conducted its business. Numerous stories in the media had documented the events leading up to the accident and the horrible consequences it had for the impoverished Indians who had made their homes near the Union Carbide plant where the accident occurred.

American chemical companies had begun to make changes in their safety policies and procedures to prevent a repeat of the disaster. Brown's employer, W. R. Grace & Company, was one of many companies reevaluating their policies for investing in LDCs.

W. R. Grace and Co.

W. R. Grace & Company was a diversified conglomerate that, in 1984, operated chemical, energy production and services, retailing, restaurant, and other types of subsidiaries in 47 states and 42 countries. The company's specialty and agricultural chemicals divisions accounted for 42 percent of its $6.728 billion in sales and 65 percent of its $322.6 million in income in 1984. At that time Grace employed thousands of workers in Latin America, the Far East, and other less-developed regions. The chemical operations in those regions accounted for 10 percent of the chemical divisions' sales and 20 percent of their profits.

The governments of some of the countries where Grace operated plants held the majority interest in the operations, much as India had controlled Union Carbide's Bhopal plant. For example, the Trinidad government owned 51 percent of Grace's Trinidad anhydrous ammonia facility and Grace owned 49 percent. The company was continuing to expand its operations in the LDCs, opening a silica gel production plant in Brazil in 1984.

John's boss, the company's vice president for environmental affairs, had asked him to attend a conference organized by the chemical manufacturers to develop, among other things, a list of guidelines for conducting business in LDCs. John opened the folder of background materials the research staff had prepared and began to read.

The Role of Chemicals in Feeding the World's People

American chemical companies had a lot to offer developing countries. John had been convinced of this even before he took his job. The agricultural chemicals like the fertilizers and pesticides that his company produced were a vital part of the Green Revolution that had increased food production dramatically in the poorer nations where additional food was so vital.

Experts estimated the number of chronically malnourished people in the world at between 0.45 and 1.3 billion in 1979, and the number was growing every year.[2] It was necessary to increase the yields of the food crops if everyone was going to be fed, since there was little unused land left to be cultivated in the developing countries. According to Nobel laureate Norman Borlaug, increases in world food supply required the use of pesticides.[3] Pesticide use had increased the average yield of corn crops grown in the tropics on research plots from 30 bushels per acre to 440 bushels per acre. Rice plots grown with the aid of insecticides in the Philippines showed yield increases of 100 percent.[4] Pesticide use also helped protect the crops after they had been harvested, when they were in storage and vulnerable to rodents and insects. Around 25 percent of the harvest worldwide would be lost without pesticide use, according to experts.[5]

Increased food production was not all that agricultural chemicals had to offer the developing nations. Economic growth necessary to raise standards of living was facilitated by the increased agricultural efficiencies chemicals made possible. Less land was needed to produce the same amount of food, and labor was freed up for other productive purposes. The sale of crops like cotton provided a valuable source of foreign exchange funds necessary to purchase advanced, modern technologies. Some experts estimate that without the use of pesticides in the United States, the price of farm products would increase by 50 percent.[6] Pesticides had proven effective in making food more affordable in developing countries as well. Finally, pesticide use had been tremendously effective in reducing the incidence of a variety of pest-borne diseases like malaria, elephantiasis, and yellow fever.[7]

The Risks of Chemical Use

There were indisputable benefits for developing countries that adopted modern technologies like agricultural chemicals. Unfortunately, as the Bhopal disaster had shown, there were also risks involved. A country like India was very different from the United States, where much of the industrial technology for producing pesticides had been developed. The Indian infrastructure was much more primitive and the culture had different norms regarding the purpose and value of human life, which meant a complex technology like pesticide production was at best an awkward fit.

The dangers of pesticide manufacture and use were not understood in third-world countries. Many third-world people perished from pesticide use. Estimates of annual pesticide poisonings ranged from a quarter to three quarters of a million people, with more than 10,000 dying annually. While LDCs used only 15 percent of the world's pesticides, they reported more than half of the accidental poisonings and more than three fourths of the deaths. Over half the fatalities were children.[8]

These fatalities occurred because people did not use the pesticides appropriately. For example, fishermen living on the shore of Lake Volta in Ghana used them to kill fish. Local people ate the fish, drank the water, and used it for other purposes. Many developed the blurred vision, dizziness, and vomiting that were symptoms of pesticide poisoning.

The boomerang effect meant that people in developed countries also were affected. They ingested excess amounts of pesticides on the fruits and vegetables that they imported from LDCs where pesticides had not been properly used. Pesticides that were banned from use in the United States, like DBCP, were sold by U.S. firms abroad and came back in the produce that foreign producers sent to the United States. This impact on people in developed nations was very hard to control.

Also, over time pesticide efficacy declined. Pesticide resistance began to appear in target insect populations, eventually becoming pesticide immunity. Consequently, more powerful pesticides, with greater toxicity to humans, animals, and the environment, were developed, marketed, and applied. This pesticide use phenomenon, called the treadmill, greatly disturbed scientists, who pointed to the increasing concentrations of very deadly pesticides throughout the biosphere.

The regulatory apparatus in third-world countries was completely inadequate to deal with these problems. They not only permitted importation of products banned in developed countries, but they failed to impose labeling or handling requirements on these dangerous substances. The pesticide regulations that they had developed were poorly enforced. Moreover, LDC regimes had insufficient awareness of the alternatives to pesticides that were available.

As a legacy of their colonial pasts, they tended to put restrictions on foreign firms operating in their countries. The Indian government, for instance, had passed laws limiting the degree of control that a foreign corporation could exercise over an Indian subsidiary. However, the government laid the blame for the Bhopal accident solely on Union Carbide, filing a $3 billion lawsuit after ruling itself the sole representative of the victims of the accident.[9]

The Bhopal Accident

A multinational corporation had much to gain and to give by expanding markets for its products and doing business in developing countries, but Bhopal made it clear that there were costs to consider as well. At the conference next week, John and representatives of other chemical firms doing business overseas would attempt to work out a set of guidelines that could be used to decide whether investment in operations in a developing country was worthwhile, and under what conditions. To refresh himself on the specific lessons to be learned from Bhopal, he reviewed the history of the accident.

The Setting.   Bhopal, the most centrally located city in India, is the capital of one of the least-industrialized states in the country. The area had a fairly good base of natural resources like water and timber, and the feudal history of the region had contributed to its status as a mainly agricultural region. Beginning in the 1950s, the Indian government had actively encouraged industrial development in the region, though it had not engaged in a particularly comprehensive planning effort, and consequently the infrastructure of services like roads, utilities, and communications services were poor.

By the 1980s, stagnation in agricultural production in the country's rural areas had driven thousands of people to the cities to look for work. Bhopal's population grew sixfold between 1961 and 1981, almost three times the average for the country as a whole. The resulting severe housing shortage forced the migrants to build shantytowns wherever there was open space, and areas near industrial plants where work might be found were favorite choices.

The walls of Union Carbide's Bhopal plant were crowded with such squatters' dwellings. The plant was originally built in the 1960s in open fields within two miles of the local commercial and transportation center. At the time of start-up, the plant was used to mix chemical components that had been manufactured overseas and shipped to Bhopal into the final pesticide formulations that would be marketed, and the plant did not pose much threat to neighboring residential areas.

However, by 1978, under pressure from the Indian government to manufacture the precursors to the pesticides in India and competitive pressures to backward-integrate its pesticide production, the company had built and begun operating the facilities necessary to manufacture the precursors. The plant was now much more of a health hazard than before, and although some local authorities objected to the continued siting of the plant at its present location, state and national government officials overruled them.[10] The plant was too important a part of the local economy to risk losing.

Among the pesticide components manufactured at the plant was a highly toxic compound called methyl isocynate (MIC). Used to make the active ingredient in the pesticide Sevin, MIC is highly unstable. It was manufactured at Bhopal in batches and stored in three refrigerated tanks set in concrete. Each tank was equipped with pressure and temperature gauges, a high-temperature alarm, a level indicator, and high- and low-level alarms.[11] There were several safety systems designed to handle accidental leaks: a vent-gas scrubber that neutralized toxic gases with a caustic soda solution, a flare tower that could burn off the gases, the refrigeration system to keep the chemical at low, stable temperatures, and a set of water-spray pipes that could control escaping gases or extinguish fires.[12]

The Evening of December 2, 1984.   When Suman Dey, a control room operator at the Bhopal plant, came on duty at 11:00 P.M. on the evening of December 2, 1984, everything seemed normal. He performed a routine check of the gauges in the control room and noticed that the pressure in the MIC storage tanks was within the normal range of 2 to 25 pounds per square inch (psi). At about 11:30, however, a worker noticed an MIC leak near the vent gas scrubber and notified Dey. A tea break was due at 12:15 A.M. and the workers planned to fix the leak afterwards. By the time the break was over at 12:40 A.M. it was too late. The pressure in one of the tanks, labeled E610, shot up to 30 psi shortly after the break began and minutes later exceeded the gauge's upper limit, 55 psi.

Dey ran outside to the storage area to investigate. He heard a tremendous rumbling sound beneath the concrete, and as he watched 60 feet of concrete six inches thick cracked open, unleashing heat so intense that Dey couldn't get close.[13] A white cloud of MIC began to shoot out of the vent gas tower attached to the tank and settle over the plant.

Within a few minutes the fire brigade arrived and began to spray a curtain of water in the air to knock down the cloud of gas. The tower from which the gas was escaping was 120 feet high, however, and the water only reached about 100 feet in the air. The system of water spray pipes was also too low to help.

Dey ran inside the control room and turned on the vent gas scrubber. It did not work. The scrubber had been under maintenance and had not been charged with a caustic soda solution. Experts later noted that even if the scrubber had been operational it would have been ineffective since the temperature of the escaping gas was at least 100 degrees fahrenheit hotter than the system was designed to handle.

By this time the plant superintendent had raced to the plant on his bicycle and he and Dey conferred on what to do next. They were afraid to turn on the flare tower for fear of igniting the large cloud of gas that had enveloped the plant. The superintendent then remembered that the flare tower was also being repaired and was missing a four-foot section. Likewise, the coolant in the refrigeration system had been drained weeks before to be used in another part of the plant. They considered routing the escaping gas into an empty MIC storage tank, but contrary to established safety procedures, no empty tanks were available. There seemed to be nothing to do.

As the gas began to escape, a warning alarm was sounded but was shut off shortly afterwards. Four buses parked near the entrance that were intended to be used for emergency evacuations of plant workers and nearby residents were left sitting as workers fled by foot in panic. By 1:30 A.M. the gas had permeated the control room and Dey dashed for his gas mask and oxygen tank. The few remaining control room workers fled, one of them breaking his leg as he scrambled up and over the barbed-wire-topped fence surrounding the plant. Dey left the control room and waited upwind for the cloud of gas to disperse, periodically putting on his mask to enter the control room and check the pressure gauge. By 2:30 A.M. the gas had stopped shooting out of the vent stack. By 3:30 A.M. the gas had dispersed from the plant.

Meanwhile, in the shantytowns and neighborhoods outside the plant, chaos reigned. The gas seeped into the rooms of the sleeping population, suffocating hundreds in their sleep and driving others out into a panicked run through the narrow streets where they inhaled even more of the gas. Blinded by the cornea-clouding effect of the gas, lungs on fire, thousands of people fled the city. Forty-five tons of MIC spread over 25 square miles of the city, killing nearly 3,000 residents and seriously injuring 40,000 more.[14]

The Costs of the Accident.   Long after the accident, victims continued to suffer from breathlessness, coughing, lung diseases, eye disorders, abdominal pain and vomiting, and menstrual disorders, as well as psychological trauma. The psychological problems were most severe for women of childbearing age, many of whom suffered from reproductive illnesses as a result of the accident. These women were afraid to tell their families or spouses about the problems because of the cultural prejudices against infertile women.[15]

The economic consequences of the accident were as devastating as the physical consequences. Many victims were physically unable to work and their families suffered as a result. Estimates of business losses ranged up to $65 million. The Union Carbide plant was closed and 650 high-paying jobs were lost, as well as 1,500 government jobs that were peripherally related to the presence of the plant. In addition, the business reputation of the city and the whole developing world suffered as a consequence of the accident.[16]

Union Carbide was hard hit by the accident. Besides the $3 billion lawsuit filed against the company by the Indian government on behalf of the victims, the company's reputation came under attack from the worldwide news media. Activist groups undertook a variety of campaigns against the company, and communities where UC had proposed building plants canceled the plans.[17] The company's stock dropped from $48 per share to a low of $32–3/4 within a few weeks (though it rallied to $52 by the end of August 1985).[18] The company's debt rating was reduced to the lowest investment grade by Standard & Poors. The company was sued by its own stockholders for not informing them of the risks of doing business abroad. Further damaging the company's and the industry's reputation was the revelation in early 1985 that there had been 28 major MIC leaks at the Union Carbide plant in Institute, West Virginia, during the five years preceding the Bhopal accident.[19]

The Investigation.   In the weeks and months after the accident a horde of reporters, Indian government officials, and Union Carbide technical experts descended on the plant to find out what had gone wrong. Gradually it became apparent that the accident resulted not only from technical malfunctions in the plant's equipment, but also stemmed from human errors and organizational shortcomings.[20] Also, the unpreparedness of the emergency infrastructure of the local government further exacerbated the problem.

The Union Carbide scientists that analyzed the residue that remained in tank E610 after the accident determined that the chemical reaction that led to the leak was caused when approximately 1,100 pounds of water was somehow introduced into the tank. Water reacts exothermically with MIC to produce a hot, highly pressurized mixture of liquid, foam, and gas. The pressure in the tank had reached 180 psi, more than enough to blow open the safety valve and allow the deadly gas to escape. The question that remained was how the water had gotten into the tank.

There were two main theories. Most experts believe the water leaked into the tank on the evening of December 2nd when an employee washed out some of the pipes leading to the tank. Investigations revealed that the employee had failed to use a device called a slip blind to ensure that water could not leak past a series of valves leading to the tank. Union Carbide argued that the accident was the result of sabotage by an unhappy employee who deliberately unscrewed a gauge and stuck a water hose into the tank. As support for this theory, Carbide cited the statements of some employees who remembered seeing a running water hose near the tank after the accident. The company also argued that it wouldn't have been possible for the large quantity of water introduced into the tank to have leaked past the series of valves between the pipes being washed and the tank.

Whatever the proximate cause of the accident, it was clear that the magnitude of deaths and injuries was the result of more than a few leaking valves or an act of sabotage. The safety policies and procedures intended to prevent such an accident were not followed, and the reasons why were rooted partly in the deteriorating financial condition of the Bhopal plant.

Simply put, the Bhopal plant was an unprofitable unit in an unimportant division of the company.[21] Competitors in the country's pesticide market had introduced new, inexpensive products and the Indian economy had been in a downturn for a few years. The Bhopal plant had lost money for three years in a row. As profits fell and the plant's budgets were cut, maintenance was deferred, employees were laid off, and training programs were scaled back. Half the operators in the MIC unit were laid off between 1980 and 1984, leaving only six. Because of the layoffs and because of rumors that the plant was a candidate for divestment, morale was low and many of the best employees quit. Labor-management conflicts were common. A 1982 company safety inspection determined that many basic safety rules were being ignored; for example, maintenance workers were signing permits they were unable to read and others were working in prohibited areas without permission.[22] Safety training was inadequate—there had been many small accidents and one death in the past—and workers had no training in dealing with emergencies. There were in fact no emergency plans for the plant at all, so when the MIC leak occurred, employees reacted in a disorganized manner, shutting off the warning siren, for example. The plant management and workers knew little about the toxic effects of MIC and could not supply the local authorities with any information on how to deal with the accident.[23]

The plant relied on manual operating systems to a much greater degree than its counterparts in the United States. The construction and final technical engineering of the plant had been done by Indian workers and engineers, and the Indian engineers had designed the plant to use more manual labor than comparable plants overseas, partly to generate more jobs. The communications system of the plant relied heavily on runners to bring messages between parts of the plant or outside the plant. The local police were not notified of the accident until 3 A.M., more than two hours after the gas release began, partly because the phones weren't working, and partly because the plant management had an informal policy of not involving the local authorities with gas leaks.[24]

The Indian Government's Role.   While the Indian government laid responsibility for the accident completely at the door of Union Carbide, it played a significant role in contributing to the conditions that created the disaster. Like many developing countries, India had strict rules regarding the degree to which foreign companies were allowed to own and operate businesses within its borders. Intent on developing the self-sufficiency of Indian industry, the government placed restrictions on the equipment that could be imported, the source of the raw materials used in manufacturing processes, and the makeup of the labor force.

Because of these regulations, control of the Bhopal plant was turned completely over to its Indian subsidiary, Union Carbide India Limited (UCIL) in 1982, and the plant was operated solely by Indians. However, UC's top management in Connecticut received monthly reports concerning the plant and continued to make major decisions concerning financial, maintenance, and personnel decisions. The Indian personnel were responsible for making safety inspections and operating the plant, including the MIC unit, according to the processing manuals supplied by headquarters.

Many aspects of the relatively primitive local and national infrastructure also contributed to the severity of the accident. The Department of Labor of the state where the accident occurred was responsible for safety inspections of the industrial facilities located there. Grossly understaffed, the Department had only 15 inspectors to cover the more than 8,000 industrial plants in the state, and some of the inspectors lacked even typewriters and telephones to assist them in their duties.[25] The two inspectors responsible for the area where the Bhopal plant was located were trained as mechanical engineers and had little understanding of the hazards of a chemical plant. The government, fearful of discouraging job-producing industries, was reluctant to place a heavy burden of safety and environmental regulations on business.

When a journalist from the Bhopal area wrote a series of articles in 1982 detailing the death of an employee that was caused by a chemical leak at the plant and warned of the possibility of a catastrophe, neither the plant management nor the government took action, even after the journalist wrote a letter to the Chief Minister of the state to warn him of the danger. A top government bureaucrat who requested that the plant be moved to another location because of the threat it posed to neighboring slum residents was transferred to another post.[26] When migrants began building dwellings adjacent to the plant, government officials allowed them to do so and in 1984 issued deeds allowing the squatters the right to stay for 30 years.

Besides an indifferent bureaucracy, the primitive state of the local social services infrastructure contributed to the severity of the accident. There was only one telephone per 1,000 residents, and dead lines were common. Running water was available only for a few hours per day and was of poor quality. The only radio station was government operated. The streets in the older parts of the city were only 12 feet wide and were crammed with animals, carriages, scooters, cars, buses, bicycles, and people, making evacuation difficult. The hospitals and dispensaries were unequipped to handle the flood of victims.

Inappropriate Technology?

Some critics argue that a highly complex technology like pesticide production is inappropriate for a country like India whose people are largely unfamiliar with the hazards of such technologies. The squatters who lived around the plant thought that it produced some kind of beneficial plant medicine and had no idea that there was any threat to their safety.[27] The employees of the plant were unfamiliar with the nature of the health threat posed by MIC and were unable to advise the doctors treating the injured. Further, preventive maintenance is a somewhat foreign concept in a subsistence economy where the idea of spending money now in order to save money later is unfamiliar.

Others argue that modern technologies like pesticides are the developing world's best hope of achieving a better standard of living and that without such technologies to increase the food supply, millions would die. A Bhopal-like accident, they contend, is part of the price developing societies pay for modernization.

When Is It Worth the Risk? John closed the folder and began to gather his thoughts. Under what circumstances was it worthwhile to invest in a developing nation like India? The Bhopal disaster demonstrated that the actions of one small plant in a distant subsidiary could threaten the survival of a whole multinational corporation. There was a definite need for a list of guidelines for corporate involvement in the developing world that would help ensure that mistakes such as those that contributed to the Bhopal disaster would not be repeated.

Discussion Questions

1. What did American chemical companies have to offer developing countries?
2. What were the risks of chemical use in developing countries?
3. Why did the Bhopal accident take place?
4. What lessons can be learned from the Bhopal accident?
5. What should John Brown say to the management of W. R. Grace about investing in less-developed countries?

Endnotes

1. Written by Mark Jankus with the editorial guidance of Alfred Marcus.
2. From D. E. Whiteside, "Note on the Export of Pesticides from the United States to Developing Countries," case 384–097, Harvard Business School, 1983, p. 127.
3. Cited in ibid., p. 128.
4. Ibid.
5. Ibid.
6. Ibid., p. 129.
7. Ibid.
8. Ibid., p. 129.
9. Shrivastava, *Bhopal: Anatomy of a Crisis* (Cambridge, Mass.: Ballinger Publishing Co., 1987), p. 59.
10. Ibid., p. 41.
11. Ibid.
12. Ibid., p. 45.
13. S. Diamond, "Workers Recall Horror," *The New York Times*, January 30, 1985, p. I1.
14. Shrivastava, *Bhopal*.
15. Ibid., p. 74.
16. Ibid., p. 72.
17. Ibid., p. 76.
18. Ibid., p. 78; see also A. A. Marcus and R. Goodman, "Corporate Adjustments to Catastrophe: A Study of Investor Reaction to Bhopal," *Industrial Crisis Quarterly* 3, 1989, pp. 213–34.
19. Shrivastava, *Bhopal*, p. 77.
20. Ibid., p. 48.
21. Ibid., p. 51.
22. Ibid., p. 49.
23. Ibid., p. 50.
24. Diamond, "Workers Recall Horror."
25. Ibid.
26. S. Hazarika, "Indian Journalist Offered Warning," *The New York Times*, December 11, 1984, p. I9.
27. "Slumdwellers Unaware of Dangers," *The New York Times*, January 31, 1985, p. I8.

CASE VC
AUTO SAFETY POLICY AT FORD
Revisiting the Pinto[1]

Karen Carlson, the newest staff member of Ford's automotive safety department and a recent M.B.A. graduate, had a lot on her mind. She had been assigned to review the facts of the Pinto controversy and to develop some ideas about what the company could learn from it in order to avoid similar situations in the future. Her presentation was scheduled for the next week.

Auto Safety Today

The issue of auto safety did not seem to go away at Ford. On April 5, 1990, the company again was hit with a huge settlement in a personal injury lawsuit. It had to pay $6 million in a case involving the safety of lap-only rear seat belts.[2] This problem had been emerging for many years as an important product liability issue for the automobile manufacturers, and a number of companies had reached multimillion-dollar settlements with litigants, but the Ford settlement was one of the largest ever in such a case.

The case presented Ford with many of the same dilemmas it had confronted nearly 15 years earlier in the Ford Pinto case. The company believed that in good faith it was adhering to state-of-the-art technology with regard to safety only to be challenged by attorneys for victims who afterward claimed that the company knew that certain features of its automobiles could not adequately protect occupants, but that it did not want to spend the extra money to do something about the problem. This claim had been made in the Pinto case and again was being made in the case of "three-point" lap and shoulder belts. Attorneys for the plaintiffs were arguing that they should have been installed in Ford's Escort model cars.

Ironically, the Escort was the successor to the Pinto. Just as the reputation of that car had been destroyed by the controversy over its safety, so now the reputation of the Escort was threatened. In both instances, Ford's subcompact challenge to Japan's dominance in this part of the market was being put to a test on account of a safety issue.

The similarity between the cases did not end there. In both instances, when the vehicles were first marketed, no government regulations required Ford do anything other than what it was doing, either in regard to the placement of the gas tank with the Pinto or the installation of three point belts with the Escort. Only in December of 1989 did the government mandate such a safety feature in the rear seats of vehicles. In the meantime, more than 140 million vehicles had been sold in the United States with lap-only rear belts.

The fact that the government did not mandate rear-seat three-point belts, however, did not prevent attorneys for the plaintiffs from bringing many successful suits. The Institute for Injury Reduction, a Maryland-based organization founded by trial lawyers to put together information on product safety cases, was predicting that the rear-belt issue would be one of the biggest sources of auto litigation in history.

Ford was very concerned. It understood that the issue was serious not only for itself but for the auto industry as a whole, which faced increased competition from the Japanese and continued loss of market share. In March of 1990, Toyota's share of the U.S. auto market was 9.2 percent, up from 6.2 percent a year earlier, while Ford's share of the U.S. market had declined from 22.6 percent a year earlier to 21.1 percent. To maintain sales, Ford had to offer $500 rebates on many of its 1990 models.

Most American automobile executives had concluded that safety did sell. Since Ralph Nader's 1963 book *Unsafe At Any Speed*, consumers had obtained a great deal of information about the relative safety of various cars from consumer groups, government regulatory agencies, and insurers. Foreign automakers had been the first to introduce high-tech safety features when similar benefits were not found in American-made products.

Autos that had poor safety records consistently were shunned by consumers. For instance, when charges were made against the Audi 5000 luxury sedan that it tended to self-accelerate, sales rapidly plummeted. Similarly, Suzuki's Samurai sport's utility vehicle lost 70 percent of its sales after claims were made that it easily rolled over during sharp turns.

No one disputed the contention that safety sells, but auto executives were asking how much safety and at what cost. What types of safety policies did they have to use in new-auto design to assure consumers they were obtaining the safety they wanted?

The Pinto History

Shortly after Lee Iacocca took over as Ford's president in 1967, Ford started the accelerated development program to bring Pinto to the market in 1971. Ford had a fairly strong position in the small-car market with its Falcon and Mustang models. Iacocca knew something about small cars and their appeal, having masterminded the introduction of the highly popular Mustang in 1964, and he wanted a new, competitive small car brought to the market quickly.

By 1967 it appeared that foreign imports like the Volkswagen were posing a threat to Ford's small-car niche. The company needed an inexpensive, fuel-efficient subcompact in order to be fully competitive. According to the Ford executives, who believed the company should compete in the small-car market, doing so was the socially responsible thing to do. It saved American jobs, conserved energy, and reduced pollution. It gave people the chance to obtain inexpensive transportation, people who might otherwise not be able to afford an automobile. Introducing a small car added to the convenience of their lives. In suburban America, where a car was a necessity, providing an inexpensive option to the standard-size American vehicle was important. Single people and families needing a second car would find the Pinto attractive. Of course, other managers thought Ford should stick to producing the large models where the profit margins were much higher.

To help clearly define what Iacocca wanted, he developed the "rule of 2,000." The car wasn't to weigh more than 2,000 lb or cost more than $2,000. Even at that price the car would be more expensive than the subcompacts offered by foreign producers, who didn't have to deal with high labor costs.[3]

Pinto's product objectives were as follows:

1. True subcompact:
   a. Size.
   b. Weight.
2. Low cost of ownership:
   a. Initial price.
   b. Fuel consumption.
   c. Reliability.
   d. Serviceability.

3. Clear product superiority:
   a. Appearance.
   b. Comfort.
   c. Features.
   d. Ride and handling.
   e. Performance.

Critics later pointed out that passenger safety was not on this list.

The Successful Introduction of the Pinto

Pinto made it into production in time for the 1971 model year as Iacocca had demanded. Rather than the usual 43-month development period, it was in dealer showrooms in 38 months. In the six years following its introduction in August 1970, it fulfilled many of the company's expectations and became one of Ford's all-time best-selling models. The 2 million Pintos sold between 1970 and 1977 helped retain Ford's market position during a period of rapidly escalating gas prices. The Arab oil embargo had caught the other major American auto manufacturers without an adequate line of small, fuel-efficient cars, and the Pinto sold well among cars in its size range.[4]

The first public criticism of the Pinto came not from consumers but from Byron Bloch, an independent auto safety expert. He warned on national television in 1973 that the fuel system was very vulnerable to even minor damage and called for the recall of Pintos to repair this hazard. The Nader-funded group, the Center for Auto Safety, demanded that the newly formed National Highway Traffic Safety Administration (NHTSA) investigate the Pinto. It claimed that attorneys engaged in liability lawsuits and that its own research provided grounds for a defect investigation, but NHTSA reviewed the complaints and found no investigation necessary. NHTSA felt that statistical studies did not show a greater problem with Pintos than with other vehicles.

The Insurance Institute for Highway Safety, however, then released a 1975 study showing a growth in the number of fire-related incidents. Ford had a disproportionate share. Twenty percent of vehicles on the road were manufactured by Ford, while the company's cars had 35 percent of the fire-related incidents.

"Pinto Madness"

In August 1977, precisely seven years after production of the Pinto began, the popular, muckraking journal, *Mother Jones* called a news conference in Washington to announce the publication of a piece called "Pinto Madness."[5] Although not the first published article to suggest that Ford executives had known about the Pinto's explosive defects before the car was produced (columnist Jack Anderson had written on the subject in late 1976), it generated additional attention to the issue.[6] The article contained a number of serious allegations which can be summarized as follows:

1. The Pinto's accelerated development schedule meant that crash tests were conducted after assembly tooling had already begun, making changes in design prohibitively expensive.

2. The safety of the car was not a serious consideration in its design because top executives like Iacocca believed "safety doesn't sell."

3. The Pinto's designers knew of the car's defects but chose not to remedy them (even though the modifications might have cost as little as $1 per car for materials) based on a cost/benefit analysis that crassly assigned a dollar value to human life.

4. Ford mounted a concerted campaign to delay implementation of the relevant safety standards, succeeding in postponing their final adoption until the 1977 model year.

Stories in the press quoted top Ford officials as saying that the article was "unfair and distorted."[7] The article made no pretense of objectivity, concluding, for example, with this question: "One wonders how long the Ford Motor Company would continue to market lethal cars were Henry Ford II and Lee Iacocca serving 20-year terms in Leavenworth for consumer homicide."[8] Still, the article did raise some troubling questions about the company's behavior.

A Public Relations Disaster

Ford management considered the allegations misrepresentations and the controversy a public relations disaster. They viewed the charges as being grossly unfair, yet the public believed them. Opponents of the car's design suggested that it might be more likely than the average car to explode into flames when rear-ended by another vehicle and asserted that many Ford customers had died fiery deaths. But how many people actually had died?

Mark Dowie claimed 500 deaths in the *Mother Jones* article. But the National Highway Traffic Safety Administration (NHTSA) in its investigations of the Pinto counted only 38 cases of rear-end collisions of Pintos that resulted in fuel tank damage, leakage, and ensuing fires, and in these 38 cases, NHTSA reported 27 fatalities and 24 instances of nonfatal burns.

Ford's argument was that its placement of the car's gas tank between the rear bumper and the differential housing on the rear axle was *state-of-the-art* for the period in which the car was introduced. Legally, that is all that was required of the company—to meet a state-of-the-art standard.

It was well into the design process that an engineering study suggested an alternative, that the "safest place" for the fuel tank might be directly above the rear axle. This option, which was diligently considered by Ford, was rejected for very sound *safety* reasons.

- First, Ford rejected it because moving the tank closer to passengers actually increased the threat that they would be consumed by fire.
- Second, doing so required the use of a circuitous filler pipe that could be easily dislodged in an accident.
- Third, if the fuel tank was placed further to the front, it would change the car's center of gravity, making it more difficult to control, precisely the problem with the Corvair that Nader so vigorously protested in *Unsafe At Any Speed.*
- Finally, if the fuel tank placement was different, then the car could not be serviced as easily, which presented another safety hazard.

In addition, moving the fuel tank would reduce trunk size and make it harder to offer a station wagon or hatchback option in the future.

Not Violating Regulations

Ford was not violating any existing government regulations when it placed the fuel tank where it did. In January 1969, under NHTSA's *proposed* rear-end safety standard, the vehicle was tested striking a 4,000-lb moving barrier at 20 MPH. The vehicle was supposed to leak less than an ounce of fuel per minute. In the four tests Ford conducted, the vehicles slightly exceeded this limit in three cases, and in the fourth there was massive leakage because of improper welding (the fuel tank split at the seams). However, before production began Ford *made modifications* so that its car would conform to the 4,000-lb moving-barrier test.

The government, though, did not go with this standard. It had no standard. Instead, it contemplated pushing the limit upward to a 4,000-lb fixed-barrier test, which Ford considered to be the equivalent of a 4,000-lb moving-barrier test at 40 MPH. Auto engineers believed that such a standard was highly unrealistic. More than 85 percent of rear-end collisions took place at speeds less than 20 MPH. The cars did not strike stationary objects, but hit other moving vehicles. In any case, only 0.45 percent of all auto injuries were a result of ensuing fires. At speeds of 40 MPH or more, the occupants would die or be hurt because of the impact, not because of the fire.

At that time (1971), Pinto already was on the market and many Pintos already were being driven. Ford did not want to unduly alarm people about a contentious issue that still was in the very early stages of consideration. Still, it retested the Pinto using the 20 MPH and 30 MPH fixed-barrier tests that the government was proposing. When it found excessive leakage and concluded that it would have to completely tear up the car and modify the design, it decided to stick to the 20 MPH moving-barrier standard for current models and to do the engineering work that would enable it to meet a future 30 MPH moving-barrier test, which it believed NHTSA ultimately would adopt.

In early 1971 a junior engineer (Pricor) conducted a study that explored various ways to meet the 30 MPH moving barrier standard. Almost all the options (an over-the-axle gas tank, a repositioned spare tire, installation of body rails, and a redesigned filler pipe) involved extensive redesign of the vehicle. Only a rubber bladder (estimated to cost $5.80 per vehicle) could be installed without extensive redesign, but it would not work in cold weather, when it became stiff making it difficult to fill the gas tank, or hot weather, when it simply failed.

Wide Media Coverage

Nonetheless, though the incidents were few, when Pintos were struck from behind at closing speeds between 30 and 35 MPH, the accidents received wide media coverage. In these occurrences, the gas tank was smashed between the bumper and differential housing, and fuel sprayed over the pavement and inside the vehicle. It ignited from a spark, perhaps from sheet metal scraping the pavement, and it caused enormous fires, killing or maiming the vehicle's occupants in a hideous way.

Two such incidents were reported very widely:

· In a 1972 accident a Pinto was rear-ended on a California freeway at 30 to 50 MPH. The woman driving the car, Lily Gray, died from the subsequent fire. Her 13-year-old passenger, Richard Grimshaw, suffered burns over 80 percent of his body, losing his nose, an ear, and much of a hand as a result. The boy underwent scores of reconstructive skin grafting operations and was scarred for life. A California jury awarded the boy $2.8 million in February 1978 for wrongful injuries and set punitive damages at $125 million, the largest punitive damage award ever at the time. The court later reduced the punitive damages to $3.5 million.[9] The jury was strongly influenced by the films of the Pinto crash tests performed before the car went on the market in 1970. The tests showed a Pinto being backed into a wall at 20 mph and the nonflammable liquid in the car's gas tank spraying into the passenger compartment as a result. A juror told a reporter that "it looked like a fireman had stuck a hose inside the car and turned it on. In my mind, that film beat the Ford Motor Company."[10]

· In a 1978 accident in Indiana three teenaged girls were burned to death in a Pinto when they were struck from behind by a van. A part-time prosecutor for the county where the accident occurred brought charges of reckless homicide against the company (the first time a corporation had been charged with murder), and the subsequent trial drew national attention. A jury found the company not guilty of the charges, but significant harm had been done by the publicity to its reputation.[11]

NHTSA's Investigation

Under pressure from consumer advocate Ralph Nader and others who expressed outrage over the Pinto's explosive potential, NHTSA finally opened an investigation into the Pinto in the fall of 1977. Dowie claimed that NHTSA would "never force the company to test or recall the more than two million pre-1977 Pintos still on the highway. Seventy or more people will burn to death in those cars every year for many years to come. If the past is any indication, Ford will continue to accept the deaths."[12] In late 1977 Ford issued a press release responding to the Dowie article and the issues it raised. In part, it said that

> the truth is that in every model year the Pinto has been tested and met or surpassed the federal fuel system integrity standards applicable to it. . . . It is simply unreasonable and unfair to contend that a car is somehow unsafe if it does not meet standards proposed for future years or embody the technological improvements that are introduced in later model years.[13]

NHTSA informed Ford that a public hearing on what it had determined were safety defects in the fuel system would be held in June 1978. Shortly before the hearing was to begin, Ford announced a recall of all 1971–1976 model Pintos in order to remedy the defect. NHTSA canceled the planned hearing after the recall announcement, since the repairs Ford would be making would eliminate the fire danger to the degree required by law. The cost to Ford of the recall was estimated at $20 million. This cost was borne by a company that had earned $1.5 billion after taxes the previous year.[14]

"60 Minutes"

Shortly after the recall announcement, the CBS news program "60 Minutes" aired a segment on the Pinto controversy. Correspondent Mike Wallace discussed the Grimshaw accident and interviewed a former Ford engineer who said Ford had known of the safety defect but hadn't remedied the problem because of the cost involved. Wallace's interview with Ford's executive in charge of environmental and safety engineering, Herbert Misch, made Misch appear unable to answer pointed questions about the controversy.[15] A public image of Ford as a company that willfully sacrificed the safety of its customers in return for larger profits began to take hold.

Production of the Pinto ceased in 1980. The company's top executives during the controversy, CEO Lee Iacocca and chairman Henry Ford II, both had left by then, and the company began developing an emphasis on quality (its advertising theme was "At Ford, Quality Is Job One"). It tried to reduce damageability and increase the safety of its vehicles.[16]

Charges and Contercharges

To help clarify the policy questions involved, Karen Carlson, Ford's new safety staff member, again scanned her informational materials and scrutinized the facts relevant to the situation. She reviewed the charges that had been brought against Ford.

Charge 1: The accelerated development program was responsible for the design flaws. According to Mark Dowie, the author of the "Pinto Madness," the Pinto was rushed into production in 25 months instead of the usual 43. Ford records indicated that it actually took 38 months to bring the Pinto into production, and that the early introduction of the vehicle provided competitive advantage—five months of market dominance when the car's leadership was uncontested by any rival.[17] That the car was developed more quickly than normal to meet the competition meant that assembly tooling (where the machines that will make the parts of the car are themselves made) had to start before crash tests occurred.[18] Tooling usually took place after crash tests were completed. Still, Ford was able to make adjustments in the gas tank design before production, which allowed the car to meet the federal safety standard for rear-end collisions that was designed to protect passengers from rear-end fires.[19]

According to Dowie, secret company documents showed that the company had also crash-tested 11 Pinto prototypes before production at an average of 31 MPH, and that only 3 had escaped with gas tanks intact. Dowie argued that Ford refused to adopt modifications because assembly tooling had already begun, and modifications to the machine tools would cut into profits.

The preproduction test-crash films introduced as evidence in the Grimshaw trial, which showed Pinto gas tanks spraying fuel profusely when backed into a wall at 25 MPH, suggested that engineers within the company were aware that the tanks were vulnerable. Still, at that time the applicable proposed federal standard (there was no actual standard) was for a moving 20 MPH test, not a fixed 25 MPH test. According to Ford, the physics involved with crash tests meant that a car backing into a solid object (as in the fixed tests) was subjected to almost twice the stress of a car struck by a moving object.[20]

According to Ford, Pinto was involved in fewer fire-related collisions than would be expected given the number of Pintos on the road.[21] Dowie, however, claimed that the studies commissioned by NHTSA showed that more than 3,000 people were burning to death in 400,000 auto fires per year and that the rate was increasing five times faster than building fires. He asserted that Ford made 24 percent of the cars on the road, yet these cars accounted for 42 percent of the collision-ruptured gas tanks.[22]

Charge 2: Ford placed little importance on safety considerations in its design process. According to Dowie, design engineers who learned of the Pinto's explosive faults were loathe to inform Lee Iacocca of their findings. He quoted several former company officials on the subject, one of whom told him: "Safety wasn't a popular subject around Ford in those days. With Lee it was taboo. Whenever a problem was raised that meant a delay on the Pinto, Lee would chomp on his cigar, look out the window and say, 'Read the product objectives and get back to work.'"[23] The emphasis was on styling and price considerations, not safety, said another engineer. And another recounted how no one showed up when he gave a presentation on safer gas tank design.[24] The company's design departments seemed to take to heart a maxim attributed to Iacocca: "Safety doesn't sell."

Undoubtedly, the Pinto controversy helped bring the importance of automobile safety design into the public consciousness, as did Ralph Nader's book on automobile safety, *Unsafe at Any Speed.* Still, there may have been some truth to Iacocca's adage that safety doesn't sell between 1967 and 1970 when the Pinto was being developed.

Charge 3: The Pinto's designers chose not to incorporate inexpensive design modifications that could have saved the lives of many of the burn victims, and made this decision on the basis of a cost-benefit analysis that assigned a value to human life. Dowie's article claimed that four design changes the company tested in preproduction could have reduced the chances of fatal fires occurring. First, a $1 plastic device could be placed between the tank and the differential housing, shielding the tank from the sharp bolts on the housing that tended to pierce the tank in crashes. Second, a piece of metal could be placed between the tank and the rear bumper to absorb some of the impact of a crash. Third, a $5.08 rubber liner could be placed inside the gas tank to keep gas from spilling out if the tank was pierced. Fourth, the gas tank could be placed above the drive shaft, away from the rear axle and bumper altogether. Ford had a patent on this tank design and used it on its Experimental Safety Vehicle, which had withstood rear-end impacts of 60 MPH. Ford denied that these were the options it considered in the preproduction stage. Still, a former engineer testified at the Grimshaw liability trial that 95 percent of the people who had died as a result of the Pinto fires would have survived if an alternative tank placement had been used. He estimated the additional cost at $9.95 per car.[25]

Ford never explicitly used cost-benefit analysis in evaluating different methods for containing damage from rear end collisions. Yet Dowie attacked Ford in a deceptive way by using the 1973 NHTSA proposed standard for fuel leakage in *rollover accidents* as an example of where Ford did use cost-benefit analysis. As part of its case against this standard, Ford presented a cost-benefit analysis purporting to show how the money spent to put an $11 valve on every car it made to prevent leakage in a rollover would greatly exceed the social benefit that would occur as a result. The analysis assumed that 180 people would die in auto fires if the valve were not installed, and that another 180 would be seriously burned. Using a NHTSA-supplied figure of $200,000 in dollar damages per death (including $10,000 for the victim's pain and suffering), and $67,000 in lost dollar damages for a surviving burn victim, Ford calculated that requiring installation of the valves on the 12.5 million vehicles sold that year would mean at net loss to society of $87.5 million.[26]

The rollover cost-benefit calculations were widely publicized in the press and made the company appear to be valuing profit over human suffering and death. The fact that NHTSA approved of this method of calculating the social costs of a proposed regulation did not receive much attention, nor did the fact that this cost-benefit analysis had nothing to do with the controversy about exploding rear fuel tanks with which it was associated.

Charge 4: Ford mounted a campaign against the rear-end safety standards that delayed their adoption for eight years. When a federal agency like NHTSA proposes a new regulation, it requests public comment on the effects and feasibility of the regulation. During the evolution of Standard 301, Ford submitted evidence supporting its contentions that various aspects of the standard were unnecessary, unrealistic, or otherwise excessive. Dowie characterized Ford's actions with regard to the standards as cynical:

> There are several main techniques in the art of combating a government safety standard: (*a*) make your arguments in succession, so the feds can be working on disproving only one at a time; (*b*) claim that the real problem is not X but Y . . . ; (*c*) no matter how ridiculous each argument is accompany it with thousands of pages of highly technical assertions it will take the government months or, preferably years, to test.[27]

There was no doubt that Ford's top management was hostile toward some aspects of federal safety regulation. NHTSA was a new, inexperienced agency. Its leadership during the Carter administration came from the ranks of ex-Naderites (Joan Claybrook), and it lacked not only the capacity to be objective but the technical competence to do a good job. Combined with the effects of inflation, foreign price competition, and the cost burden of complying with other regulations concerning fuel efficiency and pollution controls, the costs of safety regulations added significantly to the automakers' competitive worries.

Conclusion

Having finished her review of the Pinto controversy, Karen had a number of questions she still was considering and some ideas on how company policy with regard to automobile safety could be better handled in the future:

· Was the company negligent for not voluntarily improving its gas tanks to a higher standard than had been proposed by NHTSA?

· Should Ford allow a compressed development schedule that requires assembly tooling to begin before crash tests occur?

· If potential customers were in fact more concerned with a car's style, fuel efficiency, and price than with safety features that could make the car more expensive, was Ford at fault for not incorporating the state-of-the-art in safety design anyway, regardless of the cost?

• Was Ford behaving wrongly by trying to fight the adoption of standards that would cost the company and the car buyer money and that might hurt the company's competitive position, eventually costing employees and communities jobs?

• How should society determine whether the good arising from a proposed regulation outweighs the costs to society that would be required to satisfy the regulation?

• If statistics showed that even one person's life could be saved by requiring a design change, would it be worth any cost, no matter how high?

• If cost-benefit analyses are necessary, what is the appropriate way to value human life and suffering?

Karen was considering the possibility of some type of internal standard of reasonableness where Ford would proceed with the development of a new vehicle if the income generated was likely to exceed the probability of a safety recall times the cost, but she was aware that such a reasonableness standard might be considered by some to be a form of cost-benefit analysis and that it would be repugnant to them on ethical grounds. She also wondered about its legality and if it would stand up well in the courts.

Discussion Questions

1. Why did the Pinto controversy take place?
2. What lessons should Ford learn from Pinto?
3. What should Karen Carlson say in her presentation?

Endnotes

1. This case was prepared by Mark Jankus and Alfred Marcus.
2. Neal Templin, "Ford Settles Big Lap Belt Injury Suit," *The Wall Street Journal*, April 5, 1990, p. B1.
3. D. L. Davidson, "Managing Product Safety: The Ford Pinto," case 383–129, Harvard Business School, 1984, p. 114.
4. Ibid., p. 14.
5. M. Dowie, "Pinto Madness," *Mother Jones*, September/October 1977, pp. 18–32.
6. J. Anderson and L. Whitten, "Auto Maker Shuns Safer Gas Tank," *Washington Post*, December 30, 1976, p. B7.
7. "Ford is Recalling Some 1.5 Million Pintos, Bobcats," *The Wall Street Journal*, June 12, 1978, p. 2.
8. Dowie, "Pinto Madness," p. 32.
9. R. Mokhiber, *Corporate Crime and Violence: Big Business and the Abuse of the Public Trust* (San Francisco: Sierra Club Books, 1988) p. 378.
10. R. J. Harris, Jr., "Why the Pinto Jury Felt Ford Deserved $125 Million Penalty," *The Wall Street Journal*, February 14, 1978, p. A1.
11. See F. T. Cullen, W. J. Maakestad, and G. Cavender, *Corporate Crime under Attack: The Ford Pinto Case and Beyond* (Cincinnati: Anderson Publishing Co., 1987), pp. 245–308.
12. Dowie, "Pinto Madness," p. 32.
13. Cited in Davidson, "Managing Product Safety," p. 117.
14. Ibid., p. 118–19.
15. Cullen et al., "Corporate Crime and Violence," p. 167.

16. Ford 1982 annual report, cited in G. Starling and O. W. Baskin, "Ford Pinto," in *Issues in Business and Society: Capitalism and Public Purpose* (Boston: Kent; 1985) p. 439.
17. Davidson, "Managing Product Safety," p. 114.
18. Ibid.
19. Ibid., p. 115.
20. Ibid.
21. Ibid., p. 115, 117.
22. Dowie, "Pinto Madness," p. 28.
23. Ibid., p. 21.
24. Ibid., p. 23.
25. Mokhiber, *Corporate Crime and Violence*, p. 377.
26. Dowie, "Pinto Madness," p. 24, 26.
27. Ibid., p. 27.

BIBLIOGRAPHY

Further Reading for Part II

Ackerman, R. W., and R. Bauer, eds. *Corporate Social Responsiveness: The Modern Dilemma*. Reston, Va.: Reston, 1976.

Anderson, J. W. *Corporate Social Responsibility: Guidelines for Top Management*. New York: Quorum, 1989.

Ansoff, H. I., ed. *Business Strategy*. New York: Penguin Books, 1977.

Bennett, A. "Ethics Codes Spread Despite Skepticism." *The Wall Street Journal*, July 15, 1988, p. 13.

Berger, P. L. "New Attack on the Legitimacy of Business." *Harvard Business Review*, September–October 1981, pp. 82–89.

Carroll, A. B., ed. *Managing Corporate Social Responsibility*. Boston: Little, Brown, 1977.

Donaldson, T. *The Ethics of International Business*. New York: Oxford University Press, 1989.

Fahey, L., and V. K. Narayanan. *Macroenvironmental Analysis for Strategic Management*. St. Paul: West Publishing Company, 1986.

Galbraith, J. K. *The Affluent Society*. Boston: Houghton Mifflin, 1958.

Hughes, J. R. *The Governmental Habit: Economic Controls from Colonial Times to the Present*. New York: Basic Books, 1977.

Leone, R. *Government Regulation of Business: Developing the Managerial Perspective*. Boston: Harvard Business School, 1981.

Marx, T., ed. *Business and Society: Economic, Moral, and Political Foundations*. Englewood Cliffs, N.J.: Prentice Hall, 1985.

Matthews, J. B., K. E. Goodpaster, and L. L. Nash. *Policies and Persons: A Casebook in Business Ethics*. 2nd ed. New York: McGraw-Hill, 1991.

Olson, M. *The Logic of Collective Action*. Cambridge, Mass.: Harvard University Press, 1965.

Post, J. E., ed. *Research in Corporate Social Performance and Policy: Vol. 11*. Greenwich, Conn.: JAI Press, 1989.

Post, J. *Corporate Behavior and Social Change*. Reston, Va: Reston Publishing, 1978.

Romano, R., and M. Lehman. *Views on Capitalism*. Beverly Hills, Calif.: Glencoe Press, 1970.

Starling, G., and O. Baskin. *Issues in Business and Society: Capitalism and Public Purpose*. Boston, Mass.: Kent Publishing, 1985.

Steiner, J. F. "The KKR-RJR Nabisco Blockbuster Leveraged Buyout." In *Industry, Society, and Change*. New York: McGraw-Hill, 1991.

Tuleja, T. *Beyond the Bottom Line*. New York: Penguin Books, 1985.

Further Reading for Part III

Ashford, D. E. *Policy and Politics in France: Living with Uncertainty.* Philadelphia: Temple University Press, 1982.

———. *Policy and Politics in Britain.* Philadelphia: Temple University Press, 1981.

Badaracco, J. L. *Loading the Dice: A Five-Country Study of Vinyl Chloride Regulation.* Boston, Mass.: Harvard Business School Press, 1985.

Bluestone, B., and B. Harrisonn. *The Deindustrialization of America: Plant Closings, Community Abandonment, and the Dismantling of Basic Industry.* New York: Basic Books, 1982.

Boskin, M. J. *Reagan and the Economy: The Successes, Failures, and Unfinished Agenda.* San Francisco: Institute for Contemporary Studies, 1987.

Brickman, R.; S. Jasanoff; and T. Ilgen. *Controlling Chemicals: The Politics of Regulation in Europe and the United States.* Ithaca, N.Y.: Cornell University Press, 1985.

Cohen, T. *Remaking Japan: The American Occupation as New Deal.* New York: The Free Press, 1987.

Galambos, L., and J. Pratt. *The Rise of the Corporate Commonwealth: U.S. Business and Public Policy in the Twentieth Century.* New York: Basic Books, 1988.

Ginsburg, D. H., and W. J. Abernathy. *Government, Technology, and the Future of the Automobile.* New York: McGraw-Hill, 1978.

Hardin, R. *Collective Action.* Baltimore: Johns Hopkins Press, 1982.

Heidenheimer, A. J.; H. Heclo; and C. T. Adams. *Comparative Public Policy: The Politics of Social Choice in Europe and America.* New York: St. Martin's Press, 1975.

Katzenstein, P. J. *Policy and Politics in West Germany: The Growth of a Semisovereign State.* Philadelphia: Temple University Press, 1987.

Lawrence, P. R., and D. Dyer. *Renewing American Industry.* New York: The Free Press, 1983.

Lindblom, C. E. *Politics and Markets: The World's Political-Economic Systems.* New York: Basic Books, 1977.

Lodge, G., and B. Scott, eds. *U.S. Competitiveness in the World Economy.* Boston: Harvard Business School Press, 1985.

Marcus, A. A.; A. M. Kaufman; and D. R. Beam, eds. *Business Strategy and Public Policy.* New York: Quorum Books, 1987.

Nelson, R. R. *High-Technology Policies: A Five-Nation Comparison.* Washington, D.C.: American Enterprise Institute for Public Policy Research, 1984.

Olson, M. *The Logic of Collective Action.* Cambridge, Mass.: Harvard University Press, 1965.

———. *The Rise and Decline of Nations: Economic Growth, Stagflation, and Social Rigidities.* New Haven: Yale University Press, 1982.

Pemple, T. J. *Policy and Politics in Japan.* Philadelphia: Temple University Press, 1982.

Piore, M. J., and C. F. Sabel. *The Second Industrial Divide.* New York: Basic Books, 1984.

Polanyi, K. *The Great Transformation: The Political and Economic Origins of Our Time.* Boston: Beacon Press, 1957.

Posner, R. "Theory of Economic Regulation." *Bell Journal of Economics and Management* 5, 1974, pp. 335–58.

Preston, L. E., ed. *Business and Politics: Research Issues and Empirical Studies.* Greenwich, Conn.: JAI Press, 1990.

———. *Government Regulation and Business Response: Research Issues and Empirical Studies.* Greenwich, Conn.: JAI Press, 1990.

Quinn, D. P. *Restructuring the Automobile Industry: A Study of Firms and States in Modern Capitalism.* New York: Columbia University Press, 1988.

Ramsey, D. K. "Car Wars: General Motors vs. the Japanese." In *The Corporate Warriors: Six Classic Cases in American Business.* Boston: Houghton Mifflin, 1987.

Rothschild, E. *Paradise Lost: The Decline of the Auto-Industrial Age.* New York: Vintage Books, 1973.

Schlozman, K. L., and J. T. Tierney. *Organized Interests and American Democracy.* New York: Harper & Row, 1986.

Shonfield, A. *Modern Capitalism: The Changing Balance of Public and Private Power.* New York: Oxford University Press, 1969.

Stein, H. *Presidential Economics: The Making of Economic Policy from Roosevelt to Reagan and Beyond.* New York: 1984.

Stigler, G. "The Theory of Economic Regulation." *Bell Journal of Economics and Management Science* 1971.

Tyson, L., and J. Zysman. *American Industry in International Competition: Government Policies and Corporate Strategies.* Ithaca, N.Y.: Cornell University Press, 1983.

van Wolferen, K. *The Enigma of Japanese Power: People and Politics in a Stateless Nation.* New York: Alfred A. Knopf, 1989.

Vogel, D. *Fluctuating Fortune: The Political Power of Business in America.* New York: Basic Books, 1989.

———. *National Styles of Regulation: Environmental Policy in Great Britain and the United States.* Ithaca, N.Y.: Cornell University Press, 1986.

Ward, B. *The Ideal Worlds of Economics: Liberal, Radical and Conservative Economic World Views.* New York: Basic Books, 1979.

Wilson, J. Q. *American Government: Institutions and Policies.* Lexington, Mass.: D. C. Heath, 1980.

Wilson, G. K. *Business and Politics.* 2nd ed. Chatham, N.J.: Chatham House Publishers, Inc., 1990.

Further Reading for Part IV

Allen, J., ed. *Environment 91/91.* 10th ed. Guilford, Conn.: The Dushkin Publishing Group, Inc., 1991.

Anderson, F. R.; A. V. Kneese; P. D. Reed; S. Taylor; and R. B. Stevenson. *Environmental Improvement through Economic Incentives.* Baltimore, Md.: Johns Hopkins University Press, 1977.

Bohi, D. R. *Energy Price Shocks and Macroeconomic Performance.* Washington, D.C.: Resources for the Future, 1989.

Danielsen, A. L. *The Evolution of OPEC.* New York: Harcourt Brace Jovanovich, 1982.

Dorfman, R., and N. S. Dorfman. *Economics of the Environment.* New York: W. W. Norton & Company, 1972.

Energy Information Adminstration. *Short-Term Energy Outlook: Quarterly Projections.* Washington, D.C.: Energy Information Administration, October 1989.

Energy Information Administration. *Annual Energy Outlook: 1987.* Washington, D.C.: Energy Information Administration, 1987.

Ford, D. *Cult of the Atom: The Secret Papers of the Atomic Energy Commission.* New York: Simon & Schuster, 1982.

Goldfarb, T. D. *Taking Sides: Clashing Views on Controversial Environmental Issues.* 4th ed. Guilford, Conn.: The Dushkin Publishing Group, Inc., 1991.

Kelman, S. *What Price Incentives: Economists and the Environment.* Boston, Mass.: Auburn House Publishing Company, 1981.

Kneese, A. V., and C. L. Schultze. *Pollution, Prices, and Public Policy.* Washington, D.C.: The Brookings Institution, 1975.

Rolph, E. S. *Nuclear Power and the Public Safety.* Lexington, Mass.: D. C. Heath and Company, 1979.

Rosenbaum, W. A. *Energy, Politics, and Public Policy.* Washington, D.C.: Congressional Quarterly, 1987.

Schultze, C. L. *The Public Use of Private Interest.* Washington, D.C.: The Brookings Institution, 1977.

Simon, J. L. *The Ultimate Resource.* Princeton, N.J.: Princeton University Press, 1981.

Tobin, R. J. *The Social Gamble: Determining Acceptable Levels of Air Quality.* Lexington, Mass.: Lexington Books, 1979.

U.S. Congress. House. Committee on Energy and Commerce. Subcommittee on Energy and Power. *Hearings on Advanced Reactor Technologies.* Cong., sess., 1989, H. No. 101–17.

———. *Hearings on Alernative Automotive Fuels.* Cong., sess., 1987, H. No. 100–87.

U.S. Congress. Senate. Committee on Energy and Natural Resources. *Hearings on Domestic Petroleum Industry Outlook.* Cong., sess., 1987, S. Hrg. 100–51.

———. *Hearings on the World Oil Outlook.* Cong., sess., 1987, S. Hrg. 100–39.

U.S. Congress. Senate. Committee on Energy and Natural Resources. Subcommittee on Energy and Power. *Hearings on Alternate Motor Vehicle Fuels.* Cong., sess., 1989, S. Hrg. 101–141.

———. Subcommitee on Energy Regulation and Conservation. *Hearings on Automobile Fuel Efficiency Standards.* Cong., sess., 1989, S. Hrg. 101–44.

———. Subcommittee on Energy Research and Development. *Hearings on Advanced Reactor Development Programs.* Cong., sess., 1988, S. Hrg. 100–846.

———. *Hearings on Energy Efficiency and Renewable Energy Research, Development, and Demonstration.* Cong., sess., 1989, S. Hrg. 101–168.

———. *Hearings on Renewable Energy Technologies.* Cong., sess., 1987, S. Hrg. 100–291.

Vig, N. J., and M. E. Kraft. *Environmental Policy in the 1990s.* Washington, D.C.: CQ Press, 1990.

Winter, G. *Business and the Environment.* New York: McGraw-Hill, 1988.

Wood, W. C. *Nuclear Safety: Risks and Regulation.* Washington, D.C.: American Enterprise Institute, 1983.

Further Reading for Part V

Baily, M. N., and A. K. Chakrabarti. *Innovation and the Productivity Crisis.* Washington, D.C.: The Brookings Institution, 1988.

Betz, F. *Managing Technology: Competing through New Ventures, Innovation, and Corporate Research.* Englewood Cliffs, N.J.: Prentice Hall, 1987.

Claybrook, J. *Retreat from Safety.* New York: Pantheon Books, 1984.

J. L. Coleman, *Markets, Morals and the Law.* New York: Cambridge University Press, 1988.

Crandal, R.; H. Gruenspecht; T. Keeler; and L. Lave. *Regulating the Automobile.* Washington, D.C.: Brookings Institution, 1986.

Fisse, B., and G. Braithwaite. *The Impact of Publicity on Corporate Offenders.* Albany: State University of New York Press, 1983.

Gaskins, R. H. *Environmental Accidents: Personal Injury and Public Responsibility.* Philadelphia: Temple University Press, 1989.

Hawken, P.; J. Ogilvy; and P. Schwartz. *Seven Tomorrows: Toward a Voluntary History.* New York: Bantam Books, 1982.

Hayes, R. H., and S. C. Wheelwright. *Restoring our Competitive Edge: Competing through Manufacturing.* New York: John Wiley & Sons, 1984.

Heilbroner, R. L. *An Inquiry into the Human Prospect.* New York: W. W. Norton & Company, Inc., 1975.

Hirsch, F. *Social Limits to Growth.* Cambridge, Mass.: Harvard University Press, 1976.

Jasanoff, S. *Social Research Perspectives: Risk Management and Political Culture (No. 12).* New York: Russell Sage Foundation, 1986.

Landes, W. M., and R. A. Posner. *The Economic Structure of Tort Law.* Cambridge, Mass.: Harvard University Press, 1987.

Lowrance, W. W. *Of Acceptable Risk.* Los Altos, Calif.: William Kaufman, Inc., 1976.

Mitroff, I. I., and R. Kilman. *Corporate Tragedies.* New York: Praeger, 1984.

Mokhiber, R. *Corporate Crime and Violence: Big Business Power and the Abuse of the Public Trust.* San Francisco: Sierra Club Books, 1988.

Nelson, R., and N. Winter. *An Evolutionary Theory of Economic Change.* Cambridge: Harvard University Press, 1982.

Olson, M., and H. H. Landsberg, eds. *The No-Growth Society.* New York: W. W. Norton, 1973.

Polinsky, A. M. *An Introduction to Law and Economics.* 2nd ed. Boston: Little, Brown and Company, 1989.

Posner, R. A. *Economic Analysis of Law.* 2nd ed. Boston: Little, Brown and Company, 1977.

Rosenberg, N. *Perspectives on Technology.* New York: Cambridge University Press, 1977.

Name Index

SUBJECT INDEX

A

A. H. Robins Company, 598–99, 613
Absolute liability
    first court ruling, 586–87
    Johns-Manville Case, 589
    movement toward, 588–92
Accounting measurement, 12
Acid emissions, 426–27
Acid rain, 502
    Clean Air Act provisions, 505
Activist courts, 258–59
Adaptation typology, 33–34
Ad Hoc Coalition for Competitive
    Telecommunications, 130
Administrative elite, 258
Administrative relief, 591
    in Japan, 603–9
    tort law reform without, 602–3
    victims' compensation, 601–2
Adolescents, 63–64
Advanced Micro Devices, 276
Advocacy advertising, 125–26
Aetna Life and Casualty, 126
Affirmative action programs, 153,
    162, 164–65
    court rulings, 165–67
Agency relation, 103–4
Agriculture, subsidized, 278
AgTech database, 201
Air conditioners, 525

Air pollution
    carbon dioxide buildup, 448–53
    litigation, 606–7
    ozone depletion, 446–48
Alliance for Responsible CFC Policy,
    501
Alliant Techsystems, Inc., case,
    332–40
Allied-Signal Corporation, 276
Allocation function of government,
    225–26
Alternative fuels, Clean Air Act
    provisions, 504–5
Altruism
    and egoism, 62–63
    examples, 64–66
    moral personality, 63–64
    prudential, 66–69
    sources of, 60–69
American Academy of
    Otolaryngology–Head and
    Neck Surgery, 623
American Bar Association, 600
American Express Company, 520
American Journal of Obstetrics and
    Gynecology, 598
American Law Institute, 600
    Second Restatement of Tort Law,
    588

American Management Association,
    160
American Medical Association, 623
American Motors, 353
American Petroleum Institute, 503
American political tradition, 258–59
American Speech Language and
    Hearing Association, 623
American Trial Lawyer's
    Association, 600
Ampex Corporation, 529
Anaconda copper mines, 382
Analyzers, 34, 41
Andrea McCormack v. Hankscraft, 598
Animal studies data, 550–51
Annual reports, 16
Antidiscrimination court cases,
    165–67
Apple Computer, 511
Applied Energy Services, 454
Applied Expert Systems, 520
Arab-Israeli War of 1973, 426
Arco Solar, Inc., case, 464–79
Artificial intelligence, 517
    obstacles to adopting, 519–20
Asbestos claims, 577–78
Asbestos compensation bill, 602
Asea Brown Boveri, 494, 495